Malcolm X

A Historical Reader

Edited by

James L. Conyers, Jr.

and

Andrew P. Smallwood

Library of Congress Cataloging-in-Publication Data

Malcolm X : a historical reader / edited by James L. Conyers and Andrew P. Small-
wood.
    p. cm.
  Includes bibliographical references and index.
  ISBN-13: 978-0-89089-228-2 (alk. paper)
  ISBN-10: 0-89089-228-8 (alk. paper)
  1. X, Malcolm, 1925-1965. 2. Black Muslims--Biography. 3. African Americans--
Biography. I. Conyers, James L. II. Smallwood, Andrew P. III. Title.

  BP223.Z8M35 2008
  320.54'6092--dc22
  [B]

                          2007045340

CAROLINA ACADEMIC PRESS
700 Kent Street
Durham, North Carolina 27701
Telephone (919) 489-7486
Fax (919) 493-5668
www.cap-press.com

Malcolm X

We dedicate this volume to the memory and spirit of
Mrs. Jacqueline Irene Pierce-Conyers (1961–2006)
Mrs. Lillian Shouse Vilabrera (1915–2002)
Mr. Demetrius Matthews Wharton (1967–2002)
Dr. Asa G. Hilliard (1933–2007)
Mr. William A. Dunston Sr. (1942–2002)
Mr. Adrian Williams (1965–2005)

Malcolm X. Courtesy of LOOK Magazine, December 1969.

Contents

Preface   ix
Acknowledgments   xi

Part One
Africana Studies Appraisal of Malcolm X

1   The Legacy of Malcolm X's Leadership:
In the Tradition of Africana Social Movements
Andrew P. Smallwood   3

2   "Message to the Grass Roots":
Malcolm X's Analysis of Africana Culture and History
James L. Conyers, Jr.   17

3   From Malcolm X to Omowale Malik Shabazz:
The Transformation and Its Impact on the Black Liberation Struggle
Akiniyele K. Umoja   31

4   The Legacy of Malcolm X as a Framework for Social Welfare
Interventions in Black Communities
Mekada Graham   55

5   Methodology and Meaning: The Sociology of Malcolm X
Rhett Jones   67

Part Two
Black Nationalism and Pan-Africanism

6   The Sociopolitical Philosophy of Malcolm X
Maulana Karenga   93

7   Malcolm X and the Economic Salvation of African Americans
James B. Stewart   111

8   Malcolm X: Human Rights and the United Nations
Robert L. Harris, Jr.   125

9   Black Nationalism and Garveyist Influences
Shirley N. Weber   131

10   "To Unbrainwash an Entire People": Malcolm X, Cultural
Nationalism, and the US Organization in the Era of Black Power
Scot Brown   137

11   Malcolm X and Pan-Africanism
Paul Easterling   147

Part Three
Malcolm X's Intellectual Leadership

12   Literary Malcolm X: The Making of an African American Ancestor
      Christel N. Temple   167

13   In the Age of Malcolm X: Social Conflict and the Critique of
      African American Identity Construction
      Katherine O. Bankole   187

14   Reflections on Omowale Malcolm X and Martin Luther King, Jr.:
      Afrikan Liberation Struggle and the Political and
      Psychocultural Critique of Civil Rights
      Ahati N. N. Toure   205

15   Malcolm X: An Apostle of Violence or an Advocate for
      Black Human Rights?
      Victor O. Okafor   215

16   Malcolm X and Human Rights: An Afrocentric Approach to Reparations
      Malachi D. Crawford   227

17   Malcolm X in the Company of Thinkers
      Maghan Keita   235

Part Four
Black Artistic Expression

18   Malcolm X: Internet Resources and Digital Media
      Larry Ross   263

19   The Work of Fifty African American Poets on the Life and
      Career of Malcolm X (1925–1965)
      Julius E. Thompson   267

20   Malcolm X and Africana Critical Theory: Rethinking Revolutionary
      Black Nationalism, Black Radicalism, and Black Marxism
      Reiland Rabaka   281

21   The Media's Assault on Malcolm X
      Adisa A. Alkebulan   299

22   Malcolm X: A Study of the Power of Transformation
      Miriam Ma'at-Ka-Re Monges   309

23   Malcolm X-isms and the Protest Poetry of Blas Jiménez:
      Liberation by Any Means Necessary
      Antonio Tillis   315

24   Globalizing African American Political Thought:
      A Case Study of Malcolm X
      Godwin Ohiwerei   329

25   Public and Shadow Values in the Thought of Malcolm X
      Rhett Jones   337

26   "You Don't Call the Kittens Biscuits": Disciplinary Africana
      Studies and the Study of Malcolm X
      Greg Kimathi Carr   353

Contributors   377
Index   381

Preface

The idea and task of taking on the topic of examining the life and work of Malcolm X is stupendous and encyclopedic. Nonetheless, as we compiled records and communiqué, our knowledge grew, posture advanced, swagger oscillated, and we became reflexive of ourselves and of Africana history and culture, with regard to space, place and time. Simply put, we understood with humility and spirit that this volume was to make a singular contribution to the larger ongoing body of literature on the topic of Malcolm X.

Indeed, Malcolm X is studied inside canons within the humanities, social sciences, and professions. Yet, very few scholars have been able to locate the subject as human—African diasporan and equally important, posit ideas and analyses within the framework of a global Pan Africanist—Afrocentric symmetry.

Subsequently, creative space, energy, time, and forward progressive motion has softened contemporary domestic and international bipartisan social forces, to tolerate the political philosophy of Malcolm X. Endurable is the perquisite to explain the subject as an enigma, hostile Black man, or sometimes as a kickback radical. To many, this allows the subject of Malcolm X to be appealing, whereas, scholars can capriciously existentialize his lasting contributions.

Consequently, far from the illusion of Malcolm X being a reactionary protagonist—he was a scholar who evoked a pro-active and assertive pose. In this sense, he was able to review an issue and then offer a reflexive analysis, pertaining to the direct and indirect cause and consequence of a dispatch. This inquiry entrapped long and short term outcomes to political and economic designs confronting Africana phenomena on a global and national level. Phrased another way, his probes were saturated in appraising patterns of the creation and consequences of subordinate group status (i.e., the oppression of Africana people on a global and continental basis).

As we have congregated this assembly of essays, which amass this volume, our objective and liturgy is simple and straightforward. First, to challenge scholars in the discipline of Africana Studies to organize, prepare, and comport audits on Africana leadership of the nineteenth and twentieth century. Certainly, the idea of reclamation is aesthetically historic and incumbent to examining agency and sovereignty of African people. Second, espouse the necessity for implementation of Afrocentric meta-theories, to describe and evaluate Africana phenomena. Lastly, engage the requisite for scholars to exercise interdisciplinary tools and research methods for triangulating the: nexus, retention, and cultural milieu of Africana prodigies.

In conclusion, we have enjoyed numerous social outings to brief and debrief about the social construction of this text. Even more important, with loyalty, respect for the sacredness of the HOUSE, advocation of brotherhood-sisterhood, and our love for people of African descent, we have been blessed to see our ideas become a published reality. In memoriam and libation, we evoke the name of El Hajj Malik Shabazz and the countless other Africana leadership figures whose shoulders we stand on. So shall it be said—AGOO-AMEN (**response for attention**).

YAA ASANTEWAA, YIMHOTEP, NKRA!

Dr. James L. Conyers, Jr., University of Houston
Dr. Andrew P. Smallwood, Austin Peay State University

Acknowledgments

When I think about the passage of time since the inception of this project, I am reminded of one of many sayings used in the Smallwood household, this one that my mother used to share with us stand out: "The more things change the more they remain the same." As a young child I never fully grasped what this meant and yet it stayed with me over the years and now with the completion of this project I am reminded of my mother's words. Much has changed in the world and yet there are some things that remain constant. One of constants, is the power of people who at their best help to inspire us to achieve our goals and ultimately our dreams. There have been various individuals, we have come in contact with during the course of this project, whose influence and contributions whether directly or indirectly have been helpful to completing this project and we would like to acknowledge them at this time. We start here with our family members:

From the Conyers family: Mrs. Agnes Conyers, James L. Khalfani Sekou Conyers, III, Fredrick Kamau Abotare Conyers, Chad Anthony Hawkins, Gwen Woods, Khalis Woods, Shaheed Woods, and Khalil Amir Woods. From the Smallwood family: Mr. David P. Smallwood and Mrs. Grace F. Smallwood, Mr. Lawrence D. Smallwood and Mr. Mark C. Smallwood, Shomari Smallwood, Lauryn Smallwood and various uncles, aunts, cousins and family friends.

I would also like to acknowledge various colleagues for their collegiality and general assistance and support: We would also like to acknowledge other individuals for their support: Dr. Julius Thompson, Dr. Gerald Davis, Dr. William Nick Nelson, Mr. Zane Corbin, Mr. Anthony Robinson, Mr. James Jamison, Ms. Beth Johnson, Dr. Shawn Donaldson, Dr. Melanie E. Bratcher, Dr. Gerald Horne, Dr. John Antel, Dr. John Rudley, Dr. Molefi Kete Asante, Dr. Abu Abarry, Dr. Jay Katsley, Dr. Clara Meek, Dr. James B. Stewart, Dr. Sundiata Cha Jua, Dr. Shawn O. Utsey, Mrs. Angela Williams Phillips, Mrs. Sheneka Stewart, Dr. Robert L. Harris, Dr. James Turner, Dr. Phyllis M. Cunningham, Dr. Harold Cheatham, Dr. Leila V. Moore, the late Dr. Earl E. Thorpe, Dr. Arthell Sanders, The late Dr. Ernest Mason, Mr. Lawrence W. Young, The Friends of African American Studies at the University of Houston, Dr. Sherry Hoppe, Dr. Bruce Speck, Dr. James Diehr, Dr. Dewey Browder, Dr. Alvin Hughes, Dr. Richard Gildrie, Dr. Thomas Dixon, Dr. Michelle Butts, faculty in the History Department at APSU, Dr. Dwonna Goldstone, Dr. Jill Eichhorn, Dr. Karen Sorensen, Dr. Gail Robinson-Oturu, Dr. Dixie Dennis, Mrs. Debbie Shearon, Mrs. Pam Allen, Mrs. Tonya DeShon, Mr. Lantz Biles, Mr. David Davenport, Mr. Phil Petrie, Mr. Richard Jackson, Ms. Carol Bennett, members of the African American Staff and Faculty Organization at APSU, faculty in the College of Arts and Letters at APSU, Mrs. Eileen Cummings, Mr. Lacy DeBerry, Mrs. Daphne Dunston-Wharton, Dr. Kevin Jones, Mr. Gary Crumpler, Mr. Lyndon Perkins, Mr. Brian T. Davis, the former Ms. Vanessa Heyward, Ms. Althea Greene, Dr. Don-Terry Veal, Dr. Wilodean Burton, President Timothy Hall, Prof. Joyce Hargrove, Dr. David

Kanervo, Dr. George Pesley, Dr. Charles Pinder, Dr. Mark Michael, Dr. Jeffrey Mirel, Dr. Elwood Robinson, Dr. Brenda Scales, Dr. Brenda Shaw, Dr. Gregory Zieren, Ms. Karenthia Barber, Ms. Adrienne Brown, Mrs. Dennie Burke, Mrs. Patricia Dunston, Mr. William A. Dunston Jr., Ms. Keisha Dunston, Ms. Helen Chin, Ms. Darlene Cooley, Ms. Jan DeJean, Ms. Denise Edwards, Mrs. Saundra Edwards, Mrs. Kathleen Evans, Ms. Theresa Flick, Ms. Gillian Furbert, Ms. Shelley Hicks, Mrs. Charlotte Jacque, Mr. David Johnson, Ms. Gina Johnson, Ms. Monica Johnson, Mrs. Sharon Johnson, Ms. Alicia Kincaid, Ms. Kimberly Maultsby, Mrs. Una Mulzac, Mrs. Betty Osborne, Ms. Tonya Pendleton, Ms. Darlene Roper, Ms. Debra Starks, Mrs. Terry Stringer-Damron, Ms. Lysa Teal, Ms. Terri Teelucksingh, Mr. John E.Thomas, Ms. Stefeni Thomas, Mrs. Michelle Tyndall, Ms. Dana Wade, Ms. Stacey Walker, Ms. Patricia Washington, Miss Deme Wharton, Miss Desne Wharton, Mr. Dimitros Wharton, Mrs. Murielle Wharton, Ms. Enid Wharton, Ms. Kember L. White, Ms. Stephanie White, Ms. Karoletta Woodhouse and if we left out the names of other individuals this was unintentional and we thank you as well.

Finally, we would like to thank many of our former students over the years and particularly those individuals from various walks of life whose, energy, enthusiasm and intellectual curiosity have been inspirational and serve to remind us that our work is not finished.

Part One

Africana Studies
Appraisal of Malcolm X

1

The Legacy of Malcolm X's Leadership: In the Tradition of Africana Social Movements

Andrew P. Smallwood

> If you stick a knife in my back nine inches and pull it out six inches there's no progress. Progress is healing the wound.
>
> —Malcolm X (2006)

Introduction

As we move forward into the twenty-first century, our society is still trying to grasp both the extent and the quality of changes that have occurred over the last fifty years. The social movements of the 1950s, 1960s, and 1970s resulted in the collective struggles of various groups of people that had often been dehumanized and marginalized in mainstream American society. It was within these movements that generations of African Americans sought their liberation from systematic oppression within that society. Through the efforts of brave individuals working with local and national organizations, African Americans began to integrate into existing public institutions and to create shifts in how these institutions responded to them.

Generally, this essay addresses the leadership of Malcolm X in the tradition of African American leaders as part of social movements. Specifically, it explores his significance as an African American leader in the context of Africana Social Movements. Regarding Social Movement Theory, Rhoda Blumberg states: "A social movement is a type of behavior in which a large number of participants consciously attempt to change existing institutions and establish a new order of life. A new order of life, in this case, would be a system in which African Americans have an opportunity to share all the country has to offer on an equal basis with others. A broader definition of social movements would include not only persons who engage in group action for a cause but also those who agree with them on the need to change" (1991, 191).

Furthermore, in my view, an Africana Social Movement can not only include but also go beyond the issue of social equality to address issues of social sovereignty. Pan-African/Black sovereignty in the diaspora includes political, economic, and cultural dimensions expressed in collective behavior and in resistance to institutional racism and

3

cultural discrimination, with a leadership working in conjunction with a larger collective toward social action.

Twentieth-Century African American Leadership

African American leaders have fought against racial discrimination throughout American history. The formation of the African Methodist Episcopal Church in 1812 by Richard Allen; Nat Turner's rebellion against enslavement in 1831; Frederick Douglass's public discourse condemning slavery; and Booker T. Washington's program to relieve Black suffering through vocational education were attempts by African American leaders to organize their people to fight injustice during the nineteenth century.

In 1903 W. E. B. Du Bois wrote that a "Talented Tenth" of educated African Americans would serve to advocate full equality for the masses of Black people (W. E. B. Du Bois 1968, 236). Du Bois's call for Black leadership to voice the concerns of the Black masses underscored the need for liberating Black leadership to address societal injustice by advocating social change.

In the early 1900s, Black leaders such as Ida B. Wells-Barnett and Marcus Garvey used vastly different approaches in addressing race relations in America. As a journalist and one of the early members of the National Association for the Advancement of Colored People (NAACP), Wells-Barnett worked vigorously for the passage of laws against lynching and segregation. She advocated social integration as the way toward equality and respect for African Americans. Arriving in the United States from Jamaica in 1916, Garvey was very critical of the conditions for Blacks in America and advocated social separation between Whites and Blacks. Garvey adopted part of Booker T. Washington's self-help philosophy and his emphasis on improving the Black masses. He also embraced the philosophy found in Black Nationalism to address the problems of racial discrimination faced by African Americans.

Garvey's influence on African Americans in the 1920s and 1930s was significant: his Black Nationalist philosophy and racial pride was evident in the formation of other organizations, such as the Nation of Islam, which posed alternative socioreligious solutions to the struggle for Black liberation (Smallwood 2001, 36).

Many of the key leadership figures in the Civil Rights Movement came from the African American churches, Black colleges and universities, and grassroots organizations across the United States. These individuals borrowed tactics rooted in the teachings of Mohandas Gandhi and in the historical struggles of the labor movement. (Colaiaco 1993, 2; Cone 1991, 77–78) Often a small group of individuals sought to address discrimination and injustice in American society. As one of the few kinds of organizations controlled by African Americans in their communities, Black churches served as an important resource to them historically (Karenga 2002, 264–265).

The Origins and Evolution of Malcolm X's Leadership

In his youth Malcolm X exhibited natural qualities of leadership, as recognized by his peers in middle school (e.g., he was elected class president in the eighth grade) and as a self-proclaimed "hustler" during his time in Boston (Malcolm X 1992, 108–150). During his incarceration in prison for petty crimes, Malcolm would discover an outlet to express his innate leadership qualities.

While in prison from 1946 to 1952, Malcolm underwent an intellectual reawakening and spiritual conversion that began with his participation in the Nation of Islam (NOI). Though information about this time in Malcolm's life is less extensive, the oratorical powers he displayed during his later public career were surely incubated then. In fact, in his *Autobiography* Malcolm mentions he was already a voracious reader while incarcerated and wanted to expand his vocabulary by copying an entire dictionary word for word. While in prison, Malcolm's leadership qualities were expressed by his leading the prison debate team in victories over students from elite eastern colleges near the prison. (Branham 1995, 121). Malcolm's early leadership skills were also expressed in his recruitment activity in prison for the NOI and then as an advocate for improving the treatment of NOI inmates by requesting that they be given cells facing eastward to accommodate their prayer ritual. Further, Malcolm voiced the dietary restrictions of NOI members and requested that prison officials offer an alternative meal plan. These actions eventually resulted in a nonviolent prison protest led by Malcolm, during which he wrote the local newspapers to criticize prison conditions (Perry 1991, 133–134; Strickland 1994, 62, 64).

After his release from prison, Malcolm X's rise to power in the Nation of Islam took place in only four years: he organized numerous temples throughout the United States (see Table 1) and eventually became the National Representative for the organization.

Several characteristics of Malcolm X's prominent role in the NOI are evident: his ministerial leadership, including the training of ministers; his organization of temples across the country; and his offering classes to local members in public speaking, the origins of human civilization, and eastern philosophy. (Karim 1992, 89–98).

In the early and mid-1950s, Malcolm viewed himself in a role similar to that of noted Christian evangelist Billy Graham, whose spirit of evangelical zeal he would emulate to promote Elijah Muhammad's message and the NOI as the best solutions for Black people in 1950s America. (Jenkins and Tryman 2002, 241–242)

During this important period in Malcolm X's development, Malcolm incorporated domestic and international issues into his public statements and ministry. His concern for violence against African Americans in the South was a consistent theme in his leadership as he placed his public statements in the context of the international and political climate of African and Asian independence.

As I have stated earlier, an Africana Social Movement addresses specific political, economic, and cultural concerns of Black people in their communities. The legacy of Malcolm X's leadership can be found in several Africana Social Movements: the African Independence Movements of the 1950s and 1960s; the Civil Rights, Black Power, Black Nationalist, Black Studies, and Black Arts Movements of the late 1960s; and the Hip-Hop Movement of the 1980s and 1990s. Members of each movement became familiar

**Table 1.   Malcolm X's Organization of
Temples in the Nation of Islam**

West Coast	Upper South
San Francisco, CA	Baltimore, MD
Los Angeles, CA (Temple No. 27)	Washington, DC
San Diego, CA	
	New England
Midwest	Boston, MA (Temple No. 11)
Milwaukee, WI	Boston/Roxbury, MA
Chicago, IL	Springfield, MA
St. Louis, MO	Hartford, CN (started by Rosalee
Dayton, OH	Bey in her home in 1955)
Detroit, MI (Temple No. 1)	
Cleveland, OH	**Mid-Atlantic Region**
Youngstown, OH	New York, NY (Temple No. 7)
Cincinnati, OH	Philadelphia, PA (Temple No. 12)
	Pittsburgh, PA
Lower South	Camden, NJ
Houston, TX	Atlantic City, NJ
New Orleans, LA	Buffalo, NY
Atlanta, GA	Albany, NY

Source: New York City Public Library, Schomburg Center for Research in Black Culture 2005a

with Malcolm X's leadership in the NOI and were attracted to his uncompromising public criticism of systematic social oppression and world imperialism as well as his advocacy of cultural pride and unity in a way that went beyond other NOI representatives. Various organizations would later focus on self-determination, social empowerment, cultural celebration, and community uplift, as evidenced in the Black Panther Party, the US organization, the Republic of New Africa, the Revolutionary Action Movement, and local grassroots organizations.

Malcolm X: Civil Rights, Black Power, and Black Nationalist Movements in America, 1953–1964

When examining the origins of the Civil Rights Movement, we find various local and national organizations of the twentieth century that were advocating full equality and first-class citizenship for African Americans. In the period after World War II, especially during the 1950s, economic prosperity and optimism led to various challenges of racial segregation in the United States. The Supreme Court decision, *Brown et al. vs. Board of Ed. Topeka, Kansas*, in May 1954; the slaying of Emmett Till in Money, Mississippi, in August 1955; and the protest and arrest of Rosa Parks in Montgomery, Alabama, in December 1955 were three significant events that helped to galvanize African Americans to fight racial segregation in the southern United States.

From 1953 through early 1964, Malcolm was restricted to nonengagement in civil rights and other social issues affecting African Americans. As leader of the NOI, Elijah

Muhammad had forbidden all members from participation in civil rights organizations, marches, or any political activity in general (Clegg 1997, 149–157; Perry 1991, 207–212; Essien-Udom 1962, 177–178) Through most of this period, Malcolm X was very critical of civil rights leadership and tactics, while the NOI moved increasingly away from the political rhetoric of Black Nationalism and international events and focused more on religious theology to address social problems facing Black people in their communities.

However, the harassment and arrest of NOI member Johnson Hinton in Harlem in 1957; the killing of Ronald Stokes in Los Angeles by members of the LAPD in 1962; the arrest and criminal trial of two NOI members in New York City in January 1963; and the police harassment of NOI members in New York City and Rochester in February 1963 led Malcolm to organize and mobilize NOI members to protest and, in several instances, to march with placards reminiscent of the civil rights marches of the day (Strickland 1994, 81, 83, 103–105, 127–128, 138, 139).

The emphasis of the Civil Rights Movement on desegregating southern institutions and the growing poverty in the Black communities in northern U.S. cities were two factors that led to the ideological shift of some Black leaders away from nonviolent ideology toward the Black Power Movement of the mid- to late-1960s. Organizations such as the Student Nonviolent Coordinating Committee (SNCC) and the Congress of Racial Equality (CORE) were major advocates of Black unity, Black consciousness, and cooperation among Blacks themselves instead of interracial cooperation. The issue of Black empowerment has roots in Black people seeking political power within mainstream American society. However, as Alphonso Pinkney (1975) observes:

> The Black Power movement, on the other hand, went beyond social reform. If the demands for political, economic, and social control by black people over the institutions which are responsible to them, along with the other changes necessary for the liberation of American blacks were achieved, American society will have undergone revolutionary changes. The civil rights movement did not address itself to the complex, deeply rooted problems facing black people in the slums of the United States. The Black Power movement did. (195)

This emphasis on self-help and community empowerment, reminiscent of the views of Marcus Garvey in the 1920s, was revisited by Elijah Muhammad in the NOI, starting in a socioreligious context in the 1930s, and was increasingly transformed by Malcolm X into a sociopolitical context in the late 1950s and early 1960s.

During the early 1960s, Malcolm X began to privately question the role of the NOI in improving the conditions of African Americans. Malcolm believed that the organization, with all its resources, could do more to address the plight of *all* African Americans, not just Black Muslims. His views were probably influenced in part by key action-oriented civil rights organizations such as the Southern Christian Leadership Conference (SCLC) and by student groups such as the Student Nonviolent Coordinating Committee (SNCC), both of which were at the forefront of social action. In 1963 Malcolm began to change his public discourse, aligning himself more with Black Nationalist philosophy, and in 1964, after leaving the NOI, he sought cooperation with the politically active organizations of the Civil Rights Movement (Goldman 1979, 115–116).

The origins of Black Nationalist expression are evident in the nineteenth-century colonization movement, which addressed Black emigration from the United States to

Africa and Latin America. Though emigration in the early nineteenth century was neither financially feasible nor widely popular among Black people, Black Nationalism did provide an ideological perspective on Black political thought that surfaced in the twentieth century with the Marcus Garvey movement. As James Turner (1977) correctly points out, Garvey viewed verbal protest and marches as useless without the power to support Black Nationalism and identified the problems of Africans in America with colonialism in Africa. Turner further states: "In the final analysis Garvey must be considered a race-conscious nationalist whose pride in Africa was founded on his knowledge of Africa's great history and culture" (176). It is clear from research that both Malcolm X and the Nation of Islam were influenced by Black Nationalist expression either directly or indirectly (Malcolm X 1992, 3–7; Essien-Udom 1962, 18).

Expressions of International Independence and Pan-Africanism, 1964–1965

Because both of Malcolm's parents were members of Marcus Garvey's UNIA and his mother had come from Grenada, Malcolm saw himself at an early age as part of an international community (DeCaro 1996, 41–43). Through this background, his self-study in prison, and the religious teachings of Elijah Muhammad, Malcolm brought an international, historical, political, and cultural worldview into the Nation of Islam.

Malcolm's repeated public statements referring to the Bandung Conference held in Indonesia on April 15, 1955, showed that he was aware of the independence movements of African and Asian nations and that he sought to locate African Americans in the larger context of the international sociopolitical struggle from colonial rule. As Jenkins and Tryman (2002) note, African and Asian people of different religions and political ideologies came together at the Indonesian Bandung Conference to fight European colonialism and to address the need for progress and nationalism that would lead to sovereignty. In 1959, Malcolm called for a "Bandung Conference of Negro Leaders" to be held in Harlem to fight American injustice (Jenkins and Tryman 2002, 90–91). (According to Baba Zak Condo [1993, 56], Malcolm was invited to "The Afro-Asian Conference in Algiers scheduled for June 29, 1965, and according to FBI files, Malcolm X was invited to the March 1965 Bandung Conference in Indonesia, though he had not made a decision to attend because his two organizations were in need of financial support [Federal Bureau of Investigation 1995]).

C. Eric Lincoln (1961), whose book *The Black Muslims in America* was the first sociological study of the NOI, discusses Malcolm X's involvement in providing widespread visibility to the organization in the late 1950s. After being named the National Representative from 1957 through 1963, Malcolm used public platforms to address the conditions of African Americans and of Africans in the diaspora. Malcolm's participation in public events in Harlem gave him two opportunities. First, it allowed him to promote the teachings of Elijah Muhammad and the mission of the NOI in order to recruit new members. Second, it allowed him to expand the organization ideologically into international events—an expansion that would lay the foundation for Pan-African explorations for several years and that may have later justified his being forced out of the organization on ideological grounds. Yusuf Shaw, former NOI associate and FOI captain in Temple Number 7, observed: "Oh, Malcolm is fitting in, but he's changed. Changed from religious talk to nationalistic talk" (Strickland 1994, 132).

During his time as National Representative of the NOI, Malcolm X's impact was also made in a variety of other ways. For example, his columns in *The New York Amsterdam News*, the *Pittsburgh Courier* and *The Los Angeles. Herald-Dispatch* eventually led Malcolm to found *Muhammad Speaks* in 1960. The main periodical of the NOI, it provided the organization an opportunity to reach an even wider audience (Lincoln 1961, 134; Jenkins and Tryman 2002, 406; Strickland 1994, 78).

In his book *From Civil Rights to Black Liberation*, William Sales (1994) attempts to redefine Malcolm X's political legacy by examining his evolution from Black Nationalism to Pan-Africanism (84–85). It is important to note that Malcolm X traveled extensively throughout the world in 1959, in 1964, and early in 1965. Other examples of Malcolm's expression of Pan-Africanism are his talks with African revolutionaries and his engaging in a dialogue of revolutionary action to combat European colonialism in Africa (Turner 1977, 180).

Malcolm X's public statements concerning international events and the independence of African colonies can be traced back to the early 1950s. His interest in internationalism and African independence had a powerful impact on the Civil Rights Movement and on the traditional civil rights organizations. First, Malcolm laid out an international agenda that civil rights leaders would have to respond to. Second, he advocated cultural pride and community empowerment as demonstrated in the Black Power Movement. Malcolm's impact on civil rights organizations during his lifetime is evident when we consider the comments of John Lewis and Donald Harris on their trip to Africa for SNCC in 1964:

> Among the first questions we were continually asked was, "What's your organization's relationship with Malcolm's?" We ultimately found that this situation was not peculiar to Ghana; the pattern repeated itself in every country. After a day of this we found that we must, immediately on meeting people, state our own position in regards to where we stood on certain issues—Cuba, Vietnam, the Congo, Red China and the U.N. and what SNCC's role, guidelines, and involvement in the Rights Struggle was. Malcolm's impact on Africa was just fantastic. In every country he was known and served as the main criteria for categorizing other Afro-Americans and their political views. (Carson 1991, 196).

Malcolm's public speeches and international travels provided him with a platform to voice the concerns of the people in the African diaspora about uniting on the basis of a common heritage as well as their shared colonialism and cultural hegemony. Indeed, Malcolm X's writings (e.g., his autobiography published in 1965); many of his public speeches in 1964 and 1965; his trips to Africa, Europe, and the Middle East; and his founding of two organizations, the religious Muslim Mosque Incorporated (MMI) in March 1964 and the political Organization of Afro-American Unity (OAAU) in June 1964, clearly placed his thought in the traditions of African liberation and sovereignty. In all of these activities, he expounded a Pan-Africanist view, which included political and economic independence, cultural celebration, and unity among all people of African descent. Malcolm's public discourse included statements in 1964 in support of the Congo's struggle for independence from the ongoing influence of Western colonial powers on its sovereignty. He also held clandestine meetings with the Cuban revolutionary Che Guevara and worked to recruit volunteers to fight in the Congo's civil war in 1965 (Condo 1993, 51). In speaking with a group of high school students from Mc-

Table 2.   Malcolm X's Selected International Travels in Africa, Europe, and the Middle East, 1964–1965

Africa	Europe
Alexandria and Cairo, Egypt	London, England
Accra, Ghana	Paris, France
Conakry, Guinea	Frankfurt, Germany
Monrovia, Liberia	Geneva, Switzerland
Ibadan & Lagos, Nigeria	
Dakar, Senegal	**Middle East**
Khartoum, Sudan	Beirut, Lebanon
Addis Ababa, Ethiopia	Kuwait
Nairobi, Kenya	Jedda and Mecca, Saudi Arabia
Dar es Salaam, Tanzania	

Source: New York City Public Library, Schomburg Center for Research in Black Culture 2005b

Comb, Mississippi, in January 1965, Malcolm X stated: "In my opinion, the greatest accomplishment that was made in the struggle of the Black man in America in 1964 toward some kind of real progress was the successful linking together of our problem with the African problem or making our problem a world problem." (Malcolm X 2001, 67). This theme provided a foundation from which the next generation advanced the struggle for liberation from global imperialism.

Black Studies Movement and Black Arts Movement Assessments, 1966–1969

Malcolm X's message of cultural pride, self-study, critical analysis, and social protest reflects the concerns of many minority groups that would object to a history of racial, ethnic, gender, and class discrimination. Malcolm's public rhetoric served as a pedagogical approach for Black people that foreshadowed educational reforms which occurred after his death.

During the mid- to late-1960s came the call for curriculum reform that eventually led to the founding of Black/Africana Studies Departments and programs throughout the United States (Karenga 2002, 13–26). Such programs included the reexamination of ancient Africa and its contribution to world civilization. James Stewart accurately points out three key reasons for studying classical African civilizations: the problematic aspect of traditional research on this period, the rich intellectual history and traditions of Africa prior to those in Europe, and the importance of modern Black thought as it emanated from these past traditions. (Stewart 1997, 117–118) Because of information that has been lost, grossly distorted, or misinterpreted, an important aspect of the mission of Black/Africana Studies is to research the contributions of Africans in the diaspora as part of a reclamation project to address decades of neglect regarding the study of African people.

The demand for a Black Studies department at San Francisco State College (SFSC) in 1968 arose from both a student and a community need for education that would accurately address Black life and the problems facing Black people in their communities. As I have posited previously, Malcolm X was clearly a forerunner of the modern

Black/Africana Studies Movement (Smallwood 2001, 161–162; Smallwood 2005, 248–263).

Malcolm X laid a foundation of uncompromising Black cultural expression for Black people to follow. This became a significant influence on the Black Arts Movement of the late 1960s (Neal 1989, ix). It was Malcolm's charge that inspired a generation of Black artists to examine African American life. Malcolm also stated:

> Our cultural revolution must be the means of bringing us closer to our African brothers and sisters. It must begin in the community and be based on community participation. Afro-Americans will be free to create only when they can depend on the Afro-American community for support, and Afro-American artists must realize that they depend on the Afro-American community for inspiration. (Malcolm X 1970, 55)

In the article "The Social Background of the Black Arts Movement," Larry Neal (1987) vividly describes emerging Black artists and their function and purpose in documenting the Black experience. Neal first discusses the embrace of African philosophy and language by Leroi Jones (now Amiri Baraka) in *MUNTU* and his exploration of the blues in *Blues People*, making a broad statement about African American culture (Neal 1987, 12). Neal, later in his article, calls for academic research about the great street orators in Harlem during the 1960s, who "educated a lot of people" about their politics, history, and sociology in the urban areas of the northern United States. Neal sees this Harlem oral tradition as originating from Marcus Garvey and then continuing through Ed Davis and Malcolm X (Neal 1987, 13).

The Hip-Hop Movement and the Emergence of Rap Music, 1970s–1990s

When examining the origins of rap music, Maulana Karenga (2002) cites current research placing rap in the traditions of African culture and Black music, with the emphasis on oratory:

> The form clearly evolves in the tradition of oratorical modes such as "signifying" and "playing the dozens" as well as "rapping" in both the sense of political discourse and romantic "programming," in a word, the sense of skilled word use to achieve given ends. (412)

In his discussion of the jazz vocalists of the 1940s and 1950s, Karenga (2002) mentions that their combination of talking and singing laid the foundation for Black musicians in the 1960s to utilize oral tradition in music.

Rap as a modern-day musical genre originated from hip-hop culture. Hip-hop came initially from house and block parties attended primarily by Black and Latino youth in New York City's South Bronx during the mid-1970s. It then spread to other parts of the city and eventually to the larger metropolitan area. Artists such as Kool Herc, Africa Bambataa, D. J. Grandmaster Flash, and Kurtis Blow helped popularize the music locally and gain the attention of record companies (Jones 1994). Though only mildly popular during the 1970s, in the 1980s rap music became a major form of Black musical expression and gained worldwide popularity (Karenga 1994, 412). The emergence of rap music outside New York City has contributed to both the growth and the diversity of the genre.

The early twentieth-century expression of Black Nationalism and Pan Africanism was restated and explored by young African Americans of the 1950s and 1960s seeking social change. Then, after the civil rights era, the legacy of the Black liberation struggle found its way in the creative self-expression of urban social commentary in the hip-hop culture of the 1980s and 1990s, when early rap artists were introduced to and then gravitated toward Malcolm X's discourse—both his message and his oratorical style. We hear Malcolm's message (e.g., samples of his speeches) used by early Black musicians ranging from rapper Keith LeBlanc's "Malcolm X: No Sell Out" (1983) to the collaboration of popular hip-hop artists aka the *Stop the Violence Movement* and their single "Self-Destruction" (1989) to even the L.A. jazz group Black/Note's album *Jungle Music* (1994). His image was also used in several rap videos, including two by Public Enemy, "Night of the Living Baseheads" (1988) and "Fight the Power" (1989), and one by MC Hammer, "Help the Children" (1990). Malcolm would also be referred to or quoted by artists such as NWA, Wu-Tang Clan, and Lauryn Hill, among others (Marable 2002, 61). Some research has linked themes in the life and work of Malcolm X to themes found in the rap music of this era (e.g., the life of a hustler, being incarcerated, Islam, violence in Black communities, and the importance of Africa (Sales 1994, 5).

This resurgence of interest in Malcolm X coincided with the reexploration in current popular culture of the major events, music, and Black activists and artists from the 1960s. Some researchers and students of hip-hop culture have successfully argued that the development of rap music essentially opened the door for the sampling of music and spoken words by lesser-known Black musicians, poets, and political leaders/martyrs of the 1960s and then for introducing these individuals to the current generation. In the African tradition of the *griot*, or storyteller, the spoken word in songs by rap artists coming out of hip-hop culture helped to introduce the name and image of Malcolm X to another generation of Black youth, many of whom were born after his lifetime. The resurgence of Malcolm X in Hip-Hop culture also paved the way for filmmaker Spike Lee's *Malcolm X* (1992). In addition, it placed Malcolm X for the better (and quite probably for the worse) in the consciousness of mainstream popular culture via the mass media—which used him for mass-market consumption while failing to examine his ideology, both political and cultural.

Conclusion

Based on the extensive literature, including his autobiography and speeches, research by academicians, colleagues, contemporaries, community members, opponents, and, yes, some enemies, it is abundantly clear that Malcolm X's life represents the work of a significant leader, intellectual, and activist of the twentieth century. His public career and public statements have left a profound impact on understanding Black life in the twentieth and twenty-first centuries. Through Malcolm X's intelligence, the charisma of his leadership, the sincerity of his commitment, and his struggle for and service to African people, he deeply influenced the lives and thoughts of many others and gained attention as an agent of social change.

In addressing his legacy several weeks after his assassination, Shirley Graham Du Bois, the widow of W. E. B. Du Bois, whom Malcolm had met several months earlier in Ghana, read a statement from the *Los Angeles Herald-Dispatch* on Ghana Radio:

Malcolm X was in Los Angeles ten days ago organizing throughout this nation to teach black people unity, organization and authentic Islam. Malcolm X was assassinated because he was teaching the black man the Arab is your brother. "Don't fight the Arab! Don't allow yourself to be drawn into a bloody war in the Middle East which is inevitable!" (S. Du Bois 1965)

In her last radio interview in 1997, Malcolm's widow Betty Shabazz made several observations about her late husband:

Got to walk in his footsteps … when you look at what he was about: International sisterhood and brotherhood, still valid. Human rights for our people. And not just singularly for our people but for all people but somehow our people are always left out when we get to the finish line.… Our ability to understand self-defense and self-determination. Educational skills and professional career development for men as well as women and that we should take responsibility for our lives.

Malcolm garnered an even wider universal appeal in death than he had in life. The memories of his profound work ethic; of his respect for education; and of his dedication to liberation, social analysis, personal reassessment, and critical inquiry continue to make a profound global impact. Malcolm's influence, both during his life and after his death, has become evident in the different ideological positions expressed in the Africana Social Movements from the 1950s to the present.

References

Blumberg, Rhoda Lois. 1991. *Civil rights: The 1960s freedom struggle*. Rev. ed. Boston: Twayne Publishing.

Branham, Robert J. 1995. 'I was gone of debating': Malcolm X's prison debates and public confrontations. *Argumentation and Advocacy* 31 (3): 117–137.

Carson, Clayborne, David Garrow, Gerald Gill, Vincent Harding, and Darlene Clark Hine, eds. 1991. *Eyes on the prize: The civil rights reader*. New York: Penguin Books.

Clegg, Claude A. 1997. *An original man: The life and times of Elijah Muhammad*. New York: St. Martin's Press.

Colaiaco, James A. 1993. *Martin Luther King Jr.: Apostle of militant nonviolence*. New York: St. Martin's Press. (Orig. pub. 1988.)

Condo, Baba Zak. 1993. *Conspiracies: Unraveling the assassination of Malcolm X*. Washington, DC: Nubia Press.

Cone, James H. 1991. *Martin & Malcolm & America: A dream or a nightmare*. Maryknoll, NY.: Orbis Books.

DeCaro Jr., Louis A. 1996. *On the side of my people: A religious life of Malcolm X*. New York: New York University Press.

Du Bois, Shirley Graham. 1965. The beginning—not the end. Radio talk. March 17. Ghana Radio, Accra. Transcript, the John Henrik Clarke Papers. New York: New York City Public Library, Schomburg Center for Research in Black Culture.

Du Bois, W. E. B. 1968. *The autobiography of W. E. B. Du Bois*. New York: International Publishers.

Essien-Udom, E. U. *Black Nationalism: A search for identity*. Chicago: University of Chicago Press.

Federal Bureau of Investigation. 1995. File on Malcolm X. Microform. File CG 100-33593, slide 67D. Wilmington, DL: Scholarly Resources.

Goldman, Peter. 1979. *The death and life of Malcolm X*. Urbana, IL.: University of Illinois Press.

Jenkins, Robert L., and Mfanya Donald Tryman, eds. 2002. *The Malcolm X encyclopedia*. Westport, CT.: Greenwood Press.

Jones, J. T. IV. 1994. Kool Herc stakes claim to original Hip-Hop beat. *USA Today*, April 26, 4D.

Karenga, Maulana. 2002. *Introduction to Black Studies*. 3rd ed. Los Angeles: University of Sankore Press.

Karim, Benjamin. 1992. *Remembering Malcolm*. With Peter Skutches and David Gallen. New York: Carroll and Graff.

Lincoln, C. Eric. 1961. *The Black Muslims in America*. Boston, MA: Beacon Press.

Malcolm X. 1992. *The Autobiography of Malcolm X*. With Alex Haley. New York: Ballantine Books. (Orig. pub. 1965.)

Malcolm X. 1970. *Malcolm X: By any means necessary*. Ed. George Breitman. New York: Pathfinder Press.

Malcolm X. 2001. *Malcolm X talks to young people: Speeches in the U.S., Britain, and France*. Ed. Steve Clark. New York: Pathfinder Press. (Orig. pub. 1965.)

Malcolm X. 2006. Archival news footage from the *Seventy-Eighth Annual Academy Awards*, ABC TV, March 5, 2006.

Marable, M. 2002. Malcolm's life after death. *American Legacy* 8 (3): 45, 46, 49, 53, 54, 56, 61.

Neal, Larry. 1987. The social background of the Black Arts Movement. *The Black Scholar* 18 (1): 11–30.

_____. 1989. *Visions of a liberated future: Black Arts Movement writings*. New York: Thunder's Mouth Press.

New York City Public Library, Schomburg Center for Research in Black Culture. 2005a. The growing Nation of Islam: Selected Nation of Islam mosques organized by Malcolm X. Poster on display at exhibit *Malcolm X: A Search for Truth*, May 19, 2005–December 31. New York: New York City Public Library, Schomburg Center for Research in Black Culture.

_____. 2005b. Malcolm X's international and U.S. travels. Poster on display at exhibit *Malcolm X: A Search for Truth*, May 19–December 31. New York: New York City Public Library, Schomburg Center for Research in Black Culture.

Pinkney, Alphonso. 1975. *Black Americans*. 2nd ed. Englewood Cliffs, NJ.: Prentice Hall.

Perry, Bruce. 1991. *Malcolm: The life of a man who changed Black America*. Barrytown, NY: Station Hill Press.

Sales, William. 1994. *From civil rights to Black liberation: Malcolm X and the OAAU*. Boston, MA: South End Press.

Shabazz, Betty. 1997. Interview by Bernard White and Amy Goodman. *The Morning Show*. May 19. Pacifica Radio and WBAI, New York.

Smallwood, Andrew P. 2001. *An Afrocentric study of the intellectual development, leadership praxis and pedagogy of Malcolm X.* Lewiston, NY: Edwin Mellen Press.

_____. 2005. The intellectual creativity and public discourse of Malcolm X: A precursor to the modern Black Studies Movement. *Western Journal of Black Studies* 36 (2): 248–263.

Stewart, James B. 1997. Reaching for higher ground: Toward an understanding of Black/Africana Studies. In *Africana studies: A disciplinary quest for both theory and method*, ed. J. L. Conyers. Jefferson, NC.: McFarland.

Strickland, William. 1994. *Malcolm X: Make It Plain.* New York: Viking Press.

Turner, James E. 1977. Historical dialectics of Black Nationalist Movements in America. *Western Journal of Black Studies* 1 (3): 164–183.

2

"Message to the Grass Roots": Malcolm X's Analysis of Africana Culture and History

James L. Conyers, Jr.

Introduction

Whenever discussing Malcolm X, one may wonder about the paucity of research concerning his activism. Malcolm X is considered one of the most prominent black leaders of the twentieth century.[1] Indeed, Frederick Harper acknowledges the impact of Malcolm X on the Black Power and Black Arts Movements: "Great leaders also influence the time in which they live and the people around whom they live. Along the same line, it appears that Malcolm X had a significant influence on black militant leaders and on the philosophy of black militancy."[2] Additionally, Manning Marable claims:

> Malcolm X was the Black Power generation's greatest prophet, who spoke the uncomfortable truths that no one else had the courage or integrity to broach. Especially for young Black males, he personified for us everything we wanted to become: the embodiment of Black masculinist authority and power, uncompromising bravery in the face of racial oppression, the ebony standard for what the African-American liberation movement should be about.[3]

Richard Brent Turner adds:

> Even Malcolm X must be considered in the context of this process. After his death, he became an icon in African American culture; black artists, intellectuals, and celebrities tended to commodify his image and political ideas in a way that makes it easy to forget that Islam was at the center of his spiritual-political

---

1. Peter Goldman, "Malcolm X: Witness for the Prosecution," in *Black Leaders of the Twentieth Century*, eds. John Hope Franklin and August Meier, 305–330 (Urbana and Chicago: University of Illinois Press, 1982). (A journalist's review of the life and times of Malcolm X.)
2. Frederick D. Harper, "The Influence of Malcolm X on Black Militancy," *Journal of Black Studies* 1, no. 4 (1971): 387–402.
3. Manning Marable, "Rediscovering Malcolm's Life: A Historian's Adventure in Living History," *Souls* 7, no. 1 (2005): 20–35.

journey, beginning as Malcolm Little and progressing through Malcolm X to El-Hajj Malik El-Shabazz.[4]

In writing religious history or biography, the writer must locate his or her subject in place and time. Therefore, this essay is organized as follows: 1) a historical overview; 2) theory application; 3) methodology; and 4) conclusion and commentary. The essay asserts that Malcolm X's "Message" not only analyzed the operation of Africana culture as it pertains to blacks living in today's society but also (and simultaneously) attempted to develop a cursory analysis of past African phenomena. In his lecture "Message to the Grass Roots," Malcolm X was cognizant of allegory, metaphor, and symmetry in providing a common-sense perspective. For example, he narrates:

> We want to have just an off-the-cuff chat between you and me, us. We want to talk right down to earth in a language that everybody here can easily understand. We all agree tonight, all of the speakers have agreed, that America has a very serious problem. Not only does America have a very serious problem, but our people have a very serious problem. America's problem is us. We're her problem. The only reason she has a problem is she doesn't want us here. And every time you look at yourself, be it black, brown, red, yellow, a so-called Negro, you represent a person who poses such as a serious problem for America because you're not wanted. Once you face this as a fact, then you can start plotting a course that will make you appear intelligent, instead of unintelligent.[5]

This essay is also organized biographically—even as it analyzes the 1963 lecture. Bashir El Beshti compares an analysis to an autobiography, with emphasis on the latter's subject: "The autobiography, as a genre, is characterized by what might be called 'a double focus,' a split between the identity of the person whose life is being recounted and the voice of the person recounting."[6] Of interest is the analysis of Marable, who states that Malcolm X was the "ecumenical ebony standard for collective Blackness."[7] Furthermore, Michael Eric Dyson presents an intriguing evaluation:

> In large measure, the literature on Malcolm X has missed the mark, losing its way in the murky waters of psychology devoid of history, culture, and politics, substituting—given racial politics in the U.S.—necessary but defensive praise for critical appraisal, or becoming entrapped in insular ideological frameworks which neither illuminate nor surprise.[8]

---

4. Richard Brent Turner, *Islam and the African American Experience* (Bloomington: Indiana University Press, 2003), 239.

5. Malcolm X, *Malcolm X Speaks: Selected Speeches and Statements*, ed. George Breitman (New York: Grove, 1990), 4.

6. Bashir M. El Beshti, "The Semiotics of Salvation: Malcolm X and the Autobiographical Self," *Journal of Negro History* 82, no. 4 (1997): 359–367.

7. Marable, "Rediscovering Malcolm's Life," 20–35.

8. Michael Eric Dyson, "X Marks the Plots: A Critical Reading of Malcolm's Readers," *Social Text*, no. 35 (1993): 25–55.

Historical Overview

Malcolm X was born Malcolm Little at University Hospital in Omaha, Nebraska, on May 19, 1925. He was also known later in life by his Muslim name, El-Hajj Malik El-Shabazz. His parents, Earl Little and Louise Norton Little, were both active members of Marcus Garvey's Universal Negro Improvement Association, and they wrote for the UNIA newspaper, the *Negro World*.

The Little's home was reportedly attacked by Ku Klux Klansmen in December 1926, and the Littles immediately left for Milwaukee, Wisconsin. In January 1928, they moved to Lansing, Michigan. There, Earl Little, as an organizer for the Garvey movement, continued his community activism. In September 1931, his body was found beside the town's trolley tracks, cut in half by a trolley car. Historical accounts differ: some have claimed that local white-supremacist organizations committed the murder; others have speculated that his death was a suicide. Whatever the case, from 1931 to 1939, the Little family disintegrated. In 1939 Malcolm's mother, Louise, was diagnosed as legally insane and committed to the state mental hospital in Kalamazoo, Michigan, where she remained for more than twenty years. Malcolm began having problems with the social welfare system and was placed in foster care. He also spent time in juvenile detention homes.

By 1941 Malcolm had moved to the Roxbury section of Boston to live with his sister Ella. He held various jobs—as a laborer and a porter on the New Haven Railroad, for example. From 1944 to 1946 Malcolm was continually involved in illegal activity, resulting in a prison sentence of eight to ten years for burglary at the Charlestown (Massachusetts) Prison. There, he began to teach himself reading and writing. After being relocated to the Concord Reformatory in 1947, Malcolm was exposed to the teachings of Elijah Muhammad by a fellow inmate. His life was transformed: he was converted to Islam. Malcolm's siblings were also converted, and they, along with Malcolm, accepted membership into the Nation of Islam.

After fifteen months at the Concord Reformatory, Malcolm was transferred to Norfolk Prison Colony and then sent back to Charlestown to serve the remainder of his sentence. Paroled in 1952, he went to live with his brother Wilfred in Inkster, Michigan, where he worked as a furniture salesman. That same year he changed his last name to "X" to replace the "Little" that had been used by his slave ancestors and became an active member of the Nation of Islam.

From this point on, Malcolm X's activity in the Nation of Islam intensified. In the fall of 1953, he became first minister of Boston Temple No. 11; in March 1954, he was appointed acting minister of Philadelphia Temple No. 12; and in June of that year, he was appointed minister of New York Temple No. 7. His message in the temple and on the streets of Harlem stressed Black Nationalism and lambasted integration as a hoax.

At the same time, Malcolm X also made an important transition in his family life. In 1958, he married Betty Sanders. In November his first daughter, Attallah, was born. By 1965, Malcolm and Betty had six daughters.

Taking on the responsibilities and duties as a national spokesperson for the Nation of Islam, Malcolm traveled widely, expressing his views in television interviews, court cases involving civil rights, and forums on black equality and leadership. By 1963, however, his status was beginning to deteriorate within the leadership circle of the Nation of Islam. That year in Detroit, he gave one of his most influential lectures, "Message to the Grass Roots," arguing for Black Nationalism and thereby challenging Elijah Mohammad's conception of the Nation of Islam as a purely religious movement. Days later, he referred to the death of President John F. Kennedy as "chickens coming home to roost." Immediately after making this comment, he was suspended from his position as national spokesperson for the Nation of Islam and banned from public speaking for ninety days. In March 1964, after his period of suspension, he announced that he was leaving the Nation of Islam to establish Muslim Mosque Incorporated and the Organization of Afro-American Unity. He also moderated his views and moved toward accommodation with Martin Luther King, Jr.'s crusade for civil rights.

In April 1964 Malcolm made a hajj to Mecca to fulfill the religious requirement of all Muslims. This period also served as time for self-reflection and meditation. When he returned to the United States and founded the Organization of Afro-American Unity, he hoped to link the freedom struggles of blacks in Africa with those in the United States. The end came on February 21, 1965, when he was assassinated by four gunmen while giving a speech at the Audubon Ballroom in Harlem.

Malcolm X was only thirty-nine years old when he died, but in that brief lifespan, he became one of the most important African American leaders of the twentieth century. Although often out of step with civil rights leaders because of his separatist views and his refusal to eschew violent means of change, he nurtured pride and self-respect in African Americans, and more than anyone else, he reestablished their connection to Africa.[9]

Theory Application

This essay employs a theory called the Ujima paradigm, which focuses on the description and evaluation of Africana phenomena by using variables such as cosmology, ontology, epistemology, axiology, and social ecology. Using this paradigm will assist the researcher in organizing, sifting, and examining data by means of an alternative kind of analysis. According to Creswell, the basic stages of such an analysis are as follows: developing a theory; discerning patterns of theories; categorizing data and information; posing queries to shape and format research; and gathering data to prepare research findings.[10]

On the other hand, communication scholars may opt to examine Malcolm X's "Message to the Grass Roots" by means of Structuration theory.[11] However, this theory, with its sole emphasis on connecting to the culture of involuntary immigrants, may not be appropriate for examining phenomena with a multilayered approach. Such an approach provides fresh perspectives and analyses concerning Malcolm X—especially his "Message" in November 1963. Indeed, Dyson asserts: "Malcolm X was too complex a historic figure ... to be viewed through a monocular theoretical gaze or narrow cultural prism."[12] Gerald Horne agrees with Dyson when, in reference to researching the historiography of Malcolm X, he defines the term *myth* as "useful parables and allegories containing

---

9. The following sources were used in compiling this section of the essay: David Gallen, ed., *A Malcolm X Reader* (New York: Carroll and Graf Publishers, Inc., 1994); Malcolm X (with Alex Haley), *The Autobiography of Malcolm X* (New York: Grove, 1965); and Theresa Perry, ed., *Teaching Malcolm X* (New York: Routledge, 1996).

10. John W. Creswell, *Research Design: Qualitative and Quantitative Approaches* (Thousand Oaks, CA: Sage, 1994), 96.

11. Oscar H. Gandy, Jr., *Communication and Race* (New York: Arnold, 1998), 32.

12. Dyson, "X Marks the Plots," 25–55.

Table 1. Biographical Profile of Malcolm X

May 19, 1925	Malcolm Little is born in Omaha, NE.
1929	The family's Lansing, MI, home is burned to the ground.
1931	Malcolm's father is found dead on the town's trolley tracks.
1946	Malcolm is sentenced to 8–10 years for armed robbery; serves 6½ years at Charlestown, MA State Prison.
1948–49	Malcolm converts to the Nation of Islam while in prison.
1953	Malcolm changes name from Malcolm Little to Malcolm X and becomes assistant minister of the Nation of Islam's Detroit Temple.
1954	Malcolm X is promoted to minister of the Nation of Islam's New York Temple.
1958	Malcolm X marries Betty Sanders in Lansing, Michigan.
1959	Malcolm X travels to the Middle East and Africa.
1963	The Nation of Islam orders Malcolm X to be silent, allegedly because of his remarks concerning President Kennedy's assassination.
1964	Malcolm X leaves the Nation of Islam and starts his new organization, Muslim Mosque, Inc., in March.
1964	Malcolm X travels to the Middle East and Africa in April.
1964	Malcolm X starts the Organization of Afro-American Unity (OAAU), a secular political group, in May.
1965	Malcolm X's home is firebombed on February 14.
1965	Malcolm X is assassinated as he begins speaking at the Audubon Ballroom, New York, February 21.

lessons for today [that] help to explain the world."[13] In addition, Nancy Clasby, in order to describe and evaluate the intellectual ideas of Malcolm X, presents an alternative paradigm from Franz Fanon's three-stage model of development: "1. The native identity evolves from a numbing violence of colonialism, 2. Dream state of the native, and 3. Emotional sensitivity of the native."[14] Furthermore, Hank Flick provides a paradigm in order to examine the historical and political stereotypes (or "myths") concerning African Americans and the correctives which Malcolm X used to "counteract" such stereotypes:

The myths Malcolm identifies were, (1) blacks were animals, (2) blacks were a minority, and (3) integration was a concept that served and was supported by a majority of Black Americans. In regard to the presence of these myths, Malcolm designed his own model to examine and counteract them. His paradigm of myth inversion involved a series of steps that involved him in, (1) identifying the myth, (2) locating its purpose, author, and origin, and (3) noting the antidote needed in order to counteract such a myth.[15]

Finally, Molefi Asante affirms Flick's paradigm:

13. Gerald Horne, "'Myth'" and the Making of 'Malcolm X,'" *American Historical Review* 98, no. 2 (1993): 440–450.

14. Nancy Clasby, "The Autobiography of Malcolm X: A Mythic Paradigm," *Journal of Black Studies* 5, no. 1 (1974): 18–34.

15. Hank Flick, "Malcolm X: Destroyer and Creator of Myths," *Journal of Black Studies* 12, no. 2 (1981): 166–181.

In reality, Malcolm was an astute observer of the historical conditions of African Americans and he saw that in the serious reconstruction of African culture, the struggle for power and the ability to create categories which are accepted by others frequently played a much more important role than economic necessity.... By virtue of its affirming posture this new view of culture became, in Malcolm's theory, a critique of oppressive reality. This critique was presented in Malcolm's rhetoric as a missile against the enemies of the African American people.[16]

Cosmology

The concepts of worldview and praxis are essential when one examines humans' interaction with one another. Throughout his "Message to the Grass Roots," Malcolm X first showed common sense as well as an ability to think critically. By this, I mean that he not only made his subject plain but also presented it using metaphor and simile. Second, he addressed the dilemma of commonalities in America, regarding culture, religion, and world politics. Third, directly and indirectly, he assessed issues and schemas concerning the enslavement of Africana people. George Breitman states:

> When some people speak of integration, they mean any action, court ruling or law that eliminates segregation or discrimination in one or more areas. They call it integration if one Negro is added to a police force or if five Negro children are admitted to a previously all-white school. Some in the group assert that integration already exists in the North, and that the task is to make the South like the North, but that it will become integrated by the addition of separate acts of desegregation, one by one, over an indefinite period of time. Integration, thus defined, is condemned and rejected by many black people as tokenism and gradualism. It is not that they object to the desegregation of any one or more areas, but that they see this concept of integration as a trick or device for denying them genuine and complete freedom now or in the foreseeable future.[17]

Ontology

By assessing the nature of being, one can locate a number of points that reflect problems and issues concerning the systematic subordination of Africana people. However, Malcolm X defined *humanism* holistically. In fact, he felt that humanism is so effortlessly cultivated that ideas about privilege and systematic and institutional racism provide a context for raising alternative queries and ideas. For example, Malcolm X once discussed the 1954 Bandung Conference, which addressed directly and indirectly how people of color were able to develop alliances to examine political, social, and economic issues on an international basis. Additionally, when Malcolm X founded the Organiza-

---

16. Molefi Kete Asante, *Malcolm X as Cultural Hero and Other Afrocentric Essays* (Trenton, NJ: Africa World Press, 1993), 29.

17. George Breitman, *The Last Year of Malcolm X: The Evolution of a Revolutionary* (New York: Schoken Books, 1968), 52.

tion of Afro-American Unity in 1964, he provided an alternative praxis for people of Africana descent to organize for long-term planning. Concerning the Bandung Conference, Malcolm stated:

> In Bandung back in, I think 1954, was the first unity meeting in centuries of black people. And once you study what happened at the Bandung conference, and the results of the Bandung conference, it actually serves as a model for the same procedure you and I can use to get our problems solved. At Bandung all the nations came together, the dark nations from Africa and Asia. Some of them were Buddhists, some of them were Muslims, some of them were Christians, some were Confucianists, and some were atheists. Despite their religious differences, they came together. Some were communists, some were socialists, some were capitalists — despite their economic and political differences, they came together. All of them were black, brown, red or yellow.[18]

Epistemology

Developing bodies of knowledge is an important aspect relevant to discourse. In his "Message to the Grass Roots," Malcolm X provided an alternative body of knowledge based on the historical and cultural experiences of Africana people. He addressed this basis through two comparative analyses. First, he pointed out similarities and differences in "the Black and Negro Revolution." Malcolm contended that one of the priorities of warfare is to acquire land. To some, this priority can be examined within the entangled contexts of colonialism and imperialism. Malcolm offered three examples in support of his contention: the American Revolution, the French Revolution, and the Russian Revolution. All three wars, Malcolm claimed, eventually led to the acquisition of land. Malcolm's second comparative analysis focused on the House Negro and the Field Negro. The House Negro empathized (and thus may have felt at least some equality) with the oppressor, while the Field Negro felt only subordinate to the suppressor and experienced the consequences of genocide. As an even more important aspect relevant to Malcolm's discourse, Robin D. G. Kelley points out that Malcolm classified Black leadership into three categories:

> When it came to attacking and ridiculing the black bourgeoisie, Malcolm was perhaps the least charitable of the NOI leadership. He called them "house slaves," "Uncle Toms," "Nincompoops with Ph.D.s," "Quislings," "sell-outs," and, of course, "bourgeois negroes." And all of these terms did not necessarily mean the same thing. Malcolm essentially spoke of different categories. First, there were the elite he knew as a teenager: working-class black folk with upper-class pretensions. By trying to adopt the mannerism of the authentic bourgeoisie, this nouveau riche (without the wealth!) carved out for themselves a whole black elite culture. Second, there were the truly wealthy blacks whose social and cultural lives were inseparable from that of the white elite. He excoriated such people. And, finally, there were the self-proclaimed black leaders, the "handkerchief heads" who ran integrationist organizations and begged for Civil Rights. In Malcolm's view, all three categories of the black bourgeoisie shared a common disdain for the culture of the black masses. Indeed, Malcolm

---

18. Malcolm X, *Malcolm X Speaks*, 5.

usually identified the black bourgeoisie by its culture rather than its income or occupation.[19]

Interestingly, Celeste Condit and John Lucaites classify Malcolm's oratory and rhetoric into four categories: (1) dissent with vision; (2) dissent with a mystic vision—speaking in; (3) a dissenting rhetoric—Malcolm X speaks out; and (4) beyond dissent—the search for a constructive rhetoric.[20] Furthermore, Harper lists four features of Malcolm's expressive commentary: (1) leadership, (2), intelligence, (3), charisma, and (4) creativity.[21] In addition, Nancy Clasby addresses the evolution of Malcolm's discourse: "Malcolm's effort to create himself anew necessitated the breakdown of the old master-slave relationship which characterized the ties of the black minority to white society. In order to break the relationship and cleanse himself overt resistance was essential."[22]

Axiology

Regarding the relativity of values, one might ask: How did Malcolm X describe, and differentiate between, the values, norms, and mores of Africana people? To answer the question: Malcolm X focused his political philosophy on Africana Nationalism. Indeed, he used the terms "Black Nationalism" and "global Pan-Africanism" interchangeably throughout his "Message to the Grass Roots." Equally important, Malcolm X surveyed independence movements in Africa during the 1950s and 1960s. He began his survey by assessing the independence movement in the Gold Coast. In 1957, the British colony obtained its independence from Great Britain and changed its name to Ghana (land of gold). Y. N. Kly claims:

> On the other hand, socialist scholars rightly realize that after his break with The Honorable Elijah Muhammad, Malcolm developed a distinct political philosophy of national liberation, but they confuse his development of a distinctly political philosophy with having dropped Islam as a guiding orientation, and thus in aspersing him they tend to ignore too much the Islamic as well as pre-Islamic background and depth of his thinking. This results in a confused understanding of his view of national liberation and revolution and a tendency to interpret his concept of national liberation as interchangeable at all points with his concept of revolution.[23]

Darren Davis and Christian Davenport express a similar assessment concerning this confused understanding of Malcolm's views: "The influence of Malcolm X may also be seen in the alteration in attitudes about politics and Malcolm himself."[24]

---

19. Robin D. G. Kelley, "House Negroes on the Loose: Malcolm X and the Black Bourgeoisie," *Callaloo* 21 no. 2 (1998): 419–435.

20. Celeste M. Condit and John L. Lucaites, "Malcolm X and the Limits of the Rhetoric of Revolutionary Dissent," *Journal of Black Studies* 23, no. 3 (1993): 291–313.

21. Harper, "The Influence of Malcolm X on Black Militancy," 387–402.

22. Clasby, "The Autobiography of Malcolm X," 18–34.

23. Yusuf Naim Kly, *The Black Book: The True Political Philosophy of Malcolm X (El-Hajj Malik El-Shabazz)* (Windsor, Ontario: Clarity International, 1986), 22.

24. Darren W. Davis and Christian Davenport, "The Political and Social Relevancy of Malcolm X: The Stability of African American Political Attitudes," *The Journal of Politics* 59, no. 2 (1997): 550–54.

Social Ecology

When using the term *social ecology*, I am referring to the social and environmental factors that shaped and perhaps influenced the landscape of 1963, the year in which Malcolm X delivered his "Message to the Grass Roots." Table 2 provides a chronological listing of events during the calendar year 1963, which include both African and American history.

In addition, Diagram 1 provides a synthesis of four theories that can be used to examine Malcolm's celebrated lecture. The images in the diagram are those from the Akan culture: the Asante stool and the Djembe drum. The data, as presented in the diagram (and as represented by images of the Asante stool), show that in his "Message to the Grass Roots," Malcolm X intended to analyze Africana culture and history.

Methodology

Methodology means the kind of research used in secondary analysis. Therefore (of course), in order to examine Malcolm X's "Message to the Grass Roots" methodologically, I employed triangulation by using tools from historical analysis and the ethnography of communication. *Triangulation* can be defined in many ways. As Bruce L. Berg puts it: "[Triangulation is] a form of multiple operationalism or convergent validation.... .[It is] used largely to describe multiple data collection technologies designed to measure a single concept or construct.... For many researchers, triangulation is restricted to the use of multiple data gathering techniques (usually three) to investigate the same phenomenon. This is interpreted as a means of mutual confirmation of measures and validation of findings."[25] This particular study is organized according to what Abbas and Charles Teddlie call "parallel/simultaneous studies."[26] Still, with the query centered on methodology and the outline plan of study, this part of the essay is a qualitative assessment of the examination of Malcolm X's "Message to the Grass Roots." The advantages of using a qualitative approach are numerous. Moreover, in a survey component, John Creswell addresses this point by writing: "Criteria: Researcher's World View; Qualitative Paradigm—A researcher's comfort with the ontological, epistemological, axiological, rhetorical, and methodological assumptions of the qualitative paradigm."[27]

Indeed, emphasizing a precise rhetorical assessment of Malcolm X, Table 2 provided a socioecological landscape of the calendar year 1963. With this landscape, we were able to review the social climate and the political issues as they related to Malcolm X. In Table 3, the emphasis on collecting data is directed to examining the topics of discussion Malcolm X presented during the calendar year 1963. Admittedly, this table is not exhaustive; however, it reflects the invited lectures given by Malcolm X. In fact, the "Message to the Grass Roots" attempts to discuss the issues of dialectical materialism in examining Africana phenomena. *The Columbia Encyclopedia* defines *dialectical materi-*

25. Bruce L. Berg, *Qualitative Research Methods for Social Science*, 3rd ed. (Boston: Allyn and Bacon, 1989), 5.

26. Abbas Teddlie and Charles Teddlie, *Mixed Methodology: Combining Qualitative and Quantitative Approaches*, Applied Research Methods Series (Thousand Oaks, CA: Sage, 1998), 18.

27. Creswell, *Research Design*, 9.

Table 2.   Social Ecology of the Civil Rights Movement in 1963

January 14, 1963	George C. Wallace becomes Governor of Alabama (Democrat).	Alabama
January 28, 1963	Harvey Gantt, an African American student, desegregates Clemson University, in South Carolina.	Clemson, SC
February 8, 1963	United States places bans on financial, travel, and commercial transactions with Cuba.	Washington, DC
February 13, 1963	Malcolm X leads an Islamic demonstration in Times Square.	New York, NY
February 17, 1963	Michael Jordan, NBA Basketball Player is born.	Brooklyn, NY
March 18, 1963	United States Supreme Court rules that the poor must have legal representation. (*Gideon vs. Wainwright*)	Washington, DC
March 27, 1963	Alcatraz, a federal penitentiary, is closed.	San Francisco, CA
April 16, 1963	Dr. Martin L. King, Jr., is arrested and writes his "Letter From A Birmingham City Jail."	Birmingham, AL
May 4, 1963	City Commissioner Eugene "Bull" Connor unleashes dogs on Black protestors.	Birmingham, AL
	Sidney Poitier wins the Academy Award for his performance in "Lilies of the Field."	
	Free jazz improvisation movement takes shape with artists such as Ornette Coleman, Eric Dolphy, and Sun Ra.	
May 15, 1963	Mercury Program: NASA launches the last mission of this space program.	Houston, TX
May 23, 1963	Fidel Castro, dictator of Cuba, visits the Soviet Union.	Moscow, Russia
May 25, 1963	The Organization of African Unity is established under the leadership of Haile Selassie.	Addis Ababa, Ethiopia
May 28, 1963	Sit-ins, Mississippi Summer Freedom.	Mississippi
June 11, 1963	George C. Wallace, then Governor of Alabama, blocks a door at the University of Alabama in an attempt to stop desegregation by two Black students, Vivian Malone and James Hood.	Tuscaloosa, AL
June 12, 1963	Medgar Evers is assassinated outside his home.	Jackson, MS
August 10, 1963	Malcolm speaks at Unity rally in Harlem.	New York, NY
August 18, 1963	James Meredith becomes the first African American to graduate from the University of Mississippi.	Oxford, MS
August 27, 1963	Dr. W. E. B. Du Bois makes his eternal transition.	Accra, Ghana
1963	Throughout 1963, more than 100 of the 130 AFL-CIO chapters and affiliates pledge to abolish segregation.	
August 1963	Imam Warith Deen Mohammed is released from serving a two-year prison sentence for evading the draft; months later he leaves the Nation of Islam.	

Table 2. *Continued*

August 28, 1963	March on Washington, DC.	Washington, DC
August 28, 1963	Malcolm X attends March on Washington as a critical observer; he comments that he can't understand why Negroes should become so excited about a demonstration "run by whites in front of a statue of a president who has been dead for a hundred years and who didn't like us when he was alive."	Washington, DC
August/Sept. 1963	Max Roach records album titled, "Freedom Now Suite."	New York, NY
Sept. 15, 1963	16th Street Church is bombed.	Birmingham, AL
October 7, 1963	SNCC organizes Freedom Day.	Selma, AL
October 9, 1963	Uganda becomes a republic.	Uganda
October 22, 1963	Malcolm X delivers speech to students at Wayne State University.	Detroit, MI
November 2, 1963	South Vietnamese President Ngo Dinh Diem is assassinated.	Saigon
November 6, 1963	Coup leader General Duong Van Minh takes over leadership of South Vietnam.	Saigon
Nov. 10, 1963	Malcolm X delivers his lecture, "Message to the Grass Roots."	Detroit, MI
Nov. 16, 1963	Newspaper strike.	Toledo, OH
Nov. 22, 1963	President John F. Kennedy is assassinated.	Dallas, TX
Nov. 24, 1963	Alleged assassin Lee Harvey Oswald is shot by Jack Ruby.	Dallas, TX
Nov. 29, 1963	President Lyndon B. Johnson establishes the Warren Commission.	Washington, DC
December 1, 1963	At an NOI rally in New York, Malcolm states that Kennedy "never foresaw that the chickens would come home to roost so soon," despite a directive from Elijah Muhammad that no Muslim minister comment on the assassination.	New York, NY
December 4, 1963	Malcolm is suspended and silenced by Elijah Muhammad from his ministry for ninety days for his remark on the death of the president.	Chicago, IL
Dec. 12, 1963	Kenya declares its independence from Great Britain.	

Diagram 1

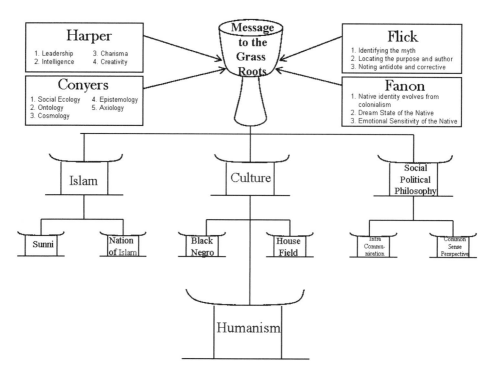

alism as follows: "In theory dialectical materialism is meant to provide both a general world view and a specific method for the investigation of scientific problems. The basic tenets are that everything is material and that change takes place through 'the struggle of opposites.'"[28] However, Africana socialism refers to the collective expression and communication centered on Africana cultural values and thought.

Conclusion and Commentary

The purpose of this article was to examine Malcolm X's "Message to the Grass Roots," a lecture presented on November 10, 1963. First, I addressed the thematic points of points in the lecture. Second, I applied theory and method in order to describe and evaluate the lecture. Third, I provided tables and a diagram to enumerate the ideas expressed in the lecture and to show how scholars have attempted to describe Malcolm X's paradigmatic approach in addressing the systematic subordination of Africana people at both national and international levels. To some, this lecture was considered one of the most significant ever given by Malcolm, even though his "Message" was delivered near the end of his association with the Nation of Islam as its national spokesperson. In addition, given the climate of controversy and hate in America during and before his lifetime, he addressed issues which some referred to as prophetic. Last,

---

28. *The Columbia Encyclopedia*, Sixth Edition, s.v. "Dialectical Materialism," www.bartleby.com/65/di/dialcti-mat.html.

Table 3. Lectures by Malcolm X in 1963

Mosque #7, New York, NY	January 1, 1963	A Night with the NOI.
East Lansing, MI	January 23, 1963	Malcolm X speaks on the Race Problem in America at the invitation of the African Students Association and the campus chapter of the NAACP, Michigan State University, East Lansing, MI.
Hi-Fi Country Club Charlotte, NC	January 30, 1963	Lecture at the Hi-Fi Country Club.
New York, NY	February 13, 1963	Muslim Demonstration in Times Square.
New York, NY	June 29, 1963	Muslim rally in Harlem, 115th Street and Lenox Avenue.
HARLEM Unity Rally	August 10, 1963	Malcolm X speaks on the Black Revolution at the invitation of Adam Clayton Powell, Abyssinian Baptist.
Philadelphia, PA	September 1963	The Old Negro and the New Negro.
Wayne State University, Detroit, MI	October 22, 1963	Malcolm X delivers lecture to students at Wayne State University.
Northern Grass Roots Leadership Conference Detroit, MI	Nov. 10, 1963	Malcolm X delivers "Message to the Grass Roots."
OAAU Rally, Audubon Ballroom, New York, NY	Dec. 13, 1963	Malcolm X speaks on the Afro-American problem as a world problem, with Dick Gregory and Babu.
Harvard Law School Forum	Dec. 16, 1963	Malcolm X speaks on the African Revolution and It's Impact on the American Negro.*

* Malcolm X Research Web Site, http://www.brothermalcolm.net/mxtimeline.html

the events that occurred in 1963, the year in which the lecture was presented, constituted a period of protest and activism by Africana people.

In closing, my goal was not to present a rhetorical analysis of Malcolm X's "Message to the Grass Roots" but to examine the lasting contributions of Malcolm X himself by borrowing some tools from communication ethnography, by using secondary analysis and historical analysis as major methods of research, and by triangulating data. Perhaps, as scholars study the life and contributions of Malcolm X, they might become cognizant that Malcolm X had a shadow cabinet of officials who provided information to him and that he used social science and humanistic approaches in describing and evaluating information.

3

From Malcolm X to Omowale Malik Shabazz: The Transformation and Its Impact on the Black Liberation Struggle

Akiniyele K. Umoja

On March 12, 1964, Malcolm X publicly made his break with the Nation of Islam (NOI) and eleven months later began to chart a new political course. Malcolm's new political agenda represented not only a break with the politics of the NOI but with elements of North American Black Nationalism. Malcolm became the ideological father of a new nationalist movement, often called the Black Power movement, which began to emerge during the late 1960s. Organizations such as the Revolutionary Action Movement (RAM), the Black Panther Party (BPP), the Provisional Government of the Republic of New Afrika (PGRNA), the Congress of African People (CAP), the US Organization, the League of Revolutionary Black Workers (LRBW), and the Student Non-Violent Coordinating Committee (SNCC) (during its Black Power period) all cite some ideological and inspirational connection with Malcolm X. This essay argues that after leaving the Nation of Islam, Malcolm X began to articulate and attempt to develop a new model for Black Nationalism. Aspects of his new model were incorporated into the political culture of Black Power organizations of the 1960s and are institutionalized in contemporary nationalist groups.

This essay also argues that Malcolm's new nationalist model was quite different from the old, or fundamental, Black Nationalism. Influenced by anticolonial national liberation movements in Afrika,[1] Asia, and the Americas, Malcolm began to develop ideological positions that challenged the perceptions and practices of the fundamental Black Nationalists in North America in previous eras. The new nationalist model differed from fundamental Black Nationalism in ways such as leadership and decision-making style, the perspective on the role of women in the liberation movement, the ideological orientation of social change, and the view of Afrikans in Afrika.

In his seminal work *Black Nationalism: A Search for an Identity in America*, E. U. Essien-Udom describes the character of Black Nationalism in the United States from the nineteenth century until the early 1960s. From the post-World War I era to the early

---

1. As a form of cultural self-determination and in order to be consistent with the practice of many Afrika-centered intellectuals and activists since the early 1970s, this author spells *Afrika* with a *k* rather than with a *c*. (In many written Afrikan languages, *Afrika* is spelled with a *k*.)

1960s, he identifies two basic forms of Black Nationalism. One is the Islamic-oriented nationalism of the Moorish Science Temple and the Nation of Islam. The other is the more secular Afrikan Nationalism of the Universal Negro Improvement Association (UNIA) and other similar organizations. The Moorish Science Temple and the Nation of Islam rejected Christianity as the "white man's religion" and acknowledged Islam as the "Black man's religion." The Islamic-oriented nationalists emphasized a rejection of the Negro American identity in favor of an Asiatic one.[2] Both the Moorish Science Temple and the Nation of Islam established separatist institutions for Black people. In addition, both organizations criticized "the White man" with rhetoric rather than political activity that would confront American polity. Whereas the political objective of the Moorish Science Temple was ambiguous, the Nation of Islam desired political separation from the United States. Its political program called for the repatriation of Blacks to Afrika or the establishment of an independent territory for Blacks in North America.[3]

Unlike Islamic-oriented Black Nationalists, the UNIA was an ecumenical movement. While most of its members were Christian (affiliated with the Christian African Orthodox Church that was prominent in the organization), Muslims, Hebrews, and atheists were also active in the UNIA. The Christians in the UNIA were from a variety of denominations. While the UNIA leader Marcus Garvey promoted a Christian message that included Black images of biblical personalities, he also recognized his spiritually diverse constituency by promoting religious tolerance.[4] The UNIA's focus was uniting Afrikan people on the basis of racial nationalism, with an emphasis on political and economic independence. The long-range political objective of the UNIA was to establish a strong racial empire in Afrika that would protect the interests of Afrikan people worldwide.[5] The establishment of such an empire was to be based upon the European patriarchal and capitalist model of nation building through "science and religion."[6]

In his early youth, Malcolm X was politically influenced by Black Nationalism. His parents were local officers in Marcus Garvey's Universal Negro Improvement Association.[7] During Malcolm's incarceration, his siblings recruited him into Elijah Muhammad's Nation of Islam. His membership in the NOI transformed him from his former life of crime to that of a Black Nationalist. After leaving the NOI, Malcolm initiated practices and ideological positions that distinguished his perspectives from those of his nationalist predecessors.[8]

---

2. E. U. Essien-Udom, *Black Nationalism: A Search for an Identity in America* (Chicago: University of Chicago Press, 1969), 33–36.

3. Ibid., 258–64.

4. Tony Martin, *Race First: The Ideological and Organization Struggle of Marcus Garvey and the Universal Negro Improvement Association* (Dover, MA: The Majority Press, 1986), 69–77.

5. Essien-Udom, *Black Nationalism*, 36–38.

6. Marcus Garvey, "African Fundamentalism," Marcus Garvey.com, http://www.marcusgarvey.com/african.htm.

7. Jan Carew, *Ghosts in Our Blood: With Malcolm X in Africa, England, and the Caribbean* (Chicago: Lawrence Hill, 1994), ix–x, 130–31; Spike Lee, with Ralph Wiley, *By Any Means Necessary: The Trails and Tribulations of the Making of* Malcolm X (New York: Hyperion, 1992), 47. Malcolm's parents, Earl and Louise Little, were both active members of the UNIA. They met each other at a UNIA meeting in Montreal, Canada. Earl was a UNIA organizer, and Louise wrote articles for the UNIA publication, the *Negro World*.

8. William Sales, *Malcolm X and the Organization of Afro-American Unity* (Boston: South End Press, 1994), 59–73.

Malcolm's Split from the NOI

Brother Malcolm first received national and international attention as an organizer, minister, and national spokesperson for the Nation of Islam. With Malcolm as a major force within the NOI, the organization grew from three temples to over one hundred during the eleven years he was a member of the organization.[9] There is no doubt that Malcolm's determination, his organizational and oratorical ability, and his sincerity helped develop the NOI into the premier Black Nationalist organization of the 1950s and early 1960s.

Malcolm's militant rhetoric and radical stands threatened the hierarchy of the NOI that surrounded the organization's leader Elijah Muhammad. They feared Malcolm's radical nationalist statements brought too much attention to the organization by the U.S. government. Still others were jealous of the close relationship Malcolm shared with Muhammad, of the respect and love he had developed in the Black community, and of the attention he had gained from the American media. Members of the national leadership, including members of Muhammad's family, had begun to live comfortable lives as the organization expanded and prospered. Since Elijah Muhammad was aging and his health was beginning to deteriorate, those who had become comfortable because of the success and growth of the movement felt threatened by the possibility of Malcolm's replacing Muhammad as the supreme leader of the NOI.[10] Malcolm's enemies within the NOI hierarchy included Raymond Sharrief, Supreme Captain of the Fruit of Islam (FOI) (the men's society and paramilitary wing of the NOI), John Ali, National Secretary of the NOI, and Elijah Muhammad, Jr., Assistant Supreme Captain of the Fruit of Islam. Other ministers and officials, including New York FOI Captain Joseph X. Gravitts (aka Yusuf Shah) participated in covert attacks on Malcolm X in internal organizational struggles.[11]

Elements of the hierarchy moved to isolate Malcolm within the organization. Eventually Malcolm was placed on a ninety-day suspension for having made a statement regarding the death of U.S. President John F. Kennedy. In violation of an order by Elijah Muhammad that Muslims remain silent on the death of the President, Malcolm claimed that Kennedy's assassination was an example of the "chickens coming home to roost." In other words, the violence that America had perpetrated against Afrikans and other colonized peoples had come home to haunt white America. Malcolm stated further:

> I said the hate in white men had not stopped with the killing of defenseless black people, but that hate, allowed to spread unchecked, finally had struck

9. Clifton Marsh, *From Black Muslims to Muslims: The Transition from Separatism to Islam, 1930–1980* (Metuchen, NJ: The Scarecrow Press, 1979), 73; Martha Lee, *The Nation of Islam, An American Millenarian Movement* (Lewiston, NY: The Edwin Mellen Press, 1988), 53–55.

10. M. Karenga, "Malcolm and the Messenger: Beyond Psychological Assumptions to Political Analysis," *Black News* 4, no. 21 (1982): 4–7; Benjamin Karim, with Peter Skutches and David Gallen, *Remembering Malcolm: The Story of Malcolm X from Inside the Muslim Mosque by His Assistant Minister Benjamin Karim* (New York: Carroll and Graf, 1992), 128–148.

11. Zak Kondo, *Conspiracy: Unraveling the Assassination of Malcolm X* (Washington, DC: Nubia Press, 1993), 65.

down this country's Chief of State. I said it was the same thing as had happened with Medgar Evers, Patrice Lumumba, with Madame Nhu's husband.[12]

After his ninety-day suspension for his statement and violation of Muhammad's order, Malcolm's suspension (along with his silence) was extended indefinitely. During the initial ninety-day suspension, Malcolm sensed a conspiracy against him within the leadership of the NOI and decided that he could best work toward the liberation of Afrikans inside the U.S. if he was unfettered by the increasingly conservative organization.[13]

Convinced he would never be allowed to function meaningfully within the NOI again, in January 1964 Malcolm began to meet with others for the purpose of forming a new organization: Muslims dissatisfied with the NOI hierarchy's corruption and lack of political activism; and intellectuals and activists inclined toward Pan-Afrikanism, nationalism, and radical politics. Those involved in these early meetings included historian John Henrik Clarke, author John Oliver Killens, television producer Lynn Shifflet, and writer Peter Bailey.[14] In March 1964, when Malcolm declared his independence from the NOI, he also announced the formation of a new organization, the Muslim Mosque, Incorporated (MMI). Like the NOI, the MMI would provide "a religious base and the spiritual force necessary" to attack vices which "destroy the moral fiber" of Black communities in America.[15] While the name "Muslim Mosque, Incorporated" suggested a religious organization, Malcolm initially intended that membership be open to any person of Afrikan descent, regardless of his or her religion. In a fund-raising and recruitment letter (signed, "Malcolm X, Minister of Muslim Mosque, Inc."), the MMI membership was described as open to anyone "who is sincerely interested in creating a better life and a better world for 22 million Afro-Americans."[16] The MMI was designed to have a Black Nationalist political, economic, and social program. Despite Malcolm's nondenominational intentions, the Islamic name discouraged some non-Muslims from joining the MMI.[17] After returning from his trip to Afrika in May 1964, he announced the formation of the Organization of Afro-American Unity (OAAU) on June 28.

With the creation of the OAAU, Malcolm envisioned the two organizations (the MMI and the OAAU) as possessing different functions. While the MMI continued as a religious organization propagating orthodox Islam in the United States, the OAAU was to serve as a united front, as a vehicle of political action, and as a nationalist/Pan-Afrikanist agenda for people of Afrikan descent in the United States and throughout the Western Hemisphere. After his trip to Mecca, Malcolm described the Muslim Mosque,

12. Malcolm X, as told to Alex Haley, *Autobiography of Malcolm X* (New York: Ballantine, 1973), 307. Medgar Evers, a Mississippi civil rights activist, was assassinated in 1963. Patrice Lumumba, the elected head of state of the Congo, was assassinated in 1960, in supposed cooperation with the Central Intelligence Agency. "Madame Nhu's husband" was Ngo Dinh Diem, the anti-Communist head of state of South Vietnam. Since his policies seemed ineffective in containing Communist and other opposition forces, South Vietnamese generals, with alleged American approval, assassinated Diem.

13. John Henrik Clarke, introduction to *Malcolm X: The Man and His Times* (Trenton, NJ: Africa World Press, 1990).

14. A. Peter Bailey, "I Remember Malcolm," *Black Collegian* 19, no. 3: 66; William W. Sales, *From Civil Rights to Black Liberation: Malcolm X and the Organization of Afro-American Unity* (Boston: South End Press, 1994), 104–105.

15. Malcolm X, "Statement to Press Conference on the Break from the Nation of Islam: March 12, 1964," in *Two Speeches by Malcolm X*, ed. Kroonm Thompson and Richard L. Thompson, 5 (New York: Pathfinder, 1987).

16. Malcolm X, "Letter from Malcolm X, Minister of Muslim Mosque, Inc." (n.d.).

17. Kondo, *Conspiracy*, 41.

Inc. as "an authentic religious group … which practiced the religion of Islam as it is practiced and taught in Mecca and Cairo and Lahore and other parts of the Moslem world."[18] The MMI offered religious instruction, prayer services, martial arts instruction, and classes in the Arabic language. Composed primarily of former NOI members with Fruit of Islam defense training, the MMI also provided a security force for OAAU activities.[19] Malcolm stated that, while the MMI promoted Islam, "we realized that we were Black people in a white society. We were Black people in a racist society." Speaking on the reason for establishing the OAAU, he argued: "[W]e knew that this was a problem beyond religion and we formed another organization that was nonreligious." The OAAU was described by Malcolm as "designed after the letter and spirit of the Organization of African Unity." Malcolm saw the Organization of African Unity (OAU) as a vehicle to enable the "coming together," or solidarity, of continental Afrikans. The OAAU would serve as a vehicle for unity and solidarity of Afrikans in America.[20] While Malcolm desired a separation between MMI and OAAU activities and leadership, MMI member James Shabazz would play a leadership role in the OAAU, and Benjamin Kareem, former NOI assistant minister to Malcolm, and other MMI members would serve as speakers at OAAU rallies.[21]

For clarity, I will distinguish between Malcolm's ideology before and after his leaving the NOI: his NOI period will be labeled the "Malcolm X period"; his post-NOI period will be labeled the "Omowale Malik Shabazz period." Omowale ("a child returns home") is a Yoruba name given to Malcolm by Nigerian Muslim students during his first trip to Afrika.[22] Malik Shabazz is an Arabic name given to Malcolm X by Elijah Muhammad. Malcolm used Malik Shabazz in his international travels. The name Omowale Malik Shabazz represents Malcolm's development after his pilgrimage to Mecca and his travels in Afrika.

Popular accounts of Malcolm's life have emphasized the influence of his trip to Mecca on his ideology during his last years—especially the two most widely circulated media on his life, Alex Haley's Autobiography of Malcolm X and Spike Lee's feature film Malcolm X. While Malcolm certainly made a spiritual transformation, his corresponding political transformation is often underemphasized. Indeed, his primary role in the last eleven months of his life was not primarily as a cleric but as a political spokesperson and leader. While his trip to Mecca was a significant spiritual event in his life, his travels to Afrika played a major role in his political and ideological transformation and development. Even before leaving the Nation of Islam, Malcolm was in contact with and influenced by the anticolonial freedom fighters from Afrika, Asia, and Latin America. Immediately after leaving the NOI, Malcolm sought to build a Black Nationalist agenda with his establishment of the MMI as the "'working base' for an action program designed to eliminate the political oppression, economic exploitation and social degradation suffered daily by 22 Million Afro-Americans."[23] In late March 1964, at the second

18. Malcolm X, "Prospects for Freedom in 1965," in Two Speeches by Malcolm X, ed. Kroonm Thompson and Richard L. Thompson, 32–34 (New York: Pathfinder, 1987).

19. Louis DeCaro, On the Side of My People: A Religious Life of Malcolm X (New York: New York University Press, 1996), 232; Sales, Civil Rights to Black Liberation, 112.

20. Malcolm X, "Prospects for Freedom in 1965," 33–34.

21. DeCaro, On the Side of My People, 232; Sales, From Civil Rights to Black Liberation, 112–3.

22. Malcolm X, Autobiography, 357; Ruby M. Essien-Udom and E. U. Essien-Udom, "Malcolm X: An International Man," in Malcolm X: The Man and His Times, ed. John Henrik Clarke, 247 (Trenton, NJ: Africa World Press, 1991).

23. Malcolm X, "Letter from Malcolm X."

MMI rally, Malcolm dropped the opening prayer to Allah in order to avoid alienating non-Muslims.[24] In Afrika, he dialogued with progressive heads of state and Afrikan nationalist freedom fighters, and he regarded certain Afrikan leaders as political mentors. He also engaged in discussions with revolutionaries from Asia and Latin America. He considered the Black liberation movement in North America linked with anticolonial national liberation movements. After he returned from Mecca and while he was establishing the MMI as a religious organization based on orthodox Islam, most of his public life emphasized organizing the OAAU around social and political concerns. When former NOI members contacted Malcolm and his associates about joining the new efforts, he encouraged them to join the OAAU, not the MMI.[25]

During the Omowale Malik Shabazz period, Malcolm developed a new approach to leadership and ideology. This new approach was his contribution to developing a radical nationalist movement in the United States. While there were other nationalist organizations that reflected the nationalism of the previous period, by the early 1960s the NOI was the preeminent Black Nationalist organization in the United States. At the same time, the growing activism in the United States, particularly concerning de jure segregation in the South, and the anticolonial struggles of people of color worldwide inspired new nationalist tendencies in the Black freedom movement and the new viewpoints of Malcolm. Direct action campaigns, such as the bus boycott in Montgomery, Alabama, in 1955 and the sit-ins and Freedom Rides of the early 1960s, inspired a new momentum in the Black freedom movement in the United States. NOI policy prevented Malcolm and other militant NOI members from involving themselves in desegregation campaigns that captured the hearts and minds of millions of Afrikans in North America. While a minister in the NOI, Malcolm lamented that he had not been involved in the confrontation with segregation. In his *Autobiography* he reflects on that period:

> If I harbored any personal disappointment whatsoever, it was that privately I was convinced that our Nation of Islam could be an even greater force in the American black man's overall struggle—if we engaged in more action. By that, I mean I thought privately that we should have amended, or relaxed our general non-engagement policy. I felt wherever black people committed themselves, in the Little Rocks and the Birminghams and other places, militantly disciplined Muslims should also be there—for all the world to see, and respect and discuss.... I felt the real potentiality that considering the mercurial moods of the black masses, ... the labeling of Muslims as "talk only" could see us, powerful as we were, one day suddenly separated from the Negroes' frontline struggle.[26]

Malcolm's reflection demonstrated his dilemma as militant action in the civil rights movement advanced and gained more attention from the masses of Afrikans in the United States, particularly Black youth. New forces, such as the Revolutionary Action Movement (RAM), also began to emerge. Organized in 1963, RAM described its politics as "somewhere between the Nation of Islam (Black Muslims) and SNCC (Student Nonviolent Coordinating Committee."[27] In other words, RAM's political stance was not

---

24. Peter Goldman, *The Death and Life of Malcolm X* (New York: Harper and Row, 1973), 137.

25. Ibid., 137–8, 243; Sales, *From Civil Rights to Black Liberation*, 147. Malcolm's emphasis on a secular Black Nationalism created tension within the MMI—mostly among former NOI members. Some MMI members wanted a re-creation of the NOI under Malcolm's leadership.

26. Malcolm X, *Autobiography*, 295–96.

27. Max Stanford, "Towards a Revolutionary Action Movement Manifesto," in *Black Nationalism in America*, ed. John Bracey, August Meier, and Elliot Rudwick, 508 (Indianapolis: Bobbs-Merrill, 1970).

only nationalist, like that of the NOI, but also confrontational and activist, like that of the SNCC. RAM did not identify with the nonconfrontational political stance of the NOI and the integrationist orientation of the SNCC. Describing its ideology as "revolutionary nationalism," RAM represented a growing trend in the insurgent Black movement of the 1960s.[28]

In the 1950s and early 1960s, Malcolm was also living in an international environment that included anticolonial revolutions. While a minister in the NOI, Malcolm often noted developments in Afrika, Asia, and Latin America. The first Afro-Asian diplomatic gathering, the Bandung Conference of 1955, greatly inspired Malcolm. The Muslim leader often referred to the Mau Mau Rebellion against British colonialism in Kenya and the French defeat in Vietnam.[29] As an NOI minister and Black community leader in New York, Malcolm often came in contact with leaders of progressive governments and anticolonial movements visiting the United Nations. When newly independent Ghana's head of state Kwame Nkrumah visited the UN in 1958, Malcolm hosted a reception along with other community leaders, including Congressman Adam Clayton Powell.[30] In September 1960, Malcolm facilitated the accommodation of Fidel Castro and the Cuban delegation at the Hotel Theresa in Harlem. On September 20, 1960, Fidel and Malcolm held a historic midnight meeting at the Hotel Theresa.[31] That these national liberation struggles and their leaders were often mentioned in Malcolm's speeches reflected their strong influence on his ideology.

The Shift from the Model of Divinely Chosen Leadership to the Model of Leadership Based on Merit

When Malcolm split from the NOI, he also began to shift his leadership style from the model of messianic leadership. Like most fundamentalist Black Nationalist movements, the NOI was based upon the messianic leadership model through which the leader was considered commissioned by divine forces to lead his people. Such a model would legitimize the leader's unquestioned authority. Essien-Udom argues that both the Islamic-oriented and the Afrikan nationalists possessed messianic leadership styles. In the "old" fundamental Black Nationalist movements, Essien-Udom asserts, the leader served as a "national messiah" and a divinely "chosen 'vessel'" for the redemption of Black people.[32]

The messianic leader also possessed solutions for the problems of an oppressed people, solutions which were generally revealed to him by divine forces. Noble Drew Ali of the Moorish Science Temple was a "prophet" with a divine commission sent by Allah.

28. Robert Brisbane, *Black Activism: Racial Revolution in the United States, 1954–1970* (Valley Forge, PA: Judson, 1974), 171.

29. Karl Evanzz, *The Judas Factor: The Plot to Kill Malcolm X* (New York: Thunder's Mouth Press, 1992), 50.

30. Ibid., 74–76.

31. Rosemarie Mealy, *Fidel and Malcolm X: Memories of a Meeting* (Melbourne, Australia: Ocean, 1993), 11–12, 41–44.

32. Essien-Udom, *Black Nationalism*, 59–61.

In the UNIA, many considered Marcus Garvey a prophet, and his followers often compared him to Jesus Christ and John the Baptist.[33] After attending a UNIA meeting in 1960, Essien-Udom later mentioned UNIA speakers who referred to Garvey as "one sent by God who is now one of the 'saints' in His Kingdom."[34]

In the NOI, Malcolm believed in and advocated the divinity of Elijah Muhammad. Elijah was the Moses, the great prophet who would lead his people to the Promised Land. He was selected by Allah to lead the NOI and the Black Nation. When Malcolm established the Muslim Mosque, Inc., he knew that his primary asset was his reputation as a leader. He realized that he had the support of younger, activist Muslims and militant, urban, non-Muslim Blacks. He maintained a religious component within the MMI and initially continued to pay deference to Elijah Muhammad. But when Malcolm established himself as a leader independent of the NOI, he did not base his qualifications for leadership on having been the chosen representative of a divine being.

> I do not pretend to be a divine man, but I believe in divine guidance, divine power, and in the fulfillment of divine prophecy. I am not educated, nor am I an expert of any particular field—but I am sincere and my sincerity is my credential.[35]

Malcolm also realized that during his years as an NOI spokesman, he had developed other leadership credentials as well. He was an international media figure as well as a Black community leader in New York. In addition, he could speak to middle-class intellectuals as well as to the grassroots of the ghettos. Indeed, he understood that most national civil rights figures did not hold the respect he held in the urban ghettos.

> Time and again when I spoke at street rallies, I would draw ten and twelve times as many people as most other so-called "Negro leaders." I knew that in any society a true leader is one who earns and deserves the following he enjoys.... I knew the ghetto people knew that I never left the ghetto in spirit.[36]

Malcolm's assessment of his assets focused on the reputation he had developed based upon his work and advocacy on behalf of the ghetto masses. Thus, he did not perceive or project himself as chosen by a divine being but as chosen by the black masses because of his efforts.

In the Omowale Malik Shabazz period, Malcolm did not refer to himself in language and titles that would distinguish him from the majority of Afrikan descendants inside the United States. As a result, in his speaking engagements in Black communities, he was introduced as "Brother Malcolm X" or just plain "Malcolm." Also, in a radio interview on December 27, 1964, Malcolm had the following conversation with Bernice Bass:

> BASS: Our guest here is the son of a Baptist minister, the Honorable Minister Malcolm X.
>
> MALCOLM: I never accept the term honorable.... Most people I've seen really end up misusing it, and I'd rather just be your Brother Malcolm.[37]

33. Ibid., 43; Martin, *Race First*, 68–69.
34. Essien-Udom, *Black Nationalism*, 43.
35. Malcolm X, *Malcolm X Speaks: Selected Speeches and Statements*, ed. George Breitman (New York: Grove, 1990), 20.
36. Malcolm X, *Autobiography*, 70.
37. Malcolm X, *Malcolm X: The Last Speeches*, ed. Bruce Perry (New York: Pathfinder, 1989), 95.

The Shift toward Radical Democracy

In the Malcolm X period, Malcolm was a loyal follower of the Messenger, Elijah Muhammad. Elijah, the leader chosen by Allah, was the ultimate authority regarding NOI policy and program, and all NOI Muslims were obligated to obey Allah's Messenger or face God's "chastisement."[38] This belief leads to an organization that discourages dissent, critical thinking, and democratic decision-making processes.

In the Omowale Malik Shabazz stage, after leaving the NOI, Malcolm worked in a collective fashion to build an organization based on principles different from those of the NOI. For example, the program of the OAAU was developed not by Malcolm but by an ad hoc committee consisting of community activists, scholars, artists, students, professionals, Black Nationalists, and Muslims. William Sales argues that besides the meetings which Malcolm, John Clarke, John Killens, Lynn Shiflet, and others were holding in New York, discussions were taking place among activists in Cleveland and Detroit and among expatriates in Ghana.[39] Thus, the program of the OAAU reflected not only Malcolm's ideas but the consensus of the ad hoc committee and the activist and expatriate communities committed to the freedom of Afrikan people. Peter Bailey, a participant in the New York meetings, aptly summed up their members' consensus: "[W]ith enthusiasm and occasional disagreements, but no rancor, we hammered out the Organization of Afro-American Unity's positions on collective economic development, self-defense, community control of schools, international affairs, and other key areas."[40]

Malcolm and the OAAU did not claim to possess "the solution" to "the dilemma" of Black people. His new leadership methodology moved beyond authoritarian collectivism and embraced democratic participation. At an OAAU rally on January 24, 1965, Malcolm made the following appeal to members and potential recruits:

> [W]e're trying to get ourselves organized in such a way that we can become inseparably involved in an action program that will meet the needs, desires, likes or dislikes of everyone that's involved. And we want you involved in it.... We are attempting to make this organization one in which any serious-minded Afro-American can actively participate, and we welcome your suggestions at these membership meetings.... We want your suggestions; we don't in any way claim to have the answers to everything, but we do feel all of us combined can come up with an answer.... With all of the combined suggestions and the combined talent and know-how, we do believe that we can devise a program that will shake the world.[41]

Although Malcolm emphasized Black unity, his interpretation of it was not solely based upon Black people united behind his leadership. His understanding of unity differed from that of the NOI, in which questioning the authority of the Messenger or leaving the organization to follow a new path was treachery. While in Afrika during the summer of 1964, Malcolm received letters from several dissatisfied members of the OAAU and the MMI. Malcolm responded to them in an open letter to both organizations. The let-

---

38. Malcolm X, *Autobiography*, 191–92. Malcolm speaks of his brother Reginald losing his sanity after disobeying the NOI leader's orders. If NOI members disobey the will of the Messenger of Allah, Allah chastises them by attacking their senses and sanity.

39. Sales, *From Civil Rights to Black Liberation*, 99–100, 104–105.

40. Bailey, "I Remember Malcolm," 66–67.

41. Malcolm X, *Malcolm X on Afro-American History* (New York: Pathfinder, 1970), 43.

ter, written in Cairo, Egypt, on August 29, 1964, shows an example of Malcolm's democratic style in the Omowale Malik Shabazz stage.

> I believe in human rights for everyone, and that none of us is qualified to judge each other, and that none of us should therefore have that authority. We don't have the right to force anyone to walk with us, nor do we have the right to condemn those who want to leave, those who become impatient when they don't see us getting results and therefore want to try another way. We can't blame them, and we have no right to be angry with them. If we ourselves produce results, people will stay and they will all support a good program that is getting results.
>
> If brothers want to establish another organization, even that is their right. We must learn to wish them well, and mean it. Our fight must never be against each other. No matter how much we differ over minor things, our fight must always be directed against the common enemy.... I've never sought to be anyone's leader.... When I return I will work with anyone who thinks he can lead ... and I only pray to Allah that you will work with me likewise."[42]

Thus, it would not be considered sinful if one left the MMI or the OAAU. Malcolm's experience with the hierarchy of the NOI may have made him sensitive to the need for flexibility in maintaining one's allegiance to the two organizations.

Malcolm also began to encourage critical thinking. When he was a follower of Elijah Muhammad, he feared questioning the decisions and ideas of the Messenger. Even doubting the Messenger or harboring dissatisfaction with him could lead to divine chastisement. But Malcolm's political and psychological divorce from the NOI allowed him to think and speak for himself. During the Omowale Malik Shabazz stage, Malcolm also encouraged others to adopt this independent style of discourse. In a December 1964 speech to teenagers from Mississippi while on a tour sponsored by the Student Nonviolent Coordinating Committee, Malcolm encouraged independent thinking:

> One of the first things I think young people, especially nowadays, should learn is how to see for yourself and listen for yourself and think for yourself. Then you can come to an intelligent decision for yourself. If you form the habit of going by what you hear others say about someone, or going by what others think about someone, instead of searching that thing out for yourself and seeing for yourself, you will be walking west when you think you're going east, and you will be walking east when you think you're going west.[43]

The Shift in the Role of Women in the Freedom Movement

In the Omowale Malik Shabazz stage, Malcolm broadened his democratic ideas as he began to change his attitude concerning the participation of women in the Black freedom movement. The fundamental Black Nationalists did not provide a specific pro-

---

42. Malcolm X, *By Any Means Necessary*, ed. George Breitman (New York: Pathfinder, 1970), 111–112.
43. Malcolm X, *Malcolm X Speaks*, 137.

gram whereby females could rise to leadership positions in the liberation movement. Female leaders did arise in the UNIA and in the Moorish Science Temple, but in neither organization was there a formal program to achieve gender balance and female representation in the leadership. The NOI institutionalized female leadership both nationally and locally by appointing female captains for its women's organization, the Muslim's Girls Training (MGT). Locally, a woman was also eligible to become a secretary or an investigator—two significant positions in local temples. However, women were excluded from the ministry, and unless one of them was the national captain of the MGT, they were not represented in the national leadership.[44] Moreover, according to NOI policy, females could never act as leaders in the liberation struggle; they could act only as wives and mothers.

In the Malcolm X stage, as an NOI minister, Malcolm regarded women as inferior to men. Indeed, his view on gender roles is exemplified in the following passage from his *Autobiography*:

> Every month, when I went to Chicago, I would find that some sister had written complaining to Mr. Muhammad that I talked so hard against women when I taught our special classes about the different natures of the two sexes. Now, Islam has very strict laws and teachings about women, the core of them being that the true nature of a man is to be strong, and a woman's true nature is to be weak, and while a man must at all times respect his woman, at the same time he needs to understand that he must control her if he expects to get her respect.[45]

During Malcolm's travels in Afrika during the Omowale Malik Shabazz period, his observations profoundly changed his thinking about the status of women. Malcolm traveled to countries developing democratic, progressive principles as well as to those relying on traditional, patriarchal customs reinforced by neocolonial rulers. In November 1964, he spoke of his new awareness to a group of Afrikan students in Paris:

> One thing that I became aware of in my traveling recently through Africa and the Middle East, in every country you go to, usually the degree of progress can never be separated from the woman. If you're in a country that's progressive, the woman is progressive. If you're in a country that reflects that consciousness towards the importance of education, it's because the woman is aware of importance of education. But in every backward country you'll find the women are backward and in every country where education is not stressed it's because the women don't have education. So one of the things I became thoroughly convinced of in my recent travels is the importance of giving freedom to the woman, giving her an education, and giving her incentive to get out there and put that same spirit and understanding in her children. And frankly I am proud of the contributions that our women have made in the struggle for freedom and I'm one person who's for giving them all the leeway possible because they've made a greater contribution than many of us men."[46]

In the OAAU, Malcolm began to promote the advancement of female leaders in the organization. One female OAAU member commented:

> Among the core of people in the OAAU, some of the most hard-working were women who had skills.... He [Malcolm] had no problems with women having

44. Essien-Udom, *Black Nationalism*, 145–49.
45. Malcolm X, *Autobiography*, 225–226.
46. Malcolm X, *By Any Means Necessary*, 179.

ideas or asserting leadership.... Perhaps Malcolm's attitude was a bit unusual than that which typified ... the nationalists, but he was a very open-minded person.[47]

In fact, Malcolm recruited Lynn Shifflet, a Black female producer at NBC, to assist him in establishing the OAAU. Shifflet chaired its early organizational meetings and thus clearly served in the OAAU's leadership. When male chauvinists in the OAAU challenged Shifflet's authority, Malcolm supported her position and the right of women to play critical roles in the liberation movement.[48]

In sum, Malcolm's perspective concerning women's participation in the freedom movement changed radically during the last period of his life. In the Malcolm X stage, he saw women as inferior to men and thus incapable of leadership. In the Omowale Malik Shabazz stage, he saw the liberation of women into leadership roles as a necessity in the struggle for Black liberation—and he began to act on his new perspective.

The Shifting View of Continental Afrikans

From the early nineteenth century until the late 1950s and the 1960s, most manifestations of Black Nationalism in North America held a condescending view of their "Brothers and Sisters" in Afrika. By the beginning of the nineteenth century, the number of Afrikan-born residents in the Black population in North America had significantly decreased. During the century, a significant portion of the Black population had been influenced by white-supremacist images of Afrika that had been designed to justify racial slavery. Consequently, throughout the century, Black Nationalists intending to repatriate to Afrika indicated that one of their missions was to bring "civilization" to Afrika.[49] In some ways, this condescending view of continental Afrikans was held by fundamental Black Nationalists in the twentieth century. While Islamic-oriented Black Nationalists often invoked the glorious past of ancient Black civilizations, they rarely mentioned Afrikan peoples south of the Sahara—or so-called Black Afrika. In addition, the UNIA stated that one of its aims was to "assist in civilizing the backward tribes of Afrika."[50]

The independence movements in Afrika after World War II inspired new sentiments among Black Nationalists and Black people in the United States in general. Continental Afrikans fighting for independence and seizing the mantle of state power created images that challenged white-supremacist stereotypes. Malcolm and his contemporaries began to see continental Afrikan nationalists as peers or even role models

---

47. Muriel Feelings, quoted in Lisa Chapman Jones, "Talking Book: Oral History of a Movement," *Village Voice: The Weekly Newspaper of New York* 30, no. 10 (March 5, 1985): 19.

48. Sales, *From Civil Rights to Black Liberation*, 104–105, 210.

49. Wilson Jeremiah Moses, *Classical Black Nationalism: From the American Revolution to Marcus Garvey* (New York: New York University Press, 1996), 9, 12, 26; Wilson Jeremiah Moses, *The Golden Age of Black Nationalism: 1850–1925* (New York: Oxford University Press, 1988), 20–21.

50. "Aims and Objects of the UNIA," in *Marcus Garvey: Life and Lessons*, ed. Robert Hill and Barbara Bair, 207 (Berkeley: University of California Press, 1987).

51. Robert Harris, Nyota Harris, and Grandassa Harris, *Carlos Cooks and Black Nationalism* (Dover, MA: The Majority Press, 1992), 16, 43–50, 73–75. Carlos Cooks, leader of the African Pioneer Nationalist Movement, was a contemporary of Malcolm in Harlem. Some consider the African nationalism of Cooks as an influence on Malcolm. In a reverent tone, Cooks speaks in support of

and advisors.[51] Even prior to the Omowale Malik Shabazz period, Malcolm did not see Afrika as a place to be "civilized." Rather, he found in Afrikan independence movements lessons that could be applied in North America. After leaving the NOI, he sought to develop reciprocal relationships with progressive Afrikan states and liberation movements. Concerning global Afrikan solidarity, he stated "that we [Afrikans in America] reach out to them [continental Afrikans] and they reach out to us."[52] In the spirit of Pan-Afrikan solidarity, Malcolm sought to build support for Afrikan freedom struggles. Some even suggest that Malcolm sought to mobilize Blacks from the United States with military training to fight neocolonialists and imperialist-supported mercenaries in the Congo.[53] In the Omowale Malik Shabazz period, he also sought advice and support from progressive Afrikan heads of state and Afrikan freedom fighters.

Malcolm not only respected his counterparts on the Afrikan continent; he also appreciated indigenous Afrikan culture. In the Omowale Malik Shabazz stage, rather than calling for the "civilization" of Afrika, Malcolm called for a migration "back to Africa culturally, philosophically and psychologically."[54] Malcolm believed that if Afrikan people grounded themselves in an Afrikan culture, they would produce new Afrika-centered philosophical approaches and social structures. In January 1964, at the OAAU founding rally, Malcolm shared his belief with Nana Nketsia, the Minister of Culture in Ghana.

> He said that as an African his concept of freedom is a situation … in which he is free to give vent to his own likes or dislikes and thereby develop his own African personality. Not a condition in which he is copying some European cultural standard or some European cultural pattern.[55]

In addition, Malcolm mentioned the tradition of improvisation used by a Black classical (or so-called jazz) musician. He argued that the same kind of creativity could be applied to political, economic, and social matters.

> Well, likewise he [any Afrikan person] could do the same thing if given the intellectual independence. He can come up with a new philosophy. He can come up with a philosophy that no one has heard of yet. He can invent a society, a social system, an economic system, a political system, that is different from anything that exists or has existed anywhere on this earth.[56]

Thus, Malcolm believed in an Afrikan worldview that could create social and economic structures distinct from those based on European and American capitalism or Soviet socialism.

Another indication of Malcolm's new perspective of Afrika was his choice of designation for Black people in North America. During a period when most Black leaders chose to call themselves "Negroes," Malcolm identified himself as an "Afro-American" or as an "Afrikan." Malcolm felt that if Blacks in the United States chose to identify themselves as Afrikans, they would be linked with continental Afrikans and Afrikan descendants throughout the diaspora.

---

such continental Afrikan leaders as Patrice Lumumba, Kwame Nkrumah, Jomo Kenyatta, and Gamal Nasser.

52. Malcolm X, *Malcolm X Speaks*, 211.

53. Carlos Moore, *Castro, Blacks and Africa* (Los Angeles: UCLA Center for Afro-American Studies, 1988), 186–187.

54. Malcolm X, *Malcolm X Speaks*, 210.

55. Malcolm X, *By Any Means Necessary*, 63.

56. Ibid., 64

The Shift from Mysticism to Insurgent Confrontation

The Islamic-oriented Black Nationalists often claimed that some divine intervention would eliminate the oppression of Blacks in the United States and bring about true freedom, justice, and equality. Neither the Islamic-oriented nationalists nor the Afrikan nationalists advocated insurgent confrontation with the American state to bring about social change. While acknowledging the racism of American political institutions, fundamental Black Nationalists often chose the tactic of accommodation as opposed to confrontation with the white power structure and white supremacists.

While in the NOI, Malcolm X believed that God Allah himself taught Elijah Muhammad. He not only believed in the great wisdom and knowledge of the divinely chosen Messenger but also converted others to this belief. Minister Malcolm also taught that God Allah himself would eventually intervene to destroy the white devil. God Allah would insure that the Asiatic Black man would rule the planet Earth. The NOI believed in separation—either through the formation of an independent Black National state or through repatriation to Afrika. Separation was to be achieved not through political or military conflict but through divine intervention.

Even before his split from the NOI, Malcolm X advocated armed revolution as a means to obtain land and independence. On November 10, 1963, Malcolm made the following statement during a speech to militant activists in Detroit:

> Revolution is bloody, revolution is hostile. Revolution knows no compromise. Revolution overturns and destroys everything that gets in its way.... A revolutionary wants land so he can set up his own nation, an independent nation."[57]

In Malcolm's last speech as a representative of the NOI on December 4, 1963, Malcolm identified traditional NOI beliefs:

> It is only a matter of time before White America too will be utterly destroyed by her own sins and all traces of her former glory will be removed from the planet forever.
>
> The Honorable Elijah Muhammad teaches us that as it was divine will in the case of the destruction of slave empires of the ancient and modern past, America's judgment will also be brought about by divine will and divine power."[58]

While still an NOI minister, Malcolm also expounded a metaphysical view of history. The Asiatic Black tribe of Shabazz consisted of "the Original Man." The white race was "grafted" by an evil scientist, Yacub. The uncivilized whites were driven to the hills and caves of Europe because of their wickedness. The prophet Moses was sent to Europe to civilize the white devils.[59]

In the Omowale Malik Shabazz stage, Malcolm demystified his approach to leadership and ideology. Unlike Drew Ali or Elijah Muhammad, Malcolm did not claim his message was provided him by a divine being. He was well read and encouraged others

---

57. Malcolm X, *Malcolm X Speaks*, 9.
58. Malcolm X, *The End of White World Supremacy: Four Speeches by Malcolm X* (New York: Arcade, 1971), 121–22.
59. Malcolm X, *Autobiography*, 167–71.

to read and acquire an education. After leaving the NOI, he encouraged intellectuals and students to do the research necessary to solve problems and develop plans. Malcolm also encouraged travel, since his trips to Afrika and the Middle East had greatly expanded his thinking.

Another example of Malcolm's changing epistemological perspective is his analysis of the cause of slavery. In a speech on January 24, 1965, Malcolm did not propound a divine cause for the enslavement of Afrikans. Rather, he argued that the development of gunpowder for military uses by Europeans was a technical advantage, which allowed the West to control Afrika and Asia.[60] While a more sophisticated analysis is necessary to understand the enslavement of Blacks and the underdevelopment of Afrika, Malcolm was not seeking metaphysical answers to political and economic questions. In the Omowale Malik Shabazz stage, he demystified his nationalism.

After leaving the NOI, Malcolm articulated the necessity of a short-range program to initiate the long-range objective of independent Black nationhood. He felt a short-range program was necessary to answer immediate concerns of voting rights, housing, education, employment, and racist violence. In the Omowale Malik Shabazz stage, he began to articulate a long-range program, which included revolutionary nationalism, Pan-Afrikanism, anti-imperialism, and socialism. While he became increasingly non-committal on the separate Black state in public, he had not dismissed the idea of independence through revolution. Late in his life he told the writer Alex Haley, "It may be that the American Black Man does need to become involved in a revolution. What it means is a complete overturn—a complete change.... [A] true Negro revolt might entail, for instance, fighting for separate Black states."[61]

Malcolm also sought to empower the liberation movement of Afrikans inside the United States by developing links with anticolonial, national liberation movements and with anti-imperialist nation states. As a Pan-Afrikanist, Malcolm struggled to establish working relationships among peoples of Afrikan descent worldwide in a common front against racism in the United States. Brother Malcolm consistently criticized the role of western imperialism in Afrika and sought to build a militant movement inside the United States in solidarity with the continental Afrikan liberation struggle. He reminded newly independent Afrikan states of their responsibility to support the human-rights struggles of their brothers and sisters inside the United States. Specifically, in a memorandum to the delegates of an Organization of African Unity summit on July 17, 1964, he reminded representatives of thirty-four, mostly newly independent Afrikan states that "African problems are our problems and our problems are African problems." In seeking a commitment of Afrikan states to become involved in the affairs of Afrikans in the United States, Malcolm proposed the following:

> Some African leaders at this conference have implied that they have enough problems here on the mother continent without adding the Afro-American problem.
>
> With all due respect to your esteemed positions, I must remind all of you that the good shepherd will leave ninety-nine sheep, who are safe at home, to

---

60. Malcolm X, *Malcolm X on Afro-American History*, 28–29.

61. Malcolm X, *Autobiography*, 366. Malcolm probably made this statement to Alex Haley in December 1964. According to George Breitman, Malcolm added material to the *Autobiography* in the spring of 1964 and again in December of the same year. This chapter of the *Autobiography*, titled "1965," refers to events in the summer of 1964, which rules out that the statement was made during the spring of 1964. See George Breitman, *The Last Year of Malcolm X: The Evolution of a Revolutionary* (New York: Pathfinder, 1967), 4.

go to the aid of the one who is lost and has fallen in the clutches of the imperialist wolf.[62]

Malcolm also supported anticolonial and national liberation movements in Asia and Latin America. Malcolm viewed each victory against western imperialism and domination as the creation of one more progressive zone of power. He understood that the success and growth of national liberation in Asia, Africa, and Latin America changed the international balance of power and created favorable conditions for the liberation of the Afrikan nation in North America.

In the Omowale Malik Shabazz stage, Malcolm also attacked the system of capitalism. He compared capitalism to a vulture, which was sucking the blood of the weak and the oppressed. In addition, he increasingly combated the capitalist propaganda against the system of socialism. In a speech at the Audubon Auditorium in Harlem on December 20, 1964, he used his vulture metaphor to criticize capitalism: "You can't operate a capitalistic system unless you are vulturistic; you have to have someone else's blood to suck to be a capitalist."[63]

After his split from the NOI, Malcolm no longer expounded the metaphysical view that the Asiatic Black tribe of Shabazz consisted of "the Original Man" and that the white race was "grafted" by an evil scientist and driven to the hills and caves of Europe because of its wickedness. Rather, he continued to contend that people of color were rising while the white world was declining. To support his contention, he relied on the existence of anti-imperialist, anticolonial revolutions in Africa, Asia, and Latin America. After his travels to Afrika and the Middle East, he no longer attributed the decline of the white world to divine intervention but to the actions of men and women. His speeches referred to an "action program" and to alliances with newly independent developing nations in Afrika, Asia, and Latin America in order to neutralize the power of western imperialism.[64]

Malcolm's Impact on the Afrikan Liberation Struggle in North America

Malcolm began to develop positions and practices that distinguished him from fundamental Black Nationalism. Indeed, he was considered the ideological and spiritual father of a new nationalism that accelerated in the late 1960s. Some aspects of Malcolm's transformation in the Omowale Malik Shabazz stage served as ideological models during the Black Power movement. But some of his ideological changes were not consolidated within the new nationalist movement.

One aspect of Malcolm's transformation that failed to become a dominant feature of the new nationalism was his attempt to move away from messianic leadership. Malcolm

62. Malcolm X, "Memorandum to Their Excellencies, First Ordinary Assembly of Heads of States and Governments, Organization of African Unity, Cairo, U.A.R., from Malcolm X, Chairman of the Organization of Afro-American Unity," news release of the Organization of Afro-American Unity, July 17, 1964.

63. Malcolm X, *Malcolm X Speaks*, 121.

64. Malcolm X, *Malcolm X on Afro-American History*, 43; Malcolm X, *Malcolm X Speaks*, 119–130.

was indeed beginning to challenge messianic leadership, but he had not developed the OAAU to the point where the organization was independent of his personality. While many of Malcolm's statements indicated that he had challenged messianic leadership and the lack of organizational democracy, the OAAU had not incorporated his challenges sufficiently, prior to his assassination, so that it could serve as an example for future movements. Though Malcolm had begun to reject certain trappings of messianic leadership, the cult of personality and the pattern of hierarchal organization were well entrenched in the Black Power movement. The messianic model in Black American culture had a greater influence on Black Power leadership styles than the model that Malcolm had preferred.

The existence of sexism in the Black Power movement has been well documented.[65] Though there was strong female leadership in the movement and women participated on every level of it, misogyny and sexism were common. While patriarchy still persists, some Black activists followed Malcolm's example of fighting for the inclusion of Afrikan women in the leadership of the freedom struggle. Some contemporary Black liberation organizations have institutionalized gender balance in their positions of leadership. For example, according to the bylaws of the National Coalition of Blacks for Reparation in America (NCOBRA), there "shall be one woman and one man serving as Co-Chairperson."[66] In addition, the Malcolm X Grassroots Movement states in its principles of unity: "We will struggle to end sexist oppression: We actively oppose any form of oppression that limits women from reaching their full potential, as manifested in our cultural, economic, political and social institutions, practices and beliefs."[67]

An important aspect of Malcolm's political legacy has been the Pan-Afrikan solidarity demonstrated by Afrikans in the United States with liberation movements on the Afrikan continent. In the 1970s, Blacks in North America increased their support for liberation movements in Guinea Bissau, Mozambique, Angola, Zimbabwe, and South Africa. The mobilization of over 100,000 people for Afrikan Liberation Day in 1972 and 1973 exemplified this growing Pan-Afrikan solidarity. The anti-imperialist Afrikan solidarity movement emphasized that continental Afrikans should determine their own political destinies without being "civilized" by western customs and beliefs or Islamic-oriented Afrikans from the United States.

Malcolm's embrace of Afrikan culture and his call for Afrika-centered cultural innovation helped inspire a cultural revolution in the Black Power movement. Cultural nationalists and artists developed new intellectual and aesthetic creations to galvanize the struggle for Black consciousness. The Black Arts Movement expressed the politics of the Black Power movement through poetry, plays, music, visual arts, and other artistic forms. Cultural nationalists promoted holidays such as Kwanzaa and developed Afrika-centered educational institutions. Indeed, Malcolm X can be regarded as an ideological influence on today's Afrika-centered intellectual movement.

Another aspect of Malcolm's ideological legacy was the development of an insurgent nationalist activism. Malcolm became the national spokesperson for the emerging mili-

---

65. Paula Giddings, *When and Where I Enter: The Impact of Black Women on Race and Sex in America* (New York: Bantam, 1984), 314; Robert L. Allen, *Black Awakening in Capitalist America* (Garden City: NJ: Anchor Books, 1970), 168–70.

66. Linda Allen Eustace and Imari A. Obadele, *Eight Women Leaders of he Reparations Movement U.S.A.: An Intimate Glimpse* (Baton Rogue, LA: The Malcolm Generation, 2000), v.

67. "Principles," Malcolm X Grassroots Movement, http://hometown.aol.com/mxgm/principles/htm.

tant, revolutionary, and nationalist trend that later became known as the Black Power movement. He also became the spokesperson and the central personality for the insurgent nationalist trend in the Black freedom movement. In the northern urban centers of the United States, this trend included the Revolutionary Action Movement (RAM), UHURU, and the Group on Advanced Leadership (GOAL) in Detroit; elements of the Afro-American Association in California; the Afro-American Institute in Cleveland; the National Afro-American Organization in Chicago; and the literary group and forerunner of the Black Arts Movement, UMBRA, in New York. The young militants of these groups identified with the direct-action and confrontational tactics of the civil rights movement, but they rejected nonviolence and integration as a solution to racism. They also identified with the economic program and the image of self-respect projected by the NOI, but they were critical of the NOI's noninvolvement in political action confronting American racism and white-supremacist terrorism inflicted upon Afrikan people. Malcolm's legacy gave these young militants a national voice.[68]

Malcolm also helped accelerate the radicalization and militancy of the pre-1964 desegregation movement in the South. Malcolm spoke to and dialogued with workers of the Student Nonviolent Coordination Committee (SNCC) and toured Alabama. Malcolm's emphasis on self-defense and self-determination influenced many civil rights workers before 1964 to abandon nonviolence and integration and instead call for Black Power. The Black Power movement in the South was part of the insurgent nationalist trend.[69]

Within the civil rights movement Malcolm planned to change the emphasis of the movement to one of human rights. If the movement was redefined as a *human* rights movement, it could, under the United Nations charter and international law, bring charges in the UN against the United States for human-rights abuses and thereby gain international support. In an article titled "Racism: A Cancer That Is Destroying America," originally published in the *Egyptian Gazette* on August 25, 1964, Malcolm outlined his distinction between civil rights and human rights:

> As long as the freedom struggle of the 22 million Afro-Americans is labeled a civil rights issue it remains a domestic problem under the jurisdiction of the United States, and as such, bars the intervention and support of our brothers and sisters in Africa, Asia, and Latin America, as well as that of the well-meaning whites of Europe. But once our struggle is lifted from the confining civil rights label to the level of *human rights*, our freedom struggle has been *internationalized*.[70]

Malcolm's position on human rights began to influence the activists of the southern freedom struggle. SNCC activist Cleve Sellers remembered Malcolm's influence on the organization's thinking:

> SNCC's members were becoming increasingly aware of the international implications of domestic black oppression. Malcolm X had a lot to do with this new awareness. Although we didn't have much personal contact with him, his ideas

---

68. Maxwell Curtis Stanford, "Revolutionary Action Movement (RAM): A Case Study of an Urban Revolutionary Movement" (master's thesis, Atlanta University, 1986), 82, 100–107.

69. Clayborne Carson, David Garrow, Gerald Gill, Vincent Harding, and Darlene Clark Hine, eds., *The Eyes on the Prize Civil Rights Reader: Documents, Speeches and First Hand Accounts from the Black Freedom Struggle, 1954–1990* (New York: Penguin, 1991), 244–46.

70. Malcolm X, "Racism: A Cancer that is Destroying America," in *Malcolm X: The Man and His Times*, ed. John Henrik Clarke, 305 (Trenton, NJ: Africa World Press, 1990).

about the international struggle for human rights made a big impression on our thinking.

Throughout the latter portion of 1966, Malcolm's speeches were frequently discussed at SNCC gatherings. Before his assassination most of us were convinced that his awesome charisma and brilliant insights would have resulted in his becoming one of the first men in history to lead a multi-continental revolutionary movement.[71]

In his movement memoir, SNCC leader James Forman reflected on Malcolm's ideological influence:

I read *Malcolm X Speaks* carefully. His criticism of the term *civil rights*, and his advocacy of the term *human rights* in its place, led me to formulate a resolution that was adopted at the June 1967 staff meeting of SNCC.

This resolution declared that the SNCC considered itself a human rights organization working for the liberation of black people in the United States but of all oppressed peoples, especially those in Africa, Asia, and Latin America.[72]

Malcolm's influence on Forman and the SNCC indicates his ideological influence on the liberation struggle in the United States, particularly regarding the linking of the Afrikan fight for freedom in North America to the international fight for human rights and self-determination.

The insurgent nationalist trend was generally described as "revolutionary nationalism." The revolutionary nationalists utilized confrontational methods—from demonstrations to armed resistance—to achieve their political goals. They generally believed that armed struggle was inevitable in order to achieve Black liberation from racism and to prevent the genocide by violent white supremacists of Afrikans in North America.[73] The Revolutionary Action Movement (RAM), a part of this trend, worked closely with Malcolm X during his last year.[74] One RAM member, Herman Ferguson, helped run the OAAU liberation school, the educational component of the organization.[75] Furthermore, RAM members believed that Malcolm played a central role in the Black liberation movement. In the words of Akbar Muhammad Ahmed, former field chairman of RAM:

The pivotal personality and force in the development of revolutionary nationalism unmistakably is Malcolm X.... Malcolm's break with the religious black nationalism of the Nation of Islam was an important development because it provided the movement with a public center for black nationalism.[76]

After Malcolm's assassination, a spokesperson for the Revolutionary Action Movement articulated the political significance of the martyred leader by comparing Malcolm to Patrice Lumumba, the assassinated prime minister of the newly independent Congo:

[H]e [Malcolm] was to black America what Lumumba was to the Congo. In this way, his spirit should be to black revolutionary nationalists what Lu-

---

71. Cleveland Sellers, with Robert Terrell, *The River of No Return: The Autobiography of a Black Militant and the Life and Death of SNCC.* (Oxford, MS: University of Mississippi Press, 1973), 187–88.

72. James Forman, *The Making of Black Revolutionaries* (New York: MacMillan, 1972), 480.

73. John Bracey, August Meier, and Rudwick, eds., *Black Nationalism in America* (Indianapolis: Bobbs-Merrill, 1970), 504; Brisbane, *Black Activism*, 177–181.

74. Stanford, "Revolutionary Action Movement," 90–92,

75. Sales, *From Civil Rights to Black Liberation*, 120–21.

76. Ibid., 96–97, 100–107.

mumba's spirit is to the Congolese National Liberation Front. In the Congo the word is "Lumumba lives." In Black America the word must be: "Malcolm lives! Keep on pushin'!" "Change gonna come!"[77]

The Black Panther Party for Self-defense (BPP) was another insurgent nationalist organization that identified itself as part of the legacy of Malcolm X. Indeed, political prisoner Mumia Abu-Jamal, who joined the BPP at fourteen years old, stated:

> Malcolm X, seen as "one of the great prophets of black liberation" at the time of his 1965 assassination, so deeply inspired Huey P. Newton that he would refer to the Black Panther Party as the "heirs of Malcolm."[78]

Insurgent nationalists Huey Newton and Bobby Seale organized the Black Panther Party in Oakland, California, in 1966. They adopted the black panther symbol from the Lowndes County Freedom Organization, which had been founded the previous year in Alabama.[79] Newton and Seale defined the BPP's ideology as "revolutionary nationalism." The BPP's advocacy of armed self-defense was one of the features that made Newton refer to the group as the "heirs of Malcolm." Furthermore, Newton said that the program of the BPP was "a living testament" to Malcolm's life's work.[80] Inspired by Malcolm X while he was incarcerated, Eldridge Cleaver formed a prison group called the Organization of Afro-American Unity. After his release Cleaver met Newton, Seale, and the Oakland-based Panthers and decided to join the BPP. To the BPP political program, Cleaver introduced the concept of a plebiscite, or vote, concerning the political relationship of Blacks to the United States. Point Ten of this Ten-Point program called for a plebiscite, supervised by the United Nations, to determine if Afrikans in the United States would remain under U.S. jurisdiction or form an independent nation-state. The BPP believed that Cleaver's proposed Black plebiscite was linked to Malcolm's emphasis on human rights.[81]

Another insurgent nationalist organization, the Provisional Government of the Republic of New Afrika (PGRNA), had several links to Malcolm X. The PGRNA was founded on March 31, 1968, at the Black Governmental Conference, a national convention of Black Nationalists in Detroit, Michigan. The Black Governmental Conference had been organized by the Malcolm X Society, which was headed by a former associate of Malcolm, attorney Gaidi Obadele (Milton Henry), and by his brother, Imari (Richard).[82] The Obadele brothers were organizers of the Detroit-based militant civil rights organization Group on Advanced Leadership (GOAL). GOAL had sponsored three of Malcolm's speaking engagements in Detroit. That Malcolm had influenced GOAL to become a Black Nationalist organization is evidenced by the decision to

77. Revolutionary Action Movement, "Why Malcolm X Died," *Liberator*, April 1965, 10.
78. Mumia Abu Jamal, "A Life in the Party: An Historical and Retrospective Examination of the Projection and Legacies of the Black Panther Party," in *Liberation, Imagination and the Black Panther Party*, ed. Kathleen Cleaver and George Katsiaficas, 40 (New York: Routledge, 2001).
79. RAM and SNCC chapters created Black Panther parties in other major cities, including San Francisco, Los Angeles, Chicago, and New York.
80. Huey P. Newton, with J. Herman Blake, *Revolutionary Suicide* (New York: Harcourt Brace Jovanovich, 1973), 71, 113.
81. Bobby Seale, *Seize the Time: The Story of the Black Panther and Huey P. Newton* (New York: Random House, 1968), 63.
82. Gaidi Obadele (Milton Henry) traveled with Malcolm to the OAU Summit in Afrika in August 1964; he spoke at a OAAU meeting on December 22, 1964. See Malcolm X, *Malcolm X Speaks*, 77–84; Clayborne Carson, ed., *Malcolm X: The FBI File* (New York: Carroll and Graf, 1991), 308–309.

change the name of the group to the Malcolm X Society after Malcolm's death in 1965.[83] Other founders of the PGRNA included Malcolm's widow, Betty Shabazz (who later served as vice president of the organization); OAAU liberation school organizer Herman Ferguson; associates and supporters of Malcolm X; and founders of the Los Angeles-based Malcolm X Foundation, Obaboa Owolo (aka Ed Bradley) and Hakim (Allen) Jamal. Founding officers of the PGRNA also included scholar and founder of Kwanzaa, Maulana Karenga; poet and playwright Amiri Baraka (aka Leroi Jones); SNCC chairman H. Rap Brown (aka Jamil Al-Amin); the leader of the Yoruba movement in North America, Oserjiman Adefumi; former Garveyite and Reparations advocate Queen Mother Moore; and RAM leader, Max Stanford.[84] At the Black Governmental Conference, five hundred Black Nationalists, including the above-named associates of Malcolm X, declared their independence from the United States and demanded that five Deep South states (South Carolina, Georgia, Alabama, Mississippi, and Louisiana) be granted to the descendants of enslaved Afrikans as partial reparations. This territory would be the basis of an Afrikan nation on North American soil and would be named the Republic of New Afrika.

Many of the PGRNA founders described themselves as "Malcolmites."[85] Imari Obadele was the theoretical architect of what was called "the Malcolm X Doctrine." The Doctrine called for Black Nationalist mobilization in the North and the South, organized Black Nationalist defense forces, disruptive guerilla warfare, international support for the Republic of New Afrika, and a plebiscite supervised by the United Nations (similar to the one proposed by the BPP).[86] One of the PGRNA's foundation documents, the "New Afrikan Creed," states:

> We believe in the Malcolm X Doctrine: that We must organize upon this land, and hold a plebiscite, to tell the world by vote that We are free and our land independent, and that after the vote, We must stand ready to defend ourselves, establishing the nation beyond contradiction.[87]

While Obadele was the author of the Malcolm X Doctrine, he credited Malcolm for inspiring him and others to move in a nationalist direction. Obadele stated: "[M]ore than any man the late Malcolm X … gave it [the Malcolm X Doctrine] to me to see it as I have seen it."[88]

During the mid- and late-1960s, the FBI launched its Counterintelligence Program (COINTELPRO) in order to infiltrate and thereby seriously weaken insurgent Black Nationalist organizations such as the SNCC, RAM, the BPP, the PGRNA, and other na-

---

83. Chokwe Lumumba, *Roots of the New Afrikan Independence Movement* (Jackson, MS: New Afrikan Productions, 1991), 9.

84. Ibid., 9–10; United States Senate (91st Cong.), *Riots, Civil and Criminal Disorder: Hearing Before the Permanent Subcommittee on Investigations of the Committee on Government Operations*, pt. 20, 4246–4270, 4352–4376 (Washington, DC: U.S. Government Printing Office, June 26 and June 30, 1969). This Senate investigation report focuses on Black Nationalist organizations, including the Republic of New Afrika, the Revolutionary Action Movement, the Black Panther Party, and the SNCC. Owolo's and Jamal's relationship to Malcolm is mentioned in Alex Haley's epilogue to Malcolm's *Autobiography* (432). Hakim Jamal also details his relationship to Malcolm X. See Hakim Jamal, *From the Dead Level: Malcolm X and Me.* (New York: Random House, 1971).

85. Imari Obadele, *War in America: The Malcolm X Doctrine* (Chicago: Ujamaa Distributors, 1968), 4, 42.

86. Ibid., 33–42.

87. "New Afrikan Creed" in *Roots of the New Afrikan Independence Movement*, Chokwe Lumumba, 41 (Jackson, MS: New Afrikan Productions, 1991).

88. Obadele, *War In America*, 42.

tionalist groups. The strength of the FBI's counterintelligence methods, combined with a lack of discipline, sophistication, and resources, as well as the ideological weaknesses of the new Black Nationalist movement, caused a significant retreat in the struggle for national self-determination and human rights throughout the 1970s and most of the 1980s. Many Black Nationalist organizations have struggled since the 1980s, winning limited victories and sometimes suffering defeats.[89]

Conclusion: The Legacy of Omowale Malik Shabazz Today

Malcolm's ideological legacy has played an important role in the development of the Black Power movement and in the continuing contemporary struggles for Afrikan liberation. In order to maintain Malcolm's legacy and his contribution to the struggle of Afrikan people, intellectuals and activists should critically analyze and interpret his statements and actions.

With the resurrection of Afrikan national and political consciousness in the late 1980s and into the 1990s, Afrikan youth have kept alive the image of Brother Malcolm. Contemporary rap artists have evoked his name and used quotations from his speeches in their rhythmic songs. Malcolm X T-shirts, medallions, and buttons have become popular fashion statements among Blacks on campuses and in the community. "By any means necessary" has become a rallying cry for greater numbers of Afrikan youth both in challenging racist violence, the Ku Klux Klan, and white supremacy and in demanding basic human rights and self-determination.[90]

One factor in the resurrection of Malcolm's image was the continual promotion of him as a symbol of struggle by the Black liberation movement he had inspired when he was alive. In the 1970s, Dr. Mutulu Shakur, health activist, member of the PGRNA, and political prisoner, initiated a campaign in Harlem to "bring Malcolm back." On February 21, 1978, thirteen years after Malcolm's assassination, thousands of people came to a "Malcolm X Commemoration" at the Audubon Ballroom in Harlem, the site of his assassination.[91] In 1990, the New Afrikan Peoples Organization and other Black Nationalist, Pan-Afrikanist, and activist groups organized a campaign to have Lenox Avenue in

---

89. Imari Obadele, Kwame Afoh, Chokwe Lumumba, and Ahmed Obafemi, "A Brief in Support of Black Political Prisoners and Prisoners of War Unlawfully Jailed by the United States during the Course of Their Lawful Struggles in the United States for Freedom from Oppression," in *A Brief History of the Black Struggle in America*, ed. Imari Obadele, 19–62 (Baton Rogue, LA: House of Songhay, 1991).

90. Sales, *From Civil Rights to Black Liberation*, 3–19.

91. Chokwe Lumumba (speech), in *Perspectives on Black Liberation and Social Revolution: Radical Tradition and a Legacy of Struggle*, ed. Abdul Alkalimat, 4–5 (Chicago: Twenty-First Century Books, 1990). Dr. Shakur is currently a political prisoner. For information on his case, see Akinyele Umoja, "Set our Warriors Free: The Legacy of the Black Panther Party and Political Prisoners," in *Black Panther Party Reconsidered*, ed. Charles E. Jones 429–31 (Baltimore: Black Classic Press, 1998); Akinyele Umoja, "Repression Breeds Resistance: The Black Liberation Army and the Radical Legacy of the Black Panther Party," in *Liberation, Imagination, and the Black Panthers*, ed. Kathleen Cleaver and George Katsiaficus 15–19 (New York: Routledge, 2001).

Harlem renamed Malcolm X Boulevard. Efforts such as these kept Malcolm's image in the minds of Afrikans in America and helped introduce him to Black youth.[92]

As Malcolm's image continues to remain the central symbol of struggle, a critical interpretation of the general direction and principles he struggled for will help Afrikans in America to develop a national, political, and social consciousness. Any movement continuing the legacy of Omowale Malik Shabazz must include the principles of collective leadership and progressive democracy. Also, continuing the political legacy of Omowale Malik Shabazz means a commitment to New Afrikan self-determination, Pan-Afrikanism, cultural revolution, anti-imperialism, antisexism, and social justice. In addition, continuing the legacy of our martyr Brother Malcolm means a commitment to one of his main principles—the internationalization of the New Afrikan struggle for self-determination, national liberation, and a new global economic order. Finally (and especially important for Black communities in the United States), internationalizing the struggle in the tradition of Malcolm X means working for the international support of the Afrikan fight for human rights and self-determination in North America.

---

92. Sales, *From Civil Rights to Black Liberation*, 3.

4

The Legacy of Malcolm X as a Framework for Social Welfare Interventions in Black Communities

Mekada Graham

Introduction

Black communities have been an integral part of British society for several centuries, yet they have occupied a peripheral or hidden position in social welfare discourse. As a result, social welfare in black communities has been neglected as a field of study and important contributions to the well-being of black communities and the relief of human suffering have rarely been documented or discussed. The life stories, histories, and intellectual agendas emerging from the experiences of blacks and their cultural heritage open up lines of enquiry where a group's own interpretation of social life is revealed. Consequently, a more inclusive picture of social welfare emerges to provide an invaluable source of material across the spectrum of human experiences.

The history of social welfare and social work includes black men and women who founded various organizations to serve the needs of their communities. Many of these activists were guided by principles of self-help, cultural pride, solidarity, and mutual aid where community-defined aspirations became the focal priority at the grass-roots level (Carlton-LaNey, 2001).

Historically, social welfare activities have been tethered to social, religious, and political organizations and have been a major source of support for individuals and families as they have struggled to survive and resist the hardship and deep-seated racism in Britain. The history of their struggle and resistance is the context in which contemporary black-community organizations have asserted the rights of black people in order to meet their needs.

The unfolding of the hidden histories of black communities reveals the ways in which black activism played a pivotal role in defending the rights of black people in Britain. Black activism consists of several strands that chart the struggles of black communities over time.

The Pan-African movement emerged as an important political and social institution that advocated unity among African people throughout the world. As a form of modern political and social thought for the self-definition and self-determination of black people, Pan-Africanism advocated a physical and spiritual reconnection with Africa. The first Pan-African conference, held in London in 1900, set the agenda for strategies of resistance to racism and imperialism in order to forge social, political, and cultural renewal in Africa and throughout the African diaspora. Such international conferences and meetings, as well as the production of literature, helped to create a web of affiliations between black people in Britain and in the United States. These close associations—across political, social, and religious groups—empowered black communities to meet their social, psychological, and intellectual needs.

One important area of study is the close association between black people and the civil rights and black power movements in the United States and England. These social and political movements exerted a powerful influence on developing strategies of resistance to the historical burdens of racism in British society.

Black communities have sought inspiration and ideas from black politics, cultural institutions, and the philosophies of Marcus Garvey and Malcolm X. As Small (1994) contends, "blacks in England have used their perceptions of black success in the United States as a yardstick, implicit or explicit, against which to evaluate their own progress" (p. 4). The struggles of African Americans have had a profound influence on the ways in which black communities have resisted racism and oppression to create new futures and set intellectual agendas and priorities. It is within this context that the legacy of Malcolm X continues to be an important force in shaping and guiding social welfare activities in many black communities.

Social welfare activities have also been shaped and defined by forms of solidarity, mutuality, and reciprocity grounded in the cultural antecedents of self-determination and community personhood. These historical and cultural influences have emerged from a sense of collective struggle against experiences of racism in the wider society. Within this context, communities have reflected on the ways in which racism continues to play an important part in the life chances of individuals and families and have constructed strategies of resistance to racism. Within these communities, critical discussions and debate take place about normative beliefs and ways of knowing, as people in the communities search for models of human excellence and possibilities in the context of liberation practices. Such forms of resistance to racism strengthen African identities and a spiritual sense of being and are manifested in a wide range of social interventions that set the thematic parameters of social welfare activities.

Within the context of empowerment, black community organizations have embraced the legacy of Malcolm X as a cultural focal point in establishing a human agency expressed in interventions and activities guiding social welfare interventions and activities. Malcolm X proposed a collective, proactive response by black people that would recognize their need for a self-defining attitude in order to change their situation and predicament. Malcolm's proposal was particularly important in the British context because, in whatever way black people choose to define themselves, there are still more powerful stereotypes embedded within the wider society that define their status and identities (Stanfield, 1994; Graham, 2002b).

The cultural disparagement of Africa, its people, and their descendants continues to be a powerful force across the cultural landscape of British society. Consequently, for many black communities, British society can be a hostile place. It is important, then, for black individuals and families to understand the nature of this hostility, as well as its institutions, social structures, and practices, in order for them to make choices freely (Dei, 1999).

Within this context, black communities face important challenges that invite a creative discourse grounded in critical consciousness. Statistics have indicated a sustained over-representation of black people in social welfare agencies at the beginning of a new century—for example, the number of black children in the public-care system, in the juvenile-justice system, and in official school-exclusion data, as well as the number of black people subject to compulsory admissions to psychiatric units (Barn, Sinclair, & Ferdinand, 1997; Skellington & Morris, 1992; National Association for the Care and Resettlement of Offenders, 1991). Indeed, this overrepresentation has remained constant for many decades, even before the turn of the century, and no specific plan has yet been put into action to deal with it. Despite the rhetoric and veneer of equal opportunities in multicultural Britain, multiple levels of institutional racism continue to affect the life chances of families and individuals. These dimensions of racism have been widely acknowledged by the wider society and articulated in the recent Macpherson Report (1999). This influential report substantiated what black people had been voicing for many years: racism permeates the structures and institutions of British society (Graham, 2002a).

In fact, social welfare institutions often reinforce patterns of discrimination and disadvantage, which are compounded by a lack of support services for black families and communities. Moreover, there is growing research evidence that many black families seek support from voluntary organizations and community networks, which offer a more holistic approach. Black community-based organizations have responded to these challenges by acquiring critical knowledge as the tool for social transformation in shaping and defining social welfare activities. The legacy of Malcolm X has played an important role in expressions of critical consciousness that assist in maintaining forms of resistance which impede the severing of past histories and cultures from black communities.

This essay presents the history of black activism and social welfare in Britain in order to provide the context in which the intellectual legacy of Malcolm X provides a reference point in shaping community-oriented action strategies for social change. This essay, therefore, speaks of the processes of critical consciousness in which the phrase often used in black communities, "freedom from mental slavery," is considered a means of social transformation in the pursuit of community regeneration and spiritual renewal.

Black Activism in Social Welfare

In order to appreciate the importance of Malcolm X, it is necessary to briefly chart a history of black activism in social welfare. The beginnings of such activism can be traced to the enslavement of African men, women, and children in Britain, who were bought and sold as chattels or commodities (Lorimer, 1992; Shyllon, 1977; Fryer, 1984).

The growing African community in London during the 1700s consisted of many enslaved and some "free" African people. Historian Shyllon (1977) notes that until 1772 most African people were enslaved except for some "free" African people who had evaded recapture. The population of African people was estimated as approximately 10,000 to 15,000 (Shyllon, 1974). According to Banton (1972), toward the end of the eighteenth century, 2 percent of the population in Britain were people of African descent. The majority of the enslaved African population consisted of children and young people, a pattern reflected within the enslaved populations in the Americas and the Caribbean (Myers, 1993; Braidwood, 1994). The enslaved community also included African people who had arrived in Britain after having enlisted to fight for the nation during the American War of Independence—an act for which they had been promised their freedom (Gerzina, 1995).

The enslavement of African people and its impact on social welfare have been well-documented in the United States and elsewhere within the African diaspora, yet the enslavement and its impact have remained unacknowledged in the history of British social welfare (Billingsley & Giovannoni, 1972; Graham, 2002a).

During the eighteenth and nineteenth centuries, the social welfare needs of African people in Britain were regarded as satisfied through the institution of slavery, and therefore access to poor relief was largely denied (Graham, 2002a). Myers (1993) confirms the precarious position of black people in that "they failed to be cushioned by the safety net of poor relief and the law consistently ruled that blacks brought to England were not hired servants and therefore not entitled to wages" (p. 53). These experiences of racism, grounded in the contours of early social welfare, demonstrate that enslaved and "free" African people elicited different responses from the state and its instruments of welfare. These Africans' attempts to access social welfare were firmly linked to their status as "property" and therefore did not necessarily entitle them to any amelioration of their circumstances.

Early examples of community responses to social needs are seen in efforts to secure emancipation from the tyranny and brutality of enslavement. The African community in London established "clubs to support those who were 'out of place'" (Fryer, 1984, p. 70). The term *out of place* refers to those without employment—probably enslaved African people who had evaded capture. They were offered support and assistance from these clubs.

There is very little direct testimony about the lives of enslaved or "free" African people in Britain. However, in the absence of this material, the narratives (later transcribed) from formerly enslaved African people offer written proof of their protests against enslavement and their affirmation of African humanity in the face of atrocity. These personal and subjective narratives confirm an African heritage expressed within the social practices and formations in black communities.

African solidarity was inextricably bound to and expressed within the resistance to enslavement and the self-emancipation of the African community. It is difficult to imagine successful leadership within the African community, given the oppressive forces present in eighteenth-century Britain. Yet a group of African men calling themselves "sons of Africa" emerged during the late eighteenth century as a potent force, possibly the first named Africa-centered political organization in Britain. The sons of Africa included Olaudah Equiano (already known as a leader of the African community), Ottobah Cugoano, Broughwar Jogensmel, Yahne Aelane, Cojoh Ammere, George Mandeville, William Greek, Bernard Elliot Griffiths, and Thomas Cooper (Shyllon, 1977).

The sons of Africa set about planning ongoing resistance through mobilizing the African community and establishing political and social gatherings. Olaudah Equiano published his narrative in 1789. His book became a best seller and preceded a lecture tour throughout Britain, during which he spoke on the evils of enslavement.

In 1787 Ottobah Cugoano published his narrative, with the help of Olaudah Equiano. Cugoano was forthright in his condemnation of enslavement and demanded the total freedom of African people. He also declared that African people had a moral duty to resist enslavement. Furthermore, he believed that every person in Britain was, in some degree, responsible for the enslavement of African people. The sons of Africa mounted a sustained campaign, writing to newspapers, publishing statements, lobbying Parliament, and addressing meetings on the abolition of enslavement. Besides taking part in many public debates, they collaborated with each other, writing letters and narratives, as well as working in the interests of the African community. They used their influence to support their brothers and sisters in many ways. For example, they supported the community in its demands for wages for work, and as a result of their efforts, many enslaved Africans were able to "buy" their freedom. They also celebrated legal victories in their struggle against enslavement.

Fryer (1984) describes the visit of about three hundred African people to support two black men who had been imprisoned for the crime of begging. During their confinement, the community contributed toward their upkeep.

The sons of Africa became the focal point for news and information gathered from the dockside about rebellion and enslavement in the Caribbean and the Americas. African people met whenever they could, in taverns and organized social gatherings, sometimes celebrating the victories of their kin. As Fryer (1984) points out, "a few days later this partial victory was celebrated by a gathering of about 200 blacks, with their ladies, at a Westminster public house" (p. 69). People such as the sons of Africa highly regarded others like themselves, who sought to relieve the suffering of Africans in Britain by drawing strength from their ancestral past.

The unfolding of the hidden histories of black communities provides the context in which black activism has shaped and defined some models of social welfare in those communities. These early forms of resistance to racism and oppression continued to be expressed in Pan-African organizations and groups at the beginning of the twentieth century. Fryer (1984) alludes to the importance of Pan-Africanism as a major political force of the twentieth century that "was largely created by black people living in Britain" (p. 272). Although the Pan-African movement was concerned with wider issues of colonialization, imperialism, racism, and inequalities throughout the African diaspora, it also played a pivotal role in defending the rights of black people living in Britain. The movement's struggles for a better and fairer society gave rise to concerns about the social and welfare needs of black people and their families in efforts to forge greater self-determination.

Many organizations emerged during this period—for example, the African Progressive League, the African Children's Fund; the Coloured Seaman's Industrial League, The League of Coloured Peoples, and the Pan African Federation. These organizations raised funds for various social welfare activities, held conferences, actively supported black rights, provided assistance for families in need, organized family days, gave help in finding accommodations, and provided ongoing support. A significant number of these organizations had close links with black churches and religious affiliations.

Black Communities Asserting Agency and Creating Successful Futures

Black scholars and activists have criticized the way in which knowledge is constructed about black communities. Black communities have conceptualized knowledge as an emancipatory process sometimes referred to as "freedom from mental slavery." This intellectual endeavor seeks to engage in critical consciousness to undo any form of intellectual enslavement (Dei, James, James-Wilson, Karumanchery, & Zine, 2000). Black organizations and groups have created strategies to address the social and intellectual needs of black individuals and families in order to empower them. This is an integral part of the decolonization process that must take place and that draws upon cultural antecedents as a way of creating new visions of the future. By researching and interpreting his philosophy, one can reveal the impact of Malcolm X on the various aspects of black people's lives.

Malcolm X advanced the importance of learning about the past in order to recover hidden histories as a means of creating new futures and possibilities. He engaged in the restoration of histories, philosophies, and cultures in the African diaspora and advocated the systematic study of black civilizations in the diaspora as a way of conceiving new paradigms for humanity. These activities were not merely confined to intellectual endeavors; they also represented the possibilities of social transformation where African men and women would acquire the power to think and act as a people connected to an African past with identity and purpose (Davis, 1993). Thus, African agency has become central to theories of social change. Randolph (2002) uses the term *cultural capital* to describe "the sense of group consciousness and collective identity that serves as an economic resource to support collective ... philanthropic efforts" (p. 182). Group consciousness is expressed through reconnecting with cultural products and ways of knowing that challenge existing hegemonic ideas (Dei, 1999). The affirmation of cultural knowledge can be empowering in providing people with choices and options in order for them to break away from the dominant ideologies that have shaped and defined their social realities.

Within the dynamics of power relationships, black organizations have drawn attention to the imposition of power on subjugated communities by dominant groups. Foucault (1977) observed that "power and knowledge directly imply one another" and are inextricably linked in the processes of the acquisition and dissemination of knowledge (p. 175). These insights draw attention to the ways in which Eurocentric knowledge is positioned and institutionalized as a powerful construct in defining the realities of black communities. This process is maintained through conduits where a group's culture, language, and history is often misrepresented, discounted, or eradicated and the dominant group's culture is imposed.

Consequently, for black communities power and knowledge are inextricably bound in an emancipatory process towards intellectual freedom and empowerment. It is within this context that Afrocentric knowledge affirms and maintains the authority and agency of black communities.

Black community organizations are a focal point in understanding the cultural and political contributions of Malcolm X. The legacy of Malcolm X provides a pivotal example of human agency in the acquisition and dissemination of knowledge. These processes permit criticism of the falsehoods that have been told about black people and provide the vehicle for cultural realignment in "placing African ideals at the centre of any analysis that involves African culture and behaviour" (Asante, 1987, p. 9). The cultural aspects of Africanness and the critical consciousness manifested in the social formations and practices of black families, communities, and organizations continue to be powerful resources in assisting black people to affirm their spiritual, emotional, and intellectual potential and experiences in the African diaspora. Malcolm X questioned the futility of attempting to adopt the standards of a society that "historically rejected their [Africans'] worth as human beings" and stressed the need for Africans to identify with Africa and African peoples throughout the world (Harris, 1982, p. 108).

One of the greatest challenges facing black communities and their knowledge systems, such as Africa-centered worldviews, is maintaining their spiritual as well as material realms of life in the face of continuing marginalization, exclusion, and insidious aspersion. The subjugation of African identities has become more problematic than ever before as the modern world denigrates and dismisses the African past and the importance of its legacy in the lives of people of African descent (Dei, 1999).

Community activism has been pivotal in advocating black rights, social action, and the struggle for a just society. Small (1994) refers to the determination and resilience of black communities in "not passively [accepting] racialised hostility which bombards them; communities and cultures of resistance have been forged to oppose and overturn such hostility" (p. 42). These experiences have provided the impetus for black communities to reach "deep into their culture, religion, heritage and personal experiences to employ various tactics and strategies" of resistance (Small, 1994, p. 13).

These struggles have involved not only critique and resistance but also the exploration of new and creative ways to ensure the well-being of black communities. Black communities have employed cultural capital in order to set intellectual agendas for discussing social issues and concerns surrounding their everyday lives. They have drawn upon the legacy of Malcolm X as a source of strength and community empowerment.

For example, books, magazines, and newspapers have provided the means by which "black" writing is presented in various forms. The wider society has generally ignored the perspective of black peoples' understandings, perceptions, and interpretations of social issues and experiences that shape their everyday lives. As a result, a written expression of histories and ways of knowing and theorizing about the concerns and issues within black communities takes on new meanings. These concerns are often located in the need to analyze the social conditions, the experiences of living, and the dynamics of discrimination from the point of view of black people themselves. For Malcolm X the need for black communities to determine their own life conditions and opportunities was paramount.

How can this self-determination be achieved in light of British social welfare policies that sometimes have a detrimental impact upon the life chances of individuals and families in black communities? Magazines such as *Afrikan Business and Culture* have provided an important means of theorizing about the pressing social welfare concerns within black communities as well as offering practical solutions to these concerns. Such magazines and newspapers often discuss the "undiscussed" and seek to break with dominant ideologies and present new understandings by drawing upon the spectrum of views and concerns across black communities.

Literature produced within black communities theorizes about the ways in which black communities have been historically disempowered in their interactions with societal institutions. Moreover, black community organizations and groups give space and voice to cultural values and knowledge, forging a way out of colonial mentalities and reaffirming pride in black cultural heritage. These community projects assist in institutionalizing the cultural values and visions of black people, in initiating social exchanges, and in offering opportunities to network in the exchange of goods and services.

The intellectual legacy of Malcolm X provides an anchor whereby community empowerment means taking charge of the community and creating new ways of meeting the needs of black people. This legacy, as well as efforts to acquire, strengthen, and increase knowledge of cultural resources, invites opportunities to incorporate ways of knowing and living at an interpersonal level. As a result, black community organizations, groups, and families make important contributions toward creating new futures, visions, and possibilities.

Rites of Passage:
Life Cycle Development Programs

In what ways has the intellectual legacy of Malcolm X been realized in social welfare interventions? Black communities have theorized about their situations and have created practical strategies for social change.

For example, in recent years Africa-centered theories of social change have provided the framework for rites-of-passage or life-cycle-development programs to facilitate transitions in families and to regenerate communities. Black communities have designed such programs to help stem negative pathways and self-destructive behaviors among young black people. Black parents, elders, and responsible adults and activists have been conscious of the need for an orderly process of maturation to nurture and develop the physical, intellectual, emotional, and spiritual needs of young black people in order to prepare them for adulthood. This action-oriented approach provides an important and effective tool in promoting human agency and a sense that successful futures can be created. Bernard (2001), in her research study, draws attention to the ways in which racism "inhibits our ability to dream and to set goals; it often leads to dreams deferred or lost. The men in the study have stated that in order to survive, they have first to have a dream, an ambition, a goal and then work to realise it, breaking through many barriers to do so" (p. 64). Graham (2001) has discussed elsewhere the importance of cultural knowledge, which can operate as a buffer "that protects you and holds you together and propels you to plan for the future and be creative about the future."

Life-cycle-development programs (or rites-of-passage programs) often embrace the concept of personhood through a process of becoming. This is achieved through understanding and appreciating the self and one's community, as well as through cooperation with the larger community, having a purpose in life, creativity, and spirituality. Rites-of-passage programs provide a vehicle for self-development and growth toward self-empowerment — a vehicle in which communities are involved.

Spiritual knowing is cultivated to facilitate the individual's sharing of experiences of the universal meaning of human existence through being in a community and in a relationship with other people. The complex link between the spiritual and emotional well-being of the individual is nurtured and made relevant to everyday living. Consequently, cultural connections are brought to the fore as an action-oriented communal strategy for social transformation. Thus, the learner shares in a sense of community and belonging within an integrated community process.

These programs take place in black community organizations at the grass-roots level, where young black people are offered opportunities to connect with the community and with each other and to create a way of being and thinking that parallels African value systems and ways of knowing that have emerged from the historical and contemporary struggles and experiences of black people.

Although rites-of-passage programs have tended to focus upon young people, researchers such as Glynn (1998) have developed a fatherhood prison program that seeks to empower black men and their parenting role through the use of drama, as well as the written and spoken word. The process of exploring life's journey has parallels to the process and journey of transformation. The need for Africans to redefine themselves and thus become liberated within is one of the gifts from the legacy of Malcolm X: "[Y]ou teach yourself, and stand up for yourself, and respect yourself, and know yourself, and defend yourself, and be yourself" (Davis, 1993, p. 22). For Africans, cultural knowledge then becomes a framework for empowerment through agency and self-determination.

Social welfare programs and activities have given voice to and the opportunity to enact various strategies and make choices as black people come to know their life worlds. Social welfare activities have invited opportunities for black people to become self-conscious agents, creating strategies of empowerment and empowering each other through social action-oriented programs, meetings, and study groups. Through such activities, black people construct spaces to move beyond mere survival and to strive toward success "by any means necessary."

Conclusion

Black communities have continued to draw upon the legacy of Malcolm X for the betterment of African people living in European societies. Critical consciousness and cultural products have stood the test of time and are important strands of historical continuity for black communities. Black community organizations, through social welfare activities, are engaged in revitalizing past traditions, histories, philosophies, and cultures that have been disparaged by the wider society. Through the use of these cultural values to explain human behavior, empowerment for blacks can be realized through a more culturally centered approach to reality. In seeking to interpret their experiences, black communities have used their own creative endeavors to address social problems and difficulties by shaping social interventions, from their point of view, as sources of their empowerment. Their strengths, skills, and capacities have contributed to the successes of black communities over time. The influence of the philosophy of Malcolm X has been pivotal in assisting communities to meet the needs and challenges of social welfare. In order to create new visions and new futures, power, agency, and resistance are necessary tools for African empowerment.

References

Asante, M. (1987). *The Afrocentric idea*. Philadelphia: Temple University Press.

Banton, M. (1972). *Racial minorities*. London: Fontana.

Barn, R., Sinclair, R., & Ferdinand, D. (1997). *Acting on principle: An examination of race and ethnicity in social services provision for children and families.* London: British Agencies for Adoption and Fostering.

Billingsley, A., & Giovannoni, J. (1972). *Children of the storm.* New York: Harcourt Brace Jovanovich.

Braidwood, S. (1994). *London's black poor and the foundation of the Sierra Leone settlement 1786–1791.* Liverpool: Liverpool University Press.

Carlton-LaNey, I. (Ed.). (2001). *African American leadership, an empowerment tradition in social welfare history.* Washington, DC: NASW Press.

Davis T. (1993). *Malcolm X: The great photographs.* New York: Workman Publishing.

Dei, G. (1999). Why write black? Reclaiming African cultural knowledge in diasporic contexts. Toronto: University of Toronto, Department of Sociology and Equity Studies in Education, OISE.

Dei, G., James, I. R., James-Wilson, S., Karumanchery, L., & Zine J. (2000). *Removing the margins.* Toronto: Canadian Scholars' Press.

Foucault, M. (1977). *Discipline and punish.* London: Allen Lane.

Fryer, P. (1984). *Staying power: The history of black people in Britain.* London: Pluto Press.

Gerzina, G. (1995). *Black England: Life before emancipation.* London: John Murray.

Graham, M. (2001). Exploring African centered knowledge in social welfare. PhD thesis, University of Hertfordshire, England.

Graham, M. (2002a). *Social work and African-centered worldviews.* Birmingham, UK: Venture Press (BASW).

Graham, M. (2002b). Creating spaces: Exploring the role of cultural knowledge as a source of empowerment in models of social welfare in black communities. *Journal of Social Work, 32* (1), 35–49.

Harris, R. (1982). Coming of age: The transformation of Afro-American historiography. *Journal of Negro History, 67* (2), 107–121.

Lorimer, D. (1992). Black resistance to slavery and racism in eighteenth century England. In J. Gundasra & I. Duffield (Eds.), *Essays on the history of blacks in Britain.* Aldershot, UK: Ashgate Publishers.

Macpherson, W. (1999). Stephen Lawrence inquiry: Report of an inquiry by Sir William Macpherson of Cluny. London: The Stationery Office, CM4262-I.

Myers, N. (1993). Servant, sailor, tailor, beggarman: Black survival in white society 1780–1830. *Immigrants and Minorities, 12* (1).

National Association for the Care and Resettlement of Offenders. (1991). *Race and criminal justice: NACRO briefing.* London: Author.

Randolph, A. (2002). Building upon cultural capital: Thomas Jefferson Ferguson. *Journal of African American History, 87* (Spring).

Shyllon, F. (1977). *Black people in Britain 1555–1833.* London: Oxford University Press.

Skellington, R., & Morris P. (1992). *Race in modern Britain today.* Newbury Park, CA: Sage.

Small, S. (1994). *Racialised barriers, the black experience in the United States and England in the 1980s.* London: Routledge.

Social Exclusion Unit. (1998). *Truancy and school exclusion report*, cmt. 3957. London: Author.

Stanfield, J. (1994). Ethnic modeling in qualitative research. In N. Denzin & Y. S. Lincoln (Eds.), *Handbook of qualitative research*. Thousand Oaks, CA: Sage.

5

Methodology and Meaning: The Sociology of Malcolm X

Rhett Jones

Near the end of the introduction to her edited volume, *The Death of White Sociology*, Joyce Ladner observes:

> Hence, Black sociology must become more political than mainstream sociology has been. Black sociology must also develop theories that assume the basic posture of eliminating racism and systematic class oppression from the society. The myth of "value-free" sociology becomes relevant to the Black sociologist, because he must become "pro-value," by promoting the interests of the Black masses in his research, writings and teachings. (Ladner 1971, xxvii)

Sociologists and other black scholars of the time, as Ladner's anthology makes so clear, questioned whether systems of thought developed originally in Europe (Anderson 1993, 113) could adequately analyze or understand, much less explain, the position and behavior of blacks in the United States. Ladner placed the term "value free" in quotation marks because many black intellectuals had long concluded that, far from being neutral in their study of Afro-Americans, white American intellectual structures were hostile. Far from being part of the solution, establishment sociology was—as the tagline of the 1960s ran—part of the problem.

This essay begins by examining some of the problems in understanding Malcolm X's sociology and then discusses the methodology he developed and the changes he thought were necessary to use it. These changes encouraged more black people to participate in observation, study, and reflection and in sharing conclusions with one another. Malcolm focused on a system of thought derived from these efforts—a system developed from black people's own insight and work, not from some idea of what their viewpoint ought to be. The essay next examines Malcolm's emphasis on the genuine resources available to or denied blacks, not the specious resources so many Afro-Americans had been tricked into accepting as central. It concludes with an exploration of racial status—not in the American context (as most sociologists have narrowly applied the term) but in the international arena. As in so many things, Malcolm X anticipated most social scientists by adopting an international rather than a national perspective.

Constructing the Sociology of Malcolm X

Malcolm was among the many Afro-Americans (his preferred term) in the 1960s who had grave reservations about the racial and political neutrality of American social science. He did not believe most white scholars were capable of shedding their racist baggage in studies of society. Of course, Malcolm X was not formally trained in sociology, but none of the founding fathers of sociology in either the United States or Europe were formally trained in the discipline. They shared with Malcolm a deep interest in human affairs, a tireless capacity for watchful observation, and the intellectual powers to synthesize many observations and emerge with new insights into the workings of society. Malcolm X also shared with them a powerful anger against injustice, a resultant commitment to change, and a willingness to use his insights to bring about change.

There are at least three related problems in understanding Malcolm X's sociological thought. First, he was a speaker not a writer (Breitman 1967, 3; Clarke 1969, 271). With the exception of his letters and a few other written documents, such as his work on the Organization of Afro-American Unity, his views on societal machinery and its operation must be drawn from his speeches. By all accounts he was an outstanding speaker. His political biographer, George Breitman, noted that his best talks to black audiences were direct, simple, serious, humorous, and unsurpassed in both educating and inspiring those who heard him (Breitman 1970, 35). While reaching diametrically opposite conclusions concerning Malcolm X's contributions to the black struggle, Breitman (1971, 22) and Asante (1987, 28) agree that he was the master of the aside, or, in Asante's words, the "rhetorical pause." Epps (1969, 10), though disagreeing with Malcolm X on much, acknowledged that he was "an extraordinarily clear thinker," adept at synthesizing philosophical and political ideas and superior in the art of rhetoric. His long time foe, Roy Wilkins, conceded Malcolm was a mesmerizing speaker, and "the toughest man in debate that I've ever seen. None of us could touch him, not even Dr. King" (Wilkins 1982, 317). Part of Malcolm's success as a speaker is found in his ability to relate to his audience. According to Breitman (1972, 1), he always adapted his speaking style to the audience, employing the vocabulary and using the rhythm that best suited its needs. The give-and-take between the man and his audience was often remarkable for the impact it had on both parties. Malcolm X took his audiences seriously, for, as will be seen below, dialogue with them was part of his strategy. And they seemed to understand that he took them seriously and responded accordingly. Despite the many different audiences to which he spoke, his thought was consistent. He was a speaker, not a writer, but there are few contradictions in his ideas.

This is not to say that Malcolm never disagreed with himself. The second problem in understanding his sociological thought is that it was constantly evolving (Barnes 1971, 23). Although Breitman (1967, 22) divides Malcolm X's life into three periods, for the purpose of this essay it is divided into four: his early childhood, his life as a petty criminal and prisoner, his experiences as a follower of Elijah Muhammad and the Nation of Islam both inside and outside prison, and finally, his emergence as an independent theoretician. In this last stage, cut short by his assassination on February 21, 1965, he was in the process of developing his own perspective on history, culture, and society, though, as Malcolm always made clear, his ideas were much influenced by dialogue with others. Even his opponents recognized these changes. Levine (2000, 174), sympathetic biographer of black democratic socialist Bayard Rustin, notes that while Rustin had considered some of Malcolm's earlier ideas "ridiculous," he understood that by the time of his death, Malcolm X had altered his perspective on whites. Roy Wilkins (1982, 317) also believed that Malcolm had moved toward the idea of peaceful coexistence with whites. While this paper focuses on the last stage, the stages are not distinct. They blend into one another, and themes important at one stage may be temporarily eclipsed, only to strongly reemerge at a later stage. In order to understand how Malcolm X interpreted social realities, it is necessary to freeze them, but it should be emphasized that his thought was in the process of constant change. These changes were influenced by his dialogues with others, so that his exchanges with others in the course of his talks had a great impact on his ideas, just as these ideas naturally shaped his talks.

The third problem in understanding Malcolm's sociological thought is similar to the problems in understanding the thought of the first sociologists. He is claimed by so many of his intellectual progeny—of varied (and even opposite) political positions—that it is difficult to track his ideas through the thick, tangled ideological underbrush. Each of his "disciples" claims that, since Malcolm is one of them, Malcolm's thought is best and most correctly interpreted in their framework. Malcolm's philosophy, argues Talmadge Anderson (longtime editor of *The Western Journal of Black Studies*) attracted blacks in the 1960s who had grown weary and cynical over the gradual and nonviolent strategies of traditional civil rights leaders (Anderson 1993, 104). But these Afro-Americans were united only in their rejection of mainstream tactics, for, as Jones (2001, 124–126) makes clear, they were themselves divided into nationalists and Marxists. Writing from a nationalist perspective, Karenga (1993, 175), views Malcolm as the center of the Black Nationalist movement, while the leftist-oriented Alkalimat (1984, 304) finds him central in the worldwide interracial workers' struggle against "capitalism and imperialism."

Further complicating the political battles of Marxists and nationalists over the intellectual legacy of Malcolm X is their awareness of the significance of their battles. Asante (1988, 18), for example, decries attempts by those who would reduce his ideas to a "footnote in Marxism." But Breitman (1967, 39) believes that the best way of describing Malcolm is as a "revolutionary internationalist," and in Breitman's many writings on Malcolm, he makes clear that the man was not antisocialist but was in agreement with many socialist positions. The Socialist Workers Party, of which Breitman was a member, was an early, clear, and strong supporter of the post-Black Muslim Malcolm X, a position for which it was strongly criticized by other Marxist parties such as Progressive Labor (King 1969). Similarly, in a talk given in 1967, James E. Jackson, then a member of the Central Committee of the Communist Party of the United States, denounced Black Nationalism as incompatible with revolutionary Marxism: "The opposite of racial nationalism is interracial equality and justice, not the change of white nationalism to black nationalism" (Jackson 1974, 210). While Asante (1988, 18) believed Malcolm merely "used Socialism" as a way to sharpen his nationalism, other black activists/intellectuals (Alkalimat 1984, 304; Karenga 1993, 250) concluded that at the time of his death, Malcolm X was well on his way to constructing a revolutionary Black Nationalism in opposition to both racism and imperialism. It was these conflicting interpretations of Malcolm's thought that make it so difficult for students of Malcolm to place him in either the nationalist or Marxist box. Black Nationalists, such as members of the Nation of Islam, and virtually all leftists tied the emergent black struggle to the anticolonialist movements of the time. In seeing colonialism and racism as tied to capitalism, Malcolm X was drawing on and contributing both to Black Nationalism and to Marxism (Bell 1968, 176). He was not simply a Black Nationalist *or* a Marxist.

Because Malcolm's talks were so clear and so consistent despite these three central problems, it is possible to see a sociological understanding emerging in his thought and to argue, without much effort, that this understanding, if properly framed, can contribute to the evolution of sociology as a discipline. More important, if properly utilized, this understanding can contribute to the worldwide black struggle.

In framing Malcolm's thought for the purposes of this essay, one can divide society into four distinct, though related, levels by using the concepts *values, norms, statuses,* and *resources. Values* are the principles which most members of society believe are good, right, and proper. Values are worth striving for, and in contemporary America they include such ideals as democracy, love, success, and happiness. While values are, by definition, accepted by most members of society, they are, by this same definition, vague and abstract. *Norms* are more concrete, since they specify how one *ought* to behave to realize one's values. For example, to be successful, one ought to work hard; to maintain a democracy, one ought to vote. Of course, persons need not necessarily follow the norms, which only indicate how persons ought to behave. Some persons may seek success by cheating—in clear violation of the norms. A *status* refers to one's position in society and determines which norms one ought to follow or how one ought to follow them in order to realize one's values. Most societies specify different norms for men and women, for children and adults, or in multiracial societies, for those of different races. One's status, in turn, provides one with differential access to resources. A factory owner, for example, has greater access to resources than the person who works for her. If values are located at the highest level of abstraction, then *resources*—money, land, skills—are located at the most concrete or basic level. It is possible to read the causal connections among the four levels either of two ways. One may read the connection from the most basic to the most abstract. So, for example, control of labor gives one a status, which opens up certain norms, which, in turn, make possible the achievement of values. Or one may read the link of causation from the most abstract to the most basic so that beliefs, or values, lead one to select certain norms, which, in turn, lead to a particular status, which, in turn, gives access to resources. Most Marxist sociologists read from the bottom up, arguing that access to the means of production (the control of resources) determines what happens in society. In their view, art, science, media, law, military, government, and religion—collectively called by Marxists "the superstructure"—are all shaped by control of economic resources. Other sociologists take the position that the relationship is not one way but that these other aspects of society have an impact on economics, just as economics has an impact on them.

One way of interpreting the shift in Malcolm's view of society is to claim that Malcolm moved from reading society from the top down to analyzing it from the bottom up. While a member of the Nation of Islam, Malcolm attributed the problems of blacks in the United States to the evil beliefs and resultant evil machinations of whites and to the failure of blacks to understand, and utilize in struggle, their history and themselves. The solution to these problems was for black Americans to return to Islam—their true and ancestral religion— since using its values would lead them to a new set of norms, thereby giving them an improved status, which, in turn, would give them better access to society's resources. After breaking with the Black Muslims, Malcolm stood this idea on its head, focusing less attention on religious values and more on economic and political solutions to the problems of Afro-Americans. Archie Epps, one of his critics, claimed that Malcolm was moving "toward a kind of primitive Marxism" (Epps 1969, 92), but he never styled himself a communist, or even a socialist.

Malcolm did, however, make favorable statements about *The Militant*, the publication of the Socialist Workers Party, and in the last months of his life clearly shifted his ideas on Black Nationalism (Malcolm X 1971, 15) and on the significance of race itself.

In a 1965 interview, after first explaining how he had once described Black Nationalism, Malcolm continued:

> But when I was in Africa in May, in Ghana, I was speaking with the Algerian ambassador who is extremely militant and is revolutionary in the true sense of the word (and has his credentials as such for having carried on a successful revolution against oppression in his country). When I told him that my political, social and economic philosophy was Black Nationalism, he asked me very frankly, well, where did that leave him? Because he was white. He was an African, but he was Algerian, and to all appearances he was a white man. And he said if I define my objective as the victory of Black Nationalism, where does that leave him? So he showed me where I was alienating people who were true revolutionaries, dedicated to overturning the system of exploitation that exists on this earth by any means necessary. So, I had to do a lot of thinking and reappraising of my definition of Black Nationalism. Can we sum up the solution to the problems confronting our people as Black Nationalism? (Alkalimat 1984, 303–304)

This question was not rhetorical. Malcolm X, who, even after his break with the Nation of Islam, often praised its Black Nationalist contributions to African American communities, was genuinely in search of answers. Before turning to those he found, it is useful to briefly examine the means he employed in his search, since the two are closely linked.

Rooting Methodology in Reality

Methodology and theory are reciprocally linked. Theory needs methodological strategies to find answers to questions it poses. The methods used to find these answers shape new questions and (often) alter the taken-for-granted orientation of theory itself. How the question is asked determines the answer, while the answer can lead to the question being posed in a different, and more useful, way. This was clearly the case with Malcolm X's ideas about society. To understand its workings, Malcolm did not turn to the ideas of historians, philosophers, social scientists, and other scholars who had studied the social order, though he made clear in *The Autobiography of Malcolm X* (1965a) that he had learned a great deal from reading their work. Instead, he turned to the ideas of people themselves, folk who, while they seldom wrote about the society in which they lived, always reflected on it and continually revised their reflections. As he listened with such care to these people, it is not surprising that Malcolm was emerging at the time of his death with a perspective on society from the bottom up, rather than one shaped by social theorists and hence built from the top down. His focus was what Americans, white and black, were doing and saying, not what they claimed to believe.

As he saw it, the new generation of African Americans looked at America not as they wanted it to be, but as it actually was. Malcolm X's view was like Marcus Garvey's. In fact, a number of scholars (Alkalimat 1984; Asante 1987; Anderson 1993; Karenga 1993) saw great similarities between the two. Omali Yeshitela, then chair of the African People's Socialist Party (despite its name, based in the United States), could have been referring to Malcolm X's methodology when he observed that members of Garvey's United Negro Improvement Association understood perfectly that any understanding of how black people will be liberated must necessarily come from an analysis of the actual conditions of existence for black people in the real world. These were not people who went to school

and accidentally stumbled upon a book which revealed to them that there are contradictions and injustices in life that had to be rectified (Yeshitela 1982, 42).

   Like Garvey and his followers, Malcolm centered his work on the "actual conditions"
of Afro-American life, noting that while some may have been surprised at his changed
position on white people, he had always "tried to face facts, and to accept the reality of
life" (Malcolm X 1965a, 60). According to Asante (1988, 18), Malcolm understood the
significance of blacks living in the very center of imperialism and so brought his analysis to bear on blacks in the United States.

   As to how blacks living in the United States should regard whites and the larger world
of people of color, Malcolm insisted they should examine issues and events for themselves. Listening and thinking were all important, and Afro-Americans should never base
their "impression of someone on what someone else has said or written" (Malcolm X
1965b, 91). He urged his listeners to listen, see, and think for themselves, reaching their
own conclusions as to who were their friends and who were their enemies (Malcolm X
1965b, 102, 137). They should not, simply and uncritically, accept the word of others.
According to Black Panther leader Eldridge Cleaver (1968, 60), "The truth which Malcolm uttered had vanquished the whole passel of so-called Negro leaders and spokesmen
who trifle and compromise with the truth in order to curry favor with the white power
structure." Malcolm was killed, Cleaver argued, because he was uncovering ideas about
America that seemed to many blacks to have the ring of reality. Berry and Blassingame
(1982, 385) suggest that Malcolm had such a great impact on black Americans because
his observations seemed to be reasonable and reflect reality, while those of such mainstream leaders as Martin Luther King, Jr., Roy Wilkins, and Whitney Young seemed be
utopian, expecting good things of whites, many of whom could be seen on nightly television savagely attacking peaceful demonstrators. These and other mainstream black leaders seemed, as Malcolm X saw it, sadly out of touch with reality, expecting racists to treat
blacks humanely, while nothing in either their history or the current reality suggested
they were capable of such behavior. The most cursory study of white American actions,
Malcolm often declared, revealed how futile it was to appeal to the good will and humanity of many whites. Shortly after Malcolm's death, Stokely Carmichael and Charles V.
Hamilton wrote that political clashes result from "a conflict of interests, not of con-
sciences" (1967, 75), a sentiment with which Malcolm would certainly have agreed.

   The key to Malcolm's methodology was therefore a careful examination of, and reflection on, the realities of black life in the United States and elsewhere in the world.
The focus had to be the conflict of interests between the races, which Malcolm came to
argue was not so much based on race itself but on the control that whites had long exercised over the world's resources and on the challenges that Africans, Asians, Latin
Americans, and black citizens of the United States were now mounting against it.
Morality and conscience had nothing to do with Malcolm's argument. For blacks to
come to an understanding of how this international system of exploitation and oppression operated, Malcolm concluded, would not be easy—for three reasons. First, blacks
were accustomed to listening to what many whites told them rather than seeking out
answers for themselves. Therefore, as noted above, Malcolm continually urged Afro-
Americans to undertake their own studies and to listen carefully to one another. Second, Malcolm had concluded that many whites in positions of power had created structures and ideologies which deliberately obscured the realities that black people needed
to understand. So successful had many white Americans been in using this tactic that
Afro-Americans often ended up hating their friends and loving their enemies (Malcolm
X 1965b, 91). This tactic was especially well used by the American government, which

Malcolm described as "deceitful and tricky" (Malcolm X 1965b, 91) and which was adept at shifting blacks' attention away from the crucial issues of political control and economic power. In this tactic the government was aided by Christian churches that were handmaidens to colonialism, imperialism, and racism and were therefore rightly regarded with suspicion by the colored peoples of the world. The great counterbalance to political and religious deceit should have been the universities, but Malcolm had little faith in them: "Just because you have colleges and universities, doesn't mean you have education" (Malcolm X 1971, 16). From his point of view, the universities were far from encouraging African Americans to reach conclusions for themselves and were instead skillfully employed to miseducate blacks and make it difficult for them to understand basic realities.

The third problem that needed resolution before black Americans could begin to understand how the system worked was that they come to understand the nature of Africa and Africanity. Grasping the nature of Africanity was difficult for the general reason that Africa and Africans were held in contempt by many white Americans and for the specific reason that the continent, rich in material resources and great civilizations, as well as the origin of mankind itself, was systematically ignored or seldom mentioned at every level of American education. According to a number of scholars (Harris 1990, 11; Lewis 1994, 11–12; Okunor 1996, 5–6; Okoli 1999, 36), it is hardly surprising that many white American educators have prevented the understanding of Africa in general and African history in particular. In Malcolm's view, knowledge of Africa and of the linkages between Africans and African Americans was deliberately distorted. Yet if black Americans were to understand their past, present, and future roles on the planet, they would realize that they were themselves Africans. Malcolm declared to black audiences that it was impossible to "have a positive attitude toward yourself and a negative attitude toward Africa at the same time" (Malcolm X 1965b, 168).

Central to the exploitation of blacks in North America, argued Malcolm, was the near destruction of African history and culture in the Americas (Malcolm X 1970, 53). Without knowledge of their past, black Americans could understand neither their position in the United States nor how this position was linked to the worldwide oppression of peoples of color (Malcolm X 1972, 4). Before they could begin to understand this position, they had to first understand themselves. Parenthetically, it may be noted that nationalists and Marxists alike agreed on the need for black people to reject mainstream scholarly interpretations of their life, though they disagreed on what the alternative should be to these distortions of black culture. Africans and Afro-Americans were similar, and in order to fully comprehend the heart and mind of blacks in America, one had to understand the heart and mind of blacks in Africa, "[b]ecause it is the same heart and the same mind, though separated by 400 years and the Atlantic Ocean" (Malcolm X 1965b, 168). Recognition of this tie, Malcolm's studies suggested, would lead African Americans directly to the kind of research they needed to undertake to better understand themselves and, through this understanding, to lay the foundation for black liberation.

While overcoming these three barriers and employing Malcolm's methodology were difficult, they were not, he often declared, impossible. The insight his approach produced "was so explosive" and impressive because it demonstrated the falseness of much that was routinely taught in the schools (Barnes 1971, 24). In short, his approach worked. While blacks listened to what he had to say, many of them also adopted his tactics and began to develop, and, more important, to articulate, original perspectives on America. According to Malcolm, this occurred because (despite the campaign of disinformation) blacks actually knew a great deal about whites. It was only a matter of systematically organizing and then applying this knowledge. Many Afro-Americans had been servants in America for over 300 years, during which time their insight into white Americans, crucial to their very survival, had been sharply developed (Malcolm X 1965b, 77). However, because of white power, this insight could not be publicly and politically applied. What blacks knew about whites—as studies of the nineteenth-century slave community and the twentieth-century black community revealed—often had to be taught indirectly to their children and shared covertly with other blacks, usually by means of songs and folklore. Malcolm X boldly dragged all this accumulated Afro-American wisdom out into the light, where blacks could see it more clearly, publicly discuss it with one another, and reshape it for better use in the black struggle. "I spend my time out there in the streets with people, all kinds of people, listening to what they have to say," Malcolm reported, arguing that his approach was the key to understanding blackness (Malcolm X 1965b, 175).

Malcolm also said that as a result of living in the United States, he had learned it was important to study whiteness (Malcolm X 1965b, 173). One consequence of his study was the knowledge that while most white Americans were hostile to African Americans, not all of them were. It was important for blacks to observe, study, and reflect on whites, and then to distinguish between whites who were supportive, those who were indifferent, and those who were hostile. "I have analyzed whites with my own understanding," Malcolm declared (Malcolm X 1965b, 189), and when his analysis was complete, he intended to approach them with the same intensity he devoted to his study. This strategy he recommended to his audiences, suggesting that it was important to distinguish among whites, and even to search among them for allies in the struggle, rather than simply dismissing them out of hand. For, as he often said, if you condemn a man because he is white, you leave him no options, no out, for he cannot help being white (Malcolm X 1965b, 213). Whites should be condemned and fought when their actions warrant it. But they first need to be understood by means of observation, reflection, and analysis. This understanding would not inevitably lead to conflict, but as Malcolm indicated in a 1964 lecture at Harvard, it could well lead to possible interracial cooperation. Once blacks understood whites, they might be able by means of "honest, sincere, realistic communication" devise a solution to America's racial problem (Malcolm X 1965b, 160). But this solution required genuine understanding by both races and honest discussion, not the submissive, self-effacing, specious dialogue most blacks used—not because they did not understand whites but because they were unwilling to publicly confront white Americans by militantly acting on their understanding. Without such frankness, blacks would never get whites to face up to the ugly realities of racism.

Besides the individual insights into the workings of American racist thought most African Americans gained simply by growing up in the United States, Malcolm's methodology assumed that new insights could be gained through deliberate, collaborative, systematic efforts. These were insights, he explained, that could be developed by groups of people working together that would far exceed and considerably enrich the insights of one person. In essence, his research strategy called for black Americans to do in public what their slave ancestors had long done in private: to share their insights into the racist structures of society with one another. He denied that he was an expert in any particular field and called for ideas and tactics from all—most especially from young people (Breitman 1971, 9). Young people, whether or not they were college students, had much to contribute to such study and analysis because they had less of a stake in the reward structure of American society, were more flexible, and therefore could be more objective in their approach to solutions for bigotry (Malcolm X 1965b, 143). In his talks Malcolm strongly and repeatedly called on all to involve themselves in the new search for solutions (Malcolm X 1971, 5), announcing his plan to hold seminars and discussions and declaring his intention to listen to everyone (Malcolm X 1965b, 41). With all the "combined suggestions and talent and know-how," he expected a program to be devised "that will shake the world" (Malcolm X 1972, 43).

He had given some thought as to how these discussions ought to be organized:

> I frankly think it is always better to be informal. As far as I am concerned, I can speak to people better in an informal way than I can with all this stiff formality that ends up meaning nothing. Plus, when people are informal, they are relaxed. When they are relaxed, their mind is more open, and they can weigh things more objectively. Whenever you and I are discussing our problems we need to be very objective, very cool, calm and collected. That doesn't mean we should always be. There is a time to be cool and a time to be hot. (Malcolm X 1965b, 161–162)

Deliberate, objective explorations were not, as Malcolm saw it, necessarily incompatible with the political passion necessary to eradicate racial prejudice. In the seminars he envisioned, persons would be deliberate in their discussions, yet they would accept as legitimate the expression of anger and other strong emotions. Informality, placing folk at their ease, was his preferred method, since in a supportive environment, they would be more likely to share new ideas frankly rather than simply repeat those that had already failed.

Anger was acceptable, perhaps essential, in Malcolm's methodology because the purpose of all this organized study, reflection, reading, and sharing of ideas was to bring about change. Malcolm's sociology was like that of sociology's founders: applied sociology, which was intended to redress society's ills. However, by the time Malcolm had outlined these ills and encouraged his listeners to devise new ways to cure them, courses in applied sociology, once the backbone of American sociology curricula, were disappearing, rapidly melting away under the strong sun of "value-free" sociology. But there were sociological movements seeking to bring the insights of the discipline to bear on America's many pathologies. Marxist sociologists—some of whom organized themselves into the Red Feather Institute for Advanced Studies in Sociology—made no pretense of being neutral and used the sociological perspective against the ruling class and its lackeys. An entire group of nonestablishment sociologists, many of whose works appeared in *Radical Sociology* (Colfax and Roach 1971), similarly rejected mainstream sociology. The populist sociologist, C. Wright Mills, declared of his work: "I have tried to be objective, I do not claim to be detached." Malcolm's societal thought obviously fit into the framework suggested by Mills's statement, but Malcolm placed less emphasis on objectivity and more on achieving racial justice.

Still he insisted that those of "us who are at the bottom" must devise our own system of "reason and logic" if the black struggle was to be successful (Malcolm X 1965b, 133). For, "if you give people a thorough understanding of what it is that confronts them, and the basic causes that produce it, they'll create their own program. And when people create a program you get action" (Malcolm X 1965b, 118–119). Black tactics in America's ongoing race wars needed to be based on ideas developed by black people through a methodology of study and discussion. Only these black-derived strategies could defeat racism, and then only if Afro-Americans were bold enough to take the steps their own analyses urged (Malcolm X 1970, 155). Indeed, as Malcolm pointed out, armed with this "intellectual independence," "the black man can come up with a new philosophy. He can come up with a philosophy that nobody has heard of yet. He can invent a society, a social system, an economic system, a political system, which is different from anything that exists or has ever existed anywhere on earth. He will improvise; he'll bring it from within himself. Once we can sit down and think as we please, and do as we please, we will show people what pleases us. And what pleases us won't always please them" (Malcolm X 1970, 44) — because, as he said in a 1964 speech delivered in New York City, "you can bet that when you write the script for yourself, you're always doing something different than you'd be doing if you followed somebody else's script" (Malcolm X 1965b, 119). Black people needed to do this work themselves. No one else could do it for them. Only Afro-Americans could generate the script that would energize them because it would be derived from their own experience as refracted through their own thought. Like Malcolm, other scholars (Gwaltney 1980; Jones 1980; Duneier 1992) interested in constructing a black social science have focused on how Afro-Americans themselves interpret their lives.

While Malcolm's methodology rested primarily on blacks coming to understand whites, themselves, history, and Africanity, Malcolm did not mean that they should not make use of other sources. Malcolm himself read widely and utilized much of his (largely Eurocentric) readings in developing his own paradigm for the study of society. For example, as a great admirer of things African, Malcolm urged his African American listeners to model themselves on their continental sisters and brothers. Many African intellectuals had made use of the socialist perspective, but they had concluded that "the African has to use a form of socialism that fits into the African context; whereas the form that is used in the European country might be good for that particular country it doesn't fit as well into the African" reality (Malcolm X 1970, 181). African activists/intellectuals had learned much from socialism, but instead of slavishly importing it unchanged to Africa, they had adapted it creatively to their own needs. Afro-Americans ought to have done the same thing. They needed not only to be open to all forms and sources of thought but also to filter these through the knowledge they had acquired in the United States. Clearly, one of the reasons why there was not greater agreement and cooperation between American Marxists (white and black) and Malcolm at the time of his death was the failure of these Marxists to adequately address racial realities in the United States. They based their perspectives on Marx's teachings on Europe, sometimes supplementing his teachings with Lenin's, Trotsky's, Stalin's, and Mao's writings on nationalism, all of which were woefully inadequate for an understanding of the black dilemma in America. They even insisted on carrying European Marxist party divisions into the United States, where such divisions usually made little sense. While blacks frequently admired the courage of Marxists in their willingness to publicly confront many racist American authorities and the violence so readily employed by their quasi-fascist front men such as the Ku Klux Klan, most black Americans rejected Marxist ideology.

Malcolm X was as open to leftist ideas as to all others, always insisting that black Americans had the responsibility of evaluating ideas from nonblack sources and integrating them into their own experientially derived ideas. From his viewpoint reality always trumped theory, never the other way around. Later nonestablishment black movements were much influenced by this argument. As Howard Zinn wrote of the SNCC, its mostly young members did not commit themselves to any particular ideology but developed their own ideas freely, often changing them to fit their understanding of racial reality in the United States (Zinn 1965, 7). These changes eventually transformed the organization from one that was biracial and integrationist to one that was all black and committed to black power.

Identifying Real Resources

Though he did not use the term *black power* in the way it was employed by later activists, Malcolm (as already noted) increasingly focused his work on the system of exploitation upon which much of American society rested. There are, he observed in the 1964 founding rally of his Organization for Afro-American Unity, only two kinds of power that count in America, economic and political, with social power derived from them (Malcolm X 1970, 45–46). The American value system, with its celebration of freedom, justice, and equality under law, turned out to be a sham that confused and misled. Instead of shaping a society committed to fair play and equal opportunity, this ideology papered over oppression and exploitation. The basic causes of racism in the United States were, Malcolm declared, ignorance and greed (Malcolm X 1965b, 196). Because these were the driving forces of the way of life of most Americans, it was a waste of time—and therefore it made no sense—to enter into dialogue with most whites, to appeal to their conscience and sense of fairness, or to practice nonviolence. None of these actions had any relevance to most whites' central determination to obtain more wealth and power for themselves. In an address in November 1964, Malcolm explained:

> You know you can't communicate if one man is speaking French and the other one is speaking German. They've both got to speak the same language. Well, in this country you're dealing with a man who has a language. Find out what that language is. Once you know what language he speaks in, then you can talk to him. And if you want to know what his language is, study his history. His language is blood, his language is power, his language is brutality, his language is everything that's brutal. And if you can't talk that talk, he doesn't even hear you. You can come talking that old sweet talk, or that old peace talk, or that old nonviolent talk—that man doesn't hear that kind of talk. (Malcolm X 1970, 154)

By pretending a commitment to democracy, many white Americans in positions of authority aimed to confuse Afro-Americans, to keep blacks talking, petitioning, demonstrating, and begging instead of directly challenging whites for economic and political power.

Malcolm was not fooled. "Well, I am one who doesn't believe in deluding myself. I'm not going to sit at your table and watch you eat with nothing on my plate and call myself a diner. Sitting at the table doesn't make you a diner, unless you eat some of what's on that plate" (Malcolm X 1965b, 26). From this comment, one can easily see that Malcolm's social thought was determined not by American beliefs but by what he perceived to be American realities. Blacks were told that they were Americans, allowed to sit at the table and encouraged to defend the table in the nation's wars, but they were never given anything to eat. They were not, as Malcolm saw it, genuine diners; nor were they genuine Americans. One can also easily see that Malcolm's theory was shaped by his methodology. His ideas were based on what he had learned from his own observations and from listening to blacks at the very bottom of the nation's social system. Afro-Americans had long understood that they did not have access to the resources of the United States, though their passports declared them American citizens. In a riveting, lengthy, fact-filled book, Swedish sociologist Gunnar Myrdal, brought over by the Carnegie Corporation to study America's race problem from an outsider's perspective, concluded that most white Americans were also well aware that blacks were seated at the dinner table with nothing on their plates. They felt guilty, Myrdal argued—caught in a dilemma in which they recognized that African Americans were being denied the country's resources and yet unwilling to act against this injustice (Myrdal 1944).

Malcolm X denied that white Americans felt any of the guilt observed by Myrdal, so asking whites to do the right thing was certain to fail. The American system, Malcolm contended, was made possible by the enslavement of blacks and therefore was incapable of producing justice for blacks (Malcolm X 1970, 116). You could not, he argued, expect a chicken to produce a duck egg unless you totally transformed the chicken. As Malcolm saw it, the chicken would not transform herself since she liked things pretty much the way they were. Nor could you appeal to the chicken's (nonexistent) guilty conscience. You had to force it to change. The country exercised power, crushing anything that got in its way (Malcolm X 1965b, 119), and the only way to end its oppression of blacks was with power (Malcolm X 1965b, 150).

To confront and eventually defeat white power, blacks needed to understand exactly how it worked. This understanding required, as has already been noted, that they look beyond the image which the nation projected of itself: a democracy rooted in Judeo-Christianity and holding lofty beliefs concerning the dignity of all human beings. Blacks also needed to recognize that white power was international. Malcolm's sociology was quite different from the establishment sociology of his era, which focused not on societies in general but on modern American and Western European societies in particular. In the introduction to his book, *Comparative Sociology*, Robert Marsh wrote: "Many sociological propositions are, of course, stated as if the relationships and generalizations hold true for all societies, social systems, and even social actions. However, such propositions have rarely been tested outside of modern American and Western European societies" (Marsh 1967, 6). In short, sociologists claimed to be uncovering the general rules of all societies when, in fact, most of their data was derived from a relatively small percentage of the world's societies. Virtually all of the societies on which American sociologists based their theories were white. Malcolm X anticipated, by at least two decades, the interrelationships among societies now seen as commonplace by most social scientists and insisted that neither the United States nor any other society operated in a vacuum. All the world's societies were interdependent. Malcolm declared that the power structure which practiced racism in the United States and imperialism abroad was not only ruling America; it was ruling the world (Malcolm X 1971, 27). For blacks to challenge this racist power, they would need to master and break existing international linkages.

The best way to begin doing so was to master and break the relationship between black Africa and most of western Europe, which had been deliberately subjugating Africa for economic reasons. Most of western Europe had exploited Africa to feed its factories and was therefore directly responsible for the low standard of living prevalent on the continent (Malcolm X 1965b, 127). The system seized raw materials in Africa, shipped them to Europe "to feed the machines of the Europeans and make jobs for them." The resulting manufactured goods were then turned around and sold back to the Africans as finished products (Malcolm X 1965b, 127). It was pointless to morally appeal to the white world to share such wealth with Africans; the white world was simply too greedy. The only effective response would be for Africa to industrialize and to make and sell its own products. Control of the economic system also made it possible for the Western world to misrepresent Africa and African realities. Much of the negative press about blacks in the Congo, Malcolm argued, stemmed not from their actual savagery and inability to govern themselves but was intended to justify what the Western powers were doing to the Congolese (Malcolm X 1970, 128).

According to Malcolm, Afro-Americans should understand that African problems were their problems and their problems were African problems (Malcolm X 1965b, 73). The link between black Americans and Africans was regularly demonstrated, he observed, reporting that three Kenyan students were mistaken for African Americans and brutally beaten by New York City policemen. And shortly after that, two Ugandan diplomats were also beaten by police officers who thought they were American blacks (Malcolm X 1965b, 74). It was not sufficient, Malcolm often declared, for Africans to struggle separately for independence in Africa while black Americans fought separately for racial justice in the United States. Black peoples had to confront international power with international power (Malcolm X 1965b, 129). Understanding how the white world's social order operated would lead black people throughout the world to realize that they had to work together.

This need to work with other blacks worldwide did not mean African Americans should neglect their struggle in the United States; they also needed to understand that America was not isolated from the rest of the planet and to conduct their struggle in the light of this understanding. "Any power that's local, if it is real power, is only a reflection or a part of that international power" (Malcolm X 1965b, 129). A battle against local power could, at the same time, be a battle against the international power behind it, but only if Afro-Americans grasped the nature of the relationship between the two. It was therefore legitimate for American blacks to battle for land, because without it they remained beggars—economically, politically, and socially (Malcolm X 1965b, 57). In addition, as was the case with Africans, they needed to establish industry, creating businesses for themselves so that they did not have to beg whites for jobs (Malcolm X 1965b, 39). Securing land and developing industry was, from Malcolm X's perspective, the key to genuine power for black Americans. Speaking at a Harlem church in 1964, he insisted: "There's only one way to be a first-class citizen. There's only one way to be independent. There's only one way to be free. It's not something that someone gives to you. It's something that you take" (Malcolm X 1965b, 111). The American power structure—indeed, the international power structure of which America was the center—was about that: power. Malcolm X knew not only how it worked but also that it would only respond to genuine power—organized, developed, and applied on an international scale. Malcolm frequently suggested, in the last months of his life, that African Americans should bypass the federal government of the United States and take their case directly to the United Nations. Or, as he often insisted, black people ought to stop talking about civil rights and start talking about human rights. They were, he argued, millions of Africans, Asians, and Latin Americans who were sympathetic to the plight of America's blacks, but as long as Afro-Americans themselves insisted on framing their problems in a national context, these folk were powerless to help them. In its treatment of blacks, America was clearly in violation of the United Nations' many statements on human rights; therefore, Afro-Americans should find ways to make use of UN power.

For black Americans to undertake such a struggle they would, in the social paradigm for action Malcolm was developing, have to carry out three measures. First, they would have to stop relying on whites for needed resources and instead rely on themselves. Second, they would have to arm themselves with knowledge of their own African past, a weapon that would empower them in their challenge to the international western cartel.

And third, they would have to ignore America's false, self-serving values and instead focus on America's ugly, oppressive realities.

Blacks need not wait for full development of their own economic resources to begin to support one another. Malcolm set the example by taking up collections after his talks. By encouraging Afro-Americans to support the rental of halls in which he made his presentations, Malcolm thereby asked them to assume responsibility for the institution they supported. In defending his approach, he publicly declared he was modeling himself on Garvey, noting that the great black leader was able to take a militant stance because he relied on blacks, not whites, for financial support (Malcolm X 1970, 59). African American activists who followed in Malcolm's wake also sought black support. So, as Bell observed (1968, 190), the Congress of Racial Equality signaled its break with whites by plastering posters in northern ghettos which read: "Support Black Power; send $1 to CORE." Only by rejecting white money, Malcolm X and those who followed him insisted, could blacks develop a truly independent policy. If blacks bettered their own communities, "[we would not] be running around here trying to knock our way into a social circle where we're not wanted" (Malcolm X 1965b, 29). For black Americans to be socially comfortable in their own circles, these circles would have to be financially free from whites.

The second key to a successful black struggle was for Afro-Americans to develop knowledge of their past. The absence of such knowledge had "crippled" black Americans (Malcolm X 1972, 3). One of the reasons for the success of the Nation of Islam among black folk was the organization's willingness not only to reveal the true African American past (not the false one constructed and taught in the schools) but to link it to the African past. The Black Muslims discovered that deep within the subconscious of the black man in the United States, "he is still more African than he is American. He thinks he is more American because whites have been lying to him" (Malcolm X 1965b, 172). Indeed, according to Malcolm X (1972, 14, 15), the black past was deliberately distorted so that the black history which whites taught emphasized "down home" (the black experience in the slave states of the Old South) rather than "back home" (the black experience in precolonial Africa). For those blacks who were persistent in wanting to know what had happened before all that cotton picking, whites had prepared an image of black Africa populated with ignorant savages who did not even understand their own lands. These folk were stupid and cruel, and they lacked any civilization save that brought to them by whites. And for blacks who stubbornly pushed beyond these falsehoods, they found waiting for them the rigid divisions of humankind into races. Jones (1971) demonstrates white scholars had proved as early as the nineteenth century (at least to their own satisfaction) that blacks were inferior to whites. European and white American scholars divided human beings into a number of different races (the exact number depended on who was doing the classifying and for what purpose) which were then ranked according to their immutable intellectual abilities. Although this scholarship was already becoming obsolete at the time Malcolm spoke, it was tenaciously hanging on and indeed has survived into the twenty-first century.

These racial divisions, according to Malcolm, had no existence in the reality on which his social thought rested; instead, they were fictions organized by imperialists (with support from their anthropology lackeys) to justify European domination of Asians and Africans (Malcolm X 1972, 18). As far as blacks were concerned, Malcolm concluded that the so-called immutable racial lines were shifted about to make certain no civilized persons would be classified as black (Malcolm X 1972, 18). If necessary, as was the case with the Egyptians, civilized persons were classified as white, or as an alternative, they were classified as a people of mixed race who had been civilized by whites. Most black Americans lacked the education to pierce the screen of these conceptual lies because the cruelties of American slavery had cut the link between black Africans and black Americans. Once blacks in the New World lost their languages and their names, "our roots were cut off with no history, we became like a stump, something dead, a twig over here in the Western hemisphere. Anybody could step on us, trample upon us or burn us, and there would be nothing we could do about it" (Malcolm X 1972, 17). African Americans could embark aggressively on liberating themselves only if they were willing to smash the image racists had created of black folk and relearn their own past. Malcolm once responded to a question by suggesting the greatest mistake the Civil Rights movement had made was trying to organize people for the achievement of a specific goal; it was a mistake, he said, because "[y]ou have to wake the people up first, then you'll get action. [Question: Wake them up to their exploitation?] No, to their humanity, to their own worth, and to their heritage" (Malcolm X 1965b, 198).

For black Americans to begin their struggle, they would not only have to finance it themselves and destroy racist lies; they would also have to stop centering their strategies on America's values—which were a deliberately misleading public-relations sham—and instead focus on how the nation's resources were really allotted. Blacks should also stop believing in phony resources—things which they had long considered important but which in fact had given them no real power. Skin color was one of these "resources." It clearly gave some blacks privilege, and "there was a time when you would find American Negroes" who were proud of their white blood (Malcolm X 1970, 119). Malcolm was clearly wrong in relegating what some scholars such as Russell, Wilson, and Hall (1993) call "the color complex" to the black past, since some Afro-Americans still remain strongly committed to light skin color. But he was clearly right in pointing out that there is no real power in skin color and that those black Americans who think otherwise are reaching for the wrong resource. In his view, the limitations of skin color were parallel to the limitations of white patronage. Virtually all of the insightful social science studies of the black community over the course of the 1930s and into the 1950s emphasized that some blacks, in the North as well as in the South, derived considerable influence from their links with well-to-do whites. But Malcolm understood that such power was not only racially limited (it usually gave such black folk power only over other blacks) but also temporally limited. It could be withdrawn virtually at will by the white patron.

Unfortunately, space does not permit full exploration of the relationship between skin color and ties to powerful white patrons or of the relationship between these two and black church membership, but from Malcolm's sociological perspective, none of these were particularly important anyway. In general, as Malcolm saw it, Christianity, whether Catholic or Protestant, had buttressed, supported, and encouraged racism. For example, members of the Catholic establishment, he said, "[are now trying] to act like everything is all right. They made a few black Cardinals and a couple of bishops," and they expected that support from blacks would follow (Malcolm X 1972, 40). Neither skin color nor white patronage nor religion gave black Americans any more access to genuine economic and political power than similar pseudoresources gave their colonized African brethren. In all three cases, they gave prestige in the eyes of some, but no power. In *Black Bourgeoisie* (1957), a scathing portrait of the African American middle class, black sociologist E. Franklin Frazier pointed out how few economic and political resources its members actually had. In both Africa and the Americas the prestige this middle-rung group held was important to them and demonstrated their closeness to their white patrons and their distance from the black masses. The crucial clash between the status so important to them and their powerlessness in the international arena is key in understanding Malcolm X's approach to their position.

Playing the Race Role

In sociology, a *status* is the position an individual occupies, while a *role* is the way she actually functions within the parameters of this status. So, for example, being sworn into the force gives a person the status of police officer, but how he actually carries out the duties that go along with this status involves playing its role. In a race-conscious society such as the United States, the races are assigned different statuses: white Americans are placed at the top, followed by Asian Americans, Latinos, and Native Americans; African Americans are firmly mired at the bottom. How persons act (that is, play their role) within the framework of their assigned racial status clearly varies, and because many Americans are racist, no one can escape one's status. Even whites who are antiracist benefit from their status of whiteness. The system of social thought Malcolm X was developing at the time of his death was based on this racist reality, not on some ideological dream that the United States ought to ignore or discount race. Archie Epps wrote, correctly, that the black world within which Malcolm lived and thought was the underside of America (Epps 1969, 109). Malcolm X wanted and worked for black unity, but looking from the bottom up, he understood that blacks were divided. Among the most powerful forces dividing them, and shaping how they played their racially assigned roles, was class.

As in so much of his social thought, Malcolm's approach to class among black Americans had little to do with such factors as skin color, religion, links to whites, or other pretensions to prestige. It centered on economic and political power. Malcolm worked to strip away false divisions, insisting there is "no such thing as an upper class Negro," since all blacks catch the same hell (Malcolm X 1965b, 174). According to Asante (1988, 19), Malcolm defined class among blacks according to the level of identification with the white power structure. Those who most identified with whites were at the top of the system, those who least identified with them at the bottom. The black American middle class did not control the black community but was used by white folk to control it for white people (Malcolm X 1970, 72–73). As a result, Malcolm insisted in a December 1964 impromptu talk at the Audubon Ballroom, while there are black oppressors of blacks, they are doing just what whites have taught them (Malcolm X 1965b, 92). Or, put more simply, the white power structure controls the black community through the black "establishment" (Malcolm X 1965b, 203).

This intermediate position between the white ruling classes and the black masses, while it may have provided middle-class blacks with psychological satisfaction, did not eradicate their knowledge that middle-class blacks remained subject to racism. In fact, Malcolm claimed such black folk were more "disillusioned, frustrated, and disenchanted" than lower-class blacks because they could better appreciate what they were denied (Malcolm X 1965b, 158–159). But just as they sought to enjoy their status, so, too, did they want to be regarded by whites as respectable and responsible (Malcolm X 1965b, 134). Like many black sociologists, Malcolm X understood the intense determination of middle-class blacks to separate themselves from the ignorant masses of black folk and to demonstrate their commitment to the civilized world of white people. This psychological orientation carried over into and shaped their participation in politics, since, according to Malcolm, they did not want to be looked upon by "the white man" as extremist, violent, or irresponsible (Malcolm X 1965b, 134). Their determination to be "black Europeans," to use Maquet's term (Maquet 1972, 7), had a powerful impact on their lives. Less than a month before the day on which he was killed, Malcolm, applying his own methodology (listen, learn, reflect, conclude, then listen again), said of the black middle class:

> You ever watched them? You ever watched one of them? Do that — watch them, watch the real bourgeois black Americans. He never wants to show any real sign of emotion. He won't even tap his feet. You can have some of that real soul music, and he'll sit there, you know, like it doesn't move him. I watch him, and I'm telling you. And the reason he tries to pretend like it doesn't move him is that he knows it doesn't move them [whites]. And it doesn't move them because they can't feel it, they've got no soul. And he's got to pretend he has none just to make it with them. This is a shame, really. (Malcolm X 1972, 13)

While a shame, it was, sadly, a reality, as black Americans who sought to get ahead in white America chose to act like whites. In bettering their status by playing a role in which they emulated white people, these middle-class blacks often cut any meaningful tie between working-class blacks and themselves. Speaking of New York City, Malcolm said that the blacks who came downtown to dialogue with white radicals did not know how to talk with blacks that remained uptown in Harlem (Malcolm X 1965b, 206).

While middle-class blacks sought to distinguish their position in American society from that of other blacks, in fact, argued Malcolm, all blacks occupied the same status in the eyes of most whites. By favoring some blacks at the expense of others, most whites kept blacks divided, thereby preventing them for exercising the kind of unified action that would end European and white American control. Whenever blacks made the effort to unify on the basis of their racial identity, many whites quickly termed such common action racism (Malcolm X 1972, 11). But, argued Malcolm, when whites ruled the world, they did not term this racism, preferring instead to call it imperialism (Malcolm X 1972, 9). Nor did they publicly acknowledge that the European Common Market was racist, even though it only served Europeans. Black folk needed to shrug off the charges of racism made by the world's original racists and instead develop strategies that would bring blacks together.

Such action would take considerable effort since the American and European power structures relied on more than just name-calling to keep blacks divided. For example, U.S. officials sent American Uncle Toms to black Africa, where these men often succeeded in widening the gap between blacks on either side of the Atlantic, for the image they left behind them was so obnoxious that black Africans ended up not wanting to identify with Afro-Americans (Malcolm X 1965b, 152). The United States Department of State, Malcolm often indicated, tried to convince Africans that black Americans were not interested in Africa's struggles, while other branches of the American government tried to convince the nation's blacks that black Africans were a savage and inferior people not worth their concern. Yet the two peoples were linked and needed to act in unity. In November 1964, in a rally held after his return from Africa, Malcolm stated that Africans might have won their independence but that independence meant little to them if blacks had no respect in the United States, since they would be treated not as independent Africans but as subservient black Americans (Malcolm X 1970, 146). For Africans to be respected, Afro-Americans had to be respected. Similarly, Afro-Americans could expect no respect as long as Africa remained subservient to imperialism.

However, persons of African descent could begin gaining respect not by begging whites for it but by respecting one another. Sadly, Malcolm noted, African Americans often celebrated their nonviolence, but they meant they were nonviolent with whites, not with one another (Malcolm X 1965b, 138). They were not nonviolent, loving, or forgiving with one another.

Malcolm X considered the violence blacks inflicted on one another shameful, for by such action they accepted a status—but not one they had created for themselves. They were acting out the position the white power structure assigned them as they thuggishly attacked and preyed on one another. At the same time, they were rejecting their commonality and undermining their own struggle. Of the rejection of unity between American blacks and black Africans, Malcolm said: "But when you have people who look exactly like you, and you are catching hell, to boot, and you still are reluctant or hesitant or slow to identify with them, then you need to catch hell. You deserve all the hell you get" (Malcolm X 1965b, 130). In a sense blacks all occupied the same status in that they were given no real power by whites, but they were not using the common position assigned them as the basis for unity. On the contrary, they were accepting the various superficial divisions created by whites—skin color, religion, patronage, birthplace—and drawing away from one another on the basis of them. Malcolm urged black peoples to focus on what really bound them to one another, to stop fighting each other, and in particular to end public battles.

Many ruling-class whites encouraged blacks to battle one another and gave maximum publicity to conflicts between black peoples, whether focusing on local black-on-black crime or international conflicts among African nations. These tactics had an impact not only on whites but on blacks themselves. Malcolm urged black folk to stop fighting among themselves and instead focus on their common enemy (Malcolm X 1970, 111). Of course, he was not so naïve as to believe that blackness in itself was sufficient to impose unity. The central purpose of the study, reflection, and dialogue he urged on his listeners was to sort out their differences to determine which of the differences among black people were genuine, and therefore needed to be resolved, and which were false. These false differences were, more often than not, created by white oppressors and, once identified, could be discarded. But only blacks could do this. Discovery of false divisions could not be imposed by fiat, but false divisions could be uncovered by blacks as the result of their study. Genuine differences should be examined "in the closet," Malcolm pointed out. "[W]hen we come out in front, let us not have anything to argue about until we get finished arguing with the man" (Malcolm X 1965b, 25). First should come study, then discussion, then frank resolution of differences. And only then, as a unified group, should blacks confront the racist powers.

In their study and struggle, blacks would have to grapple with the meaning of blackness. As Malcolm himself saw it, blackness was not a status limited to the United States:

> Because when we say Afro-American we include everyone in the Western Hemisphere of African descent. South America is America. Central America is America. South America has many people in it of African descent. And everyone in South America of African descent is an Afro-American. Everyone in the Caribbean, whether it's the West Indies, or Cuba, or Mexico, if they have African blood, they're Afro-Americans. If they're in Canada and they have African blood, they're Afro-Americans. (Malcolm X 1970, 38)

Present-day readers might not be comfortable with Malcolm's terminology since it is doubtful that Canadians of African heritage would want to be termed Afro-Americans, but the basis of his argument remains as clear now as it was then. Blacks were bound together, whether they lived in Mexico, Canada, or that imperialistic nation between the two. Many whites treated all blacks as if they were one people; blacks therefore needed to understand the ways in which they actually were one people. They could then draw on this knowledge to create not a false unity imposed by a bogus, racist science but a genuine unity constructed by blacks themselves.

To become aware of this commonality did not mean that African Americans had to return to Africa. Some might choose to do so and, as Malcolm often declared, his experiences in Africa suggested that those who came to Africa with skills and commitment would be welcome. Others could choose to remain in the United States, win the rights the Constitution guaranteed all Americans, yet achieve "a working unity" with Africa (Malcolm X 1965b, 63). According to George Breitman, in Malcolm's belief blacks needed to focus on this working unity, for the black revolt was not "simply a racial conflict of black against white" but a global rebellion of the oppressed against their oppressors. Afro-Americans needed to understand how their position in the world was linked to that of other peoples. It was important to understand blackness, Malcolm seemed to argue, but it was equally important to understand how blackness was related, through the action or inaction of black peoples, to others on the planet. Afro-Americans had an urgent need to understand that they ought to be in solidarity with Africans, Asians, and Latin Americans who were "seething with bitterness, animosity, hostility, unrest, and impatience" (Breitman 1967, 39). There indeed ought to be "a working unity" between these peoples and black Americans, but on what should it be based?

As with so many of the questions Malcolm posed in the last months before his death, the answers were complex, never simple. They were to be uncovered only by means of long study and the patient sharing of ideas. But Mary Frances Berry and John W. Blassingame simplistically linked Malcolm X with Algerian revolutionary Frantz Fanon by claiming that both men thought violence was the revolutionary's solution to the worldwide problem of racism (Berry and Blassingame 1982, 17). Eldridge Cleaver, in writing about the link between Malcolm X and Black Panther leader, Huey P. Newton, agreed:

> Malcolm saw all the way to national liberation, and he showed us the rainbow and the golden pot at its end. Inside the golden pot, Malcolm told us, was the tool of liberation. Huey P. Newton, one of the millions of black people who listened to Malcolm, lifted the golden lid off the pot and blindly, trusting Malcolm, stuck his hand inside and grasped the tool. When he withdrew his hand and looked to see what he held, he saw the gun. (Cleaver 1969, 38)

But not quite. Malcolm often criticized nonviolence, but he never placed exclusive emphasis on violence as the solution. He frequently insisted that, whether under the laws of the United States, the Judeo-Christian tradition, or plain old common sense, African Americans had the right to defend themselves when attacked.

Violence was not the only solution, especially since in Malcolm's internationalist sociological paradigm, much more was involved than a simple confrontation between whites and blacks in the United States. There were many variables that needed sorting out before blacks could act. To be sure, Malcolm said, whites treated Native Americans differently than they treated blacks because Indians were willing to use violence. And, to be sure, the United States was directing an imperialist and racist war in Vietnam. But the U.S. was having difficulty with its lackeys in the South Vietnamese government (Malcolm X 1972, 41), and as Malcolm pointed out, "[y]ou know, when the puppet starts talking back to the puppeteer, the puppeteer is in bad trouble" (Malcolm X 1965b, 219). Events were also complicated by struggles among the Western powers. France, instead of being a satellite to the United States, wanted the United States to be its satellite (Malcolm X 1965b, 120). Yet another barrier to settling for a simple answer was what most Americans then called "Red China." According to Malcolm, the People's Republic of China (governing, according to his figures, 700 million Chinese) was not officially recognized by the United States government, which claimed that the real government of China was located in Taiwan, to which the Chinese nationalists had retreated after losing to the Communists (Malcolm X 1965b, 200). Malcolm considered this claim a manifest fiction and refused to accept it (Malcolm X 1965b, 187). When asked what he thought about "Red China" in relation to black Americans, he replied: "Well, I think that it is good to have centers of power on this earth that aren't controlled from either Paris, London or Washington, D.C." (Malcolm X 1965b, 215). The United States had its own fictions, which were heightened when placed in an international context. South Africa, declared Malcolm in a 1964 address to the Organization of African Unity, practices segregation and preaches segregation: "She, at least practices what she preaches. America preaches integration and practices segregation. She preaches one thing while deceitfully practicing another" (Malcolm X 1965b, 75).

The statuses occupied by these varied groups (as well as by many others) and how they related to one another had to be understood by Afro-Americans if their own battle was to be successful. Such understanding was not some luxury, something to which black Americans might turn their mind as a respite from their own struggles, but an integral part of their own struggles. Racist imperialists understood the linkages among France, China, South Africa, Vietnam, and the United States, and in order to continue their domination of world, they had created a distorted interpretation of these ties. The refusal of the United States to recognize the government of mainland China was the silliest and most obvious example of these distortions. For blacks to effectively combat this domination, they had to construct their own interpretation of these complicated interrelationships and then use it. The status held by peoples of color had been assigned them by racists and imperialists, but the new roles peoples of color would play could shatter that status and make possible a new world order.

Conclusion

Malcolm X's sociological ideas about the links among resources, statuses, norms, and values were not complete at the time he was killed. Nor was it clear how a full understanding of these relationships should be employed in the Afro-American struggle. Malcolm X might have made the task easier by simply focusing on bigotry in the United States, but his own methodology led him to conclude that while the United States was the center of modern racism, the nation did not exist in isolation from the rest of the world. In a speech he gave in Detroit less than two weeks before his assassination, Malcolm explained:

> I might point out here that colonialism or imperialism, as the slave system of the West is called, is not something that is just confined to England or France or the United States. The interests in this country are in cahoots with the interests in France and the interests in Britain. It's one huge complex or com-

bine, and it creates what's known not as the American power structure or the French power structure, but an international power structure. This international power structure is used to suppress the masses of dark-skinned people all over the world and exploit them of their national resources. (Malcolm X 1965b, 160)

There could be, he concluded, no separatist solution for American blacks in which they won equality with American whites while the rest of the nonwhite world remained subordinate. Similarly, the so-called independence of Africa would remain a political sham unless Afro-Americans, having gained freedom in the United States, used their freedom to help achieve genuine autonomy for Africa.

Malcolm's methodology was linked to his provisional conclusions. He worked from the bottom up, learning from black experiences and from the insights black folk discovered and developed from them. As a result, he focused on resources linking these experiences and insights to the positions Afro-Americans claimed for themselves and to those into which they were shoved by the power of whites. He gave less attention to white American values, which he viewed as misleading, false, and hypocritical, and even less attention to the normative system on which they were, in his view, supposedly based. For that reason, this essay has focused on resources and statuses. Malcolm X's ideas on norms and values were equally original and insightful, though in the system he was constructing, not as important.

Methodology and meaning were, as talks in the last months of his life make so clear, tied to action. Malcolm X's sociological thought was not some disconnected system to be dispassionately debated by students and professors who also examined other forms of sociological thought. His ideas were meaningless unless they were applied and used by black people (whose experiences, readings, and dialogues had created the ideas) in the cause of their own liberation. Malcolm's sociology was a closed circle. It was rooted in the realities of Afro-Americans, developed though their reflections on those realities, and then, having been modified through Malcolm's consultations with blacks, applied with ferocious energy to transform the realities of black life.

References

Alkalimat, Abdul. 1984. *Introduction to Afro-American studies.* Urbana, IL: Peoples College.

Anderson, Talmadge. 1993. *Introduction to African American studies.* Dubuque, IA: Kendall/Hunt.

Asante, Molefi Kete. 1987. *The Afrocentric idea.* Philadelphia: Temple University Press.

———. 1988. *Afrocentricity.* Trenton, NJ: Africa World Press.

Barnes, Jack. 2001. In tribute to Malcolm X. In *Malcolm X talks to young people: Speeches in the U.S., Britain, and France.* Ed. Steve Clark. New York: Pathfinder Press. (Orig. pub. 1965.)

Bell, Inge Powell. 1968. *CORE and the strategy of non-violence.* New York: Random House.

Berry, Mary Frances, and John W. Blassingame. 1982. *Long memory: The black experience in America.* New York: Oxford University Press.

Breitman, George. 1967. *The last year of Malcolm X: The evolution of a revolutionary*. New York: Merit Press.

_____, ed. 1970. *By any means necessary: Speeches, interviews and a letter by Malcolm X*. New York: Pathfinder Press.

_____. 1971. *Malcolm X: The man and his ideas*. New York: Pathfinder Press.

_____. 1972. Introduction. In *Malcolm X on Afro-American history*. Malcolm X. New York: Pathfinder Press.

Carmichael, Stokely, and Charles V. Hamilton. 1967. *Black Power: The politics of liberation in America*. New York: Vintage Books.

Clarke, John Henrik, ed. 1969. *Malcolm X: The man and his times*. Assisted by A. Peter Bailey and Earl Grant. New York: Collier Books.

Cleaver, Eldridge. 1968. *Soul on ice*. New York: Delta Books.

_____. 1969. *Post-prison writings and speeches*. Ed. Robert Scheer. New York: Vintage Books.

Colfax, J. David, and Jack L. Roach. 1971. *Radical sociology*. New York: Basic Books.

Duneier, Mitchell. 1992. *Slim's table: Race, respectability, and masculinity*. Chicago: University of Chicago Press.

Epps, Archie, ed. 1969. *The speeches of Malcolm X at Harvard*. New York: William Morrow.

Frazier, E. Franklin. 1957. *Black bourgeoisie: The rise of a new middle class in the United States*. New York: Collier Books.

Gwaltney, John Langston. 1980. *Drylongso: A self-portrait of black America*. New York: Vintage Books.

Harris, Robert L., Jr. 1990. The intellectual and institutional development of Africana studies. In *Black studies in the United States: Three essays*. New York: The Ford Foundation.

Jackson, James E. 1974. *Revolutionary tracings in world politics and black liberation*. New York: International Publishers.

Jones, Rhett S. 1971. Proving blacks inferior, 1870–1930. *Black World* 20 (February): 4–19.

_____. 1980. Finding the black self: A humanistic strategy. *Journal of Black Psychology* 7 (August): 17–26.

_____. 2001. From ideology to institution: The evolution of Africana studies. In *Color-line to borderlands: The matrix of American ethnic studies*, ed. Johnnella E. Butler. Seattle: University of Washington Press.

Karenga, Maulana. 1993. *Introduction to Black Studies*. Los Angeles: University of Sankore Press.

King, Don. 1969. Attack bosses' stronghold. *Progressive Labor* 7 (August): 36–47.

Ladner, Joyce, ed. 1971. *The death of white sociology*. New York: Random House.

Levine, Daniel. 2000. *Bayard Rustin and the civil rights movement*. New Brunswick, NJ: Rutgers University Press.

Lewis, Stanford. 1994 The political agenda of the Hamitic hypothesis. *The Afrocentric Scholar* 3 (December): 1–17.

Malcolm X. 1965a. *The autobiography of Malcolm X*. With Alex Haley. New York: Grove Press.

_____. 1965b. *Malcolm X speaks: Selected speeches and statements*. Ed. George Breitman. New York: Grove.

_____. 1970. *By any means necessary*. Ed. George Breitman. New York: Pathfinder Press.

_____. 1972. *Malcolm X on Afro-American history*. New York: Pathfinder Press.

_____. 2001. *Malcolm X talks to young people: Speeches in the U.S., Britain, and France*. Ed. Steve Clark. New York: Pathfinder Press. (Orig. pub. 1965.)

Maquet, Jacques. 1972. *Africanity: The cultural unity of black Africa*. Trans. Joan R. Rayfield. New York: Oxford University Press.

Marsh, Robert M. 1967. *Comparative sociology*. New York: Harcourt, Brace and World.

Myrdal, Gunnar. 1944. *An American dilemma: The Negro problem and modern democracy*. New York: Harpers.

Okoli, Emeka J. 1999. Ethnicity, the press, and integration in Nigeria. *The International Journal of Africana Studies* 5 (December): 32–48.

Okunor, Shiame. 1996. The unconscious carriers of monoculturalism: The process of real assimilation. *The Griot* 2 (Fall): 1–6.

Russell, Kathy, Midge Wilson, and Ronald Hall. 1993. *The color complex: The politics of skin color among African Americans*. New York: Harcourt Brace Jovanovich.

Wilkins, Roy. 1982. *Standing fast: The autobiography of Roy Wilkins*. With Tom Mathews. New York: The Viking Press.

Yeshitela, Omali. 1982. *Not one step backward! The black liberation movement from 1971–1982*. Oakland, CA: Burning Spear Publications.

Zinn, Howard. 1965. SNCC: The new abolitionists. Boston: Beacon Press.

Part Two

Black Nationalism and Pan-Africanism

6

The Sociopolitical Philosophy of Malcolm X

Maulana Karenga

Background and Significance

No single person, with the exception of Marcus Garvey, has captured Black minds and hearts with the same intensity and enduring influence as Malcolm X. His bold stands, organizational ability, and the severe incisiveness of his analysis of American society made him the definitive symbol of the Black liberation movement in the 1960s. Malcolm was born in Omaha, Nebraska, on May 19, 1925, in a Garveyite family. The racist murder of his father for his strong nationalist views eventually led to the destruction of Malcolm's family, hard times and hard work, and a lumpen life of hustle and survival. At twenty, Malcolm was sentenced to ten years in captivity (or "in prison," as the white establishment calls it), where his lumpen life came to an end and the difficult and disciplined process of self-reconstruction began (Malcolm X 1964).

In captivity, he read voraciously and began to build the intellectual basis for the work in which he would eventually become involved and the social analysis he would eventually develop and offer Black America. Moreover, while in captivity, he heard of Elijah Muhammad and the Nation of Islam (NOI) and discussed Muhammad's teachings with his brother Reginald, who was a member of the Nation. The teachings reminded Malcolm of the childhood sessions with his father on Garvey and Garveyism; of the vision of Africa, free, proud, and productive again; of Black men once again active and respected on the stage of human history. Malcolm began to correspond with Muhammad, and upon his release from captivity in 1952, he went to meet him and work with him.

After his period of preparation and training, Malcolm became a minister and organizer for the Nation of Islam. From his main base in Harlem at Mosque No. 7, he systematically expanded the membership, structure, and influence of the Nation. He introduced the Nation to Black students, the petty bourgeoisie, the country, and eventually the world. He not only built the structural basis for the Nation's expansion but also founded *Muhammad Speaks,* which became, at one point, the most widely circulated Black paper in the country. In 1963, he was suspended from the organization as a direct result of a lecture, "God's Judgment on White America," in which he described the Kennedy assassination as a historical case of "chickens coming home to roost," i.e., historical payback for U.S. complicity in assassination plots throughout the world (Malcolm

X 1971, 121–148). However, as Malcolm contended, such an assertion was not out of character for him or the Nation and would not have, in ordinary circumstances, merited censure. The real problem centered on leadership struggles and considerations and the NOI's ruling group's concern for the image and continuation of the organization.

In 1964, seeing that he had no chance of reentering the Nation, Malcolm disassociated himself from it and organized the Muslim Mosque, Inc., an orthodox Islamic organization. Later the same year, he organized the Organization of Afro-American Unity (OAAU), modeled after the Organization of African Unity (OAU) and dedicated to the defense, unity, and liberation struggle of African peoples in the Western hemisphere. He traveled to Africa and the Middle East, presented a document to the OAU, and met with various heads of state in a calculated thrust to internationalize the Afro-American liberation struggle and win allies for it around the world. In 1965, the year of his assassination, he was working on building support among heads of state and diplomats for a petition to the United Nations which charged the U.S. government with genocide against Afro-American people. There is considerable speculation that Malcolm's effort to internationalize the Afro-American struggle and his fiercely uncompromising stand on the right and responsibility of Black self-defense were contributing factors to his assassination. The death of Malcolm was a great loss to the Black liberation movement, for he was unique, committed, and resourceful. Indeed, Pinkney (1976, 65) observes:

> The depth of Malcolm X's understanding, his leadership ability, and his keen intelligence were such that if he had lived and developed his ideas and organization skills, he could very well have become the most important Black man in American history.

Still, the legacy Malcolm left is awesome and instructive. Malcolm's greatness lies not only in his accomplishments—organizational and theoretical—but equally in the models he left for emulation.

Malcolm's practical legacy revolved around the models he left through his practice of what Blacks can and should strive to be. Malcolm was a model on various levels—and was therefore the symbol and substance of the best of Black Nationalist thought and practice. First of all, he was a *model revolutionary.* He boldly stepped out beyond the religious context of Islam and challenged the system for its brutality, exploitation, and oppression of Black people. He lived a Zulu-disciplined and self-sacrificing life, defying both death and danger. His call was not for reform and integration but for Black power and liberation through organization and through struggle—armed and otherwise. His motto, "freedom by any means necessary," summed up his thought and practice and placed him in the company of all serious freedom fighters.

Malcolm was also a *model of Black manhood.* In a eulogy delivered at Malcolm's funeral, Ossie Davis stated: "Malcolm was our manhood, our living Black manhood. This was his meaning to his people and in honoring him we honor the best in ourselves" (Clarke 1969, xii). Speaking to the enemies of Black and human freedom concerning manhood and liberation, Malcolm claimed:

> I'm the man you think you are. And if it doesn't take legislation to make you a man and get your rights recognized, don't even talk that legislative talk to me. No, if we're both human beings we'll both do the same thing. And if you want to know what I'll do, figure out what you'll do, I'll do the same—only more of it.

Third, Malcolm was a *model Maulana, a model Master-Teacher.* He had an uncanny ability to redefine the world in Black and simple yet profound terms rich in imagery and figurative language. He often taught by metaphor, exposing the mystifying power relations of society and the world. Speaking of the historical decline of capitalism, Malcolm compared it to a once-strong eagle turned into a weak, cowardly vulture preying on the helpless (Malcolm X 1965, 10). Likewise, his use of the metaphors of the field and the house to depict Blacks as models of class behavior and class consciousness that exist and divide Blacks today (Malcolm X 1965, 10*ff.*) is profound and fitting in both conception and analytical application. It was Malcolm's capacity to demystify the world for the masses which, among other qualities, so endeared him to them.

Malcolm was not just a model master-teacher; he was also a *model student.* It is undoubtedly his dedicated and disciplined study which eventually made him a master-teacher. Before he was twenty, Malcolm could hardly read and write. But while in captivity, he began to study English, penmanship, etymology, and Latin (Malcolm X 1964, 156). He was also determined to build an operational vocabulary and embarked on a long, difficult project of copying every word in the dictionary to do this (Malcolm X 1964, 173). Moreover, each night he slept only three or four hours and read the rest of the time, even though the lights of the cell were turned out and he had only the glow of the corridor light by which to read (Malcolm X 1965, 175). When he came out of captivity, he continued to study and read diligently even while traveling, never feeling he knew or had read enough.

Malcolm especially liked to study history and saw it as the key social science for understanding causes and tendencies of social processes and phenomena, as well as for learning lessons and possibilities inherent in the Black and human condition (Malcolm X 1970b). As he often said, "of all our studies, history is best qualified to reward our research" (Malcolm X 1965, 8).

Fifth, Malcolm was a *model organizer.* As mentioned above, he laid the structural basis for the organizational expansion of the Nation of Islam. Moreover, he assisted in the training of ministers for the Nation, organized its newspaper, and set up its organizational and functional links with the Black community. He built the basis for countless Black United Front rallies and efforts and, after leaving the Nation, established the Organization of Afro-American Unity to serve as a model for other organizations like the Black United Front.

Finally, Malcolm was a *model critical thinker.* His presentations were not merely articulate, like those of so many Black spokesmen friendly to the media; they were also profound and well constructed. Furthermore, his logic was incisive, and he enjoyed the meticulous development of each point he made. While in captivity, he had joined the debating society in order to express the wealth of knowledge his abundant reading and rich and instructive experience had given him. The fierce and engaging debates he participated in sharpened his analytical ability, accustomed him to meticulous detail in argumentation, and tested and tempered him for the more demanding practice he would eventually pursue. It is this model of the critical thinker, as opposed to the legendary "rapper," that stands at the heart of Malcolm's contribution, which will be explored below in view of its value and meaning for Black Nationalist thought and practice.

Theoretical Development: Process and Problems

It is appropriate here to note the problem of selecting, synthesizing, and categorizing the essential concepts, theories, and themes of Malcolm X's sociopolitical thought. There are, as others have observed, seemingly contradictory assertions which are difficult to reconcile within the overarching framework of his thought. Moreover, these contradictions—some real, others imagined—have produced various claimants to his political legacy and have helped to confuse further his essential theoretical thrusts. Thus, when reading or studying Malcolm, one must examine his assertions and contentions in the context of four factors that shaped his theoretical development after he had left the Nation and had begun to develop his own unique contribution in clearer terms.

The first and perhaps the definitive factor shaping Malcolm's post-NOI thought is the profound *crisis of faith and theory* he faced as a result of his ouster and subsequent hostile treatment by the NOI. The factor is so critical because, in essence, it involved his disassociation from a structure and theory which had molded and dictated the course of his life for twelve years and his reconstruction of a viable alternative in a matter of months. The urgencies of the time did not allow Malcolm long-term contemplation and reevaluation; rather, they demanded an almost instant self-redefinition which would reflect his continuing strength and leadership capacity yet distinctness of doctrine.

A second factor which shaped Malcolm's theoretical development—and which complicated the effects of his crisis of faith and theory—was that *he was not a theorist or an ideologist.* Essentially, he was an interpreter and master-teacher, not a constructor of a system of thought. It was Muhammad who had constructed the system of thought and had commissioned Malcolm to teach it to the Black masses in North America. As a social critic and analyst rather than a system builder or theorist, Malcolm discovered that it is easier to interpret and reinterpret an old message than develop a new system or body of thought which is coherent, comprehensive, and relevant to the urgencies of the day.

A third factor which shaped Malcolm's theoretical assertions and development was *the need to attract new adherents and allies.* As a practical and active man, Malcolm faced the task of building a new base of followers and supporters who could offer the kind of practical assistance necessary to launch and complete newly proposed social projects. It was obvious that unless he wanted even more hostile confrontations with the NOI, he would have to construct an alternative philosophical framework which had at least two characteristics. First, it would have to clearly disassociate him from the limited religious appeal and emphasis of the NOI; second, it would have to be broad and various enough to draw the maximum number of' adherents and allies.

Thus, the philosophy of the OAAU is eclectic and conducive to flexibility in interpretation and application. It allows for the reformism of voting as well as the revolutionary emphasis on armed struggle. Its focus and essence is the liberation of Blacks in the United States, but it urges the creation of allies in the Third World as well as among sincere revolutionaries of any color. It is essentially this thrust and search for the operational and inclusive analysis of and position on vital issues that gives Malcolm's theoretical development much of its unevenness and makes it seem contradictory in parts.

A fourth factor which shaped Malcolm's theoretical development was his *commitment to growth and expansion* and the constant developmental change this commitment required. In his autobiography, he writes that his life has been a "chronology of *changes*" (Malcolm X 1964, 344) and that he knew that, because of this tendency, people would criticize and condemn him. However, he argues, even if his policies and programs changed, he would not change his ultimate objective—the liberation of Black people "by any means necessary":

> Policies change, and programs change, according to time. But the objective never changes. You might change your method of achieving the objective, but the objective never changes. Our objective is complete freedom, complete justice, complete equality, by any means necessary. (Malcolm X 1965, 116)

Indeed, his policy and program after he left the NOI did change—from a policy and program advocating an organization of Blacks for limited religious and nationalist purposes to an attempt to build a broad-based organization and movement of the oppressed many to defy and defeat the ruling few.

The project first involved a focus on *Black* and a thrust toward interclass Black unity; it then extended to a campaign for Third World solidarity and a possible alliance with whites who had committed racial and/or class suicide and demonstrated a capacity for common revolutionary struggle. Thus, the labels "contradictory," "revolutionary internationalist," "Third World socialist," etc., are too facile to be profound or definitive, too rigid to reflect the adaptive vitality and creative versatility of the man. Malcolm prided himself on his open-mindedness and ability to change in the light of new evidence and analysis. A failure to recognize and respect such adaptive vitality reduces analysis of Malcolm's thought and practice to mere labeling and thus deprives Black America and the world of the rich variety in his life and legacy.

The Ideological Legacy

Nationalism

At the core of Malcolm X's social and political thought is the fundamental concept of Black Nationalism. Regardless of the new names and purposes Malcolm has been given since his death, he was above all a nationalist—an unashamed partisan for his own people, Afro-Americans. In redefining his philosophy after his disassociation from the NOI, he stated: "Our political philosophy will be Black nationalism. Our economic and social philosophy will be Black nationalism. Our cultural emphasis will be Black nationalism" (Malcolm X 1965, 21). To Malcolm nationalism was an inescapable consciousness and practice if Blacks were to liberate, defend, and develop themselves. He argued that the key identity of Blacks was not organizational but social and racial:

> You don't catch hell because you're a Methodist or Baptist; you don't catch hell because you're a Democrat or a Republican; you don't catch hell because you're a Mason or an Elk; and you sure don't catch hell because you're an American; you catch hell because you're a Black man. (Malcolm X 1965, 4)

The need, then, was to recognize this fundamental fact and respond creatively to it.

Malcolm's nationalism was concerned not merely with defense but also with development. He understood that

> [a] race of people is like an individual man; until it uses its own talent, takes pride in its own history, expresses its own culture, affirms its own selfhood, it can never fulfill itself. (Malcolm X 1970a, 53)

To Malcolm collective achievement yielded self-confirmation and self-respect, as well as recognition and respect from others.

Malcolm's nationalism also recognized and urged the need for a cultural revolution. Malcolm, like other Black leaders, appreciated the importance of culture in the liberation struggle. He observed in the charter of the OAAU: "Culture is an indispensable weapon in tile freedom struggle. We must take hold of it and forge the future with the past" (Malcolm X 1970a, 56). Thus, "[w]e must recapture our heritage and our identity if we are ever to liberate ourselves from the bonds of white supremacy. We must launch a cultural revolution to unbrainwash an entire people" (Malcolm X 1970a, 55). Malcolm's view was, in fact, *cultural nationalism*—the recognition and appreciation that until Black history and humanity are rescued and reconstructed, until the oppressor's monopoly on Black minds is broken, liberation on any other level is impossible.

Orthodox Muslims, socialists, and integrationists often deny Malcolm's Black Nationalist position and picture him as a one-dimensional reflection of their own philosophies. For them, Malcolm was in the last years of his life a changed man, having seen a great light and evolved to a "higher" level of Islamic, socialist, or integrationist consciousness. However, these contentions must be seen for what they are. First, they are essentially wishful distortions, understandable attempts to appropriate from Black history a man of such great meaning and magnitude not only to Black people but also to human history and development. Second, such contentions are abstractions of quotations from the rich variety of Malcolm's thought without appreciation for context, motive of assertion, and overall theoretical consistency and emphasis.

Orthodox Muslims, socialists, and integrationists make two assertions which they feel justify their contentions that Malcolm had abandoned Black Nationalism as a core principle of his social and political thought. The first is that his hajj to Mecca caused him to see white folks in a different light, i.e., that they were capable of fraternity with Black folks through Islam. Indeed, Malcolm did say: "The true Islam has shown me that a blanket indictment of all white people is as wrong as when whites make blanket indictments against Blacks" (Malcolm X 1964, 368). From this position, he eventually argued that it was social context which created evil white men rather than their genetic makeup. The white man, he concluded, "is *not* inherently evil, but America's racist society influences him to act evilly. The society has produced and nourishes a psychology which brings out the lowest, most base part of human beings" (Malcolm X 1964, 377).

The second assertion emerges from an incident in which the Algerian ambassador in Ghana asked Malcolm where Malcolm's philosophy of Black Nationalism left the ambassador and other "white revolutionaries" who were Malcolm's potential allies in the struggle for liberation. Malcolm claimed that he was forced to reconsider the use of the term *Black Nationalism*, though he later admitted that he could find no word as definitive to describe his overall philosophy (Malcolm X 1965, 212).

Although Malcolm's religious experiences on the hajj to Mecca influenced his decision to lift his blanket indictment of whites, other factors also shaped the decision and merit discussion. As mentioned above, Malcolm was confronted with the need to break away from the biological interpretation of white racism, which he had inherited from the NOI, in order to develop a new image and ideological thrust and thus win new adherents and allies. It is only logical that his reevaluation of this position took place within an Islamic context and was explained in religious terms. Such a religious reevaluation not only won him new allies among the orthodox Muslims but also justified, or at least facilitated, his reinterpretation of white humanity in a way that a purely political reevaluation never could—especially for a nationalist.

Moreover, it is important to note two assertions made by Malcolm regarding his religious reevaluation of whites. First, Malcolm pointed out that he made a distinction between Muslims and ordinary white men and between the world of Islam, where the brotherhood of men was possible and practiced, and the United States, where the brotherhood of men was both nonexistent and problematic to achieve:

It was in the Holy World that my attitude was changed by what I experienced *there,* and by what I witnessed *there,* in terms of brotherhood—not just brotherhood toward me, but brotherhood between all men, of all nationalities and complexions, who were *there.* And now that I am *back* in America, my attitude *here* concerning white people has to be governed by what my Black brothers and I experience *here,* and what we witness *here*—in terms of brotherhood. (Malcolm X 1964, 362; emphasis added)

Thus, Malcolm did not confuse a religious experience in Saudi Arabia with the social experience in the United States. One was an experience of religious fraternity and the other an experience of social oppression.

Moreover, Malcolm made it clear on his return from Mecca that his letter from there was not a signal of a change from Black Nationalist to integrationist Muslim but a broadening of perspective through travel and the exchange and learning which it engenders. "Travel broadens one's scope," he observed. "It doesn't mean you change—you broaden" (Malcolm X 1965, 70). Although he saw Islam as contributive to this new insight and position, he was careful to point out that it in no way meant he had abandoned his commitment to Black liberation by becoming more religious than Black, more Muslim than nationalist.

Speaking directly to this question, he stressed:

No religion will ever make me forget the condition of our people in this country. No religion will ever make me forget the continued fighting with dogs against our people in this country. No religion will make me forget the police clubs that come up 'side our heads. No God, no religion, no nothing will make me forget it until it stops, until it's finished, until it's eliminated. I want to make that point clear. (Malcolm X 1965, 70)

Thus, the point is clear that the move to redefine his image and ideology, to win new adherents and allies and to communicate a possibility of human fraternity in and through Islam was not for Malcolm either a denial or a diminishing of his clear and unshakeable commitment to Black people and their liberation. As Malcolm points out, he was concerned, after discussion with the Algerian ambassador, that he perhaps "was alienating people who were true revolutionaries" (Malcolm X 1965, 212) and potential allies. Moreover, he did not want to appear as if he were simply rephrasing the NOI's racial emphasis and thus limit his appeal and audience. Yet, as he noted, he was "hard pressed" to provide a more specific or definitive expression to characterize the overall philosophy he felt necessary for Black liberation.

Malcolm's response to the Algerian ambassador, however, would undoubtedly have been different if two conditions had prevailed: (1) if Malcolm had already consolidated his organizational base and felt more secure in his direction toward liberation, and (2) if his ideological thrusts had been less eclectic and had already assumed a solid systematic form resistant to external challenges such as the one the Algerian posed. The fluid and broad character of Malcolm's social thought was a reflection and result of both this concern for adherents and allies and the fact that he was not a builder of an alternative system of thought. Moreover, the urgencies and the brevity of the time in which he had to build were also limiting and deprived him of the conditions he needed to develop an operational ideological framework even at the level of which he was capable.

Under different circumstances and with an alternative body of nationalist thought resistant to conflicting variations, Malcolm could have taught the Algerian ambassador a lesson in ideology and struggle as he had taught others so often. A consolidated system of Black Nationalist thought would have allowed and encouraged Malcolm to challenge the ambassador's position rather than accept it or be overly influenced by it.

After all, all revolutions are nationalist, i.e., directed toward the liberation of a given nation. Black Nationalism is, thus, a social consciousness and practice dedicated to the liberation of Blacks, just as Algerian nationalism was dedicated to the liberation of Algerians. Moreover, *Black* and *Afro-American* are used interchangeably just as the Algerians and French used *Arab* and *Algerian* interchangeably—and, according to Fanon, even *nigger*. In addition, the term *Black* has a social as well as a racial connotation. From a social perspective, it refers to an oppressed as well as potentially the most revolutionary national community in the United States. Thus, if the Algerian could not have identified with the racial connotation of *Black*, he should have had no problem identifying with its social connotation—and therefore with the struggle of Blacks in the United States—if indeed he was for the oppressed and against the oppressor.

Finally, when the Algerian ambassador said he was white, he unwittingly showed the social and political importance of color in a world where Europe once ruled minds as well as bodies and made race an essential category of identification and human worth throughout the world. During the French rule of Algeria, the Algerians were designated as "niggers" and, at best, "miserable Arabs." Thus, it is interesting to note that even after Algeria had achieved its independence, this Algerian revolutionary would still use a racial category—even to counter Malcolm's use—and then would choose *white* as the most appropriate racial category in which to place himself. Even if he had problems with being considered (by the previous French colonialists) as a "nigger" (or "socially" *Black*), for the sake of alliance and common identity, he could have eschewed racial categories altogether and said he was, like Malcolm, *African*. After all, in spite of what his former colonial rulers told him before independence, Algeria is not a part of France or Europe but a nation-state in Africa. It is this kind of contradiction that Malcolm, *under different circumstances*, would have enjoyed exposing and challenging.

In conclusion, then, it is important to establish that Malcolm was above all a nationalist who saw nationalism as a correct and indispensable social consciousness and practice necessary to achieve Black liberation. Malcolm, however, did caution nationalists not to be dogmatic or narrow and urged them not to condemn people for their race but to condemn then for their social thought and practice. "It's smarter," he observed, "to say you're going to shoot a man for what he is doing to you than because he's white. If you attack him because he's white, you give him no out … [because] he can't stop being white" (Malcolm X 1965, 213). In the same statement, however, he stressed, "I haven't changed. I just see things on a broader scale.… We got to be more flexible" (Malcolm X 1965, 213). Open-mindedness and flexibility, yet constant commitment to the overriding objective of Black liberation "by any means necessary," defined the development and direction of Malcolm's social thought. In essence, these characteristics make up Black nationalism, in spite of the opportunistic labeling that emerges from the marketplace of distorted ideas and of deficient analysis of Malcolm's thought.

Islamic Regeneration

A second aspect of Malcolm's social thought was his stress on *Islam as a key to Black moral regeneration and spiritual elevation.* He was not simply a Black Nationalist; he was a Black *religious* Nationalist. As a religious nationalist, he posed moral and spiritual development as fundamental to social and political development. Linking Islam and Black Nationalism, he explained the liberation process as one that moves from the mental and moral to the political. For Malcolm, the need was for the Black man (and by logical extension, the Black woman) to become aware of his and her potential and responsibility; then he and she would ostensibly become able to contribute to the nationalist thrust toward racial dignity and economic and political self-determination and development. Malcolm contended:

> [T]he religion of Islam makes him morally more able to rise above the evils and the vices of an immoral society. And the political, economic, and social philosophy of Black nationalism instills within him the racial dignity and the incentive and the confidence that he needs to stand on his own feet and take a stand for himself. (Malcolm X 1970a, 9–10)

Malcolm was fond of saying, "Wake them up, clean them up and then, stand them up." Also, at the founding of the Muslim Mosque, Inc., Malcolm again stressed the need for moral reformation in the Black community and linked nationalism with Islam in the overall project of liberation:

> The Muslim Mosque, Inc. will have as its religious base the religion of Islam, which will be designed to propagate the moral reformation necessary to up the level of the so-called Negro community by eliminating the vices and the other evils that destroy the moral fiber of the community—this is the religious base. But the political philosophy of the Muslim Mosque will be Black nationalism, and the social philosophy will be Black nationalism. (Malcolm X 1970a, 5)

It is important to note here that Malcolm stressed religion as a *social practice* rather than a *spiritual ritual*. He rejected the white-oriented, heaven-centered Christianity taught to Blacks, declaring:

> Here in race-torn America, I am convinced that the Islamic religion is desperately needed, particularly by the American Black man. The Black man needs to reflect that he has been America's most fervent Christian—and where has it gotten him? In fact, in the white man's hands, in the white man's interpretation where has Christianity brought this world? (Malcolm X 1964, 369)

For Malcolm, religion was a support of social struggle, not a substitute for it. It was a call to struggle against social evil and the evil men who created and sustained it. He explained this social interpretation of religion as follows:

> When I talk like this, it doesn't mean I'm less religious, it means I'm more religious. I believe in a religion that believes in freedom. Any time I have to accept a religion that won't let me fight a battle for my people, I say to hell with that religion. (Malcolm X 1970a, 140)

Such a religion, then, which had enabled him to raise and reconstruct himself "from the muck and mire of this rotting world" (Malcolm X 1964, 287), was for Malcolm a clear asset to the Black liberation struggle on both a spiritual and a practical level.

Community Unity

A third fundamental principle of Malcolm's social thought was the stress on community unity as an indispensable condition for the building of an effective united Black front against oppression and exploitation. Malcolm argued continuously that the fundamental reality of Blacks was their Blackness. It was their Blackness which caused them to "catch hell," not their identity as Elks, Masons, Baptists, or Methodists. Thus, he concluded, "What you and I need to do is learn to forget our differences. When we come together, we don't come together as Baptists or Methodists" (Malcolm X 1965, 4), but as Black people with a common enemy and a common objective.

It is in the spirit of this drive for an effective operational unity that Malcolm established the OAAU in 1964, modeled after the OAU on the continent. In building this intra-Black unity, Malcolm stressed that this effort should not be interrupted or diverted by a premature attempt to forge an alliance with whites. He argued that there could be no real and effective solidarity with others until there was solidarity among Blacks. Speaking directly to this issue, he stated:

> There can be no Black-white unity until there is first some Black unity. There can be no workers' solidarity until there is first some racial solidarity. We cannot think of uniting with others, until after we have first united among ourselves. We cannot think of being acceptable to others until we have first proven acceptable to ourselves. One can't unite bananas with scattered leaves. (Malcolm X 1965, 21–22)

Obviously, he saw that the premature alliances and unequal relations which Blacks were quick to form with whites were another form of white hegemony and Black dependence.

Moreover, he recognized such an arrangement as another excuse by some escapist Blacks not to organize and work in their own community. As long as such groups and individuals could cling to the edge of white achievement, they could and often would, he felt, use that as a substitute for their own achievement and shirk their responsibility to their community. For those whites who proved or wanted to prove themselves sincere, Malcolm urged them to work among the racists in their own community and convert them to nonracist and nonviolent positions:

> I tell sincere white people, "Work in conjunction with us—each of us working among our own kind." Let sincere white individuals find all other white people they can who feel as they do—and let them form their own all-white groups, to work trying to convert other white people who are thinking and acting so racist. Let sincere whites go and teach non-violence to white people! (Malcolm X 1964, 377)

Thus, he concluded: "Working separately, the sincere white people and sincere Black people actually will be working together" (Malcolm X 1964, 377).

Community Organization

Fourth, Malcolm argued for total community organization as a necessary part and requirement of community unity. He urged everyone to join an organization of his or her choice, to get mobilized and organized, and to stand ready for the hour of action. Nationalism, he argued, demands such total organization. Thus, he said, join the NAACP, CORE, SNCC, the church or "any organization, that has a gospel that's for the uplift of the Black man...." And if the organization is not practicing the Black upliftment it preaches, disassociate yourself from it and join another. "And in this manner, the organizations will increase in number and in quantity and in quality." (Malcolm X 1965, 41).

Malcolm stressed group tolerance and cooperation. Perhaps remembering and responding to his experience with the NOI, he stated: "We don't have the right to force anyone to walk with us, nor do we have the right to condemn those who want to leave" (Malcolm X 1970a, 111). Thus, he concluded:

> If brothers want to establish another organization … that is their right. We must learn to wish them well, and mean it. Our fight must never be against each other. No matter how much we differ on minor things, our fight must always be directed against the *common enemy*. (Malcolm X 1970a, 111)

After all, he reasoned, "If our own program produces results, then our work will speak for itself. If we don't produce results, then we have no argument anyway" (Malcolm X 1970a, 112). In conclusion, then, Malcolm reasoned that once each group was organized around its own interests and everyone was in a group of his or her choice, then each group and each person could be linked in the common struggle for Black liberation and a higher level of human life.

Redefinition of the Struggle

A fifth theoretical contribution of Malcolm's social thought was his redefinition of the Black struggle as one for human rights rather than one for civil rights. Malcolm engaged in this effort for four reasons. First, Malcolm argued that, in essence, the Black struggle was more of a human struggle than a civil rights struggle. He contended:

> We are fighting for recognition as human beings. We are fighting for the right to live as free humans in this society. In fact, we are actually fighting for rights that are even greater than civil rights and that is human rights. (Malcolm X 1965, 51)

Blacks, thus, were not fighting for civil rights as much as they were for rights they had from birth as human beings—human rights. Given this redefined struggle, Malcolm argued: "[T]he Black problem has ceased to be [simply] a [Black] problem. It has ceased to be an American problem and has now become a world problem, a problem for all humanity" (Malcolm X 1969, 173).

Such assumption and assertion logically led to a broadening of the moral and political appeal of the Black struggle. For they had been posed in human terms and goals all nations could identify with and support. Malcolm observed:

> Human rights are something you were born with. Human rights are your God-given rights. Human rights are the rights that are recognized by all nations of this earth. (Malcolm X 1965, 35)

Thus, being denied rights vital to the defense and development of the human personality was a moral and political question which extended in importance and impact beyond the United States, winning more new allies for the Black struggle.

A third reason Malcolm argued for the redefinition of the Black struggle was to effect a clear rupture between Blacks and the American system and to expose the system for what it really was. Indeed, Malcolm contended:

> Uncle Sam's hands are dripping with the blood, dripping with the blood of the Black man in this country. He's the earth's number-one hypocrite … posing as the leader of the free world. (Malcolm X 1965, 35)

Thus, it was incumbent on Blacks to "[l]et the world know how bloody his hands are [and to] [l]et the world know the hypocrisy that's practiced over here" (Malcolm X 1965, 35).

Finally, Malcolm sought to redefine the Black struggle as essentially a human rights struggle in order to internationalize it in scope and content and thus to avoid the UN-sanctioned international prohibition against interference in domestic affairs. He asserted: "Whenever you are in a civil-rights struggle, whether you know it or not, you are confining yourself to the jurisdiction of Uncle Sam" (Malcolm X 1965, 34). Given the restrictions under Chapter 1, Article 2, Section 7 of the UN Charter, "[a]ll our African brothers and our Asian brothers and our Latin American brothers cannot open their mouths and interfere in the domestic affairs of the United States" (Malcolm X 1965, 34). However, he reasoned, once "you expand the civil-rights struggle to the level of human rights, you can then take the case of the Black man in this country before the nations in the UN" (Malcolm X 1965, 34) and argue on two levels. First, Blacks could argue that the case is a violation of the UN Covenant on Human Rights. Second, they could argue that Black oppression is a threat to world peace under Chapter VII, which deals with threats to peace, breaches of peace, and acts of aggression. In light of these provisions, Malcolm contended: "We have to make the world see that the problem with which we're confronted is a problem for humanity," not just a Black problem. For, in fact, "there'll be no peace on this earth as long as our human rights are being violated in America" (Malcolm X 1970a, 86).

Third World Solidarity

A sixth core principle of Malcolm's social and political thought was his commitment to *Third World solidarity,* the unity and collective struggle of the people of color, the "have-nots," whose collective liberation struggle was for him the main force behind the history of this era. Three factors shaped his thought on this focus and concern: (1) his background in the NOI; (2) his study and appreciation of the Bandung Conference; and (3) his travels in Africa and Asia, which placed him in contact and exchange with Third World peoples, their leaders, and movements.

As mentioned above, a fundamental assumption and contention of the NOI was that the world is divided into only two peoples—the Original Men and their diabolical derivatives, in other words, divine Blacks and white devils. Thus, although the Blacks in the United States are the chosen, Africans, Asians, and Latin Americans are all one people—variations of the Original Man (Lincoln 1961, 75; Essien-Udom 1962, 147).

A second factor which helped shape Malcolm's concept of the Third World was his study and appreciation of the possibilities projected by the Afro-Asian Bandung Conference held in 1955 in Bandung, Indonesia, where nineteen African and Asian states took their first major step toward defining themselves as an independent force in the world. As early as 1959, Malcolm had posed Bandung as a united-front model for the Harlem Black leadership. Within the framework of the NOI, he saw Bandung and subsequently all-African and Afro-Asian conferences as indicative of the increasing "unity of Black mankind" (Essien-Udom 1962, 156). Again, in 1963, in his "Message to the Grass-roots," he posed Bandung as a model for uniting in opposition to a common enemy and using the struggle against this enemy as a method of overcoming petty differences among Black peoples (Malcolm X 1965, 5*ff.*).

Finally, Malcolm's concept of the Third World was shaped by his travels, which, as he said, broadened his perspective and made him see the international dimension of power and oppression. Speaking in 1964 at an OAAU meeting to honor Fannie Lou Hamer and brief the Black community on his trip to Africa and Asia, Malcolm stressed the need to identify with the Third World and to see power and oppression as global. He argued: "Today, power is international, real power is international; today, real power is not local" (Malcolm X 1965, 129). Thus, Blacks here must look beyond the United States and discover where they "fit in the scheme of things" (Malcolm X 1965, 117).

Blacks, he continued, are not alone but have natural allies, Third World peoples— Africans, Asians, and Latin Americans. The need then is for Blacks to see that in the struggle against European oppression, "We are all brothers of oppression and today brothers of oppression are identified with each other all over the world" (Malcolm X 1970a, 13). Thus:

> When the 22 million Black Americans see that our problem is the same as the problem of the people who are being oppressed in South Vietnam and the Congo and Latin America, then—then oppressed people of this earth make up a majority, not a minority—then we approach our problem as a majority that can *demand,* not as a minority that has to beg. (Malcolm X 1965, 218)

Malcolm further reasoned: "[W]e are today seeing a global rebellion of the oppressed against the oppressor, the exploited against the exploiter" (Malcolm X 1965, 217). And in this "era of revolution ... the revolt of the American [Black] is part of the rebellion against oppression and colonialism which has characterized this era" (Malcolm X 1965, 217). History, according to Malcolm, has thus thrust upon Third World peoples a collective task of global liberation, and Afro-Americans must recognize their central role in this project, not as an American minority but as a world majority. In this way, he reasoned, Blacks would self-consciously assume their essential role as part and parcel of the rising tide and the main force behind the history of this era, thereby freeing themselves and in the process contributing to human liberation on a world scale.

Finally, it is important to note that Malcolm's identification with and support of Third World struggles led him to the conclusion that socialism was a basic aspect of Third World struggles for liberation. He noted that almost every one of the African and Asian countries "that has gotten independence has devised some kind of socialistic system" (Malcolm X 1965, 120). It follows then, according to Malcolm, that if Blacks find that the nations in Africa and Asia are developing socialist systems to solve their problems, Blacks might find it advantageous to emulate them. He asserted:

> Before [Blacks] start trying to be incorporated or integrated, or disintegrated, into this capitalistic system, [they] should look over there and find out what [system] are the people who have gotten their freedom adopting to provide themselves with better housing ... better education ... better food ... and better clothing. (Malcolm X 1965, 121)

It is these and other similar assertions which lead to the conclusion that Malcolm had begun to extend his position to include a socialist solution to Afro-American and other Third World problems.

Pan-Africanism

Pan-Africanism formed a seventh pillar in the social and political thought of Malcolm X. For within the overarching framework of his early emphasis on Third World solidarity, Malcolm placed special stress on Afro-American solidarity with other African peoples — both those in Africa and those in the Diaspora. All Blacks, he maintained, are African peoples and thus need to build an active and effective unity which would increase their power. "Can you imagine," he pondered, "what can happen, what would certainly happen, if all of these African-heritage people ever *realize* their blood bonds, if they ever realize they all have a common goal — if they ever unite" (Malcolm X 1964, 363). Moreover, to harness at least a part of this potential energy among African peoples, Malcolm, emulating the Organization of African Unity, asserted that he had formed with others

> an organization known as the Organization of Afro-American Unity which has the same aim and objective — to fight whoever gets in our way, to bring about the complete independence of people of African descent here in the Western Hemisphere, and first here in the United States, and bring about the freedom of these people by any means necessary. (Malcolm X 1970a, 37)

For Malcolm, the establishment of the OAAU was a step toward organizing Africans in the Diaspora and uniting them with Africans in Africa in the collective project of Black liberation on a world scale — in the tradition of Marcus Garvey.

Repeatedly, Malcolm stressed the need for Africans in the Diaspora to identify and unite with Africans in Africa. Even in the NOI, which focused more on the Arab and Islamic worlds, Malcolm wrote from Africa in 1959:

> Africa is the land of the future ... definitely the land of tomorrow, and the African is the man of tomorrow.... Africa is the New World, a world with a future ... in which the so-called American Negroes are destined to play a key role. (Lincoln 1961, 225–226)

Although Malcolm stressed the need for Afro-Americans to identify and unite with Africans in Africa, he equally stressed the need for them to identify and unite with themselves in the United States. Moving from his earlier position that Afro-Americans should physically return to Africa, Malcolm argued in the end that it would be more prudent for Afro-Americans to return spiritually and culturally to Africa while building a power base for Blacks in the United States (Malcolm X 1970a, 104).

The Pan-Africanism Malcolm argued for also contained at its core the assumption and urgency of mutually beneficial relations between Africans in Africa and Africans in the Diaspora. But he also stressed the need for Africans in Africa to recognize their responsibility to Africans in the United States in solving a problem which might seem unique to them but was, in fact, a problem of all African peoples. Thus, in his appeal to the African heads of state at the OAU Conference in Cairo, July 17–21, 1964, he argued:

> Your problems will never be fully solved until and unless ours are solved. You will never be fully respected until and unless we are also respected. You will never be recognized as free human beings until and unless we are also recognized and treated as human beings. (Malcolm X 1965, 75)

Given this reality, Malcolm continued, it would be to the interest of Africans in Africa to support the Afro-American struggle against racist exploitation and oppression by assisting in bringing the Black problem to the UN. After all, Malcolm chided the heads of state, if Jews could find legal grounds for threatening to bring Russia before the UN for violating Russian Jewish human rights, Africans in Africa and in the UN should be able to do — and should not hesitate to do — the same for their African relatives in the United States. He hoped that they would not submit to the economic coercion of neocolonialism—or in his words, "that our African brothers have not freed themselves of European colonialism only to be overcome and held in check now by American *dollarism*" (Malcolm X 1965, 76).

Accent on Youth

An eighth core concept in Malcolm's social thought was his accent on youth. Malcolm saw Black youth as the fundamental element in the construction of Black people's future. "This generation," he said, "especially of our people, has a burden, more so than any other time in history … [and] the most important thing that we can learn to do today is think for ourselves" (Malcolm X 1965, 137). Speaking of the directions his new movement would take, he noted:

> [O]ur accent will be upon youth. We've already issued a call for the students in the colleges and universities across the country, to launch their own independent studies of the race problem in the country and then bring their analyses and their suggestions for a new approach back to us so that we can devise an action program geared to their thinking. The accent is on youth because the youth have less stake in this corrupt system and therefore can look at it more objectively, whereas the adults lose their ability to look at it objectively because of their stake in it. (Malcolm X 1970a, 6)

Malcolm urged Black adult responsibility to Black children—specifically, adult responsibility to teach the children history, respect, and collective responsibility. He stressed:

> We must provide constructive activities for our children. We must set a good example for our children and must teach them always to be ready to accept the responsibilities that are necessary for building good communities and nations. We must teach them that their greatest responsibilities are to themselves, to their families and to their communities. (Malcolm X 1970a, 52)

For Malcolm, youth had a special role in making revolution and building a new world. He saw "a powerful example in the Young Simbas in the Congo and the young fighters in South Vietnam" (Malcolm X 1965, 222), and he urged Black youth to follow their example in initiative and daring as agents of both continuity and profound social change.

Freedom By Any Means Necessary

Finally, at the front, center, and end of Malcolm's social thought was his stress on the right and responsibility of Black people to struggle for freedom using any means necessary. Within the framework of this overarching concept were two constant themes: self-defense and self-liberation through revolution. The theme of self-defense began for Malcolm even in the NOI and stayed with him throughout his life. For Malcolm, it was a moral right and responsibility for Blacks to defend themselves and "criminal to teach any man not to defend himself when he is the constant victim of brutal attacks" (Malcolm X 1965, 22). The tactic of nonviolence used by the civil rights movement was to him both dangerous and deceptive. For it assumed the morality of an amoral or immoral oppressor. "Tactics based solely on morality," he stated, "can only succeed when dealing with people who are moral or a system that is moral" (Malcolm X 1970a, 43). However, history had proved, he concluded, that the United States could claim neither.

Malcolm further argued that self-defense was also a political right guaranteed by Article 2 of the Constitution, which prohibits infringement on the right of the people to bear arms (Malcolm X 1970a, 11). For Malcolm, then, inherent in the right to bear arms was the right to self-defense against citizen and government abuse and threats.

Moreover, Malcolm reasoned that Black assumption of this responsibility would provoke more responsive action from the government. Using as an example the president's ordering of troops to Birmingham during the Black revolt in 1963, Malcolm observed:

> The only time he sent troops into Birmingham was when the [Blacks] erupted, and then the President sent the troops in there, not to protect the [Blacks] but to protect them white people down there from those erupting [Blacks]. (Lomax 1964, 178–179)

Finally, Malcolm saw government abuse of its coercive power as a threat to Black life and rights; thus he realized the need of Blacks for the capacity to defend themselves against such abuse. He noted that police are in the Black community not to protect Blacks but to oppress and check them. Not only, he concluded, do they not protect Blacks; "in fact, sometimes we need protection against *them*" (Malcolm X 1970a, 30). Thus, for Malcolm, the need for a self-defense capacity among Black folks was imperative—in fact, indispensable.

It seems only logical that a man of such daring assertiveness and righteous indignation against oppression and exploitation would eventually argue not only for self-defense but also for revolution. Revolution, Malcolm argued, was, in the final analysis, the price people pay for human rights, and their dignity leads to the struggle that individuals make as human beings to secure and defend them. To him, revolution was a right and a process in the pursuit and defense of human freedom. Moreover, revolution, Malcolm observed, was a cause that, of necessity, involved the loss of life on both sides. Thus, he claimed, Blacks must be ready not only to lose their lives but to take the oppressor's life also, for "any cause that can cost you your life must be the type of cause in which you yourself are willing to take life" (Malcolm X 1970a, 84).

Malcolm warned Blacks against the fatalism that would make them feel incapable of this historical task. For if they could fight wars against great odds for whites overseas, they could fight for themselves. As he put it, "if you can be brave over there, you can be brave right here.... And if you fight here, you will at least know what you're fighting for" (Malcolm X 1965, 25). Also, he warned against letting the charge of violence and the negative image it carries in this society deter those who dare struggle. Indeed, according to Malcolm, "[n]obody who's looking for a good image will ever be free" (Malcolm X 1965, 134).

Finally, Malcolm linked the right of the oppressed to freedom to the privilege of the oppressor to peace, arguing that if Blacks could not have freedom, the oppressor would have no peace. He contended that "if we can't be recognized and respected as human beings, we have to create a situation where no human being will enjoy life, liberty, and the pursuit of happiness" (Malcolm X 1970a, 86). Malcolm summed up his position as follows:

> We declare our right on this earth to be a man, to be a human being, to be respected as a human being, to be given the rights of a human being in this society, on this earth, in this day, which we intend to bring into existence by any means necessary. (Malcolm X 1970a, 56)

In this statement, Malcolm posed the Afro-American question again as, in essence, a human struggle. It is this focus and stress on the human character and importance of the Black liberation struggle that makes his contribution to his people at the same time his contribution to humanity, to every effort for national liberation, and to every struggle for human freedom and dignity in the world.

References

Clarke, John H., ed. 1969. *Malcolm X: The man and his times.* New York: Macmillan.

Essien-Udom, E. U. 1962. *Black Nationalism: A search for identity in America.* New York: Dell.

Lincoln, C. Eric. 1961. *The Black Muslims in America.* Boston: Beacon Press.

Lomax, Louis. 1964. *When the word is given.* New York: New American Library.

Malcolm X. 1964. *The autobiography of Malcolm X.* New York: Grove.

_____. 1965. *Malcolm X speaks: Selected speeches and statements.* Ed. George Breitman. New York: Grove.

_____. 1969. *The speeches of Malcolm X at Harvard.* Ed. Archie Epps. New York: William Morrow.

_____. 1970a. *By any means necessary.* Ed. George Breitman. New York: Pathfinder.

_____. 1970b. *Malcolm X on Afro-American history.* New York: Pathfinder.

_____. 1971. *The end of white supremacy: Four speeches.* Ed. George Breitman. New York: Merlin House.

Pinkney, Alphonso. 1978. *Red, black and green: Black Nationalism in the United States.* New York: Cambridge University Press.

7

Malcolm X and the Economic Salvation of African Americans

James B. Stewart

Introduction

This paper examines the foundations of the proposals advocated by Malcolm X (born Malcolm Little, aka El-Hajj Malik El-Shabazz) to foster the economic liberation of African Americans. It argues that his proposals originated, in part, from his difficult personal experiences in coping with an exploitative economic system. The analysis builds on this author's previous investigations that identified three interrelated political-economic models in Malcolm's thought (Stewart 1990, 1992). The first of these models focuses on the economics of a separate Black nation-state; the second analyzes the economics of "urban-community-based" development in the United States; and the third explores macrointernational economic relations.

Although there are three distinct models in Malcolm's thought, as his understanding of the global economic order deepened, they merged into a synthesis that linked the plight of African Americans to that of peoples of African descent worldwide. The present study devotes comparatively little attention to a critique of the internal logic of the models. Rather, it emphasizes identifying those aspects of Malcolm's personal experiences that shaped his perceptions of how to stimulate sustained economic empowerment for peoples of African descent. The *Autobiography of Malcolm X* (1966) and the controversial biography by Bruce Perry (1991) are used here to identify the experiences salient for understanding Malcolm's economic philosophy. However, Malcolm's economic thought itself must be culled from an examination of his speeches, since he left no treatises addressing it.

The hypotheses that undergird the present investigation are (a) that a basic pattern of limited attachment to mainstream economic institutions characterized Malcolm's experiences and those of his family throughout his formative years and (b) that this pattern of economic alienation and the process of developing survival strategies were a major force shaping Malcolm's general ideas about political economy and his specific proposals for empowering African Americans.

Malcolm's experiences led him to adopt a theory of economics that advocates wholesale changes in the economic order rather than small adjustments to the status quo. His emphasis on the need to change existing structures led him to concentrating on the political component of the political-economic nexus. Consequently, his discussions of economics describe general tendencies of systems rather than specific details. At the same time, Malcolm continually integrated insights from new experiences into his system of thought, eventually leading him to a comparatively sophisticated understanding of the complexities of the contemporary domestic and international economic orders.

The experiential foundations of each of the three models are explored in the next three sections, beginning with the model of the separate Black nation. The contemporary relevance of Malcolm's perspectives is explored in the final section.

The African/African American State Solution

Malcolm's early exposure to the teaching of Marcus Garvey facilitated his advocacy of Elijah Muhammad's proposal for a Black nation-state during the early period of his association with the Nation of Islam. The vision of a separate nation-state for African Americans was rooted in the drive to establish a geographic space where African Americans could exercise political, economic, and social control over their own destinies. This drive found concrete expression in the individual lives of Black families, including Malcolm's:

> My father wanted to find a place where he could raise our own food and perhaps build a business. The teaching of Marcus Garvey stressed becoming independent of the white man. We went next for some reason to Lansing, Michigan. My father bought a house and soon, as had been his pattern, he was doing free-lance Christian preaching in local Negro Baptist churches, and during the week he was roaming about spreading word of Marcus Garvey. (Malcolm X 1966, 3)

This account documents the strong emphasis on self-sufficiency in the provision of basic needs (i.e., food and shelter), as well as the need for independence from exploitative labor markets. For Earl Little, independent preaching was a form of self-employment. The forces that led Earl Little to supplement his income through odd jobs generated similar responses from other Black ministers. Odd jobs were not, however, Earl Little's only extraministerial venture. Malcolm related that the family also raised rabbits and sold them to whites (Malcolm X 1966, 9). This experience helped cultivate the idea that small businesses were an important foundation upon which to build larger cooperative economic ventures. To illustrate, Malcolm was asked in 1963 about the smallness of the businesses operated by members of the Nation of Islam. In response, he argued:

> [Y]ou have to start small and develop into that which you ultimately will become. And the Honorable Elijah Muhammad has actually shown his business ingenuity by showing how to start out small and develop our businesses — make them grow — and then our business ability grows right along with that business. (Malcolm X 1963b, 84)

Earl Little used the family homestead to raise a portion of the food consumed as part of his strategy for independence. Malcolm recalled developing an attachment to that homestead by participating in the process of planting and raising foodstuffs (Malcolm X 1966, 8). This symbiotic relationship with the land is diametrically opposed to the exploitative relationship between African Americans and landowners in the share-tenancy system that constituted the modal experience of African Americans in the rural South. Home ownership and, more generally, land ownership provided some insulation from the traditional patterns of exploitation. Many African Americans planted large vegetable gardens in their back yards after migrating to the North and purchasing homes.

Earl Little was able to interweave his commitment to traditional Christian religion with active advocacy of Black Nationalism. Malcolm related: "I knew that the collections [monetary offerings] my father got for his preaching were mainly what fed and clothed us, and he did other odd jobs, but still the image of him that made me proudest was his crusading and militant campaigning with the words of Marcus Garvey (Malcolm X 1966, 6). Later, Malcolm would argue that adherence to the philosophy of Black Nationalism did not require renunciation of Christian beliefs (Malcolm X 1964a).

For Earl Little, the critical ingredient integrating his various activities was the vision of Marcus Garvey—whose efforts were directed toward preparation for an emigration of African Americans back to Africa. Malcolm's exposure to the Garvey ideology through his father probably created a subliminal attraction to an "African solution" to the political-economic problems of African Americans. As a result, early in his association with the Nation of Islam, Malcolm was able to argue forcefully for Elijah Muhammad's proposal that African Americans emigrate to Africa:

> [T]he only lasting and permanent solution is complete separation on some land that we can call our own. Therefore, The Honorable Elijah Muhammad says that this problem can be solved and solved forever just by sending our people back to our own homeland or back to our own people, but that this government should provide the transportation plus everything we need to get started again in our own country. (Malcolm X 1963b, 74)

The emigration proposal of the Nation of Islam implicitly assumed the existence of an Africa controlled by Africans—an assumption consistent with Garvey's dream as communicated by Malcolm's father:

> I can remember hearing of "Adam driven out of the garden into the caves of Europe." "Africa for Africans." "Ethiopians, Awake!" And my father would talk about how it would not be much longer before Africa would be completely run by Negroes—"by black men," was the phrase he always used." (Malcolm X 1966, 6)

But such a massive emigration would require a substantial financial base and the logistical capabilities to undertake it. Malcolm came to understand these prohibitive constraints, and his father's (and Garvey's) vision was changed to a domestic alternative:

> He [Elijah Muhammad] says that if the American government is afraid to send us back to our own people, then America should set aside some separated territory, right here in the Western hemisphere where the two races can live apart from each other, since we certainly don't get along peacefully while we are together. (Malcolm X 1963b, 74)

Malcolm's alternative was the origin of the well-known position of the Nation of Islam that five Southern states should be turned over to African Americans for establishing a separate African American nation. The rationale for the five-state proposal was based on two criteria: (a) relative population size and (b) the ability of the land to sustain necessary levels of agricultural production:

> The Honorable Elijah Muhammad says that the size of the territory can be judged according to our population. If a seventh of the population of this country is black, then give us a seventh of the territory, a seventh part of the

country. And that is not asking too much because we already worked for the man for four hundred years. (Malcolm X 1963b, 72)

Both Malcolm X and Elijah Muhammad understood that even if the domestic proposal were implemented, there would be a long transition period during which African Americans would remain engaged principally in the American political economy. However, the economic functioning of African Americans in the American political economy would be undertaken as preparation for eventual disengagement from the country rather than as a strategy for achieving economic integration with it.

> The Honorable Elijah Muhammad says ... [b]etter jobs won't solve our problems. An integrated cup of coffee isn't sufficient pay for four hundred years of slave labor. He also says that a better job, a better job in the white man's factory, or a better job in the white man's business, or a better job in the white man's industry, or economy is, at best only a temporary solution. He says that the only lasting and permanent solution is complete separation on some land that we can call our own. (Malcolm X 1963b, 73–74)

The use of the term *slave labor* in the preceding passage is noteworthy. Malcolm typically referred to the menial jobs that African Americans were relegated to as those of "slaves" (Perry 1991, 59). Malcolm was well aware, however, that there were substantial differences in occupational status among Black workers. Thus, in commenting on the status of Black workers in Lansing, he observed:

> Back when I was growing up the "successful" Lansing Negroes were such as waiters and bootblacks. To be a janitor at some downtown store was to be highly respected. The real "elite," the "'big shots," the "voices of the race" were the waiters at the Lansing Country Club and the shoeshine boys at the state capitol.... No Negroes were hired then by Lansing's big Oldsmobile plant, or the Reo plant. (Malcolm X 1966, 5)

Differences in occupational status among Black workers created a significant barrier for convincing more affluent African Americans that the separate nation-state was a viable proposition.

Malcolm was able to argue forcefully for the importance of a nation-state because he could extrapolate from the individual struggles of his father and others to envision a successful, massive collective effort. Following his break with the Nation of Islam, however, Malcolm repudiated the separate nation-state model, particularly the African solution. He also rejected the vision of a separate Black nation in the South and signaled his emergent emphasis on international political economy. The factors associated with this shift in position are discussed in Stewart (1992).

While Malcolm's break with the Nation of Islam precipitated his rejection of the separate nation-state model, both before and after the rift he maintained an unswerving commitment to an urban, community-based development model, as discussed below.

Ghetto Economic Development

The economic problems that Malcolm had observed among many Black families in Lansing, Michigan, came home to roost with the death of his father. This event initiated an irreversible downward spiral in the economic fortunes of the Little family. Malcolm's subsequent views about the economic plight of African Americans were profoundly shaped by his own increasingly weakened attachment to the legal economy and experiences that engendered a profound distrust of governmental support agencies, specifically, and governmental authorities, in general.

One insurance company refused to pay the contracted death benefits following his father's death, precipitating a cash crisis in the household. Malcolm's brother, Wilfred, quit school and found a job to help support the family. Malcolm's mother, Louise, reluctantly resorted to purchasing on credit and seeking employment as a day worker (Malcolm X 1966, 11–12). Eventually, however, despite her efforts, the family had to resort to public assistance to survive. Thus, despite monumental efforts to manage finances frugally, the Littles' dependence on public assistance increased. This growing dependency enabled social workers to intervene aggressively in the family's affairs. Malcolm recalled that his mother would confront the state welfare people in an effort to keep them from "coming around so much, meddling in our lives" (Malcolm X 1966, 13). Malcolm attempted to contribute to the family's coffers by obtaining paid employment, but with little success. His negative experience with the labor market stimulated him to undertake his first experiments with illegal activities, such as theft, to augment the family's resources.

Malcolm and the other Little children were dispersed to foster homes. The break with his family ties catalyzed Malcolm's growing involvement in illegal activities. His adaptive coping style developed into a pattern of behavior that was at odds with his earlier socialization. "The more I began to stay away from home and visit people and steal from the stores, the more aggressive I became in my inclinations. I never wanted to wait for anything" (Malcolm X 1966, 15). He began to develop "hustling" skills through association with older adolescents. At the same time, however, Malcolm was simultaneously maintaining involvement in the legal economy. As an example, he recalled: "I picked strawberries, and though I can't recall what I got per crate for picking. I remember that after working hard all one day, I wound up with about a dollar, which was a whole lot of money in those times" (Malcolm X 1966, 16).

An interaction with his eighth grade English teacher ensured that Malcolm would become increasingly involved in the illegal underground economy. The teacher urged Malcolm to give up his dreams of becoming a lawyer. Malcolm recalled the following advice: "A lawyer—that's no realistic goal for a nigger. You need to think about something you *can* be. You're good with your hands—making things. Everybody admires your carpentry shop work. Why don't you plan on carpentry?" (Malcolm X 1966, 36.)

The effect on Malcolm was devastating. "It was then that I began to change—inside. I drew away from white people." Malcolm made a critical choice at this point. He refused the option of staying in Lansing and strengthening his attachment to the labor market in favor of relocating to Boston. Malcolm's migration to Boston cemented his connection to the underground economy. Here he was able to combine legal and illegal entrepreneurial activities to carve out a more comfortable life style. He started working in a pool hall as a "racker" and soon graduated to the Roseland State Ballroom, where he obtained legitimate employment such as shining shoes and providing other personal services in order to enter more profitable, but illegitimate, activities such as hustling liquor and marijuana. As he learned the ropes, he was also able to boost his income by serving as a go-between for johns and prostitutes. This experience provided the foundation for Malcolm's activities as the pimp "Detroit Red" in Harlem.

Malcolm's growing involvement in hustling continued to catalyze a transformation in his character, values, and lifestyle. Recalling this transformation, he observed: "The first liquor I drank, my first cigarettes, even my first reefers, I can't specifically remember. But I know they were all mixed together with my shooting craps, playing cards, and betting my dollar a day on the numbers, as I started hanging out at night with Shorty and his friends" (Malcolm X 1966, 51). His friends encouraged him to abandon earlier values and pursue immediate, hedonic satisfaction. Malcolm related the following exchange with Shorty regarding plans to purchase a zoot suit: "I remarked that I had saved about half enough to get a zoot. 'Save?' Shorty couldn't believe it. 'Homeboy, you never heard of credit?'" (Malcolm X 1966: p. 51.) As mentioned above, Malcolm's only previous experiences with credit purchases occurred during the period of his mother's struggles to keep the family intact. Given the nature of those experiences, it is wholly understandable that Malcolm would have avoided such entanglements until enticed by Shorty to upgrade his wardrobe.

Two aspects of the various experiences described above are especially noteworthy. First, even as Malcolm became increasingly integrated into the illegal underground economy, he maintained significant attachment to the legal labor market. The beginning of World War II provided new employment opportunities for African Americans. Malcolm found work as a porter on a train route between Boston and New York. But even while holding this job, Malcolm found a way to increase his income by manipulating the rules. Perry (1991, 60) observes:

> Malcolm learned many things on the railroad. The sandwiches that were sold by the "kitchen car crews" were accounted for by the number of sandwich bags expended. With the connivance of the dining car stewards, who supervised the food preparation, the sandwich salesmen retrieved as many of the used food bags as possible. The cooks filled them with new sandwiches, which were sold in the old wrappers. The profits went into the pockets of the crewmembers.

When Malcolm was fired, he expressed little concern because "in those days such jobs as I could aspire to were going begging" (Malcolm X 1966, 78). In fact, he was able to obtain several jobs after his termination from the New Haven Railroad line.

The second significant aspect of his experiences during this period is the collective character of both his legal and illegal activities. Both types of activities required a network of colleagues. Malcolm learned the tricks of the hustling trade from more experienced street men. His ability to obtain legal jobs resulted from inside information provided by friends. He was able to find good deals in purchasing goods and services because of his involvement in informal information networks. His drug-pushing activities were initially financed by one of his compatriots (Perry 1991, 70–71). During his incarceration, in addition to establishing himself as the bookmaker for his cellblock, Malcolm was able to use his experience pushing drugs (Perry 1991, 111). Perry (1991) observes, later quoting Malcolm:

> The oscillatory character of Malcolm's involvements in hustling, legitimate employment, and entrepreneurial activities coupled with his experiences in cooperative ventures significantly influenced his approach to urban economic development. In the first instance, Malcolm believed that it would be possible to channel the energies and resources devoted to hedonic pursuits, both legal and illegal, into a comprehensive development program:
>
> [T]he money that we used to throw away when we were Christians—nightclubbing and drinking and smoking and participating in these other acts of immorality—the money we save when we become Muslims—we channel it into

these small business enterprises and try to develop them where they can provide some job opportunities for the rest of our people. (Malcolm X 1963b, 84–85)

It is significant to note that most of the small businesses started by Elijah Muhammad's followers were not owned by the Nation of Islam but by individual Muslims. At this time, neither Malcolm nor Elijah Muhammad was able to conceive of a cooperative model of business organization to serve as a foundation for a community-wide economy.

To illustrate, one of the most comprehensive statements of Malcolm's theory of a community-based economy is found in the speech "Ballots or Bullets," in which Malcolm describes the economic philosophy of Black Nationalism. For him, such a philosophy "only means that we should own and operate and control the economy of our community" (Malcolm X 1964a, 38). The failure to follow such a strategy leads to a situation where Black communities become slums (Malcolm X 1964a, 39). Malcolm maintained that the economic philosophy of Black Nationalism "helps African Americans become conscious of the importance of controlling the economics of our community" (Malcolm X 1964a, 39). He further emphasized the need for a reeducation campaign to accomplish this objective (Malcolm X 1964a, 39). He claimed that the principal outcome of this strategy would be "a situation wherein '[i]f we own the stores, if we operate the businesses, if we try and establish some industry in the community, then we're developing to the position where we creating employment for our own kind'" (Malcolm X 1964a, 39). The use of *we* in Malcolm's argument is a rhetorical tactic rather than a suggestion for strategies of collective ownership.

Malcolm's commitment to the expansion of small-enterprise community development was reinforced by his experiences in establishing and operating temples for the Nation of Islam. In fact, his experiences could have served as a foundation for urban development based on collective rather than individual ownership.

In addition, Malcolm was successful in stabilizing the financial situation of several NOI temples. According to Perry (1991, 145), Malcolm's "perseverance, plus his knowledge of ghetto psychology, enabled him to attract a slow, steady stream of converts that made it possible for Temple Number One to triple its membership within a few months." Malcolm became Elijah Muhammad's chief fundraiser. Each temple under Malcolm's control was required to submit to him weekly and monthly financial reports (Perry 1991, 163). Malcolm's financial acumen, "perseverance," and "knowledge of ghetto psychology" indicate that, in addition to providing for the spiritual needs of its members, the Black church has always been the major economic institution in Black communities (Stewart, 1986). Malcolm also honed his entrepreneurial and business skills through his role in founding *Muhammad Speaks,* the official organ of the Nation of Islam (Perry 1991).

This vision of indigenously controlled community development was maintained as Malcolm attempted to establish the Organization of Afro-American Unity (OAAU) after his break with Elijah Muhammad. In discussing the organization's program and its activities in Harlem, he emphasized: "Harlem is our house: we'll clean it up. But when we clean it up, we'll also control it. We'll control the politics. We'll control the economy. We'll control the school system and see that our people get a break" (Malcolm X 1965, 133). Malcolm also articulated the willingness of the OAAU to work with all groups involved in promoting constructive change, an offer that subtly backed away from his earlier criticism of such institutions as the Christian church. Most important, however, Malcolm envisioned the OAAU as a bridge between African Americans and other peoples of African descent, thus emphasizing his growing commitment to a global approach to solving the economic problems of African Americans.

Not Just an American Problem

Malcolm's early recognition of the global character of economic exploitation was couched in religious metaphor. For example, in the 1963 speech "God's Judgment of White America," he argued:

> The Honorable Elijah Muhammad teaches us that as it was the evil sin of slavery that caused the downfall and destruction of ancient Egypt, and Babylon and of ancient Greece, as well as ancient Rome, so it was the evil sin of colonialism (slavery, nineteenth-century European style) that caused the collapse of the white nations in present-day Europe as world powers.... It is the rise of the dark world that is causing the fall of the white world.... Our present generation is witnessing the end of colonialism. (Malcolm X 1963a, 121)

In contrast, the global vision articulated by Malcolm following his visit to Mecca and various African countries was grounded in both a specific knowledge of the developmental state of individual countries and a concrete view of the interconnection among the conditions of peoples of African descent throughout the world.

The OAAU was intended as a bridge between African Americans and other peoples of African descent in support of Malcolm's emergent global vision. This vision was reflected in an interview with Bernice Bass in December 1964, entitled "Our People Identify with Africa." Malcolm spoke of "the tendency on the part of Africans to identify completely with what is happening to the Black man in this country" (Malcolm X 1964b, 93). Similarly, he noted "an increasing tendency on the part of our people to identify with what's going on or happening to our people on the African continent" (Malcolm X 1964b, 93–94). In his *Autobiography*, Malcolm related that he came to realize during his visits abroad that "the single worst mistake of the American black organizations, and their leaders, is that they have failed to establish direct brotherhood lines of communication between the independent nations of Africa and the American black people" (Malcolm X 1966, 347). Malcolm argued that there was an integral connection between the growing role of the United States in exploiting the peoples of Africa and the plight of African Americans.

In the Bass interview, Malcolm reported that Egypt and Ghana were developing very rapidly and remarked that "Ghana is a remarkable country, a remarkably progressive country" (Malcolm X 1964b, 96). In his *Autobiography* as well, Malcolm reported that he had been especially impressed with the pace of development in Egypt, particularly in its manufacture of transportation vehicles (Malcolm X 1966, 321).

Malcolm was fascinated by the development in Ghana for several reasons. He admired the leadership of Kwame Nkrumah in having made the country the "fountainhead of Pan-Africanism" (Malcolm X 1966, 352). In addition, he supported Nkrumah's efforts to avoid becoming embroiled in a neocolonial relationship with Western nations. Malcolm contrasted Ghana's developmental path with those of Senegal and Nigeria, both of which he suggested had become quasi colonies of the United States (Malcolm X 1964b, 99).

Malcolm's views on the role of women in the development of nations are of special interest because they conflict directly with the role ascribed to women in the Nation of Islam. He asserted: "[I]n every country that was progressive, the women were progressive. In every country that was underdeveloped and backward, it was to the same degree that the women were undeveloped, or underdeveloped, and backward" (Malcolm X 1964b, 98). His elaboration on the link between the status of women and national development amplifies the contradiction with the views of women characteristic of the Nation of Islam:

> It's noticeable that in the type of societies where they put the woman in a closet and discourage her from getting a sufficient education and don't give her the incentive by allowing her maximum participation in whatever area of the society where she's qualified, they kill her incentive. And killing her incentive, she kills the incentive in her children. And the man himself has no competition so he doesn't develop to his fullest potential. So in the African countries where they opt for mass education, whether it be female or male, you find that they have a more valid society, a more progressive society. (Malcolm X 1964b, 98)

One cannot help wondering whether Malcolm's positive vision of the role of women in national development was influenced by his mother's struggles to keep the family intact after his father's death. As mentioned above, Louise Little was forced to become involved in economic activities outside the home to supplement the family income. Her lack of marketable skills, coupled with the limited employment opportunities for women generally, frustrated her efforts to avoid dependency on public assistance. The events that unfolded in Malcolm's early life correspond closely to the scenario which he projected for societies that deny women the right of full participation.

Malcolm became increasingly specific in analyzing the global political economy. His analysis included a sharp assessment of the role of the United States as an agent of neocolonialism. Malcolm observed: "The countries that are identified with America the most are the ones that are the most backward and the ones that have the most problems" (Malcolm X 1964b, 100). But he also observed:

> [I]n no time can you understand the problems between Black and white people here in Rochester or Black and white people in Mississippi or Black and white people in California, unless you understand the basic problem that exists between Black and white people—not confined to the local, but confined to the international, global level on this earth today. When you look at it in that context, you'll understand. But if you only try to look at it in the local context, you'll never understand. (Malcolm X 1965a, 155)

These two conclusions exemplify Malcolm's call for a strategy that links the struggles of Africans in Africa with those of African Americans in the United States. But have subsequent developments rendered Malcolm's global strategy obsolete? Or, alternatively, are strengthened connections between Africans and African Americans, based on an understanding of commonalities in their respective roles in the global economic order, still a useful approach for the pursuit of economic liberation? These issues are addressed below.

Contemporary Relevance

While the foundations of both the separate-nation model and the small entrepreneur-based model of urban development have eroded considerably since Malcolm's death, the power of his global perspective has increased significantly. More frequently, inner-city communities led by African American mayors have related to the larger polit-ical-economic order like African nations trapped in a neocolonial network. Thus, the process of change in urban inner-city communities has weakened the infrastructure of predominantly Black communities, even though many mayors of African descent have been elected in large cities. This phenomenon provides a foundation for urban develop-ment, but there are serious questions as to whether the small-entrepreneur develop-ment proposed by Malcolm is viable.

The belief that competition with monopoly capitalism can be beaten by a network of small Black-owned businesses is associated with what has been called the "Myth of Black Capitalism" (Ofari 1970). Although Black-owned businesses are indeed more likely to sell to Black customers and to hire Black employees than businesses owned by members of any other group, their impact on monopoly capitalism is minimal. The term *Black capitalism* was, in fact, coined during the 1968 Presidential campaign by Richard Nixon, hardly a supporter of economic empowerment for African Americans (Allen 1969; Blaustein and Faux 1972). Despite numerous programmatic initiatives such as Minority Small Business Investment Companies (MSBICs) and set-asides for Black suppliers, underdevelopment of the Black capitalist sector as well as external eco-nomic control and exploitation persist. Moreover, Black-owned businesses generate rel-atively few employment opportunities. To illustrate, although the number of Black-owned businesses doubled between 1969 and 1982, the number with salaried employees remained constant—about 38,000. This pattern indicates that businesses of African Americans increasingly consist of sole proprietorships involved in retail trade and the provision of services but have few employment opportunities for community residents.

For business development to contribute meaningfully to collective liberation, it is re-quired that communities be organized to manage both the internal economy and the links to the economic institutions operating outside predominantly Black communities. This requirement means that Black-owned firms must be treated as social property rather than the private property of individuals or limited groups of individuals (Allen 1969). Community-development corporations constitute one vehicle for involving the community more broadly as owners in business enterprises. The initiatives of Reverend (Dr.) Leon Sullivan in Philadelphia during the 1960s provide a concrete example. Through contributions of church members, several projects, including Progress Plaza Shopping Center and an apartment building, were completed. There was also a connec-tion to Sullivan's other major initiative—Opportunities Industrialization Centers (OICs), a self-help vocational training operation that created some job opportunities for those undergoing training. The key elements of this model are collective ownership and control that create organic incentives to support the enterprises and their imple-mentation through established community-based organizations (Stewart 1984). This model was, in fact, accessible to Malcolm both temporally and experientially. His expe-riences in managing temple finances and in founding *Muhammed Speaks* were an ideal foundation for movement in directions similar to Sullivan's.

Community-level development is not sustainable, however, unless the larger political economy nurtures such development. Unfortunately, cities are junior partners in the overall metropolitan economic structure in a manner similar to the neocolonial rela-tionship between "developed" and "developing" countries. In both cases, while political control may be a necessary condition for pursuing development, it is far from sufficient to guarantee that development will, in fact, occur. For example, Black mayors can di-rectly influence economic flows to African American communities through several channels, including selective purchasing from minority contractors often formalized in local versions of set-aside programs. However, cities are creatures of the state, and state legislatures and governors have tended to allocate public resources disproportionately to rural areas. Moreover, elections in several cities, including Chicago and Charlotte, North Carolina, demonstrate that the staying power of Black mayors is not guaranteed. A variety of factors contribute to the potentially tenuous status of Black mayors. These include reinvestment displacement and suburbanization of many African Americans, especially those of the middle class.

Despite these limitations, some observers have suggested that the political control exercised by Black mayors offers the potential to implement a more formalized Black economic network that cuts across geographical boundaries. Such an interurban economic network was proposed at the 1982 Black Economic Summit under the rubric of a "Black Common Market." In support of such a market, a Black Development Fund and Reconstruction Finance Corporation was also proposed. In addition, it was recommended that a Black Religious Consortium be established to pool resources across denominational lines in support of economic development (National Summit Conference on Black Economic Survival & Development 1982). Two other recommendations of the Conference were the creation of an Afro-American-Caribbean and Afro-American International Development Services Fund and an African Business Information Exchange. These recommendations are consonant with Malcolm's views about the need for an international strategy to address domestic problems.

Malcolm's attraction to Ghana, discussed previously, stemmed in part from the development strategy employed by Kwame Nkrumah. As noted earlier, Nkrumah advocated nonalignment as a political strategy to avoid the worst manifestations of neocolonialism. He recognized that neocolonial control could be exercised by financial interests not identifiable with a particular country. He also foresaw a process producing increasingly worsening conditions in neocolonial territories, thus precipitating revolts by the masses that would be suppressed through the use of military power by neocolonial nations. The subsequent record of the proliferation of coups and military regimes in postindependence Africa is a testimonial to the accuracy of Nkrumah's vision (Nkrumah 1966). Pan-African unity was, for Nkrumah, both the key to overcoming neocolonialism and a stage of organization that would develop more fully following the defeat of neocolonialism. He maintained that "[t]he only way to challenge this economic empire and to recover possession of our heritage is for us also to act on a Pan-African basis, through a Union Government" (Nkrumah 1966, 256).

Efforts at both continental political unity and regional and continental economic integration have proved to be false starts. The Organization of African Unity has come under criticism for corrupting the vision of Nkrumah (M'Buyinga 1982). In addition, efforts to pursue noncapitalist developmental paths in individual countries have only produced limited escape from the forces of global imperialism (cf. Obinde, 1988). The most ambitious effort to pursue national self-reliance was that of Julius Nyerere in Tanzania. Malcolm appeared to have little knowledge of the developmental trajectory of Tanzania, and Nyerere's major initiatives occurred after Malcolm's assassination. Nyerere attempted to implement Tanzanian socialism with the Ujamaa village as the cornerstone. The introduction of new technologies was to be adapted to the traditional societal values (Nyerere 1968). The goal of Nyerere's unsuccessful policies was to create "an up-to-date and larger version of the traditional African family" (Nyerere 1968, 456).

Many of the same issues that confronted the first generation of postcolonial African leaders still hamper development efforts and are manifested in a continuing debate regarding the relationship between underdevelopment in Africa and neocolonialism. Two competing explanations for the persistence of underdevelopment in Africa currently dominate the literature. The World Bank has assigned principal responsibility for this pattern to mismanagement of African economies by African leaders and continuing political instability. In contrast, the leaders of African countries have attributed underdevelopment to the continuing operation of the forces of neocolonialism (Browne and Cummings 1984). The most obvious example of the persistence of neocolonialism is the current policy used by the International Monetary Fund and the World Bank in making development loans. Countries are now required to make major structural changes in their economies in order to qualify for loans as part of a structural adjustment program. The required changes are designed to expand the role of market mechanisms. However, structural adjustment programs have weakened the public sector and intensified the foreign domination of individual economies (see Obinde 1988).

Even in the specter of neocolonialism, some possible directions for developing a global liberation strategy for peoples of African descent are crystallizing. To illustrate, the growing "Africanization" of African American popular culture may provide an opportunity to forge an authentic Pan-African consciousness. The large-scale impact of African symbols on the popular culture of African Americans is evident in attire, music, and rituals. The current growing identification of African Americans with the motherland appears to be more rooted in an understanding of Africa than was the case during the 1960s. The Black Power movement of the 1960s adopted stylized symbols such as the Afro that were not based on any specific African cultural artifact or practice. The current reassertion of African identity is manifested through display of a variety of authentic artifacts—for example, Kente cloth. This "Africanization" has proceeded concurrently with a growing identification of the younger generation with Malcolm X. This identification is shown in popular culture in various ways—particularly through the widespread use of the symbol X on attire. To date, the interest in Malcolm has focused primarily on his unrelenting assault on domestic racism, as symbolized by the phrase "by any means necessary." However, as interest in Malcolm increases, his relationship to Africa should provide a foundation in popular culture for the exploration of Pan-African strategies.

Malcolm's views about the role of women in economic development were clearly prescient, as demonstrated by international recognition of the need to mobilize the untapped resources of women in development efforts. This recognition crystallized when the United Nations designated the 1980s as the decade to focus on this issue. The culminating event reflecting this focus was a major conference in Nairobi, Kenya, in 1985. In the spirit of Malcolm's insistence on the interconnections between the circumstances facing African Americans and peoples of color throughout the world, elevating and expanding the role of women must be an integral component of a comprehensive development strategy for African Americans. The resurgence of interest in Malcolm can be useful in laying the foundation for continuing progress in this area. Malcolm's views of the role of women in economic development, extended into the African American milieu, provide a critical counterbalance to religious and secular ideologies that seek to reinforce male dominance. As a Muslim, Malcolm's words gain even greater force because many associate Islam with restricted roles for women.

The current activities of Reverend Leon Sullivan constitute one example of efforts to establish formal links between African Americans and Africans in Africa. Sullivan, in cooperation with President Houphouet Boigny of the Ivory Coast, cohosted the first African American Summit in Ibadjan, Ivory Coast, in 1991. Over three hundred African American delegates attended the Summit. A second summit was held in Gabon in May 1993. These efforts should be understood as an extension of Sullivan's community-based economic development program in Philadelphia, discussed previously. Sullivan's developmental concerns are channeled through the International Foundation for Education and Self Help (IFESH), an organization he founded to promote African development. A major goal of this organization is to generate debt relief for African countries, thereby making them less vulnerable to the policy dictates of the World Bank and the International Monetary Fund. Sullivan's initiative is a concrete example of extending the domestic agenda of peoples of African descent into the international arena.

As we continue to learn the lessons that Malcolm taught regarding the need for a Pan-African global economic strategy and as we implement programs consistent with that view, the meaning of his pregnant observation that our problem is "not just an American problem" will become increasingly clear (Malcolm X 1965b).

References

Allen, R. 1969. *Black awakening in capitalist America, An analytic history.* Garden City, NJ: Doubleday.

Blausten, A., and G. Faux. 1972. *The star spangled hustle.* Garden City, NJ: Doubleday.

Breitman, G., ed. 1989. *Malcolm X speaks: Selected speeches and statements.* New York: Pathfinder Press.

Browne, R., and R. Cummings. 1984. *The Lagos Plan of Action vs. The Berg Report: Contemporary issues in African American economic development.* Washington, D.C.: The African Studies and Research Program of Howard University.

Goodman, B., ed. 1971. *The end of white supremacy: Four speeches by Malcolm X.* New York: Merlin House.

Malcolm X. 1963a. God's judgment of white America (The chickens are coming home to roost). In *The end of the white world supremacy: Four speeches by Malcolm X*, ed. B. Goodman, 121–148. New York: Merlin House, 1971.

_____. 1963b. The Black revolution. In *The end of white world supremacy: Four speeches by Malcolm X*, ed. B. Goodman, 67–80. New York: Merlin House, 1971.

_____. 1964a. Ballots or bullets. In *Malcolm X speaks: Selected speeches and statements*, ed. G. Breitman, 23–44. New York: Pathfinder Press, 1989.

_____. 1964b. Our people identify with Africa. Interview by B. Bass. December 27. In *Malcolm X: The last speeches*, ed. B. Perry, 91–107. New York: Pathfinder Press, 1989.

_____. 1965a. Not just an American problem but a world problem. In *Malcolm X: The last speeches*, ed. B. Perry, 151–181. New York: Pathfinder Press, 1989.

_____. 1965b. There's a worldwide revolution going on. In *Malcolm X: The last speeches*, ed. B. Berry, 111–149. New York: Pathfinder Press, 1989.

_____. 1966. *The Autobiography of Malcolm X.* With Alex Haley. New York: Grove Press.

M'buyinga. E. 1982. Trans. Michael Pallis. *Pan-Africanism or neo-colonialism?: The bankruptcy of the O.A.U.* London: Zed Books.

National Summit Conference on Black Economic Survival & Development. 1982. Report to the Closing plenary session. Mimeograph, July 28.

Nkrumah, K. 1966. *Neo-colonialism: The last stage of imperialism.* New York: International Publishers.

Nyerere. J. 1968. *Freedom and socialism.* London: Oxford Press.

Obinde, B. 1988. *The political economy of the African Crisis.* London: Zed Books.

Ofari, E. 1970. *The Myth of Black capitalism.* New York: Monthly Review Press.

Perry, B., ed. 1989. *Malcolm X: The last speeches.* New York: Pathfinder Press.

Perry, B. 1991. *Malcolm: The life of a man who changed Black America.* Barrytown, NY: Station Hill Press.

Stewart, J. B. 1984. Building a co-operative economy: Lessons from the Black experience. *Review of Social Economy* 42:360–368.

_____. 1986. The Black church as a religion-economic institution. Report prepared for research project *The Black Church in America*, Director and Principal Investigator C. E. Lincoln.

_____. 1990. "More than an American problem": The economic thought of Malcolm X. Mimeograph.

_____. 1992. Experimental foundations of the economic thought of Malcolm X. Mimeograph

8

Malcolm X: Human Rights and the United Nations

Robert L. Harris, Jr.

Even in three hours and twenty minutes, it is difficult to capture on the screen a life as rich and complex as the thirty-nine years of Malcolm X. Indeed, the epic film by Spike Lee (released in 1992) opens only a small window into Malcolm's life and thought. Although one cannot expect a biographical film to be comprehensive, *Malcolm X* gives short shrift to some very important aspects of Malcolm's life, especially during his last years.

Cinematographically, the movie beautifully captures Malcolm's pilgrimage to Mecca. However, the film focuses more on Malcolm as a tourist than as a leader of Black America: one fails to sense how heads of state received him while he was out of the United States. For example, the film never shows that King Faisal of Saudi Arabia honored Malcolm as a guest of the country after his hajj.[1] In addition, except for pictures on the wall of reputed FBI agents who wiretapped his conversations, the film never portrays the time that Malcolm spent in Africa seeking support for his position that the problem for Afro-Americans was one of "human rights," not "civil rights."

Central to Malcolm's thought, after his break with the Nation of Islam, was the idea that the Afro-American struggle for liberation in the United States was being waged on a false premise. He maintained that African Americans would never receive civil rights as citizens of the country until their human rights were restored. He believed that slavery and oppression had stripped Afro-Americans of their human rights and that therefore many white Americans did not regard them as human beings worthy of civil rights.[2] The history of racism in the United States gave much credence to Malcolm's argument. As justification for enslavement and in response to the abolitionist movement, apologists for slavery in the United States had argued that African Americans were beings of a lower order—that in the great chain of being, the white man came first, then the yellow man, the red man, and the black man at the bottom.[3] For Malcolm, the issue was not that African Americans were not recognized as first-class citizens of the United States but that they were not even considered full human beings.

---

1. Clayborne Carson and David Gailen, eds., *Malcolm X: The F.B.I File* (New York: Carroll & Graf, 1991), 75.
2. John Henrik Clarke, ed., *Malcolm X: The Man and His Times* (New York: Macmillan, 1969), 305.
3. Thomas F. Gossett, *Race: The History of an Idea in America* (Dallas: Southern Methodist University Press, 1963), and George M. Fredrickson, *The Black Image in the White Mind: The Debate on Afro-American Character and Destiny, 1817–1914* (New York: Harper & Row, 1971).

After his hajj and his stay with King Faisal, Malcolm spent three weeks in Africa (May 2 to May 19, 1964). He visited Nigeria, Ghana, Liberia, Senegal, and Morocco. In Ghana, he addressed the Parliament, an honor usually reserved for visiting heads of state. He also had an audience with Kwame Nkrumah, President of Ghana. Malcolm sought support for his human rights position and charged that the United States had colonized African Americans in a way similar to the European colonization of Africa and Asia. Despite the decline of colonization in Africa and Asia and the abolition of slavery in the United States, neocolonization perpetuated a subordinate position for Africans, Asians, and African Americans. Malcolm warned African nations in particular not to substitute "American dollarism" for European colonialism.[4]

Malcolm returned to Africa two months later and attended the Organization of African Unity (OAU) Conference in Cairo, Egypt—as the only American allowed to attend. Although he was not permitted to address the Conference, he was allowed to circulate a memorandum in which he reminded the African heads of state that the 22 million Black people in the United States were originally African and that they resided in the United States not by choice but by a cruel accident in history. The problems of Africans and African Americans, he claimed, were inextricably related. Also, he called the heads of independent African states the "shepherds of all African people everywhere, whether they are still at home here on the mother continent or have been scattered abroad."[5] In addition, he described the position of African Americans as defenseless before American racists, including racist police officers, who either mistreated or even murdered them because they were Black and of African descent. Africans from the continent, moreover, were often mistaken in the United States for American Negroes and were also subject to police brutality. He cited examples of three students from Kenya and two diplomats from Uganda who had been mistreated by the police in the United States.

Africans, Malcolm declared, would never gain respect until African Americans had respect. "Our problem is your problem," he told them. It was not a Negro problem or an American problem but a world problem. And it was not a problem of civil rights but of human rights. He considered the United States worse than South Africa because the United States preached "liberty and justice for all" while it practiced the opposite. "If South Africa is guilty of violating the human rights of Africans here on the mother continent," he wrote, "then America is guilty of worse violations of the 22 million Africans on the American continent. And if South African racism is not a domestic issue, then American racism is not a domestic issue."[6] He characterized the 1964 Civil Rights Act, which outlawed discrimination in public accommodations and transportation, among other racist practices, as a propaganda maneuver to keep the African nations from condemning the United States' racist practices before the United Nations as they had condemned the same practices in South Africa.

Malcolm informed the African heads of state that the newly formed Organization of Afro-American Unity (OAAU), which he represented, had decided to raise the freedom struggle in the United States above the domestic level of civil rights to the international level of human rights. He asked them to assist the OAAU in bringing the African-Amer-

---

4. Malcolm X, *The Autobiography of Malcolm X*, with the assistance of Alex Haley (New York: Ballantine Books, 1973), 370, and Peter Goldman, *The Death and Life of Malcolm X* (New York: Harper & Row, 1974), 226–27.

5. Clarke, ed., *Malcolm X*, 288–92.

6. Clarke, ed., *Malcolm X*, 288–92.

ican problem before the United Nations on the grounds that the United States was "morally incapable of protecting the lives and property of 22 million African Americans" and "on the grounds that our deteriorating plight is definitely becoming a threat to world peace."[7] He concluded that African Americans asserted the right to self-defense and retaliation against racist oppression. If they must die anyway, he promised that they would do so fighting back. Such a situation could "escalate into a violent, worldwide, bloody race war" which could therefore become a threat to world peace and security.

The Organization of African Unity passed a resolution praising the United States Congress for having enacted the 1964 Civil Rights Act but expressing concern about continued racial oppression and urging the United States government to intensify its efforts against racial discrimination.[8] Malcolm remained in Africa for four months. He attended the second African Summit Conference in Cairo, on August 21, 1964, and issued a press release reaffirming his position that just as the violations of human rights in South Africa were an international issue, so, too, were the violations of human rights in the United States. He stressed the importance of seeing the problem as an international issue. As long as the racial oppression of African Americans in the United States remained a domestic problem (i.e., one confined to the jurisdiction within its borders), their brothers and sisters in Africa, Asia, and Latin America, as well as well-meaning whites in Europe, would not be able to intervene and to help them.[9]

Over the next two months, Malcolm traveled to fourteen African nations and talked with the heads of state in seven countries about his plans to bring racial oppression in the United States before the United Nations. He spent time with Prime Minister Jomo Kenyatta of Kenya and Prime Minister Milton Obote of Uganda, and was the house guest of President Sekou Toure of Guinea.[10]

During the Conference of Independent African States in Accra, Ghana, in 1958, African nations had sought to pressure South Africa into respecting human rights as enunciated in the Charter of the United Nations and the Universal Declaration of Human Rights. As more African countries joined the United Nations, increasing from three in 1950 to thirty-five in 1964 (or roughly 30 percent of the international organization), the problem of racial oppression in South Africa gained greater salience.[11]

Before 1960, primarily because of opposition from the United Kingdom and France, the United Nations did not consider the apartheid question in South Africa on the grounds that it was a problem within the domestic jurisdiction of that nation and was therefore not a threat to international peace and security. However, the Sharpeville Massacre of March 21, 1960, forced a reconsideration of the question.[12] About five thousand Africans had gathered around the police station in a peaceful demonstration to protest the pass laws, low wages, and high rents. They had also been expecting to hear an important statement regarding the passes. But the police panicked and opened their weapons on the demonstrators, killing 67 and wounding 186. The wanton shoot-

---

7. Clarke, ed., *Malcolm X*, 288–92.

8. Goldman, *The Death and Life of Malcolm X*, 227.

9. Clarke, ed., *Malcolm X*, 305.

10. Malcolm X, *Autobiography*, 370.

11. Moses E. Akpan, *African Goals and Diplomatic Strategies in the United Nations* (North Quincy, MA: Christopher Publishing House, 1976), 84, and David A. Kay, "The Impact of African States on the United Nations," *International Organization* 23, no. 1 (1969): 21.

12. Wellington W. Nyangoni, *Africa in the United Nations System* (Rutherford, NJ: Fairleigh Dickinson University Press, 1985), 162.

ing of unarmed civilians, many of whom had assembled merely out of curiosity, shocked the world.[13] Four days after the slaughter, eight African nations and twenty Asian nations requested a United Nations Security Council session to consider the massacre as a situation creating international friction and threatening international peace and security. For the first time, the United Nations Security Council voted (9 to 0, with 2 abstentions, France and the United Kingdom) for a resolution condemning apartheid and requesting that the government of South Africa take measures to bring about racial harmony and to end its policies of apartheid and racial discrimination.[14]

From 1960 to 1967, the major concerns of African countries in the United Nations were decolonization and South Africa. African countries pressed the General Assembly (and continued to press the Security Council) to take measures to end apartheid in South Africa. On November 6, 1962, the General Assembly, by a vote of 67 to 16 (with 23 abstentions), resolved that member nations should break off diplomatic relations with South Africa, close their ports to its vessels, prohibit their own ships from trading with South Africa, and refuse landing facilities to South African aircraft. African countries argued that Article 56 of the United Nations Charter bound member nations to promote "universal respect for, and observance of, human rights and fundamental freedom for all without distinction as to race, sex, language, or religion." Finally, on December 4, 1963, the Security Council unanimously adopted a resolution condemning apartheid, calling for freedom of political prisoners, and requesting an embargo of arms sales to South Africa. In addition, the United Nations assisted the victims of apartheid and established various committees to study how to resolve the problem.[15]

While the African nations had the power to secure passage of resolutions against South Africa, they lacked the influence to persuade the major Western powers (France, the United Kingdom, and the United States) to commit their own resources to change the South African social and political system.[16] For Malcolm, the measures taken by the United Nations against apartheid in South Africa were sufficient to warrant pressing his case for a similar condemnation of racial oppression in the United States. Prior to his assassination on February 21, 1965, Malcolm had planned to petition the United Nations for a charge of genocide against 22 million African Americans.

The petition, an outline of which was completed before his death, resembled the 1951 *We Charge Genocide* petition of the Civil Rights Congress. That petition was presented by a delegation headed by Paul Robeson to the Secretary General during the Fifth Session of the United Nations General Assembly convened in Paris, France, and simultaneously in the United States. The petition was based on the Convention on the Prevention and Punishment of the Crime of Genocide adopted by the General Assembly of the United Nations on December 9, 1948. The Genocide Convention prohibited "acts committed with intent to destroy, in whole or in part, a national, ethnical, racial or religious group as such." The petition, with ample evidence from the years 1945 to 1951, sought to demonstrate the deliberate killing of African Americans by the police, gangs, and the Ku Klux Klan, an organization chartered in several states as a semiofficial arm of state government and given state tax exemption as a benevolent society. The Black Belt, a crescent extending from Virginia, through twelve Southern

---

13. Ambrose Reeves, *Shooting at Sharpeville: The Agony of South Africa* (Boston: Houghton Mifflin, 1961).
14. Akpan, *African Goals*, 89.
15. Akpan, *African Goals*, 94–101.
16. Kay, "The Impact of African States," 35.

states, to Texas, contained a third of the Black population of the United States and was the scene of most of the genocidal practices against African Americans. The struggle for the ballot was the central issue around which revolved most of the incitement to genocide. According to the petition, elected officials in many Southern states justified genocide in statements denying the rights of African Americans.[17]

The *We Charge Genocide* petition consisted of five parts: an opening statement, a section on genocide law and the indictment, the evidence, a summary, and an appendix. The outline for Malcolm's petition was more chronological and reflected the time period in which it was written. Its second paragraph asserts: "We have appealed to the conscience of America, but her conscience slumbers."[18] This statement is probably a reference to the civil rights movement and an appeal to conscience to end racial discrimination and segregation. The petition thus contends that after more than three centuries of wrongs against African Americans, it was only fair to conclude that America's conscience was not able to accord human beings whose skin was not white the rights of life, liberty, and the pursuit of happiness. Malcolm's petition corresponded with his position on human rights and departed from the *We Charge Genocide* petition in its focus on the Universal Declaration of Human Rights as well as the 1948 Genocide Convention. It argued that there was no recourse but to petition the United Nations, given the many years of "supplication, petitioning, pleading and agitation for affirmation of basic human rights, all to no avail."[19]

Malcolm's petition drew on the following articles of the Universal Declaration of Human Rights. Article 2 stipulates that everyone is entitled to all the rights and freedoms set forth without regard to race, color, sex, language, religion, political or other opinions, national or social origin, property, birth, or status. Under Article 5, no one shall be subjected to torture or to cruel, inhuman, or degrading treatment or punishment. Article 6 affirms that everyone has the right to recognition everywhere as a person before the law. Article 7 acknowledges that all are equal before the law and are entitled without any discrimination to equal protection of the law. Article 16 recognizes that men and women of full age have the right to marry and to found a family without any limitation due to race, nationality, or religion. (His charge against the United States for violation of Article 16 was a major departure for Malcolm, who had opposed interracial marriage.) Article 17 states that everyone has the right to own property alone as well as in association with others. And Article 23 notes that everyone has the right to work, to free choice of employment, to just and favorable conditions of work, and to protection against unemployment. Everyone without any distinction has the right to equal pay for equal work. Malcolm's petition planned to provide brief explanations of violations of these basic human rights in the United States.[20]

In addition, Malcolm's petition would provide evidence of economic genocide in a list of conditions of life calculated to bring about the physical destruction of African Americans in whole or in part. The segregation that imprisoned African Americans from birth to death by cutting them off from adequate education, health care, and housing was a source of bodily and mental harm. Like the *We Charge Genocide* petition, Malcolm's would focus on the South, where most African Americans lived and where conditions were most oppressive. His petition would compare conditions with the rest

17. William L. Patterson, ed., *We Charge Genocide* (New York: International Publishers, 1970).
18. Clarke, ed., *Malcolm X*, 343.
19. Clarke, ed., *Malcolm X*, 344.
20. Clarke, ed., *Malcolm X*, 345.

of the population in education, employment, housing, hospital facilities, incarceration, medical care, disease and infant mortality, confinement to mental institutions, and adult life expectancy. In one major difference from the earlier petition, Malcolm's recognized the triple oppression of Black women and planned to examine the slavery antecedents of such oppression. In many other respects, the petitions were similar: both linked the murder of black people to seeking their right to vote, and both revealed the complicity of public officials, especially in the South, in killing African Americans for trying to exercise their rights. Part Two of the *We Charge Genocide* petition (the section on genocide law and the indictment) is almost identical to the section in Malcolm's petition, "The Law." However, Malcolm's petition placed more emphasis on the history of racial oppression in the United States than the previous petition, which concentrated primarily on the years between 1945, when the United Nations was founded, and 1951, when the petition was issued.[21]

Malcolm's proposed petition to the United Nations reveals his own keen interest in and deep appreciation of African American history. He knew that African Americans had been accorded civil rights during Reconstruction with passage of the Thirteenth, Fourteenth, and Fifteenth Amendments to the Constitution. The Civil Rights Acts of 1866 and 1875 supposedly granted African Americans racial equality. Despite the constitutional amendments and civil rights laws, African Americans still suffered from racial oppression, especially in the South. The 1896 U.S. Supreme Court decision, *Plessy v. Ferguson*, established the doctrine of "separate but equal" and virtually nullified previous civil rights legislation. Therefore, civil rights could be given and could be taken away. For Malcolm, human rights were natural rights affirmed by the world community in the Charter of the United Nations and in its Universal Declaration of Human Rights. He brought a different perspective to the struggle for racial equality in the United States. Unfortunately, his tragic death removed the prospect of a different route to freedom—one based on a firm understanding of the African American past, an inextricable connection to Africa, and a grounding in international politics.

---

21. Clarke, ed., *Malcolm X*, 345–6.

9

Black Nationalism and Garveyist Influences

Shirley N. Weber

> The Negro people of the Western world have dissipated their love for self; they have lost apparently all attachment to home. Whether through propaganda or otherwise, the Negro seems to be the only individual who has no personal national love, no personal national patriotism. Propaganda has been so scattered among us that we have been taught to love, to respect, to worship, to adore everything other than those things that are native to us, that are dear to us as people.[1]
>
> Marcus Garvey
> Washington, D.C., 1921

Nationalism is a sense of national consciousness, exalting one nation above all others and placing primary emphasis on the promotion of its culture and interests as opposed to those of other nations or multinational groups. In his 1964 speech "Ballots or Bullets," Malcolm X defined the ideology of Black Nationalism in terms of three broad categories: political, social, and economic:

> The political philosophy of Black nationalism only means that the Black man should control the politics and the politicians in their own community....
>
> The economic philosophy of Black nationalism only means that we should own and operate and control the economy of our community....
>
> The social philosophy of Black nationalism only means that we have to get together and remove the evils, the vices, alcoholism, drug addiction, and other evils that are destroying the moral fiber of our community. We ourselves have to lift the level of our community, the standard of our community to a higher level, make our own society beautiful so that we will be satisfied in our own social circles and won't be running around here trying to knock our way into a social circle where we're not wanted.[2]

Complementing this definition of the ideology of Black Nationalism, Stokely Carmichael and Charles V. Hamilton, in *Black Power: The Politics of Liberation in Amer-*

---

1. Shirley N. Weber, "The Rhetoric of Marcus, Leading Spokesman of the Universal Negro Improvement Association in the United States, 1916–1929" (PhD diss., University of California, 1975), 164.

2. Malcolm X, "Ballots or Bullets," in *Selected Speeches and Statements*, ed. G. Breitman (New York: Grove Press, 1966), 38–39.

ica, write of the political, social, and economic aspects of Black power that can work together to bring about Black liberation.[3] (In their volume, the terms *Black power* and *Black Nationalism* are synonymous.)

Additionally, Alphonso Pinkney presents some characteristics associated with nationalist movements:

> The beliefs and circumstances identified with such movements usually include common cultural characteristics such as language and customs; a well defined geographic territory; belief in a common history or origin; closer ties among fellow nationals than with outsiders; common pride in cultural achievements and common grief in tragedies; mutual hostility toward some outside group; and mutual feelings of hope about the future.[4]

The first portion of this quotation usually provides the most difficulty for students of Black Nationalism because the "language" of Afro-Americans is not easily recognized as a language separate from American English and the customs of Afro-Americans are not seen as different from American traditions. However, within the last three decades, as a result of J. L. Dillard's *Black English*, Blacks have come into a full awareness and appreciation of their language as an identifiable and traceable one.[5] Also, authors such as Janheinz Jahn have proven the "African-ness" of the culture of the Afro-American.[6] In addition, because Blacks have been taught not to acknowledge Africa as their homeland, they have felt there was no territory that Afro-Americans could claim and defend physically, emotionally, and financially against foreign attacks. Although these issues may have been resolved sufficiently for Black scholars to easily identify the Black Nationalist movement, it must be pointed out that even if Blacks do not meet all of Pinkney's characteristics, his other characteristics are so easily observable and strong in Black movements that they can outweigh and counteract the arguments concerning territory, language, and custom.

In identifying the important factors that give rise to nationalism, John Stuart Mill categorizes them into three basic groups. They are (1) an identity of political antecedents; (2) the possession of a national history and a consequent community of recollections; and (3) collective pride and humiliation, pleasure and regret, connected with the same incidents in the past.[7] From Mill's categorization, one can see that the common struggle of Afro-Americans against systematic forms of humiliation and degradation clearly explains the development of nationalist movements within the Black community, past and present.

Implied within discussions of Black Nationalism is a sense of pride and dignity coupled with the desire for self-determination. With this implication in mind, it can easily be shown that Black Nationalism is one of the oldest ideological struggles of Afro-Americans, even before the ideology of integration. For example, reactions of Africans to oppressive slave catchers, such as committing suicide by starvation, jumping overboard slave ships, and staging rebellions and revolts aboard these same ships, are clear

---

3. Stokely Carmichael and Charles V. Hamilton, *Black Power: The Politics of Liberation in America* (New York: Vintage, 1967).

4. Alphonso Pinkney, *Red, Black, and Green: Black Nationalism in the United States* (New York: Cambridge University Press, 1976), 1–2.

5. J. L. Dillard, *Black English* (New York: Random House, 1972).

6. Janheinz Jahn, *Muntu: An Outline of the New African Culture* (New York: Grove Press, 1961).

7. John Stuart Mill, "Representative Government," in *The Dynamics of Nationalism*, ed. Louis L. Snyder (Princeton, NJ: Princeton University Press, 1964), 2–4.

indications that the principles of nationalism (self-determination against forces designed to destroy the culture, heritage, and humanity of the African) were the motivating factors. Although there were no established institutions that specifically spoke of "nationalism," the revolts against the forces that sought to take away the national identity of the African implied nationalist tendencies. This refusal to surrender was the genesis of Black Nationalism for the African American.

In the New World, the Black struggle before 1865 was primarily concerned with the emancipation of slaves. Even when free Blacks met to discuss their situation, as they did in 1800 at the Negro Convention in Philadelphia, the threat of slavery was always present and was therefore a major concern. Free Blacks realized that the line between "free status" and "slave status" was very thin. Consequently, all efforts were directed toward achieving the initial step—emancipation—so that other reforms could take place within the society. Blacks who did not concentrate solely on emancipation were Paul Cuffee, Martin Delaney, and others, who were of the "Back-to-Africa" persuasion. Even after emancipation and the 1877 Compromise (ending Reconstruction), when Blacks realized that the promise and dreams of freedom were in actuality nightmares of deceptions and quasi slavery, they concentrated their efforts on either integration, with W. E. B. Du Bois; or separation, with Henry Turner; or accommodation, with Booker T. Washington.

In 1916, one form of Black Nationalism was established in New York City by Marcus Garvey under the organizational names of the Universal Negro Improvement Association (UNIA) and the African Communities Leagues. Marcus Garvey, a native of Jamaica, became the leader of the largest all-Black Nationalist organization, with over 3 million members representing over nineteen countries. While many scholars attempt to dismiss Garvey as an advocate of emigration who was only interested in going back to Africa, the eight-point platform of the UNIA clearly reveals its larger nationalist scope. The goals were as follows:

1) To champion Negro nationhood by the redemption of Africa.

2) To make the Negro race conscious.

3) To breathe ideals of manhood and womanhood in every Negro.

4) To advocate self-determination.

5) To make the Negro world conscious.

6) To print all the news that will be interesting and instructive to the Negro.

7) To instill racial self-help.

8) To inspire racial love and self-respect.[8]

From these eight points, one can see that the philosophy of the UNIA was structured to encompass cultural/social, political, and economic nationalism.

Garvey viewed the Afro-American's lack of political influence as a result of his poor relationship with his homeland. Therefore, he advocated "Africa for the African" (not "Back to Africa"). Garvey hoped that the shift of Africa from white rule to African rule would give the African, whether at home or abroad, the necessary international influence to demand equal treatment. In an address entitled "Africa, A Nation for the Negro Peoples of the World," presented in Washington, D.C., on November 20, 1921, Garvey stated:

---

8. Weber, "The Rhetoric of Marcus, 44.

We are hopelessly outnumbered and therefore we are weak, and because there is no organization to bring us together to make us numerically strong we are weak, and we reflect our weakness the world over. I say, "Get strong over there and you can transfer part of the strength over here.... Now, if America or West Indian Negroes will concentrate upon the building up of Africa and make it strong, a strong African republic will make you strong in America, even though you are a thousand miles away. There was a time when the Japanese at home was weak. He was a weak man in Japan, and therefore, he was weak everywhere. The Japanese concentrated upon the building up of Japan and now that it has become a strong nation the Japanese is strong anywhere, whether in America or Japan; touch him and you will see how strong he is.[9]

Economic nationalism was promoted in Garvey's UNIA program in order to achieve economic independence for Blacks. The UNIA engaged in various economic ventures on a large scale. The most noted of the enterprises was the Black Star Line, a steamship company whose primary purpose was to promote commerce among people of African descent in the Americas and Africa. The ships purchased were the SS *Yarmouth* (which Garvey intended to rename the SS *Frederick Douglas*), the SS *Kanawha*, the SS *Phyllis Wheatley* (which was never delivered to the UNIA), and the SS *Shadyside*. Because this enterprise threatened the profits of some major white corporations in the United States, the Black Star Line was allegedly sabotaged by the Federal Bureau of Investigation through paid infiltrators.[10]

In addition to the Black Star Line, other UNIA business ventures provided jobs and significant economic independence for Blacks. The purchase of Liberty Hall in New York City, as well as the establishment of the Negro Factories Corporation, the Universal Restaurants, the United Chain Stores, various millinery shops, a hat factory, a moving company, a printing plant, and many other enterprises provided jobs for UNIA members. Of all the businesses, the printing enterprise proved the most successful. The printing plant was responsible for the publishing of *Negro World*, *African World*, and *Negro Times*—periodicals that kept the Black population accurately informed of the activities of the UNIA and of the local, national, and international issues affecting the lives of Black people throughout the African Diaspora.

The cultural component of the UNIA attempted to reorient the values of Blacks. In Garvey's opinion, Blacks were apprehensive about their physical features, a feeling which contributed toward their lack of self-respect and self-love. Garvey violently opposed the use of skin-bleaching creams and hair straighteners. He glorified in the dark, bold features of African peoples:

Take down the pictures of white women from your walls. Elevate your own women to that place of honor. They are for the most part the burden-bearers of the Race. Mothers! Give your children dolls that look like them to play with and cuddle.... Men and women, God made us as his perfect creation. He made no mistake when he made us Black with kinky hair. It was Divine Purpose for us to live in our natural habitat—the tropical zones of the earth. Forget the

---

9. Weber, "The Rhetoric of Marcus, 174.

10. Tony Martin, *Race First: The Ideological and Organizational Struggles of the Universal Negro Improvement Association* (Westport, CN: Hypernon Press, 1976) (Martin writes of the tremendous involvement of the FBI in UNIA affairs).

white man's banter, that He made us in the night and forgot to paint us white.... Now take these kinks out of our minds, instead of out of your hair.[11]

Further, Garvey called for Black churches to create positive images for Blacks in their worship and in their symbols. Specifically, he called for pictures of Christ and the Madonna and the Manchild with bold African features and skin color. He also advocated the teaching of Black history in schools and a reclamation of Africa as the ancestral and cultural home of the Afro-American. Finally, he instituted ceremonies and celebrations into the Afro-American culture that reflected Black values for Black survival. A flag (red, black and green), a national song, and specific ceremonies were a vital part of the UNIA's program to reestablish African culture and heritage among Afro-Americans.

Historically, the UNIA was the most formally structured Black Nationalist organization in America, and it has had a tremendous impact on all subsequent Black Nationalist organizations and ideologies. Adam Clayton Powell, Jr., believed that the Garvey movement had a powerful impact on his life and work. However, it must be noted that Garvey had an ardent opponent, Adam Clayton Powell, Sr., who participated in a "Garvey Must Go" campaign in 1922. The younger Powell often stood outside his father's tent meetings and heard Garvey's influential teaching next door in Liberty Hall. Consequently, during Adam Clayton Powell, Jr.'s civil-rights activities of the early 1940s, his "Don't Buy Where You Can't Work" campaign had overtones of Garvey's nationalism.

The Nation of Islam (NOI) was also greatly influenced by Garvey. According to some accounts, Elijah Poole (Elijah Muhammad), the late Messenger of the Nation of Islam, was once a Garveyite of low rank. In addition, as noted in *Black Muslims in America* by C. Eric Lincoln, most of the initial members of the NOI were once Garveyites who had been dispersed after Garvey's deportation.[12] However, the organization called for a new social status for the Black man. It advocated that the Black man should improve his own status by learning how to respect himself, his woman, and his race. It also developed economic ventures in the Black community—including banks, schools, restaurants, stores, and farms—to provide for the total needs of its people and to provide them with gainful employment.

The issue of territoriality was very evident in the Nation of Islam. It advocated total physical separation from white society and also attacked traditional Christianity. As a result, before the arrival of Malcolm X into its membership, it did not participate in the traditional politics of the United States. In addition, the Depression, World War II, and the highly publicized civil rights movement of the 1960s were heavy competition for the NOI. Today, now known as the World Community of Islam, it has no nationalist program and has become mostly a religious organization.

The most renowned nationalist after Marcus Garvey is perhaps Malcolm X, who, like the younger Powell and the NOI, was also highly influenced by Garvey. In his *Autobiography*, Malcolm remembers his father, a Garveyite, as a proud Black man who loved to talk about Black people and Africa. Malcolm's father was eventually slain because of his beliefs in Garvey's teachings.[13] Thus, there exist close parallels and similarities between the ideologies of Malcolm X and those of Marcus Garvey. In his 1964 speech, "Ballots or Bullets," Malcolm introduced the term *Black Nationalism* and defined its social, po-

---

11. Amy J. Garvey, *Garvey & Garveyism* (New York: Macmillan, 1963), 29.

12. C. Eric Lincoln, *The Black Muslims in America* (Boston: Beacon Press, 1961).

13. Malcolm X, *The Autobiography of Malcolm X*, with the assistance of Alex Haley (New York: Ballantine Books, 1973).

litical, and economic components within the context of the Black experience.[14] Unfortunately, before Malcolm had an opportunity to develop fully his Organization of Afro-American Unity, he was assassinated. Those who followed Malcolm's teachings usually did not emphasize his total program of Black Nationalism. Even though Stokely Carmichael and Charles Hamilton advocated *Black Power* and defined its scope to encompass economic, social, and political components, they developed no programs to bring about the reality of self-determination.[15]

Various Black Nationalist groups have focused on one aspect of nationalism while deemphasizing others. For example, the Black Panther Party, in its initial stages, spent its energies arming and preparing for self-defense as a form of political readiness for physical revolution. The Party, while emphasizing the need for land, food, and community control, was initially active in a political struggle against police brutality. Whenever altercations or imprisonment occurred, the victims were seen as political prisoners. However, after much confrontation with the local, state, and federal police forces, the Party began to organize local improvement programs to build Black community support for their political struggles. These programs included voter-registration drives, free breakfasts, and health-care facilities.

Since the demise of Marcus Garvey and the Universal Negro Improvement Association in 1929, there has been no organization with a total program of nationalism where the economic, social, and political elements have had equal influence and development.

---

14. Malcolm X, "Ballots or Bullets."
15. Carmichael and Hamilton, *Black Power.*

10

"To Unbrainwash an Entire People": Malcolm X, Cultural Nationalism, and the US Organization in the Era of Black Power

Scot Brown

The Black Nationalist resurgence of the late 1960s and 1970s, known as the Black Power movement, even though Black Nationalism had already been part of a long-standing tradition, found a central theoretical and inspirational source in the legacy and thought of Malcolm X. Malcolm's death in 1965 did not thwart his rapid ascendancy as a common reference point for diverse ideological expressions of Black Nationalism and radicalism during this period. As a leader in the Nation of Islam and the Organization of Afro-American Unity, his political stances on a wide range of issues—including support for independent African American statehood, the right of self-defense, and anti-colonial movements abroad—would inspire a range of Black Nationalist activists and organizations.[1] This phenomenon has been described as the workings of a "spiritual advisor in absentia" for a generation of "revolutionaries" convinced of their authentic stewardship of Malcolm's legacy.[2]

The recent wave of published histories of Black Power organizations and figures has stimulated a fresh dialogue on the critical nuances and complexities inherent in the epistemological journey of those dedicated to confronting sociopolitical order of the day.[3] Accordingly, an assessment of Malcolm's impact on a diverse body of Black

---

1. William Sales, *From Civil Rights to Black Liberation: Malcolm X and the Organization of Afro-American Unity* (Boston: South End Press, 1994), 167–204; James Cone, *Martin & Malcolm & America: A Dream or a Nightmare* (Maryknoll, NY: Orbis Books, 1992), 213–314; Molei Kete Asante, *Malcolm X as Cultural Hero & Other Afrocentric Essays* (Trenton, NJ: Africa World press, 1993), 25–36; Mumia Abu-Jamal, "A Life in the Party: An Historical and Retrospective Examination of the Projections and Legacies of the Black Panther Party," in *Liberation, Imagination and the Black Panther Party: A New Look at the Panthers and Their Legacy*, ed. Kathleen Cleaver and George Katsiaficas (New York: Routeledge, 2001), 40–47.

2. William Van Deburg, *New Day in Babylon: The Black Power Movement and American Culture, 1965–1975* (Chicago: University of Chicago Press, 1992), 3.

3. Peniel Joseph, "Black Liberation Without Apology: Reconceptualizing the Black Power Movement," *Black Scholar* 31, nos. 3–4 (Fall/Winter 2001): 3–20.

groups—the Black Panther Party, the Revolutionary Action Movement, the League of Black Revolutionary Workers, the Congress of African Peoples, etc.—reveals an intricate web of intersecting ideas and personal relationships. This essay will explore Malcolm's influence on the US Organization, a leading group in promoting the cultural component of Black Nationalism.

Historically, Black Nationalist ideologies have maintained that people of African descent share a common history and life chances in a white-dominated political, economic, and social order. Studies of Black Nationalism have made use of varied categories to distinguish the disparate, and sometimes competing, tendencies within nationalism. In broad terms, different nationalisms have been defined by a relationship to a dominant or notable area of emphasis—for example, politics, economics, culture, and religion, to name a few.[4]

Black cultural nationalism has been broadly defined as the view that African Americans possess or need to cultivate a distinct aesthetic, a sense of values, and a communal ethos emerging from their contemporary folkways and/or their continental African heritage. This collective identity informs, from a cultural nationalist perspective, African Americans' historical and prospective missions and unique contributions to humanity.[5] Categories of nationalism provide significant insights into specific dimensions of Black political thought but tend to fall short of capturing the complexity of a given personage or organization. Historians have situated the literary works of nineteenth-century nationalist Martin Delaney, for instance, in the cultural nationalist tradition, while his pursuit of Black nationhood finds company among those associated with territorial nationalism.[6] The ideas espoused by the US Organization during the late 1960s and early 1970s were similarly multifaceted. The organization's leader Maulana Karenga was distinct, however, in that he defined himself, and the organization, as "cultural nationalist" and explicitly embraced the term to identify the organization's philosophy.

US Organization: Overview

During the early 1960s, Maulana Karenga (then Ron Everett-Karenga) was a graduate student in political science with a focus on African affairs at the University of Cali-

---

4. Alphonso Pinkney, *Red, Black, and Green: Black Nationalism in the United States* (New York: Cambridge University Press, 1976); E. U. Essien-Udom, *Black Nationalism: A Search for Identity in America* (New York: Dell, 1964); William Van Deburg, *New Day in Babylon: The Black Power Movement and American Culture, 1965–1975*; William Van Deburg, *Modern Black Nationalism: From Marcus Garvey to Louis Farrakhan* (New York: New York University Press, 1997); John Bracey, August Meier, and Elliot Rudwick, eds., *Black Nationalism in America* (Indianapolis and New York: Bobbs-Merrill, 1970); August Meier, *Negro Thought in America, 1880–1915* (Ann Arbor: University of Michigan Press, 1966); Howard Brotz, ed., *Negro Social and Political Thought, 1850–1920, Representative Texts* (New York: Basic Books, 1966).

5. Essien-Udom, *Black Nationalism*, 39–44; Meier, *Negro Thought in America*, 51; Brotz, *Negro Social and Political Thought*, 19–24; for a comparative discussion of cultural and political nationalisms, see Avishai Margalit, "The Moral Psychology of Nationalism," in *The Morality of Nationalism*, ed. Robert McKim and Jeff McMahan (New York: Oxford University Press, 1997), 77.

6. Sterling Stuckey, *Slave Culture: Nationalist Theory and the Foundations of Black America* (New York: Oxford University Press, 1987), 274; Also see example in Martin Delany, "The Political Destiny of the Colored Race," in *The Ideological Origins of Black Nationalism*, ed. Sterling Stuckey (Boston: Beacon Press, 1972), 195–236.

fornia at Los Angles. He helped to found the US Organization in 1965—"US" meaning Blacks as opposed to "them" whites. Karenga was convinced that enslavement and other forms of oppression in the United States had robbed African Americans of the basic elements that constitute a people's or a group's culture. He asserted that "Black people don't have a culture, they have elements of a culture."[7] In his view, African Americans imitatively embraced the culture of their oppressors. His organization set out to construct and propagate a new Black culture based on selected African traditions for the purpose of launching a cultural revolution among African Americans. In the midst of preparing for this revolution, US saw itself as the vanguard and archetype of how the entire Black nation would appear in the future.

US members used the African language Kiswahili, and sometimes other African languages, to express the organization's cultural concepts and rituals. The *Nguzo Saba* (seven principles) comprise a value system that Karenga developed as a main component of the organization's ideology: *Umoja* (Unity), *Kujichagulia* (Self-determination), *Ujima* (Collective Work and Responsibility), *Ujamaa* (Cooperative Economics), *Nia* (Purpose), *Kuumba* (Creativity), and *Imani*(Faith).[8] These principles became even more popular in the post-Black Power period as a result of the growing popularity of Kwanzaa, a week-long holiday originally established by US in 1966 as a way of commemorating the Seven Principles.

Politically, US advocates regarded themselves as organizers of organizations. Specifically, they attempted to "programmatically influence" the political and cultural projects within the Black community in a nationalist direction—by leading interorganizational caucuses (e.g., the Temporary Alliance of Local Organizations and the Black Congress); by working for self-determination, regional autonomy, and Black representation in electoral politics; by agitating against United States' military aggression in Vietnam; and by organizing a series of local and national Black Power conferences to spread Black Nationalism and build united fronts. In its view, US saw no need for recruiting mass membership. Rather, its goal was to ideologically influence other organizations with its united-front approach and thus direct the course of the coming "cultural revolution." This strategy corresponded with the organization's independent involvement in urban uprisings, school walkouts, and student strikes.

Minister Malcolm X and the Nation of Islam

As a national representative and principal organizer in the Nation of Islam (NOI) in the late 1950s and early 1960s, Malcolm X had encounters and personal relationships with many of his would-be "heirs." Karenga found in Malcolm a model of moral fortitude and disciplined commitment to the Black liberation struggle when he met Malcolm sometime in 1961 or 1962. Malcolm, Karenga reflected, "was moral in terms of self-denial.... He was never 'comfort corrupt.'"[9] Karenga met frequently with the min-

---

7. Maulana Ron Karenga, *The Quotable Karenga*, ed. Clyde Halisi and James Mtume (Los Angeles: US Organization, 1967), 7.

8. Imamu [Clyde] Halisi, ed., *Kitabu: Beginning Concepts in Kawaida* (Los Angeles: US Organization, 1971), 7–8; for an earlier reference to the *Nguzo Saba*, see Clay Carson, "A Talk with Ron Karenga: Watts Black Nationalist," *Los Angeles Free Press*, 2 September 1966, p. 12.

9. Maulana Karenga, in discussion with the author, October 11, 1994, transcript, p. 18.

ister whenever he visited the Los Angeles mosque and worked to bring Malcolm to lecture on the UCLA campus in 1962.[10]

Beyond the ethical and inspirational realm, Malcolm's assessment of African American culture had a profound impact on the young student-activist in pursuit of the theoretical building blocks for his own concept of cultural nationalism. At UCLA in 1962, Malcolm told the audience of 600 that "the American Negro is a Frankenstein, a monster who has been stripped of his culture and doesn't even know his name." This assertion resonated with Karenga as he grappled with the theories of postcolonial cultural renewal and revolution in the works of Leopold Senghor, Frantz Fanon, Jomo Kenyatta, Julius Nyerere, Sekou Toure, and others. Malcolm's remarks also reminded his audience of a conclusion held historically in Black Nationalist thought that the enslavement of Africans in the Diaspora had catastrophically eliminated the fundamental attributes of an African identity and culture. Malcolm often grounded the case for the NOI's religious propositions on the presumption of a collective African American cultural deficiency caused by the Black diasporic odyssey.[11] As US chairman, Karenga would later embrace the same position, and like Malcolm, he would use it as a basis for the argument for his organization's alternative proposals, which broke radically from mainstream African American cultural life. Indeed, such a posture offered added urgency and justification for the US Organization's self-conception as the initiator of the "[t]he first time Blacks have gotten together to create a new culture based on revolution and recovery."[12]

When he met Malcolm X, Karenga was already in the midst of an extensive study of African languages, taking classes and independently learning Kiswahili and Zulu. Karenga did not concur with many of tenets of the NOI's historical narrative, especially those locating Black evolutionary origins in the Middle East or Asia rather than Africa. However, his own focus on African languages and culture was based on the NOI's previous rupture from nineteenth- and early twentieth-century nationalist reverence for Western civilization.[13] Furthermore, the NOI's promotion of Arabic as Black people's authentic language and Islam as their religion valorized non-Western cultural ideals and thus appealed to Karenga's early critique of European hegemony.

Karenga recollected that Malcolm had "tried to convert" him to Islam during their initial meeting. But Karenga responded, "I don't really believe in religion."[14] Looking back at his reasoning at the time, Karenga recalled: "I separated myself from the Christian church, and so I didn't see the need for that kind of organized expression of spirituality."[15] Nevertheless, Karenga concurred with the Malcolm's sharp criticism of Christianity as a doctrine supporting enslavement, colonialism, and imperialism.

The NOI's view that Christianity has inextricable connections to an inordinate degree of suffering and oppression for people of color throughout the world spoke to Karenga's earlier studies of works by British philosopher Bertrand Russell.[16] Russell's

---

10. Karenga, discussion, pp. 14–20; "'Negro Monster Stripped of His Culture,'—Malcolm X," *UCLA Daily Bruin*, 29 November 1962, p. 1.

11. Malcolm X, "Twenty Million Black People in a Political, Economic and Mental Prison," in *Malcolm X: The Last Speeches*, ed. Bruce Perry (New York: Pathfinder Press, 1989), 33.

12. Tiger Slavik, *Human Rights Interview: Ron Karenga* (audio recording, side 1) (Los Angeles: Pacifica Radio Archive, June 6, 1966).

13. Wilson Jeremiah Moses, *Classical Black Nationalism: From the American Revolution to Marcus Garvey* (New York: New York University Press, 1996), 1–4, 33–35.

14. Karenga, discussion, pp. 16–17.

15. Karenga, discussion, pp. 16–17.

16. C. Eric Lincoln, *Black Muslims in America* (Boston: Beacon Press, 1961), 28, 78.

essay "Why I'm Not A Christian" linked Christianity to a large measure of historical violence, warfare, and general intolerance. During the early 1960s, this theme would
reemerge, Karenga remembered, in a more concrete form through his contact with the
NOI, in which "Malcolm and the Muslims criticize [Christianity] in even more definitive ways, because they would speak from the Black position."[17]

The NOI also played a key role in the politics of Black identity, contributing its
standpoint to the historic debate over the appropriate name for African Americans.[18]
NOI ministers argued against the use of the term *Negro*, preferring *Black* as the rightful
name for African Americans. From this perspective, *Negro* was invalidated by a lack of
any relationship to land, language, or situational relevance. *Black*, on the other hand,
more appropriately suggested a binary opposition to whiteness—a pan-European identity formed out of a collective opposition to Africans in America and other people of
color in the United States and the African Diaspora. "No matter how light or dark a
white man is," Malcolm preached, " he's 'white.'" He added: "[It's the] [s]ame way with
us. No matter how light or dark we are, we call ourselves 'black'—different shades of
black—and we don't feel we have to make apologies about it!"[19]

Malcolm X popularized the phrase "the so-called Negro" as a reference to Black
people who had not arrived at a proper identity consciousness. "The so-called Negro"
was often derided for backwardness and a pathological attachment to the ways and
worldview of the oppressor. Karenga embraced this Negro/Black distinction and it
eventually became a part of the US Organization's doctrine. It was reflected in the
song "Mama, Mama," which was taught to children at the organization's School of
Afroamerican Culture. The child in the song wonders, "Mama, mama Negroes are insane / They straighten their hair and don't know their name. / They bleach their skin
and act so white. / They don't even have any purpose in life." The mother responds,
"You see my child it's a pity and a shame, / that your sick brother doesn't even know
his name. / It's not his fault, he's not to blame / The white man robbed him of his
Black brain." This victimized and self-hating Negro is then juxtaposed with the US
Organization's definition of *Blackness*. After the child asks, "Mama, mama, what does
it mean to be Black? / Is it like a color so lovely and dark?" the mother states, "To be
Black my child is much more than that. / It's the way you think and the way you
act."[20]

Even though Karenga and his radical contemporaries were ideologically indebted to
Malcolm X during his tenure in the NOI, many also felt that the Black Muslims were incapable of meeting the new political demands of that era. In 1966, just a year after US
was founded, Karenga asserted that although "[t]he Muslims have made a very positive
contribution" in that "[t]hey did a lot of groundwork among the masses in terms of
creating consciousness," the movement required an assertion from a new generation of
leaders.[21] Karenga saw the NOI as a part of an older nationalist trend and considered

17. Bertrand Russell, "Why I Am Not a Christian," in *Bertrand Russell on God and Religion*, ed.
Al Seckel (Buffalo, NY: Proetheus Books, 1986), 57–71. (This essay was first published in 1927.);
Karenga, discussion, p. 6.
18. Stuckey, *Slave Culture*, 193–244. In these pages, Stuckey explores how the names controversy
raged as early as the nineteenth century.
19. Lincoln, *Black Muslims in America*, 69.
20. School of Afroamerican Culture, "Mama, Mama," song, n.d., papers of Maulana Karenga
and the US Organization, African American Cultural Center, Los Angeles.
21. Carson, "A Talk with Ron Karenga," p. 12.

himself and other 1960s activists as generationally distinct from the Nation, stating that "it is up to us, the younger people to go on from where they [the NOI] left off."[22]

The contention that the NOI had not kept pace with the demands of a new era was reinforced by the dramatic series of events in 1965. The turbulent year opened with the assassination of Malcolm X in February and moved on to endure a massive Black uprising in the Watts section of Los Angeles in August. Those two events paved the way for the formation of the US Organization and made a deep imprint on its formative period. Militancy was widespread: a yellow sweatshirt with an imprint of Malcolm X's face and the phrase "St. Malcolm"—worn by various Black activists in L.A., including Karenga, during the uprising's aftermath—came to symbolize the close connection between the two events.

For many young Black Nationalists throughout the United States, the advocacy of self-defense and armed resistance became a litmus test for organizational or individual activist legitimacy. Karenga felt that the NOI's focus on religion had undermined its capacity to pass this test. When talking about this generational difference, Karenga exclaimed that "we're young and our main attraction is to the people who would make the revolt." He concluded: "The Muslims ... are not a political organization, they are a religious organization."[23] He then distinguished them from his own group: "We [the US Organization] engage in some type of political expression.... [T]o be an action organization you have to take some stand politically and the Muslims have not done that."[24]

Malcolm's brief political career after he left the NOI came to overshadow whatever reservations Karenga had about the limitations of Malcolm's religious orientation. As leader of the Organization of Afro-American Unity, Malcolm advocated a secular solution to the same cultural crisis of the "Frankenstein" identified in his 1962 speech at UCLA. In fact, Malcolm's view of culture—as expressed in the "Statement of Basic Aims and Objectives of the Organization of Afro-American Unity"—was a precursor to Karenga's assertion: "You must have a cultural revolution before the violent revolution. The cultural revolution gives identity, purpose and direction."[25] With a similar conception of culture as a foundation for African American collective consciousness, Malcolm wrote: "We must recapture our heritage and our identity if we are ever to liberate ourselves from the bonds of White supremacy."[26]

The US Organization and Malcolm X

The founders of US saw their organization as a revolutionary vessel, carrying out Malcolm's cultural mandate. In the fall of 1965, Maulana Karenga, Hakim Jamal, Dorothy Jamal, Tommy Jacquette-Mfikiri (Halifu), Karl Key-Hekima, Ken Seaton-Mse-

---

22. Carson, "A Talk with Ron Karenga," p. 12.
23. Ron Karenga and others, "What Is Black Power?" (audio recording of panel discussion, tape 2, side 1) (Los Angeles: Pacifica Radio Archive, July 23, 1966). Other panelists present were Benjamin Wyatt, Albert Burton, Clifford Vaughs, Benjamin Handy, and Arnett Hartsfield.
24. Karenga and others, "What Is Black Power?"
25. Karenga, *The Quotable Karenga*, 11.
26. Malcolm X, "Statement of Basic Aims and Objectives of the Organization of Afro-American Unity" in *New Black Voices: An Anthology of Contemporary New Black Literature*, ed. Abraham Chapman (New York: New American Library: 1972), 563.

maji, Samuel Carr-Damu (Ngao Damu), Sanamu Nyeusi, and Brenda Haiba Karenga were among the early members of this newly formed group.[27] According to Hakim Jamal, the organization was not formed in a single meeting but grew out of a study group called the Circle of Seven, led by Karenga, which had met regularly at the Black-owned Aquarian Bookstore in Los Angeles. Jamal also asserted that he had selected the name "US" for the group. Prior to his association with Karenga, he had printed and locally distributed a "magazine" called *US*, intended "for all the black people [and] to be put in markets, free." He also noted that the US Organization's motto, "Anywhere we are, US is," had originally been "a caption for the magazine."[28]

Jamal had been a close associate of Malcolm—from Malcolm's days as a Boston hustler to his political career with the Nation of Islam and the Organization of Afro-American Unity. Upon joining forces with the study group, he led a push to situate the martyred Black Nationalist leader as the US Organization's main ideological and inspirational reference. The organization's first newspaper, *Message to the Grassroots*, which appeared in May 1966, designated Karenga as the "chairman" of US and Jamal as its "founder." The first issue was dedicated to "Mrs. Betty Shabazz, the widow of our slain nationalist leader."[29] By the summer 1966, Jamal had parted company with US. The split likely resulted from differences over the organization's philosophy and leadership directions. Jamal's preference for a political program based on the teachings of Malcolm X seems to have ultimately clashed with Karenga's rapidly expanding dominance over US. By the late summer of 1966, Karenga had become the organization's central ideologue and leader.[30]

On February 22, 1966, US convened its first public event, a memorial observance for Malcolm X, who had been assassinated the previous February. US called the event a *Dhabihu* (Sacrifice) service and declared the day a special holiday to pay homage to Malcolm's sacrifice of his life for the cause of Black liberation.[31] Karenga was featured as the keynote speaker at the service, which was attended by about 200 people.[32] The *Dhabihu* gave Karenga a platform to introduce the organization's political views to a larger community, especially the basis for what would become his organization's opposition to the Vietnam War.

The anti-imperialist service also included a candle lighting ritual, an activity also associated with the first Kwanzaa celebration to occur some ten months later. An account

---

27. C. Batuta, "US—Black Nationalism on the Move," *Black Dialogue* 2, no. 7 (Autumn 1966): 7; Karenga, discussion, p. 44; Karl Key-Hekima, in discussion with the author, November 11, 1996, transcript, pp. 4–5.

28. "An Interview with Hakim Jamal," *Long Beach Free Press*, 17 September 17–1 October 1969, p. 12.

29. *Message to the Grassroots*, 21 May 21 1966, pp. 1, 5. This newspaper was short-lived and may have folded just after the first issue went into print. It had certainly been discontinued by the time that Jamal left US in the late spring or summer of 1966. In August 1966, US introduced a new official newspaper called *Harambee*—its first edition commemorating the anniversary of the Watts uprising. This author was able to locate one edition of the paper in the personal papers of Terry Carr-Damu.

30. By 1968, Jamal had founded the Malcolm X Foundation, based in Compton, California. The Foundation, he argued, was the true heir to Malcolm's revolutionary legacy. Jamal also became a critic of the US Organization's cultural nationalism, contending that its emphasis on African culture diverted its members from participating in revolutionary action. See "'Operational Unity' Leaves Jamal Cold," *Los Angeles Sentinel* 18 April 1968, sec. A, p. 11; "An Interview with Hakim Jamal," pp. 6, 12, 14.

31. Carson, "A Talk with Ron Karenga," 12.

32. "First Annual Memorial Staged for Malcolm X," *Los Angeles Sentinel*, 3 March 1966, sec. A, p. 11.

of the ceremony noted that "[t]wo candles burned at the foot of the lectern" and that "[t]hey were blown out and re-lit, but not before the audience was informed that one burned for Malcolm X and the other for Patrice Lumumba."[33] US and other local nationalists were openly defying the NOI by organizing this public event—especially since the *Dhabihu* took place at a time when the NOI vehemently argued that Malcolm was a befallen traitor. Just over a year after US introduced the *Dhabihu*, its second annual celebration of Malcolm X's birthday, now called *Kuzaliwa* (birthday), stood at the center of student protest in Los Angeles.

In December 1966, US initiated the first *Kwanzaa* celebration. Those in attendance remember it as a small, intimate gathering. However, the organization's members likely felt that diligent activism would bring forth a wider acceptance of their "new" Black culture. This feeling was indicated in the organization's call in the following spring for African Americans not to go to work or school on May 19, or the closest weekday to it, in observance of a new Black national holiday, *Kuzaliwa*—the birthday of Malcolm X. The response in Los Angeles was overwhelming and was partly responsible for the organization's growing appeal to African American youth in that city.

Beyond California, the activism of US throughout the Black Power years was shaped by a continuous effort to participate in, form, or lead African American umbrella organizations modeled on Malcolm's united-front ideal. Historian Komozi Woodard maintains that independent politics and the goal of nationality formation were key developments in the cultural nationalism of the Black Power era. A centerpiece in these developments was the launching of what Woodard has called the Modern Black Convention Movement: the 1966, 1967, and 1968 Black Power Conferences; the 1970 and 1972 conventions of the Congress of African People; the 1972 National Black Political Convention in Gary, Indiana; and a series of other major political gatherings. From 1966 through 1968, the US Organization led the initiating phase of the Modern Black Convention Movement. For example, along with other organizations, it played a leadership role in the planning and direction of the 1967 and 1968 Black Power Conferences.

Malcolm X was a source of inspiration not only for the US Organization's aboveground community organizing and political agenda but also for its underground participation in violent resistance. After leaving the ranks of the NOI, Malcolm's support for the right of Black self-defense was surpassed by his open endorsement of armed resistance to oppression. US (like the Revolutionary Action Movement, the Black Panther Party, the Black Liberation Army, and other groups) responded to Malcolm's call for the development of an African American "Mau Mau" or guerilla fighting force as a complement to the efforts of such groups as the Mississippi Freedom Democratic Party and the Student Nonviolent Coordinating Committee in electoral politics and desegregation.[34]

Unlike radicals dedicated to the application of the guerrilla-warfare theories of Mao Zedong and Che Guevara to the United States, Karenga was skeptical of the notion that a political party could instigate revolution by initiating a guerrilla war with the state. Armed struggle, if it was to be effective, could not be achieved by a small group of revolutionaries alone, but a broad-based African American consensus, he felt, could sustain an organized, protracted armed struggle for political objectives. "What we should concentrate on is not the weapons but the people," Karenga stated, and then he asked: "How can we win the people?" He further asserted that "it is not a question of how can

---

33. "First Annual Memorial Staged for Malcolm X."
34. Malcolm X, *Malcolm X Speaks: Selected Speeches and Statements*, ed. G. Breitman (New York: Pathfinder Press, 1993), 105–107.

we kill the enemy, for the people must decide that that is necessary themselves, or the vanguard will vanish and the revolutionary party which has placed itself in a front position will fall flat on its face and history will hide all of them."[35]

Underground resistance was the quiet companion of the US Organization's campaign to "win" African American hearts and minds through the introduction of alternative African-inspired rituals and cultural practices. This approach mirrored Malcolm's concept of guerilla warfare as a measure corresponding with electoral politics and community organizing. Accordingly, US did not embrace revolutionary violence as a part of its public discourse, but its paramilitary wing took part in regular underground activities such as bank robberies, raids of armories, and sabotage.[36]

The aspirations of nationalist organizations committed to actualizing Malcolm's vision of revolutionary change were stifled, though not extinguished, by the onslaught of United States government repression, peaking in the late 1960s and the early 1970s. By the late 1960s, the FBI had accumulated a great deal of experience in infiltrating and disrupting Black political organizations with a broad range of ideological persuasions. As early as 1919, the decade-old, Bureau of Investigation (the word *Federal* was added in 1935) had institutionalized a system of infiltrating and disrupting organizations such as the National Association for the Advancement of Colored People, the African Blood Brotherhood, and the Universal Negro Improvement Association.[37] In the late 1960s the FBI was in the midst of a protracted campaign, known as COINTELPRO, to disrupt and neutralize Black nationalist and radical organizations in the United States.[38]

As a result of a replay of government tactics used to disrupt the Nation of Islam and the Organization of Afro-American Unity—ultimately laying the basis for Malcolm's assassination—the US Organization's influence declined, alongside that of most radical organizations of the period, as the group succumbed to factional violence, sectarian rivalry, and a leadership breakdown in the early 1970s.[39] (The US Organization continues to operate to this day, but on a comparatively smaller scale—as an influential cultural nationalist cadre based in Los Angeles.) Post-Black Power decades did not foster a climate of mass mobilization, which was conducive to the flourishing of cultural nationalism in the 1960s. However, manifestations of Malcolm's precepts on culture continue to impact the tenor and tone of Black resistance.

---

35. Maulana Karenga, "Revolution Must Wait for the People," *Los Angeles Free Press*, 16 May 1969, p. 14.

36. "L.A.P.D. Raids US Headquarters; Arrests Two," *Los Angeles Sentinel*, sec. A, p. 1, sec. D, p. 2; Federal Bureau of Investigation, "Everett Leroy Jones," FBI file # 100-425307, 24 December 1967, p. 12, Amiri Baraka Papers, Moorland-Spingarn Research Center, Howard University, Washington, D.C.; "Bank Robbery Nets US Member 25 Years," *Los Angeles Sentinel*, 14 August 1969, sec. A, p. 3; "2 'US' Members Guilty of Crime," *Los Angeles Sentinel* 6 March 1969, p. 1; Ngoma Ali, in discussion with the author, November 10, 1996, transcript, pp. 24–25.

37. Kenneth O'Reilly, *"Racial Matters": The FBI's Secret File on Black America, 1960–1972* (New York: Free Press, 1989), 1–14.

38. Federal Bureau of Investigation, Director to SAC Albany, "Black Nationalist Hate Groups," FBI file # 100-448006, 4 March 4 1968, section 1 pp.1–6, *COINTELPRO: The Counter Intelligence Program of the FBI* (Wilmington, DE: Scholarly Resources, 1978), microfilm.

39. "Karenga Denies Shooting of UCLA Black Panthers," *Los Angeles Free Press*, 31 January–7 February 1969, p.1; "2 Former US Members Ambushed in View Park," *Los Angeles Sentinel*, 27 August 1970, sec. A, pp. 1, 8; "Ron Karenga Rebuffs Charges Against US," *Los Angeles Sentinel*, 30 September 1970, sec. A, pp. 1, 8; "Karenga, 2 Others Found Guilty of Torturing Woman," *Los Angeles Times*, 30 May 1971, p. 26; Amiri Baraka, *The Autobiography of Leroi Jones* (Chicago: Lawrence Hill Books, 1997), 392–393, 404; Komozi Woodard, *A Nation within a Nation: Amiri Baraka (LeRoi Jones) and Black Power Politics* (Chapel Hill: University of North Carolina Press, 1999), 165.

Conclusions

The politics of collective identity stand at the forefront of the African American freedom struggle, given the history of enslavement and the systematic assault on diasporic connections to an African cultural identity. In the early 1960s, neither Malcolm X nor Maulana Karenga had access to a future paradigm shift in African American historiography which refuted the notion that enslavement had completely shattered the African cultural foundations of its captives. Historians of enslavement in the United States—Sterling Stuckey, Margaret Washington, Vincent Harding, and others—have uncovered the deep rootedness of the Black struggle to maintain various African cultural practices in religion, philosophy, music, and dance as a form of resistance to slavery. However, Malcolm's characterization of African Americans as a people suffering from a debilitating cultural void helped inspire a dynamic counterresponse from cultural nationalists.

The US Organization's pursuit of the cultural revolution—with its alternative life-cycle ceremonies, holidays, and united-front political formations—spoke directly to the politics of twentieth-century American institutional racism and the persistent defamation of African history and culture in American mass media and popular culture. The cultural nationalist thrust gave rise to the production of aesthetic conceptions, philosophical paradigms, and ritual representations of Africa and African American cultural possibility that contested established notions of Western triumphalism.

Categories of nationalism have traditionally compartmentalized politics and culture. Malcolm's impact on the US Organization and the wider Black cultural nationalist movement highlights their unavoidable intersection amid the history of African American resistance. Cognizant of this relationship between politics and culture, Malcolm declared, "We must launch a cultural revolution to unbrainwash an entire people."[40]

---

40. Malcolm X, "Statement of Basic Aims and Objectives of the Organization of Afro-American Unity," 563.

11

Malcolm X and Pan-Africanism

Paul Easterling

Introduction

> My father, the Reverend Earl Little, was a Baptist minister, a dedicated orga-
> nizer for Marcus Aurelius Garvey's U.N.I.A. (Universal Negro Improvement
> Association). With the help of such disciples as my father, Garvey, from his
> headquarters in New York City's Harlem, was raising the banner of black race
> purity and exhorting the Negro masses to return to their ancestral African
> homeland—a cause which had made Garvey the most controversial black man
> on earth. (Malcolm X 1965a, 1)

During his childhood Malcolm X was nurtured in a home that taught and believed
in Pan-Africanism and the struggle of African people on a worldwide scale. Early in
his adulthood, he abandoned the values which his parents, through Garvey, had
taught him, and entered a life of crime. In prison he discovered the Nation of Islam
(NOI) and began to recover the Black Nationalist ideology and ultimately the Pan-
African values by which he was reared. The NOI trained him and helped him wean
himself from alcohol and drugs; in return, he gave the NOI national recognition and
helped the organization grow into the religious belief system for the African American
community it is today. Because of a natural evolution in his ideology and a moral split
with the leaders of the NOI, Malcolm continued to return to the Pan-African roots
from which he was raised and became a dangerous ideological force against American
and Western oppression. Some argue that this and other issues ultimately led to his assassination.

This essay contends that Malcolm was returning to his Garveyite roots of Pan-
Africanism throughout his life. In support of this argument, the essay will first examine
the major motif of Garveyism. Then it will analyze Pan-Africanism as it was espoused
by Malcolm, especially over the last two years of his life. Finally, it will make a comparative analysis of the Pan-Africanism of Garvey and Malcolm. The ultimate purpose of
the essay is to present a deeper understanding of Pan-Africanism as it was espoused by
Malcolm in his attempt to forge new strategies for the collective liberation of African
people.

Methodology

This essay will employ a qualitative research methodology as well as historical analysis. *Historical analysis* is

> the means by which the researcher deals with the latent meaning of history. History is a phenomenon. It is a transcript of the relentless surge of events, the sequential and meaningful record of human activity. The historical method aims to assess the meaning and to read the message of the happenings in which men and women, the events of their lives, and the life of the world around them related meaningfully to each other. (Leedy 1989, 125)

Given this definition, this essay will examine the earlier Pan-Africanist ideology that Malcolm experienced as a phenomenon that led to his involvement with the NOI and that ultimately led to the later Pan-Africanist ideology he expressed prior to his untimely death. Through this analysis (emphasizing the latter part of his life), it is hoped that the reader will gain an in-depth view of Malcolm's personal history as it related to Pan-Africanism and how that relationship led to his becoming the historical figure who best expressed Pan-Africanism. Using the historical method, the essay will also examine the evolution of Pan-Africanism as an ideology and as a strategy for liberation.

Garveyism and Malcolm Little

> Since childhood, Malcolm Little's life had been characterized by all of the essential themes that would later underscore his message to a generation of Black people engulfed in crisis. In the particular sense of racism, Malcolm would come to know from his youth the reality of white racial animosity and insouciance toward the black struggle. That reality would increasingly press in on his human experience as he grew from childhood into manhood. (DeCaro 1996, 38)

This excerpt, from Louis A. DeCaro, Jr.'s *On the Side of My People: A Religious Life of Malcolm X*, indicates that Malcolm's ideology was formed during an early stage of his life. These "essential themes" were the teachings of Marcus Garvey that Malcolm's parents had brought into their household and many other households in the area in which they lived—since Malcolm's father, Earl Little, was a part of Garvey's organization, the Universal Negro Improvement Association (UNIA).

> Earl Little traveled around preaching Garvey's ideas, often from behind the pulpits of African American churches—the memory of which left the mistaken impression in the mind of a young Malcolm that his father was an itinerant, unordained Christian preacher. (DeCaro 1996, 39)

Indeed, in his *Autobiography* Malcolm remembers:

> My father bought a house and soon, as had been his pattern, he was doing free-lance Christian preaching in local Negro Baptist churches, and during the week he was roaming about spreading word of Marcus Garvey. (Malcolm X 1965a, 3)

Malcolm's early memories and teachings of his father shaped Malcolm's Pan-African philosophy. They stayed with Malcolm his entire life and grew in strength as he neared his death.

The entire Little family was immersed in the Garvey movement. Earl Little was "president of the Omaha branch of the U.N.I.A" (DeCaro 1996, 40). Louise Little, Malcolm's mother, who was from the Caribbean Island of Grenada, supported her husband in his teachings and in his involvement in the organization. She also wrote articles for the UNIA's paper the *Negro World*, in the News of Divisions section. However, Earl's and Louise's membership in the UNIA brought the Little family harassment from the local Ku Klux Klan.

Earl and Louise Little's involvement in the UNIA had an impact on both Malcolm and his siblings. DeCaro explains:

> To say Malcolm and his siblings were reared in a Garveyite home is no exaggeration. The Little children were undoubtedly accustomed to hearing their father's powerful baritone voice leading the Garveyites in prayers and hymns; likewise, they regularly enjoyed sitting around the stove while Louise told them stories about their proud ancestry as black people. "She told us we came from great people that were onetime rulers," Malcolm's brother Philbert recalled. (DeCaro 1996, 42)

DeCaro further discusses two aspects of Garvey's philosophy which had a profound impact on the Little family: "First, the self-help emphasis of Marcus Garvey was not taken merely as a model for the masses, but as a principle of the household" (DeCaro 1996, 42). For example, Earl Little lived his life very independently. He worked as a freelance craftsman, a job in which he was not greatly successful because of his political views. He and his wife also grew food in their own garden and owned cows, chickens, and rabbits—which they used for the family as well as for retail purposes. Given his Garveyite "self-help" ideology, Earl Little indeed practiced what he preached. Not only was this ideology the collective philosophy of the Little family; it can also serve as an example for all African people who desire a sense of solidarity and independence from the oppressive system (DeCaro 1996, 42–43).

This mind-set filtered down to the younger Littles, who were encouraged to grow and nurture their own gardens: "[A]ll of Earl and Louise's children were allocated ground for personal gardens" (DeCaro 1996, 42). By tending to their gardens and performing other chores, the children were taught the strict discipline necessary for self-help. Such discipline would stay with Malcolm throughout his life (DeCaro 1996, 42).

The second aspect of Garvey's philosophy that profoundly influenced the Little household was Afrocentrism. Malcolm claimed

> that his childhood conception of Africa was much like that of other children in the United States, picturing it as the stereotypical dark continent—a place of steaming jungles filled with natives and wild animals. (DeCaro 1996, 43)

However, in the Little household, he was quickly sensitized to "black internationalism" when he noticed that his mother, born in Grenada, was not like the rest of the Black people he had come into contact with. DeCaro continues:

> The Littles received not only *Negro World*, but they also regularly read other black publications, including newspapers from the Caribbean. At the dinner table, the Little children would hear their parents discuss the philosophy and

concerns of Garvey's "scattered Africa," undoubtedly making Malcolm sensitive to Afrocentrism. (DeCaro 1996, 43)

Thus, through the Garveyite philosophy of his parents, Afrocentrism and Pan-Africanism became a solid part of Malcolm's psyche—as well as the foundation of an ideology which allowed him to accept the teachings of Elijah Muhammad. Moreover, after his split from the NOI, the Garveyite ideology formulated Malcolm's strategy regarding the African world (DeCaro 1996, 42–43).

Marcus Garvey and Elijah Muhammad

Before Elijah Pool became Elijah Muhammad and before he became the leader of the Nation of Islam, he was a soldier in Marcus Garvey's UNIA regiment: "For Garvey and his followers, who included the young Elijah Pool, black nationalism was as much a religion as a political philosophy" (Evanzz 1999, 57). As a child, Elijah Pool was already familiar with many of Garvey's teachings. Indeed, according to Evanzz (1999, 57), "Garvey espoused many concepts that Elijah was introduced to as a child, and much of his philosophy echoed Turner."

Evanzz is referring to Bishop Henry Turner, who was one of the earliest Black Nationalists/Pan-Africanists. Evanzz describes Pool's introduction to Turner's teaching and its effect on Pool's young mind:

> At the turn of the century, black children in Cordele attended one of two "colored-only" schools. Children whose parents attended the colored Methodist Episcopal Church went to the Holsey-Cobb Institute, while Presbyterians sent their children to the Gillespie-Selden Institute. However, it was distance more than religion that dictated the choice for Elijah. The Methodist school, overseen by Bishop Turner, was closer to the Pool's home, so Elijah attended Holsey-Cobb. "I walked five miles to school every day," Elijah recalled. Shortly after he started school at the age of six, Elijah's demeanor changed. Once a very active child, he suddenly became quiet and introverted, often parking himself in a corner of the living room with the Holy Bible the minute he finished his homework and after-school chores. (Evanzz 1999, 22)

Thus, as Evanzz indicates, Malcolm and Elijah were similar in two fundamental ways. First, as children they were both exposed to the ideology of Pan-Africanism—Malcolm through his Garveyite parents and Elijah through Bishop Turner at the Holsey-Cobb Institute. This similarity ultimately led to their close interaction during the 1950s and 1960s. Second, both of them were connected with the Garvey movement. Elijah was more directly connected with the movement since he was able to work with Garvey in person before Garvey was deported. Malcolm, however, had a more distant connection—through the ideology and activities of his parents.

The link between Garvey and Elijah was significant but did not last long, because "[by] the time Elijah joined the U.N.I.A., Garvey was caught in … [a] counter-intelligence web" (Evanzz 1999, 59) which eventually led to his deportation. After Garvey was deported, Elijah had to search for a new way to cultivate his ideologies of Pan-Africanism and Black Nationalism. His search led to his interactions with Noble Drew Ali, founder of the Moorish Science Temple, and Master Ford Muhammad—and ultimately to the founding of the Nation of Islam.

Malcolm and Elijah

Malcolm and Elijah became closer—in ideology as well as personality—after Malcolm spent time in prison for armed robbery. Indeed, Malcolm's foundation in Pan-Africanism enabled him to matriculate into Elijah's organization very easily. The only element new to Malcolm was the NOI's religion of Islam. He soon embraced it, however, and his new religious stance eventually reignited the teachings of his mother and father from his childhood.

After leaving prison as a convert to Islam, Malcolm met with Muhammad personally, and from that point, he began his tireless work in Muhammad's name. During this time, he gave the NOI a new and vibrant life it did not have before. The NOI grew exponentially and spread across America. The fire and charisma that Malcolm brought to the NOI inspired many to join the organization and to seek the teachings of Muhammad. Consequently, the NOI was forever indebted to Malcolm, for without him, it would arguably have never made the strides it did (Malcolm X 1965a).

Much of what Malcolm taught through the NOI was not new to him: the ideas of Black solidarity and fearless, tireless work were a part of Malcolm's life before he was sentenced to prison. But now, with his new religious stance and the backing of the NOI, Malcolm was able to project his message to African Americans and eventually to the world (Malcolm X 1965a).

> If I harbored any personal disappointment whatsoever, it was that privately I was convinced that our Nation of Islam could be an even greater force in the American black man's overall struggle—if we engaged in more action. By that, I mean I thought privately that we should have amended, or relaxed, our general non-engagement policy. I felt that, wherever black people committed themselves, in the Little Rocks and the Birminghams and other places, militantly, disciplined Muslims should also be there—for all the world to see, and respect and discuss.
>
> It could be heard increasingly in the Negro communities: "Those Muslims *talk* tough, but they never *do* anything unless somebody bothers Muslims." (Malcolm X 1965a, 295)

This excerpt is crucial in any discussion of Malcolm's attitude toward NOI strategy. It shows that Malcolm was a man of action and that he had African peoples' well-being at heart regardless of their religious affiliation. The excerpt is also crucial in any discussion of liberation strategies for African people. To use a religion only in its narrow meaning for effecting liberation will not address *all* the needs of *all* African people. Malcolm emphasized this point in a speech he delivered at Tuskegee University:

> Elijah believes that God is going to come and straighten things out. I believe that too. But whereas Elijah is willing to sit and wait, I'm not willing sit and wait on God to come. If he doesn't come soon it will be too late. I believe in religion, but a religion that includes political, economic, and social action designed to eliminate some of these things, and make a paradise here on earth while we're waiting for the other. (Malcolm X 1992, 22)

This excerpt indicates that Malcolm was not satisfied with the lack of political, economic, and social action in the NOI. It is also indicates that Malcolm saw the importance of the involvement of a religion in politics, economics, and society. If a religion does not address all these areas of life, especially within an oppressive system, the religion becomes problematic.

For most of Malcolm's interaction with the Nation of Islam, he was a loyal soldier and leader. However, this loyalty was compromised when Malcolm became aware of the infidelity of his teacher and religious father Elijah Muhammad. That Malcolm voiced his concern about Muhammad's infidelity made him a mark for those in the Nation who were envious of his success. It also opened the way for the counterintelligence maneuvers that were later initiated against Malcolm and the NOI. However, it was Malcolm's comments about the assassination of John F. Kennedy that ultimately drove Malcolm from the organization. Yet it can argued that, with the increasing violence against African Americans, the nonengagement policy of the NOI would eventually have caused a split between Malcolm and the organization (Malcolm X 1965a).

Malcolm and Pan-Africanism

> Africa is the land of the future ... definitely the land of tomorrow, and the African is the man of tomorrow. Only yesterday, America was the New World, a world with a future—but now, we suddenly realize Africa is the New World—the world with the brightest future—a future in which the so-called Negroes are destined to play a key role. (DeCaro 1996, 142)

These words of Malcolm's were spoken to the Black press, and, once again, they reflect his Garveyite upbringing. They indicate not only the importance of African Americans investing in Africa but also the importance of connecting African Americans with Africans on the Continent. Malcolm's words constitute a significant Pan-African strategy for liberation. The linkage between Africans in America and Africans in Africa, each of whom experienced similar types of oppression, amounts to a collective unity—which, in turn, leads to power. In indicating the importance of collective unity, Malcolm also stated:

> Thus, African's [sic] consider American's [sic] treatment of Black American's [sic] a good yardstick [by] which they can measure the sincerity of America's offer of assistance here, and many young Africans are openly stating that what America practices at home does not coincide with what she preaches abroad, and are thus suspicious of her overtures here. (DeCaro 1996, 143)

Malcolm's statement indicates that the United States has been consistent in its treatment of African people on a global scale. For example, the involvement of the CIA in the assassination of Patrice Lumumba is matched by the FBI's COINTELPRO infiltration of the civil rights movement and the NOI in an effort to destroy both of them.

That Malcolm saw and made the connection among Africans on a global level indicated not only his Garveyite roots but also his role as a leader of Africans throughout the world. Not since Garvey himself did Africans throughout the world have a leader who stressed the importance of the global unity of Africans.

James Cone discusses the influence of Malcolm's Pan-African message:

Africa emerged as the continent of preference in defining the identity of African-Americans. "It's nation time" and "We are an African people" could be heard in political meetings, casual conversations, and the classrooms of newly founded educational institutions, many of which derived their names from Malcolm. So pervasive was Malcolm's influence that even mainstream civil rights leaders, preachers and politicians acknowledged his insight and integrity.... Blacks today who are proud to claim their African heritage should thank Malcolm. (Cone 1999, 291)

Malcolm's profound influence on Africans must once again be attributed to his Garveyite roots. However, Garvey's influence was not as wide as Malcolm's—largely because of the growth in the media from Garvey's time to Malcolm's. Through the media of the 1960s—radio, television, and the press—Malcolm was able to reach not only Africans but all people throughout the world.

Garvey did have access to media. Indeed, *The Negro World*, his avenue to the masses, helped him reach people he could not speak to directly. However, Malcolm also had access to radio and television so that people as far as Cairo, Egypt, were able to hear and see his passion and fire. Consequently, the Pan-African movement penetrated the masses more effectively and widely—and won the hearts and minds of more African people—than Garvey's movement.

The following sections will focus on Malcolm's interaction with various African leaders at home and abroad and on his political strategy in bringing charges against the United States to the United Nations.

Malcolm and African Leaders

Malcolm made two important journeys to the Middle East and Africa. The first lasted from April 13 to May 21, 1964. Egypt, Arabia, and Lebanon were the first countries he visited (Cone 1999, 313). During his stay in Arabia, he made his historic pilgrimage to Mecca, where he saw the true face of Islam. There he experienced brotherhood between races that he had never witnessed while in America. The experience profoundly influenced his political advocacy of human rights throughout the world (Malcolm X 1965b, 59–60).

The fourth African country he visited was Nigeria, where he spoke to students at Ibadan University. Here Malcolm was given the affectionate name Omowale (in Yoruba, "the son who has come home") because continental Africans, in general, and Nigerians, in particular, viewed Malcolm as a representative of Africans in America. In a personal letter he writes:

Here in Africa, the 22 million American blacks are looked upon as the long-lost brothers of Africa. Our people here are interested in every aspect of our plight, and they study our struggle for freedom from every angle. Despite Western propaganda to the contrary, our African brothers and sisters love us, and are happy to learn that we also are awakening from our long "sleep" and are developing strong love for them. (Malcolm X 1965b, 61)

Since Malcolm was a representative of Africans in America, his words above comprised the crux of the Pan-African movement. Unity between Africans on the Continent and

Africans in the Diaspora was a necessity, for without that unity the movement would be powerless. The United States (and nations like it) have tried to disseminate lies and misinformation that would create a rift between continental and diasporic Africans. Such lies are what Malcolm called "western propaganda"—which goes hand in hand with the divide-and-conquer strategy the Western world has used for centuries in dealing with people of African descent. This strategy can be seen in the writings of Willie Lynch, an African enslaver who preached that control of Africa could emerge from disunity. It can also be seen in W. E. B. Du Bois's aid in the efforts to deport Marcus Garvey as well as in the fabricated dichotomy of Malcolm versus Martin Luther King, Jr., which is still heatedly debated today. Therefore, since it is obvious that disunity has been the main strategy of the oppressor, unity must be the main strategy of Africans. Malcolm himself predicted the result of such a strategy when he said: "Unity between the Africans of the West and the Africans of the father land will well change the course of history" (Malcolm X 1965b, 62).

Near the end of Malcolm's first journey abroad, he traveled to Ghana, where he met with fellow liberation fighter and Prime Minister Kwame Nkrumah. During his visit, he addressed the Ghanaian Parliament and university students (Cone 1999, 313) and spoke further about the plight of Africans in American and the need for unity between diasporic and continental Africans. His enthusiasm for Pan-Africanism he carried back to the States, where he continued to speak of the importance of unity with liberation movements around the world (Cone 1999, 313). In his speeches, Malcolm suggested that liberation movements do not happen in a vacuum: the movements are connected with other peoples' oppression in different parts of the world.

Malcolm's second journey abroad was much more extensive. From July 9 to November 24, 1964, he visited eighteen countries: Egypt, Arabia, Kuwait, Lebanon, Khartoum, Ethiopia, Kenya, Zanzibar, Tanzania, Nigeria, Ghana, Liberia, Guinea, Senegal, Algeria, Switzerland, France, and Britain. During his travels, he gave many speeches and spoke with many heads of the nations. He also spoke privately with leaders of the liberation movements that were operating during this time.

These meetings and speeches allowed Malcolm to push for greater awareness of the problems Blacks were facing in the United States. Africans in America and Africans in Africa have had similar oppressors; however, there have been differences in their respective struggles. Awareness of these differences is key in Pan-African liberation strategy (Cone 1999, 313).

These meetings and speeches also allowed Malcolm to plan new strategies regarding the struggles of African Americans. Cone explains:

> By linking the black struggle in the United States with a worldwide revolution among Third World nations, Malcolm was able to challenge the typical assumption of the civil rights movement: Since blacks were a minority, they had no other options than to negotiate their freedom through nonviolence. (Cone 1999, 313)

This issue of minority status is also addressed by Malcolm himself:

> I don't believe in this outnumbered business.... You're only outnumbered when you're in Mississippi and New York and that's it. But when ... black Americans see that our problem is the same as the problem of the people who are being oppressed in South Vietnam and the Congo and Latin America ... then—the oppressed people of this earth make up a majority, not a minority—then we approach our problem as a majority that can demand, not as a minority that has to beg. (Cone 1999, 313–314)

Once again, Malcolm indicates that unity among all "oppressed people" in their struggle for liberation is of the utmost importance. Arguably, a lack of unity may be the reason why many of the freedom struggles of African Americans have not yet led to complete liberation. In future struggles for liberation, the importance of unity must be seriously considered.

> In this great partnership with Africa, Malcolm maintained it was necessary for African Americans to go back mentally, culturally, spiritually, philosophically and psychologically to Africa.... Malcolm sought a two-way bridge between Africans and African Americans. He challenged Africans that they would never be respected until "the black man in America is also recognized and respected as a human being." ... "So I say that we must have a strong Africa, and one of my reasons for going to Africa was because I know this. You waste your time in this country, in any kind of strategy that you use, if you're not in direct contact with your brother on the African continent who has his independence." (De-Caro 1996, 224–225)

Malcolm's continuing advocacy of Pan-Africanism makes the movement—and its philosophy—embraced by Africans throughout the world. It has been perceived that Africans in Africa do not care about Africans in America, and vice versa. Thus, in the passage above, Malcolm is appealing to Africans on both sides of the ocean. Specifically, he is calling for a sense of responsibility and brotherhood between Africans in America and Africans on the Continent, and he is asking each group not to place blame upon the other.

Also in this passage, Malcolm is calling for a mental, cultural, spiritual, philosophical, and psychological emigration back to Africa. Obviously, Africans in the United States, many of whom have lived here for generations, would not want to make a *physical* return to Africa—and Malcolm is fully aware of this. So his words suggest the importance of *some* connection with Africa—one that need not be physical. Such a linkage is primary in the struggle for liberation because if African Americans are connected to Africans on the Continent, they will always have the strength and spirit of Africa to support them.

Malcolm and the United Nations

> According to Malcolm, the struggle of African Americans for their freedom should not be perceived at all as a domestic issue, and indeed the intent of the OAAU is "to 'internationalize' it by placing it at the level of human rights." Thus he beseeches the Independent African States to place this issue before the United Nations because, firstly, the United States government is "morally incapable of protecting the lives and property of twenty-two million African Americans" and, secondly, their "deteriorating plight is definitely becoming a threat to world peace." (Carson and Gallen, 1991, 300)

This excerpt is taken from the FBI files on Malcolm, which were collected and edited by Clayborne Carson and David Gallen. The files contain Malcolm's plan to appeal to the United Nations concerning the problems faced by Africans in America. Malcolm's appeal suggested that the United States had neither the capability nor the desire to change the actions of its government and citizens in their treatment of African Americans. Malcolm's appeal also suggested the hopelessness felt by African Americans. In the present day, this hopelessness must be seriously considered, and two questions must be asked: Were the problems that evoked this sentiment ever seriously addressed and solved? Is there evidence that this sentiment still exists within the minds and hearts of African Americans today? If the first question cannot be answered positively and the second cannot be answered negatively, then one must ask: Why, in the nearly forty years since Malcolm addressed these concerns, do the conditions still exist which make the problems that evoked this feeling of hopelessness a reality for people of African descent in America? Malcolm further clarifies this sentiment:

> If the federal government does not find within its power and ability to investigate a criminal organization such as the Klan, then you and I are within our rights to wire Secretary-General U Thant of the United Nations and charge the federal government in this country, behind Lyndon B. Johnson, with being derelict in its duty to protect the human rights of twenty-two million Black people in this country. And in their failure to protect our human rights, they are violating the United Nations Charter, and they are not qualified to continue to sit in that international body and talk about what human rights should be done in other countries on this earth [Applause]. (Malcolm X 1992, 26–27)

Malcolm's charge against the U.S. government was a charge of accountability. In addition, his charge was an act of courage because he was the first to call for accountability of the actions of the U.S. government on an international level. Implicit within this call for accountability were UN sanctions against the United States if its government did not take seriously the lives of Africans within its borders. Malcolm felt that the charge of accountability had to be placed against the United States especially if it claimed to be the vanguard of morality among the rest of the world's nations. Without a sense of accountability, the United States and its defenders were hypocrites.

To clarify the need for human rights as opposed to civil rights, Malcolm explained the stipulations within the charter of the United Nations:

> All of the nations that signed the Charter of the UN came up with the Declaration of Human Rights, and anyone who classifies his grievances under the label of human rights violations, those grievances can then be brought into the United Nations and can be discussed by people all over the world. For as long as you call it "civil rights," your only allies can be the people in the next community, many of whom are responsible for your grievance. But when you call it "human rights," it becomes international. And then you can take you troubles into the World Court. You can take them before the world. And anybody anywhere on this earth can become your ally. (Malcolm X 1992, 170)

Malcolm's words suggest that the United States, throughout its history, has violated not merely the civil rights of its African American citizens but also their human rights. Indeed, this nation has violated its African-descended people with a blatant disregard of their humanity. Malcolm was correct in considering the racism faced by African Americans in the United States as a violation of their *human* rights. Otherwise, the humanity of Africans would continue to be marginalized in the courts of America and the world.

Also of great importance is that African Americans should acquire allies in their struggle for liberation. If Malcolm had lived and if his appeal to the United Nation had spoken to the humanity of the world's leaders and to the oppressed of the world, there would have been a much greater chance of victory in this struggle.

Conclusion

It has been shown that the development of Malcolm X as a child was key to his actions and strategy in his adult years. Nurtured in a Garveyite home, he was taught to love and respect his African heritage. In turn, this love and respect gave him the philosophical and psychological tools necessary to combat all that he faced throughout his life. In addition, his background created a strong link and interaction with the Honorable Elijah Muhammad. This connection and interaction placed him on the world's stage as a voice of Africans in America and beyond it. Consequently, he is still praised, honored, and studied by many in the realms of politics, religion, law, and academia, and by those engaged in the continuing struggle for worldwide African liberation. In addition, because of his adherence to his Garveyite foundation throughout his life, he continually advocated strengthening the unity of the world's African population. This advocacy placed him in the dual role of prosecutor of the United States government and defender of African people in the world's court.

Students of Malcolm's words and actions—his whole philosophy and sagacity—will gain a solid foundation and strong weapons with which to stand and fight for liberation. Without such study, Africans in America and on the Continent would be doing themselves a disservice by robbing future generations of a fighting chance to carry on Malcolm's legacy.

References

Carson, Clayborne, and David Gallen, eds. 1991. *Malcolm X: The FBI file*. New York: Carroll & Graf.

Cone, James H. 1999. *Martin & Malcolm & America: A dream or a nightmare*. New York: Orbis Books.

DeCaro, Jr., Louis A. 1996. *On the side of my people: A religious life of Malcolm X*. New York: New York University Press.

Evanzz, Karl. 1999. *The messenger: The rise and fall of Elijah Muhammad*. New York: Vintage.

Leedy, Paul D. 1989. *Practical research: Planning and design*. New York: MacMillan.

Malcolm X. 1965a. *The autobiography of Malcolm X*. As told to Alex Haley. New York: Grove.

————. 1965b. *Malcolm X speaks: Selected speeches and statements*. Ed. George Breitman. New York: Grove.

————. 1992. *February 1965: The final speeches*. Ed. Steve Clark. New York: Pathfinder.

Dr. Martin Luther King, Jr. and Malcolm X waiting for press conference. Courtesy of the Library of Congress, 1964 March 26.

Dr. Martin Luther King, Jr. Courtesy of the Library of Congress, 1964.

Malcolm X waits at Dr. Martin Luther King, Jr.'s press conference. Courtesy of the Library of Congress, 1964 March 26.

Malcolm X being interviewed by reporters. Courtesy of the Library of Congress, 1964.

Malcolm X at Queens Court. Courtesy of the Library of Congress, 1964.

Black Manhattan mural at 135th Street and Lenox Ave. IRT subway station in New York, NY. Courtesy of David P. Smallwood (2005).

Courtesy of Charles "Boko" Freeman, 2007.

Malcolm X lecturing. Courtesy of LOOK Magazine, December 1969.

Honorable Elijah Muhammad lecturing. Courtesy of the Library of Congress.

Campus of the University of Ghana at Legon. Malcolm X gave a lecture in the Great Hall (located in the tower) on May 13, 1964 as part of a week long trip in the country sponsored by the Malcolm X Committee. During the trip Malcolm X met President Kwame Nkrumah, ambassadors from foreign nations in Africa, Asia and Latin America and established a chapter of the OAAU in Ghana. Courtesy of Andrew Smallwood (August, 2005).

Part Three

Malcolm X's Intellectual Leadership

12

Literary Malcolm X: The Making of an African American Ancestor

Christel N. Temple

In Africana American Studies, Black cultural heroes are easily distinguished by their contributions to the discipline's areas of history, religion, politics. However, the significance of Black cultural heroes, or *mythoforms*, has not been sufficiently analyzed in the content area of literature, which lies within the category of creative production and which is therefore the most creative, speculative, and expressive arena for the masses to affirm, to record, and to promote the legacy of their ancestors. Although preceded by the legacies of Frederick Douglass and Nat Turner (among others) and succeeded by the legacies of leaders such as Martin Luther King Jr. and Medgar Evers, Malcolm X continues to be the most significant mythoform in Black literature. Attention to Malcolm as a mythoform even exceeds attention given to modern-day cultural heroes, both living and deceased, such as Angela Davis, Gwendolyn Brooks, and Nelson Mandela, who have also been nurtured and promoted in the literature. The process whereby Malcolm has emerged as the inspiration for literature written during his lifetime, for literature created following his assassination, and for reflective literature of the contemporary era indicates a collective cultural response. This essay will define this process as a continuation of African-derived literary forms.

Afrocentric scholars have an exhaustive task ahead of them as they forge ahead to uncover, record, and disseminate evidence that defines the culture created by Africans on America's shores within the culture's traditional, African-derived forms and paradigms. The way the Black community responded to Malcolm X's death reflected an African paradigm of ancestor creation and emerged in the form of the *funeral dirge*, which is the ritual action of public emotion and affirmation that permits an individual's ascendance into perpetual communal myth and remembrance. As expected, the cultural adaptations that Blacks in America have made will require that the terms *funeral dirge* and *creation of ancestors* remain flexible. In addition (and unfortunately), the task of uncovering an African past encounters barriers in the most unexpected places. For example, even in such exhaustive reference guides as *The Oxford Companion to African American Literature* (1997), there is no entry for "dirge"; and the closest reference is the heading "Funeral and Mourning Customs." Neither is there an entry for "eulogy," "elegy," or "praise poem." We cannot assume that the genre of the funeral dirge, so central to the African oral tradition, ceased to exist among African Americans because of several centuries of enslavement. Obviously, there is a need for more research into narratives and other sources chronicling cultural practices of Africans during enslavement.

J. H. Nketia, in *Funeral Dirges of the Akan People* (1955), states that the funeral dirge as an oral form is central to the funeral ceremony because the Akan, who are representative of West Africa peoples, in general, are concerned with maintaining harmony in their universe, which consists of the living, the ancestors, and those yet to be born. African Americans are no less concerned with a similar universe, so one has to wonder: What happened to their understanding of the importance of the funeral dirge and its relationship to sustaining the community through the eventual creation of ancestors? One answer is that the funeral dirge and ancestor creation did not disappear at all; the example of Malcolm X (although there may have been others before him for whom we do not have records) demonstrates that a substantial portion of the African American community has been attentive to these foundations of its cultural existence. Another answer is that the environment of the United States has been so racially oppressive and restricting that African Americans did not have the freedom, the resources, and the inspiration to be their African cultural selves until one hundred years after Emancipation.

The Oxford Companion to African American Literature (1997) does, however, give sustained treatment of Malcolm X in the section "Poetry," where it defines Malcolm's influential role in the flowering of the late 1960s Black Arts Movement. Malcolm is also mentioned under the heading "Character Types." Here he is defined as a moral guide and as a vessel of cultural values. Although the *Oxford* essay focuses on female moral guides in Black literature, it does highlight the importance of Black male figures in fiction and in history who are either freedom fighters or rebels. The prerequisite for being a moral guide is based on the life journey of the individual. Malcolm X's *Autobiography* (1965), a nearly biblical account of Malcolm's path toward awakening and social consciousness, is also responsible for Malcolm's hero dynamic.

In the African American literary tradition, there is a fine line between speculation and myth making. Many nonliterary scholars do not realize the existence of *speculative fiction*, which includes not only science fiction but also the hypothetical literary scenarios "what if … ?" or "what would life be like if … ?" Douglas Turner Ward's play *Day of Absence* (1966), in which white people wake up one day and Blacks have disappeared, is a well-known example of this genre. The cultural experience of African Americans is wrought with speculation because their existence in America, since enslavement, has required them to live a life preoccupied with race and problem solving. The nature of such problem solving requires that an African American constantly think of scenarios that will lead to absolute freedom and equality. In fact, not only has the cultural experience of African Americans preordained speculation about how to obtain freedom in the present and the future; it has also been preoccupied with defining and reconstructing their past. It is this preoccupation in which the uniqueness of the culture of African Americans diverges from the traditional African culture they brought with them prior to enslavement.

The oral traditions of African Americans when they arrived as enslaved became insufficient to counter the new hostile environment they faced. The African oral traditions functioned "as an informal education that prepared youth for their responsibilities as adults in the community" (Boateng 1990, 110). In addition, fables, myths, legends, and proverbs were agents of intergenerational communication. For example, fables, most often in the form of trickster narratives "conveyed moral lessons … [and] were carefully constructed to inculcate the values of the societies into the children without necessarily and formally telling them what to do and how to do it. In most of these stories, a catalogue of likely tricks are set out in story forms and successful countermoves to them are described" (Boateng 1990, 111).

The enslavement experience of African Americans demanded that their environmental point of reference shift with their introduction to a new world order. The premises of their indigenous culture were, of course, relevant, but they had to adapt the contexts in order to react to and to survive among a society hostile to them. For example, fables transmitted the values of the "superiority of brilliance over steadiness," the "unity of the clan," "cooperative effort," the "merits of group solidarity," and the "dangers of individualism" (Boateng 1990, 112). However, in the new environmental context of Africans forging their way toward freedom in America, the traditional education that youth received in the home or in the community necessitated the learning and reinforcement of new and additional lessons and strategies that were direct responses to enslavement, racism, injustice, life or death situations, and various responses to attacks by racist and silent, skin-color-benefiting whites.

This discussion of adaptations in culture relates to the literary treatment of Malcolm X because his life is the material for new, timeless, distinctly African American myths. It is not a contradiction that a real person can also be a useful myth because, as Boateng reminds us (1990, 115), "much history contains myth, and many myths contain historical truths." If we tied together all of the poems, dramas, and narratives about Malcolm X into one story, we would have an epic. It would be a tool that, like a myth, "sustains morality, ritual, law, and sanctions against offenders" (Boateng 1990, 115). It would be artistically African in the most traditional sense because no single artist could claim authorship of the total work. That such a body of material exists and continues to be generated about Malcolm X elevates him as an indisputable legend and ancestor. The record assumes a supernatural quality about the man, and in time, legend will be fully exalted into a mythoform, a functional mythology, or a collection of sacred stories about the people. These notions relate specifically to Asante's definition of *mythoform*: "[It is] the all-encompassing deep generator of ideas and concepts in our living relationship with our peers, friends, and ancestors. As a productive force, it creates discourse forms that enable us to use cultural sources effectively" (Asante 1987, 96).

If African Americans can suspend a narrow, self-absorbed, linear concept of time that does not include their individual lifetimes, they may realize that their African American heritage represents an emerging cultural reality for a people of African descent that was dispersed. Their cultural legacy in America is richer than they realize yet still more uncovered than they realize. The recuperation from catastrophic events such as the Maafa and from the global racist oppression of people of African-descent may take hundreds of years to be completely accomplished. Malcolm's story and development as an ancestor through literary documents could, in hundreds of years, become a classic, community-validated epic (like the *Sundiata*) or a legend that sustains the functional oral (and now written) tradition of the African American experience. The work of ancestor creation that Black Arts writers began in the 1960s, and which continues even today, can be the foundation of myths and legends that will sustain descendants of African Americans in hundreds of years to come.

Introduction: Why Malcolm X

In the afterword to *Black Fire: An Anthology of Afro-American Literature* (1969), Larry Neal reminds African Americans of the significance of their literature when he writes: "Black literature must become an integral part of the community's lifestyle. And I believe that it must also be integral to the myths and experiences underlying the *total*

history of black people" (Neal, 1969, 653). This is a final critical message to bring together the ideas presented in a seminal volume of Black revolutionary literature—
mostly poetry. Ten of the poems, as well as much of Neal's afterword (an essay entitled
"And Shine Swam On"), suggest that Malcolm X has emerged as the much-anticipated
leader who could merge history, rhetoric, and functional mythology with a "hip" revolutionary message that creative artists, scholars, and leaders would honor and attempt
to reproduce for decades to come.

Malcolm's assassination is an acknowledged indicator of a shift in Black poetry.
Scholars agree that the shift resulted in a "furious flowering" of revolutionary Black
writing because the assassination captured the imagination of younger poets and became the catalyst for the Black Arts Movement. Neal states the reasons why the radical
and philosophical framework for the movement is based largely on the vision and empowering message of Malcolm:

> [Malcolm] touched all aspects of contemporary Black nationalism. His voice
> sounded the tough urban street style, and his life became a symbol and inspi-
> ration. With his words resonating in their consciousness and his image inspir-
> ing a revolutionary world vision, poets such as David Henderson, James A.
> Emmanuel, Robert Hayden, and Etheridge Knight paid tribute to him after his
> death. (Neal 1989, ix)

In the afterword to *Black Fire*, Neal also discusses the similarities among and the significance of Black mythological figures, or mythoforms—including "Nat Turner, Martin Delaney, Booker T. Washington, Frederick Douglass, Malcolm X, Garvey, Monroe
Trotter, Du Bois, Fanon, and a whole panoply of mythical heroes from Br'er Rabbit to
Shine" (Neal 1969, 639). Inevitably, Neal extols Malcolm X from the panel of 1960s
leadership because "a Malcolm, finally, interprets the emotional history of a people
better than the others" (Neal 1969, 639). For Neal in 1968 when *Black Fire* was first
published, as well as for us in 2007 as we review the literary legacy of Malcolm X, it is
clear that

> Malcolm covered everything—nationhood, manhood, the family, brother-
> hood, history, and the Third World revolution. Yet it always seemed that he
> was talking about a revolution of the psyche, about how we should see our-
> selves in the world. But just as suddenly as he was thrust upon us—he was
> gone. Gone, just as Black America was starting to understand what he was talk-
> ing about. (Neal 1969, 645–46)

Any discussion of Malcolm X is twofold (at least). We praise his vision, and then we
lament losing him. This process is a mystery, and even a puzzle, that keeps us wondering— and working to recreate and revive a spirit and a message that showed the greatest
promise and potential for Black America, in particular, and for humanity, in general.

One year later, in 1969, two of Neal's Black Arts comrades, Dudley Randall and Margaret G. Burroughs, released the first edition of a collection of poems dedicated to Malcolm X—*For Malcolm: Poems on the Life and Death of Malcolm X*. This text was conceived in April 1966 at the Fisk University Writers' Conference. Randall and Burroughs
recall that after "[h]earing Margaret Walker read her poem on Malcolm X [at the con-
ference] … we were reminded of the great number of poems that had been written in
his memory, and we decided to make a selection from them and to publish it" (Randall
and Burroughs 1969, xix).[1]

---

1. Citations to poems in this collection will be designated as *FM*.

Randall and Burroughs noticed that the entries they received "grouped themselves by certain themes," and they subsequently arranged the poems in the same pattern—in four sections, each covering an aspect of Malcolm's life: The Life, The Death, The Rage, and The Aftermath (Randall and Burroughs 1969, xix). There are similarities between this structure and Nketia's structural elements of the dirge: the ancestor, the deceased, the domicile of the ancestor, the domicile of the deceased, reflections, and messages. Although not in perfect traditional dirge structure, *For Malcolm* contains all of the elements of the dirge.

There is one other literary volume on Malcolm X—*Malcolm X: Justice Seeker* (1993), by James B. Gwynne. Smaller in scope than *For Malcolm*, it includes reprints of poems, personal narratives, historical pieces, essays, and one play. In addition, although not a collection of poetry, Malcolm's own *Autobiography* (1965) is an accurate literary document that makes it possible for us to know his life well. The *Autobiography* has fostered the establishment of patterns of affirming and remembering Malcolm X.

Reintroducing and Defining the Dirge

This section of the essay examines in detail how the dirge has been documented among the group of Africans who evolved in the United States since enslavement. Models of the dirge come mostly from Nketia's 1955 seminal work on the Akan, which covers traditions of the Twi-speaking (Asante, Akyem, Kwawu, Akuapem) and the Fante-speaking groups of present-day Ghana. Another model of the dirge, examined by Ode S. Ogede in "Context, Form and Poetic Expressions in Igede Funeral Dirges" (1995), is practiced by the Igede (also called Egedde or Igedde), who reside in the Benue State of Nigeria. All the models and examples of the dirge in this essay originate from West Africa, the region from which most African Americans descend. Since there are many dirge practices among West Africans, this essay may seem to oversimplify a complex oral literary tradition. Therefore, the seminal text by Nketia, the full article on the Igede dirge by Ogede, and other sources highlighted in their bibliographies should complement this essay.

According to Ogede (1995, 80–81), a *dirge* is the "primary means by which mourners express their grief." In addition, it is "an immediate response" of "lamenting the loss of human life" and contains an element of storytelling. Furthermore, it contains literary material that has "expressive power with which dirge composers stimulate their listeners emotionally and intellectually." Finally, in order for the dirge to move its audience sufficiently, the "performer should feel the pathos of the occasion and sentiments embodied in the dirge."

The dirge is a mournful song or poem, but it is more complex than many realize. Indeed, according to Nketia (1955, 50), it

> is generally not preoccupied with Death personified or with the pathos of mortality in general.... As the funeral dirge is concerned with mourning particular individuals, it tends to reflect on the significance of particular events of death to the bereaved or their effect on those left behind.... The building up of associations between the present and the past by means of references to Ancestors and events, the singing of praises and the identification of individuals in terms of their group affiliations are also a major concern of the Akan funeral dirge.

The primary difference in the dirge between the African American poetry tradition and traditional West African practice is that in the latter, the genre is customarily taught to girls, who continue to practice and perform the songs and lyrics throughout their adult lives. Obviously, in African American culture, the dirge can be performed by either gender.

Most of the literature created in response to Malcolm X is poetry. African American poetry, characterized by its brevity, figurative imagery, appropriation of rhythm and music, and lyricism, is most similar to song, which follows the structure of the dirge. Modern circumstances of African American culture disallow, or have removed, the rituals of performance and ceremony (and their cyclic repetition) from the lyrical expressions that constitute the African American dirge. However, Black poetry has a vibrancy and life of its own in the tradition of Nommo, by evoking powerful images and truth with the written and spoken word.

Some cultural considerations uniquely define the African American experience, and it is possible that the challenges and stresses of African existence in America since enslavement would allow flexibility in the African community's conceptualization of terms and conditions for performing a dirge and for becoming an ancestor. For example, if culture can be generally defined as the way of life of a group of people based on their successful methods of surviving within a given environment, it is logical to suggest that the parameters and meanings of traditional key concepts related to "becoming an ancestor" would undergo reinterpretation that would account for the new worldview that Africans faced as an enslaved and oppressed group in the United States.

Defining the ancestor's "type of death," for example, would require flexibility in the culture of African Americans. In Igede funeral dirges, deaths are classified as either "good" or "bad," and "only a good death is by custom fit to be mourned on an elaborate scale calling for dirge compositions" (Ogede 1995, 80). Therefore, this essay must critically redefine Malcolm's death—which was, technically, a homicide (a "bad" death)— as a "battle death" (a "good" death). For survival reasons, the Black cultural experience in America presupposes that every Black person is constantly under attack by and, therefore, engaged in a war against racist institutions and their representatives.

Another definition that may require alteration in the context of African American culture is that of an "elder" or "old age." Given the shift in mortality rates for Africans during and after enslavement, African Americans have had to mature quickly. Malcolm underwent a transformation while in prison. He had time to reflect and meditate on the frivolous nature of the first phase of his life. He corrected his misuse of those early years by embarking upon an accelerated learning process. Coming full circle, Malcolm used his time in prison to seek and find wisdom, spirituality, and perspective. His defined his sordid past as a tool of experience that gave him enough insight to be a speaker and leader capable of reaching the masses, many of whom were identical to his old self. This process of Malcolm's life, amply documented in his *Autobiography* (1965), confirms that he was wise and therefore acts as public proof of his worthiness to become an ancestor. Malcolm was indeed prepared for leadership, and this preparation presupposes a maturity, or "elderhood," which, in an African American experiential context, prepares the leader for the likelihood of death in battle—a "good" death.

This lengthy discussion of Malcolm's advancement in wisdom and his inevitably reconstructed life span (based on the challenges of his being a Black man in a violent and racist society) is imperative in the process of adapting the traditional definition of *ancestor* to the African American cultural experience. Ephirim-Donkor's explanation of the requirements for becoming an ancestor suggests the possible dilemma in the context of African American culture:

> [T]he beginning must be lived in anticipation of the end. The individual must therefore accrue material opulence as well as virtues that are extolled by the matrikin. This is what the individual will be judged by at old age and upon his or her demise.
>
> At old age an elder is apt to reminisce as to whether or not he or she has successfully integrated all states of existence. The reflexivity of this period is spurred largely by the imminence of death, the race against time, and accountability before the ancestors. (Ephirim-Donkor 1997, 130)

The "material opulence" mentioned here is another condition of becoming an ancestor that would require flexibility in its application to the African American cultural experience. The politics of institutional racism in America have traditionally placed limitations on the economic opportunities for Blacks in America.

This essay consists of exploratory cultural research that can only speculate on possibilities of cultural practice. Even Ogede confirms that research has only begun to explore the depth of the oral tradition among African people:

> The publication of Nketia's *Funeral Dirges of the Akan People* (1955) was a quantum leap forward in the study of the African dirge, and since that time elaborate attention has been paid to the genre. Nevertheless, there are still real gaps that need to be filled in the rather copious scholarship in the field, particularly because, in the collection of African oral literary materials generally, it is the larger ethnic groups that have usually dominated the field, and the dirge study is no exception. (Ogede 1995, 79)

Ogede's description of the dirge provides even more possibilities for contextualizing the dirge tradition in African American literature, in general, and for honoring Malcolm X, in particular:

> Because each mourner tends to improvise his/her own words, in the performance of the Igede dirges much talent is involved, and the pieces contain many layers of condensed poetic material. Embedded in the dirges, moreover, are cultural beliefs and practices that should speak to the interest of historians, anthropologists, sociologists, even psychologists and philosophers. (Ogede 1995, 80)

In their poems, Black poets honoring Malcolm use all the elements of the Igede dirge.

Another connection with Malcolm is that in the Igede tradition, there are performance groups, such as the Idoma Alekwu troupe, which "perform dirges copiously and by that means call all their neighbours to attend every scene where a death has occurred. They believe that this is necessary in order to involve everyone in the community in sharing the sorrow occasioned by the loss of life" (Ogede 1995, 81). African American poets provide the same function as that of the professional mourners. However, considerations of flexibility must allow for adaptations by Black poets since they live in an era of writing and technology and in a larger geographic area than the Igede local unit. Consequently, it impractical for them to feature a strictly oral dirge to honor a national hero.

The dirge, in the Igede tradition, is performed immediately after the death is announced and continues for a two-week period after death. There are also memorial ceremonies that mark the first calendar year after the death, but they do not use the dirge form. (It is noteworthy that Etheridge Knight composed a poem for Malcolm entitled "For Malcolm, A Year After" [*FM*, 43]). The dirge itself is reserved only for the period of two weeks after death—a period involving an immediate public display of mourning. A reflective, ritualistic remembrance of the individual for years to come may be served by the praise poem, which is another genre in the oral tradition that permits ancestors to be honored during and after deaths. That dirges to Malcolm X were *written* (as well as sometimes performed) and, therefore, recorded for posterity differs somewhat from the traditional West African dirge tradition. However, the immediate outpouring of poetry to Malcolm that expressed grief and mourning qualifies the literature as a modern transposed form of the dirge. Because these dirges were recorded as written documents; because Malcolm exhibited an effective, unprecedented leadership style; and because Black America has longed for leadership like Malcolm ever since his death, African Americans have continued to mourn, praise, and seek wisdom and direction from Malcolm's life. The early poems (dirges) to Malcolm appropriately showed that the poets felt "the pathos of the occasion and the sentiments embodied in the dirge" (Ogede 1995, 81), and the consistency in the poetic reflection of Malcolm's life, death, and legacy share the same sort of pathos.

Ogede provides another description of the dirge that is relevant to comparison to the literature mourning Malcolm X:

> Thus, in mourning a death, a dirge performer may identify a distinct quality (possessed by a dead person or by his family) and praise it, employing a proverb or a riddle to enliven the praise and alluding in the process to an event that occurred either in the deceased's own life or in earlier family history, or to a folk-tale incident. (Ogede 1995, 81)

The content of the poetry written about Malcolm verifies the relevance of this aspect of the Igede dirge. Larry Neal's "Malcolm X—An Autobiography" hails Malcolm's father as a Garveyite, "silhouetted against the night-fire, gun in hand" (*FM*, 9). In "Looking Homeward, Malcolm" Conrad Kent Rivers describes Malcolm's mind at death: "He remembers Betty dressing the kids, and Alex pushing for words against time" (*FM*, 66). James Patterson, in "Ballad to the Anonymous," sings of the distinct quality in Malcolm that emboldened him to discard his "slave name" and replace it with "X" as his last name. Patterson defines Malcolm as kin by comparing him to his own great-grandfather:

> His name was simply X,
> Malcolm, just like yours;
> And just like you, he did not know
> His origin, of course.
> His dad was X, his grand-dad too,
> And all his ancestors. (*FM*, 77).

Nketia presents a context for the relationship between death, the dirge, and ancestor acknowledgment, particularly concerning the death of a leader. He claims that "premature death, the death of a useful or important member of a community may call for a good deal of wailing" (Nketia 1955, 6). Concerning the afterlife, he adds:

> It is believed that there is a world of the dead built on much the same pattern as that of this world and that when a person dies he goes to his Ancestors. There are beliefs in the visitations of the dead, in invisible participation of the dead in the life of this world and in the continuation of ties of kithship and kinship after death. Consequently, the living are anxious to keep up good relations with the dead, to remember them to show concern for them, to identify themselves with them and to ask their favour. (Nketia 1955, 6)

Margaret Burroughs, in "Brother Freedom," places Malcolm among the ancestors:

> Immortal now, he sits in fine company
> With L'Ouverture and Joseph Cinque
> With Vesey, Turner and Prosser
> Lumumba and Evers and others. Brother Freedom. (*FM*, 22)

Margaret Walker, in "For Malcolm X," understands that our cyclical universe includes the living, the ancestors, and those yet to be born. For this reason, she asks of Malcolm, "When and Where will another come to take your holy place?/Old man mumbling his dotage, or crying child, unborn?" (*FM*, 33).

According to Nketia's description of Akan funeral dirges, they necessarily contain references to the ancestors. What makes the Akan dirge structure empowering as a cultural legacy for African Americans is that although every dirge mentions several persons from the deceased's lineage, the Akan consider that such persons do not always live in the same locality: "Migrations due to war, famine, expansion, marriage and slavery have caused a dispersion" (Nketia 1955, 20). Because the names and details of the lineage of African Americans were stolen and not recorded, it would have been difficult for the community of mourners to invoke the names of Malcolm's ancestors. Ironically, Malcolm was the first major Black cultural icon to take the last name "X" to designate this loss. Nonetheless, Nketia's description of what is done when such a dispersion has taken place corroborates that Black poets recall Malcolm among a pantheon of leaders, such as Frederick Douglass, Nat Turner, Gabriel Prosser, Marcus Garvey, and others. Nketia explains:

> These facts of lineage segmentation and clan dispersions are important in dirges, for they determine the choice of forebears that are to be associated with the deceased. As those in the minimal lineage are closer to the deceased than those of the maximal lineage or the clan and may be better known to the mourner, naturally the inclination of a dirge singer would be to associate as many of the prominent members with the deceased as possible. (Nketia 1955, 20)

Thus, the ancestors that poets have associated with Malcolm run the gamut from the above-mentioned national Black ancestors to Malcolm's parents and siblings who supported his development. In fact, Nketia clarifies that the funeral dirge marks the last time when the deceased is privileged to hear about the deeds of his ancestors; hence, he has enough information to find his way to them in the next world (Nketia, 1955, 25). The list of prominent members of society and of ancestors with whom poets have associated Malcolm is extensive—and includes Ida B. Wells, Sojourner Truth, Martin Delany, Rosa Parks, David Walker, Patrice Lumumba, Michael Schwerner, James Chaney, Andrew Goodman, Stokely Carmichael, Amiri Baraka (formerly LeRoi Jones), H. Rap Brown, Martin Luther King, Jr., Toussaint L'Ouverture, Jean-Jacques Dessalines, Nelson Mandela, Fannie Lou Hamer, Muhammed Ali, Alex Haley, Betty Shabazz, Denmark Vesey, Nat Turner, Gabriel Prosser, Robert Williams, Medgar Evers, James Meredith, Marcus Garvey, and Malcolm's father. This list is generated from twelve separate poems in Randall and Burroughs's 1969 anthology.

Nketia also points out: "Once he [the deceased] sets foot in it [the underworld or afterlife], he cannot and should not come back except as a divine Ancestor spirit. But if he had been partially wicked in his lifetime, or something had gone wrong before his journey or in the course of it, he might not be admitted to the world of the spirits" (Nketia 1955, 44). For this reason, mourners may wish him well, wish him a good journey, and "tell him to announce himself at the outskirts of town" (Nketia 1955, 44). In "The Solitude of Change," Jay Wright believes that Malcolm is still attentive to our world after his death. Wright asks:

> Do you listen now
> as we debate our judgments?
> Whatever others say of you, no matter,
> take this talisman to sail briefly
> over whatever dark depths you discover there. (*FM*, 29)

Wright wishes Malcolm well once he arrives into the afterlife. James Worley, in "Sleep Bitter, Brother," wishes Malcolm peace:

> Fall yearning down, my hopes shall compass yours.
> Be done seeking, you will share my search.
> Keep fingers crossed when you give up the ghost,
> And strings attached; there's work for ghosts to do. (*FM*, 23)

Bravery, determination, and skill in war are attributes particularly highlighted in Akan funeral dirges (Nketia 1955, 23). The wisdom, wealth, longevity, and physical characteristics of the deceased are also acknowledged. Nketia admits that "there is no limit to what a mourner can mention," but he does highlight such virtues as "[b]enevolence, sympathy for others, readiness to give advice, to listen to others, to share with others" and "endurance, slowness to anger, [and] patience" (Nketia 1955, 37). The topics of Ogede's study of dirges foster values such as "honesty, hard work, fair play, solidarity, generosity and humility" (Ogede 1995, 82). All of the poems to Malcolm highlight these qualities, but several stand out for their effectiveness. The poem by Amiri Baraka (formerly LeRoi Jones), "A Poem For Black Hearts," captures Malcolm's spirit. Baraka sings of "Malcolm's hands raised to bless us/all black and strong in his image/of ourselves" and of "Malcolm's/ heart, raising us above our filthy cities" (*FM*, 61). Finally, Baraka sings of Malcolm's "pleas for your dignity, black men, for your life,/black men for the filling of your minds with righteousness" (*FM*, 61–62).

In the traditional Akan dirge, the deceased is also called by several names because, when alive, the individual had multiple names on the basis of the day he or she was born and other qualities. The African American tradition lacks a similar method of naming the deceased, but that does not prevent poets from honoring Malcolm with a variety of identities. Amiri Baraka (formerly LeRoi Jones) calls Malcolm a "Fire Prophet." Some poets identify Malcolm by his birth name, Malcolm Little; by the name he took while in the Nation of Islam, Malcolm X; and by the name he took upon his return from Mecca, El Hajj Malik Shabazz. Other poets address Malcolm as "Seventh Son," "Big Red," "Ghetto Flower," "A Giant," an artist, a landscape, a portrait, "Black Prince," "sweet singer," "hurricane man," "Elijah's Right Hand," "Detroit Red," "Brother Freedom," and, simply, "Malik."

Nketia (1955) observes that "the dirge also recalls the home, the common place of origin of the deceased with his Ancestors, and mention of a town, village, [or city or state] that is significant in the history of the deceased or his kin." Several poets mention Malcolm's affiliation with Africa, with the North and Midwest, and with towns that were significant in his life—Omaha, Detroit, Boston, Chicago, and Harlem, New York. K. William Kgositsile, in "Brother Malcolm's Echo," connects Malcolm with the fury of protest and freedom seen in Watts and in the Sharpeville Massacre (*FM*, 55).

Finally, Nketia highlights the significance of reflections and messages in the dirge:

> The last important component of the dirge is the body of expression portraying the mourner's reaction or her attitude to the event of death and to the loss

of the deceased. Her reflections of her own plight, her messages and utterances to the dead as well as the living may be incorporated. There are traditional expressions for these, but there is scope for originality of sentiment and expression. (Nketia 1955, 44)

In Randall and Burroughs's anthology, Malcolm's death is described as a catastrophic event for Black America. Indeed, Sonia Sanchez laments:

Do not speak to me of living.
life is obscene with crowds
of white on black.
death is my pulse.
what might have been
is not for him/or me
but what could have been
floods the womb until I drown. (*FM*, 39)

In "Days After," Helen Quigless grieves the loss: "On the silent eve of history's grief/Rejection whirs sedately in the air" (*FM*, 66). Le Graham, in "The Black Shining Prince," sighs:

He's gone. his
death lingers on. &
so
does he. (*FM*, 57)

However, Edward S. Spriggs, in "Stillborn Pollen Falling," combines his grief with a promise to remember Malcolm:

Malik's flowers fade
among the weeds (too many
winds disperse his seeds,
robbing them of April rain,
crowding them in a cement,
choking off another generation).
O our tomorrow poets:
stillborn pollen falling
s i l e n t l y
at the feet of our dead
& exiled poets. Wait!
The waters are rising
& the ritual begins again. (*FM*, 73)

Spriggs reminds us that death is not the end of Malcolm, and Nketia provides the best summary of the significance of the traditions of the dirge and of understanding the ancestors:

From the point of view of lineages, the theme of the Ancestor emphasizes that the members are not a people without a tradition, without a history of which they could be proud. The deceased and the living are not "displaced" persons or people having no bonds ... they can call their kinsmen. Hence lineage sentiments are aroused in the dirge, sentiments which bind the living and the dead together in fellowship, sentiments which give meaning and emotional depth to the dirges which are otherwise, in the main, catalogues of words and deeds. (Nketia 1955, 25)

Drama and Other Literary Genres

This essay is primarily concerned with the poetry written to Malcolm X, but the analysis would be incomplete without a review of other literary genres based on Malcolm's life, death, and legacy. Drama is the next largest literary genre that pays tribute to Malcolm X.

Two of the first three plays published about Malcolm X are found in the anthology *New Plays from the Black Theatre* (1972), edited by Ed Bullins. Amiri Baraka (formerly known as LeRoi Jones) wrote *The Death of Malcolm X*, and N. R. Davidson, Jr., wrote *El Hajj Malik: A Play About Malcolm X*—both first published in 1969. The third play, also first published in 1969, is Colin Hodgett's *We Will Suffer and Die if We Have To: A Folk Play for M. L. King*. Hodgett's drama is about the legacies of both Dr. King and Malcolm X.

Baraka's *The Death of Malcolm X* is a scathing, satirical history pageant. Baraka constructs upper and lower scenes on several areas of the stage, and these scenes represent different ideological groups in the United States. The groups range from bohemian whites, a slick-talking U.S. president with a Klansman on his cabinet (called "Uncle Sam Central"), to an "operating room" of the "Institute for Advanced Black Studies," where Blacks are drugged and kept in bondage. The scenes also include a "war room," where a white instructor is training Black agents A, B, and C in how to stage the commotion in the Audubon Ballroom, where they will eventually kill Malcolm. The climax of the play is Malcolm's assassination. Instead of a resolution or falling action to end the play, there is only a brief sardonic celebration by representatives of white supremacy. Baraka's final description is clear:

> Last image is of all the featured ofays together at a party in U.Sam suits, celebrating and making jokes, later going through a weird historic ritual, with the Viking, Conquistador, Caveman, Roman, Greek, leading a slow dance as they put on U.Sam suits, making growling unintellible noises, but ending each phrase rhythmically with "White!" "AWhite!" "AWhite!!" "AWhite!!" &. (Jones 1969, 19–20)

The play suggests that white supremacists plotted to kill Malcolm because he had told them and the world: "[Y]ou are evil. Evil. It is that simple fact that will animate the rest of the world against you! That simple alarming fact of your unredeemable evil! You are disqualified as human beings ... disqualified by your inhuman acts" (Jones 1969, 9). These lines refer to Malcolm's decision to take the United States before the United Nations for human-rights offenses. Baraka also reminds us that Malcolm was a hero for all people of color. After Malcolm's death in the play, the next scene shows "black people (and Africans and Asians and Latin-Americans) clutching their breasts, as if shot, at the same time" (Jones 1969, 19).

Davidson's play, *El Hajj Malik: A Play About Malcolm X* is a pageant that uses ten actors (Actor One, Actor Two, etc.) who chant in ensemble and in call-and-response patterns to dramatize the important events of Malcolm's life. Davidson uses poetry, lyrical expressions, figurative language, exclamation, storytelling and Baptist preaching to create a fast-paced, vibrant narrative. The play also uses passages from Malcolm's *Autobiography*. The stage is set with a retractable screen that projects slides of multiple aspects of the Black experience in America, including images of enslavement, lynchings, singing, and crying. The Harlem sequence of the play uses jazz rhythms and the structure of the folk ballad to elevate Malcolm to the status of a folk hero—much like Slim Greer or

Stagolee. Davidson also uses blues poems and brass instruments to enhance the energy of his pageant. Yet Davidson is attentive to shifts in tone as the play chronicles the years of Malcolm's religious conversion, the development of his political platform, and his eventual death.

To write *El Hajj Malik*, Davidson relied on *The Autobiography of Malcolm X* (1965) and George Breitman's edited collection *Malcolm X Speaks: Selected Speeches and Statements* (1965). In his 1972 screenplay *One Day When I Was Lost*, James Baldwin also used the *Autobiography* as his primary resource. In writing this successful screenplay, Baldwin employed the same dramatic skill to interpret complex racial predicaments of Black life in America as he employed in writing *Blues for Mister Charlie* (1964). Since the narrative follows Malcolm's *Autobiography* closely, it is sufficient to rely on Baldwin's own description of what he attempted to do in his version. He introduces *One Day When I Was Lost* as follows:

> The legal complexities created by Malcolm X's rupture with the Nation of Islam Movement have dictated, in part, the structure of this scenario. The estate of Malcolm X and The Nation of Islam Movement can be considered at war, and I have, therefore, been forced to invent what is here called The Movement, without more specifically naming it; and, of course, I have not been able to use the actual names of any of the people in the Nation of Islam Movement, particularly not that of the Honorable Elijah Mohammed. I have, in short, discarded some characters and invented others. But I think I have remained faithful to the thrust and intention of Alex Haley's book, on which this scenario is based, and to the truth of the stormy, much maligned, groping and very moving character of the man known as Malcolm X. (Baldwin 1973, 6)

Baldwin and Davidson both address the possibility that the Nation of Islam participated in Malcolm's death, but Baraka's drama strictly holds U. S. white supremacy responsible. The literature, much of which is historical fiction, allows readers to explore diverse speculative possibilities of truth and meaning surrounding Malcolm's life.

Charles Gordon's dramatic treatment of Malcolm X, *The Breakout* (1972), was published the same year as Baldwin's screenplay. *The Breakout* has fifteen characters, including Malcolm X, and it is a fictionalized tale of the forces responsible for Malcolm's death. The play attacks Uncle Tomism and promotes themes of Black unity and cooperative economics, as two main characters, Slim and Feet, seek ways to break out of the prison of welfare, segregation, and poverty that America has prepared for Blacks. Gordon defines *jail* as "wherever white people run black people's lives" (Gordon 1972, 411).

As Slim and Feet plan their "breakout," they encounter other Blacks, some with more privileges, who are also in "jail." One prisoner, Reverend J. P. Jackson, is treated very well. Whites cater to him; he has been rewarded with money and amenities for his Tomism; and he recently received an award from the American government for "the elimination of divisive factors in the Negro community" (Gordon 1972, 423). The Reverend suffers from recurring nightmares, and the two men use juju to creep into his dreams to find out what is bothering him. They discover that he murdered Malcolm X in exchange for money and prestige. At first glance, the Reverend appears to be a symbol for the integrationist politics of Dr. Martin Luther King, Jr., but the character is not an exact personification of Dr. King. Gordon uses the character as a symbol for all the unhealthy and self-defeating behaviors that prevent Black Americans from being free on their own terms. The Reverend is also the antithesis of Malcolm X.

The dramatists, including Gordon, who have used Malcolm X as an icon or resource in their texts are well-read on Malcolm's ideas and beliefs. Gordon quotes from several of Malcolm's speeches, including "Message to the Grassroots." In fact, this play's premise that America is a type of prison comes directly from Malcolm's ideology. For example, Malcolm says in the play, "[D]on't be shocked when I say I was in prison — you still in prison. That's what America means, prison. All black people in prison" (Gordon 1972, 427).

In literature, Malcolm X is frequently compared and contrasted with Dr. Martin Luther King, Jr., both directly and indirectly. Chronologically, the next play which refers to Malcolm X was written not by an African American but by a Nigerian. In *A Play of Giants* (1984) Wole Soyinka satirizes the neocolonial African leaders of the 1970s and 1980s. Soyinka presents an African American character, Dr. Batey, a naive, idealistic sociologist who is ignorant of the true nature of leaders such as Idi Amin of Uganda and Mobutu Sese Seko of Zaïre, who are satirized in the play. In sentimental, idealistic outbursts, Dr. Batey tries to warn the African leadership about the perils of cheating the black masses. In his soliloquy, he laments the loss of Dr. King and Malcolm X:

> And sometimes even the people you serve must betray you; that is the unkindest cut of all. Bought, or simply misguided, blinded by their own greed or incapable of transcending their own petty clan loyalties, they desert the lofty heights of your vision and burrow busily beneath the mountains of your dreams. Do you think our experience is any different, those of us from the mother continent who were settled here as slaves? We had a man here, a king among men who once declared, I have a dream. He revealed that he too had been to the summit of the mountain of his dreams, your mountain, the Kilamanjaro of every black man's subconscious.... He was cut down by the bullets of an assassin.... You don't understand. It was a conspiracy. And in such another conspiracy, who do you imagine pulled the trigger that felled Malcolm X? Who provided the guns? (Soyinka 1984, 53)

Soyinka's *A Play of Giants* is a complex satire whose meanings are beyond the scope of this essay. However, Soyinka has a global readership, and he mentions Dr. King and Malcolm with a familiarity presuming that readers are well aware of the importance of these two men. In a sense, Soyinka's mention of African American leaders demonstrates the international, or at least Pan-African, exposure of 1960s Black leadership.

The most recent play published about Malcolm X is Jeff Stetson's *The Meeting: A One Act Play* (1990), which is frequently performed, particularly on college campuses. Stetson continues the comparison between the leadership ideologies of Dr. King and Malcolm, but by presenting a less-sensationalized and less-abstract encounter between the two leaders and their ideologies, Stetson invites audiences to listen, to learn about, and to evaluate different approaches to leadership. *The Meeting* is respectful of both leaders in its dramatic process.

Sustained treatment of Malcolm is found in all genres of African American literature, not just poetry and drama. Two additional texts stand out — one nonfiction, one fiction. The first is Maya Angelou's literary memoir, *All God's Children Need Traveling Shoes* (1991), a chronicle of her years in Ghana during the 1960s. Angelou dedicates the memoir to "Julian [Mayfield] and Malcolm and all the fallen ones who were passionately and earnestly looking for a home." She spends approximately twenty-five pages describing the expatriates' interactions with Malcolm as he passed through Ghana and several other African countries after his visit to Mecca. The expatriates had been working diligently to obtain an audience between Malcolm and President Kwame Nkrumah. Angelou describes Malcolm as "the stalking horse for the timid who openly denied him but took him, like a forbidden god, into their most secret hearts, there to adore him" (Angelou 1991, 129). She also praises his humor, his wit, his intelligence, and his ability to shock and enthrall an audience. However, she was totally unprepared for the shock that Malcolm had planned for her.

For weeks, Angelou had verbally scorned Shirley Graham Du Bois, the widow of the late Dr. W. E. B. Du Bois, who had recently died in Ghana. Angelou and the other Black Americans in Ghana were hoping that Shirley Graham Du Bois would help them arrange a meeting between Malcolm and President Kwame Nkrumah. Malcolm eventually spent some time with the president, but he made certain to teach Angelou a lesson about sensitivity and patience. Angelou drove Malcolm to the airport, and records his reprimand at length:

> Malcolm broke the silence. "Now, Sister, what do you think of Shirley Du Bois?" The question gave me a chance to articulate my anger, and I let loose. I spoke of her lack of faith, her lack of identity with Black American struggle, her isolation from her people, her pride at sitting in the catbird seat in Ghana. Malcolm let me continue until my tirade wound down.
>
> "Now, Sister, I thought you were smart, but I see you are very childish, dangerously immature." He had not spoken so harshly before to anyone in Ghana—I was shocked.
>
> "Have you considered that her husband has only been dead a few months? Have you considered that at her age she needs some time to consider that she is walking around wounded, limping for the first time in many years on one leg?"
>
> Tears were bathing my face, not for the sad picture Malcolm was drawing of Shirley, but for myself as the object of his displeasure.
>
> Malcolm said, "Sister, listen and listen carefully.... We need people on each level to fight our battle. Don't be in such a hurry to condemn a person because he doesn't do what you do, or think as you think or as fast. There was a time when you didn't know what you know today." His voice became more explanatory and less accusatory.
>
> He said...."I wanted to ride with you to encourage you to broaden your thinking. You are too good a woman to think small. You know we, I mean in the United States and elsewhere, are in need of hard thinkers. Serious thinkers, who are not timid. We are called upon to defend ourselves all the time. In every arena." Malcolm had lost his harshness and seemed to be reflecting rather than addressing me. (Angelou 1991, 144–146)

Even though her work is a memoir, Angelou chronicles this encounter with Malcolm with the language and expression of a novel. The lessons that Malcolm taught her during this period of her life are those that African Americans must pass down from one generation to the next.

The second text (not poetry and not drama) that features Malcolm is Ghanaian Kofi Awoonor's novel *Comes the Voyager At Last: A Tale of Return to Africa* (1992). Malcolm is an influence on the spiritual development of the main character (a nameless Black American), who journeys aimlessly through life in America and then finds himself drawn to Africa to eventually participate in a ritual of spirit possession and return.

While in America, he spends time in prison and meets Brother Aboud, a member of the Nation of Islam. Awoonor structures the novel so that the main character's exposure to Islam while in prison parallels Malcolm's exposure to the religion under the same circumstances. However, Awoonor's protagonist hears about Malcolm from another prison inmate, Harlemite Henry Sullivan:

> But Henry said there was the Minister Malcolm who was head of the mosque in Harlem who was a serious dude. He'd done time, used to be a pusher in Harlem, had run quite a good number of rackets like women, dope and had been in all major hustles in Harlem. Now, Henry said, this brother was a minister in the Nation of Islam and everyone said he was a helluva preacher. He himself hadn't heard this dude but he had a cousin who had attended all the religious sessions in the mosque. (Awoonor 1992, 58)

Malcolm is not a primary character in the novel, but his influence on the other characters is notable. The protagonist eventually reaches the mosque in Harlem where Malcolm is preaching, but it is not completely clear why Awoonor has included this scene in his novel, since its action involves the theme of returning to Africa and being guided by ancestral spirits. Perhaps the purpose of Malcolm's presence in the narrative is to give credibility to the transition of the protagonist, who eventually experiences an epiphany concerning his African identity and his purpose in life. The character is changed from a self-centered, egocentric criminal to a visionary who embraces a spiritual Pan-Africanism.

Conclusion

Cheikh Anta Diop writes: "The role of History in the life of a people is vital: History is one of the factors that ensure the cohesion of the diverse elements of a community, a kind of social cement. Without historical consciousness, people cannot be called on to assume its destiny of greatness" (Diop 1996, 119). If we add to Diop's explanation of history Bruce Perry's observation from *Malcolm X: The Life of a Man Who Changed Black America* (1991), the revolutionary predicament of the African American nationalist becomes clear: "Revolutionaries are not required to succeed. Usually they end up deflated or dead, martyrs to their chosen cause" (Perry 1991, 280). This observation reminds African Americans that many of their cultural heroes knew that they would likely die for their beliefs, their courage, and their activism. Malcolm felt that an early death was imminent; Dr. King and others spoke of similar premonitions. However, if the activism of great leaders will necessarily be temporary because of racist and government-sponsored assassinations, then the future memory of the legacies of these assassinated leaders is more important to the success of Black Culture than the leaders' brief life spans. In this sense, Black leaders who have emerged as mythoforms have lived properly as ancestors, knowing that their legacies and memory will foster more change than their brief lives did.

Thus, Malcolm's literary record, ranging from his *Autobiography* to the attention given to him in many other works, proves that Malcolm, despite his assassination, has been one of the most successful activists in the history of African Americans. As a critical analysis of the literature confirms in detail, Malcolm X lives on boldly—as an ancestor.

References

Andrews, William L., Trudier Harris, and Frances Smith, eds. 1997. *The Oxford companion to African American Literature*. New York: Oxford University Press.

Angelou, Maya. 1991. *All God's children need traveling shoes*. New York: Vintage Books.

Asante, Molefi K. 1987. *The Afrocentric idea*. Philadelphia: Temple UP.

Awoonor, Kofi. 1992. *Comes the voyager at last: A tale of return to Africa*. Trenton, NJ: Africa World Press.

Baldwin, James. 1964. *Blues for Mister Charlie*. New York: Dial Press.

_____. 1973. *One day when I was lost: A screenplay based on The Autobiography of Malcolm X*. New York: Dial Press.

Boateng, Felix. 1990. African traditional education: A tool for intergenerational communication. In *African culture: The rhythms of unity*, ed. Molefi K. Asante and Kariamu Welsh Asante, 109–122. Trenton, NJ: Africa World Press.

Breitman, George, ed. 1965. *Malcolm X speaks: Selected speeches and statements*. New York: Grove/Atlantic.

Bullins, Ed., ed. 1969. *New plays from the Black theatre*. New York: Bantam Books.

Davidson, Jr., N. R. 1972. *El Hajj Malik: A play about Malcolm X*. In *New plays from the Black theatre*, ed. Ed Bullins, 201–246. New York: Bantam Books.

Diop, Cheikh Anta. 1996. *Towards the African renaissance: Essays in culture and development, 1946–1960*. London: Karnak House.

Ephirim-Donkor, Anthony. 1997. *African spirituality: On becoming ancestors*. Trenton, NJ: Africa World Press.

Gordon, Charles (OyomO). 1972. *The breakout*. In *Black drama anthology*, ed. Woodie King and Ron Milner, 407–429. New York: Columbia University Press.

Gwynne, James. 1993. *Malcolm X: Justice seeker*. New York: Steppingstones Press.

Hodgett, Colin. 1971. *We will suffer and die if we have to: A folk play for M. L. King*. Valley Forge, PA: Judson Press.

Jones, LeRoi (Amiri Baraka). 1972. *The death of Malcolm X*. In *New plays from the Black theatre*, ed. Ed Bullins, 1–20. New York: Bantam Books.

Malcolm X. 1965. *The autobiography of Malcolm X*. As told to Alex Haley. New York: Grove Press.

Neal, Larry. 1969. And shine swam on. In *Black fire: An anthology of Afro-American writing*, ed. LeRoi Jones and Larry Neal, 638–656. New York: William Morrow.

_____. 1989. *Visions of a liberated future: Black Arts Movement writings*. New York: Thunder's Mouth Press.

Nketia, J. H. 1955. *Funeral dirges of the Akan people*. New York: Negro Universities Press.

Ogede, Ode. S. 1995. Context, form and poetic expression in Igede funeral dirges. *Africa* 65 (1): 79–96.

Perry, Bruce. 1991. *Malcolm: The life of a man who changed Black America*. Barrytown, NY: Talman.

Randall, Dudley, and Margaret G. Burroughs, eds. 1969. *For Malcolm: Poems on the life and death of Malcolm X*. Detroit: Broadside Press.

Soyinka, Wole. 1984. *A Play of Giants*. New York: Metheun.

Stetson, Jeff. 1990. *The Meeting: A One Act Play*. New York: Dramatists Play Service.

Ward, Douglas Turner. 1966. *Day of absence*. New York: Dramatists Play Service.

Additional Literature on Malcolm X

Dumas, Henry. 1969. Mosaic Harlem. In *Black fire: An anthology of Afro-American writing*, ed. LeRoi Jones and Larry Neal, 345–346. New York: William Morrow.

Giovanni, Nikki. 1972. For a while progress. In *Black judgment*, 18. Detroit: Broadside Press.

_____. 1972. POEM (no name no. 3). In *Black feeling, Black talk*, 18. Detroit: Broadside Press.

Haynes, Jr., Albert E. 1969. ECLIPSE. In *Black fire: An anthology of Afro-American writing*, ed. LeRoi Jones and Larry Neal, 406–409. New York: William Morrow.

Hodges, Frenchy Jolene. 1971. Dreams, common sense and stuff. In *Black Wisdom*, 16. Detroit: Broadside Press.

Jackmon, Marvin E. 1969. That old time religion. In *Black fire: An anthology of Afro-American writing*, ed. LeRoi Jones and Larry Neal, 268. New York: William Morrow.

Kgositsile, K. Wm. 1969. The awakening. In *Black fire: An anthology of Afro-American writing*, ed. LeRoi Jones and Larry Neal, 226–227. New York: William Morrow.

Neal, Larry. 1969. Malcolm X—An autobiography. In *Black fire: An anthology of Afro-American writing*, ed. LeRoi Jones and Larry Neal, 315–317. New York: William Morrow.

_____. 1969. The narrative of the black magicians. In *Black fire: An anthology of Afro-American writing*, ed. LeRoi Jones and Larry Neal, 312–314. New York: William Morrow.

Public Enemy. 1994. Party for your right to fight. In *In search of color everywhere: A collection of African-American poetry*, ed. E. Ethelbert Miller, 58. New York: Stewart, Tabori & Chang.

Sanchez, Sonia. 1971. Rite on: Wite America 2. In *We a badddDDD people*, 26. Detroit: Broadside Press.

_____. 1993. For Black History Month/February 1986. In *Under A Soprano Sky*, 95–97. Trenton, NJ: Africa World Press.

_____. 1993. Notes from a journal. In *Under A Soprano Sky*, 98–100. Trenton, NJ: Africa World Press.

_____. 1993. On listening to Malcolm's "Ballot or the Bullet." In *Under A Soprano Sky*, 51. Trenton, NJ: Africa World Press.

_____. 1993 Malcolm. In *Malcolm X: Justice seeker*, ed. James B. Gwynne, 20. New York: Steppingstones Press.

_____. 1995. Poem. In *Wounded in the House of A Friend*, 29–30. Boston: Beacon Press.

Smith, Welton. interlude. 1969. In *Black fire: An anthology of Afro-American writing*, ed. LeRoi Jones and Larry Neal, 289–290. New York: William Morrow.

_____. 1969. Malcolm. In *Black fire: An anthology of Afro-American writing*, ed. LeRoi Jones and Larry Neal, 283–285. New York: William Morrow.

Snellings, Rolland. 1969. SUNRISE! In *Black fire: An anthology of Afro-American writing*, ed. LeRoi Jones and Larry Neal, 322–323. New York: William Morrow.

Spriggs, Edward. 1969. Every Harlem face is AFROMANISM surviving. In *Black fire: An anthology of Afro-American writing*, ed. LeRoi Jones and Larry Neal, 341. New York: William Morrow.

13

In the Age of Malcolm X: Social Conflict and the Critique of African American Identity Construction

Katherine O. Bankole

Introduction

The foundation of African American Studies was built upon the struggle to explicate the history of people of African descent in the United States and in the world. The main features of the discipline have been advocacy, assertiveness, and the call to reexamine issues of human equality with respect to access to knowledge. Another important feature has been the drive to make the discipline relevant to the needs of the masses of African Americans.[1] Indeed, the discipline could not exist as an integral function of the academy without addressing the needs of the Black community. Many content factors have influenced the development and direction of African American Studies in higher education. Specifically, African American Studies has been developed and has advanced through several main foci, including, but not limited to, classical African Civilization studies; the study of the liberation history of the African people; and the role of key historical personages among African Americans. The development of African American Studies has been significantly influenced by the historical legacy of such personalities as Malcolm X (El-Hajj Malik El-Shabazz). The importance of Malcolm X cannot be taught in the academy without concurrent attention to such critical concepts as human transformation and evolution; Black Nationalism; human rights and civil liberties;[2] a rootedness in life-affirming values and ethical behavior; the social confrontation of African Americans with racism and white supremacy; and queries and analysis of the deep structure of African American identity formation. Malcolm is remembered largely be-

---

1. Among the excellent sources for studying the origins and development of the discipline of Africana Studies is Delores P. Aldridge and Carlene Young, eds., *Out of the Revolution: The Development of Africana Studies* (Lanham, MD: Lexington Press, 2000).

2. An early 1970s review of these concepts is Charles G. Hurst, Jr., *Passport to Freedom, Education, Humanism, and Malcolm X* (Hamden, CT: Linnet Books, 1972).

cause of his ability to define these and other concepts in African American terms. In addition, he provided a comprehensive understanding of the complex issues related to the African American experience and the global plight of people of color, or in his language, the "non-white" people of the world. Using his life experience as a primary teaching tool, he established a specific method of speaking as well as proposals for and solutions to the problems cited in his severe criticism of American society and the African American experience. As Karenga notes, Malcolm "use[d] his context as text."[3] More than three-and-a-half decades since his assassination in 1965, Malcolm X is still acknowledged as a force to be reckoned with in the national and popular culture of the United States — especially in higher education.

The study of Malcolm X (as well as that of other personages of the protest movements of the 1960s) is a complex project for some instructors, scholars, and researchers because of the political interpretations of his life and his legacy and the assumptions about them in the popular culture. In 1968 Trout asked: "Should the Protest Movement be taught?" She concluded: "Studying the Protest Movement each day is an act of discovery for the teachers and for the students."[4] In addition to courses on the protest movements, courses on Malcolm X are being taught in higher education. They bring a host of challenges to the professor, which include the issues that Black and white students bring to the classroom.[5] Since the late 1960s, many scholars from across disciplines have argued in favor of the importance and efficacy of teaching Malcolm X.[6] Americanists do not need to ask the question: Should the American Revolution or the Civil War be taught? However, we scholars in Africana Studies are expected to pose ideologically based questions about the study of Malcolm X that do not routinely appear in the investigations of other historical personages. Such questions include the following: Why should Malcolm X be studied? Was Malcolm X a racist? Rarely do we ask the questions: What were Malcolm X's observations about knowledge and information systems? What was the intellectual basis for his criticism of racial domination? Too often our analyses in Western culture are overshadowed by reductionist generalities as to whether Malcolm X was a superhero or a militant, ultimately providing more of a glimpse into the analyst's perspective than that of Malcolm himself. The more simplistic characterizations of Malcolm include the highly subjective and emotionally charged labels "Black hater," "Black racist," and "Black radical." Malcolm himself predicted such labeling: "[W]hen I am dead … the white man, in his press, is going to identify me with 'hate.'"[7]

The broad and growing research on Malcolm X since his assassination also includes works focusing on the important mythic interpretations of his life and legacy.[8] Time has revealed that Malcolm was often viewed as a major voice of African Americans during

---

3. Maulana Karenga, "The Oppositional Logic of Malcolm X: Differentiation, Engagement and Resistance," *Western Journal of Black Studies* 17, no. 1 (1993): 14.

4. Lawana Trout, "The Teaching of Protest and Propaganda Literature," *Black American Literature Forum* 2, no. 3 (Autumn 1968): 52; see also Carl Moore, "A Course in the Rhetoric of Black Power," *Journal of Black Studies* 2, no. 4 (June 1972): 511–515.

5. See Michael Eric Dyson, preface to *Making Malcolm: The Myth and Meaning of Malcolm X* (New York: Oxford Press, 1995), vii–xxvi ("Teaching Malcolm").

6. See Theresa Perry, ed., *Teaching Malcolm X* (New York: Routledge, 1996) and Andrew P. Smallwood, *An Afrocentric Study of the Intellectual Development, Leadership Praxis, and Pedagogy of Malcolm X* (Lewiston, NY: Edwin Mellen Press, 2001).

7. Malcolm X (with Alex Haley), *The Autobiography of Malcolm X* (New York: Grove Press, 1965), 381.

8. See Albert Cleage, "Myths About Malcolm X," in *Malcolm X The Man and His Times*, ed. John Henrik Clarke, 13–26 (Trenton, NJ: Africa World Press, 1990).

the first half of the 1960s. This voice, out of so many others of the period, was cause for concern in American society. Before his assassination in 1965, Malcolm had become a public icon (today we use the term "public intellectual"). Even in his open-air addresses in Harlem, Malcolm commanded audiences of one thousand people and more.[9] He was also considered a major national and international leader[10]—primarily because of his unequivocal rejection of racism and white supremacy through his philosophical ideas and because of his ability to mobilize people. In addition, his high regard resulted from the attention given him by the mass media as well as from his ability to manage his own public image. As Lincoln notes, Malcolm represented the Nation of Islam's "fiery polemicist, [who] dominated black interest in the press and on television with his frequent public debates and lectures on the teachings of Elijah Muhammad."[11] The life of Malcolm X provides an opportunity for scholars to continue to evaluate him as an individual with a style of engagement that far exceeded the traditional leadership skills and abilities of his contemporaries. There is no doubt that Malcolm proffered one of the most widely observed analyses of American society and that he influenced the life and work of countless people.[12] The discipline of Africana Studies—and the disciplines of American Studies and History in particular—must challenge the media's stock image of Malcolm X[13] as well as continue the critiques of his important legacy by encouraging students to raise the level of discussion about his life and work.

The Malcolmian Method in the Age of Malcolm X

Malcolm X was a "people's historian/cultural analyst" at a time when the idea that African Americans had a concrete and credible history and culture was subject to sustained racial attack. Asante described him as "pre-eminently a cultural spokesperson, a cultured person, an analyst and theorist of culture, a revolutionary cultural scientist."[14] While studies on Malcolm X continue to grow in the examination of his life and work, the interpretations regarding his impact upon American and world societies seem inexhaustible. Indeed, his legacy is recent; the interpretations are vast; and his criticisms of society are still relevant. Thus, we are still living in the "Age of Malcolm X." This essay briefly reviews one of Malcolm's most significant arguments—central to his thesis as a leader and as an individual: the question of identity among African Americans. Malcolm spoke often about the issue of Black identity: "[V]ery few of our people really look upon themselves as being black. They

9. The *New York Times* often reported on Malcolm X and the Nation of Islam. In 1963, it reported that 1,000 people had gathered to hear Malcolm X discuss racial integration. See "Malcolm X Assails Racial Integration," *New York Times*, 14 July 1963, p. 50.

10. Robert L. Harris, Jr., "Malcolm X: Human Rights and the United Nations," *Western Journal of Black Studies* 17, no. 1 (1993): 1–5.

11. C. Eric Lincoln, *Race, Religion, and the Continuing American Dilemma* New York: Hill and Wang, 1999), 110.

12. Molefi Kete Asante, *Afrocentricity* (Trenton, NJ: African World Press, 1989), 18–19.

13. See Clyde Taylor, "The Malcolm Ghost in the Media Machine," review of *Malcolm X*, by Spike Lee, *The Black Scholar* 22, no. 4: 37–41.

14. Molefi Kete Asante, *Malcolm X As Cultural Hero and Other Afrocentric Essays* (Trenton, NJ: Africa World Press, 1993) 25.

think of themselves as practically everything else on the color spectrum except black."[15] As Franklin notes, the question of identity was often characterized by Malcolm's adoption of African and Arabic names.[16] The question was further addressed when Malcolm built a strong rhetorical construct for oppositional analysis—a Malcolmian Method—to discuss not only the relationships between Blacks and whites but also the intragroup relationships among African Americans (e.g., his "House and Field Slave" analysis).[17] Malcolm's critique was also informed by his early commitment to the teachings of the Honorable Elijah Muhammad, the work of the Nation of Islam, his understanding and treatment of global and Pan-African issues, the development of Muslim Mosque, Inc., and the Organization of Afro-American Unity (OAAU). However, Malcolm asserted that a change in identity perceptions among African Americans was already occurring: "[Y]et just yesterday you would have to admit that it was very difficult to get our people to refer to themselves as black. Now all of a sudden our people of all complexions are not apologizing for being black but bragging about being black."[18]

According to Benjamin Karim in his edited volume *The End of White World Supremacy: Four Speeches by Malcolm X*, Malcolm X did not become a threatening force until he was noticed by white Americans through the modern press. He came to national attention because of his altercations with the police and the notion that he was a Black man with "too much power"—referring to his leadership in the Nation of Islam and the discipline exhibited by its membership.[19] Indeed, as Ossie Davis notes, Malcolm was a descendant of "slaves" who chose to be a man, and therefore, he posed a terrifying force against racial injustice in America.[20] Malcolm X came to national attention because he employed a distinct rhetorical style that he used *consistently* to clarify the position of the Nation of Islam in his speeches to the masses. His rhetorical style has been analyzed by several scholars, including Asante, Flick and Powell, Karenga, and Gray.[21] Malcolm used his rhetorical style to present a kind of argumentation called *oppositional analysis*. Karenga defines it as "oppositional logic" which is "self-consciously distinct from established-order logic."[22] In his oppositional analyses, Malcolm provided the most definitive responses to racism and the condition of African Americans through the use of opposing terms and positions and the contrasting placement of two ideas, issues, people, and so forth. Gray, in his examination of Afrocentric theory and praxis, locates Malcolm's style among the following areas of argumentation: Sankofan, Nommoic, Maatic, Political-Intellectual, African collective memory-perception, and Explicit locational.[23]

---

15. Malcolm X, *The End of White World Supremacy: Four Speeches by Malcolm X*, ed. Benjamin Karim (New York: Merlin House, 1971), 24. See also Benjamin Karim (with Peter Skutches and David Gallen), *Remembering Malcolm* (New York: Carroll and Graf, 1992).

16. John Hope Franklin, *From Slavery to Freedom: A History of African Americans* (New York: Knopf, 1994), 553–554.

17. Malcolm X, *The End of White World Supremacy*, 87.

18. Malcolm X, *The End of White World Supremacy*, 24.

19. Malcolm X, *The End of White World Supremacy*, 1.

20. Malcolm X, *Autobiography*, 457–460.

21. Molefi Kete Asante, *The Afrocentric Idea* (Philadelphia: Temple University Press, 1987), 51–52; Hank Flick and Larry Powell, "Animal Imagery in the Rhetoric of Malcolm X," *Journal of Black Studies* 18, no. 4: 435–451; Karenga, "The Oppositional Logic of Malcolm X," 6–16; Cecil Conteen Gray, *Afrocentric Thought and Praxis: An Intellectual History* (Trenton, NJ: Africa World Press, 2001), 143–155.

22. Karenga, "The Oppositional Logic of Malcolm X," 6.

23. Gray, *Afrocentric Thought and Praxis*, 28–47.

Table 1. The Malcolmian Method of Oppositional Rhetoric

Step 1	State the opposing terms and/or concepts.
Step 2	Define the terms and concepts.
Step 3	Locate the terms and concepts in a historical context.
Step 4	Locate the terms and concepts in a theological and/or humanistic context.
Step 5	View the arguments both for and against the issues on the basis of the terms and concepts.
Step 6	Consistently use logical analysis and reasoning rooted in ethical thought and practice.
Step 7	Keep the interaction focused on the opposing terms and concepts.
Step 8	Use clear and concise language, phrases, images, etc.
Step 9	Speak from a position of power and authority.
Step 10	Refocus any dialogue which moves away from the subject terms and concepts. (In other words, avoid being "baited" into any kind of nonproductive dialogue.)

This discussion acknowledges these frameworks as exceptional tools for understanding Malcolm X, and it adds the observation of a *Malcolmian Method*—an oppositional rhetorical process used by Malcolm in conjunction with a direct argument for the principles of American democratic equality and human rights (see Table 1). This process should be included in the pedagogy not only as a reflection of the persona of Malcolm X but also as an important strategy of engagement for the civil rights and Black Power movements. The Malcolmian Method includes the overlapping interactive steps in Table 1.

For example, if *racism* and *human equality* are the two oppositional terms being addressed, then each term poses such questions as the following: What is it? Where does it exist? Where can it be found? How can it be realized? Malcolm X uses this method of oppositional rhetoric in making speeches, during interviews, and in other public-dialogue forums. The Malcolmian Method is rooted in the oral tradition and rhetorical styles of African people; is informed by the historical and contemporary experiences of Africans and other people of color; and is significant because Malcolm used words and imagery economically to guide the public toward logical conclusions relative to truth seeking.

Condit and Lucaites note that while there were limits to Malcolm's revolutionary rhetoric (including those Malcolm imposed upon himself), these limits were related to the tools necessary to effect fundamental change in contemporary racist society.[24] Malcolm and his close aides recognized that he was outgrowing not only the doctrine of the Nation of Islam but also his need for the organization when weighed against the needs of people of African descent throughout the world.[25] With such needs in mind, Malcolm used this Malcolmian Method in every argument he posed, including those regarding reparations and racial separation. Malcolm was most adept at using oppositional rhetoric in discussing the African American experience regarding identity construction: the lack of historical knowledge; the psychosocial control of the Black

---

24. Celeste Condit and John Lucaites, "Malcolm X and the Limits of the Rhetoric of Revolutionary Dissent," *Journal of Black Studies* 23, no. 3 (March 1993): 291–313.

25. Karim, *Remembering Malcolm*, 146–161.

masses; the criticism of the term *Negro*; the historical experiences of Blacks in America; the personal reformation project of the Nation of Islam; the position of Black middle-class; and the leaders in the civil rights movement. Malcolm X was unrelenting regarding the issue of identity among persons of African descent in the Americas. His attitude toward it is a critical subject for students of Africana Studies, American Studies, and History.

The Black Crucible of Knowledge

In his speech "The Black Man's History," Malcolm X argues that since Blacks knew little about their own history, they accepted other interpretations of their history and culture and were thus provided a false history—and a flawed sense of themselves. He asserts: "The thing that has made the so-called Negro in America fail, more than any other thing, is your, my lack of knowledge concerning history. We know less about history than anything else."[26] Yet, as scholars of Malcolm X have noted, over time he challenged his own ideas about Black history with respect to identity formation. However, he never departed from his earlier argument: "[O]f all the things that the Black man, or any man for that matter, can study, history is the best qualified to reward all research. You have to have a knowledge of history no matter what you are going to do; anything that you undertake you have to have a knowledge of history in order to be successful in it."[27] Malcolm used the experiences of Blacks born in Africa to support his claim that, in contrast with African Americans, continental Africans possessed a deeper knowledge and appreciation of their own history and experienced a different form of colonial subjugation.

In addition, Malcolm noted that even highly skilled and intellectually gifted Blacks in American society—those who had graduated from America's most prestigious colleges and universities—suffered from a lack of knowledge of their history and culture. Indeed, as Malcolm echoed one of the main theses of Carter G. Woodson, the "Negro is mis-educated" away from himself and away from developing and sustaining meaningful relationships with his or her people. One of the more comprehensive conceptualizations of Malcolm's emphasis on the importance of historical knowledge is advanced by Karenga: "Malcolm saw history as a field for both human and divine action and a need for African and other oppressed people to unite in solidarity and to self-consciously struggle to regain their history and humanity and build an new world."[28] Malcolm's insistence on the necessity of alliances among Africans and other people of color rested upon their common histories as well as a sense of human connectedness and a common identity.

Psychosocial Control of the Black Masses

There has been a long discussion of the history of psychosocial control of Blacks in the United States. The enslavement and forced migration of Africans was predicated

---

26. Malcolm X, *The End of White World Supremacy*, 26.
27. Malcolm X, *The End of White World Supremacy*, 26.
28. Maulana Karenga, *Introduction to Black Studies* (Los Angeles: University of Sankore Press, 2002), 281.

upon the ability of American slaveholders to physically and mentally control the source of slave labor. In his *Police and the Black Community*, Wintersmith examines theories on the issues of violence, the relations between police and Black citizens, and, most important, the historical legacy of psychological manipulation that coincided with the period of enslavement.[29] Malcolm X believed that there existed a psychosocial control over African Americans from the past to the present and that this kind of control prevented Blacks from discovering their own identity. He also claimed that propaganda reinforced this kind of control—especially through mass media in the United States, which affected the perceptions that Blacks had of themselves. He criticized the power of the establishment over the media as follows: "[W]ith skillful manipulating of the press they're able to make the victim look like the criminal and the criminal look like the victim."[30] He also discussed many propagandistic tactics of the press in its coverage of the civil rights and Black Power movements. He described such a tactic in his speech "The Old Negro and the New Negro": "Oftentimes a propagandist who is shrewd will tell just enough truth to make you believe that he is being objective and to get you to listen and then he starts injecting the negative side, and this is where we become resentful."[31] This observation, and ones similar to it, gave African Americans an opportunity to explore the "marketing" aspect of our society, especially in terms of their status when confronted with racism. In this observation, Malcolm moved the notion of identity beyond geography and politics to the realm of mental aptitude. In doing so, he asserted that there was an attitudinal or behavioral component to Black identity. In "The Black Revolution," he stated:

> I'm black first, America doesn't even come into my mind. I don't think of myself as an American so I don't try to act like one. Which means they don't mistake me for a white man. But as a Muslim, when we go back among Africans, our feelings are the same as the Africans'; our objectives are the same as the Africans'. We are one people, so we get along well with each other. Usually the only so-called American Negroes whom the Africans see are the ones that have been sent over by the State Department, Uncle Toms, stool pigeons.[32]

Malcolm's social commentary also included economic and political disfranchisement as a tool for the psychosocial control of Blacks. In his speeches, he pointed out the deplorable living conditions of the masses of Blacks in such areas as housing and education, noting that these conditions contributed to the tendency of Blacks to surrender to racist practices. In addition, he criticized middle-class Blacks for denying their "Blackness" while using it as a tool to curry favor in white circles of power and for failing to establish an industrial and entrepreneurial basis for development in the Black community. Furthermore, he criticized Black ministers for their willingness to build more and more churches instead of retail stores and educational centers.

Malcolm cited the legacy of the enslavement of African people in the United States as a major factor influencing the attitudes and behaviors of Blacks. In his analysis, enslavement not only debilitated the sensibilities of the Black masses but also contributed to

---

29. Robert Wintersmith, *Police and the Black Community* (Lexington, MA: Lexington Books, 1972). See particularly Chapter 2, "Police-Black-Community Relations: A Historical Account"; Chapter 3, "Theoretical Factors Related to This Investigation" (addressing the antebellum period); and Chapter 4, "Blacks During Reconstruction and After."

30. Malcolm X, *Malcolm X Speaks: Selected Speeches and Statements*, ed. George Breitman (New York: Grove Press, 1966), 165.

31. Malcolm X, *The End of White World Supremacy*, 83.

32. Malcolm X, *The End of White World Supremacy*, 77.

the destructive behavior patterns among African Americans. Regarding his premise on Black identity formation, he argued that Blacks had not established more businesses and schools because they had been programmed, from the period of enslavement, not to accomplish those goals on their own but to ask white America to fulfill their needs. Despite some of the successes of the boycotts of the civil rights era,[33] the violent intimidation of Blacks who sought to establish rival businesses and educational institutions induced a fear-based climate which affected widespread and consistent community building other than the development of churches. To combat the mind control of Blacks, Malcolm noted the role that Islam played in undoing "the type of brainwashing that we have had to undergo for four hundred years at the hands of the white man in order to bring us down to the level that we're at today."[34] In addition, speaking as much about the media attacks on himself as about the collective Black experience, Malcolm related intellectual acumen to the ability to perceive the psychosocial control of Blacks: "[T]his man shows great intelligence in being able to analyze the news and show how the white press, as soon as the black man begins to take a militant and uncompromising stand, whether it be in America or Africa, will begin to project that man either as a dictator or as a black supremacist or teacher of hate."[35]

After Malcolm X left the Nation of Islam, he did not significantly alter his beliefs about the psychosocial control of Blacks, but it was no longer necessary for him to assert that the Nation of Islam was the only vehicle for achieving awareness.

The Criticism of the "So-Called Negro"

Malcolm X, using the technique of oppositional analysis in his public speaking, was preeminent in his criticism of the term *Negro* as a designation for Black people. In most of his speeches, he referred to Blacks as the "so-called Negro" people in order to highlight the dilemma of who controls vast categories of human nomenclature. He also used the phrase "so-called Negro" to point out what the concept has meant in American history over time. According to Malcolmian logic, why would Blacks refer to themselves as Negroes when Negroes are being oppressed and brutalized? In addition, the acceptance and use of the term was not a part of the teachings of the Nation of Islam. Malcolm also noted that other Blacks classified as Negroes, such as those from the continent of Africa, were given special privileges and consideration while "regular Negroes" were subjected to Jim Crow practices. The crowning argument in Malcolm's criticism of the term *Negro* concerned the "X" factor—the Nation of Islam's use of the X to signify the lost names of African people through the holocaust of enslavement. As Malcolm noted: "I received my 'X'—which of course is substituted for the slave name given to our forebears by the plantation owners, 'X' being the unknown factor, since we did not know what our rightful names were."[36] Since

---

33. Robert E. Weems, Jr., "African-American Consumer Boycotts During the Civil Rights Era," *Western Journal of Black Studies* 19, no. 1 (1995): 72–79.
34. Malcolm X, *The End of White World Supremacy*, 26.
35. Malcolm X, *The End of White World Supremacy*, 113.
36. Malcolm X, *The End of White World Supremacy*, 9.

the Nation of Islam was at its height, this system of naming caused widespread debate, among individuals both white and Black, about the status of African Americans and about Black identity—a debate that was framed by the Nation of Islam. According to Malcolm, there was an "old and new Negro." He defined the two in opposition to each other, noting that the "old Negro" was reminiscent of the personality taught to capitulate to racism and white supremacy while the "new Negro" rejected the legacy of dehumanization and actively sought liberation on the same terms as members of white society.

In his speech "The Old Negro and the New Negro," Malcolm went on to define the *house slave* and the *field slave*. In his analysis of a concept found in the narratives of formerly enslaved Africans, Malcolm asserted that the "house slave" (the "old Negro") was a familiar person to the slaveholder while the "field slave" (the "new Negro") was an unfamiliar person, a stranger to the slaveholder. An important aspect of Malcolmian logic as demonstrated by his speeches is the significance of what he leaves out (or alludes to) as much as the significance of what he says. For example, in his comparison of the house slave with the field slave, Malcolm X points out the characteristics of the house slave: loyalty to the slaveholder; a lack of independent thought processes; and, ultimately, a complete devotion to the needs of white society. With these characteristics, the house slave establishes patterns of behavior which indicate that he or she will betray other Blacks to show support for the slave master. The field slave is the opposite of the house slave. The field slave is not conditioned to accept the circumstances of enslavement. The field slave wants freedom and expresses this want through attitude and behavior. If the field slave gets the opportunity to run away to freedom, he or she will take it. In this seminal speech, Malcolm stated:

> Now just as you have the house Negro and the field Negro a hundred years ago, in America today you have a house Negro and a field Negro. You have a modern counterpart of that slavery-time Uncle Tom, only the one today is a twentieth-century Uncle Tom. He doesn't wear a handkerchief around his head, sir. He wears a top hat. He speaks with a Harvard accent. Sometimes he is lawyer or a judge or a doctor or he is an ambassador to the UN ... This is the twentieth-century house Negro. He wants to live with his master ... Now then, you have the masses of black people in this country who are the offshoot of the field Negro, during slavery. They are the masses.[37]

Furthermore, Malcolm pointed out the incongruity that the house negro continually discusses the "we-ness" of American society when he or she does not share in the benefits of American society. In addition, he asserted that it is the persona of the "house negro" (the "responsible Negro," the "system Negro," or the "Good Black") whom the established order hand-selects because it knows (is familiar with) these characteristics in persons classified as Black—because it, in fact, created the persona. Therefore, in his analysis, the term *Negro* per se is not necessarily a designation to criticize; a human being should be judged by virtue of his or her behaviors, character, actions, and attitudes. Malcolm represented the overt "anti-Negro," who, as Hoyt notes, was "too much of a man to be a good nigger. For the two things are truly incompatible."[38]

---

37. Malcolm X, *The End of White World Supremacy*, 89–90.
38. Charles Hoyt, "The Five Faces of Malcolm X," *Black American Literature Forum* 4, no. 4 (1970): 108.

The African, History, and American Nationality

Malcolm X stated that, of all of his school subjects as a youth, he liked English and history the most. As a young person of African descent in the segregated North, he suffered the constant diminishment of his intellect and being, noting that the entire history of Black Americans in his textbook consisted of only one paragraph.[39] Later, Malcolm read widely in history while in prison. In his autobiography, he states:

> I found books like Will Durant's *Story of Civilization*. I read H. G. Wells' *Outline of History*. *Souls of Black Folk* by W. E. B. Du Bois gave me a glimpse into the black people's history before they came to this country. Carter G. Woodson's *Negro History* opened my eyes about black empires before the black slave was brought to the United States, and the early Negro struggle for freedom.
>
> J. A. Rogers' three volumes of *Sex and Race* told about race-mixing before Christ's' time.[40]

Malcolm linked history with American nationality. He understood that American whites knew their history and appreciated it but that African Americans knew and appreciated little of their own history: "You can hardly show me a black adult in America—or a white one, for that matter—who knows from the history books anything like the truth about the Black man's role."[41] Throughout the rest of his life, Malcolm continued to pursue an understanding of the connection between history and national identity.

The Honorable Elijah Muhammad had laid the basis for Malcolm's use of what Asante calls "[o]bjectivism"—that is, "the use of our cultural artifacts as symbols in all reproductive work."[42] With such "objectivism," Malcolm linked the historical experiences of African Americans with Islamic teachings and used them together as a tool for liberation. Malcolm was also concerned with how the historical experiences of Blacks informed their identity with respect to the concept of nationality. His primary concept of a Black identity had much to do with how African Americans were treated by American society. This concept included the historical and contemporary condition of African Americans. From the standpoint of history, Malcolm cited the enslavement of Africans as proof of their noncitizenship status. As further proof, he cited the postslavery experiences of racial violence—including lynching, debt-peonage, and the concerted psychological tools used against African Americans. When asked by Adam Clayton Powell if he "hated the white man," Malcolm replied:

> How can you ask us do we hate the man who kidnapped us four hundred years ago, brought us here and stripped us of our history, stripped us of our culture, stripped us of our language, stripped us of everything that you could use today to prove that you were ever part of the human family, brought you down to the level of an animal, sold you from plantation to plantation like a sack of wheat, sold you like a sack of potatoes, sold you like a horse and a cow, and then hung

---

39. Malcolm X, *Autobiography*, 27–29.
40. Malcolm X, *Autobiography*, 175.
41. Malcolm X, *Autobiography*, 174.
42. Asante, *Afrocentricity*, 14.

you up from one end of the country to the other, and then you ask me do I hate him? Why, your question is worthless![43]

With this form of logic, Malcolm X distinguished between the concept of national citizenship (birth) and the circumstances related to actualized democratic equality (experience). A citizen was an individual who was accepted as a citizen, acknowledged as a citizen, and treated as a citizen. Malcolm did not establish a fine distinction between one's country of origin and one's treatment in that country: "Just because you're in this country doesn't make you an American. No, you've got to go farther than that before you can become an American. You've got to enjoy the fruits of Americanism."[44] Malcolm's connection of history and equality as a component of national identity is also related to his presentation of people of African descent, particularly African Americans, as original or first-world peoples of the planet. Knowing this would free Blacks from the degradation that comes with second-class citizenship, allowing for a new mind-set to take place.

Healing the "Sin Sick": The Reformation Project of the Nation of Islam

Malcolm X made great use of his time discussing the platform of the Nation of Islam and the organization's ability to make an impact on the individual. In describing the personal reformation project of the Nation of Islam, Malcolm noted that Islam provided substance to the Black man and woman. He also discussed the ways in which the Nation of Islam reached out to Black men and women in prisons, to those on the street—indeed, to any Black person in need of direction and a sense of purpose. The Nation of Islam also provided a distinct sense of personal identity. Indeed, the rationale behind the organization's platform was clear. The legacy of slavery, the historical oppression, segregation, lynching, disfranchisement, unemployment, underemployment, illiteracy, and so forth—all resulted in the devaluation of a specific race and class of persons. As Malcolm stated: "The Honorable Elijah Muhammad teaches us to reform ourselves of the vices and evils of this society, drunkenness, dope addition, how to work and provide a living for our family, take care of our children and our wives."[45] Membership in the Nation of Islam was an entrée into a new sense of self identified by a new name. In addition to its spiritual teachings, the organization taught the Black individual that he or she was no longer a degraded "Negro" in American society but a first-world person.[46] Indeed, the Black man or woman was no longer an object of scorn and pity but an inherently important individual prepared to take full responsibility for the development of his or her life. The reformation project of the Nation of Islam also demonstrated the oppositional rhetoric of Malcolm X. Islam became the "antidote" to the ills of American society which plagued African Americans. Benjamin Karim details how he was affected by the Nation of Islam and Malcolm X on a personal level:

> Inside, what struck me immediately was the "brightness," the sobriety of the brothers walking around ... I was spellbound. Now I understood for the first

---

43. Malcolm X, *The End of White World Supremacy*, 79–80.
44. Malcolm X, *Malcolm X Speaks*, 172.
45. Malcolm X, *The End of White World Supremacy*, 83.
46. See C. Eric Lincoln, *The Black Muslim Movement in America* (Boston: Beacon Press, 1973).

time why brother Leo had been after me to learn black history. I had never in my life heard a man speak like that, and I knew then that something in my life had changed or was about to change. I had been like a boat adrift, and I had found my course … I got up and followed the brothers toward the rear. There the secretary of the mosque explained to us what we had to do, in a very simple manner. There was no ritual.[47]

The reformation project of the Nation of Islam filled a deep need in the African American community. The project was spiritual in dimension—and it also included the historical experience of African Americans, by African Americans, and for African Americans. One of the most widely discussed aspects of the reformation project is the transformation of Malcolm X. His transformation is considered a paradigm of the African American experience and speaks to the changes human beings undergo over time. As El-Beshti notes, "Malcolm might seem like a different man in each of his incarnations, but his essence—of fluidity, of emergence, of growth—always remained intact."[48] Therefore, while the reformation project of the Nation of Islam was a defining factor in the emergence of Malcolm X, he did not change the substance of who he was—from El-hajj Malik El-Shabazz to Omowole ("the son who returns").

In his *Autobiography* and in his many speeches, Malcolm featured his own life as evidence of the successful reformation project of the Nation of Islam. Certainly individuals of all backgrounds with interest in the words of Malcolm X found his life a case study in the possibilities of consciousness and awareness. Indeed, Malcolm laid his life bare to the world: the aspects of his life that he himself found unsavory and regrettable he discussed openly. While there were no secrets to be discovered and held over his head, much of the pedagogy on Malcolm X examines more of the world of "Detroit Red" and "Big Red" and less of Malcolm as a human being within his time. American popular media specialists avoided Malcolm's central criticism of white domination of the Black masses and the discussion about his ability to argue effectively against racism while at the same time confronting it. This avoidance was the media's major strategy for discrediting Malcolm X while he was alive and in the years after his death. After his death, Sann provided the standard liberal observation regarding Malcolm X: "He lives on today as something of a cult figure, but he had preached violence—there can be no revolution without bloodshed—and he died by it."[49] However, Malcolm X, while living, prepared for his critics beyond the grave. The "live by the sword"-"die by the sword" admonition didn't seem to apply to white racial violence and systemic discrimination against Blacks. Malcolm was succinct: "Not a single white person in America would sit idly by and let someone do to him what we black men have been letting others do to us. The white person would not remain passive, peaceful, and nonviolent. The day the black man in this country shows others that we are just as human as they in reaction to injustice, that we are willing to die just as quickly to protect our lives and property as whites have shown, only then will our people be recognized as human beings."[50] The outcomes of Malcolm's observations serve as an anatomy of the system of racism itself. As Malcolm surmised, when an argument for such concepts as racism, white supremacy, and discrimination is indefensible, it cannot be legitimately sustained through logical dis-

---

47. Malcolm X, *The End of White World Supremacy*, 8–9.

48. Bashir M. El-Beshti, "The Semiotics of Salvation: Malcolm X and the Autobiographical Self." *Journal of Negro History* 82, no. 4 (Autumn, 1997): 363.

49. Paul Sann, *The Angry Decade: The Sixties* (New York: Crown Publishers, 1979), 158.

50. Malcolm X, *The Speeches of Malcolm X at Harvard*, ed. Archie Epps (New York: Apollo Editions, 1969), 161–175.

course. Therefore, the first course of action is to redefine the terms of the discourse to one's advantage and simply, but consistently, to avoid the key issues. Malcolm X used the reformation project of the Nation of Islam and his commitment to his own personal redemption as tools to address racism, white supremacy, and discrimination. In doing so, he showed that the Nation of Islam could not be viewed as a fringe or a cult group in the Africana community.

The Black Middle Class and Civil Rights Leaders

Not all members of the Black middle class were leaders in the civil rights movement, and vice versa. In 1969 Bailey noted the two main group strategies during the civil rights movement: "the middle-class strategy" was led by the NAACP; the "nonviolent direct action strategy" was led by the Southern Christian Leadership Conference (SCLC), The Congress of Racial Equality (CORE), and the Student Nonviolent Coordinating Committee (SNCC).[51] However, Malcolm X defined key issues within the Black middle class in the liberatory struggle, and he identified profound problems in the strategies and tactics of civil rights workers. As a social critic he was interested in fully examining the challenges inherent in the rise of the Black middle class and Black leaders in the civil rights movement. E. Franklin Frazier had suggested earlier that the Black middle class ("Black Bourgeoisie") consisted of a masked bundle of frustrations, insecurities, delusions, self-hatred, and guilt. For example, Franklin felt: "[T]he chief frustration of the middle-class Negro is that he can not escape identification with the Negro race and consequently is subject to the contempt of whites. Despite his 'wealth' in which he has placed so much faith as a solvent of racial discrimination, he is still subject to daily insults and is excluded from participation in white American society.... They constantly repress their hostility toward whites and seek to soothe their hurt self-esteem in all kinds of rationalizations."[52] Malcolm X was generally dissatisfied with the work of such individuals and with what they represented. Indeed, he saw them as self-serving "house Negroes."

This participatory exploitation, according to Malcolm X, was a product of racism. He defined it as the opportunity for racists to select and identify key Black individuals who would a) be thrust into the national leadership of African Americans and then challenge and nullify the Black radical position; b) be an entity easily controlled by the establishment; c) be always responsive to material rewards for opportunities for their service; and d) be prepared to attack radical Black leaders and other Blacks who were not selected by the establishment. For example, in their study of Black leadership in 1950s Tallahassee, Florida, Killian and Smith found the following: "[M]ost of these white leaders indicated that they were unwilling to deal with these New Leaders because the militant spokesmen were uncompromising in their opposition to segregation. It is only in this sense that communication has broken down between the races. The New Leaders are unwilling to communicate and negotiate with whites in the circumscribed, accommodating fashion of yesterday."[53] Killian and Smith's findings are important be-

---

51. Harry A. Bailey, Jr., "Negro Interest Group Strategies" *Urban Affairs Quarterly* 4, no. 1 (September 1969): 26–38.

52. E. Franklin Frazier, *Black Bourgeoisie* (New York: Collier, 1962), 176–195.

53. Lewis M. Killian and Charles U. Smith, "Negro Protest Leaders in a Southern Community," in *The Making of Black America*, ed. August Meier and Elliott Rudwick, 2:334–341 (New York: Atheneum, 1976).

cause of the variety of ways by which Malcolm X was attacked throughout his public career—from the time he was a member of the Nation of Islam until his assassination in 1965. He was the public figure who fit perfectly the historic stereotype of the "bad nigger" leader. However, as Henry has noted, the term "bad nigger" could have been applied to any number of Black leaders or individuals of the time, regardless of whether their rhetoric was perceived as moderate or militant.[54] The "bad nigger" is one of many postslavery images which were used as a social and political buffer between the Black middle class and white American society.[55] Yet in 1973, Borden asserted that the Black rhetoric of the sixties shifted at times—particularly after the assassination of Malcolm X.[56] It is believed that this event (and the assassinations of Medgar Evers, Martin Luther King, Jr., and Robert and John F. Kennedy) catapulted many Black middle-class and civil rights movement individuals from pragmatic gradualism to Malcolmian militancy.

Malcolm X made Martin Luther King, Jr. representative of what he thought about the strategies of the Black middle-class and civil rights movement leaders. Malcolm was quick to point out that the typical response to King's nonviolent approach was violence. He used the startling evidence of white abuse of peaceful Black protestors to support his ideas on the right of Blacks to defend themselves in the face of violent conflict. Both Malcolm X and Martin Luther King, Jr. were each characterized as an "enemy" of the other, except that their differences with each other often appear more ideological—and certainly much less visceral than the those between W. E .B. Du Bois and Marcus Garvey. Brown, like other eyewitnesses of the time, noticed the salient feature of strategically maneuvering the "good Blacks versus bad Blacks." In her autobiography, she details the reason why it was necessary for American society to sustain such a dichotomy:

> It had been the embrace of reputed opponents Martin Luther King, Jr., and Malcolm X in 1964 that had most alarmed Hoover. It was not a strong embrace, but it had certainly signaled a red alert.... Hoover saw that the union of Malcolm and Martin was the worst possible threat to the internal security of America. The synthesis of their philosophies and, even worse, their forces, directed toward an aggressive campaign to gain "freedom" for black people, was a real danger. Both men were assassinated not long after that embrace.[57]

A whisper of such an alliance suggested that more Blacks would have been brought to some type of liberatory consciousness. Many have researched and written about the government-supported factionalism among Black leaders and organizations of the time.[58] These scholars continue to suggest that the internal struggles have layers of questions about how Black leaders, members of the Black middle class, and the heads of the civil rights movement were viewed and manipulated by the United States government. Malcolm's disdain for the self-interest of the Black middle class was unapologetic. How-

---

54. Among the scholarly discussions of such negative stereotypes, see also Charles Henry, "The Political Role of the 'Bad Nigger,'" *Journal of Black Studies* 11, no. 4 (June 1981): 461–482.

55. See also William H. Wiggins, Jr. "Jack Johnson as Bad Nigger: The Folklore of his Life," in *Contemporary Black Thought*, ed. Robert Chrisman and Nathan Hare, 53–70 (New York: Bobbs-Merrill, 1973).

56. Karen Wells Borden, "Black Rhetoric in the 1960s: Sociohistorical Perspectives," *Journal of Black Studies* 3, no. 4 (June 1973): 423–431.

57. Elaine Brown, *A Taste of Power* (New York: Pantheon, 1993), 236.

58. See Clayborne Carson, *Malcolm X: The FBI File* (New York: Carroll & Graf, 1991), 83; Karl Evanzz, *The Judas Factor: The Plot to Kill Malcolm X* (New York: Thunder Mouth Press, 1992), xix; Manning Marable, "By Any Means Necessary: The Life and Legacy of Malcolm X" (speech, Metro State College, Denver, CO, February 21, 1992, http://www.lbbs.org/zmag/articles/barmarable.htm (accessed February 2, 2000).

ever, he left room for a dialogue with those who he felt had neglected the masses of poor African Americans and who were therefore part of the exploitation of Black people in the United States. He did acknowledge the brave struggle of civil rights workers, but he criticized their efforts within the context of a more effective unified Black struggle. He also understood that all Black leaders were suspected of engaging in activities that could be viewed as threat to the security of the nation. However, since he frequently discussed his beliefs in "the brotherhood of all men,"[59] he understood that the Black middle class and the civil rights workers had the responsibility and, more important, the capability of working together. This sentiment is best shown in the development of the Organization of Afro-American Unity (OAAU). The OAAU statement resolved: "[We are] [c]onscious of our responsibility to harness the natural and human resources of our people for their total advancement in all spheres of human endeavor."[60]

"The Urgent Spirit"[61] of Malcolm X and African American Identity Formation

In his speeches and writings, Malcolm X used various terms to refer to the people of African descent born in the United States. He used the term *Negro*, which was common at the time. More often than not, he critiqued the term *Negro*, and the identity of Blacks, by using the phrase the "so-called Negro." This critique culminated in "Malcolm's challenge—that we were Africans," and "it became clearer that 'Negro' was dead."[62] The death of the term *Negro* was also evident in his use of the terms *original, Asiatic, Afro-American, Black, African-American*, and then, finally, *African*. While he made distinctions between continental Africans and African Americans, he made no distinction about the ancestral connectedness. He spoke collectively for the Black nation and the search for Black identity in his queries:

> "[W]e want to know what are we? How did we get to be what we are? Where did we come from? How did we come from there? Who did we leave behind? Where was it that we left them behind, and what are they doing over there where we used to be? This is something that we have not been told. We have been brought over here and isolated—you know the funniest thing about that: they accuse us of introducing "separation" and "isolation." No one is more isolated than you and I."[63]

These and similar sets of questions show that Malcolm X was making an Afrocentric assessment regarding the agency and collective state of being of Blacks. Part of the purpose of the Malcolmian Method of oppositional rhetoric was to demonstrate to Blacks the existence of something that had been hidden; another part of its purpose was to uplift something that had been torn down. For Malcolm X the issue of identity formation

---

59. Malcolm X, *The Speeches of Malcolm X at Harvard*, 162.

60. George Breitman, *The Last Year of Malcolm X: The Evolution of a Revolutionary* (New York: Merit Publishers, 1967), 105.

61. Gray describes the quality of Malcolm X as "an urgent spirit" openly dedicated to the liberation of African people. See Cecil Conteen Gray, *Afrocentric Thought and Praxis: An Intellectual History* (Trenton, NJ: Africa World Press, 2001), 155.

62. Asante, *Malcolm X As Cultural Hero*, 27.

63. Malcolm X, *Malcolm X Speaks*, 118.

was a matter of consciousness among Black people. Jones (Amiri Baraka) surmised that "Malcolm X's greatest contribution … was to preach Black Consciousness to the Black Man."[64] In his analysis of the "so-called Negro" as presented to the African in America, Malcolm's central theme was self-knowledge and the power inherent in the collective possessed of such knowledge.

Malcolm X did not passively accept the decisions of white American society concerning who or what the Black person was. The Organization of Afro-American Unity (OAAU) addressed the issue of identity in its charter. According to Section I, "Establishment," the OAAU was designed to "include all people of African descent in the Western Hemisphere, as well as our brothers and sisters on the African Continent."[65] In Malcolm's speeches, and in this document, there were no debates about "mixed blood theories," "hybridization," or such related concerns as to whether Black Americans were an African people.[66] Yet, unlike that of his contemporaries, Malcolm's approach to the Africanity of Blacks was not a concept to be argued for or against. For him it was an undisputed fact that did not imbue the individual with any special, or even superior, qualities. Rather, it was, as he noted, a reality subject to generations of concerted distortion and negative inculcation. The ultimate essence of Malcolm's message, like the observations of Jones, was African identity among Black people and how to fuel this identity into a unified victory over racism. Malcolm X took the warrior's position ("[E]ach day I live as if I am already dead"[67]) by using the sense of his own mortality as a catalyst to live fully. As an African in a community, Malcolm X summarized the warrior mission of his life and work: "Anything I do today, I regard as urgent. No man is given but so much time to accomplish whatever is his life's work. My life in particular never has stayed fixed in one position for very long."[68] This understanding of human mutability was meant to be a catalyst for African Americans to begin systematically addressing all of the legacies of racism and racial domination—especially the issue of African identity among Blacks.

Summary and Conclusion

A review of the life and work of Malcolm X reveals a tightly woven argument that addressed the issue of Black identity construction in the United States. This argument stayed consistent during Malcolm's time with the Nation of Islam and continued after his split with the organization and the beginning of the Organization of Afro-American Unity (OAAU). The study of Malcolm X tasks us to examine his uses of historical knowledge. In his life-long critique of the question of identity, beginning with his own life as a point of departure and then expanding his critique to the African world collective, Malcolm continued the dialogue on African American liberation. In this dialogue with life, he chose to be an activist and advocate for people of African descent and other people of color. After his separation from the Nation of Islam and the bombing of his

---

64. Leroi Jones, *Home* (New York: Morrow, 1966), 241.
65. Breitman, *The Last Year of Malcolm X*, 106.
66. See Katherine Bankole, *You Left Your Mind In Africa: Journal Observations and Essays on African American Self-Hatred* (Dellslow, WV: Nation House, 2001).
67. Malcolm X, *Autobiography*, 381.
68. Malcolm X, *Autobiography*, 378.

home, he could have assumed a different position. However, as Smallwood has argued, he made a conscious decision to be a "cultural educator."[69] Furthermore, he made informed decisions about the nature of history. In doing so, he demonstrated how the African must actively engage racism as a past and a current phenomenon. For the African, there is little benefit in musing about the vagaries of history, for there are multiple contemporary challenges taking place simultaneously. Carew states that Malcolm "made it clear that his role as a leader was not just to analyze the world, but to change it."[70] In addition, for African people he set goals for the use of historical knowledge. One use was to locate oneself in relationship to similar historical experiences without being a victim of history. Finally (and most important), he understood his own participant-observer role in the making of history. In the end, he defined the overall struggle of African Americans as a "cultural revolution," a "journey to our rediscovery of ourselves ... [so that] [a]rmed with the knowledge of the past, we can with confidence charter a course for our future."[71] As Ford notes in his text on Africana heroes, Malcolm's life is indeed placed in the realm of epic lives—the lives of heroic figures who quest after what others perceive as impossible.[72]

The Malcolmian Method of oppositional rhetoric was used in Malcolm's dialogues to address African Americans on such issues as their lack of knowledge about their own history; the psychosocial control of the Black masses; his criticism of the term *Negro*; how the historical experiences of Blacks have informed their identity; the personal reformation project of the Nation of Islam; the manipulation of the Black middle class and of the leaders of the civil rights movement; and Black identity formation. We can discuss a Malcolmian Method within the contexts of Malcolm's journey through redemption to reflection as a self-conscious activity. Included in this method are the necessary tools of discipline, an awareness of an unfolding process of awakening, the commitment to the ultimate goal, and, finally, the ability to exhibit strength in the face of overt and covert forms of racial attack. Scholarly critiques of Malcolm X consistently relate the need to view him as a product of the total African world experience. For example, Asante delineates him as a son of history:

> To truly understand Malcolm we must understand him in the context of his particular time and space. As heir to resistance, nationalism, pride, knowledge, and nobility, it was destined that he would be a cultured person as well as a teacher of culture.[73]

Such a view of Malcolm X places him within the framework of the legacy of Marcus Garvey and that of the Black Nationalists and Pan-Africanists who came before him.[74] When Malcolm X is placed within this framework, people of African descent understand him—whether they accept his views or not—and they reject the traditional Western mainstream view of him as an aberration among his own people and a threat to white people.

---

69. Andrew P. Smallwood, *An Afrocentric Study of the Intellectual Development, Leadership Praxis, and Pedagogy of Malcolm X* (Lewiston, NY: The Edwin Mellen Press, 2001).

70. Jan Carew, *Ghosts in Our Blood: With Malcolm X in Africa, England, and the Caribbean* (Chicago: Laurence Hill Books, 1994), xi.

71. Breitman, *The Last Year of Malcolm X*, 111.

72. See Clyde W. Ford, *The Hero With an African Face: Mythic Wisdom of Traditional Africa* (New York: Bantam Books, 2000).

73. Asante, *Malcolm X As Cultural Hero*, 31.

74. See Oba T'Shaka, *The Political Legacy of Malcolm X* (Chicago: Third World Press, 1983), chap. 6, 167–206.

In addition, the subtleties of the critiques on the life and work of Malcolm X, especially with respect to his rhetorical style, continue to be limited to whether or not he had the right to say what he said and whether he had the right to say it the way he said it. As a result, while Malcolm X is fully engaged in much broader terms than before, we are still tasked to move beyond the apologia of blackness. Karenga would call this "exposing unreasonable reasoning" within his ten essential aspects of the oppositional logic of Malcolm X.[75] It constitutes the last stages of the unmasking of the critical language of racial domination. This aspect of Malcolm X's logic presumed the existence of human rights in the face of racial double standards. This aspect also defined the warrior archetype of Malcolm X. His legacy is as transcendent as the legacy of the warrior who journeyed to forbidden territory and came back enlightened and immortal.

---

75. Karenga, "The Oppositional Logic of Malcolm X," 9.

14

Reflections on Omowale Malcolm X and Martin Luther King, Jr.: Afrikan Liberation Struggle and the Political and Psychocultural Critique of Civil Rights

Ahati N. N. Toure

Omowale Malcolm X (El-Hajj Malik El-Shabazz) and Dr. Martin Luther King, Jr., are typically contrasted as the ideological poles of the Afrikan struggle in the United States of the mid-twentieth century. To a great extent this polarization is true, despite attempts by some propagandists to harmonize their differing objectives and definitions of the U.S. Afrikan liberation struggle.[1] Both leaders did agree that the citizenship-rights (civil-rights) struggle had yielded only token, negligible results.[2] Moreover, both were religious clerics who agreed on the imperative of revolutionary change, embraced an in-

---

1. The basic problem here is the propaganda that asserts that Malcolm became an integrationist after his break from the Nation of Islam and his pilgrimage to Mecca, which marked his embrace of Arab-centered Islamic orthodoxy. See the late Reverend Albert Cleage's very cogent analysis on this and related issues in "Myths About Malcolm," in *Malcolm X: The Man and His Times*, ed. John Henrik Clarke, 13–26 (Toronto: Macmillan, 1969).

2. Malcolm addressed this question numerous times. As an example, see Malcolm X, "God's Judgement of White America," in Clarke, ed., *Malcolm X*, 283.

King, in a very revealing admission of the actual gains of the citizenship-rights movement, stated: "When millions of people have been cheated for centuries, restitution [another word for reparations] is a costly process. Inferior education, poor housing, unemployment, inadequate health care—each is a bitter component of oppression that has been our heritage. Each will require billions of dollars to correct. Justice so long deferred has accumulated interest and its cost for society will be substantial in financial as well as human terms. *This fact has not been fully grasped, because most of the gains of the past decade were obtained at bargain rates. The desegregation of public facilities cost nothing; neither did the election and appointment of a few black public officials* [my italics]." Further, he asserted: "White America must realize that *justice for black people cannot be achieved without radical changes in the structure of our society* [my italics]. The comfortable, the entrenched, the privileged cannot continue to tremble at the prospect of change in the status quo." See Martin Luther King, Jr., "A Testament of Hope," in *A Testament of Hope: The Essential Writings and Speeches of Martin Luther King, Jr.*, ed. James M. Washington, 314–315 (New York: HarperSanFrancisco, 1986). One should note that this essay was published posthumously, in 1969, and that, therefore, it represented King's latest thoughts—just before his assassination. One should also note that King supported reparations.

ternationalist focus, opposed U.S. imperialism, and were assassinated very likely by individuals hired by U.S. government counterintelligence agencies (such as the FBI's
COINTELPRO).[3] Yet their theological, philosophical, ideological, and methodological
differences were profound and, fundamentally, diametrical. According to the late historian John Henrik Clarke, Malcolm was "an astute revolutionary theoretician" and "the
finest revolutionary theoretician and activist produced by America's black proletariat in
this century."[4] According to American church historian James M. Washington, King, by
contrast, "certainly was an Americanist."[5] From the southern U.S. Afrikan petty bourgeoisie, King was a Christian philosopher and an activist of great erudition, but he was
much steeped in the European tradition. From the perspective of official U.S. propaganda, Malcolm is negatively—and falsely—portrayed as the exponent of wanton violence against and hatred of American white people of European descent, whereas King
is extolled as the premier representative of nonviolence, universalism, and reason. But
there are, of course, numerous problems with these Eurocentric and propagandistic
characterizations.[6]

---

3. Malcolm was assassinated on 21 February 1965. King was assassinated three years later, on 4
April 1968.

4. John Henrik Clarke, "Preface to Part V," in Clarke, ed., *Malcolm X*, 271–272.

5. James M. Washington, "Editor's Introduction: Martin Luther King, Jr., Martyred Prophet for
a Global Beloved Community of Justice, Faith, and Hope," in Washington, ed. *A Testament of Hope*,
xix.

6. On this matter of universalism, note the brilliant critique offered by the Afrikan cultural an-
thropologist Marimba Ani, *Yurugu: An African-Centered Critique of European Cultural Thought and
Behavior* (Trenton, NJ: Africa World Press, 1994). See especially Chapter 2, "Religion and Ideology,"
where Ani notes: "Christianity is only universal in that European cultural nationalism is characterized by universal or international imperialistic ambition.... The international character of the European political ambition or objective has been continually and tragically (for its 'objects') confused
with the spurious universalism of European cultural and ideological identification.... The proselyti-
zation of Christianity has perhaps the greatest culturally immobilizing and demoralizing effect on
its 'objects'" (150).

She adds: "It is a moot question as to whether any such 'universalism' is desirable even if it were
possible. Nationalistic, i.e. (self) group identification, is positive because it is humanly feasible and
originates in concrete circumstances of cultural definition. Hope for humankind lies in the possibilities for fashioning nationalistic ideologies that are not definitionally predicated on the destruction
of other cultural groups. European nationalism and above all its Christianism are therefore 'negative' from this viewpoint. Second, even if the ability to identify with others is accepted as a normative goal, it is neither Christian thought nor European ideology that makes such identification possible. The European concept of self is an isolating one....

"In other words, from the African-centered perspective, it is not nationalism (cultural particu-
larism) that is negative, but the content that a particular nationalist ideology is given that makes it a
threat to the survival of others. In this regard, it is clearly European nationalism, of which Christianity is an example, that has been most destructive of the peaceful coexistence of divergent cultural groupings. The projection of so-called 'universalism' as an assumed goal of human behavior is
not desirable or culturally meaningful, but it allows Europeans to thereby project European particu-
larism as something other than it is....

"Europeans simply discovered the political value of not verbally identifying 'god and nation';
that is not to say that this identification ceased to exist. Most other cultures have had no political
ambitions that required such rhetoric, and when they have, they were certainly not as successful or
as 'well-equipped' to carry them out. They therefore speak of 'a god' in necessary relationship to
'their nation' or culture" (191–194).

Nineteenth-Century U.S. Afrikan Liberation Movements: Nonviolence versus Armed Struggle

One of the most compelling problems is simply that from a historical and cultural vantage point, nonviolence as an ideological approach to liberation struggle, or as a tactical methodology, has never resonated deeply in Afrikan culture in the United States. This was especially so in the eighteenth and nineteenth centuries, when the Afrikan masses enslaved in the South and the Afrikan intellectuals and activists in the North organized themselves in opposition to the white-supremacist slave states and slaveholders by means that included clandestine operations and open, armed revolution. In some instances, independent Afrikan settlements, created by those who had escaped enslavement by slaveholders in slave states, defended themselves against reenslavement through sustained guerrilla warfare.[7] As the U.S. Afrikan historian, novelist, and human-rights activist William Wells Brown told audiences in London and Philadelphia in 1854: "Already the slave in his chains in the rice swamps of Carolina and the cotton fields of Mississippi, burns for revenge."[8] Indeed, note the historians John Hope Franklin and Alfred A. Moss, Jr., "Revolts, or conspiracies to revolt, persisted down to 1865."[9]

Furthermore, the dominant view among U.S Afrikan intellectuals and activists in the antebellum period of the nineteenth century was that armed struggle against American enslavement and oppression was not only moral but an imperative of the liberation struggle and a necessary vindication of Afrikan humanity.[10] Northern Afrikan activists

---

7. The examples are legion. See Walter C. Rucker, "'The River Floweth On': The African Social and Cultural Origins of Slave Resistance in North America, 1712–1831" (Ph.D. diss., University of California-Riverside, 1999) and Yvonne Tolagbe Ogunleye, "An African Centered Historical Analysis of the Self-Emancipated Africans of Florida, 1738 to 1838" (Ph.D. diss., Temple University, 1995). For her extensive discussion of the Afrikan war of liberation in Florida, see pp. 260–352. See also Steven H. Shiffrin, "The Rhetoric of Black Violence in the Antebellum Period: Henry Highland Garnet," *Journal of Black Studies* 2 (September 1971): 45–56; Leslie Friedman Goldstein, "Violence as an Instrument for Social Change: The Views of Frederick Douglass (1817–1895)," *Journal of Negro History* 61 (January 1976): 61–72; Moses Dickson, *Manual of the International Order of Twelve Knights and Daughters of Tabor containing general laws; regulations, ceremonies, drill and landmarks*, 8th ed. (Glasgow, MD: Moses Dickson Publishing Co., 1911); Katharine DuPre Lumpkin, "'The General Plan Was Freedom': A Negro Secret Order on the Underground Railroad," *Phylon* 28 (Spring 1967): 63–77; and Herbert Aptheker, "Resistance and Afro-American History: Some Notes on Contemporary Historiography and Suggestions for Further Research," in *In Resistance: Studies in African, Caribbean, and Afro-American History*, ed. Gary Y. Okihiro, 10–20 (Amherst: The University of Massachusetts Press, 1986).

8. William Wells Brown, *St. Domingo: Its Revolutions and its Patriots. A Lecture, Delivered before the Metropolitan Athenaeum, London, May 16, and at St. Thomas' Church, Philadelphia, December 20, 1854*, ed. Maxwell Whiteman (Philadelphia: Rhistoric Publications, 1969), 38.

9. See John Hope Franklin and Alfred A. Moss, Jr., *From Slavery to Freedom: A History of African Americans*, 7th ed. (New York: Knopf, 1994), 144. See also Franklin and Moss, *From Slavery to Freedom*, 140–147; Lerone Bennett, Jr., *Before the Mayflower: A History of the Negro in America, 1619–1964* (Baltimore: Penguin, 1964), 96–126; and Peter H. Wood, "Strange New Land, 1619–1776," in *To Make Our World Anew: A History of African Americans*, eds. Robin D. G. Kelley and Earl Lewis, 90–95 (New York: Oxford University Press, 2000).

10. Herbert Aptheker notes that in the 1850s, support for the legitimacy of U.S. Afrikan armed struggle was "so frequently expressed [by U.S. Afrikan and American human-rights activists alike] that one is justified in declaring that, among anti-slavery folk, ... [such support] became common-

and intellectuals in the United States saw an ineradicable interrelationship between their defense of Afrikan humanity, or manhood, and the moral and ethical sanctions of Protestant Christianity. In their view, it was a correlation that necessitated armed retaliation to counter the violation and humiliation of American subordination and to conclusively establish for white supremacists the irrefutable credentials of their humanity as Afrikan persons in America. Thus, as Protestant Christians, and in many instances as clergymen, northern U.S. Afrikan intellectuals such as David Walker, Henry Highland Garnet, Frederick Douglass, and William Wells Brown, among numerous others, advanced the notion that armed struggle was the Afrikan's God-approved obligation.

"Look upon your mother, wife and children, and answer God Almighty; and believe this, that it is no more harm for you to kill a man, who is trying to kill you, than it is for you to take a drink of water when thirsty," Walker asserted in 1829. In fact, "the man who will stand still and let another murder him, is worse than an infidel."[11]

A thirty-four-year-old ordained minister in the African Methodist Episcopal Zion Church, Douglass concurred. Twenty-five years after Walker's legendary advocacy of armed struggle, Douglass urged his readers to the same in an 1854 editorial in *Frederick Douglass' Paper* titled "The True Remedy for the Fugitive Slave Bill." In the most unequivocal of terms, he declared: "*A good revolver, a steady hand, and a determination to shoot down any man attempting to kidnap* [italics in the original]. Let every colored man make up his mind to this, and live by it, and if need be, die by it. This will put an end to kidnapping and to slaveholding, too."[12] In that same year, Afrikan activists in Philadelphia held a convention during which they approved a resolution declaring, "[T]hose who, without crime, are outlawed by any Government can owe no allegiance to its enactments ... we advise all oppressed to adopt the motto, 'Liberty or Death.'"[13] Three years earlier, consistent with his fellow activists, Douglass had concluded that "common sense ... teaches that physical resistance is the antidote for physical violence."[14]

Eight years before, the Reverend Henry Highland Garnet, in an August 1843 speech to a national convention of "free colored people" in Buffalo, New York, made explicit the connection between U.S Afrikan manhood and the armed struggle against American slaveholders and slave states. "In the name of God, we ask, are you men? Where is the blood of your fathers? Has it all run out of your veins?" the twenty-seven-year-old Presbyterian minister remonstrated against the alleged passivity of enslaved Afrikans in the

---

place. It is, indeed, a moot question whether the hitherto dominant pacifist or non-resistance wing of the movement (so far, at least, as its articulate members were concerned) was not overshadowed and outweighed, in the decade of crisis [1850–1860], by activists and believers in resistance [armed struggle]." See Herbert Aptheker, "Militant Abolitionism," *Journal of Negro History* 26 (October 1941): 463.

11. David Walker, *David Walker's Appeal to the Coloured Citizens of the World, but in particular, and very expressly, to those of the United States of America*, ed. Charles M. Wiltse (New York: Hill and Wang, 1965), 26. Aptheker, who pioneered in researching what he called "militant abolitionism," noted (with some sarcasm regarding the fantastic propaganda about enslavement in the United States) that support for U.S. Afrikan armed struggle "was widespread and deep-rooted. It appears to have been particularly common among the Negro people themselves, especially those who had escaped from the delights of the patriarchal paradise." See Aptheker, "Militant Abolitionism," 484.

12. Frederick Douglass, "The True Remedy for the Fugitive Slave Bill," *Frederick Douglass' Paper*, June 9, 1854, in *The Life and Writings of Frederick Douglass*, ed. Philip S. Foner, 5:206 (supp. vol., 1844–1860) (New York: International, 1975).

13. Aptheker, "Militant Abolitionism," 465.

14. Frederick Douglass, "Is Civil Government Right?," *Frederick Douglass' Paper*, October 23, 1851, in Foner, ed., *The Life and Writings of Frederick Douglass*, 214.

South. "Let your motto be resistance! *resistance!* RESISTANCE! [Italics and small capitals in the original.] No oppressed people have ever secured their liberty without resistance."[15]

According to the historian Katharine DuPre Lumpkin, in the 1840s and 1850s, Detroit revolutionaries William Lambert and George De Baptiste were members of an Afrikan secret society which they described in recollections to Detroit newspaper reporters in the 1870s and 1880s. This underground Afrikan movement operated for a decade or more with the chief mission of assisting enslaved Afrikans to escape the South's enslavement regime. Apparently, it also secretly organized for armed struggle, and to protect its underground railroad operations, it conducted covert assassinations of the U.S. government's Afrikan informants in the South. Lambert, who had documents from the clandestine order, said it was called "African American Mysteries: Order of the Men of Oppression." De Baptiste remembered it as the "Order of Emigration" with "Men of Oppression" the highest degree. De Baptiste also said the revolutionary movement's aim was to spread the organization throughout the North, adding that it had several degrees or cells and that each worked separately from the other.

The secret order imposed elaborate rituals of initiation for each of its three degrees, which Lambert and De Baptiste stated were called "Captives," "Redeemed," and "Chosen." Within this last and highest degree, there were five levels: rulers, judges and princes, chevaliers of Ethiopia, sterling black knights, and knights of St. Domingo. This last, and highest, level, interestingly enough, "had a ritual of great length *dealing with the principles of freedom and the authorities on revolution, revolt, rebellion, government* [my italics]." De Baptiste recalled that the order had participated in the planning (and was supposed to have participated in the execution) of John Brown's 1859 raid at Harper's Ferry, the purpose of which was to facilitate an organized, armed exodus of enslaved Afrikans from Virginia to Canada that would intimidate and overwhelm the American authorities. The operation was also supposed to have served as a violent and active repudiation of the Fugitive Slave Act of 1850, which would lead to its nullification by Congress.[16]

Interestingly, whereas King believed that U.S Afrikan armed struggle was immoral, unwinnable, and counterproductive to Afrikan assimilationism,[17] integrationist intellectuals and activists of the nineteenth century assumed it was a necessary and effective means by which to achieve social and cultural assimilation in the United States. Armed retaliation against violent white-supremacist assaults was crucial in establishing U.S. Afrikan "manhood" rights and was a prerequisite for respectful acceptance in the United States. Without violence, this objective would have been an utter impossibility in the minds of such intellectuals and activists. From an assimilationist viewpoint, the accuracy of their assumption was proved when U.S. Afrikans were unilaterally incorporated into the United States after the Civil War by means of the Thirteenth, Fourteenth, and Fifteenth Amendments to the Constitution.

---

15. "Garnet's Call to Rebellion, 1843," in *A Documentary History of the Negro People in the United States,* ed. Herbert Aptheker, vol. 1, *From Colonial Times Through the Civil War,* 232–233 (New York: Citadel Press, 1979). See also Shiffrin, "The Rhetoric of Black Violence," 45–56.

16. Lumpkin, "The General Plan," 63, 70–72, 74–75.

17. As an example, see King's arguments on this matter in "Where Do We Go From Here?"—his presidential address to the Tenth Annual National Convention of the Southern Christian Leadership Conference, in Washington, ed. *A Testament of Hope,* 249. See also his essay "A Testament of Hope," in Washington, ed., *A Testament of Hope,* 323; his 1967 book *Where Do We Go From Here? Chaos or Community,* in Washington, ed., *A Testament of Hope,* 590–595; his 1968 essay "Showdown for Nonviolence," in Washington, ed., *A Testament of Hope,* 64–72; and his 1965 *Playboy* interview, in Washington, ed., *A Testament of Hope,* 365.

Outside the United States, the most celebrated example of Afrikan armed struggle for northern intellectuals and activists — and, to a significant degree, the masses enslaved in the South — was the Haitian Revolution. "Africans throughout the Americas," observes V. P. Franklin, "viewed the Haitian Revolution as a model for overthrowing the system of 'racial slavery' that accompanied the formation of the plantation economy in the Caribbean, North, and South America."[18] The U.S. Afrikan historian James Theodore Holly praised it as "one of *the noblest, grandest, and most justifiable* [my italics] outbursts against tyrannical oppression that is recorded on the pages of the world's history."[19] He further rhapsodized: "Never before, in all the annals of the world's history, did a nation of abject and chattel slaves arise *in the terrific might of their resuscitated manhood* [my italics], and regenerate, redeem, and disenthrall themselves: by taking their station at one gigantic bound, as an independent nation, among the sovereignties of the world."[20]

As an ideological approach, as a methodological tactic, and as a philosophical basis for a way of life in response to white-supremacist enslavers in the United States, advocacy of nonviolence originated with white Americans of European descent, most notorious of whom was the New England abolitionist William Lloyd Garrison.[21] Formerly enslaved U.S. Afrikans, on the other hand, felt far differently. John Henry Hill, who in 1853 had escaped enslavers in Richmond, Virginia, told fellow U.S. Afrikan activists in Philadelphia's Underground Railroad movement that he believed in the superior effectiveness of armed struggle over moral suasion and passive resistance. Citing abolitionist newspaper accounts that "contain long details of insurrectionary movements among the slaves of the South," Hill declared: "I believe [*sic*] that the fire and the sword would affect more good in this case" than pious prayers.[22] To the masses of enslaved Afrikans in the South — who far more closely adhered to Afrikan traditional culture,[23] who were also more insulated from Europeanization, and who knew firsthand the inhuman criminality of enslavement in the United States — nonviolence as a methodology of struggle was simply inconceivable.

For example, in 1812 Virginia security forces arrested and interrogated a revolutionary named Tom for having killed his enslaver. Under interrogation, Tom revealed that he was part of a liberation movement spearheaded by a traditional religious leader (a

---

18. V. P. Franklin, "'Location, Location, Location': The Cultural Geography of African Americans — Introduction to a Journey," *The Journal of African American History* 87 (Winter 2002): 2.

19. James Theodore Holly, *A Vindication of the Capacity of the Negro Race for Self-Government, and Civilized Progress, as Demonstrated by Historical Events of the Haitian Revolution; and the Subsequent Acts of That People Since Their National Independence* in *Black Separatism and the Caribbean, 1860*, James Theodore Holly and J. Dennis Harris, ed. Howard H. Bell (Ann Arbor: University of Michigan Press, 1970), 21.

20. Holly, *A Vindication*, 25.

21. See Nathan Irvin Huggins, *Slave and Citizen: The Life of Frederick Douglass* (New York: HarperCollins, 1980), 60–61. Huggins writes that Douglass had once embraced the philosophy of nonviolent passive resistance championed by the American abolitionist William Lloyd Garrison, who was his mentor when he first joined the abolitionist movement. Huggins adds, however, that as one who had been enslaved, Douglass had no profound belief in nonviolence and he grew to view enslavement by Americans as "a state of war" to which armed resistance was the only proper response. Huggins argues that the American revolutionary John Brown's influence accounted for Douglass's increasing conviction of the necessity of armed struggle.

22. Aptheker, "Militant Abolitionism," 467.

23. For insight into the dynamics of U.S. Afrikan traditional culture during the era of enslavement, see Walter Rucker, "Conjure, Magic, and Power: The Influence of Afro-Atlantic Religious Practices on Slave Resistance and Rebellion," *Journal of Black Studies* 32 (September 2001): 84–103 and Tolagbe Ogunleye, "The Self-Emancipated Afrikans of Florida: Pan-African Nationalists in the 'New World,'" *Journal of Black Studies* 27 (September 1996): 24–38.

so-called conjurer) named Goomer, from Rockingham County, North Carolina. He also told interrogators that he had been encouraged to do away with his enslaver by a fellow revolutionary named Celia, who had confessed to him that "she had rather be in hell than where she was." Tom disclosed to enslaver security forces the fierceness of U.S. Afrikan sentiment against white-supremacist enslavement in Virginia: A fire had destroyed a Richmond theater a year earlier, and local Afrikans "were glad that the people were burnt in Richmond, and wished that all the white people had been burnt with them. That God Almighty had sent them a little Hell for the white people, and that in a little time they would get a greater." Tom further revealed that U.S. Afrikans "in the neighborhood said that these British people was about to rise up against this Country, and that they [the Afrikans] intended to rise sometime in next May. *That they were buying up guns for the purpose* [my italics]. That they were not made to work for the white people, but [that] they [the white people] ... [were] made to work for themselves; and that they [the Afrikans] ... would have it so." The revolutionaries planned to break into a local store "to get the Guns, Powder, &c out of it ... *they would then raise an army* [my italics]."[24]

Yet, even when certain U.S. Afrikan intellectuals advocated nonviolence as a methodology of struggle, it was, for the most part, only applicable to the struggle *against the United States, not against the enemies of* the United States.[25] This qualified advocacy explains the posture of nineteenth-century U.S. Afrikan historians in their focus on U.S. Afrikan contributions to the war efforts of the United States. William Cooper Nell, William Wells Brown, George Washington Williams, and Joseph T. Wilson all celebrated U.S. Afrikan participation in America's wars.[26] Of the four, Brown distinguished himself by noting that the U.S. Afrikan struggle in the American Civil War was prefigured by independent, armed resistance movements that preceded the conflict between the Union and the Confederacy. "The efforts of Denmark Vesey, Nat Turner, and Madison Washington to strike the chains of slavery from the limbs of their enslaved race," he wrote, "will live in history and will warn all tyrants to beware of the wrath of God and the strong arm of man."[27] On the other side were Wilson's odd and contradictory observa-

---

24. "Confession of a Virginia Rebel, 1812," in Aptheker, ed., *A Documentary History*, 56–57.

25. An example here is the U.S. Afrikan historian and civil-rights and peace activist James W. C. Pennington. Although during the Civil War he repudiated his stance of nonviolence to advocate U.S. Afrikan armed resistance, he had formerly urged that U.S. Afrikans use moral force and arbitration and asserted that armed resistance would prove self-defeating. He had also urged: "*Colored people must bear and forbear.... Colored Christians, let it be seen that they have nothing to hate in you but good will and piety.... Let our love and pity for them be manifested in our constant prayer for their good* [Pennington's italics]." See James W. C. Pennington, *A Text Book of the Origin and History, etc. etc. of the Colored People* (Hartford, CT: L. Skinner, 1841; repr., Detroit: Negro History Press, n.d.), 87–89. Citations are to the Negro History Press reprint.

26. William C. Nell, *The Colored Patriots of the American Revolution: With Sketches of Several Distinguished Colored Persons: To Which is Added a Brief Survey of the Condition and Prospects of Colored Americans* (Boston: Robert F. Wallcut, 1855; repr., New York: Arno Press and *The New York Times*, 1968); William Wells Brown, *The Negro in the American Rebellion: His Heroism and His Fidelity* (Boston: Lee Shepard, 1867; repr., Miami: Mnemosyne, 1969); Joseph T. Wilson, *The Black Phalanx: A History of the Negro Soldiers of the United States in the Wars of 1775–1812, 1861–'65* (Hartford, CT: American Publishing Company, 1888; repr., New York: Arno Press and *The New York Times*, 1968); and George Washington Williams, *A History of the Negro Troops in the War of the Rebellion, 1861–1865, preceded by a review of the Military Services of Negroes in Ancient and Modern Times* (New York: Harper Brothers, 1888; repr., New York: Bergman, 1968). Future citations are to the reprint editions above.

27. Brown, *The Negro in the American Rebellion*, 36.

tions. According to him, U.S. Afrikans' motives for service in the military campaigns of the United States were, paradoxically, patriotic and self-interested. "[F]or the first time in the history of what is now the United States," he wrote of the year 1770, "the negro, inspired by the love of liberty, aimed a blow at the authority that held him in bondage." Yet, in a glaring non sequitur, he observed that U.S. Afrikans ultimately served and identified with the interests of their enslavers: "In numerous instances, when the Indians attacked the white settlers, particularly in the Northern colonies, negroes were summoned and took part in the defense of the settlements." Indeed, he contended: "The Indian was more of a terror to him than the boa-constrictor." Furthermore, he argued: "*[T]hough slaves*, they knew that if captured by the Indians their fate would be the same as that of the white man; consequently *they fought with a desperation* equal to that of the whites, *against the common enemy*[all italics mine]."[28]

In the final analysis, the ideological weight of nonviolence as a methodology and philosophy has tended to constrain the nature of U.S. Afrikan resistance against that white supremacy which exists in the United States and in the nation's government, but not against the nation's enemies. In other words, nonviolence—because of its ideological underpinnings—has philosophically and politically served to protect the security, stability, and survival of the United States.

Citizenship Rights, Nonviolence, and International Human Rights

No better example of the ideological underpinnings of nonviolence can be seen than in an analysis of King's rejection of Malcolm's call to escalate the U.S. Afrikan liberation struggle from the level of citizenship rights to that of international human rights. In 1964, Malcolm obtained support from Afrikan and Asian nations for a human-rights petition to the United Nations charging the United States government with genocide against U.S. Afrikans. However, the idea had originated some two decades earlier with the founding of the UN in 1945. The first effort was a petition submitted by W. E. B. Du Bois in 1947 on behalf of the NAACP titled *An Appeal to the World: A Statement on the Denial of Human Rights to Minorities in the Case of Citizens of Negro Descent in the United States of America and an Appeal to the United Nations for Redress.*[29] According to diplomatic historian Carol Anderson, the U.S. State Department undermined this effort, with the assistance of former first lady Eleanor Roosevelt, the supposed friend of Afrikans in the United States. The State Department's objective was to defeat the petition in order to prevent the United States government from suffering international embarrassment, exposure, and censure for the fraudulence of its so-called democracy.[30]

---

28. Wilson, *The Black Phalanx*, 26.

29. W. E. B. Du Bois, *An Appeal to the World: A Statement on the Denial of Human Rights to Minorities in the Case of Citizens of Negro Descent in the United States of America and An Appeal to the United Nations for Redress* (New York: National Association for the Advancement of Colored People, 1947).

30. Carol Anderson, "With Friends Like These … Eleanor Roosevelt, the NAACP's Struggle for Human Rights, and the Limits of Liberalism, 1946–1952," (paper, African American and African Studies Interdisciplinary Symposium, *Bridging the African Diaspora in the New Millennium,* African American and African Studies Program, University of Nebraska-Lincoln, February 23, 2001).

Four years later, William L. Patterson, Paul Robeson, Mary Church Terrell, and Du Bois were among ninety-four signatories to a human-rights petition submitted to the UN charging the United States government with genocide against its Afrikan citizens. The Civil Rights Congress submitted the 1951 petition to the UN secretary general in New York and to the fifth session of the UN General Assembly in Paris. This second petition came six years after the founding of the UN in 1945 and three years after the General Assembly had adopted the Convention on the Prevention and Punishment of Genocide in 1948. The petition charged that U.S. government officials were actively engaged in committing, conspiring to commit, publicly inciting to commit, attempting to commit, and complicity in committing genocide against the nation's 15 million Afrikans. Specifically, it charged that "the Government of the United States, its Supreme Court, its Congress, its Executive branch, as well as the various state, county and municipal governments, consciously effectuate policies which result in the crime of genocide being consistently and constantly practiced against the Negro people of the United States."[31]

31. William L. Patterson, ed., *We Charge Genocide: The Historic Petition to the United Nations for Relief from a Crime of the United States Government Against the Negro People* (New York: Civil Rights Congress, 1951; repr., New York: International, 1970), 6–7. Citations are to the International reprint. See also pages xii, 32, and 31–54. According to the Convention, "genocide means *any* of the following acts committed with *intent to destroy*, in whole *or in part*, a national, ethnical, racial or religious group, as such: (a) Killing members of the group; (b) Causing serious bodily or mental harm to members of the group; (c) Deliberately inflicting on the group *conditions of life* calculated to bring about its physical destruction in whole *or in part*; (d) Imposing measures intended to prevent births within the group; (e) Forcibly transferring children of the group to another group [my italics]."

15

Malcolm X: An Apostle of Violence or an Advocate for Black Human Rights?

Victor O. Okafor

> You say we hate white people; we don't hate anybody. We love our own people so much they think we hate the ones who are inflicting injustice against them.
>
> —Malcolm X

Malcolm X was one of the African American leaders who provided inspirational leadership for the Black community at a time of a great existential crisis. I am referring to the turbulent period of American history most popularly called "the civil rights movement"—but which I prefer to designate "the black protest movement." During the 1950s and 1960s, this nation witnessed a heightened phase of a centuries-old New World African struggle. It was a grassroots movement with many leaders at the local, state, and national levels. Although Martin Luther King, Jr. was the most nationally acclaimed leader of the Black protest, or civil rights, movement and won global recognition as the recipient of the Nobel peace price, Malcolm X, as numerous nascent reviews of his life and his ideas indicate, remains firmly anchored in the New World African memory of that epic struggle. Indeed, Malcolm X remains a household name in the African American community.

Born in 1925, Malcolm lived for forty years—until he was assassinated in 1965. His life was a turbulent one characterized by many ups and downs. He was a foster child, and he served a six-and-a-half-year prison term for burglary. During his childhood (like most New World Africans of his generation), he experienced incidents of white-supremacist bigotry and terrorism: the Ku Klux Klan (KKK) burned down his family's homes in Omaha, Nebraska, and in Lansing, Michigan. When his family's Lansing home was burned down in 1929 (Malcolm was four years old then), Ku Klux Klan membership was said to number at least seventy thousand in Michigan—five times more than the number of Klan members in Mississippi. Philbert Little, one of Malcolm's brothers, recaptured what happened on the day their house was consumed by fire: "The house burned down to the ground. No fire wagon came. Nothing. And, we were burned out" (Bagwell, 1994). Whereas Malcolm's father, Earl Little, blamed the fire on "local whites," "the police accused Earl and arrested him on suspicion of arson. The charges were later dropped" (Bagwell, 1994). The same Ku Klux Klan is also believed to have been behind the death of Malcolm's father—a death that was officially reported as the result of an electric-street-car accident. The loss of Earl Little—the breadwinner of the Littles—was a devastating experience for the family. Malcolm's mother,

Louise Little, apparently overwhelmed by the burden of taking care of the family alone, eventually broke down and was moved to a mental asylum. After her commitment, Malcolm and his other brothers and sister were placed in various foster homes.

Although Malcolm lost his father early in life, his influence on the little boy appears to have been long lasting—as attested by Malcolm's worldview and psychosocial philosophy in his adult life. While Malcolm's father was alive, he followed the teachings of Marcus Garvey, the leader of the popular Universal Negro Improvement Association (UNIA). In fact, Earl Little was a local leader of the Association. In addition, Malcolm's mother wrote for the Garvey newspaper, *The Negro World*. Both Earl and Louise taught Malcolm and his siblings to be proud of their African ancestry; they admonished their children not to think of themselves as "Negroes" or "niggers" but as "black people" (even though at the time, "Negro" was the term used to designate New World Africans). Philbert Little recalled that his father was a proud, independent-minded black man: "[He] didn't want anybody to feed him. He wanted to raise his own food. He didn't want anybody to exercise authority over his children. He wanted to exercise the authority and he did." But, of course, that authority evaporated once Earl died. Since both of their parents were gone (one dead, the other in a mental asylum) and they themselves were scattered in foster homes, Malcolm, his brothers Philbert and Wilfred, and his sister Yvonne grew up in the absence of that fatherly and motherly care that had been the mainstay of their early childhood.

Why was Malcolm's father a target of white rage through the terrorism of the Ku Klux Klan? Wilfred, Malcolm's older brother, answers the question in the following recollections:

> In the city where we grew up, Whites would refer to us as those uppity niggers or those smart niggers that lived outside the town. In those days whenever a white person refers to you as a smart nigger that was their way of saying this is a nigger you have to watch because he is not dumb (Bagwell, 1994).

Wilfred continues:

> [Our father] was always speaking in terms of Marcus Garvey's way of thinking and trying to get black people to organize themselves, not to cause any trouble but to work in unity with each other towards improving their conditions. But in those days, if you did that you were still considered a trouble-maker (Bagwell, 1994).

Many have assumed that the Nation of Islam profoundly (and solely) influenced Malcolm's outlook on life; however, Malcolm's background perhaps more deeply impacted his outlook. Indeed, as Alex Haley, his biographer, puts it, "All the things [Malcolm] had done in his earlier life … including, I should say, his very early encounter with white viciousness, synthesized into the Malcolm who became the spokesman for the Nation of Islam " (Bagwell, 1994).

As noted earlier, Malcolm's adult life was a checkered one, including imprisonment for burglary. While Malcolm served his prison term, his brother Philbert wrote to him about the Nation of Islam. In addition, a prison roommate encouraged him to embrace Islam. Malcolm also read widely while in prison, covering works by Will Durant, H. G. Wells, W. E. B. Du Bois, Mahatma Gandhi, Herodotus, Schopenhauer, Kant, Nietzsche, and Spinoza (Mullane, 1993, p. 661).

After Malcolm was released from prison, he joined the Nation of Islam (NOI) in August 1957 and subsequently changed his name from Malcolm Little to Malcolm X. In a television interview, he explained his reasons for joining the organization:

I was in prison. I was a very wayward, criminal, backward, illiterate, and uned-
ucated and whatever other negative characteristic type of person you can think
of until I heard the teaching of the Honorable Elijah Mohammed. [I joined]
because of the impact that it had upon me in giving me a desire to reform myself and rehabilitate myself for the first time in my life. That's what made me to
accept him....

... I noticed that after being exposed to the religious teachings of Honorable Elijah Mohammed immediately it instilled in me a high degree of racial
pride and racial dignity that I wanted to be somebody, and I realized that I
couldn't be anybody by begging the white man for what he had, but I had to
get out here and try and do something for myself and make something for myself (Bagwell, 1994).

Malcolm also admired the Nation of Islam for having created schools for the children of its members, where they were taught mathematics, science, history, and Arabic.
In those schools, women were taught nutrition, child rearing, and guidelines for relat-
ing to their husbands. Men were taught parental responsibility, history, and religion.

In the same television interview Malcolm explained his reasons for changing
his name from Malcolm Little to Malcolm X:[1]

My father did not know his last name. My father got his last name from his
grandfather, and his grandfather got his from his grandfather who got it from
the slave master....

... The real names of our people were destroyed during slavery.... The last
names of my forefathers [were] taken from them when they were brought to
America and made slaves. And then the name of the slave master was given,
which we reject (Bagwell, 1994).

Although Malcolm was historically accurate in his account of the cultural genocide
that had been visited upon enslaved Africans, he no doubt overstated his case when he
used the pronoun we in reference to those members of the New World African community who have since rejected the last names they inherited from plantation masters. Indeed, Malcolm's use of the word we could not have referred to all New World Africans.

In the Nation of Islam, Malcolm emerged quickly as an eloquent and charismatic
speaker. Within two years of joining the NOI, Malcolm assisted in organizing Muslim
temples in Boston, Hartford, and Philadelphia. Elijah Mohammed rewarded him with
an appointment as the minister of what was regarded as the most important Eastern
temple, Harlem's # 7 in New York. His brother Philbert recalled: "[W]hen Malcolm
came out [of prison], he was full of fire; he had gotten so full of fire that he got out at
the right time in the right place so he could expound."

By 1963, Malcolm's relations with Elijah Mohammed had become strained. First,
Malcolm had heard rumors that Mohammed had fathered several children though his
secretaries, and the rumors may have diminished Malcolm's reverence for the Nation's
founder. In addition, Malcolm's growing popularity, which overshadowed that of Mohammed, may have been viewed with alarm by certain members of the Nation who
nursed ambitions of succeeding the man upon his death. A contemporary of Malcolm's,
Louis X, provided the following insight on these members and their ambitions:

---

1. Malcolm addressed himself as "El-Hajj Malik El-Shabazz" in a 1965 communication from
Mecca.

Minister Malcolm was honest. He was sincere. He was dedicated to the uplift-ing of African American people. Then, you had another group of people who were officials there in Chicago who were dedicated to the uplifting of them-selves. He accused them of taking money, of buying expensive jewelry, of buy-ing furs. He accused them of converting the Nation of Islam into a criminal or-ganization (Bagwell, 1994).

Historian John Henrik Clarke provided a similar insight: "There were ... people in the Nation with aspirations towards [the] number one slot. And if Elijah Mohammed passed away and if Malcolm took over the Nation, the first thing he might do was some serious house cleaning.... So, the idea was to get rid of him before the event of the pass-ing of the old man" (Bagwell, 1994).

But perhaps the most celebrated reason for Malcolm's falling out with the leadership of the Nation of Islam was his suspension for ninety days in late November 1963, in the wake of the assassination of President John F. Kennedy. When news broke of Kennedy's death, Elijah Mohammed was reported to have instructed Malcolm not to make any derogatory public statement about the late president. But Malcolm disobeyed this order. In a speech during a temple gathering, he claimed that Kennedy's assassination was an example of the "chickens coming home to roost" (Malcolm X, 307). He meant that the assassination was a consequence of the kinds of plots that the United States government had engaged in around the world, including the masterminding of the as-sassination of foreign leaders such as Patrice Lumumba of the Republic of the Congo.

In March 1964 Malcolm announced his departure from the Nation of Islam and founded Muslim Mosque, Incorporated. This organization turned out to be a mixed blessing of sorts, for as Malcolm would later tell a news conference, he believed that the Nation of Islam did not take kindly to the emergence of a rival Islamic organization. It only exacerbated the tensions between him and the Nation.

In April 1964, Malcolm made a pilgrimage to Mecca, and after the pilgrimage, he visited fourteen African countries and met with eleven African heads of state in an at-tempt to galvanize continental African support for the ongoing Black freedom move-ment in the United States. In July 1964, he attended a meeting of the Organization of African Unity (OAU) in Cairo. He explained his mission as follows:

My purpose is to remind the African heads of state that there are 22 million of us here in America who are also of African descent and to remind them also that we are the victims of American colonialism or American imperialism, and that our problem is not an American problem; it is a human problem; it is not a Negro problem; it is a problem of humanity; it is not a problem of civil rights but a problem of human rights (Bagwell, 1994).

In fact, Malcolm attended the OAU meeting by invitation. Even then, he understood the dynamic linkage between the continental struggles and those of New World Africans. Historian John Henrik Clarke recounted: "Malcolm X saw no contradiction between the African fight and the black American fight in the United States. He thought one was an extension of the other; you can draw support from one to enhance the other " (Bagwell, 1994).

Indeed, the African tour exerted a discernible impact upon Malcolm. On returning from his tour, he announced the formation of an organization patterned after the OAU. He called it the Organization for Afro-American Unity (OAAU) and hoped it would serve as a platform for unifying New World Africans. He explained his rationale for founding the OAAU as follows: "This organization of Afro-American Unity [is designed] to bring about the complete independence of people of African descent here in the Western Hemisphere, but first here in the United States. [It is designed] to bring about the freedom of these people by any means necessary" (Bagwell, 1994). He also intended to use the OAAU to champion the cause of New World Africans before the United Nations, since the problems that confronted them were not problems of civil rights but those of human rights. During a speech before a Rochester Methodist church on February 16, 1965, Malcolm explained that the impetus for redefining the problem of civil rights as a problem of human rights had come to him from African nations' representatives at the United Nations:

> They said that as long as the Black man in America calls his struggle a struggle of civil rights ... it's domestic and it remains within the jurisdiction of the United States. And if any of them open up their mouths to say anything about it, it's considered a violation of the laws and rules of protocol.... 'Civil rights' are within the jurisdiction of the government where they are involved. But 'human rights' is part of the Charter of the United Nations. All the nations that signed the Charter of the UN came up with the Declaration of Human Rights, and anyone who classifies his grievances under the label of human rights violations, those grievances can then be brought into the United Nations and be discussed by people all over the world. For as long as you call it 'civil rights,' your only allies can be the people in the next community, many of whom are responsible for your grievance. But when you call it 'human rights,' it becomes international. And then you can take your troubles into the World Court. You can take them before the world. And anybody anywhere on this earth can become your ally (Malcolm X, 1992, p. 170).

However, Malcolm he did not live to actualize this and other goals of the OAAU, for he was assassinated a few days later, on February 21, 1965.

A casual observer may be puzzled about Malcolm's high standing among African Americans despite his unsavory early adulthood that culminated in a prison term. Furthermore, mainstream historiography seems to portray Malcolm as the polar opposite of Dr. Martin Luther King, Jr., through inferences and images that depict Malcolm as an apostle of violence in contrast with a peace-loving and nonviolent King. But is it entirely true that Malcolm advocated violence against, and even hatred of, white America? In order to explore this question, I have examined a cross section of Malcolm's speeches—the speeches themselves, not paraphrases or summaries by third parties.

Afrocentric research, analysis, and synthesis are guided by some protocols as delineated by Asante (1990). These are the functional, the categoral, and the etymological protocols—which are paradigmatic instruments based on the "assumptions of the Afrocentric approach to human knowledge" (Asante, 1990, p. 13) and which are defined as follows:

> The functional paradigm represents needs, policy, and action. In the categoral paradigm are issues of schemes, gender, class, themes, and files. The etymological paradigm deals with language, particularly in terms of word and concept origin (Asante, 1990, p. 13).

In examining Malcolm's speeches, my essay employs the etymological paradigm of Afrocentric research, analysis, and synthesis, by which the researcher and writer elucidates the historical and philosophical location of the rhetoric employed by a given author or speaker.

A 1994 television documentary on the life and speeches of Malcolm X, produced by WGBH (Boston) and Blackside, Inc., presents an early example of Malcolm's audacious rhetoric through a set of rhetorical but historically poignant questions that he asked of his all-Black audience:

> Who taught you to hate the color of your skin? Who taught you to hate the texture of your hair? Who taught you to hate the shape of your nose and the shape of your lips? Who taught you to hate yourself, from the top of your heads to the soles of your feet? Who taught you to hate your own kind? Who taught you to hate the race that you belong to so much so that you don't want to be around each other? ... You should ask yourself, Who taught you to hate being what God gave you? (Bagwell, 1994).

Those questions show Malcolm's keen sense of the well-documented impact exerted on the minds of generations of New World Africans by distorted images of Blacks in the mainstream media.

Also instructive and illuminating is a 1962 statement by Malcolm after a bloody confrontation between the police and members of the Nation of Islam's temple in Los Angeles. During that encounter, seven members of the temple were killed, including the secretary, Ronald Stokes. An all-white coroner's jury later acquitted a police officer charged with the killings, holding that his action constituted justifiable homicide. Reacting to the event, Malcolm called civil rights organizations and churches in an attempt to forge a united front against the apparent abuse of police power at the Los Angeles temple. About the Los Angeles killings, Malcolm said: "Let us remember that we are not brutalized because we are Baptists; we are not brutalized because we are Methodists; we are not brutalized because are Moslems; we are not brutalized because we are Catholics; we are brutalized because we are black people in America" (Bagwell, 1994). Two inferences can be drawn from Malcolm's powerful insights. First, theological dogmatism sometimes contradicts secular realities. For example, here we see that despite Malcolm's immersion in the religion of Islam, he retained a clear understanding of such secular realities of Black life in America as intergenerational Black phobia. Second, across human societies, some people sometimes become so intoxicated by their own theologies that they become blind to their shared humanity or shared secular concerns and interests with persons of different faiths. But, as the foregoing illustrates, Malcolm's attachment to Islam did not turn him into a zealot who could not reach out to and work with persons of different faiths to solve common secular problems.

Although the *Los Angeles Times* reported that the temple shootings were "a Moslem riot and a wild gunfight" (Bagwell, 1994), Malcolm told a different story: "I am telling you [the police] came out of those cars ... with their guns smoking.... They didn't fire any warning shots in the air. They fired warning shots point blank at innocent, unarmed, defenseless Negroes." (Bagwell, 1994).

He then added: "You say we hate white people; we don't hate anybody. We love our own people so much they think we hate the ones who are inflicting injustice against them" (Bagwell, 1994). Malcolm's statement is an example of his capacity to speak the truth in a fearless and candid fashion to those in power. In it, he answered individuals such as Mike Wallace, who had claimed he was a hater of whites. On another occasion, in 1965, he responded to similar claims:

> There are those that have accused me of being a racist. I am not a racist in any way, shape or form, and I believe in taking an uncompromising stand against any forms of segregation and discrimination that are based on race. I myself do

not judge a man by the color of his skin. The yardstick that I use to judge a man is his deeds, his behavior, and his intentions. And the press has very skillfully projected me in the image of a racist simply because I take an uncompromising stand against the racism that exists in the United States (Malcolm X, 1992, p. 37).

Did the aversion to Malcolm by the white press indeed result from his "uncompromising stand against the racism that exists in the United States"? As Asante recalls, "Malcolm was considered an extremist and a militant by most of the white press" (1993, p. 28).

Another instance of Malcolm's frankness and fearless oratory was the following statement to a Black audience:

The white man is intelligent enough. If he were made to realize how Black people really feel and how fed up we are with that old compromising sweet talk. While you are the one that makes it hard for yourself, the white man believes you when you go to him with that old sweet talk because you have been sweet-talking him ever since he brought you here. Stop sweet-talking him. Tell him how you feel. Tell him what kind of hell you've been catching (Bagwell, 1994).

That statement was vintage Malcolm, throwing a challenge at the mask by which many within the New World African community have tried to navigate the sometimes-turbulent waters of American race relations.

After he had been barred from entering France, Malcolm spoke in London by telephone to an interviewer in France in February 1965. He answered a question about whether he advocated violence:

I do not advocate violence. In fact the violence that exists in the United States is the violence that the Negro in America has been a victim of, and I have never advocated our people going out and initiating any acts of aggression against whites indiscriminately. But I do say that the Negro is a continual victim of the violent actions committed by the organized elements like the Ku Klux Klan. And if the United States government has shown itself unwilling or unable to protect us and our lives and our property, I have said that it is time for our people to organize and band together and protect ourselves, to defend ourselves against this violence. Now if that is to advocate violence, then I'm shocked at the lack of proper understanding on the part of whatever elements over there that have this attitude (Malcolm X, 1992, p. 37).

During a speech at the London School of Economics in February 1965, Malcolm again addressed the issue of violence:

We are not for violence in any shape or form, but believe that the people who have violence committed against them should be able to defend themselves.... People should only be nonviolent as long as they are dealing with a nonviolent person. Intelligence demands the return of violence with violence. Every time you let someone stand on your head and you don't do anything about it, you are not acting with intelligence and should not be on this earth—you won't be on this earth very long either. I have never said that Negroes should initiate acts of aggression against whites, but where the government fails to protect the Negro he is entitled to do it himself. He is within his rights. I have found the only white elements who do not want this advice given to [defenseless] Blacks are the racist liberals. They use the press to project us in the image of violence (Malcolm X, 1992, p. 46).

Malcolm's reference to the press in the preceding quotation reflects one of his publicly expressed concerns. On several occasions, he accused the white Western media of not only misrepresenting his own views but also consistently distorting black images both in the New World and in the Old World of Africa. He expounded on this accusation in his address to the First Congress of the Council of African organizations, which was held in London February 4–8, 1965. Exhorting African journalists to strive to portray an objective image of Africa as a counter to the Western media's distortions, Malcolm articulated what he called a "science of imagery." Charactering the Western media as "the strongest weapon of imperialism" (Malcolm X, 1992, p. 33), he explained: "The imperialist press had developed over the years a science of imagery by which and through skillful maneuvering they are able to keep the Africans on the continent apart from their brothers in America and elsewhere. By the same system the imperialists have consistently made the African freedom fighter appear like a criminal" (Malcolm X, 1992, p. 33). Thus, Malcolm accused the Western media of engaging in a deliberate distortion of African images.

Malcolm advocated both global Pan-African unity and Pan-African unity in the Western Hemisphere. He articulated his position while speaking by telephone to a meeting of African groups in France in 1965:

> The Afro-American community in France and in other parts of Europe must unite with the African community, and this was the message that I was going to bring to Paris tonight—the necessity of the Black community in the Western Hemisphere, especially in the United States and somewhat in the Caribbean area, realizing once and for all that we must restore our cultural roots, we must establish contacts with our African brothers, we must begin from this day forward to work in unity and harmony as Afro-Americans along with our African brothers. (Malcolm X, 1992, pp. 39–40).

While Malcolm X and Marcus Garvey broadly shared Black Nationalist visions, there were key tactical differences between them. For instance, they differed on the idea of a return to Africa by African Americans. While Garvey espoused the idea of talented Africans returning to Africa to help build a strong united African nation that could be a source of pride and protection for Africans all over the word, Malcolm articulated a different notion of a New World African return to Africa. To Malcolm, "back to Africa" had a different meaning from Garvey's—a symbolic meaning. To him, it did not mean the physical return of U.S. Africans to Africa. Malcolm's vision was that Africans in the United States should return to Africa culturally, philosophically and psychologically (Breitman, 1967, p. 63). A reinvigorated spiritual bond with continental Africa, he argued, would strengthen the position of Africans in America. In essence, Malcolm advocated Afrocentric consciousness for African Americans. He believed that such consciousness would make U.S. Africans more viable American citizens. Afrocentric education would give African Americans the cultural and historical "centeredness" which had been severely impaired by the systematic brainwashing that had, more or less, been the lot of the African. Such a philosophical return to Africa seems, in my view, to be a pragmatic necessity, since in the United States, education and mass communication appear, for the most part, to be characterized by a psychological orientation and philosophical underpinning which inevitably yield anti-African consciousness.

A 1959 television documentary on the activities of the Nation of Islam along with those of Malcolm X may shed light on the origins of what appeared to be a contradiction between Malcolm's own actual views and his views as presented by mainstream academe and media. Mike Wallace was the presenter of the 1959 documentary, which was entitled "The Hate That Hate Produced: A Study of the Rise of Black Racism, of a Cult of Black Supremacy among a Small but Growing Segment of the American Negro Population" (Bagwell, 1994).

Journalist Peter Goldman, who interviewed Malcolm, characterized Malcolm's words as "an act of war" on white America but noted that Malcolm was speaking for "a silent mass of black people" (Bagwell, 1994).

The impressions of Malcolm by such white, liberal American journalists as Mike Wallace and Peter Goldman differed markedly from those of African Americans in general. The following is a sample of impressions of Malcolm proffered by African American writers and scholars.

Concerning Malcolm's message to the world, Historian John Henrik Clarke stated: "He was saying something over and above that of any other leader of that day. While the other leaders were begging for entry into the house of the oppressor, he was telling you to build your own house." Concerning the Nation of Islam, which Mike Wallace had portrayed as a cult of Black supremacy, Clarke said: "[Elijah Mohammed] introduced a form of Islam that could communicate with the people he had to deal with. He was the king to those who had no king. He was the messiah to those some people thought unworthy of a messiah."

Whereas Mike Wallace interpreted Malcolm's message as hate mongering, poet Sonya Sanchez held a different view: "[Malcolm] expelled fear for African Americans. He said I would speak out loud. He said it in a very strong fashion, in a manly fashion … in a fashion to say, 'I am not afraid to say what you've been thinking all these years.' That's why we loved him. He said it loud, not behind closed doors; he took on America for us" (Bagwell, 1994). Describing Malcolm as a "cultural hero," Asante wrote that Malcolm emerged as a spokesman for African Americans "because he actually spoke what was in our hearts the way we would have spoken it if we had been so eloquent" (1993, p. 30).

In a similar tone, writer James Baldwin said: "When Malcolm talks … [he] articulates for all the Negro people who listen to him.… He articulates their suffering, the suffering which this country has long denied.… He corroborates their reality" (Bagwell, 1994).

Malcolm did more than corroborate New World African reality. He challenged African Americans to reach for new heights. For instance, in announcing the formation of the Muslim Mosque, Inc. in March 1964, he came out squarely in favor of Black political participation. Calling for the passage of an effective civil rights bill, he said: "What you and I have got to do is get involved. You and I have to be right there breathing down their throats. Every time they look over their shoulders, we want them to see us. We want to make them pass the strongest civil rights bill they ever passed" (Bagwell, 1994). Simultaneously, Malcolm announced the launching of a voter registration drive in Harlem. He asked African Americans not to register as Democrats or Republicans but as independents. In so doing, he adopted a school of thought in Black politics which contends that the African American vote can work best as a swing vote in local, state, and national elections if most African Americans are registered as independents.

Malcolm also advocated Black economic nationalism, which he described as "the black man having a hand in controlling the economy of the so-called Negro community" (Bagwell, 1994). He suggested that African Americans should develop the expertise that would enable the Black community to own and operate businesses and thereby be able to generate jobs. His social philosophy was also nationalistic: "[My] social philosophy is black nationalism, which means that instead of the black man trying to force himself onto the society of the white man, we should be trying to eliminate from our society the ills and the defects and make ourselves likeable and sociable among our own kind" (Bagwell, 1994). Indeed, his vision of race relations does not appear to fit neatly into classical racial separatism. It appears there is a "jumpy" tendency by analysts of Malcolm's visions to label him as overly separatist. Such analysts seem not to recognize his pragmatic vision that Black America would feel more comfortable with itself by eradicating what he described in the foregoing quotation as its internal "ills and defects."

As a public figure, Malcolm evolved in his thinking and in his understanding of race relations. For instance, when he returned from his pilgrimage to Mecca, he articulated a new understanding of whites—namely, that there were some angels among them. Comparing whites in the United States with the whites whom he met and interacted with during his pilgrimage, he stated that, unlike the former, the latter exhibited an air of humility and human brotherhood that he attributed to the influence of Islam. Reflecting on his new understanding, he said:

> You may be shocked by these words coming from me. But this pilgrimage, what I have seen, and experienced has forced me to re-arrange much of my thought-patterns previously held, and to toss aside some of my previous conclusions.... Despite my firm convictions, I have been always a man who tries to face facts, and to accept the reality of life as new experience and new knowledge unfolds it. I have always kept an open mind, which is necessary to the flexibility that must go hand in hand with every form of intelligent search for truth. (Mullane, 1993, p. 668)

In fact, during the remaining days of his life, Malcolm sounded more worldly in his outlook, preaching the brotherhood of humanity. For instance, in a speech to three hundred young civil rights fighters in Selma, Alabama, on February 4, 1965, he declared: "If all of us are going to live as human beings, as brothers, then I'm for a society of human beings that can practice brotherhood" (Malcolm X, 1992, p. 28). Earlier, at Oxford University in England in December 1964, Malcolm advocated a multiracial front for confronting pressing human problems of the day:

> In my opinion, the young generation of whites, blacks, browns and whatever else there is, you are living at a time of extremism, a time of revolution, a time when there is got to be a change.... People in power have misused it, and now there has to be a change and a better world has to be built; and the only way it is going to be built is with extreme methods. And I for one would join hands with anyone. I don't care what color you are as long as you want to change the miserable condition that exists in this world (Bagwell, 1994).

Indeed, Malcolm was foresighted, for those words of his would have still made sense if they had been uttered just twenty-four hours ago.

Overall, Malcolm's mission of his life after imprisonment was to advance the human interests of African peoples. Although he voiced anger toward white bigots—an anger understandable given the white terrorism he had experienced during his childhood—he was neither a hater of whites nor an advocate of wanton violence. I wonder if there exists a white American who would feel less angry than Malcolm if he or she had experienced from Blacks the same kinds of viciousness and terrorism that Malcolm and his family experienced at the hands of white terrorist groups such as the Ku Klux Klan—groups that were never brought to justice. To expect less of Malcolm is to deny and to disrespect his humanity. After nineteen Arab terrorists attacked the United States on

September 11, 2001, the nation reacted with understandable anger and later carried out a surgical military operation in Afghanistan, which, according to the U.S. government, was aimed at purging members of the group led by Osama bin Ladin that was believed to have masterminded the assault on the Word Trade Center and the Pentagon. Indeed, the world was with the United States in that military act of self-defense. The world understood nation's rage!

The horror that white bigots visited upon Malcolm's family is an apt illustration of the thesis of Madhubuti (1990) that white supremacy constitutes a potent danger to the Black family:

> I think the best word to accurately describe the impact of the white nation is having upon Black people is terror. The Black community is being terrorized by whites at all levels of human involvement.... Racism is not only alive and well in America, it is a growth industry. We need to understand that white world supremacy (racism) is a given fact of life in the world and is not vanishing. (p. vi)

Malcolm's worldview and social philosophy were a logical product of and a logical response to the existential challenges of his time, including "four hundred years of the conscious racism of the American whites" (Mullane, 1993, p. 668)—as Malcolm himself put it. He used the mythologically significant term *Nommo* (the power of the written word), or what David Howard-Pitney describes as the African American Jeremiad or political sermon (cited in Walton & Smith, 2003, p. 39), to defend the human rights of a community that was under siege by white terrorists. The African American Jeremiad, which is the political dimension of *Nommo*, constitutes a defining characteristic of Black political culture. While accurately and justly reflecting a political mood which Rueter (1995) describes as New World African "disillusionment and alienation from white America" (p. 42), Malcolm's *Nommo* was an impressive exemplar of the central thesis of Walton and Smith (2003):

> In their quest for their own freedom in the United States, [New World Africans] have sought to universalize the idea of freedom. In their attack on slavery and racial subordination, [New World Africans] and their leaders have embraced doctrines of universal freedom and equality. In doing so they have had an important influence on the shaping of democratic, constitutional government and on expanding or universalizing the idea of freedom not only for themselves but for all Americans. (p. xiv)

In his relentless crusade to force the powers that be in the United States to extend universal human rights to New World Africans, Malcolm played the role of a warrior in the sense in which Madhubuti (1990) writes about it: "As a colonized people fighting for survival and development, Afrikan Americans must see our children as future 'warriors' in this struggle for liberation" (p. 192).

References

Asante, Molefi Kete. (1990). *Kemet, Afrocentricity and knowledge.* Trenton, NJ: Africa World Press.

Asante, Molefi Kete. (1993). *Malcolm X as a cultural hero & other essays.* Trenton, NJ: Africa World Press.

Bagwell, O. (Director). (1994). *Malcolm X: Make it plain* [Documentary]. Boston: WGBH & Blackside, Inc.

Breitman, George. (1967). *The last year of Malcolm X: The evolution of a revolutionary.* New York: Pathfinder.

Madhubuti, Haki R. (1990). *Black men, obsolete, single, dangerous? The African American family in transition.* Chicago: Third World Press.

Malcolm X. (1965). *Autobiography of Malcolm X.* With Alex Haley. New York: Ballantine.

Malcolm X. (1992). *February 1965: The final speeches.* (Steve Clark, Ed.). New York: Pathfinder.

Mullane, Deidre. (1993). (Ed.). *Crossing the danger water: Three hundred years of African American writing.* New York: Anchor Books.

Rueter, Theodore. (1995). (Ed.). *The politics of race: African Americans and the political system.* Armonk, NY: M. E. Sharpe.

Walton, Jr., H., & Smith, R. C. (2003). *American politics and the African American quest for universal freedom.* New York: Longman.

16

Malcolm X and Human Rights: An Afrocentric Approach to Reparations

Malachi D. Crawford

> Indeed, how can white society atone for enslaving, for raping, for unmanning, for otherwise brutalizing *millions* of human beings for centuries? What atonement would the God of Justice demand for the robbery of the black people's labor, their lives, their true identities, their culture, their history—and even their human dignity?
>
> A desegregated cup of coffee, a theater, public toilets—the whole range of hypocritical "integration"—these are not atonement.[1]
>
> —Malcolm X, *Autobiography of Malcolm X*

Introduction

Malcolm X's approach to the issue of human rights and reparations deserves critical examination for those scholars and activists who believe that African Americans had not been articulate or thorough enough in pressing for United Nations recognition and resolution of human-rights abuses against Africans in America. His analysis of the obstacles that opposed a movement in this direction addressed issues of procedure and power.

Malcolm X, when viewed holistically, was a Pan-Africanist who argued the need for economic cooperation, political unity and self-determination among African peoples and oppressed peoples generally. This essay does not seek to explain Malcolm's approach to the struggle for recognition of African American human rights within the framework of socialism. For one, it is not necessary to do so. The historical origins of socialism neither address nor give primacy to the issue of cultural solidarity, a variable of analysis which Malcolm consistently raised when he was questioned on organizing for humanitarian purposes. He believed that the most effective means of bringing the United States before international scrutiny for its abuses of African American human rights rested with Pan-African politics. His modification of Pan-Africanism to include a

---

1. Malcolm X, with Alex Haley, *The Autobiography of Malcolm X* (New York: Ballantine, 1992), 370.

working relationship between the freedom struggles of Africans on and outside the continent of Africa and a movement away from a racialist Pan-African perspective toward the more liberating reality of African humanity provided clarity and common ground for African peoples to discuss issues of brutality and oppression. Indeed, Malcolm created a strategy of human liberation tailored to the interests and circumstances of African peoples throughout the world.

Moreover, the essentials of his interpretation of the human rights of African Americans were Afrocentric in form as well. His experience as the son of prominent Garveyites and as the former national spokesperson for the Honorable Elijah Muhammad strengthened his belief that addressing cultural issues such as self-knowledge and the necessity of a psychological and philosophical return to Africa was a prerequisite to any movement seeking to resolve the injustice done to Africans in America. Consequently, the historical context that set the stage for Malcolm's desire to petition the United Nations on the subject of African American human-rights issues substantially differed from the contexts that influenced several previous attempts by U.S. African human-rights activists.

Antecedents

World War II provided the dominant backdrop and context for the African American struggle to bring the United States before the United Nations on issues of human-rights violations. In 1946, the Detroit-based National Negro Congress (NNC) drafted the first U.S. petition on human rights. Communistic in its outlook and interests, the NNC outlined the human-rights grievances of U.S. Africans by pointing out the disparities in statistical data between U.S, Africans and whites in housing, education, family income, health, occupations, and so on. However, the petition made no specific recommendations to the UN for resolving the abuses it listed. Since the NNC did not have the broad support of the U.S. African community, the UN ignored the petition altogether.[2]

The Harvard-educated scholar-activist W. E. B. Du Bois, with the help of the National Association for the Advancement of Colored People (NAACP), attempted to bring the next petition addressing the human rights of African Americans before the UN in 1947. Before this occasion, Du Bois had utilized the outcome of World War II and the consequent unlikely continuance of Western colonialism to put forward the idea and suitability of African tutelage as a counter to African calls for immediate self-government. In several books, he addressed the need for whites to grant power on a symbolic level and share the freedom of democratic institutions with nonwhites. These books included *Color and Democracy: Colonies and Peace* (1945); *Black Reconstruction: An Essay Toward the History of the Part Which Black Folk Played in the Attempt to Reconstruct Democracy in America, 1860–1880* (1935); and *Darkwater: Voices From Within the Veil* (1920).[3] For example, *Black Reconstruction* served as a corrective to the historiogra-

---

2. Charles P. Henry and Tunua Thrash, "U.S. Human Rights Petitions Before the UN," *The Black Scholar* 25, nos. 3–4 (1996–1997): 63.

3. Earl E. Thorpe, *Negro Historians in the United States* (Baton Rouge, LA: Fraternal Press, 1958), 56. For a discussion of Du Bois's views on tutelage, see Ahati N. N. Toure, "An African-Centered Analysis of W. E. B. Du Bois' *Darkwater: Voices From Within the Veil* by Using Molefi Kete Asante's Proposed Africalogical Framework," in *African American Sociology*, ed. James L. Conyers, Jr., and Alva P. Barnett, 175 (Chicago: Nelson Hall, 1999).

phy of southern revisionists who had claimed that African American politicians were responsible for the economic failures of the South after the Civil War and that they mismanaged the democratic privileges associated with American citizenship during Reconstruction.

Consistently, at the Fifth Pan-African Congress in 1945, Du Bois and the African American historian Rayford W. Logan temporarily convinced Kwame Nkrumah, who later became the first prime minister of Ghana at its independence, to forego acting on his intention to petition Britain for the right of Ghanaian self-governance.[4] Logan wrote the closing chapter to the NAACP-sponsored human-rights petition that Du Bois brought before the UN two years later. Although the petition had broad-based support within the African American community and some international backing, the UN never addressed its contents because of the political maneuvering of U.S. delegate to the UN Commission on Human Rights and NAACP board member Eleanor Roosevelt. The former first lady believed the petition would bring international embarrassment to the United States.[5]

Interest in putting forward a document forcing the international community to address human-rights violations in the United States continued after the defeat and obstruction of the NNC's and NAACP's petitions before the UN. In 1951, the Civil Rights Congress charged the United States with genocide against African Americans. The group became the target of cold war politics and disbanded in 1956 after achieving a few successes on civil-liberty and domestic issues on the American front. In 1955, U.S. Representative Charles C. Diggs sought the help of United Nations Undersecretary Ralph Bunche in bringing the plight of African Americans to the attention of the world. Since the United States was entering into a new era of international politics at the end of World War II, U.S. officials easily sidetracked these later attempts.[6]

Many of the major organizations that had attempted to petition the UN on behalf of African Americans were frequently worried about issues of procedure and legality. Moreover, the organizations failed to address the necessity of power on a systematic basis; instead, they discussed political power in terms of procedural support. The entrance of newly independent African states into the United Nations had a dramatic influence on the balance of power within the UN General Assembly and changed the nature of the struggle to achieve recognition of African American human rights.

Pan-Africanism and Human Rights

At the time of Malcolm X's break with the Nation of Islam in 1964, Africans in the United States and in Africa articulated two dominant and competing schools of Pan-African thought. A philosophy of African unity based on race that ignored the social differences in identity between Africans in the Western Hemisphere and Africans in Africa dominated the thinking of various U.S. African intellectuals. In contrast, a school

4. Kenneth Robert Janken, *Rayford W. Logan: The Dilemma of the African-American Intellectual* (Amherst: The University of Massachusetts Press, 1993), 168.
5. Henry and Thrash, "U.S. Human Rights Petitions," 64, 65; Carol Anderson, "From Hope to Disillusion: African Americans, the United Nations, and the Struggle for Human Rights, 1944–1947," *Diplomatic History* 20, no. 4 (Fall 1996): 553–555, 558–559.
6. Henry and Thrash, "U.S. Human Rights Petitions," 60, 65–66.

of Pan-African thought shaped the thinking of Africans in Africa, who believed that the unification of Africa under a confederation of independent nation-states was the only realistic foundation for African unity.[7]

As Malcolm X grew in his spiritual and intellectual knowledge, his outlook on the struggle facing U.S. Africans underwent change as well. Three major events influenced Malcolm's perception of and approach to human rights. First, his birth into a family rooted in the ideology and demands of the Universal Negro Improvement Association (UNIA) gave him an early identification with African culture. It also helped to familiarize him with the race-based Pan-African thought of the UNIA. Second, his two trips to Africa after departing from the Nation of Islam and his experience with orthodox Islam liberated his thinking from the limits of race as a basis for human analysis. These two events and their impact on his ideology, together with the third major event, the African revolution—which consisted of the liberation struggles of African peoples in Africa and throughout the world—led him to embrace a vision of a global Pan-African struggle based on African humanity instead of race.[8]

In April 1964, Malcolm X traveled to the holy city of Mecca, in Saudi Arabia, to perform the Islamic requirement of hajj as recent convert to orthodox Islam. (Only a month earlier, immediately following his break with the Nation of Islam, he had created the Muslim Mosque Incorporated (MMI) as a center for Islamic education in the U.S. African community.) During his stay in Saudi Arabia, he observed the Islamic practice and principle of brotherhood as a basis for human interaction and retracted statements made earlier in his life that all whites were inherently evil. In a letter from Saudi Arabia, dated April 20, 1964, he wrote:

> The whites as well as the non-whites who accept true Islam become a changed people. I have eaten from the same plate with people whose eyes were the bluest of blue, whose hair was the blondest of blond, and whose skin was the whitest of white ... and I felt the same sincerity in the words and deeds of these "white" Muslims that I felt among the African Muslims of Nigeria, Sudan and Ghana.[9]

After returning from his first major trip abroad, Malcolm X announced the formation of the Organization of Afro-American Unity (OAAU) on June 28, 1964, at a public meeting of the Muslim Mosque Incorporated. The organization consisted of Africans in the Western Hemisphere, reflected the interests and spirit of the Organization of African Unity (OAU) (established in May 1963 at Addis Ababa, Ethiopia), and dealt mainly with domestic and international issues facing U.S. Africans. At the same public meeting of the MMI, Malcolm expressed his intention of advancing the human-rights case of U.S. Africans by petitioning the United Nations.[10]

On July 9, 1964, two weeks after the formation of the OAAU, Malcolm X returned to Africa and attended the Second African Summit Conference in Cairo, where he successfully lobbied African leaders to take a stance against the ill treatment of Africans in

7. Ronald W. Walters, *Pan Africanism in the African Diaspora: An Analysis of Modern Afrocentric Political Movements* (Detroit: Wayne State University Press, 1997), 55, 56.

8. Walters, *Pan Africanism*, 57; George Klay Kieh, Jr., "Malcolm X and Pan-Africanism," *The Western Journal of Black Studies* 19, no. 4 (1995): 298.

9. Malcolm X, *Malcolm X Speaks: Selected Speeches and Statements*, ed. George Breitman (New York: Grove, 1965), 60.

10. Federal Bureau of Investigation, "Malcolm K. Little," report, New York, January 20, 1965, file no. 100-399321, 5–6.

America. During this second trip abroad, Malcolm also met privately with several African heads of state, including Gamal Abdel Nasser of Egypt, Julius K. Nyerere of Tanzania, Nnaomi Azikiwe of Nigeria, Kwame Nkrumah of Ghana, Sekou Toure of Guinea, Jomo Kenyatta of Kenya, and Milton Obote of Uganda. Many of the leaders at the Conference privately agreed with Malcolm's description of the human-rights abuses which African Americans faced in the United States, and he had hoped to receive tangible support of his intention to bring the U.S. government before the United Nations for human-rights violations. Unfortunately, the Conference passed a resolution praising the United States for its humanitarian efforts, as evidenced by the passage of the Civil Rights Act of 1964, and mildly chided the nation for racial discrimination.[11]

On November 24, 1964, Malcolm X returned to New York from his second trip abroad. MMI and OAAU security officials comprised a majority of the throng that awaited him. Several African ambassadors to the United States were also on hand to receive him. After talking with friends and family, he held a brief press conference during which he spoke of the receptiveness by African countries for the issues affecting U.S. Africans and quoted statements by African leaders that they would help bring the U.S. government before the UN for human-rights violations. He also publicly denounced Moise Tshombe and expressed his belief that the recent death of twelve Americans in the Congo was a result of American aggression and interference in the affairs of the Congolese people.[12]

For various reasons, the FBI significantly increased its surveillance and intimidation of Malcolm X during and after his second trip to Africa. The FBI learned of a letter that Malcolm had allegedly written to an unnamed African delegate at the OAU Conference in Egypt, which stated that, if requested to do so, he would rally 10,000 U.S. African soldiers from Harlem in support of the Congolese nationalists against the regime of Moise Tshombe, which was backed by neocolonial powers. However, the agency could not verify whether Malcolm had suggested plans of a recruitment drive to deploy U.S. Africans in Harlem to the Congo. Nonetheless, at a meeting of the OAAU on November 29, Malcolm openly speculated on what would happen if Harlem sent U.S. African mercenaries to combat the white mercenaries in the Congo. Under the Johnson administration, the U.S. government had invested a significant amount of money and time training mercenaries and providing resources to Moise Tshombe. A memorandum concerning Malcolm's speculation was sent by the FBI to the Central Intelligence Agency (CIA) and the intelligence-gathering communities in the U.S. Army, Navy, and Air Force.[13]

Between 1960 and 1961, the United Nations provided Tshombe's illegally established separatist government with economic, diplomatic, and military support. This aid led directly to the assassination of the Congo's first constitutionally elected Prime Minister, Patrice Lumumba, and the temporary Belgian occupation of this African nation.[14] Any

11. Malcolm X, *The Autobiography of Malcolm X*, 370; Malcolm X, *Malcolm X Speaks*, 72; Federal Bureau of Investigation, "Organization of Afro-American Unity," report, New York, November 12, 1964, file no. 100-399321, 1–3.

12. Federal Bureau of Investigation, "Malcolm K. Little," report, New York, November 25, 1964, file no. 100-399321-183, 2–3.

13. Federal Bureau of Investigation, "Malcolm K. Little," report, New York, January 20, 1965, file no. 100-399321, 8; Malcolm X, *Malcolm X Speaks*, 88. It is interesting to note that during the last few months of his life, Malcolm X offered similar support to Fannie Lou Hammer of the Mississippi Freedom Democratic Party and to Dr. Martin L. King, Jr., of the Southern Christian Leadership Conference.

14. Ludo De Witte, *The Assassination of Lumumba*, trans. Ann Wright and Renee Fenby (London: Verso, 2001), 64–66, 100–103.

attempt to organize Africans outside Africa in armed struggle for Congolese self-determination would have disastrous consequences for U.S. and European (especially Belgian) objectives in Africa. Malcolm X clearly presented a problem for the neocolonial
ambitions of several Western powers. All these events caught the attention of U.S. government officials, who were increasingly concerned over Malcolm's commitment to cor-
recting the human-rights violations of African peoples and the reciprocal nature of his
Pan-African politics.

On December 2, 1964, a memorandum from FBI Director J. Edgar Hoover instructed officials in the New York City field office to follow all of Malcolm X's public activities and private correspondence. Hoover was blunt about what he needed:

> With the return of Malcolm X Little from his African trip, the possibility exists
> that additional coverage of his activities is desirable particularly since he in-
> tends to have the Negro question brought before the United Nations (UN)....
> This intensified coverage may take the form of spot check surveillance, addi-
> tional live informant coverage, and any other sources which will provide cover-
> age of his activities on a daily basis.[15]

Hoover left nothing to chance and addressed every angle that Malcolm might use:

> It is noted that Alex Quaison-Sackey, Ghanian Ambassador to the UN, has
> been elected President of the UN. Information has previously been received in-
> dicating that Little and Quaison-Sackey were on friendly terms and although
> this has not actually been verified, the possibility does exist that Little may at-
> tempt to utilize Quaison-Sackey to bring the Negro question in the United
> States before the UN. This matter should be followed closely.[16]

In fact, Quaison-Sackey arranged for Malcolm X to receive an office with the other
provisional governments in the UN. He also supported the Ethiopian petition against
South Africa. Hoover suspected that Malcolm would attempt to have his petition read
before the UN at the opening session of the General Assembly. At an OAAU meeting,
Malcolm informed an audience of over 300 people that the OAAU and MMI would
hold a protest demonstration at the United Nations on December 8, 1964, demanding
that the UN address the human-rights violations of Africans in the United States. He received encouragement for the planned demonstration from Cuban Minister of Industry
Ernesto (Che) Guevara. Malcolm X presented, therefore, a terrifying threat to U.S. authorities at the close of the year.[17]

During the remaining few weeks of his life, Malcolm X strengthened his effort to
bring international attention to the worsening predicament of U.S. Africans. In February 1965, he traveled to London at the invitation of the Council of African Organizations—a body composed of African organizations throughout Europe. He noted the
apprehension among British authorities that his presence would unite the African and

---

15. Director, Federal Bureau of Investigation, Washington, D.C., to SAC, New York, NY, "Muslim Mosque, Incorporated," memorandum, Washington, D.C., December 2, 1964, file no. 100-
399321, 1.

16. Director, FBI, Washington, D.C., to SAC, New York, NY, "Muslim Mosque, Incorporated," 1.

17. Karl Evanzz, *The Messenger: The Rise and Fall of Elijah Muhammad* (New York: Vintage,
1999), 293, 315–316; Federal Bureau of Investigation, "Organization of Afro-American Unity," report, Washington, D.C., December 2, 1964, file no. 100-399321, 1–2; Malcolm X, *Malcolm X
Speaks*, 102.

West Indian communities throughout England. The local authorities in London successfully blocked Malcolm from speaking to the group.[18]

Nevertheless, Malcolm X had received an invitation to speak to the U.S. African and resident African communities in France on the subject of human rights in the United States. A number of the French people and the French government attempted to keep Malcolm from meeting with the groups. French trade unions tried to prevent the two African communities from obtaining a venue for the meeting. When their attempt failed, the French government refused Malcolm X entry into the country and contact with the U.S. embassy in Paris.[19]

Conclusion

Before returning to New York from his second trip abroad in November 1964, Malcolm X had organized a branch of the OAAU among the U.S. African population in France. In fact, he had outlined a strategy for developing the African struggle for human rights in this country. Through the creation of OAAU pressure groups in different countries, U.S. Africans could challenge the international dimensions of America's human-rights violations with an international solution.

Malcolm X returned from London on February 13, 1965. The next day, after his home was bombed, he spoke at a rally in Detroit for the Afro-American Broadcast Company. In his speech, he described how other Africans were confronting what he called an "international power structure":

> There would be many refugees in Ghana from South Africa.... Some were being trained in how to be soldiers but others were involved as a pressure group or lobby group to let the people of Ghana never forget what happened to the brothers in South Africa.[20]

He also suggested that Africans in Europe and America were in prime strategic positions to assist the liberation struggles of Africans elsewhere in the world:

> Just as the external forces pose a grave threat, they can now see that the internal forces pose an even greater threat. But the internal forces pose an even greater threat only when they have properly analyzed the situation and know what the stakes really are....
>
> We thought that the first thing to do was to unite our people, not only internally, but with our brothers and sisters abroad. It was for that purpose that I spent five months in the Middle East and Africa during the summer.[21]

In little more than a year after Malcolm X parted ways with the Nation of Islam, he distinguished himself as the leading proponent for international recognition of the human rights of U.S. Africans. The right to life and the preservation of life (self-de-

---

18. Malcolm X, *Malcolm X: The Last Speeches*, ed. Bruce Perry (New York: Pathfinder, 1989), 113.

19. Malcolm X, *Malcolm X: The Last Speeches*, 113.

20. Malcolm X, *Malcolm X Speaks*, 159.

21. Malcolm X, *Malcolm X Speaks*, 161.

fense) were fundamental aspects of his logic in this arena. He advanced a model of Pan-African thought based on the unifying elements of African culture and the shared interests of African peoples. At all times, his actions and words reminded U.S. Africans—and civilization as whole—of mankind's inherent duty to fight for the perpetuation of African humanity. Fortunately, Malcolm also saw the direction that the upcoming generation of U.S. Africans seeking to resolve human-rights abuses would have to consider in the future. On December 20, 1964, at a meeting at the Audubon Ballroom in Harlem, he stated:

> Today, power is international, real power is international; today, real power is not local. The only kind of power that can help you and me is international power, not local power.... If you think you've got some power, and it isn't in some way tied into that international thing, brother, don't get too far out on a limb.[22]

---

22. Malcolm X, *Malcolm X Speaks*, 129.

17

Malcolm X in the Company of Thinkers

Maghan Keita

Introduction: Intellectualizing
Malcolm X/Malcolm X as "Intellectual"

" ... shotgun in hand ..." — W. E. B. Du Bois

" ... by any means necessary." — Malcolm X

He "stood guard, shotgun in hand."[1] The quotation creates quite an image: a man at his home — armed and ready to protect it at all costs. However, this man is not Malcolm X. It is William Edward Burghardt Du Bois, sixty years earlier. And the image he projects, "shotgun in hand, at his porch," is a preview of the iconographic Malcolm X, carbine in hand, peering below a window shade over the motto "By Any Means Necessary."

He "carried a gun ... and his guards were armed." Again, this man is not Malcolm X but, surprisingly, Martin Luther King, Jr.[2]

From the beginning of my attempts to conceptualize this essay, I knew I had to link Malcolm X not simply to some generalized notion of the intellect but to the intellectual medium of the time, space, and struggle of African Americans — W. E. B. Du Bois. At first blush, this is not an easy task. Nowhere do the two refer to each other;[3] and Mal-

---

1. Herbert Aptheker, ed., *The Correspondence of W. E .B. Du Bois, Volume I: Selections 1877–1934* (Amherst: University of Massachusetts Press, 1973), 123.

2. Benjamin Y. Love, "Out of King's Shadow: 40 Years after the March, the Strategist Gets His Due," *Philadelphia Inquirer*, 28 August 2003.

3. Malcolm does tell us much about Du Bois and his contemporaries in relation to his own intellectual contextualization. Indeed, he deliberately provides a very certain and specific intellectual contextualization. Interestingly enough, he *commences* with Du Bois:

    Souls of Black Folk by W. E. B. Du Bois gave me a glimpse into black people's history before they came to this country. Carter G. Woodson's *Negro History* opened my eyes about black empires before the black slave was brought to the United States, and the early Negro struggles for freedom.

    Malcolm X, with Alex Haley, *The Autobiography of Malcolm X* (1964; repr., New York: The Ballantine Publishing Group, 1999), 178.

colm's probable and tangential disregard of Du Bois can be read exponentially—ranging from his notion of the man as an "integrationist" and a "mouthpiece" for the NAACP to his unconscious affinity for Marcus Garvey by way of his father. Still, both Du Bois and Malcolm are standing guard.

In the minds of many, Malcolm X and Martin Luther King, Jr., are the juxtapositional levers of the modern civil rights movement—a movement in which King was characterized as the transcendent intellectual and spiritual figure. He, too, eschewed Du Bois, though, like Malcolm X, he could not escape the power of Du Bois's intellect.

The phrase "stood guard, shotgun in hand" seems so uncharacteristic of Du Bois. And King as a pistol packer is oxymoronic—nearly in the same way that most scholars find the notion of Malcolm as an intellectual out of character. Indeed, Malcolm has been rendered as the quintessential Black "action figure." The construction and deconstruction of Malcolm X as an icon—through an image myopically viewed and through a phrase taken out of context—has looped again and again to invent and reinforce a simplified idea and image of the man. Malcolm's refusal to disavow violence and to relinquish his right and that of his people to self-defense has been rendered as kinetic rather than cerebral. Indeed, it has been somewhat difficult to find critical analyses that link Malcolm's actions to *thought*. Consequently, the development of Malcolm's formidable intellect and its devastating force appear on a background as flat as the posters that make him an icon.

Du Bois anticipated Malcolm, and under these circumstances, within this context, he would even have celebrated him. Malcolm's conscious and deliberate ambition to craft and broaden his intellect would have excited Du Bois. As early as 1903, Du Bois acknowledged in *Souls of Black Folk* that most Black people would value such an ambition. In fact, the conscious and deliberate embrace of intellect and education became one of the most critically defining features of radical, Black identity for Du Bois, because, as Malcolm would find out in Mr. Ostrowski's eighth grade class,[4]

> above all, we daily hear that an education that encourages aspiration, that sets the loftiest of ideals and seeks an end culture and character rather than breadwinning is the privilege of white men and the danger and delusion of black.[5]

Here, Du Bois's words and Malcolm's image identify what make this kind of work so gratifying for me: it is the necessity of revisiting Du Bois and Malcolm, their contemporaries, and all those who precede them (and us) and then rereading them and rethinking of them in light of various assumptions—not simply the assumptions of my peers but those that I have carried with me for many years. The questions posed by Malcolm's life—the life of his mind—are huge in an age where the intellect dominates. My own need to place Malcolm in the company of thinkers and give him a broader intellectual context—in order to add greater weight and gravity to what is already conceived of as a grave mien—is tied to these questions. I want to see the vast intellectual foundation that supported Malcolm and the extensive *Black* intellectual community that surrounded and, ostensibly, nurtured him. This is one reason why I begin with Du Bois.

I also begin with Du Bois because, as I have written elsewhere, we do not thoroughly read those we have lionized. On that account, I posit that Du Bois and Malcolm merit

4. Malcolm X, with Alex Haley, *The Autobiography of Malcolm X* (New York: Grove Press, 1966), 36.
5. William Edward Burghardt Du Bois, *The Souls of Black Folk*, in *W. E. B. Du Bois: Writings*, ed. Nathan Huggins (New York: The Library of America, 1986), 428.

serious, critical rereadings which both acknowledge and analyze the "foundation" and "walls" of the intellectual community that spawned them—serious, critical rereadings that look as much at consonance as they do at dissonance and, in the case of Malcolm X, that explicitly acknowledge and celebrate his intellectuality and inevitably lead us to the conclusion that there is no action without thought and, *seriously*, no revolutionary action without calculation.

Let me try to refine this contextualization. In large part, the most intellectual of reflections on Malcolm X are guided by questions of popular culture. They are rooted in the physical and the kinetic. As early as Kenneth Clark's 1963 interview with Malcolm X for public television, it is Malcolm's visceral presence that Clark finds so arresting and overwhelming.

> He and his friends were immaculately dressed with no outward signs of their belonging to a separate sect or ministry.... [He was a] tall, handsome man.... *clearly a dominant personality.*

The conscious conveyance of power seems a juxtaposition to the intellect that constructs and disciplines it.[6] This is tied to a rhetorical acumen that, if left unanalyzed, conventionally leads to the conclusion that actions—the kinetics of Malcolm's speech *and* writings (especially, the vitriol of his days as a minister with the Nation of Islam)—inevitably provoke *physical* violence. Such a conclusion is the conventional analysis that conveniently allowed Henry Morganthau III to argue that Malcolm X was the "most eloquent ... apostle for *black* racism."[7] Yet, in the same set of interviews, Clark found in Martin Luther King, Jr., "the *paradox* of the *scholar* and the effective man of *social action*."[8] Morganthau is silent here, and in that silence we might read popular assent.

Contextualizing Malcolm and his racialized and racist thinking, its transcendence, and his remarkable intellectual evolution is a task historically grounded. In the latter half of the nineteenth century, the "deviltry" of white folk and their un-Christian-like nature was the stuff of both radical and conservative Black intellectual circles. In this light, Du Bois begins one of his sharpest attacks:

> What on earth is *whiteness* that one should so desire it? ... [W]e ... have been most struck ... by the utter failure of *white* religion.... [W]*hite* Christianity is a miserable failure.[9]

Du Bois, like Malcolm, *before* Malcolm, asked one of the most profound, ethical, moral, and philosophical questions of the age. The inquiry like Malcolm's in many ways, was intensified by the circumstances under which it was made: the dawning of a new media domination that would seize on sensationalism—that, for example, would deem as sensational any criticism by a Black person of whiteness and "white" civilization. As Malcolm concluded many years later, but in a much more graphic variant, Du Bois had already concluded in 1920: the possibility of white folk having souls was questionable. In a vein quite similar, Martin Luther King, Jr., implied in 1963 that most white folk were "bankrupt."

While this essay is not about William Edward Burghardt Du Bois, the shadow of Du Bois does define the intellectual context, even though both Malcolm and King sought

6. Kenneth B. Clark, *The Negro Protest: James Baldwin, Malcolm X, Martin Luther King Talk With Kenneth B. Clark* (Boston: Beacon Press, 1963), 17 (my italics).

7. Henry Morganthau III, "A Note About the Interviews," in Clark, *The Negro Protest*, 55.

8. Clark, 35 (my italics).

9. W. E. B. Du Bois, "The Souls of White Folk," in *W. E. B. Du Bois: Writings*, ed. Nathan Huggins (New York: The Library of America, 1986), 924–927 (my italics).

to avoid him. In fact, it might be argued that, politically, King was "afraid" of Du Bois, or at least of association with him, in the highly charged, Cold War years of the modern civil rights era. Malcolm, on the other hand, seemed to display a certain disregard of Du Bois. Yet both Malcolm and King were inextricably tied to Du Bois in their attempts to construct their people as morally plausible actors and in their attempts to make their case through the prodigious powers of the mind—his, theirs, and that of their race.

Malcolm's and King's minds are "moral constructions." King, in the end, addressed a new, Black Christianity, in which the "turned cheek" became the weapon of social disruption—the disruption of the status quo and of the dominant and dominating order. Malcolm began with a focus on moral deportment as the chief characterization of a new racial construction. Both of these conceptualizations are contextualized by what I articulate as the long intellectual history of Du Bois's quest to offer a "moral construction of race."

Contextualization—particularly this type of it—complicates the image and the intellectuality of Malcolm X. If the series of juxtapositions that we begin with are followed from Du Bois through Martin Luther King, Jr., then it might be argued that Malcolm's transformation was just as transcendent as King's and that it was a constant in maintaining and forwarding Du Bois's Pan-Africanism. Yet here, in terms of intellectualizing Malcolm *and* in recognizing his intellectuality, the Clark interviews become instructive. Clark introduces us to Martin Luther King, Jr., by discussing King's ability to integrate the seemingly *un-integratable*: intellect and action. King represents the juxtaposition of expectation that we might have for Malcolm. Clark, by his own admission, expects Malcolm to be a one-dimensional man of action—and here, we might read "action" as "violence." However, critical, purposeful, and in-depth reading complicates any such juxtaposition and comparison. For example, both King and his guard were told that they must put down their pistols if they were to develop a credible and powerful movement. On the other hand, in Malcolm we see violence, action, *and* intellectuality.

Clark's observation of King makes Malcolm just as much a paradox in this regard. The two of them have been constructed as such. Usually, Malcolm has been rendered for us in rather narrow and demagogic treatments. Nell Painter assesses Spike Lee's *Malcolm X* as one of the latest in a fairly long line of such renderings. This is essentially where Dyson begins as well. It is Malcolm's reduction to the demagogic—to the action hero—that must be called into question; a reduction of human intellect to a "black thing" we refuse to understand; a phenomenon we appear, for the most part, too intellectually lazy to investigate.[10] Our lack of intellectual capacity, in this case, is preconfigured by a false yet earnest dichotomy between thought and action or, as Du Bois might have put it, by another "two-ness," wholly false—the separation of mind and body.

---

10. Nell Irvin Painter, "Malcolm X across the Genres," *American Historical Review* 98, no. 2 (April 1993): 433. Michael Eric Dyson, *Making Malcolm: The Myth and Meaning of Malcolm X* (New York: Replica Books, 2000), xi. Interestingly, Painter finds in Malcolm an anti-intellectualism that becomes, for her, key to charting his intellectual growth. Since Malcolm was an *American*, his anti-intellectualism has become the stuff of national legend and identity. Without attempting to excuse Malcolm and while acknowledging that this characteristic was present—indeed, it helps make the case here—Malcolm's "anti-intellectualism"—his criticism of the Black, bourgeois intelligentsia—was more a criticism of the bourgeois interests that directed their intellectual activity than the intellectuality itself. Painter, "Malcolm X," 437–438.

Dyson has encapsulated the project in this way:

> Malcolm ... has received nothing like the intellectual attention devoted to Mar-
> tin Luther King, Jr.... [We are treated to] competing waves of uncritical cele-
> bration and vicious criticism—which settle easily into myth and caricature.[11]

If King is treated in such a manner, why not Malcolm? Here, Painter addresses the
politics of representation. She begins with the "racialized" subject and the "metonymic
stylization" that the "marketplace" dictates. For her, in all cases—Malcolm's being the
case in point—the transformation of the "individual into a racial symbol alters the
subject's life."[12] The metonymic alteration is witness to Malcolm's iconographic power.
It also means that Malcolm, the individual, will be distilled and flattened—that is, rendered more malleable—for the groups competing for his services. In many ways, some
quite nuanced, what we are witnessing resides in Amiri Baraka's [Leroi Jones's] observation of the need to have Malcolm "embrace a whole public consciousness."[13]

This politics of representation also brings to mind Sidney LeMelle's work. Malcolm's
power is recognized in the need—the necessity—of various groups to co-opt him. From
George Breitman's appropriation of Malcolm to make American Marxism/Socialism more
palatable to Black audiences and indeed give it broader credence and rationality to Tony
Thomas's use of Malcolm as the rationalizing mechanism for melding Black Nationalism
and Marxism, Malcolm and his myth find utility.[14] Perry's psychosexual treatment of Malcolm and its musings on a latent homosexuality are ironic bedfellows to the Lee/Gates attempt to create a *new* Malcolm—and, not incidentally, a *new* Nation of Islam—for a
new Black middle class.[15] This is the same middle class and its intelligentsia and their children that Painter argues Malcolm found so distasteful in his early moments in Africa.

Epps has admitted to manipulating Malcolm's texts,[16] and Dyson suspects that Haley
may have done his own "massaging" in the *Autobiography*. Horne echoes Painter's observations on the power of the marketplace. He sees this as the "commodification" of
Malcolm's image—one that can be embraced even by conservatives. In fact, Charles
Alva Hoyt recognizes—with great irony—Malcolm as a man for all causes.[17] Here,

---

11. Dyson, *Making Malcolm*, 22–23.

12. Painter, "Malcolm X," 432. Concerning the mythologies that surround both Malcolm X and
Martin Luther King, Jr., Gerald Horne notes that both neglect highly relevant and persuasive evidence because it does not necessarily comport with the contemporary lessons that one is to draw
from these mythologies. Gerald Horne, "Myth and the Making of 'Malcolm X,'" *The American Historical Review* 98, no. 2 (April 1993): 441.

13. Amiri Baraka [Leroi Jones], cited in "The Autobiography of Malcolm X: A Mythic Paradigm," *Journal Of Black Studies* 5, no. 1 (September 1974): 24.

14. Tony Thomas, "Malcolm X: His Strategy for Black Liberation," *International Socialist Review*
32, no. 5 (May 1971): 28–32. To Thomas's Marxist-Socialist analysis must be added the numerous
works of George Breitman.

15. Spike Lee and Henry Louis Gates, "Generation X," *Transition* 0, no. 56 (1992): 178–183.

16. Raymond Rodgers and Jimmie N. Rodgers, "The Evolution of the Attitude of Malcolm X toward Whites," *Phylon* 44, no. 2 (1983): 110.

17. Horne, "Myth and the Making of 'Malcolm X,'" 449. Charles Alva Hoyt, "The Five Faces of
Malcolm X," *Negro American Literature Forum* 4, no. 4 (Winter 1970). Hoyt goes on to say—in the
same way that Horne rearticulates—that Malcolm has been embraced by persons of every political
stripe—from the Black Panthers to "white racists" and "liberal white meliorists who focus on his
last, little-known, little-heeded, renunciation of racism." Hoyt, "Five Faces," 107. Here, both Hoyt
and Horne are supported—unintentionally so, in the light of history—by Joyce Nower's "Cleaver's
Vision of America and the New White Radical: A Legacy of Malcolm X," *Negro American Literary
Forum* 4, no. 1 (March 1970). Again, Nower underlines the contextual parameters outlined here:
"[B]lack vision is not a contemporary creation, however, thought up by Malcolm X, Stokely

Malcolm as the interpretive lens is interpreted, and new meaning is derived from Malcolm's own observation of his youth in Michigan: "*I was thoroughly integrated.*"

Many different public groups and their modes of consciousness have found the intellectual a bit tedious. Malcolm has been captured and interpreted by a disparate spectrum of interests, an overwhelming number of which are quite content to have him as their action hero. After all, "if Malcolm is to work as a racial symbol, it is best not to look at him too closely."[18] A closer look and contextualization might force us to deal with his intellectuality. In fact, any articulation of Malcolm must be read in context and in conjunction with the history or histories that created him.

In this regard, Gerald Horne's piece becomes a contextual lever. Horne, Painter, and Dyson have spoken to the myths of Malcolm. Horne informs us:

> [I]n common ordinary usage, to engage in myth making suggests falsification, factual inaccuracies, and the like. However, from another vantage point, *myths are not necessarily lies, they are explications.... They help to explain the world.*[19]

Yet Horne also cautions us to recognize competing mythologies and the problems inherent in the exchange of one myth for another—particularly to the degree that one might "neglect highly relevant and persuasive evidence because it does not necessarily comport with the contemporary lessons that one is to draw from these myths." The real importance of Horne's criticism relates to Malcolm's historical position as an "integral part of the scaffolding that supports a contemporary African American identity ... [and the interrogation of] circumstance [that] presents both a situation ripe for myth making and an indictment of how history is taught in this nation" in both formal and popular venues.[20] So the question that might be posed relates to how Malcolm might be realized in fuller, more human, and more intellectual dynamics: how he might be perceived as something more than an "action hero."

"Action Hero": Placing Malcolm in Intellectual Context

"It is as if W. E. B. Du Bois, Paul Robeson, Ben Davis, Claudia Jones and William Patterson did not exist."[21]

Not a few have taken exception to Carol Ohmann's Enlightenment contextualization of Malcolm and her comparison of Malcolm to Benjamin Franklin.[22] Such contextualization and comparison work when there is a critical reading of conventional Enlightenment thinkers and constructs and of the ways in which the energies of their minds gen-

Carmichael, Huey P. Newton, or Eldridge Cleaver.... [There is] a historical context." Nower, "Cleaver's Vision," 13.
  18. Painter, "Malcolm X," 433.
  19. Horne, "Myth and the Making of 'Malcolm X,'", 440 (my italics).
  20. Ibid., 441; 448.
  21. Ibid., 441.
  22. Carol Ohmann, "*The Autobiography of Malcolm X*: A Revolutionary Use of the Franklin Tradition," pt. 1, *American Quarterly* 22, no. 2 (Summer 1970): 131–149.

erated action. This contextualization and comparison also work if there is solid conceptual analysis.

How may Malcolm be understood first as Lockean and then anti- or post-Lockean? That reading can only come about through an understanding of Locke's conceptualization of *property*, particularly the property of self, and through Malcolm's fundamental, almost essentialized, understanding of "stealing" property—the property of self.[23] Such a reading gains full intellectual relief through a history of slave insurrections, the lives of Maroons and their descendants in the West Indies and Guiana in the seventeenth and eighteenth centuries, and the creation of communities of resistance by peoples of African descent in conjunction with others who were oppressed throughout the Enlightenment. These intellectual and physical acts must also be realized within the context of their impact on the Enlightenment and its thinkers. Consequently, Malcolm's historical power and intellectual inheritance are better comprehended.

Malcolm's Enlightenment heritage was concisely characterized between 1835 and 1840 when Alexis de Tocqueville wrote:

> If ever America undergoes great revolutions, they will be brought about by the presence of the black race on the soil of the United States; that is to say, they will owe their origin, not to the equality, but to the inequality of condition.[24]

According to Tocqueville, two factors presaged the Malcolms of this world. They were the intellectual and the physical: the ability first to conceptualize and then to act. It is the ability of Blacks first to discern ethical and moral issues of justice and equality and then to act on them that will revolutionize America. Thus, for Tocqueville, blacks become "representational." Such was Du Bois's premise in 1935—one that would be contested in relation to the abilities of Blacks, as slaves, first to conceptualize and then to organize around their plight.[25]

Malcolm as inheritor of the Enlightenment might be even more palatable if it were given broader yet more specific contextualization. For Malcolm, a critical, historical, and intellectual genealogy, beginning with the Enlightenment, might look as follows: Phyllis Wheatley, Olaudah Equiano, Benjamin Banneker, and David Walker. They, too,

---

23. Here, the conceptualization is not to be confused with Malcolm's street life. The intellectual endeavor associated with a life of crime, petty or not, is hardly the metaphor for this type of analysis. Central to it is this "stealing"—this reappropriation—of the Black self that moved beyond the bounds of the conventional and convenient notions of who and what Black people were. Again, in contextualizing Malcolm, we must emphasize that he was not the first in this effort, nor was he alone in it. What poises him critically is our assertion that he emphatically told Black people to think differently of themselves and that his voice, through circumstance, was magnified. The assertion that "Black is beautiful" had been articulated for decades, if not longer. Malcolm's voice gave it fuller resonance. That resonance shattered convention.

24. Alexis de Tocqueville, *Democracy in America*, ed. J. P. Mayer, trans. George Lawrence (New York: Harper Perennial, 1988), 639.

25. W. E. B. Du Bois, *Black Reconstruction in America, 1860–1880* (New York: Atheneum, 1969). Ironically, this premise was Melville Herskovits's criticism of *Black Reconstruction* in his *Myth of the Negro Past* (Boston: Beacon Press, 1958). He found Du Bois's conclusion incredible: the idea that a people, whose entire personal and collective lives were circumscribed by the physical (i.e., slave labor) could be given to intellectualizing and then acting on this condition. See Maghan Keita, *Race and the Writing of History: Riddling the Sphinx* (Oxford: Oxford University Press, 2000).

found the "souls of white folk" questionable and associated with deviltry: Christianity, as whites practiced it, was hypocritical. But Christianity, as Blacks practiced it, contained an expectant and anticipatory retribution tied to the act of liberation. Nat Turner knew that "God helped those who helped themselves." How could Malcolm or Du Bois or even King escape such a historical context and pedigree? Like the intellectual foundation of all Black people historically, Malcolm's was laid before him. He, like many of them, including Du Bois, and even King, was the product of a fiery tradition that challenged white supremacy, its morality, and its underpinnings.[26] Malcolm's racialism is historicized: Equiano calls whites "devils";[27] Du Bois questions whether they have souls. This tradition was one which, at many points, advocated separation from a morally diseased white majority. Malcolm echoes a historically grounded analysis in the Clark interview when he calls for "moral separation."[28] In itself, the rhetorical choice merits analysis in both its contemporary and historical contexts. These contexts occur within the broader context of a vibrant and extended Black intellectual life. A path is prepared.

The path prepared allowed Malcolm to further actualize and vocalize Du Bois's analytical progression from being "a problem" to identifying the problem: white folk and their "morality"—their souls. In a Harvard address in December 1964, Malcolm articulated a thesis that could readily be attributed to a 1920 Du Bois essay: whites are the source of the myriad evils Blacks have endured.[29] There is nothing new here, other than that Malcolm's address was articulated in a forum that obligated whites to hear it. The ironies of the articulation, the forum, and its hearing were that most Americans— Black as well as White—had missed the intellectual context *and* contextualization of Malcolm's address. It, along with other acts, had announced that Black folk were not all that white America, or whites in general, assumed them to be.

Even before the contextualization that Gerald Horne provides at the opening of this section, Malcolm's intellectual pedigree must be extended. What in Malcolm's demands resonates with Frederick Douglass's "The Claims of the Negro Ethnologically Considered"[30]? What linkages might be made to the observations and the calls for separation in the works of Blyden and Delany? Had Tubman and Truth left their marks? If so, many critics would claim, Tubman and Truth had not left their marks in the sense of recognizing the power inherent in Black women and their abilities to exercise it—even though, one *might* read their influence, at a stretch, in Malcolm's comments on his mother and sister and on their strengths in shaping his life. They might also be witnessed, obliquely so, in reference to his wife. In any case, I would maintain, these are contextualizations that were inescapable, even if they were not consciously recognized.

---

26. This point is illustrated anecdotally by Peter Goldman. Goldman links Malcolm and King through Elijah Muhammad. Goldman recounts an informant's recollection of a "cordial" meeting between King and the Honorable Elijah Muhammad. Their exchange constituted a "tie that binds." Peter Goldman, *The Death and Life of Malcolm X* (Urbana and Chicago: University of Illinois Press, 1979), 13.

27. Olaudah Equiano, *Narrative of the Life of Olaudah Equiano*, in *The Norton Anthology of African American Literature*, ed. Henry Louis Gates, Jr., and Nellie McKay, 206–207 (New York: W. W. Norton, 2004).

28. Clark, *The Negro Protest*, 28.

29. Rodgers and Rodgers, "The Evolution of the Attitude of Malcolm X toward Whites," 112.

30. Frederick Douglass, "The Claims of the Negro Ethnologically Considered," in *Negro Social and Political Thought, 1850–1920*, ed. Howard Brotz, 227–235 (New York: Basic Books, 1966).

By the turn of the century, before the Nation of Islam had been envisioned and be-fore Fard had made his revelation, African American clerics had made a critical as-sault on whiteness and white religiosity. The hierarchy of the African Methodist Epis-copal Church began the intellectual assault on both the racial and theological planes. It should not be lost on us that Du Bois had begun his intellectual career in the midst of all this when he took up his position at the AME Wilberforce College. The bishops' positions could not have been lost on him, either. And as the bishops' messages from the pulpits found their ways into major denominational publications, the bishops certainly gained the kind of currency that we now understand was characteristic of the word-of-mouth intellectuality that exemplified the African American community—a public intellectuality into which Malcolm's soapbox stands could be readily plugged.

The bishops had also tapped the source that would supply a fundamental element to Garvey's appeal. This had to be intimately realized in Malcolm's household and in the personal mythology that he created for himself and that has been created for him. By extension, as Painter has pointed out, the thoroughly American and then the African American appeal of the Nation of Islam and, of course, Malcolm's own appeal were rooted in a "combination of two *intellectual traditions*: ... [the] holiness religion of the black working class ... and the masculinist tradition of black nationalism."[31] Again, pains must be taken to recognize Painter's emphasis of the word *intellectual*.

These are the elements that lead us to the historically intimate contextualization that Horne wishes to make. The immediate shoulders upon which Malcolm stands—those of Du Bois, Robeson, Davis, Jones, Patterson, and others—crystallize and be-come concrete. Centering on 1948, Horne consolidates our contextualization. At the same moment that Malcolm sought admission into the Nation of Islam, "W. E. B. Du Bois had just been ousted from the leadership of the NAACP because of his re-fusal to go along with accommodation to the gathering Cold War consensus." Horne continues:

> [L]ess than a decade earlier, disputed heirs of the Enlightenment—black Marxists and radicals—were attracting adherents with a narrative [and analy-sis] that did not stint on identification with Africa but did not embrace anti-white rhetoric either.[32]

If Horne has provided the contextual lever for recognizing the intellectual Malcolm, it is Du Bois who provides the overall *conceptual* framework for its realization.

Conceptually, we are treated to Du Bois's continual forays into the construction of race and its moral and ethical parameters. What emerges from one set of analyses—my own—is a Du Boisian "*moral construction of race*," among whose central tenets are African American women and men who are dedicated to education and intellectual activ-ity, as well as their physical expression: action dedicated to the "uplift of the race." While some may find comfort in interpreting this dedication to schooling and thinking as an ab-straction, the most forceful adherents of such a racial construction—Du Bois and Mal-colm included—recognized knowledge as power, and its intelligent application as power manifest.

---

31. Painter, "Malcolm X," 436, (my italics).
32. Horne, "Myth and the Making of 'Malcolm X,'" 442.

The Moral Construction of an Intellectual Life and a Race

" ... you've got to be realistic about being a nigger."[33]

" ... cerebrating ..."[34]

"He emerged as the cold, efficient builder of a movement. His first purchases were eyeglasses, a watch, and a briefcase, apt symbols of the rigidly patterned life he would lead."[35]

In line with Du Bois's construction of African American women and men is the examination of Malcolm's intellectual life. It is, by all accounts, a life of deliberateness: discipline, preparation, and anticipation. It is a conscious and conscientious intellectual life in its purpose. It is also an intellectual life characterized by the active noun *growth*. Malcolm's 1963 interview with Kenneth Clark is contextualized by Malcolm's use of terms that explicitly speak to his intellectual growth and evolution. The conscious nature of Malcolm's engagement with his own intellectual refinement draws Clark's awestruck commentary: "[P]henomenal!"[36] Clark acknowledges that Malcolm is engaged in the deliberate act of "constructing" a mind. And by Malcolm's own admission, it is a process that he means to replicate across Black America in his quest to "rehabilitate the thinking of our people."[37] This is the theme that resounds through every major work of Du Bois: the reclamation of the African American intellect. The "souls of black folk" might rightly be read as the "minds of black folk" as well—and "hearts" as well as "minds." And Malcolm, in this context, is a logical and credible heir. Malcolm's very deliberate construction of his own intellectual prowess is an essential in Du Bois's "moral construction of race."[38]

Malcolm becomes emblematic. His deliberateness, his example of self-education par excellence, and the conscious embrace of his intellectual self within the parameters of the construction of race present Malcolm as one of Du Bois's quintessential African American men. In Malcolm lies the conscious employment of the power of the intellect on the behalf of race. "Black *is* beautiful."

In the Clark interview, Malcolm figuratively, yet clearly, enunciates the beginning of his intellectual growth and its early shortcomings. He attributes the transformation of both his spiritual and intellectual life to the Honorable Elijah Muhammad. He tells Clark: "My own *intellectual strength* was so weak, or so lacking" prior to being "taught" by Elijah Muhammad. The propaganda of the moment needs to be acknowledged. Malcolm was the voice and the *representation* of the Nation of Islam. It was a dynamic nation, but a nation under siege. His intellect originated from his loyalty to that nation and to its founder. What also must be reiterated here is Nell Painter's observations on the *intellectual* foundations of the Nation itself.[39]

---

33. Malcolm X, *Autobiography*, 36. Hoyt, "The Five Faces of Malcolm X," 108.

34. Goldman, *The Death and Life of Malcolm X*, 13. Also cited in Robert E. Terrill, " 'Colonizing the Borderlands': Shifting Circumference in the Rhetoric of Malcolm X," *Quarterly Journal of Speech* 86, no. 1 (February 2000): 67.

35. Nancy Clasby, "The Autobiography of Malcolm X: A Mythic Paradigm," *Journal Of Black Studies* 5, no. 1 (September 1974): 23.

36. Clark, *The Negro Protest*, 18–19.

37. Ibid., 28.

38. The phrase "moral construction of race" is my own appropriation.

39. Clark, *The Negro Protest*, 21 (my italics). Cf. Painter, "Malcolm X," 27 (my italics).

These two points underlie the depth of Malcolm's intellectual life—one rooted in an intellectual community that preceded Malcolm and the Nation by at least a century and a half. He had found his intellectual self in the Nation; he recognized and championed the intellectual nature of the Nation and its emphasis on the education of its members; he regarded himself as the most visible product of its efforts; and he argued that that intellectuality was personified in its leader. Such became points of propaganda—a propaganda of the mind.

Despite Malcolm's intellectual weaknesses or shortcomings before his introduction to Elijah Muhammad, he came to the Nation fully primed intellectually. He had a mission—to "rehabilitate the thinking of our people"—and the requisite tools for that mission, which he kept constantly refining. Malcolm entered the Nation enveloped in a mode where thought—"thinking"—and the mind and intellect were central to liberation in any form. The life that Malcolm articulated maintained that even the most kinetic of exercises—those which would conventionally reduce Malcolm to the status of "action hero"—had intellectual substance.

Again to Clark, Malcolm wedded action and intellect: "*Any human being who is intelligent has the right to defend himself*".[40]

Malcolm's pronouncement in the Clark interview can be seen as an Enlightenment prescription. The intellect becomes key to the "franchise" and its exercise—a franchise that can be equated to the self. The defense of the self, Malcolm clarified, is not just a matter of civil rights but also a matter of human rights—an emerging idea for Malcolm, even in 1963. The right to self-defense is an assertion for the common good. For example, in the works of intellectuals like Rousseau, Locke, and Jefferson, such a assertion can be read. Just as important, such an assertion can also be read in the works of Wheatley, Equiano, Banneker, and Walker.[41]

Malcolm is always conscious of the power of knowledge and its refinement. The Autobiography *and that famous interaction with Mr. Ostrowski underscore Malcolm's realization of the possibilities, potentials, and immense innovative qualities of the Black mind:*

> All of us ... might have probed space, or cured cancer, or built industries ... [or might have been] a lawyer, a doctor, a scientist.[42]

Yet here, just as the Ohmann/Branham Enlightenment theses need refinement, Malcolm's own conceptual and contextual limitations—are they propagandistic on his part?—need to be acknowledged. Malcolm's vision of who and what African Americans might be—their intellectual possibility, potential, and innovation—can be seen to represent a cultural and historical disconnection on his part. The vision is purposefully bound up in Malcolm's rhetorical strategy. There *are*, for Malcolm, Black

---

40. Clark, *The Negro Protest*, 25 (my italics).

41. Of course, this is Ohmann's thesis. Branham supports it in his use of George Holyoke and in his arguments on liberal revolution to contextualize his treatment of Malcolm. Robert James Branham, "'I Was Gone On Debating': Malcolm X's Prison Debates and Public Confrontations," *Argumentation and Advocacy* 31 (Winter 1995): 117–137. Again, my refinement of this thesis is that Enlightenment intellectuality extends beyond the very limited parameters of white males of European descent, and those other participants become critical to identifying, contextualizing, and then analyzing Malcolm's own intellectual inheritance. Interestingly enough, de Tocqueville would extend the thesis, in the general sense, using the American Revolution as the illustration. De Tocqueville asserts that the real revolution—"great revolutions"—would be "brought about by the presence of the black." Tocqueville, *Democracy in America*, 639.

42. Malcolm X, *Autobiography*, 90; 183. Ohmann, *"The Autobiography of Malcolm X,"* 134.

doctors, lawyers, scientists, educators, and the like. But many of them may not con-
form to what both he and Du Bois have defined as the essential characteristics of
African American men and women. They may not have, in sufficient quantities, *consciously* embraced a moral construction of race. So this point represents Malcolm's and
their and our levels of cognizance and dissonance—a cognizance and dissonance that
Painter has articulated.[43]

For Du Bois, writing in several places, that conscious embrace was symbolized in
support of education and the intellectual enterprise. Again, the deliberateness and purposefulness of Malcolm's intellectual formation and refinement have been forcefully and
explicitly analyzed in numerous quarters. His is *the* conscious embrace.

Ironically, in a space such as prison, where contrary and popular conventions envision and, therefore, necessitate the triumphs of the physical, Malcolm reconstitutes the
paradigm of the intellect and its power. The physical space of prison—the conceptualization of *physical* survival as a corporeal, active, and *kinetic* process— underscores and
rearticulates the conscious and deliberate actions of Malcolm's intellectual development. Here, as Ohmann puts it, is the conscious and deliberate direction of "all of his
energies toward a strenuous program of *self-education*."[44] This observation must be contextualized by Malcolm's remark to Kenneth Clark universalizing the Black condition in
America: "If you're born in America with a black skin, you're born in prison."[45] For
Malcolm, escape from *this* prison—liberation—becomes the conscious embrace of education and the ongoing development of the intellect—again, the rehabilitation of the
thinking of an entire people. Thus, Malcolm articulates a collective escape from the
prison of the mind. Here again, a further contextualization for Malcolm is Woodson's
The Mis-Education of the Negro and Du Bois's essays grouped under the title, *The Education of Black People*. Malcolm's possibilities and potential are witnessed in all of
these.[46]

Consciousness and the manipulation of the prison experience became a hallmark of
Malcolm's intellectual prowess. This experience made Malcolm the paradigm of *prison
intellectuals* for African Americans—and presumably in a space, both physical and conceptual, where African Americans, by and large, thought such an experience impossible. Malcolm's intellectual epiphany in prison also globalized his and their condition.
The condition of the oppressed and the dissident can be refined and honed by a physical
incarceration that cannot contain their mental and spiritual resistances.

The Western political canon is replete with grand figures whose intellectual lives are
collectively epitomized in their prison writings. In equal proportion, the prison writings
of the Third World take on equal prominence. The prison context of Malcolm's intellectual development should be associated with what has now become cliché. We need to
think of the revolutionaries whose prison experiences articulate the refinement of their
intellectual development: Gramsci, Ho Chi Minh, even King.

In the mix, however, we are hard-pressed to find any recognition or analysis of the
intellectual activity of incarceration among African Americans—not because the intel-

---

43. Painter, "Malcolm X," 437–439. See also W. E. B. Du Bois, *Philadelphia Negro* (1899; repr.,
New York: Benjamin Blom, 1967).

44. Ohmann, "*The Autobiography of Malcolm X*," 138 (my italics).

45. Clark, *The Negro Protest*, 23.

46. Carter G. Woodson, *The Mis-Education of the Negro* (1933; repr., Washington, DC: The Associated Publishers, 1969). Herbert Aptheker, ed., *The Education of Black People: Ten Critiques
1906–1960 by W. E .B . Du Bois* (Amherst: University of Massachusetts Press, 1973).

lectual activity does not exist but because of our failure to recognize it.[47] Clearly, however, Malcolm recognized it in "Bimbi, whose knowledge and skill with words represented power." Here was "a stock of knowledge as a sort of capital ... yielding a return in prestige and power." In Bimbi and in Malcolm's "*choice*" of correctional institutions were the quests for the "objective" acquisition of power.[48]

Ohmann measures that acquisition in this way:

> [F]eats of knowledge ... his [intellectual] conversion [are] a tally of words learned ... grammar rules recaptured, correspondence courses completed, debates entered and won, and books read; books of history, economics, sociology, anthropology, anything that might shed light on the history of the black man in America and illumine his way to independent power.[49]

Somewhere within Malcolm's means of acquisition was at least one slim volume of William Edward Burghardt Du Bois.[50] Ohmann recognizes in Malcolm a "drive to learn [that] was intense, consuming and effective"—a drive that was "submerged" in—contextualized by—"the black race in America."[51]

Indeed, Malcolm himself equates race and blackness in America with prison: "If you're born in America with black skin, you're born in prison."

Again, Malcolm illustrates an extended historical context. He epitomizes the deliberateness and purposefulness of the construction of the African American intellect. If America is a prison for African Americans, then education and the exercise of the intellect are the tools for liberation—one that takes on an even greater significance in what it says of the possibilities of *transcending* oppression and in its potential for altering and transfiguring the conceptual and physical structures of that oppression through analysis and critique.[52]

This transcendence and transfiguration of the confines of American life is what Robert Terrill argues was Malcolm's ability to "shift the circumference" of the physical and intellectual spaces that confined him and African Americans as a whole. On a much broader level, Terrill argues that Malcolm was capable of the "task of crafting a viable public voice while remaining unfettered of existing ideologies." While I wish that Terrill were a bit more specific in his language, he is on the mark. Malcolm's intellectual presence is witness to another shift in the recognition of the "emancipatory potential" of the change in perception that Malcolm's analysis and rhetoric elicit. Malcolm's analysis and rhetoric are nothing less than epistemological shifts; reconstructions of existing bodies of knowledge—new formulations of what is known and how it is known—in relation to African Americans, Americans, and then, the peoples of the world.[53]

---

47. Here, an interesting set of analyses might be conducted if we were to take, say, Nat Turner's prison declarations or those of John Brown's Black cohorts as indications of this kind of intellectual activity—not simply within the physical confines of prison but also within the broader sociopolitical, economic, cultural, spiritual, and intellectual incarceration within the United States. In a post-Malcolm America, the most prominent African American prison intellectuals were George Jackson and, ironically, Eldridge Cleaver. In Cleaver's pseudorevolutionary position is his attribution of revolutionary inspiration via Malcolm. See Nower, "Cleaver's Vision."

48. Ohmann, "*The Autobiography of Malcolm X*," 139.

49. Ibid., 139–140.

50. Malcolm X, *Autobiography*, 178.

51. Ohmann, "*The Autobiography of Malcolm X*," 138; 140.

52. Michelle Celeste Condit and John Louis Lucaites, "Malcolm X and the Limits of the Rhetoric of Revolutionary Dissent," *Journal Of Black Studies* 23, no, 3 (March 1993): 291–313.

53. Robert E. Terrill, "Colonizing the Borderlands: Shifting Circumference in the Rhetoric of Malcolm X," *Quarterly Journal of Speech* 86, no. 1 (February 2000): 67–68. My criticism of Terrill's

Among my preference of words to propel and compel my own conceptualization here have been *choice, manipulation,* and *deliberateness.* Up to this point, I have been arguing that Malcolm made *deliberate* and conscious efforts in embracing his intellectuality in the very manner that Du Bois articulated and championed as the obligation of African American women and men. I have also implied that Malcolm, when faced with incarceration, went so far as to *manipulate* that incarceration and to exercise *choice* in relation to the physical *and therefore* the intellectual space of his imprisonment. His choice—the choice of his family—was the Norfolk Prison Colony.

Ohmann's word "drive" suggests Malcolm's deliberate nature and that of his family and fellow inmates. From the very beginning of the Norfolk experience, there is the calculation of placement, even the implication of agency within the confines of the American penal system. This, of course, was Blassingame's analogy and comparative examination of the institutions of slavery and prison in the American context and of the ability of captives and convicts to manipulate the institutions.[54] Here, as Malcolm's experience and efforts indicate, convicts do not manipulate the system for *easy* time but for *intellectual* time—the time and space to hone that most powerful of weapons, the mind. The prison cell becomes the center for the potential intellectual and, therefore, the revolutionary refinement of its prisoner. It becomes the spawning ground for "jailhouse intellectuals," where they literally sharpen their tools—their minds.

As theoretical parameters, the notions are not far-fetched; nor are they without evidence. Malcolm's family—particularly his sister, Ella—manipulated the prison system to Malcolm's intellectual advantage. It is clear that Norfolk and its "benefits" had been thoroughly researched. The family's inquiries into the philosophical nature and physical advantages of the Colony can be considered signs of the first steps that Malcolm took toward his own conscious and deliberate intellectual development. These were the first signs that, as Michael Thewel concludes, "intellectually, [Malcolm] was in total control."[55]

In Malcolm's "total control," we can see the manipulation and mastery of the cell; the mastery and manipulation of language; and Malcolm as master rhetorician. And we can see the deliberateness and discipline that such acts entail. John Illo summarizes Malcolm's deliberateness and discipline in this way:

> [T]he man whose secondary education began privately and painstakingly at Norfolk Prison Colony was able to analyze for his people their immediate bur-

---

choice of language—e.g., the notion that Malcolm has transcended *all* "existing ideologies"—is the same that I would offer for Condit and Lucaites's implied notion that the "rhetoric of revolutionary dissent" is one-dimensional. Condit and Lucaites do address this perceptual problem by opening with the statement that Malcolm's assumed "appeal for revolution was an appeal to use violence." Condit and Lucaites, "Malcolm X and the Limits of the Rhetoric of Revolutionary Dissent," 291. However, I would have found more appealing a much more nuanced analysis of "revolution" itself. In that regard, as Terrill argues, and Bradford Stull implies, Malcolm transcended the conventional ideologies that marked both his times and ours. Bradford Stull, *Amid the Fall, Dreaming of Eden: Du Bois, King, Malcolm X and Emancipatory Composition* (Carbondale and Edwardsville, Southern Illinois University Press, 1999).
54. John Blassingame, *The Slave Community* (New York, London, Toronto: Oxford University Press, 1972), 217–226.
55. Branham, "'I Was Gone On Debating,'" 120; 128.

den, its maintenance in the system of domestic power and its relation to colonialism, more acutely than the white and black PhD's with whom he debated.[56]

The product of a "secondary education" begun "privately" and "painstakingly" caused Clark to exclaim, "Phenomenal!" and then to underscore the calculation and deliberateness of Malcolm's vocation and his dedication to the refinement of the tools necessary for the task:

[C]onscious of the ... power which he seeks to convey ... Minister Malcolm has anticipated every question and is *prepared* with the appropriate answer.... Phenomenal![57]

"Anticipation" and "preparation" became the hallmarks of the intellectual discipline that Malcolm developed in prison. He was determined that his intellect would serve him and the process of liberation for African Americans. Critics of Malcolm find fault with his intellectual prowess. They refer to the paucity of theses written by him. They mention his lost institutional legacy and the impossibility of creating one. In their limited analysis, they fail to realize and then take into account a different kind of intellectuality. In much the same way that the popular Malcolm has been reduced to "action hero," it is the dynamism of his mental processes—his kinetic intellectuality—that represents a different way of measuring intellectualism.

Malcolm's preparation, stemming from his prison days, was deliberate. It had to be if Clark's observations, as well as those of so many others, are true: he anticipated his adversaries and their arguments. This meant that he had to prepare himself for such anticipation, and that preparation, in itself, demanded discipline—conscious intellectual effort.

From Malcolm's deliberateness emerged his conscious mastery of language and his renown as a master rhetorician and orator. Malcolm's intellectuality harkens back to an earlier intellectual tradition, which celebrates oral discourse—the "active voice." In the act of thinking on his feet, Malcolm was, as Terrill puts it, "thinking orally." For Goldman, he was "cerebrating on his feet, in the heat of battle."[58] Malcolm's speech was cognitively intellectual. Indeed, in Malcolm's speech, a word was made flesh.

Malcolm's choice of intellectual delivery was even more formidable when we consider the possibilities of a conscious reciprocity between thought and speech in which both are, at once, simultaneous and catalytic. With such a reciprocity, Malcolm reclaimed the intellectual aspect of the "act"—the intellectual dynamic of rhetoric and rhetorician. In Malcolm, the oral and the orator regained their true intellectual proportions.

Even within this sense of spontaneity—in its dynamism and kinetic energy—there was a deliberateness. In many cases, as in the example of Malcolm, speech is still composed even as it is spoken. For Stull, when Malcolm spoke, he was engaged in the intellectual discipline of creating and then crafting speech.[59]

In this literally "active voice," Malcolm was morally and ethically engaged in the engineering of the escape of African Americans from the prison of America. Key to Malcolm's engagement was the intellect illumining the "way to independent power."

56. Cited in Branham, "'I Was Gone On Debating,'"136.
57. Clark, *The Negro Protest*, 17; 19.
58. Terrill, "'Colonizing the Borderlands,'" 67. Goldman, *The Life and Death of Malcolm X*, 13.
59. Stull, *Amid the Fall, Dreaming of Eden*, 3–4.

Malcolm as Epistemologist

" … Emancipatory Composition…. [E]mancipatory literacy …"[60]

" … a radical view of the Negro experience in America. "[61]

What was Malcolm "composing" or re-creating? According to Epps, whatever that might have been was the product of a "radical view." And Stull wants us to understand that in Malcolm the act of "'Composition' indicate[d] a state of intentionality." It related to the construction of knowledge; to a different way of knowing, of understanding, of interpreting, empowered by Blackness; and to the notion that this "composition"—this construction of knowledge—was intentional, and *deliberate*.[62] This relationship could have been Du Bois, and *his* people, seeing through "veils." Malcolm's vision was quite clear. His composition was the re-creation of the Black mind—the creation of a new way of thinking. But about what?

What will Black Americans think about? And what body, or bodies, of knowledge will compel that thought? And to what ends? Can there truly be a new way of thinking—of knowing? And, if so, how did Malcolm help compose this? How did he shape it? How many analytical venues have there been to make the case?

Fundamentally, Malcolm's task—the rehabilitation "of the thinking of our people"—was the re-creation of Black Americans in opposition to and in rejection and transcendence of the definitions "imposed on them by the dominant culture." Again, we might hear Du Bois in Malcolm's proposal that African Americans "remake themselves."[63] And while one might take exception to Goldman's description of Malcolm's work here as simply "dealing in symbolic action," Goldman's argument that Malcolm was "attempting the liberation of black people by altering the terms in which they thought and the scale by which they measured themselves" goes to the heart of this matter.[64] Condit and Lucaites have called this a "revolution of identity."[65] Malcolm worked this "revolution" both from and within historical contexts.

Malcolm's invitation was largely one to a re-creation along class lines. Here, Malcolm transcended Du Bois in terms of his "grassroots," working-class appeal. Yet he was in keeping with Du Bois's radical call to Black transgression in the articulation of who and what Black people are and of who and what white people might be. The invitation was also thoroughly intellectual.[66]

This transgression was participation in the re-creation of Black Americans in opposition to and in transcendence of the notions of who and what Black folk are. It began, again, with Du Bois paraphrased: "the minds of black folk"—i.e., Black folk *do* think. The "things" of oppression; the "objects" of all the studies; the "problem" that *Souls of Black Folk* opens with *do* think.

---

60. Ibid., 1; 7.
61. Archie Epps, in Terrill, "'Colonizing the Borderlands,'" 68.
62. Stull, *Amid the Fall, Dreaming of Eden*, 4.
63. Terrill, "'Colonizing the Borderlands,'" 67.
64. Goldman, *The Death and Life of Malcolm X*, 13. Also quoted in Terrill, "'Colonizing the Borderlands,'" 67.
65. Condit and Lucaites, "Malcolm X and the Limits of the Rhetoric of Revolutionary Dissent," 302.
66. Terrill, "'Colonizing the Borderlands,'" 68.

Malcolm's rehabilitation of the thinking of Black people fell in line with postmodern critique. Such is Stull's "emancipatory literacy"—Malcolm's invitation to his audience to participate in the shaping and reshaping of their intellects, their histories, themselves. As Giroux puts it, Malcolm's act was the development of

> [a]n alternative discourse and critical reading of how culture and power work within late capitalist societies to limit, disorganize and marginalize.[67]

As early as 1974, Clasby describes Malcolm as a "post-modern man":

> Malcolm … reconfigured and embodied … the emergence of a new paradigm of human awareness among the non-white peoples of the world.[68]

Amiri Baraka [Leroi Jones] describes Malcolm as the "arc-circle" that embraced "a whole public consciousness."[69] Indeed, Clasby sees Malcolm as "the American prototype," the creator of a "matrix of consciousness."[70] By this evaluation, Clasby means that Malcolm was busy constructing new ways of knowing and understanding. He was constructing new bodies of knowledge. He was an epistemologist.

But here, Du Bois as a foundation must be clearly recognized. Well before Malcolm articulated this notion of awareness and consciousness, Du Bois had acknowledged its existence and called for its cultivation. There was, he argued, "a mass of people who form a great reservoir of knowledge and information" whom we "ignore at [our] peril."[71] This reservoir, "from the point of view of the colored races … [constitutes a] knowledge of life and the meaning of life in the modern world." These were (and are) "the great streams of knowledge and experience … of black students.… [and] the knowledge and experience of the whole black world." They demand our constant, deliberate attention and nurturing. They also demand our ongoing interrogation and analysis.

That interrogation and analysis are the same theme that Toni Morrison reprises when she notes that although "I read as I was taught to read," "the way in which we *teach ourselves* to read and write, to speak and listen" are breaches with a past, shifts in consciousness.[72] Friere is conjured here as well. He evokes the "cultural capital of the oppressed." Such "cultural capital" is registered in Melville Herskovits's reference to Du Bois's *Black Reconstruction*. Herskovits was outraged that Du Bois had proposed that Black slaves—the "oppressed"—had minds, used them to organize, and constructed histories with them.[73] Malcolm's own constructions of knowledge and history are contextualized and recontextualized here.

James Baldwin and Bayard Rustin recognized this. Malcolm's intellectual and cultural dynamism—his epistemological verve—rested in the re-creation of self and identity for

---

67. Stull, *Amid the Fall, Dreaming of Eden*, 7.

68. Clasby, "The Autobiography of Malcolm X: A Mythic Paradigm," 24.

69. Cited in Clasby, "The Autobiography of Malcolm X: A Mythic Paradigm," 19.

70. Clasby, "The Autobiography of Malcolm X: A Mythic Paradigm," 19.

71. William Edward Burghardt Du Bois, "*Diuturni Silenti*," in *The Education of Black People: Ten Critiques 1906–1960 by W.E.B . Du Bois*, ed. Herbert Aptheker, 52 (Amherst: University of Massachusetts Press, 1973).

72. Toni Morrison, *Playing in the Dark* (New York: Vintage Books, 1992), 8 (my italics). Jean-François Lyotard, *Post-modernity* (Minneapolis and London: University of Minnesota Press, 1992), 75–80.

73. Paolo Friere, quoted in Stull, *Amid the Fall, Dreaming of Eden*, 8. Melville Herskovits, "Negro History," review of *Black Folk—Then and Now*, by W. E. B. Du Bois, *The New Republic*, 100 (August 10, 1939): 56.

all those who heard him. Even in his fear that Malcolm might "destroy [sic] a truth and invent [sic] a history," Baldwin had to admit that with Malcolm, the "Black Muslims" had "become the only movement in the country that you can call grassroots."[74]

Through Giroux, Friere, Morrison, and Du Bois, Malcolm can be seen as analyst—as the creator of a body of knowledge. If Malcolm's treatment is contextualized by "late capitalist societies" and their abilities to "limit, disorganize and marginalize," then his "acute" analysis "for his peoples' immediate burden ... [and] its maintenance in a system of domestic power and its relation to colonialism" are prescient of the powers that lay on the margins.[75] The linkages drawn are decidedly *Pan-Africanist*; they precede Du Bois and yet are concretized with and by him. The venues for rethinking and recontextualizing African American intellectual life and the lives of Africans and the African diaspora are completely realized here.

Malcolm's and Du Bois's notions of class also link here, if only tangentially. "Black is beautiful." Their conceptualizations are different, yet they both culminate in speculating on the potential and possibilities of Black folk, intellectually and otherwise. This beauty of blackness can certainly be interpreted intellectually, and Malcolm would be an apt interpreter: "beauty" understood as the ability of a people to think about, to analyze, and to criticize the American and then the global condition. Such an ability is a formidable power. Even more formidable is a vision which recognizes that Black Americans might be key to the resolution of their own difficulties. This vision is found in Du Bois's critical works as well: "the Negro's gift to civilization" in both "Conservation of Races" and *Souls of Black Folk*; a reiteration of a moral construction of race implied in the *Philadelphia Negro*; and the nation-shaping, convention-shattering moral actions of slaves depicted in *Black Reconstruction*.

These forces and the implications of these acts are amplified in Malcolm's choice of audience. That choice helps to produce new bodies of knowledge explicitly centered on "Blackness." In turn, there is the creation of a new body of knowledge "consumers" and "producers" for whom such notions appear novel. For these groups of Black people, Malcolm's work is a "recentering." It is the creation of new perspectives that become the keys for the generation of new knowledge. This is Malcolm's observation that, given knowledge and perspectives for interpretation, African Americans might change their condition and that of the world.

Lyotard discusses the "postmodern man." Possibly both Du Bois and Malcolm are postmodern men, particularly in light of the ways in which Lyotard helps us to understand postmodernity. Lyotard argues that the "post" is not simply the "after"; it is also the "position"—the "center"—from which the world is seen and known. It is the position or the center from which modernity, colonization, and the structures which compel them are viewed and criticized. The "post" is a perspective.[76] I argue, further, that the "after" is enjoined at the very moment and at every moment thereafter; that the position, the center, the perspective from which criticism might emerge is realized and

74. Baldwin went on to note the following about Malcolm's power—his coalescence with and then transcendence of Du Bois: "[It is Malcolm's and the Nation of Islam's] articulation of all the Negro people who hear them, who listen to them.... That's Malcolm's great authority over any audience. He corroborates their reality. He tells them that they really exist." Baldwin, in Clark, *The Negro Protest*, 11.
75. John Illo, quoted in Branham, "'I Was Gone On Debating,'"136.
76. Jean-Francois Lyotard, *Postmodern Fables* (Minneapolis and London: University of Minnesota Press, 1997), 95–96. Jean-Francois Lyotard, *The Postmodern Explained* (Minneapolis and London: University of Minnesota Press, 1993), 76.

then articulated. In this extended definition, the search for a rigid temporal marker for what might be "premodern," "modern," or "postmodern" lacks utility. The attempt to link the "post" to certain temporal or material conditions limits its possibilities; but, more important, such definitions limit the possibilities of those who participate in restructuring the world.

Lyotard also argues that this realization and articulation are also a "breach"—a break—with the modern and its structures. Both Du Bois's and Malcolm's criticisms of race as a structural device of modernity are breaks with that past, its assumptions, and their strictures. Malcolm's task and the body of knowledge he helped to create required that Black people come to grips with new ways of seeing themselves. His analysis, his articulation, and his presence were an intellectually visceral breach with the past and its constructions of who and what Black people were and are.

Malcolm's "embodiment" of the postmodern, to paraphrase Clasby, can be understood in this way for the generations that succeeded him: his resistance to the structures (i.e., race/racism) and to the vehicles (i.e., imperialism/colonialism) that have come to dominate the modern world defines his and our breach with that world. He and we become "postmodern" in terms of his and our ability to criticize modernity, its structures, and its vehicles.

These criticisms represent a new body of knowledge, a new way of knowing. This new epistemology—"a reservoir of knowledge" stemming "from [a] point of view"—can be loosely seen as an "epistemology of Blackness." Again, we must refer to Du Bois and his predecessors since these criticisms are notions of Black revolution spawned in the late eighteenth century and rearticulated in the nineteenth and twentieth centuries. They are notions and perspectives that gained and regained new and renewed demographic and, therefore, intellectual dynamism and power in the person of Malcolm. While the notions are not altogether new, we might argue that in Malcolm's time, their audience and therefore their impact were.

In that regard, these "postconceptualizations," (i.e., "postmodernity," poststructuralism," and "postcolonialism/anticolonialism/antiimperialism") and their discourses have been with us for quite some time. Articulations from the eighteenth through the twentieth centuries were preceded by *real* actions that might be, at best, *imaginatively* constructed:

> In some remote space at the beginning of the era, a woman, biting and scratching, resists captivity. Throughout each attempt to reconstruct her as a thing—an object—she asserts her humanity through resistance. The gendered stereotypes that are invented to construct her docility and pliancy are thwarted. Racial categorization created to render her as less than human and to rationalize the inhuman conditions of her enslavement—and of enslavement itself—is meaningless. Meaningless because she has refused to accept them from their very inception. Her acts challenge the modern and in that challenge initiate the postmodern. Through her acts—their continuity and consistency—she becomes its personification.

Malcolm wrote: "I knew nothing of the history of Africa." Du Bois's *Souls of Black Folk* may not have been his introduction to African history, but it may well have provided the spark in his attempt to construct a new body of knowledge that centered on Africa and peoples of African descent.[77] In Malcolm's case, his and Black Americans'

---

77. Malcolm X, *Autobiography*, 178.

need to know their history indicates a new moment and a realization of what such knowledge can do.

Conclusions: Critic and Critique — The Nature of Criticism

"You've got to be realistic about being a nigger."

"Why is it necessary to have a nigger in the first place?"[78]

".... A Social Commentary...."[79]

"Malcolm X is not ... anguished by the complexities inherent in transforming our society to one of racial equality and peace."[80]

For all her early insight, Clasby's 1974 postmodern analysis of Malcolm brings us back to convention—which is not her intent. She returns us to the conventional because of the linkages assumed in the prevailing epistemology. Brilliantly she makes her point by linking Malcolm to Frantz Fanon, whose ideas led Jean-Paul Sartre to warn that whites would be best served in expecting and anticipating the justified vengeance of Blacks—and who is too easily identified with violence as the cathartic and resurrecting force for those deemed "the wretched of the earth."[81] What a wonderful and appropriate pairing in conventional minds that have wedded Malcolm to the physical and the kinetic; in conventional minds that have rendered him as unthinking and anti-intellectual. This pairing is excellent for the mind that has reduced Malcolm to an apostle of violence—an "apostle of black racism."

Of course, this is the "reductionism" that Condit and Lucaites attempt to counter. They argue that in Malcolm's case—in this rivaled and contentious space for his reclamation[82]—there is the real need to resist this reductionism:

> [It] assumes that his appeal for revolution was an appeal to use violence to tear apart the prevailing social and political structures of the United States. It was none of the above.[83]

Condit and Lucaites are correct: Malcolm's analysis was not simply an appeal to physical violence. Such a narrow definition of tactics would indeed be antirevolutionary. However, they are wrong to assert that Malcolm's program did not include the fundamental alteration of some American social and political structures and the total destruction of

---

78. Baldwin, in Clark, *The Negro Protest*, 13.

79. Lizzie M. Thomas, "*The Autobiography of Malcolm X*: A Social Commentary on Black Urban Society," *Afro-Americans in New York Life and History*, January 1981, 41–50.

80. Clark, *The Negro Protest*, 49.

81. Frantz Fanon, *The Wretched of the Earth* (New York: Grove Press, 1963).

82. Here is one the values of the debate concerning Spike Lee's film *Malcolm X*. Dyson and Painter have weighed in. Lee and Gates go with the configuration—implying that they are not party to groups of contenders they criticize: "black neo-nationalism," "buppy nationalism," and the articulation that there is "a lot of re-education that has to go on." Lee and Gates, "Generation X," 183. The critique of the critique, however, belongs to Gerald Horne. Horne, "Myth and the Making of 'Malcolm X,'" 440–450.

83. Condit and Lucaites, "Malcolm X and the Limits of the Rhetoric of Revolutionary Dissent," 291.

others. This program is certainly implicit in the Clark epigraph that opens this section: Malcolm was intent on the radical alteration of American society. What Condit's and Lucaites' analysis does prompt, in keeping with Clasby twenty years earlier, is a much more critical reading and interrogation of Malcolm.

Clasby prompts such a critique by referring to Richard Wright, who saw the continuity inherent in resistance and the myriad forms it might take. Wright noted that as oppression "blots out one form of resistance ... another grows in its place with its own rights, needs and aspirations."[84] By including Wright's observation, Clasby rounds out the intellectual circle that *should* be assumed to have contextualized Malcolm's life. I am not privy to any interaction between Malcolm and Wright, but I do know that Malcolm debated with Baldwin; won the grudging respect of Bayard Rustin; and went so far as to offer guidance to Kenneth Clark and oversight of his son. Then there is the extrapolation that Clasby provides in presenting Wright, Fanon, and Malcolm in the same textual space. There is a critical moment of historical and intellectual coalescence here. The year is 1957. We are in Paris. The event is the International Conference of Black Writers and Artists. Wright is the keynote speaker; Fanon is in the wings. A huge array of Africa's diasporic intellectual community is there. *Malcolm is not. Du Bois is not.*[85] Wright's address is a riveting and withering indictment of racism and colonialism. Can the event be called "postmodern?" Possibly. For here resistance grows, and its strategies are understood to be multifaceted. Malcolm becomes yet another vehicle of resistance; another articulation of discontent and its power. What he has witnessed is expressed globally.[86] The astuteness of a critique which acknowledged that "chickens come home to roost" reflects the same analysis and tenor that Sartre saw in Fanon's work.

The conceptual expansion of Malcolm's argument from one of separation to a grudging acknowledgement of civil rights to a globalized articulation of the American problem as one of human rights shows the dynamism of Malcolm's thought processes and his intellectual growth. African Americans were part of a larger revolution being waged worldwide. In the end, Malcolm's efforts to "rehabilitate the thinking of our people" were directed toward expediting the realization among African Americans that they were players on a global stage.

Neither Fanon's nor Malcolm's critiques can be reduced to paeans on violence or, more important, on revolution as simply *physical* violence. So, building on Wright's observation, what are the possibilities? Whatever they are, they are revolutionary in that they cannot be anticipated: "White America, in fact, perceived that any resistance to the system would inevitably lead to violence."[87] At issue, then, was how to make resistance revolutionary; how to fuse it with *continuous* acts that could *not* be anticipated; how to render revolution as a process rather than an event. There is no claim that Malcolm accomplished this any more than Du Bois did, but that we study the two of them—and others—and try to make meaning of their lives and works may be a moment in the revolutionary process for all of us. Malcolm allowed for the intellectualization of that resis-

---

84. Richard Wright, cited in Clasby, "The Autobiography of Malcolm X: A Mythic Paradigm," 20.

85. Du Bois offered his solidarity to the gathering. The McCarthy House Committee on Un-American Activities had stripped him of his passport.

86. Here, Terrill notes Malcolm's ability to "shift the intellectual circumference" by both linking and dissolving the "border between the domestic and the global." Yet, again, we need to acknowledge that the act is not without historical precedent. Terrill, "'Colonizing the Borderlands,'" 68.

87. Clasby, "The Autobiography of Malcolm X: A Mythic Paradigm," 23.

tance for and at mass levels. In the end, there was the deliberate contemplation of act and consequence. There was tactical assessment and then the linkage of thought and action as a devastating force. There was the flexibility and fluidity of revolutionary action that could only be unleashed in and after contemplation — in its intellectual proportions.

Here, Fanon — prophet of *"revolutionary violence"* [?] — summarizes flexibility and fluidity and the vast forms that revolution might take:

> [N]on-violent [leaders] make people dream dreams.... In fact they introduce into their readers' or hearers' consciousness *the terrible foment of subversion.*[88]

In spite of his criticism of Martin Luther King, Jr., Fanon's point was not lost on Malcolm. Ironically, the power of Malcolm's criticism did not elude King, either. Peter Paris writes that King expressed a "growing appreciation for Malcolm's *social analysis.*"[89] And in this context, the idea inherent in "by any means necessary" gains larger meaning; it takes into account "the terrible ... subversion" of dreams; it points to the power of what Valentine Mudimbe calls "the surreptitious speech."[90] It also takes into account the questions of interpretation. Was it "nightmare" or "dream?" Had Malcolm given up on America? What were the possibilities inherent in a title and a conceptualization such as the "Ballot or the Bullet?" What possibilities lay in between? What were the various "ammunitions" at the disposal of Malcolm's "hearers and readers?"

If there were "violences" here, they emerged in two opposing forms that might be read in these ways. The first form is associated with a revolution whose essence is physical violence and destruction. It is to be viscerally feared. Then, there is revolution whose violence might be understood and manifested essentially in its break with the oppressions of an old order and their damages to the soul and psyche. This form of violence and the revolution it succors are constructive and renewing. Its primary and initial manifestations are intellectual and, some would argue, spiritual. For Fanon, they are cathartic; for Lyotard, they characterize a breach; for Malcolm, they are the "rehabilitation of the thinking of our people." The results are no less cataclysmic socially and politically. They are no less earthshaking in the realm of humanity. *They are liberating.* They center on what Joyce Nower has called the "re-humanization" of Black folk.[91] And they are a tradition as old as the beginning of the modern world and Black folks' part in

---

88. Ibid.

89. Peter Paris, "Review: *Malcolm and Martin and America: A Dream or A Nightmare,*" *Religious Studies Review* 20, no. 2 (April 1994); 88 (my italics). Through Cone, Paris goes on to corroborate the observations of a number of scholars concerning the closeness of both Malcolm's and King's positions at the close of their lives: "It was after Malcolm's death that Martin began to make his radical turn away from his vision of the American dream to gaze at the horror of Malcolm's nightmare." James Cone, *Malcolm and Martin and America: A Dream or A Nightmare* (Maryknoll, New York: Orbis Books, 1991), 212. Also quoted in Paris, "Review: *Malcolm and Martin and America,*" 88.

90. Valentine Y. Mudimbe, ed., *The Surreptitious Speech* (Chicago and London: University of Chicago Press, 1992).

91. Joyce Nower, "Cleaver's Vision of America and the New White Radical: A Legacy of Malcolm X," *Negro American Literature Forum* 4, no. 1 (March 1970): 12. While I might sympathize with Nower's intention here, regarding the "re-humanization" of Black folk, I am forced to return to Du Bois's life's work on the issue. Du Bois begins the all-too-famous *Souls of Black Folk* with, "How does it feel to be a problem?" He concludes the equally important but rarely cited 1920 essay, "The Souls of White Folk," with the notion that whites might *be the* "problem." Implicit in this notion, and just as intellectually cataclysmic, is the idea that it is whites who are in need of "re-humanization." One should look at this idea in relation to the famous Clark interviews and Baldwin's observation: "[T]hey [white people] have become in themselves moral monsters. It's a terrible indictment. I mean every word I say." Baldwin, in Clark, *The Negro Protest,* 8.

its construction: "[B]lack vision is not a contemporary creation … thought up by Malcolm X, Stokely Carmichael, Huey P. Newton, or Eldridge Cleaver." There is a "historical context" here. Nower's earliest reference to that historical context is Frederick Douglass.[92] The reference implies an even earlier intellectual and historical environment for Malcolm's development.

* * *

"One ever feels his two-ness."[93]

Modern life is predicated on a series of "double consciousnesses." In many ways, this schizophrenia may represent our only way of successfully negotiating it. Yet we fail, as Du Bois would admonish us, to examine the "neuroses" and put them to our advantage. Among the series of false dichotomies affecting contemporary double consciousness are the Enlightenment separations of mind and body and of intellect and action. Through them, we are led back to our preoccupation with Malcolm as the "action hero."

We come to recognize that that there is no juxtaposition between intellect and action; between mind and body. We cerebrate on our feet; the intellect is inherently kinetic—the mind is dynamic. There is no action without thought. The dynamism of Malcolm's intellectual life is a "social commentary," as Lizzie Thomas instructs us. It is a criticism of America and the modern world—from their inception to this very moment. As Thomas puts it, the "*Autobiography* … serves as a consciousness-raising device to several social and cultural phenomena."[94] The consciousness raised is "a whole movement to proclaim, if not convince Black Americans, that Black is beautiful." As I have already noted, for Malcolm, as well as for Du Bois, the physical nature of such beauty is only complemented, enhanced, and magnified by its intellectual prowess and potential. It seems that the implications here are at least threefold. First, the "beauty" of Black resistance/rebellion/revolution—conceptually, intellectually, and in actuality—gains new power and dynamism when placed against the array of systemic and institutional might intent on suppressing it. Second, "the movement" to which Thomas refers was one that Du Bois chronicled and analyzed all his life. Its conceptual brilliance—the brilliance of its organization and organized resistance—was subject of Du Bois's life of slaves in *Black Reconstruction*. Du Bois articulates the "beauty" of organization and organized resistance among oppressed people (namely, slaves of African descent) as a fundamentally *intellectual* phenomenon—one lost on some critics and a bane to others. Du Bois's articulation—particularly in *Black Reconstruction*—is one of Black folk in the acts of *construction, destruction, and reconstruction*.

Building on a historically constructed critique of "black beauty," the critiques that Malcolm provided move us in least two directions. They then bring us back to further analysis in relation to his own personal construction and image. From there, we are forced to interrogate the images many seek to construct and appropriate in relation to him. Among those are the construction and institutional dynamics of the Nation of Islam and our selective analyses of it. Malcolm criticized who and what he was to become and what was set before him in the most positive terms of race and class. Frederick Douglass, Booker T. Washington, Marcus Garvey, and Du Bois resonate here with notions of "dignity," "carriage," "deportment," "sobriety," "morality," and "courage," to name a few. However, what they and Malcolm and many, many

---

92. Nower, "Cleaver's Vision of America and the New White Radical," 13.
93. Du Bois, *The Souls of Black Folk*, 364.
94. Lizzie Thomas, "*The Autobiography*," 41.

others—with the exception of Douglass and Du Bois—do not entertain is the question of Black women and their oppression/suppression at the hands of a Black patriarchy. Here, my weak response for not having tackled this question in this essay is to plead the lack of space, time, and expertise. However, it is also to acknowledge where Malcolm's critique and our critique of him and his contemporary and historical contexts might take us.

Where is that? Where might such critiques of Malcolm and his intellectual and historical contexts lead us? They might liberate us—"emancipate" us: they might allow us to cross "borderlands" and to "shift the circumference" of our intellectual worlds. If this is Stull and Terrill speaking to us, it is also Horne pushing us to embrace the possibilities and potential of such an interrogation. Such an embrace "may help to explain the future course and the present utility of the Malcolm X myth."[95] Charles Alva Hoyt recognized this in 1970 when he wrote "The Five Faces of Malcolm X." Hoyt believed in Malcolm's "central position in the whole civil rights movement: in fact he may be said to recapitulate in his own person the fluctuating progress of the Negro in American life over the past four decades.... [Malcolm's life] categorize[s] stages which millions passed through."[96]

In Fanon's observation of what dreams might do to readers and hearers, Terrill recognizes Malcolm's invitation to his audiences to "transgress"—to transcend ascribed identity and convention. The ultimate transgression is found in the ways in which "Malcolm positions his audience to *critique* those identities imposed upon them by the dominant culture."[97] Du Bois may have prepared the way for such an act in works such as "The Souls of White Folk."[98] Du Bois, at the earliest moment, attempted to craft and recraft— to refine—the notions of what it might mean to be Black. And in that arduous and life-consuming process, he provided the space from which he, Malcolm, *and* we, might critique our own existence and the conditions that conspire to make them so. Malcolm articulated Du Bois' brilliance in a moment spanning 1903 to 1920: one moves from *being* the problem to *identifying* the problem and *critiquing* it. This is the context that was laid for Malcolm to *broadcast* within. The broadcast was a mass call to critique.[99]

So, to paraphrase Baldwin, "*What* is the necessity of the nigger?" If Malcolm's and Du Bois's lives are any indication—if the lives of the people with whom they shared dreams and souls are characteristic—the "necessity" of the nigger outstripped its conventional definition and construction. It was being constantly reworked, reinvented, and (one might even argue) "refined"—into something that the "inventors" of modernity would have hardly recognized. And when that "something" *was* recognized, it would constitute, in modern parlance, their "worst nightmare"—not the violent, physical manifestation of the spectral but its intellectual catalyst, what Frederick Douglass called the "spoiled nigger."

So what is "realistic about being a nigger?" If Malcolm is the example, it is to be "bright, industrious … talented," and, consequently, being Black works against the grain of the conventional definition of *nigger*. And this is Malcolm's legacy to all of us, particularly to our children. This is Du Bois in the 1920 "Souls of White Folk," suggesting in the personification of Malcolm that, perhaps, one needs to be "realistic" about being a *white* person, particularly in a space where so many Black people achieve against the odds.

95. Horne, "Myth and the Making of 'Malcolm X,'" 449
96. Hoyt, "The Five Faces of Malcolm X," 107.
97. Terrill, "'Colonizing the Borderlands,'" 68.
98. Du Bois, "The Souls of White Folk," 923–938.
99. Terrill, "'Colonizing the Borderlands,'" 70.

This is the company that Malcolm kept—the company that nurtured him. This is also the future company he sought to inspire—a company of thinkers.

Part Four

Black Artistic Expression

18

Malcolm X: Internet Resources and Digital Media

Larry Ross

The legacy of Malcolm X is well represented in cyberspace today; there are a number of Web sites focused on his principles, philosophies, and actions. This essay will offer a sampling of these Internet resources and provide the URLs of the most comprehensive ones. In addition, the essay will provide a few of the existing digital media resources together with a brief explanation of how electronic publications can be incorporated into a scholar's paper. (The author does not assume any responsibility for the content of these sites.)

The Malcolm X/Malik Shabazz Study Guide (http://www.brothermalcolm.net/studyguide.html) is divided into the following sections: Racial Ideology, The Autobiography, The End of White World Supremacy, The Legacy of Malcolm X, His Militant Action, and Principles for Action. In its introductory page, the site emphasizes the continuing violence and economic exclusion pervasive in African American communities. At the bottom of the page is a link to the Malcolm X Research Site. This link provides a wealth of information on Malcolm X, including a year-by-year chronology of his life, his family's genealogy, CDs and videos, words written and spoken, Ph.D. dissertations, and a "Webliography"—which lists resources on Malcolm X from around the world. The Web site at Burkina Faso, Malcolm X in World Perspective, is certainly worth a look. The designers of the site are to be commended for compiling an unprecedented Internet repository for researchers, students, or anyone interested in Malcolm X.

The recommended method for citing electronic documents and media can be found in *A Manual for Writers of Term Papers, Theses, and Dissertations* (6th edition), by Kate L. Turabian. Since Internet sites are updated quite often, it is important for one to note the date on which the site was accessed. Turabian further explains: "The citations of electronic documents can follow the same general form as citations of printed materials. The same basic information is needed: author and title of the particular item; name and description of the source cited, whether CD-ROM, some other physical form, or an online source; city of publication, if any; publisher or vendor; date of publication or access; and identifying numbers or pathway needed for access to the material."[1] It is not recommended that one use only a URL (Universal Resource Locator) to identify and locate an electronic source. In the case of electronic journals, quite often the URL becomes disassociated with the Internet publication. Turabian points out: "Electronic

---

1. Kate L. Turabian, *A Manual for Writers of Term Papers, Theses, and Dissertations* (Chicago: University of Chicago Press, 1996), 158.

journals, for example, may move to other locations on the Internet or may cease to exist as Internet publications, so a citation giving only the URL becomes meaningless."[2] A new locator, called the URN (Universal Resource Name) is being developed, and it will provide a "canonical name, not specific to machine, that applies even when the document is moved to another location."[3]

An essay on *The Autobiography of Malcolm X*, written by Marcel Schilling in September 1997, can be found at http://www.datacomm.ch/mschilling/malcolm.html. The essay discusses the book's authors, Malcolm X and Alex Haley, together with their intentions; its structure, language, and style; and its historical and political setting.

Malcolm's Life and Death features a bibliography on Malcolm X and can be found at http://www.evanston.lib.il.us/library/bibliographies/malcolmx.html.

A teaching guide for *The Autobiography of Malcolm X* that educators may find useful is featured at http://www.randomhouse.com/BB/teachers/tgs/malcolmx.html. This site also lists the sites on Malcolm X outside the United States.

An impressive site, http://www.unix-ag.uni-kl.de/~moritz/malcolm.html, features an excellent picture book on Malcolm X. Designed and maintained by Elke Moritz, the site also includes audio files of some of Malcolm's speeches. The site developed by author Benjamin Karim (http://sac.uky.edu/~jfmcdo00/bookshelf/malcolmx.html) is linked to the one by Elke Moritz and contains four of Malcolm's speeches and numerous links to sites like the Malcolm X Grass Roots Movement, the Malcolm X Institute of Black Studies, the Malcolm X E-mail Listserv, and the Malcolm X Official Site.

The site http://home.earthlink.net/~malx/malxintro.htm begins with a mission statement on teaching. At the bottom of the introductory page are links to a seven-speech set, a multimedia bibliography, a Malcolm X timeline, quotations, and more.

The URL http://www.wabash.edu/orgs/mxi/home.htm is the site for the Malcolm X Institute of Black Studies. Some of its links do not work; however, the ones that do, like http://www.cmgww.com/historic/malcolm/malcolm.html, are promising. This site leads to a new Malcolm X online store. Searching the site will probably find a number of useful items or tools for research on Malcolm X. Posters, videotapes, hats, and stamps are also available, as well as the original May 1963 *Playboy* interview conducted by Alex Haley and Ossie Davis's eulogy, presented on February 27, 1965.

The Italian site Associazione Malcolm X (http://www.malcolmx.it) indicates the global appeal of Malcolm's message.

The URL http://www.worldbook.com/fun/aajourny/html/bh096.html is a digital media resource on Malcolm X, who is featured in "The African American Journey" section of *The World Book Multimedia Encyclopedia Millennium Edition*. At the bottom of the page are links to Elijah Muhammad and Louis Farrakhan.

The Webcorp site (http://www.webcorp.com/civilrights/malcolm.htm) contrasts Malcolm's rejection of nonviolence with Dr. Martin Luther King, Jr.'s advocacy of it. All of the site's links are those to sound files, through which one can hear excerpts from Malcolm's speeches in both WAV and AU formats.

The main page on the site http://members.tripod.com/~bimcrot/alkisah/x.html is My Journey to Islam. It includes a timeline of Malcolm's life and his "Change to True

---

2. Ibid., 159.
3. Ibid.

Islam" in 1964, as well as the effect of his pilgrimage to Mecca on his beliefs and philosophies.

The site http://www.soundvision.com/racism/xletter.shtml features a letter written by Malcolm X on racism and Islam, titled "Hajj as a Shift against Racism." The site is developed and maintained by Sound Vision(r), and a number of resources on Islamic topics can be ordered from it.

The site http://www.arches.uga.edu/~godlas/malcomx.html is that of Professor Alan Godlas at the University of Georgia's Department of Religion. The Letter from Mecca page describes Malcolm's pilgrimage in some detail, and much of the text consists of the words of Malcolm himself.

The URL http://members.aol.com/klove01/malcomsp.htm is a link to the Black History page. Along with Malcolm's letters from Mecca, quotations from Malcolm X, and the eulogy of Malcolm X, the page contains a multimedia section which includes a film on civil rights versus human rights and numerous sound files with such titles as "Black Unity," "Nonviolence," "My Mission," "The Price of Freedom," "American Jail," "I Am an American," and "Inner-City Life."

By using the search engines for Lycos (http://www.lycos.com), Google (http://www.google.com), and Excite (http://www.excite.com), researchers can find a wealth of information on the life and work of Malcolm X. As a result, they will find that Malcolm's legacy is global.

At http://www.cdnow.com, Malcolm's speech "On Black Power" is available on compact disk in a boxed set titled *VA—Great Speeches of the 20th Century*. The DVD *Malcolm X—Death of a Prophet* is now available at Amazon.com (http://www.amazon.com/exec/obidos/ASIN/B000054OTB/qid%3D982710006/102-3106776-6368917). In addition, Amazon has the CD compilation *20th Century Time Capsule*, which also contains Malcolm's speech "On Black Power," and Walter Cronkite's CD compilation *I Can Hear It Now: The Sixties*, which features the same speech and Betty Shabazz's description of Malcolm's assassination.

The site http://www.vinyllives.com/politics/politics.htm contains excerpts from Malcolm's speeches (the number of the distributor is BMG 66132). A search on GetMusic.com (http://www.getmusic.com) led me to virtually all of the known recordings of Malcolm's speeches. The Excite page http://music.excite.com/album/122374 presents a review of the recording *Words from the Frontline*, the details of the CD and LP formats, and the list of tracks for the CD format.

The site http://www.thebigpicturedvd.com/cgi-bin/master/viewer.cgi/Malcolm_X contains a review, by Bob Banka, of the DVD of Spike Lee's film *Malcolm X*; the DVD is available in the wide-screen format (1.85:1, Anamorphic-Enhanced for 16 x 9 viewing). There are links to the film's fifty-two chapters, and English and French subtitles are included, along with closed-captioning.

The site http://www.wiu.edu/library/units/av/titlecatalog/avm_man.htm features the videotapes *Malcolm X: Nationalist or Humanist* and *Malcolm X—The End of White World Supremacy*.

19

The Work of Fifty African American Poets on the Life and Career of Malcolm X (1925–1965)

Julius E. Thompson

This essay explores the work of fifty Black poets on the contributions, impact, and historical significance of Malcolm X (1925–1965), one of the major African American leaders of the twentieth century. Historically, Black poets have focused much of their poetry on Black leadership figures. Today, over forty years after his death, Malcolm X remains a major force in Black poets' interpretations of his life and work, of the time during which he lived, and of modern society in general.

A random study of twenty anthologies of Black poetry and fifty single collections of Black poetry indicates an enormous number of poems on more than thirty-three important Black leaders, writers, and (especially) musicians.[1]

---

1. See Rosey E. Pool, ed., *Beyond the Blues: New Poems by American Negroes* (Kent, England: The Hand and Flower Press, 1962), 44–45, 59–61, 68, 72, 81–84, 88, 139, 161, 165–66; Ama Bontemps, ed., *American Negro Poetry* (New York: Hill and Wang, 1963), 1, 38–39, 117–118, 119, 122, 177; Langston Hughes, ed., *New Negro Poets: U.S.A.* (Bloomington: Indiana University Press, 1964), 59; Gwendolyn Brooks, ed., *Jump Bad: A New Chicago Anthology* (Detroit: Broadside Press, 1971), 45–46, 51–57, 115, 142–144; Erlene Stetson, ed., *Black Sister: Poetry By Black American Women, 1746–1980* (Bloomington: Indiana University Press, 1981), 120, 147, 197, 219; Robert Hayden, ed., *Kaleidoscope: Poems by American Negro Poets* (New York: Harcourt, Brace & World, 1967), 102, 117, 131; Dudley Randall, ed., *The Black Poets* (New York: Bantam Books, 1971), 87, 115, 133, 143, 157, 158, 172, 207, 230, 239, 262, 269, 323; John Oliver Killens and Jerry W. Ward, Jr., eds., *Black Southern Voices* (New York: Penguin, 1992), 288–89, 298–99; Black History Museum Committee, ed., *Sterling A. Brown: A UMUM Tribute* (Philadelphia: Black History Museum UMUM Publishers, 1976), 1–60; Carolyn Rogers, *Songs of a Black Bird* (Chicago: Third World Press, 1969), 15; Sonia Sanchez, *I've Been A Woman: New and Selected Poems* (Sausalito, CA: The Black Scholar Press, 1978), 10–11, 91–93 Nikki Giovanni, *My House* (New York: William Morrow, 1972), 28, 38; Don L. Lee, *Think Black!* (Detroit: Broadside Press, 1969), 14, 16–17; James A. Emanuel, *Panther Man* (Detroit: Broadside Press, 1970), 14, 21–22; Margaret Walker, *October Journey* (Detroit: Broadside Press, 1973), 14–18, 32–34; Audre Lorde, *Coal* (New York: Norton, 1976), 25; Lance Jeffers, *When I Know the Power of My Black Hand* (Detroit: Broadside Press, 1974), 23, 35, 62; Owen Dodson, *Powerful Long Ladder* (New York: Farrar, Straus and Giroux, 1946), 14–15, 73; and Keorapetse Kgositsile, *My Name Is Afrika* (Garden City, NY: Doubleday, 1971), 37, 73, 76, 85.

Among the Black leaders most often celebrated by Black poets are Harriet Tubman, Sojourner Truth, George Jackson, David Walker, Nat Turner, Jomo Kenyatta, Fannie Lou Hamer, W. E. B. Du Bois, Frederick Douglass, Marcus Garvey, Booker T. Washington, Toussaint L. Ouverture, and Martin Luther King, Jr.[2] Black writers are also celebrated by Black poets and include such figures as Richard Wright, Countee Cullen, Gwendolyn Brooks, Langston Hughes, Melvin Tolson, Hoyt W. Fuller, Ntozake Shange, Alex Haley, J. A. Rogers, and James Baldwin. Black musicians have especially inspired poems by Black poets. My essay includes such notables as Ma Rainey, Miles Davis, John Coltrane, B. B. King, Leontyne Price, Billie Holiday, Dinah Washington, Wes Montgomery, Charles Parker, Lionel Hampton, and Ray Charles. Sports figures that often appear in the work of Black poets are Joe Louis and Jackie Robinson.

Generation after generation, Black poets have been inspired to write on Black figures who have made a lasting impact on African American life and culture. Certainly Malcolm X and his contemporary, Martin Luther King, Jr., have been the dominant personalities in Black poetry, especially from 1960 to the present. Table 1 compares the historical significance of Malcolm X with that of Martin Luther King, Jr. Each leader was able to reach such large segments of the Black masses that their violent deaths have only added to their legacy: their challenging leadership roles and their contributions to Black life in America and abroad.[3]

Malcolm X holds a special place in the consciousness of Black poets because of his tremendous abilities as an orator; his radical leadership style; his critical commentaries on life in America and in the colonized world; his *Autobiography*, written with the assistance of Alex Haley (1965); his role as a religious leader; and his challenging of the status quo in the United States. Table 2 lists the fifty poets and the sixty-five poems discussed in this essay.[4] This study follows the model suggested by Dudley Randall and

---

2. For poems by Black poets on Martin Luther King, Jr., see Ebon Dooley, "A Poem To My Brother Killed in Combat or Something About a Conversation with My Father After Rev. King Was Killed," *Negro Digest*, February 1969, 90–91; Mari Evans, "A Good Assassination Should Be Quiet," *Negro Digest*, May, 1968, 24; Zack Gilbert, "Mirrors: For Martin Luther King, Jr.," *Negro Digest*, May, 1968, 37; Raymond Guidy, "Dr. Martin Luther King, Jr.," *Negro Digest*, August, 1968, 32; June Jordan, "In Memoriam: Martin Luther King, Jr.," in *Things That I Do in the Dark: Selected Poetry* (New York: Random House, 1977), 108; Marjorie King, "Ode to Revered Martin Luther King, Jr.," *Negro Digest*, August, 1968, 35; Ray McIver, "For Martin Luther King, Jr." *Negro Digest*, August 1968, 29; Arthur G. Mampel, "The King Is Dead," *Negro Digest*, August, 1968, 26; Vilhelm Oldgren, and "From Stockholm on Dr. Martin Luther King, Jr.'s First Death," *Negro Digest*, August, 1968, 33.

3. On Malcolm X, see Lenwood C. Davis, comp., *Malcolm X: A Selected Bibliography* (Westport, CN: Greenwood Press, 1984), 115–123; Theresa Perry, ed., *Teaching Malcolm X* (New York: Routledge, 1996); Louis A. DeCaro, Jr., *On the Side of My People: A Religious Life of Malcolm X* (New York: New York University Press, 1996), 272–74; and David Gallen, comp., *Malcolm A to X: The Man and His Ideas* (New York: Carroll and Graf, 1992), 82. On Martin Luther King, Jr., see David Lewis, *King: A Biography* (Urbana: University of Illinois Press, 1978); Stephen B. Oates, *Let the Trumpet Sound: The Life of Martin Luther King, Jr.* (New York: Harper & Row, 1982); and Taylor Branch, *Parting the Waters: America in the King Years, 1954–1963* (New York: Simon & Schuster, 1988).

4. Dudley Randall and Margaret Burroughs, eds., *For Malcolm: Poems on the Life and the Death of Malcolm X* (Detroit: Broadside Press, 1967), 3–16, 19–36, 38–40, 43–57, 61–62, 64–82; Leaonead Pack Bailey, comp., *Broadside Authors and Artists: An Illustrated Biographical Directory* (Detroit: Broadside Press, 1974), 1–99; Ras Baraka, "I Remember Malcolm," in *In the Tradition: An Anthology of Young Black Writers*, ed. Kevin Powell and Ras Baraka, 80–84 (New York: Harlem River Press/Writers and Readers Publishing, 1992); Samuel Allen, "From Paul Vesey's Ledger," in *Trouble the Water: 250 Years of African American Poetry*, ed. Jerry W. Ward, Jr., 181–182 (New York: Penguin Group, 1997); James A. Emanuel, "For Malcolm, U.S.A.," in *Whole Grain: Collected Poems, 1958–1989* (Detroit: Lotus Press, 1991), 131; Sarah Webster Fabio, "Night After Malcolm Xmas," in

Table 1. Differences in Politics, Principles, and Style of Leadership between Malcolm X and Martin Luther King, Jr.

Item	Malcolm X	Martin Luther King, Jr.
Background:	The street (lower class)	The seminary (middle class)
Major Theme:	Black people should embrace each other, not "love" their enemies.	Black people should transcend themselves, "love" their enemies.
Organizations:	Nation of Islam; Organization of Afro-American Unity; Muslim Mosque, Inc.	Montgomery Improvement Association; Southern Christian Leadership Conference
Politics:	Black	Multiracial
Black Struggle:	"[B]y any means necessary"	Nonviolent resistance
End Results:	Black self-determination	Assimilationism
Focus on the Future:	The American reality	The American dream
Reputation:	Whites: outlaw (created by the press?) Blacks: mixed, especially middle-class leadership; hero of the underclass	Whites: mixed Blacks: hero of the 1950s, early 1960s (loved? greatly respected)? Young black militants after 1963 had problems with him.
Program Policies:	Abstention from direct involvement with whites (until the last year of his life)	Direct involvement with whites
Religion:	Black Muslim/Islam (Sunni Muslim) Religious leader, Islam	Christian (Baptist) Religious leader, Baptist Church
Ideology:	From Black Nationalism to Pan-Africanism to Third World internationalism	Democratic humanism/ Christianity (King's last year: movement toward Third World internationalism)
Major Influences:	Black Nationalism; Marcus Garvey; Islam; Pan-Africanism; Third World socialism; decolonization	Mohandas Gandhi; Henry David Thoreau; Christianity; Negro history; decolonization
Major turning point:	Malcolm's split with Elijah Muhammad	King's concern with America's war in Vietnam
Vision of America:	Disenchantment?	Faith in the future?
Legacy:	"Hero" of the 1960s (martyrdom?)	Hero of the 1950s (martyrdom?)

Soul Ain't: Soul Is—The Hurt of It All (Oakland, CA: Sarah Webster Fabio, 1973), 23–24; June Jordan, "I Celebrate the Sons of Malcolm," in *Some Changes* (New York: E. P. Dutton, 1971), 78; Nubia Kai, "Malcolm," in *Solos* (Detroit: Lotus Press, 1988), 19–22; Jewel C. Latimore [Johari Amini], "St. Malcolm," in *Black Essence* (Chicago: Third World Press, 1968), 1; Welton Smith, "Malcolm," in *Trouble the Water: 250 Years of African American Poetry*, ed. Jerry W. Ward, Jr., 280–281 (New York: Penguin Group, 1997); Julius E. Thompson, "To Malcolm X," in *My Black Me: A Beginning Book of Black Poetry*, ed. Arnold Adoff, 57 (New York: Dutton Children's Books, 1994); Alice Walker, "Malcolm," in *Her Blue Body Everything We Know: Earthling Poems, 1965–1990* (San Diego: Harcourt Brace Jovanovich, 1991), 291; Jerry W. Ward, Jr., "Malcolm Victorious: In Time" (author's personal manuscript, Tougaloo, MS, 2001).

Margaret Burroughs in their important anthology, *For Malcolm: Poems on the Life and the Death of Malcolm X* (1969). The anthology groups its poems into four categories, each focused on an aspect of Malcolm X. Part One, "The Life," contains fifteen poets and sixteen poems. Part Two, "The Death," consists of twenty poets and twenty-two poems. Part Three, "The Rage," comprises nine poets and nine poems. Part Four, "The Aftermath," includes thirteen poets and eighteen poems.[5]

In this essay (from Table 2), fourteen Black poets offer poems which reflect upon "The Life" of Malcolm X. Two have been selected here as representative of the group: "Malcolm X," by Gwendolyn Brooks (1917–2000), and "My Ace of Spades," by Ted Joans.[6]

Malcolm X
By
Gwendolyn Brooks
For Dudley Randall

Original.
Hence ragged-round,
Hence rich-robust.
He had the hawk-man's eyes.
We gasped. We saw the maleness.
The maleness raking out and making guttural the air
And pushing us to walls.
And in a soft and fundamental hour
A sorcery devout and vertical
Beguiled the world.
He opened us—
Who was a key.
Who was a man.

My Ace of Spades
By
Ted Joans

MALCOLM X SPOKE TO ME and sounded you
Malcolm X said this to me & THEN TOLD you that!
Malcolm X whispered in my ears but SCREAMED
      on you!
Malcolm X praised me & thus condemned you
Malcolm X smiled at me & sneered at you
Malcolm X made me proud & so you got scared
Malcolm X told me to HURRY & you began to worry
Malcolm X sang to me but GROWLED AT YOU!!
Malcolm X words freed me & they frightened you
Malcolm tol' it lak it DAMN SHO' Is!!
Malcolm X said that everybody will be F R E E!!
Malcolm X told both of us the T R U T H....
                    now didn't he?

---

5. Randall and Burroughs, *For Malcolm*, 1–82.
6. Randall and Burroughs, *For Malcolm*, 3, 5.

Table 2. Fifty African American Poets Writing on the Life and Career of Malcolm X

Poet	Poem(s)	Category of the Poem
Nanina Alba	"For Malcolm X"	"The Death"
Ras Baraka	"I Remember Malcolm"	"The Life"
Gwendolyn Brooks	"Malcolm X"	"The Life"
Margaret Burroughs	"Brother Freedom"	"The Death"
Lucille Clifton	"Malcolm"	"The Rage"
Margaret Danner	"Malcolm X, A Lover of the Grass Roots"	"The Life"
James A. Emanuel	"For Malcolm, U.S.A."	"The Death"
Mari Evans	"The Insurgent"	"The Life"
Sarah Webster Fabio	"Night After Malcolm Xmas"	"The Life"
Julia Fields	"For Malcolm X"	"The Death"
Kent Foreman	"Judgment Day: For Big Red, the Darwinian Doge. R. I .P."	"The Rage"
Zack Gilbert	"Written After Thinking of Malcolm"	"The Aftermath"
Joe Goncalves	"Flight or a Warrant Is Issued for Malcolm X"	"The Death"
Carmin Auld Goulbourne	"Letter For El-Hajj Malik El-Shabazz"	"The Death"
Bobb Hamilton	"Memorial Day"	"The Aftermath"
Robert Hayden	"El-Hajj Malik El-Shabazz (Malcolm X)"	"The Life"
David Henderson	"They Are Killing All the Young Men"	"The Rage"
Theodore Horne	"Malcolm Exsiccated"; "There's Fire (For February 21)"	"The Aftermath" "The Aftermath"
Christine C. Johnson	"When You Died"; "My Brother Malcolm"	"The Aftermath" "The Life"
Ted Joans	"True Blues For a Dues Player"; "My Ace of Spades"	"The Death" "The Life"
LeRoi Jones [Amiri Baraka]	"A Poem For Black Hearts"	"The Rage"
June Jordan	"I Celebrate the Sons of Malcolm"	"The Aftermath"
Nubia Kai	"Malcolm"	"The Aftermath"
K. William Kgositsile	"Brother Malcolm's Echo"	"The Rage"
Etheridge Knight	"The Sun Came"; "For Malcolm, A Year After"; "It Was A Funky Deal"	"The Aftermath" "The Rage" "The Death"
Oliver LaGrone	"No Tomb In Arlington"	"The Aftermath"
Jewel C. Latimore [Johari Amini]	"St. Malcolm"	"The Life"
Le Graham	"The Black Shining Prince"	"The Rage"
Don L. Lee [Haki R. Madhubuti]	"Malcolm Spoke—Who Listened (this poem is for my consciousness too)"	"The Aftermath"
David Llorens	"One Year Ago"	"The Death"

Adapted from Randall and Burroughs, *For Malcolm*, 1969

Table 2. *Continued*

Poet	Poem(s)	Category of the Poem
James R. Lucas	"Caution"	"The Life"
Clarence Major	"Death of the Man"; "Brother Malcolm: Waste Limit"; "They Feared That He Believed"	"The Death" "The Life" "The Life"
Lawrence P. Neal	"Morning Raga for Malcolm"; "Malcolm X—An Autobiography"	"The Death" "The Life"
George Norman	"To Malcolm X"	"The Death"
James Patterson	"Ballad to the Anonymous"	"The Aftermath"
Raymond Patterson	"At That Moment"	"The Aftermath"
Helen Quigless	"Days After"	"The Aftermath"
Conrad Kent Rivers	"If Blood Is Black Then Spirits Neglect My Unborn Son"; "Look Homeward, Malcolm"	"The Death" "The Aftermath"
Sonia Sanchez	"Malcolm"	"The Death"
Welton Smith [Mbende]	"Malcolm"	"The Rage"
Edward S. Spriggs	"Berkeley's Blue Black"; "Stillborn Pollen Falling"; "For Brother Malcolm"	"The Aftermath" "The Aftermath" "The Aftermath"
Julius E. Thompson	"To Malcolm X"	"The Death"
Paul Vesey [Samuel Allen]	"From Paul Vesey's Ledger"	"The Death"
Alice Walker	"Malcolm"	"The Life"
Margaret Walker	"For Malcolm X"	"The Death"
Jerry W. Ward, Jr.	"Malcolm Victorious: In Time"	"The Death"
Joyce Whitsitt	"For Malcolm"	"The Death"
Reginald Wilson	"For Our American Cousins"	"The Death"
James Worley	"Sleep Bitter, Brother"; "The Cost"; "Color Schema"; "De Bustibus"	"The Death" "The Life" "The Aftermath" "The Death"
Jay Wright	"The Solitude of Change"	"The Death"

Adapted from Randall and Burroughs, *For Malcolm*, 1969

The other twelve poets noted in the category "The Life" are Ras Baraka, "I Remember Malcolm"; Mari Evans, "The Insurgent"; Margaret Danner, "Malcolm X, A Lover of the Grass Roots"; Sarah Webster Fabio, "Night After Malcolm Xmas"; Robert Hayden, "El-Hajj Malik El-Shabazz (Malcolm X)"; Christine Johnson, "My Brother Malcolm"; Jewel C. Latimore [Johari Amini], "St. Malcolm"; James R. Lucas, "Caution"; Clarence Major, "They Feared That He Believed" and "Brother Malcolm: Waste Limit"; Lawrence P. Neal, "Malcolm X—An Autobiography"; Alice Walker, "Malcolm"; and James Worley, "The Cost."

The poems above explore twelve major themes on "The Life" of Malcolm X. They are as follows: (1) the major impact of Malcolm's life both on his own time

(1950s–1960s) and on the time beyond it; (2) the exploitation of Malcolm by some elements in society who did not support him during his life; (3) Malcolm as a strong Black man of the people; (4) Malcolm's deep love for Black people; (5) his uncompromising stand for Black political, economic, and social rights; (6) Malcolm as a revolutionary leader; (7) his transformation from a "lost" individual to a "found" one; (8) the impact of Islam on Black life; (9) Malcolm as a deeply moving and loving brother; (10) Malcolm as a speaker of truth to the people; (11) his encouragement of Black pride and unity; and (12) the evil forces allied against him. In essence, the poems above emphasize the significance of Malcolm's life during his period in history and the special place he holds in the consciousness of Black people from one era to the next.

In this essay (from Table 2), twenty-two African-American poets offer twenty-three poems on "The Death" of Malcolm X in 1965. They are as follows: Nanina Alba, "For Malcolm X"; Margaret Burroughs, "Brother Freedom"; James A. Emanuel, "For Malcolm X, U.S.A."; Julia Fields, "For Malcolm X"; Joe Goncalves, "Flight or a Warrant Is Issued for Malcolm X"; Carmin Auld Goulbourne, "Letter For El-Hajj Malik El-Shabazz"; Ted Joans, "True Blues for a Dues Player"; Etheridge Knight, "It Was A Funky Deal"; David Llorens, "One Year Ago"; Clarence Major, "Death of the Man"; Lawrence P. Neal, "Morning Raga for Malcolm"; George Norman, "To Malcolm X"; Conrad Kent Rivers, "If Blood Is Black Then Spirit Neglects My Unborn Son"; Sonia Sanchez, "Malcolm"; Julius E. Thompson, "To Malcolm X"; Paul Vesey [Samuel Allen], "From Paul Vesey's Ledger"; Margaret Walker, "For Malcolm X"; Jerry W. Ward, Jr., "Malcolm Victorious: In Time"; Joyce Whitsit, "For Malcolm"; Reginald Wilson, "For Our American Cousins"; James Worley, "Sleep Bitter, Brother" and "De Bustibus"; and Jay Wright, "The Solitude of Change."[7]

Among the poets listed above, Etheridge Knight (1931–1991) best portrays "The Death" of Malcolm X in his poem "It Was a Funky Deal."[8]

It Was A Funky Deal
By
Etheridge Knight

It was a funky deal.
The only thing real was red,
Red blood around his red, red beard.

It was a funky deal.

In the beginning was the word,
And in the end the deed.
Judas did it to Jesus
For the same Herd. Same reason.
You made them mad, Malcolm. Same reason.

It was a funky deal.

You rocked too many boats, man.
Pulled too many coats, man.
Saw through the jive.
You reached the wild guys

7. Randall and Burroughs, *For Malcolm*, 19–40.
8. Etheridge Knight, "It Was a Funky Deal," in *For Malcolm*, Randall and Burroughs, 21.

Like me. You and Bird. (And that
Lil LeRoi cat.)

It was a funky deal.

As a group, the poets above express the outrage and sense of grief and loss which pervaded the Black community after the violent death of Malcolm X in the mid-1960s. Malcolm's work and historic role have often been compared to those of such giant figures in Black history as Toussaint L. Ouverture, Joseph Cinque, Denmark Vesey, Nat Turner, Gabriel Prosser, Patrice Lumumba, Medgar Evers, and Robert Williams. His death has also taken on religious tones, and some poets have captured this holy essence of his being by comparing his fate to that of Jesus. For example, George Norman's poem "To Malcolm X" laments:

> You died like the Savior, who died on the cross,
> A martyr, a prophet, your black brothers' loss.[9]

Thus, Malcolm's death has remained a major theme in many poems written by contemporary African American poets.

In this essay (from Table 2), eight African-American poets offer eight poems on "The Rage" of African Americans after the death of Malcolm X. They are as follows: Lucille Clifton, "Malcolm"; Kent Foreman, "Judgment Day: For Big Red, the Darwinian Doge, R.I.P."; David Henderson, "They Are Killing All the Young Men"; LeRoi Jones [Amiri Baraka], "A Poem for Black Hearts"; K. William Kgositsile, "Brother Malcolm's Echo"; Etheridge Knight, "For Malcolm X, A Year After"; Le Graham, "The Black Shining Prince" and Welton Smith, "Malcolm."[10] These poems portray "The Rage" (and the sorrow) of the Black community on the assassination of Malcolm X. Lucille Clifton's "Malcolm" is among the best examples of this category of poems.

Malcolm
By
Lucille Clifton

nobody mentioned war
but doors were closed
black women shaved their heads
black men rustled in the alleys like leaves
prophets were ambushed as they spoke
and from their holes black eagles flew
screaming through the streets.

Bitterness at the loss of such a great leader and thinker as Malcolm X has remained a strong current in the thought of modern-day Black poets.

Finally, from Table 2 of this essay, fifteen African American poets offer eighteen poems on "The Aftermath" of the life and death of Malcolm X. They are as follows: Zack Gilbert (1928–1997), "Written After Thinking of Malcolm"; Bobb Hamilton, "Memorial Day"; Theodore Horne, "Malcolm Exsiccated" and "There's Fire (For February 21)"; Christine C. Johnson, "When You Died"; June Jordan, "I Celebrate the Sons of Malcolm"; Nubia Kia, "Malcolm"; Etheridge Knight, "The Sun Came"; Oliver LaGrone, "No Tomb in Arlington"; Don L. Lee [Haki R. Madhubuti], "Malcolm Spoke—Who

9. George Norman, "To Malcolm X," in *For Malcolm*, Randall and Burroughs, 23.
10. Randall and Burroughs, *For Malcolm*, 43–62; Lucille Clifton, *Good News About the Earth: New Poems*, (New York: Random House, 1972), 22.

Listened (this poem is for my consciousness too)"; James Patterson, "Ballad to the Anonymous" ("Ballada O Neizvestnosti"); Raymond Patterson, "At That Moment"; Helen Quigless, "Days After"; Conrad Kent Rivers, "Look Homeward, Malcolm"; Edward S. Spriggs, "Stillborn Pollen Falling," "For Brother Malcolm," and "Berkeley's Blue Black"; and James Worley, "Color Schema."[11] Zack Gilbert's "Written After Thinking of Malcolm" and Christine C. Johnson's "When You Died" are elegant poems on the social and cultural implications of "The Aftermath" of Malcolm X's life and death.

Written After Thinking of Malcolm
By
Zack Gilbert

And if it wasn't for
All of this pressure
Perhaps, too, my art
Would be a pearls
And my songs more subtle.

But now I only know
This crude stone
In a road
Made rough with hate.

And my best song is
A beat of drums
And a shout.

When You Died
By
Christine C. Johnson

When you died, Malcolm,
Defending and speaking
For the brother that
You loved, we mourned
Your loss.
They silenced you
With shots,
But your voice
Is heard
In other youth
Who have taken up
The fight
For Freedom.
Your ringing voice
Has filled the youth
With wild desires to speak,
And from their throats
Loud and clear,
Defiant and strong,
Have come soul stirrings

11. Randall and Burroughs, *For Malcolm*, 64–82.

For Rights, for Freedoms, for Justice
Denied us
For so long, so long, so long.

You did not die in vain,
For the Freedoms you spoke of
WILL be won.
Though aggressive wars
WILL be fought,
Young men's blood
WILL stain the ground,
Anguished cries WILL rend the air,
Yet babies, victims of man's
Inhumanity and barbarism,
Will one day
Breathe the sweet pure air
Of FREEDOM.

Twelve themes radiate from the poems on "The Aftermath": (1) a celebration of Malcolm's greatness; (2) the special strength which Malcolm had given to other Black men and women; (3) the dignity with which Malcolm had stood for Black freedom; (4) Malcolm's positive work for black children; (5) that many had not understood the message which Malcolm had brought to the people (and, now that he is gone, how many will now understand it?); (6) Malcolm as a martyr for the Black struggle in America; (7) Malcolm's major role in promoting Black consciousness; (8) prayers to Allah to receive Malcolm's soul; (9) Malcolm's international role; (10) assassination as an evil act against Malcolm and the Black community; (11) lamentations for the loss of a Black son; and (12) the hope which Malcolm had given his people. Collectively, the fifteen poets have the mission to uplift the Black community, to aid its members in remembering the past struggles for freedom and justice, and to face the challenges of the future—but without Malcolm's presence. Yet the poets always suggest that his spirit and work will point a way for Blacks to follow.

This study of the work of fifty Black poets on the life and career of Malcolm X contains thirty-two men and eighteen women.[12] They are a diversified group and include some of the most noted Black poets of the twentieth century. The group is comprised of Black men such as James A. Emanuel, Zack Gilbert, Joe Goncalves, Robert Hayden, Ted Joans, LeRoi Jones [Amiri Baraka], K. William Kgositsile, Etheridge Knight, Don L. Lee [Haki R. Madhubuti], Clarence Major, Raymond Patterson, Jerry W. Ward, Jr., and Jay Wright. Black women considered major poets in this study include Gwendolyn Brooks, Lucille Clifton, Margaret Danner, Mari Evans, Sarah Webster Fabio, Julia

---

12. The men of the study are Ras Baraka, James A. Emanuel, Kent Foreman, Zack Gilbert, Joe Goncalves, Bobb Hamilton, Robert Hayden, David Henderson, Theodore Horne, Ted Joans, LeRoi Jones [Amiri Baraka], K. William Kgositsile, Etheridge Knight, Oliver LaGrone, Le Graham, Don L. Lee [Haki R. Madhubuti], David Llorens, James R. Lucas, Clarence Major, Lawrence P. Neal, George Norman, James Patterson, Raymond Patterson, Conrad Kent Rivers, Welton Smith, Edward S. Spriggs, Julius E. Thompson, Paul Vesey [Samuel Allen], Jerry W. Ward, Jr., Reginald Wilson, James Worley, and Jay Wright. The women of the study are Nanina Alba, Gwendolyn Brooks, Margaret Burroughs, Lucille Clifton, Margaret Danner, Mari Evans, Sarah Webster Fabio, Julia Fields, Carmin Auld Goulbourne, June Jordan, Christine C. Johnson, Nubia Kai, Jewel C. Latimore [Johari Amini], Helen Quigless, Sonia Sanchez, Alice Walker, Margaret Walker, and Joyce Whitsitt. On the above authors, see also Roger M. Valade III, *The Essential Black Literature Guide* (Detroit: Visible Ink, 1995), 7–8, 21–22, 32–34, 54–56, 85–87, 102, 114–115, 134, 141, 152–53, 170–172, 193–196, 203–04, 218, 231–32, 236–38, 241–43, 307, 315, 323–25, 369–72.

Fields, June Jordan, Nubia Kai, Jewel C. Latimore [Johari Amini], Sonia Sanchez, Alice Walker, and Margaret Walker. Tables 3 and 4 give a brief summary of the fifty poets' social backgrounds.[13]

The majority of the male poets (62 percent, or twenty of the thirty-two) were born between 1920 and 1939; six were born in the 1940s. On the other hand, of the female poets, seven were born between 1900 and 1919, and six were born in the 1930s. This data suggests that it usually took decades for a Black poet in this study to develop into a major American poet. Fifteen of the male poets were born in the North of the United States, seven in the South, one in the West, and two in foreign countries; the birthplace of one is unknown. Ten of the female poets were born in the North of the United States and eight in the South. Most Black poets had to leave the South in order to develop their artistry, and most of them settled in the North. The Black poets in this study were a highly educated group: twenty-seven men and seventeen women held undergraduate degrees; fifteen men and seven women held master's degrees; and six men and five women held PhDs. In order to survive financially, the Black poets in this study have often had to hold second jobs. While pursuing their vocation as poets, most of them have also followed educational careers. Thirteen of the men and six of the women have served as editors of journals and anthologies; five men and one woman have been artists; two men and two women have been musicians; others have had varied careers as attorneys, businesspersons, postal clerks, military-service personnel, social workers, and chiropractors. Such a wide range of career options have helped Black poets to survive financially in the world of work and to make their contributions to African American literature.

The poets listed in Table 2 have served as trailblazers in the ongoing assessment of Malcolm X as one of the central figures in mid-twentieth-century African American history. Their body of work denotes Malcolm's significant contributions to Black life in the areas of leadership, uplift, African affairs, Black consciousness, family and community relations, religious belief, organizational efforts among Blacks, international issues, and the continuing Black struggle for economic, political, social, and cultural freedom from one generation to the next. Perhaps scholar Oba T'Shaka summarizes Malcolm's contributions best when he observes:

> [Malcolm X,] the family man, the emotional and logical thinker, the believer in Islam, and the committed revolutionary, was a person with strengths and weaknesses like all of us. What made this man exceptional was that he was able to transform such great weaknesses into such towering strengths. He had the greatest capacity known to people, the capacity to deeply change himself. He was able to change through submerging himself in a cause greater than himself. The movements of his people changed Malcolm and Malcolm deepened the revolutionary consciousness of the people.[14]

Malcolm X holds a special place in the historical memories of the African American people, and Black poets have demonstrated with their poems that he is a central figure who must be studied and understood in the continuing struggle of Black people to move forward in the years ahead.

13. Randall and Burroughs, *For Malcolm*, 95–112; Ward, *Trouble the Water*, 539–558; Julius E. Thompson, *Dudley Randall, Broadside Press, and the Black Arts Movement in Detroit, 1960–1995* (Jefferson, NC: McFarland, 1999).

14. Oba T'Shaka, *The Political Legacy of Malcolm X* (Chicago: Third World Press, 1983), 36–37.

**Table 3.   Social Backgrounds on Thirty-Two Black Male
Poets on the Life and Career of Malcolm X**

Name	Date of Birth	Education	Major Positions
Ras Baraka	1969– Newark, NJ	Howard U.	Teacher, writer
James A. Emanuel	June 14, 1921– Alliance, NE.	BA, MA, PhD	Writer, teacher, editor
Kent Foreman	? Chicago, IL.	?	Writer, teacher, theatre director
Zack Gilbert	April 21, 1925–1997 McMullen, MO.	High School	Insurance agent and broker; writer
Joe Goncalves	1937– Boston, MA	?	Writer, editor
Bobb Hamilton	Dec. 16, 1928– Cleveland, OH	BA	Sculptor, teacher, writer, editor
Robert Hayden	Aug. 4, 1913–1980 Detroit, MI	BA MA	Teacher, writer, editor
David Henderson	1942– Harlem, NY	BA	Writer, editor
Theodore Horne	?	?	?
Ted Joans	July 4, 1928– Cairo, IL	BA	Painter, writer, teacher, musician
LeRoi Jones [Amiri Baraka]	Oct. 7, 1934– Newark, NJ	BA, MA	Writer, teacher, editor
K. William Kgositsile	Sept. 19, 1938– Johannesburg, South Africa	BA, MA	Writer, teacher
Etheridge Knight	April 19, 1931–1991 Corinth, MS	BA	Writer, teacher
Oliver LaGrone	1906– McAlester, OK	BA, MA	Sculptor, writer, teacher
Le Graham	Feb. 18, 1940– Savannah, TN	BS, MS	Teacher, writer
Don L. Lee [Haki R. Madhubuti]	Feb. 23, 1942– Little Rock, AR	BA, MFA	Writer, teacher, publisher
David Llorens	Oct. 12, 1939–1973 Chicago, IL	BA	Editor, writer
James R. Lucas	Jan. 13, 1931– Falmouth, VA	BA	Postal clerk, writer, teacher
Clarence Major	Dec. 21, 1936– Atlanta, GA	BA, honorary doctorate	Writer, teacher, editor
Larry P. Neal	Sept. 5, 1937–1981 Atlanta, GA	BA, MA	Writer, teacher, editor
George Norman	Dec. 26, 1923– Detroit, MI	BA	Post office clerk, writer, musician
James Patterson	1933– Moscow, Russia	Gorky Literary Institute	Writer, officer in the Russian Navy

Table 3. *Continued*

Name	Date of Birth	Education	Major Positions
Raymond Patterson	1929– New York, NY	BA, MA	Writer, teacher
Conrad Kent Rivers	Oct. 15, 1933–1968 Atlantic City, NJ	BA	Teacher, writer
Edward S. Spriggs	Dec. 6, 1934– Cleveland, OH	BA	Graphic artist, painter, writer, editor
Welton Smith [Mbende]	Dec. 7, 1946– Kansas City, MO	BA	Social worker, writer
Julius E. Thompson	July 15, 1946– Vicksburg, MS	BA, MA, PhD	Writer, teacher, editor
Paul Vesey [Samuel Allen]	1917– Columbus, OH	BA, LLB, MA	Teacher, writer, attorney
Jerry W. Ward, Jr.	July 31, 1943– Washington, DC	BA, MA, PhD	Writer, teacher, editor
Reginald Wilson	Feb. 24, 1927– Detroit, MI	BS, MA, PhD	Writer, editor, psychologist
James Worley	1921– Welch, WV	BA, MA	Teacher, writer
Jay Wright	May 25, 1935– Albuquerque, NM	BA, MA	Writer

Table 4. Social Backgrounds of Eighteen Black Female Poets on the Life and Career of Malcolm X

Name	Date of Birth	Education	Major Positions
Nanina Alba	Nov. 21, 1917–1968 Montgomery, AL	BA, MA	Writer, teacher
Gwendolyn Brooks	June 7, 1917–2000 Topeka, KS	AA, many honorary doctorates	Writer, teacher, editor
Margaret G. Burroughs	Nov. 1, 1917– St. Rose, LA	BAF, MIAF, honorary doctorate	Artist, writer, teacher, editor
Lucille Clifton	1936– Depew, NY	BA	Writer
Margaret Danner	Jan. 12, 1915–1984 Pryorsburg, KY	BA	Writer, teacher, editor
Mari Evans	1923– Toledo, OH	BA	Writer, musician, teacher, editor
Julia Fields	Jan. 21, 1938– Uniontown, AL	BS	Teacher, writer
Sarah Webster Fabio	Jan. 20, 1928–1979 Nashville, TN	BA, MA	Teacher, writer
Carmin Auld Goulbourne	Feb. 22, 1912– Elcristo, Cuba	High School	Writer
Christine C. Johnson	Jan. 15, 1911– Versailles, KY	BS, MA	Teacher, writer
June Jordan	July 9, 1936– Harlem, NY	BA	Writer, editor, teacher
Nubia Kai	1940s– Detroit, MI	BA	Writer, teacher, storyteller
Jewel C. Latimore [Johari Amini]	1935– Philadelphia, PA	BA, MA	Writer, editor
Helen O. Quigless	July 16, 1944– Washington, DC	BA	Writer
Sonia Sanchez	Sept. 9, 1934– Birmingham, AL	BA, MA, honorary doctorate	Writer, teacher, editor
Alice Walker	1944– Eatonton, GA	BA	Writer, teacher
Margaret Walker	July 7, 1915–1998 Birmingham, AL	BA, MA, PhD	Writer, teacher
Joyce Whitsitt	Aug. 11, 1938– Mount Clemens, MI	BS	Writer, teacher, musician

20

Malcolm X and Africana Critical Theory: Rethinking Revolutionary Black Nationalism, Black Radicalism, and Black Marxism

Reiland Rabaka

Malcolm X, Africana Studies, and (Multi) Disciplinary Decadence

For many, Malcolm X is the fountainhead of modern Black Nationalism (Baraka 1966; Draper 1970; Hall 1978; Pinkney 1976; Van Deburg 1992, 1997). His controversial and often "seemingly contradictory assertions" (Karenga 1979, 253) concerning the right of oppressed, and specifically African, peoples to self-determination and, most notably, concerning self-defensive violence have caused many commentators to focus almost entirely on Malcolm X as a critic of white supremacy and racism (Goldman 1979; Perry 1991; Wolfenstein 1993).[1] That Malcolm X criticized white supremacy is by now part of American and Pan-African public discourse (Baraka 1992; Breitman 1967; Carew 1994; Clarke 1990). However, what is little known or rarely discussed is that Malcolm's life's work and philosophical legacy are more than a mere reaction to racism. Indeed, as I shall argue in this essay, Malcolm's social and political thought, although it consistently underwent "a radical process of change and development" (Cone 1992, 211), provides us with a paradigm of the possibilities of an engaged, African-centered radical politics and social theory—a "critical theory," if you will—that is not afraid to affirm the statement of Malcolm X himself: "We declare our right on this earth to be a man, to be a human being, to be respected as a human being, to be given the rights of a human being in this society, on this earth, in this day, which we intend to bring into existence by any means necessary," (1992b, 56).

---

1. For solid critiques of psycho-biographical interpretations of and Black subject-in-reaction-to-racism approaches to Malcolm's life and legacy, and specifically regarding the work of Goldman (1979), Perry (1991), and Wolfenstein (1993), see Dyson (1995) and Rampersad (1992).

Though Malcolm's life and legacy have been analyzed, often critically, by historians, political scientists, philosophers, literary theorists, feminists, theologians, and psychologists, his life's work, to my knowledge, has never been examined as a possible influence on an Africana critical theory—that is, a theory critical of the domination and discrimination in the worlds, lives, and experiences of continental Africans and the African diaspora (Clarke 1990; Cone 1992; DeCaro 1994, 1996, 1998; Dyson 1993, 1995; Gallen 1992; Sales 1991, 1994; Wolfenstein 1993; Wood 1992). To be sure, many theorists have written on Malcolm X, but with few exceptions (Collins 1992; Lorde 1984; Karenga 1979, 1982, 1991, 1993), the bulk of this work does not attempt to relate Malcolm's social and political theory to radical political practice geared toward social transformation and human liberation in the modern moment. This essay, then, is not another nostalgic narrative of what Malcolm *did*, but in the spirit of Africana critical thought, it is a philosophical foretelling of what Malcolm can *do*.

Initially, this essay will define and explain an African-centered conception of "critical theory." It will then discuss Malcolm X as a contributor to this theory. At stake here is not whether Malcolm adhered to any strict or doctrinaire conceptions of "critical theory," "philosophy," "radical politics," or even "social theory" but that Malcolm's thought, however inchoate, represents a potential foundation upon which to forge a new "philosophy born of struggle" (Harris 1983)—a new critical theory and radical political practice. For Malcolm X, political institutions and social organizations and movements were relevant only insofar as they were "radical," which is why he stated: "I know of no group that is promising unless it's radical. If it's not radical, it is in no way involved effectively in the present struggle" (1992b, 8). The "present struggle," and ultimately the preeminent "struggle," for Malcolm— and very likely for most freedom fighters throughout human history—has always been the struggle for human rights. In exploring Malcolm's contributions to critical theory, one must keep in mind his commitment to radicalism—and Black radicalism in particular.[2]

---

2. I advance this paper, then, as a continuation of the Africana critical-theory project which was initiated in my doctoral dissertation, "Africana Critical Theory: From W. E. B. Du Bois and C. L. R. James's Discourse on Domination and Liberation to Frantz Fanon and Amilcar Cabral's Dialectics of Decolonization" (see Rabaka 2001). It need be noted at the outset, and in agreement with Held, that "[c]ritical theory, it should be emphasized, does *not* [Held's italics] form a unity; it does not mean the same thing to all its adherents" (1980, 14). For instance, Best and Kellner employ the term *critical theory* in a general sense in their critique of postmodern theory, stating: "We are using 'critical theory' here in the general sense of critical social and cultural theory and not in the specific sense that refers to the critical theory of society developed by the Frankfurt School." (1991, 33). Further, Morrow argues that the term *critical theory* "has its origins in the work of a group of German [-Jewish] scholars collectively referred to as the *Frankfurt School* in the 1920's who used the term initially *Kritische Theorie* in German to designate a specific approach to interpreting Marxist theory. But the term has taken on new meanings in the interim and can be neither exclusively identified with the Marxist tradition from which it has become increasingly distinct nor reserved exclusively to the Frankfurt School, given extensive new variations outside the original German context" (1994, 6). Finally, Best uses the term *critical theory* "in the most general sense, designating simply a critical social theory, that is, a social theory critical of present forms of domination, injustice, coercion, and inequality" (1995, xvii). He, therefore, does not "limit the term to refer to only the Frankfurt School" (1995, xvii). Thus, the term *critical theory*, along with the methods, presuppositions, and positions it has come to denote in the humanities and social sciences, a) is not the exclusive domain of Marxists, neo-Marxists, post-Marxists and Eurocentrists and b) can be operationalized to identify and encompass *radical sociopolitical theory and praxis and other emancipatory efforts and endeavors* developed by continental Africans and the African diaspora. For further discussion of the Africana Critical Theory project, see Rabaka (2006a, 2006b, 2006c, 2007, and Forthcoming).

Africana Critical Theory:
Theory Critical of Domination and
Discrimination in Continental and Diasporan
African Life-Worlds and Lived-Experiences

Malcolm X connects and contributes to critical theory in several ways, but before this essay tackles the difficult issue of what is relevant and not relevant to his social and political thought, it must develop a definition of *critical theory*. Critical theory, to put it plainly, is theory critical of domination and discrimination in both classical and contemporary society. It is a theory of social transformation and human liberation that draws from and helps to highlight the emancipatory aspects of the arts, the humanities, and the social sciences (Kellner 1989; Morrow 1994). In other words, "critical" theory can be distinguished from "traditional" theory insofar as "traditional" theory only describes or explains social phenomena (Horkheimer 1972, 1978; Marcuse 1968; Neuman 1997). Critical theory, however, not only describes or explains social phenomena; it also criticizes them, corrects them, and proposes historical alternatives based not on utopia or idealism but on the very real level of human attainment and technological advancement (Marcuse 1964, 1969, 1970, 1972). Thus, critical theory calls for a radical rejection of the established order, which, despite having the ways and means to heal the sick, feed the hungry, clothe the naked, and shelter the homeless, has refused to do so because it has confused human wants with human needs.

In calling for an Africana Studies-informed concept of critical theory, I am arguing, along with Asante (1987, 1988, 1990), that the centrality of African history and culture is inextricable to and indispensable from any analysis or proper interpretation of continental Africa and Africans and of the African diaspora. Indeed, I am concurring with Karenga that now is needed "a synthesis of tradition and reason" and that now, perhaps more than ever, persons of African origin and descent must utilize African cultures and traditions "as a resource rather than as a mere reference" (1997, 160). Africana critical theory, then, like other radical schools of thought, uses past and present critical thought to criticize "society as a whole, not some isolated, delimited realm of 'objects'" (Outlaw 1983a, 74). It is "Africana" in the sense that it is concerned with both continental and diasporan African life-worlds and life-struggles. It is "critical theory," as stated earlier, insofar as it seeks to develop a general theory critical of domination and discrimination in contemporary society and to translate that theory into a vehicle for social transformation. According to Douglas Kellner (1989, 1), a leading contemporary interpreter and exponent of the "Frankfurt School" of critical theory,

> Critical Theory is informed by multidisciplinary research, combined with the attempt to construct a systematic, comprehensive social theory that can confront the key social and political problems of the day. The work of Critical Theorists provides criticisms and alternatives to traditional, or mainstream, social theory, philosophy and science, together with a critique of a full range of ideologies from mass culture to religion. At least some versions of Critical Theory are motivated by an interest in relating theory to politics and an interest in

the emancipation of those who are oppressed and dominated. Critical theory is thus informed by a critique of domination and a theory of liberation.[3]

Turning to the social and political thought of Malcolm X, I intend to reconstruct a tradition within Africana Studies which attempts to develop "a systematic, comprehensive social theory that can confront the key social and political problems of the day." By exploring at length some of the ways in which Malcolm X attempted to "confront" such problems of his day, I will, in several senses, not merely reconstruct and comment upon an Africana critical theory; I will also criticize, correct, and offer alternatives to classical epochal issues that have mutated into contemporary epochal issues. Put another way, I do not intend to construct an Africana critical theory by simply chronicling the radical theory and praxis of Malcolm X. Rather, I intend to *do* Africana critical theory by criticizing domination and discrimination and by offering a theory of liberation in light of the key crises and issues which confront contemporary continental Africans and the African diaspora.

Far from being based simply on the "Frankfurt School" or any other brand of Western European thought, Africana critical theory is, in many senses, a direct discursive heir not merely of Malcolm's life's work and philosophical legacy but also of Kawaida theory, Afrocentric theory, and Africana philosophy. Concerning Kawaida, Karenga states: "From its inception, Kawaida has sought to be an ongoing contribution to the development of a critical theory of cultural and social change.... The two-fold thrust of Kawaida as critical theory has been and remains: 1 to offer a continuous uncompromising criticism of the established order of things; and 2 to pose correctives based on the possibilities inherent in us as people and in the social situation in which we find ourselves" (1980, 12). Africana critical theory, taking a cue from Kawaida theory, is predicated on criticism and correction.

Generously drawing from Asante's "Afrocentric idea," Africana critical theory understands the imperative and importance of engaging African phenomena "from the standpoint of the African" (1990, vi) and of "placing African ideals at the center of any analysis that involves African culture and behavior" (1987, 6). In agreement with Asante, Africana critical theory acknowledges that the critical theorists of the Frankfurt School, particularly Theodor Adorno, Max Horkheimer, Herbert Marcuse, and Jürgen Habermas, "are engaged in a somewhat similar enterprise in re-orienting thinking" (1987, 4).[4] However, Africana critical theory knows all too well that the enigmatic and epochal issues confronting Western European thinkers and European American thinkers are not the same as those that baffle and plague radical intellectuals of African descent: history, culture, and context come into play and carry a great deal of weight concerning these issues.[5] Africana and Western European critical theorists may both

---

3. On Frankfurt School critical theory, see Bernstein (1995), Bottomore (1984), Bronner (1994), Bronner and Kellner (1989), Connerton (1980), Dubiel (1985), Feenberg (1981), Friedman (1981), Guess (1981), Held (1980), Horkheimer (1972, 1978), Ingram (1990), Jay (1984a, 1996), Kellner (1984, 1989), Marcus and Tar (1984), Morrow (1994), Slater (1977), Stirk (2000), Wellmer (1974), and, by far the most comprehensive study of the Frankfurt School to date, Wiggerhaus (1995).

4. Asante refers to Frankfurt School critical theory in two of his major works on Afrocentric theory, *The Afrocentric Idea* and *Kemet, Afrocentricity, and Knowledge* (see Asante 1987, 4–5; 1990, 5, 30).

5. Best correctly contends: "[N]o understanding of history is innocent ... all 'facts' are selected and interpreted from a specific point of view" and "each interpretation of history is inevitably political in its representation of events, in its stance toward the present social reality, and in the practical implications of its narrative, method, and vision" (1995, xvi). He further claims: "Demagogues, tyrants, and mythmakers well understand the political utility of history, and exploit it for their own purposes. They know that the ability to define the meaning of the past grants the power to define the meaning of the present and future; they understand that a people without a historical memory are easily manipulated through myths of the national level and fall victim to the pseudohistorical

purport to be producing theory critical of domination and discrimination in contemporary life and society, but the contexts and confines, the historical and human horizons, the life contexts and the lived experiences of the theorists determine, in often immeasurable and unfathomable ways, what is understood to be "domination" and "discrimination."[6]

Afrocentricity exposes the Eurocentricism of many of the critical theorists of the Frankfurt School, and thus it enables radical theorists of African descent to develop critical theory without having to suffer intellectual inferiority to Eurocentric critical theory. As Asante asserts, Afrocentric critical theory does not question "the validity of the Eurocentric tradition within its context" (1987, 4). However, it does question the "ungrounded aggrandizement" of Eurocentric thought and schools of thought which claim "a universal hegemony" and applicability (1987, 4). Afrocentric critical theory is not inherently antagonistic toward Eurocentric critical theory; rather, it understands that "[w]hether one accepts a Marxist or Freudian view of reality, one is primarily participating in a limited view of reality" (1987, 4). To be sure, there are limitations in both traditions; however, a crucial difference between the two is that the Afrocentric tradition has never claimed "a universal hegemony" and applicability.

Since philosophy has often been understood as the cornerstone of critical theory, Outlaw's articulation of Africana philosophy, emerging out of the discourse of Africana Studies and paying particular attention to Asante's Afrocentricity, enables Africana critical theory to draw from the advances in philosophy from continental Africa and the African diaspora while eschewing tendencies among critical theorists to grant uncritically a prima facie prerogative to philosophy.[7] An imperative of Africana philosophy, according to Outlaw, is to "identify, reconstruct, and create traditions and repositories of thought by African and African-descended persons and peoples, in both oral and written literatures, as forms of philosophy" (1997, 63). Africana philosophy, then, is not synonymous with Africana critical theory insofar as the former is concerned primarily with identifying, reconstructing, and creating traditions and repositories for the "thought" of continental Africans and the African diaspora, whereas the latter is interested not so much in "thought" in a universal or general sense as in critical, oppositional, and emancipatory "thought" and in the ways in which the *thought processes* and *lived experiences* of continental Africans and the African diaspora

> have been influenced and corrupted by imperialism and its invasion and interruption of African history, culture, society, politics, economics, language, religion, familial structures, aesthetics, and axiology; and

---

representation of others. Each culture needs to see the present as history and to create its own narratives that secure their meaning and identities within time" (1995, xii.)

6. Best points to the complexities and contextuality of contemporary critical theory when he writes: "Critical theories ... have strong normative underpinnings which involve commitments to human freedom from forms of oppression and domination. The political vision of critical theorists relates to their understanding of what domination is, how different power systems have emerged, how they can be challenged, and how a different social world can be brought about that creates the conditions of human freedom" (1995, xv).

7. Regarding Western European critical theory, the classic statement on the relationship between philosophy and critical theory is Marcuse's 1937 "Philosophy and Critical Theory," in Marcuse (1968: 134–159). Also of interest are Adorno's "Why Philosophy?" in Ingram and Simon-Ingram (1992, 20–34) and Habermas's "Between Philosophy and Science: Marxism as Critique," in Habermas (1989, 47–54).

may be used to criticize domination and discrimination and to provide a basis for theory and praxis in the interest of liberation.

Grounded in and growing out of the discourse of Africana Studies, specifically Afrocentric theory, Kawaida theory, and Africana philosophy, Africana critical theory criticizes not only imperialism but also the anti-imperialist theory and praxis of the past—in this case the social and political thought of Malcolm X—in order to better confront, contradict, and correct domination in the present and to offer ethical alternatives for liberation in the future. It is in this sense that Africana critical theory agrees with Herbert Marcuse of the Frankfurt School of critical theory when he asserts: "Critical Theory concerns itself with preventing the loss of the truths which past knowledge labored to attain" (1968, 152) and when he further argues: "Critical Theory must concern itself to a hitherto unknown extent with the past—precisely insofar as it is concerned with the future" (1968, 158). Chiefly concerned with "preventing the loss of the truths" which radical intellectual-activists of African descent, and Malcolm X in particular, "labored to attain," this essay engages critical thought emanating from the past of continental Africa and the African diaspora with the intent to enhance and ensure African life in the present and the future.[8]

In advocating and attempting to advance Africana critical theory, my intent is twofold. First, I seek to develop and contribute to the discourse of Africana Studies. Second, I seek to engage in a tradition-construction project which envisions Africana critical theory not so much as what has been said and done by Malcolm X, among others but, even more so, as what remains to be said and done—by present and future radical intellectual-activists in continental Africa and the African diaspora. This means, then, that Africana critical theory, as an intellectual tradition or school of thought within Africana Studies, like all intellectual traditions or schools of thought, has a determinate but ever-reconfiguring constellation of texts that can be contributed to and drawn from. One of the primary purposes of this essay is to establish and elaborate on an Africana critical theory by performing an archaeology of past thought and action with the intention of addressing imperialism in contemporary continental and diasporan African life-worlds and lived-experiences.

Rethinking Malcolm X, Rethinking Critical Theory, Rethinking Black Radicalism

In order to develop an effective "Afro-American liberation movement," Malcolm X argued that African Americans needed to rethink their entire experience in the United States. Like Frantz Fanon and Amilcar Cabral in many ways, he stressed the irrefutable importance of ideology and political education. Though often overlooked, Malcolm's ideological innovations and criticisms demanded that African Americans accept that the ideological struggle was just as important as the physical struggle (1992b, 141). Fanon writes:

> Colonialism and its derivatives do not, as a matter of fact, constitute the present enemies of Africa. In a short time this continent will be liberated. For my part,

---

8. By far the best commentary on and critique of Herbert Marcuse and Marcusean critical theory have been advanced by Kellner (1984) and Schoolman (1980).

the deeper I enter into the cultures and the political circles the surer I am that the great danger that threatens Africa is the absence of ideology. (1967, 186)

Echoing Fanon, Cabral asserts:

> The ideological deficiency, if not to say the total absence of ideology, within the national liberation movement—which is basically due to ignorance of the historical reality which these movements seek to transform—constitutes one of the greatest weaknesses of our struggle against imperialism, if not the greatest weakness of all. (Cabral 1979, 122; see also Cabral 1973, 88)

Malcolm's first major contribution to Africana critical theory was an Afrocentric *ideology*—but not an ideology in a negative sense, as in "propaganda" (Schmitt 1997, 71) or a "narrow" and purportedly "normative ... collection of beliefs and values held by an individual or group for other than purely epistemic reasons" (Honderich 1995, 392). On the contrary, Malcolm cut to the ideological core of white supremacy and Eurocentrism by developing an African- and human-centered "ideological critique" of the thought, belief, and value systems of the ruling race and class.[9] Agreeing with Fanon's and Cabral's criticisms of the absence and ignorance of ideology among Africana freedom fighters, Malcolm, in January 1965, urged "young Civil Rights fighters" to "see" for themselves, to "listen" for themselves, and to "think" for themselves (1991a, 49). In doing so, Malcolm hoped to encourage the young brothers and sisters to develop oppositional and alternative ideology simultaneously. Moreover, he wanted to impress upon them the importance of viewing the world from their own perspective and on their own terms—terms based not only on the best views and values of continental Africans and the African diaspora but also on African criticisms of and contributions to human culture and civilization.

Indeed, Cabral contends: "To have ideology doesn't necessarily mean that you have to define whether you are a communist, socialist, or something like this. To have ideology is to know what you want in your own conditions" (1973, 88). Marx states that "the ruling ideas of each age have ever been the ideas of its ruling class" (Marx and Engels 1978, 489). From Malcolm's critical perspective, there is no "ruling class" but a ruling race/class. The Marxists maintain that in a class society, different classes see the world differently and consequently develop different ideologies or systems of ideas, beliefs, and values to correspond to the perceived reality (see Gottlieb 1992; Kellner 1981; Marx and Engels 1978, 1989). Class society thus gives rise to conflicting ideologies and worldviews. But when racism rears its ugly head and registers as a reality in class society, the situation changes (see, e.g., Fanon 1967, 1968; James 1992, 1994, 1996, 1999).

Malcolm's theory of social change contradicts the mainstream Marxist view that "[t]he history of all hitherto existing society is the history of class struggles" (Marx and Engels 1978, 473). Though human history is replete with innumerable instances of racial, religious, gender, and other struggles, Marxists hold fast to the belief that class struggle is the fundamental factor that shapes, defines, and deforms human existence. Typically, Marxists adhere to and advance the tenet that the capitalist class—the ruling class in Marxist theory—has the power to frame problems and determine the terms in which a problem is discussed. Malcolm's critical theory of society, which is grounded in the history and culture of African peoples as well as in their thought, belief, and value systems and traditions, simultaneously concurs with and criticizes the Marxist class-conflict theory of society.

---

9. On "ideological critique," see Adorno (2000), Gramsci (1971, 1977, 1978, 1985, 2000), Habermas (1986a, 1986b, 1986c, 1989), Horkheimer (1972, 1978), James (1992, 1994, 1999), Karenga (1976, 1978), Kellner (1981), and Marcuse (1958, 1964, 1997, 2001).

Malcolm, Marxism, and a Few Misadventures in Africana Critical Thought

Malcolm and many nationalists and Pan-Africanists agree with the Marxist argument that in a class society the ruling class holds the dominant ideology; that the dominated classes have fundamentally different experiences from those of the ruling class; that the established-order institutions in class society cater to and serve primarily the interests of the ruling class; and that these institutions do not solve the dominated classes' problems but create and exacerbate them. They also agree with the Marxist claim that the perspective of the dominated differs from that of the dominant to the degree that the life experiences of the dominated rarely afford them the opportunities to fully and freely develop that which the rich and powerful already have. Finally, they agree with the Marxist assertion that those in power have more theorists, writers, ministers, publishers, pundits, and so on, to spread their ideology; that they have control over mass media and telecommunications; and that the poor and poverty-stricken have a hard time exposing others to their life struggles because they have only word of mouth or alternative media available to disseminate their ideas.

However, dissent darts into the discussion when one understands Malcolm's conclusion that his concept of "Black Nationalism" was outright impossible—that is, wholly irreconcilable with the predatory, exploitative, and racist nature of contemporary capitalism. "I mean by Black Nationalism," Malcolm thundered, "that the Black man must control the radio, the newspaper, and the television for our communities. I also mean that we must do those things necessary to elevate ourselves socially, culturally, and to restore racial dignity" (cited in Sales 1994, 79–80). As noted above, in a capitalist society those persons or groups without capital or ways and means to generate capital are usually at the mercy of the capitalist or ruling class. And if the ruling class profits from the economic exploitation *and* racial oppression of the dominated classes, then anything less than a radical reorganization of society will not place the goods and services that Malcolm deemed necessary for Black liberation and elevation in the hands and under the control of Black people. In other words, Malcolm ultimately understood capitalism to be as a great an impediment to African American liberation as racism. Concerning capitalism, he asserted:

> It is impossible for capitalism to survive, primarily because the system of capitalism needs some blood to suck. Capitalism used to be like an eagle, but now it's more like a vulture. It used to be strong enough to go and suck anybody's blood whether they were strong or not. But now it has become more cowardly, like the vulture, and it can only suck the blood of the helpless. As the nations of the world free themselves, then capitalism has less victims, less [blood] to suck, and it becomes weaker and weaker. It's only a matter of time in my opinion before it will collapse completely. (1990, 199)

Malcolm's theory of social change concurs with the class-struggle thesis of most Marxists; yet, unlike them, it also engages the realities of racial violence and oppression. In this sense, then, Malcolm's theory of social change offers a criticism of and a corrective to the "orthodox" Marxist position in several ways.[10] First, his theory does

---

10. For a few of the more noteworthy contemporary critiques of the "orthodox" Marxist positions by neo-Marxist/New Left movement theorists, see Aronson (1995), Gottlieb (1992), Jay (1984), Kellner (1995), and Nelson and Grossberg (1988).

not exaggerate or overassert the primacy of class, whereas most Black Marxists or Marxists of African descent, in traditional Marxist fashion, tend to emphasize class and the effects of capitalism and to downplay the weight and gravity of race and racism in the contemporary worlds, lives, and struggles of continental Africans and the African diaspora (see Cruse 1967; James 1996; Marable 1996; Robinson 2000; West 1988). Second, Malcolm's theory of social change has a much broader-based and critical universe than the "orthodox" Marxist theory. This is especially evident in his Militant Labor Forum lectures, where he criticizes both capitalism *and* colonialism (1990, 1992b), and in his speeches and writings just before his assassination, where he—according to Davis (1992), Lorde (1984), hooks (1994a, 1994b), and Patricia Hill Collins (1992)—revealed that he had "altered and broadened" his views not only on race, racism, and race relations but also "concerning the role of women in society and the revolution" (Lorde 1984, 135). Finally, and in several senses, Malcolm's theory updates and offers Afrocentric alternatives to Africana Studies and other scholars interested in "insurgent intellectualism" and political activism (see hooks and West 1991). In the same spirit as Cabral (1973, 88), Malcolm knew it was not necessary for him to define himself as a "communist" or "socialist" or "Marxist" in order for him to advance an ideology or an ideological critique. Perhaps he perceived Marxism as Eurocentric and too focused on capitalist countries. Maybe he maintained his earlier wariness concerning Black/white coalitions. Whatever his reason was, when "hard pressed to give a specific definition of the over-all philosophy" which he thought was "necessary for the liberation of Black people in this country," he indicated that he "had to do a lot of thinking and reappraising of [his] definition of Black Nationalism" (Sales 1994, 88–89).

Rethinking and Reappraising Black Radicalism, Rethinking and Reappraising Malcolm X as a Black Radical

In rethinking and reappraising his definition of *Black Nationalism*, Malcolm moved his thought in the direction of both Pan-Africanism and socialism. He emphasized the connections between continental Africans and the African diaspora, criticized both capitalism and colonialism, and used his developing theory to criticize his former beliefs and to bring out what he perceived as "the best" in Black Nationalist thought. Concerning his emerging Pan-Africanism, Sales states that in "his final period of intellectual development ... [t]he role of Africa in the thinking of Malcolm was essentially political" (1994, 87). Whereas Malcolm had once advanced that African Americans should physically return to Africa, he now argued:

> The solution for the Afro-American is two-fold—long-range and short-range. I believe that a psychological, cultural, and philosophical migration back to Africa will solve our problems. Not a physical migration, but a cultural, psychological, philosophical migration back to Africa—which means restoring our common bond—will give us the spiritual strength and the incentive to strengthen our political and social and economic position right here in America, and to fight for the things that are ours by right on this continent. And at the same time this will give incentive to many of our people to

also visit and even migrate physically back to Africa, and those who stay here can help those who go back and those who go back can help those who stay here. (1992b, 152)

But before many African Americans could attain the "long-range" goals—indeed, before many of them could even value Africa and African culture and traditions, let alone visit or emigrate there—Malcolm knew what Fanon knew: "You will not be able to do all this unless you give the people some political education" (1968, 180). Whether one calls it "ideology" or "theory" or "philosophy," Malcolm, like Fanon and Cabral, emphasized the pressing need to "re-educate our people ... in regards to the science of politics, so that they will know what politics is supposed to produce," and what their "responsibilities are" (1992b, 70). In an attempt to outline the "short-range" objectives of his developing theory of social change, Malcolm declared: "Immediate steps have to be taken to re-educate our people—[to produce] a more real [concrete] view of political, economic, and social conditions, and self-improvement to gain political control over every community in which we predominate, and also over the economy of that same community" (1992b, 152).

In "re-educating" African Americans in "the science of politics," in "giv[ing] the people some political education," Malcolm admonished African Americans not to allow "anybody who is oppressing us [to] ever lay the ground rules" (1992b, 155). In fact, he stated: "Don't go by their game, don't play the game by their rules. Let them know now that this is a new game, and we've got some new rules, and these rules mean anything goes, *anything goes* [Malcolm's italics]" (1992b, 155). In other words, the "new game" and the "new rules" meant that, from Malcolm's point of view, African Americans needed to adopt and develop oppositional ideology—an alternative series of thought, belief, and value systems "black-minded" enough both to *explain* and to *criticize* their oppression and their oppressors' ideology (1992b, 104).

In normative use the term *ideology* typically involves two elements. First, it indicates "a particular style of *explanation* [italics in the original] in which the prevalence of certain beliefs and values is attributed to some significant degree to a non-epistemic role that they serve for the individuals who hold them or for society at large" (Honderich 1995, 392). Second, the term indicates a "particular style of *criticism* [italics in the original] in which beliefs and values are called into question precisely by giving this sort of interest-based or social-symbolic explanation of their prevalence—an explanation characteristically not known to the believers themselves" (Honderich 1995, 392). In investigating Malcolm's ideological contributions to Africana critical theory and keeping in mind the above assertion that ideology both explains and criticizes, African Americans must not only note Malcolm's exhortations that they explain things from their own point of view—namely, "see" for themselves, "listen" for themselves, and "think" for themselves, in short, be "black-minded," as he put it elsewhere; they must also be mindful of his emphasis on the necessity of criticism. Indeed, Malcolm mused:

> I think all of us should be critics of each other. Whenever you can't stand criticism you can never grow.... I think that we accomplish more when we sit down ... and iron out whatever differences that may exist and try and then do something constructive for the benefit of our people.... I don't think that we should be above criticism. I don't think that anyone should be above criticism. (1989, 87)

Malcolm was a major cultural critic, and he sought to utilize criticism as a tool. Like the Marxist-influenced critical theorists, Malcolm understood that his criticism was geared toward enhancing the quality of human life, which is one of the reasons he associated criticism with growth in the preceding quotation. Keeping in mind one of the cardinal concepts of critical theory—that constructive criticism can change both self and society—Malcolm criticized the ideology of the ruling race or class from the perspective of the poor, poverty-stricken Black masses, unapologetically asserting:

> The economic exploitation in the Afro-American community is the most vicious form practiced on any people in America. In fact, it is the most vicious practiced on any people on this earth. No one is exploited economically as thoroughly as you and I, because in most countries where people are exploited they know it. You and I are in this country being exploited and sometimes we don't know it ... we live in one of the rottenest countries that has ever existed on this earth. It's the system that is rotten; we have a rotten system. It's a system of exploitation, of outright humiliation, degradation, discrimination— all of the negative things that you can run into, you have run into under this system that disguises itself as a democracy, disguises itself as a democracy. (1992b, 47)

Thus Malcolm criticizes American democracy and, by default, all of American society and civilization by pointing out the inconsistency between the universal principles proclaimed by the ruling race or class and its actual practice. Indeed, Broadus Butler points out: "The preponderance of Black American philosophical inquiry, analysis, and philosophically oriented oral, literary, and political work has been directed primarily toward change in the human condition and toward social and legal change in pursuit of a clarification and perfection of the democratic ideal of justice. That pursuit always has combined ontological analysis with moral prescription—the analysis of what is with the analysis of what ought to be" (1983, 1). Over and often against the Marxist method, Malcolm employed the African American philosophical method in his efforts to "change the human condition." Drawing from traditions ranging from the critical nationalism of Martin Delany and Marcus Garvey to those of Carlos Cooks and Robert Williams, Malcolm sought consistently to combine his analysis of the present— the "what is"—with the possibilities and prospects of the future—the "what ought to be," the "what could be." He regularly reminded his people that they could "create a new society" and that they did not have to die in order to go to heaven—meaning that they did not have to stop living, physically, in order to experience happiness and attain the "good life." He stressed to them that they could "make heaven right here on this earth" (1992b, 64). Malcolm's greatest contribution to Africana critical thought lies, perhaps, in his radical commitment to continually recommit himself to end domination and discrimination and to bring into being lasting human liberation—by any means necessary!

References

Adorno, Theodor W. 2000. *The Adorno reader.* Ed. Brian O'Connor. Malden, MA: Blackwell.

Aronson, Ronald. 1995. *After Marxism.* New York: Guilford Press.

Asante, Molefi Kete. 1987. *The Afrocentric idea.* Philadelphia: Temple University Press.

_____. 1988. *Afrocentricity*. Trenton, NJ: Africa World Press.

_____. 1990. *Kemet, Afrocentricity, and knowledge*. Trenton, NJ: Africa World Press.

_____. 1993. *Malcolm X as cultural hero and other Afrocentric essays*. Trenton, NJ: African World Press.

Baraka, Amiri [LeRoi Jones]. 1966. *Home: Social essays*. New York: William Morrow.

_____. The legacy of Malcolm X, and the coming of the Black Nation. In *Home: Social essays*. New York: William Morrow.

_____. 1992. Malcolm as ideology. In *Malcolm X: In our own image*, ed. Joe Wood, 18–35. New York: St. Martin's Press.

Bernstein, Jay M., ed. 1995. *The Frankfurt School: Critical assessments*. London: Routledge.

Best, Steven. 1995. *The politics of historical vision: Marx, Foucault, Habermas*. New York: Guilford.

_____, and Douglas Kellner. 1991. *Postmodern theory*. New York: Guilford

Bottomore, Tom. 1984. *The Frankfurt School*. New York: Routledge.

Bronner, Stephen Eric. 1994. *Of critical theory and its theorists*. Malden, MA: Blackwell.

_____, and Douglass Kellner, eds. 1989. *Critical theory and society: A reader*. New York: Routledge.

Breitman, George. 1967. *The last year of Malcolm X: The evolution of a revolutionary*. New York: Schocken.

Butler, Broadus. 1983. Frederick Douglass: The Black philosopher in the United States: A commentary. In *Philosophy born of struggle: An anthology of Afro-American philosophy from 1917*, ed. Leonard Harris, 1–10. Dubuque, IA: Kendall/Hunt.

Cabral, Amilcar. 1972. *Revolution in Guinea: Selected texts*. New York: Monthly Review Press.

_____. 1973. *Return to the source: Selected speeches of Amilcar Cabral*. New York: Monthly Review Press.

_____. 1979. *Unity and struggle: Speeches and writings of Amilcar Cabral*. New York: Monthly Review Press.

Carew, Jan. 1994. *Ghosts in our blood: With Malcolm X in Africa, England, and the Caribbean*. Chicago: Lawrence Hill.

Clarke, John Henrik, ed. 1990. *Malcolm X: The man and his times*. Trenton, NJ: Africa World Press.

Collins, Patricia Hill. 1992. Learning to think for ourselves: Malcolm X's Black Nationalism reconsidered." In *Malcolm X: In our own image*, ed. Joe Wood, 58–95. New York: St. Martin's Press.

Collins, Rodnell P. 1998. *Seventh child: A family memoir of Malcolm X*. Secaucus, NJ: Birch Lane Press.

Cone, James H. 1992. *Martin & Malcolm & America: A dream or a nightmare*. Maryknoll, NY: Orbis.

Connerton, Paul. 1980. *The tragedy of enlightenment: An essay of the Frankfurt School*. Cambridge, UK: Cambridge University Press.

Cruse, Harold. 1967. *The crisis of the Negro intellectual: A historical analysis of the failure of Black leadership.* New York: Quill.

Davis, Angela Y. 1992. Meditations on the legacy of Malcolm X. In *Malcolm X: In our own Image,* ed. Joe Wood, 36–47. New York: St. Martin's Press.

DeCaro, Jr., Louis Anthony. 1994. Malcolm X and the Nation of Islam: Two moments in his religious sojourn. PhD diss., New York Univ.

_____. 1996. *On the side of my people: A religious life of Malcolm X.* New York: New York University Press.

_____. 1998. *Malcolm and the cross: The Nation of Islam, Malcolm X, and Christianity.* New York: New York University Press.

Draper, Theodore. 1970. *The rediscovery of Black Nationalism.* New York: Viking Press.

Dubiel, Helmut. 1985. *Theory and politics: Studies in the development of critical theory.* Trans. Benjamin Gregg. Cambridge, MA: MIT Press.

Dyson, Michael Eric. 1993. Uses of heroes: Celebration and criticism in the interpretation of Malcolm X and Martin Luther King, Jr. PhD diss., Princeton Univ.

_____. 1995. *Making Malcolm: The myth and meaning of Malcolm X.* New York: Oxford University Press.

Essien-Udom, E. U. 1962. *Black Nationalism: A search for an identity in America.* Chicago: University of Chicago Press.

Fanon, Frantz. 1965. *A dying colonialism.* Trans. Haakon Chevalier. New York: Grove.

_____. 1967. *Black skin, white masks.* Trans. Charles Lam Markmann. New York: Grove.

_____. 1968. *The wretched of the earth.* Trans. Constance Farrington. New York: Grove.

_____. 1969. *Toward the African revolution.* Trans. Haakon Chevalier. New York: Grove.

Feenberg, Andrew. 1981. *Lukacs, Marx, and the sources of critical theory.* Totowa, NJ: Rowman and Littlefield.

Franklin, V. P. 1995. Malcolm X and the resurrection of the dead. In *Living our stories, telling our truths: Autobiography and the making of the African American intellectual tradition.* New York: Scribner.

Friedman, George. 1981. *The political philosophy of the Frankfurt School.* Ithaca, NY: Cornell University Press.

Gallen, David, ed. 1992. *Malcolm X as they knew him.* New York: Carroll & Graf.

_____. ed. 1994. *A Malcolm X reader: Perspectives on the man and the myths.* New York: Carroll & Graf.

Goldman, Peter. 1979. *The death and life of Malcolm X.* Chicago: University of Illinois Press.

Gottlieb, Roger S. 1992. *Marxism 1844–1990: Origins, betrayal, rebirth.* New York: Routledge.

Gramsci, Antonio. 1971. *Selections from the prison notebooks of Antonio Gramsci.* New York: International.

_____. 1977. *Selections from the political writings, 1910–1920.* New York: International.

_____. 1978. *Selections from the prison writings, 1921–1926.* New York: International.

_____. 1985. *Selections from the cultural writings.* Cambridge, MA: Harvard University Press.

_____. 2000. *The Antonio Gramsci reader: Selected writings, 1916–1935*. New York: New York University Press.

Guess, Raymond. 1981. *The idea of critical theory: Habermas and the Frankfurt School*. Cambridge, UK: Cambridge University Press.

Habermas, Jürgen. 1976. *Legitimation crisis*. London: Heinemann.

_____. 1979. *Communication and the evolution of society*. Trans. Thomas McCarthy. Boston: Beacon.

_____. 1984. *Theory of communicative action*. Vol. 1. Trans. Thomas McCarthy. Boston: Beacon.

_____. 1986a. *Theory and practice*. Cambridge, UK: Polity Press.

_____. 1986b. *Knowledge and human interests*. Cambridge, UK: Polity Press.

_____. 1986c. *Toward a rational society*. Cambridge, UK: Polity Press.

_____. 1987. *Theory of communicative action*. Vol. 2. Trans. Thomas McCarthy. Boston: Beacon.

_____. 1989. *On society and politics: A reader*. Ed. Steven Seidman. Boston: Beacon.

Hall, Raymond L. 1978. *Black separatism in the United States*. Hanover, NH: University Press of New England.

Harris, Leonard, ed. 1983. *Philosophy born of struggle: An anthology of Afro-American philosophy from 1917*. Dubuque, IA: Kendall/Hunt.

Held, David. 1980. *Introduction to critical theory: Horkheimer to Habermas*. Berkeley: University of California Press.

Honderich, Ted, ed. 1995. *The Oxford companion to philosophy*. New York: Oxford University Press.

hooks, bell. 1990. *Yearning: Race, gender, and cultural politics*. Boston: South End.

_____. 1994a. *Teaching to transgress: Education as the practice of freedom*. Boston: South End.

_____. 1994b. *Outlaw culture: Resisting representation*. New York: Routledge.

_____. 1995. *Killing rage: Ending racism*. New York: Henry Holt.

_____, and Cornel West. 1991. *Breaking bread: Insurgent Black intellectual life*. Boston: South End.

Horkheimer, Max. 1972. *Critical theory*. New York: Continuum.

_____. 1978. *Dawn and decline: Notes, 1926–1931 and 1950–1969*. New York: Continuum.

Ingram, David. 1990. *Critical theory and philosophy*. New York: Paragon House.

Ingram, David, and Julia Simon-Ingram, eds. 1992. *Critical theory: The essential readings*. New York: Paragon House.

Jamal, Hakim A. 1973. *From the dead level: Malcolm X and me*. New York: Warner Books.

James, C. L. R. 1992. *The C. L. R. James reader*. Ed. Anna Grimshaw. Cambridge, MA: Blackwell.

_____. 1994. *C. L. R. James and revolutionary Marxism: Selected writings of C. L. R. James*. Ed. Scott McLemee and Paul Le Blanc. Atlantic Highlands, NJ: Humanities Press.

_____. 1996. *C. L .R. James on the "Negro Question."* Ed. Scott McLemee. Jackson: University of Mississippi Press.

_____. 1999. *Marxism for our times: C. L .R. James on revolutionary organization.* Ed. Martin Glaberman. Jackson: University of Mississippi Press.

Jay, Martin. 1984. *Marxism and totality: The adventures of a concept from Lukács to Habermas.* Berkeley: University of California Press.

_____. 1996. *The Dialectical imagination: A history of the Frankfurt School and the Institute of Social Research, 1923–1950.* Berkeley: University of California Press.

Karenga, Maulana. 1976. Afro-American nationalism: Beyond mystification and misconceptions. PhD diss., U.S. International Univ.

_____. 1977. The De-Afro-Americanization of Malcolm X. *Voice, News & Viewpoints* 17 (38): A5, A11–14.

_____. 1978. *Essays on struggle: Position and analysis.* San Diego: Kawaida Publications.

_____. 1979. The socio-political philosophy of Malcolm X. *Western Journal of Black Studies* 3 (4): 251–262.

_____. 1980. *Kawaida theory: An introductory outline.* Los Angeles: Kawaida Publications.

_____. 1981. Malcolm X: His significance and legacy. *Black News* 4 (20): 30–35.

_____. 1982. Malcolm and the messenger: From psychological assumptions to political analysis. *Western Journal of Black Studies* 6 (4): 193–201.

_____. 1991. The liberation ethics of Malcolm X: Text, context and practice. Paper, US Organization Archives, Los Angeles, CA.

_____. 1993. The oppositional logic of Malcolm X: Differentiation, engagement and resistance." *Western Journal of Black Studies* 17 (1): 6–16.

_____. 1997. African culture and the ongoing quest for excellence: Dialog, principle, practice. *The Black Collegian*, February, 160–163.

Kellner, Douglas. 1979. Critical theory, democracy, and human Rights. *New Political Science* 1 (1): 12–18.

_____. 1981. Marxism, morality, and ideology. *Canadian Journal of Philosophy*, Suppl. no 7: 93–120.

_____. 1983. Critical theory, commodities and the consumer society. *Theory, Culture, and Society* 3: 66–84.

_____. 1984. *Herbert Marcuse and the crisis of Marxism.* Berkeley: University of California Press.

_____. 1984/1985. Critical theory, mass communication, and popular culture. *Telos* 62: 196–206.

_____. 1989. *Critical theory, Marxism, and modernity.* Baltimore: Johns Hopkins University Press.

_____. 1995. The obsolescence of Marxism? In *Whither Marxism?: Global crises in international perspective*, ed. Bernd Magnus and Stephen Cullenberg. New York: Routledge.

Lincoln, C. Eric. 1961. *The Black Muslims in America.* Boston: Beacon.

Lorde, Audre. 1984. *Sister outsider: Essays and speeches.* Freedom, CA: The Crossing Press.

Malcolm X. 1967. *Malcolm X on Afro-American history.* New York: Pathfinder.

_____. 1971. *The end of white world supremacy: Four speeches by Malcolm X.* Ed. Benjamin Goodman. New York: Merlin House/Seaver Books.

_____. 1989. *Malcolm X: The last speeches.* Ed. Bruce Perry. New York: Pathfinder.

_____. 1990. *Malcolm X speaks: Selected speeches and statements.* Ed. George Breitman. New York: Grove Weidenfeld.

_____. 1991a. *Malcolm X talks to young people: Speeches in the U.S., Britain, and Africa.* New York: Pathfinder.

_____. 1991b. *Malcolm X: Speeches at Harvard.* Ed. Archie Epps. New York: Paragon House.

_____. 1992a. *The autobiography of Malcolm X.* With Alex Haley. New York: Ballantine.

_____. 1992b. *By any means necessary.* 2nd ed. New York: Pathfinder.

_____. 1992c. *February 1965: The final speeches.* New York: Pathfinder.

_____. 1992d. Chickens, snakes and duck eggs: Making history and parables with Robert Penn Warren. In *Malcolm X as they knew him,* ed. David Gallen, 145–154. New York: Carroll & Graf.

Marable, Manning. 1992. By any means necessary: The life and legacy of Malcolm X. Paper presented at Metro State College, Denver, CO.

_____. 1996. *Speaking truth to power: Essays on race, resistance, and radicalism.* Boulder, CO: Westview Press.

Marcus, Judith, and Zoltan Tar, eds. 1984. *The foundations of the Frankfurt School of social research.* New York: Transaction Books.

Marcuse, Herbert. 1958. *Soviet Marxism.* New York: Columbia University Press.

_____. 1960. *Reason and revolution.* Boston: Beacon.

_____. 1964. *One-Dimensional man: Studies in the ideology of advanced industrial society.* Boston: Beacon.

_____. 1966. *Eros and civilization.* Boston: Beacon.

_____. 1968. *Negations: Essays in critical theory.* Boston: Beacon.

_____. 1969. *An essay on liberation.* Boston: Beacon.

_____. 1970. *Five lectures: Psychoanalysis, politics, and utopia.* Boston: Beacon.

_____. 1972. *Counter-revolution and revolt.* Boston: Beacon.

_____. 1973. *Studies in critical philosophy.* Boston: Beacon.

_____. 1978. *The aesthetic dimension: Toward a critique of Marxist aesthetics.* Boston: Beacon.

_____. 1997. *Technology, war and fascism.* Ed. Douglas Kellner. New York: Routledge.

_____. 2001. *Toward a critical theory of society.* Ed. Douglas Kellner. New York: Routledge.

Marcuse, Herbert, Barrington Moore, and Robert Paul Wolff. 1965. *A critique of pure tolerance.* Boston: Beacon.

Marx, Karl, and Friedrich Engels. 1978. *The Marx-Engels reader.* Ed. Robert C. Tucker. New York: Norton.

_____. 1989. *Marx & Engels: Basic writings on politics and philosophy.* Ed. Lewis S. Feuer. New York: Anchor.

Morrow, Raymond A., with David D. Brown. 1994. *Critical theory and methodology.* Thousand Oaks, CA: Sage.

Nelson, Cary, and Lawrence Grossberg, eds. 1988. *Marxism and the interpretation of culture.* Urbana and Chicago: University of Illinois Press.

Neuman, W. Lawrence. 1997. *Social research methods: Qualitative and quantitative approaches.* Boston: Allyn and Bacon.

Outlaw, Jr., Lucius T. 1983a. Philosophy, hermeneutics, social-political theory: Critical thought in the interest of African Americans. In *Philosophy born of struggle: An anthology of Afro-American philosophy from 1917*, ed. Leonard Harris, 60–88. Dubuque, IA: Kendall/Hunt.

_____. 1983b. Race and class in the theory and practice of emancipatory social transformation. In *Philosophy born of struggle: An anthology of Afro-American philosophy from 1917*, ed. Leonard Harris, 117–129. Dubuque, IA: Kendall/Hunt.

_____. 1983c. Critical theory in a period of radical transformation. *Praxis International* 3 (2): 138–46.

_____. 1997. African, African American, Africana philosophy. In *African American perspectives and philosophical traditions*, ed. John P. Pittman, 63–93. New York: Routledge.

Perry, Bruce. 1991. *Malcolm: The life of a man who changed Black America.* Barrytown, NY: Station Hill.

Pinkney, Alphonso. 1976. *Red, black, and green: Black Nationalism in the United States.* Cambridge, UK: Cambridge University Press.

Pittman, John P., ed. 1997. *African American perspectives and philosophical traditions.* New York: Routledge.

Rabaka, Reiland. 2001. Africana critical theory: From W. E. B. Du Bois and C. L. R. James's Discourse on Domination and Liberation to Frantz Fanon and Amilcar Cabral's Dialectics of Decolonization. PhD diss., Temple Univ.

_____. 2006a. Africana critical theory of contemporary society: Ruminations on radical politics, social theory, and Africana philosophy. In *The handbook of Black Studies*, ed. Molefi K. Asante and Maulana Karenga, 130–152. Thousand Oaks, CA: Sage.

_____. 2006b. The souls of Black Radical folk: W. E. B. Du Bois, critical social theory, and the state of Africana Studies. *Journal of Black Studies* 36 (5): 732–763.

_____. 2006c. W. E. B. Du Bois's "The Comet" and contributions to critical race theory: An essay on Black Radical politics and antiracist social ethics. *Ethnic Studies Review: Journal of the National Association for Ethnic Studies* 29 (1): 22–48.

_____. 2007. *W. E .B. Du Bois and the problems of the twenty-first century: An essay on Africana critical theory.* Lanham, MD: Lexington Books/Rowman & Littlefield Publishers.

_____. Forthcoming. *Du Bois's dialectics: Black Radical politics and the reconstruction of critical social theory.* Lanham, MD: Lexington Books/Rowman & Littlefield Publishers.

Rampersad, Arnold. 1992. The color of his eyes: Bruce Perry's *Malcolm* and Malcolm's *Malcolm*. In *Malcolm X: In our own Image*, ed. Joe Wood, 117–134. New York: St. Martin's Press.

Rasmussen, David M., ed. 1999. *The handbook of critical theory*. Malden, MA: Blackwell.

Reed, Adolph, Jr. 1992. The allure of Malcolm X and the changing character of Black politics. In *Malcolm X: In our own Image*, ed. Joe Wood, 203–232. New York: St. Martin's Press.

Robinson, Cedric J. 2000. *Black Marxism: The making of the Black radical tradition*. Chapel Hill: University of North Carolina Press.

Sales, William W., Jr. 1991. Malcolm X and the Organization of Afro-American Unity: A case study in Afro-American nationalism. PhD diss., Columbia Univ.

_____. 1994. *From civil rights to Black liberation: Malcolm X and the Organization of Afro-American Unity*. Boston: South End Press.

Schmitt, Richard. 1997. *Introduction to Marx and Engels*. Boulder, CO: Westview.

Schoolman, Morton. 1980. *The imaginary witness: The critical theory of Herbert Marcuse*. New York: New York University Press.

Slater, Phillip. 1977. *Origin and significance of the Frankfurt School*. London: Routledge.

Stirk, Peter M. R. 2000. *Critical theory, politics and society*. London: Pinter Press.

Van Deburg, William. 1992. *New day in Babylon: The Black Power movement and American culture, 1965–1975*. Chicago: University of Chicago Press.

_____, ed. 1997. *Modern Black Nationalism: From Marcus Garvey to Louis Farrakhan*. New York: New York University Press.

West, Cornel. 1988. Marxist theory and the specificity of Afro-American oppression. In *Marxism and the interpretation of culture*, ed. Cary Nelson and Lawrence Grossberg, 17–34. Urbana and Chicago: University of Illinois Press.

_____. 1992. Malcolm X and Black rage. In *Malcolm X: In our own Image*, ed. Joe Wood, 48–58. New York: St. Martin's Press.

Wellmer, Albrecht. 1974. *The critical theory of society*. New York: Seabury.

Wideman, John Edgar. 1992. Malcolm X: The art of autobiography. In *Malcolm X: In our own Image*, ed. Joe Wood, 101–116. New York: St. Martin's Press.

Wiggerhaus, Rolf. 1995. *The Frankfurt School: Its history, theories, and political significance*. Trans. Michael Robertson. Cambridge, MA: MIT Press.

Wood, Joe, ed. 1992. *Malcolm X: In our own image*. New York: St. Martin's Press.

Wolfenstein, Eugene Victor. 1993. *The victims of democracy: Malcolm X and the Black revolution*. New York: Guilford.

21

The Media's Assault on Malcolm X

Adisa A. Alkebulan

Malcolm X was certainly a victim of character assassination by the white press. Probably of all African or African American figures since Marcus Garvey, Malcolm X was the most revered, feared, and misunderstood. He was revered because no other individual had inspired generation after generation of young African Americans to question and challenge the status quo; he was feared because no other individual had represented such a threat to the United States' global influence and white America's comfort zone; he was misunderstood because even after his untimely death, most Americans have not a clue as to who Malcolm really was and his impact on African Americans' struggle for human rights. His image was maligned by the white press from his early days as spokesman of the Nation of Islam (NOI) and, some might argue, is still maligned by the white press to this day. In spite of the white media's demonization of this controversial figure, Malcolm X was able to reverse that notion and offer his own criticism of and insight into the white press. However, what makes the white media's demonization of Malcolm X so disheartening is the role the intelligence community played in distorting his image. The Federal Bureau of Investigation (FBI) kept Malcolm under surveillance from the time he was in prison until his death in 1965. Furthermore, the agency was responsible for leaking bogus news stories to the press and for drawing inflammatory media attention to Malcolm's ouster from the Nation of Islam (NOI), hoping to prevent a possible reconciliation. These tactics, and others, aimed at Malcolm later formed part of the FBI's Counter Intelligence Program (COINTELPRO), which this essay will also discuss. In addition, this essay keeps in mind that Malcolm X was a member of the NOI from 1947 to 1964 and that, therefore, any discussion of Malcolm prior to his separation from the NOI *must* include a discussion of the NOI, and vice versa.

Until 1959, little national attention was given to Malcolm X and the NOI. A television documentary which aired that year in a series of five parts, *The Hate That Hate Produced*, thrust Malcolm and the NOI onto the national stage. As Malcolm put it, the documentary "cut back and forth like a two-edged sword."[1] On the one hand, it exposed the NOI, and consequently Malcolm as its spokesman, to a national audience. On the other, it helped set in motion a media onslaught that even Malcolm did not imagine. The title itself served as a justification to renounce what the NOI had set out to accomplish. Consequently, the national press began to depict the NOI (and Malcolm as

---

1. Malcolm X, with Alex Haley, *The Autobiography of Malcolm X* (New York: Ballantine, 1973), 272.

its chief "propaganda tool") as "separatists," "hate-messengers," and other disparaging epithets. This media barrage diverted attention from the general mission that Malcolm was trying to articulate.

The documentary originated at the urging of Louis Lomax, an African American reporter. Lomax eventually convinced Mike Wallace, a local New York City news anchor, to produce a special series about the little-known "Black Muslims," Black supremacists who hated whites and were completely opposed to integration.[2] At the time, the NOI did not allow itself to be covered by the white press; therefore, Lomax conducted the interviews while Wallace narrated the series and provided his own commentary. *The Hate That Hate Produced* served as a precursor of attempts by the white media to label so-called extremist organizations as "racist," "supremacist," etc., while ignoring the social conditions which created such organizations. The first part of the five-part series aired at 7:00 p.m. on July 13, 1959. Wallace opened the show with the following remarks:

> Tonight we begin a five-part series which we call *The Hate That Hate Produced*, a story of the rise of Black racism, of a call for Black supremacy among a growing segment of American Negroes. While city officials, state agencies, white liberals and sober-minded Negroes stand idly by, a group of Negro dissenters are taking to street corner stepladders, church pulpits, sports arenas and ballroom platforms across the nation to preach the gospel of hate that would set off a federal investigation if it were to be preached by southern whites.[3]

The "sober-minded Negroes," or responsible ones, to which Wallace referred were the civil rights/integrationist leaders who preached nonviolence as a means of resistance to oppression. Did Wallace's description mean that those who had chosen not to love those who oppressed them were not "sober-minded" or responsible? Of "responsible Negroes," Malcolm X said: "[The one] whom white men consider to be 'responsible' is invariably the Black 'leader' who never gets any results."[4] It is noteworthy that Wallace and others have favored nonviolence and the "love-thy-enemy" approach, since at no time in American history has any other group used nonviolence as a means of rebellion. To call the NOI anti-American is just as ludicrous. Indeed, Y. N. Kly points out that the political philosophy of Malcolm X corresponded to the American ideal in a far greater way than that of Martin Luther King, Jr.:

> It is ironic that when most Americans think of Malcolm X, they think of him as un-American or anti-American.... When we look ... at the political philosophy of Malcolm X, there can be little doubt that Malcolm's values represented a far greater integration into the American majority value system than, say, the philosophy of the honorable Dr. Martin Luther King, Jr. While King's absolute belief in non-self-defense or non-resistance against violent aggression reflected strong Hindu or Buddhist orientation, Malcolm's philosophy was really about the same as any majority American would hold, given similar circumstances or grievances—for example, the revolutionary war of 1776, the War of 1812, the Civil War, and the First and Second World Wars.[5]

2. Mike Wallace and Gary Paul Gates, *Close Encounters* (New York: William Morrow, 1984), 135.

3. Clayborne Carson, *Malcolm X: The FBI File* (New York: Carroll & Graf, 1991), 159–60.

4. Malcolm X, *Autobiography*, 439.

5. Kly, Y. N., *The Black Book: The Political Philosophy of Malcolm X* (Atlanta: Clarity Press, 1986), 2–3.

In the next segment of the documentary, Malcolm indicted the government for committing the worst crimes on earth against African Americans. Yet throughout the series, the members of the NOI were portrayed as angry, irrational racists who shocked and appalled white America. The documentary failed to reveal the rehabilitating nature of the NOI or the community service in which the organization was engaged. Of the NOI establishments, Wallace said:

> They have their own parochial schools like this one in Chicago where Muslim children are taught to hate the white man. Even the clothes they wear are anti-white man, anti-American like these two Negro children going to school. Wherever they go, the Muslims withdraw from the life of the community. They have their own stores, supermarkets, barber shops, restaurants.[6]

Wallace suggested, illogically, that the only purpose of the NOI was to teach hate of the white man. Furthermore, his suggestion that the dress of the "two Negro children" on their way to school translated into anti-anything also defied logic. Finally, what most "sober-minded" people call community development, Wallace illogically called withdrawing "from the life of the community."

In the third part of the series, which aired July 15, Wallace maintained that the NOI was in error when it returned white hate with Black hate. Yes, Wallace did make a slight reference to white racism and supremacy. But his reference was too little and too late since the series had already maintained that neither white racism nor the response to it was an issue. Rather, the issue was the alleged hateful rhetoric and preaching of the Nation of Islam. Wallace also referred to "the responsible Negro leaders" who should purge the so-called hatemongers from the ranks of Black leadership. Wallace said:

> We call this series *The Hate That Hate Produced* because it is our conviction that the hate that we have been learning about is the hatred that a minority of Negroes are returning for the hate the majority of Negroes have received.
>
> Senator Hubert Humphrey told the NAACP fiftieth-anniversary convention today that the Negro people are to be congratulated for returning love for hate, but here we are seeing tragic evidence, frightening evidence, that some Negroes are returning hate for hate. The white community must accept a good deal of the blame for the indignities the Negroes have suffered. The white community must admit its share of the blame and take corrective action. But the Negro community is not blameless. They and all of their responsible leaders must move quickly to root out the hatemongers in their midst.[7]

Wallace's refusal to provide the adequate political and social backdrop of the time prevented the American public from understanding how an organization such as the NOI could exist. Indeed, illogically, the documentary failed to acknowledge that African Americans were justified in having indicted the "white man" for crimes committed against the "Black man." As a result, it came as a surprise to white America that African Americans fired back with so much rage and anger in response to oppression. In blame-the-victim fashion, Wallace laid the groundwork for what would become years of media coverage depicting Malcolm X as a "Black supremacist," "separatist" and "hate teacher." Of this type of journalism, Malcolm said: "It will make the criminal look like he's the victim and make the victim look like he's the criminal. If you aren't careful, the newspapers will have you hating the people who are being oppressed and loving the people

6. Carson, *Malcolm X: The FBI File*, 161.
7. Carson, *Malcolm X: The FBI File*, 170.

who are doing the oppressing."[8] Fortunately for the NOI, the national attention given them by the documentary helped the organization continue to grow rather than aid in their demise.

The white press continued to try to discredit what Malcolm and his organization stood for and present it as negatively as possible. However, Malcolm recognized its tactics and at every opportunity tried to correct the media's misrepresentations. Malcolm believed that the "hate" labeling was an orchestrated attempt to discredit the NOI in the African American community. During a speech at Michigan State University in 1963, Malcolm claimed:

> Actually, this is the type of propaganda put together by the press, thinking that this will alienate masses of Black people from what he's saying. But actually the only one whom that type of propaganda alienates is this Negro who's always up in your face begging you for what you have or begging you for a chance to live in your neighborhood or work on your job or marry one of your women. Well that type of Negro naturally doesn't want to hear what the Honorable Elijah Muhammad is talking about. But the type that wants to hear what he's saying is the type who feels that he'll get farther by standing on his own feet and doing something for himself towards solving his own problem and then, at the same time, depending upon you to do something to solve them.[9]

Thus, Malcolm maintained that the media could not alienate the masses of Black people from the NOI. Indeed, Malcolm had more insight into the workings of the mass media than any other African American leader—an insight evident in many of his speeches.

It is little wonder why Malcolm could understand the way the mass media functioned and how it served as a powerful instrument. In 1957, he was sent by Elijah Muhammad to Los Angeles to organize a Temple. While there, Malcolm worked in the office of an African American newspaper, the *Los Angeles Herald Dispatch*, and was permitted to observe how the newspaper operated. From that experience, Malcolm started the NOI's own newspaper and named it *Muhammad Speaks*.[10]

Early in his association with the NOI, Malcolm X easily recognized that the media deliberately distorted views. He said: "I don't care what points I made in the interviews, it practically never got printed the way I said it. I was learning under fire how the press, when it wants to, can twist and slant. If I had said 'Mary had a little lamb,' what probably would have appeared was 'Malcolm X Lampoons Mary.'"[11]

Malcolm also understood the "image-making" power of the media. He maintained:

> They master this imagery, this image-making. They give you the image of an extremist, and from then on anything you do is extreme. You can pull a baby out of the water and save it from drowning—you're still an extremist, because they projected this image of you. They can create an image of you as a subversive and you can go out and die fighting for the United States—you're still subversive. They can paint the image of you as someone irresponsible, and you can come up with the best program that will save the Black man from the oppression of the white man.[12]

---

8. Malcolm X, *Malcolm X Speaks: Selected Speeches and Statements*, ed. George Breitman (New York: Grove, 1965), 93.
9. Malcolm X, *Malcolm X: The Last Speeches*, ed. Bruce Perry (New York: Pathfinder, 1989), 28.
10. Malcolm X, *Autobiography*, 272–73.
11. Malcolm X, *Autobiography*, 279.
12. Malcolm X, *Malcolm X Speaks*, 93.

Malcolm X also recognized that just as he and the NOI were demonized by the white press, so, too, were the African American leaders who advocated nonviolence and integration. Indeed, he argued that as long as African Americans did not stand up and fight back, the media would treat them favorably:

> You let the man maneuver you into thinking that it's wrong to fight him when he's fighting you. He's fighting you in the morning, fighting you in the noon, fighting you at night and fighting you all in between, and you still think it's wrong to fight back. Why? The press. The newspapers make you look wrong. As long as you take a beating, you're all right. As long as you get your head busted, you're all right. As long as you let his dogs fight you, you're all right. Because that's the press. That's the image-making press. That thing is dangerous if you don't guard yourself against it. It'll make you love the criminal, as I say, and make you hate the one who's the victim of the criminal.[13]

Malcolm X also showed that these same "Negro" leaders had been given the platform to launch attacks at the NOI and that "they were stumbling all over each other to get quoted."[14] The media, Malcolm realized, was serving as a tool to divide and conquer African American leadership. This tactic, inciting other African Americans to attack him, angered Malcolm more than the obvious mission of the white press to distort his views.[15] In addition to battling the misrepresentations of the white press, Malcolm knew that the media did not stand alone in demonizing him.

Malcolm revealed what the public did not grasp until several years later. The Federal Bureau of Investigation (FBI) conspired with the white press in demonizing and distorting his views. Of this unholy union, Malcolm said:

> The FBI can feed information to the press to make your neighbor think you're something subversive. The FBI—they do it very skillfully, they maneuver the press on a national scale and the CIA maneuvers the press on an international scale. They do all their dirt with the press. They take the newspapers and make the newspapers blow you and me up as if all of us are criminals, all of us are racists, all of us are drug addicts, or all of us are rioting. This is how they do it. When you explode legitimately against the injustices that have been heaped upon you, they use the press to make it look like you're a vandal.[16]

How Malcolm knew of the relationship between the white press and various government agencies perhaps we will never know. However, it is certain that he did know. During a press conference on February 17, 1965, three days after Malcolm's home was firebombed, he said: "We feel a conspiracy has been entered into at the local level, with some local police, firemen and the press."[17] Malcolm also recognized that the Central Intelligence Agency (CIA) was employing the same media tactics internationally which the FBI was employing domestically. Malcolm's 1964 speech, "Communication and Reality," further illustrates his intuitiveness:

> The American press, in fact the FBI, can use the American press to create almost any kind of image they want of any one on the local scene. And then you

---

13. Malcolm X, *Malcolm X Speaks*, 93.
14. Malcolm X, *Autobiography*, 275.
15. Malcolm X, *Autobiography*, 279.
16. Malcolm X, *Malcolm X Speaks*, 92.
17. John Henrick Clarke, "The Last Days of Malcolm X," in *Malcolm X: The Man and His Times*, ed. John Henrick Clarke, 89 (Trenton, NJ: Africa World Press, 1990).

have other police agencies of an international stature that are able to use the world press in the same manner. If the press is able to project someone in the image of an extremist, no matter what that person says or does from then on, it is considered by the public as an act of extremism. No matter how good, constructive, or positive it is, because it's done by this person who has been projected as an extremist, the people who have been misled by the press have a mental block.[18]

Malcolm's insight reveals the degree of his international consciousness. His suspicion of a media and governmental conspiracy on an international level shows that he operated on a plane that few political figures of his era could even imagine. We now know of a collusion existing between the FBI and the media, for in 1971, the Citizen's Committee to Investigate the FBI confiscated boxes of FBI files from an FBI office in Media, Pennsylvania, and disseminated the information to the press.[19] The Freedom of Information Act (FOIA) enabled the Committee to have thousands of more documents released. The Committee's actions revealed to the world the FBI's Counterintelligence Program (COINTELPRO), a secret agenda Malcolm knew of in practice if not by name.

Of course, here we are primarily concerned with the role the media played in the FBI's secret scheme to discredit Malcolm X. Malcolm, however, was not considered a formal target of COINTELPRO. This program began "officially" after his death. Nevertheless, many of the FBI's tactics later initiated under COINTELPRO were employed during their campaign against Malcolm X. William Sales points out: "The program instituted by the FBI known as COINTELPRO was not initiated until several years after Malcolm X's assassination. But from its August 1967 description of its program to disrupt and 'neutralize' so-called 'Black Nationalist hate groups,' it appears that the FBI program of discrediting Malcolm X was one of its earliest runs."[20] The FBI sought to prevent the rise of a Black "messiah" who might be successful in uniting the "militant black nationalist movement."[21] Ward Churchill and Jim Vander Wall define COINTELPRO in the following terms:

[It] is the FBI domestic Counterintelligence Program designed to destroy individuals and organizations the FBI considers to be politically objectionable. Tactics included all manner of official lying and media disinformation, systematically levying false charges against those targeted, manufacturing evidence to obtain charges against those targeted, manufacturing evidence to obtain their convictions, withholding evidence which might exonerate them, and occasionally assassinating "key leaders."[22]

Given the charisma, eloquence, and growing popularity of Malcolm X, it would only be a matter of time before the FBI considered him a "key leader."

Malcolm X first brought attention to himself through his political activity in prison. In March 1950, he began a letter-writing campaign to the local media to voice his con-

---

18. John Henrick Clarke, "Communication and Reality," in *Malcolm X: The Man and His Times*, ed. John Henrick Clarke, 308–309 (Trenton, NJ: Africa World Press, 1990).

19. Ward Churchill and Jim Vander Wall, *The COINTELPRO Papers: Documents from the FBI's Secret Wars Against Domestic Dissent* (Cambridge, MA: South End Press, 1990), xi.

20. William W. Sales, Jr., *From Civil Rights to Black Liberation: Malcolm X and the Organization of Afro-American Unity* (Cambridge, MA: South End Press, 1994), 153.

21. Carson, *Malcolm X: The FBI File*, 46.

22. Ward Churchill and Jim Vander Wall, *Agents of Repression: The FBI's Secret War Against the Black Panther Party and the American Indian Movement* (Cambridge, MA: South End Press, 1988), xii.

cerns and those of his fellow Muslims (whom he had converted) that were not being addressed by prison officials. His letters appeared in several local newspapers. He also wrote a letter to President Harry S. Truman in which he claimed that he was a Communist and that he wanted to join the Japanese army.[23] The FBI took note of these letters and began its surveillance of Malcolm in 1953, soon after he had been released from prison.[24] However, Malcolm was not designated a "key figure" by the FBI until 1958. Clayborne Carson explains:

> This designation meant that the FBI would keep "up-to-date Security Index cards on him separately [from the NOI]," an indication that the Bureau considered the Nation of Islam to be at least a potential threat to the nation's internal security. The new designation reflected Malcolm's increasing visibility as a Muslim spokesperson and the FBI's awareness of Malcolm's growing involvement in international politics.[25]

Therefore, as early as 1958, the FBI intensified its program against Malcolm X.

The FBI used tactics or tools called "friendly sources," "friendly media," "friends of the Bureau," and "gray propaganda" against Malcolm. Through such tactics, the FBI released "disinformation" to the press designed to discredit the target in the eyes of the public.[26] The FBI gave information or articles to friendly media who could be relied on to write pro-bureau stories and not reveal their sources.[27] In an FBI memo dated July 2, 1964, J. Edgar Hoover, Director of the FBI, stated: "There is indication that Little [Malcolm X] has aligned himself with subversive groups and this matter must be immediately investigated and, if feasible, a counterintelligence program will be initiated to publicly discredit him."[28] A careful examination of the media's misrepresentation of Malcolm X illustrates these tactics of the FBI.

As an example of its "gray propaganda" tactic, the FBI leaked a story to the *New York Journal American*, owned by a friend of Hoover, stating: "'Malcolm X and his Chicago headquarters' had been linked by the intelligence community in 'international intrigue with Nasser,' Castro, and Nikita Khrushchev of the Soviet Union in a 'plot to win the minds of America's 20 million Negroes to use them in winning the alliance of the newly independent dark-skinned nations in Africa.'"[29] The bogus story ran on September 25, 1960.

One of the most telling examples of the FBI's "friendly media" tactic was the story "White Man Is God For Cult of Islam" that appeared in the *New Crusader*, an African American newspaper in Chicago. The story, undoubtedly, was designed to present the NOI, the organization that Malcolm had built almost from the ground up, as negatively as possible. The article, however, was filled with inaccuracies. For example, the article claimed that Elijah Muhammad, leader of the NOI, and Wallace Dodd Fard had come up with the idea of the NOI while both were in prison together. Actually, they were not in prison together, and the NOI was founded in Detroit by Wallace Fard Muhammad. Furthermore, the story claimed that Fard was a Turkish Nazi agent during World War

---

23. Karl Evanzz, *The Judas Factor: The Plot to Kill Malcolm X* (New York: Thunder's Mouth Press, 1993), 10–11.

24. Carson, *Malcolm X: The FBI File*, 95.

25. Carson, *Malcolm X: The FBI File*, 148.

26. Churchill and Vander Wall, *Agents of Repression*, 43–44.

27. Muhammed Ahmed, "We Charge Genocide" (unpublished manuscript), 5.

28. Sales, Jr., *From Civil Rights to Black Liberation*, 153.

29. Evanzz, *The Judas Factor*, 87.

II.[30] The issue resurfaced in 1963, when the FBI released Fard's criminal record to the press. Karl Evanzz writes:

> The FBI's dossier on Fard was mailed to several large newspapers on Independence Day, 1963. On July 28, the story broke in the *Los Angeles Evening Herald-Examiner* … under the headline: "Black Muslim Founder Exposed As A White." Two days later, Hoover received a memo from Chicago advising him that the story had the desired impact on Elijah Muhammad. According to the memo, Muhammad "was quite riled up about the story and had ordered John Ali, national secretary of the NOI, to hire a good lawyer who is "one hundred percent for us" to sue the *Herald-Examiner*.[31]

In response to this article, Malcolm claimed: "[The Kennedy administration] 'planted the story to enhance the image of the so-called Negro civil rights leaders' who were scheduled to lead the March on Washington on August 28. 'The source of this slander is the government itself.' "[32]

As another example of the FBI's feeding false information to the media, Malcolm X was linked to an assassination plot against President Lyndon Johnson. Evanzz explains:

> First, the media had deliberately distorted his comment on the assassination of President Kennedy. Now, apparently, the intelligence community was manipulating the media in an attempt to frame him for conspiracy to murder the new president.… The report of the alleged assassination attempt was broadcast and published nationwide.[33]

Nothing materialized from this bogus "report." However, it did further associate Malcolm X and the NOI with violence.

These tactics against Malcolm and the NOI were employed not solely to discredit their targets. The FBI also used its "friendly media tactic" for other reasons. For example, not only did the FBI leak information on Fard to make Malcolm X and the NOI look foolish; it also leaked that information in an effort to force Malcolm out of the organization. Evanzz asserts:

> Malcolm's prominence in the national media had risen sharply, so much so that he now overshadowed Elijah Muhammad. By July [1964], Hoover had firm evidence that Malcolm X's popularity had precipitated intense jealousy on the part of Muhammad's sons Herbert and Wallace. Hoover decided that it was time to take advantage of the rivalry, and by doing so, to force Malcolm X out of the Nation of Islam.[34]

This tactic, the FBI thought, would be an extra push for Malcolm to sever ties with the organization.

To further widen the "rift" between Malcolm and the NOI, the FBI released a story announcing that this "rift" was growing. Evanzz suggests that because of this article, any chance that Malcolm had in returning to the NOI had been completely eliminated: "The draft was forwarded to [the] Assistant FBI Director … on February 13 'for his consideration,' and on February 21, the 'tip' was mailed to major newspapers, promi-

---

30. Evanzz, *The Judas Factor*, 132.
31. Evanzz, *The Judas Factor*, 145.
32. Evanzz, *The Judas Factor*, 146.
33. Evanzz, *The Judas Factor*, 173–75.
34. Evanzz, *The Judas Factor*, 145.

nent gossip columnists, and radio and television stations in New York. It was also sent to every black-owned newspaper in the United States."[35] In part, the article read:

> The rift ... appears to be widening.... It is no secret that Little would not hesi-tate one moment to take over the leadership of the Nation of Islam.... Muhammad is reportedly fuming at the temerity Little had exhibited in ques-tioning the "Messenger's" judgment and it would not surprise anyone at all fa-miliar with the works of the NOI to see Little summarily expelled from this or-ganization if he continues to buck the orders and wishes of Elijah Muhammad.[36]

Evanzz further points out that just four days before this fabricated story was sent out, Malcolm wrote a letter to Elijah Muhammad requesting reinstatement. The request was denied, and Malcolm was informed that his ninety-day suspension would not be lifted because he continued to be a "rebel."[37]

To further illustrate the connection between the white media and the FBI, on Febru-ary 3, 1963, Malcolm X appeared on a television show, *Black Muslims*, during which he criticized the FBI for infiltrating the NOI. About this show, Evanzz writes:

> The agent from FBI headquarters who monitored the program advised Hoover that he had contacted the station to see why it had given Malcolm X free adver-tising for new recruits. A representative replied, in an obvious effort to placate him, that the show was intended to present Malcolm X and the Black Muslims in a "bad light."[38]

However, in a memo to Hoover, the field agent wrote:

> The program did not put Malcolm X or the "Black Muslims" in a "bad light." ... The answers given by Malcolm X were not questioned. He was al-lowed to expound the NOI program in such a way that he created an interest in the NOI. This is another example of the effect of publicity concerning the NOI. While it is intended to have an adverse affect, it created an interest in the organization which was out of proportion to its importance.[39]

Although the television program was a failed attempt to discredit Malcolm and the NOI, it nonetheless revealed, first, that the media did, in fact, attempt to demonize Malcolm. The program's purpose was to present the views Malcolm espoused as racist. Fortunately for Malcolm, the show's host was not prepared or sophisticated enough to challenge Malcolm on his positions. Second, the program revealed that the FBI and the white media did have a relationship that calculated and plotted opportunities to dis-credit Malcolm X. The field agent who had written the memo to Hoover had no prob-lem contacting the television station and questioning the content of the show. Further-more, the station had no problem conceding to the FBI's demands. Nevertheless, neither the FBI nor the station obtained the intended results.

Just as the FBI leaked fraudulent stories to the media, it also used the press as a sur-veillance tool. Carson claims that the FBI tracked Malcolm's moves by documenting television and radio appearances and by making note of their contents.[40] For example,

---

35. Evanzz, *The Judas Factor*, 186.
36. Evanzz, *The Judas Factor*, 185–86
37. Evanzz, *The Judas Factor*, 186.
38. Evanzz, *The Judas Factor*, 150.
39. Evanzz, *The Judas Factor*, 150.
40. Carson, *Malcolm X. The FBI File*, 62–85, 316–25.

the FBI documented that on June 8, 1964, Malcolm X attempted to make arrangements with an unnamed source at CBS Television to discuss the entire story of Elijah Muhammad's alleged fathering of "illegitimate" children.[41] Much to the pleasure of the FBI, Malcolm X was successful in getting the story out by using several radio and television outlets.[42]

Malcolm X never rejoined the Nation of Islam. The FBI was successful in fostering the split between Malcolm and the organization that he almost single-handedly built. When we look back at the intelligence community's targeting of Malcolm, we must also analyze the role the media played.

Once Malcolm stepped on the national stage in 1959, he stumbled into a whirlwind that he would weather until the day he died. The white media was bent on vilifying him. However, we now know that the media's portrayal of Malcolm X was not simply a difference of views between African Americans and mainstream America. Rather, it was a systematic campaign on the part of the FBI and the white press to demonize and distort Malcolm's image. Malcolm X was, indeed, a victim of character assassination. When news agencies agreed to release slanderous articles about Malcolm X, they entered into a mercenary relationship with the FBI. Perhaps the split between Malcolm X and the NOI was inevitable, but the FBI and the white media made sure that a reconciliation would never happen.

---

41. Carson, *Malcolm X: The FBI File*, 318.
42. Carson, *Malcolm X: The FBI File*, 319.

22

Malcolm X: A Study of the Power of Transformation

Miriam Ma'at-Ka-Re Monges*

Mecca

Mecca, a city in Saudi Arabia, rests deeply within the consciousness of all Muslims. The Prophet Muhammad, the founder of Islam, was born in Mecca. Five times each day, Muslims must face Mecca when they pray. At least once in their lives, all physically well adult Muslims who can afford it are required to make a pilgrimage to Mecca during the last month of the Islamic calendar. Each year approximately two million Islamic pilgrims make this *hajj*, which means "voyage to a sacred place" (Microsoft Corporation 1997–2005). The purpose of the hajj is to bring the Muslim faithful closer to Allah.

In 1964, Malcolm X joined the hajj to Mecca, which caused a major spiritual transformation in his life. It also caused international reverberations. Malcolm's hajj forever changed the African American's perception about Mecca and Islam. In addition, Malcolm's hajj forever changed the Islamic world's view about African Americans.

This was not the first time that such a hajj had an international impact. In 1324, Mansa Musa made a pilgrimage to Mecca, which forever changed the Arabian and European world's perception of Western Africa. Mansa Musa also brought back knowledge that transformed the educational system of Mali. Mansa Musa's and Malcolm's hajjes are two of the most famous in history.

Mansa Musa's Hajj

Mansa Musa ruled the prosperous and powerful West African nation of Mali from 1321 to 1337 (Boahen 1966, 17). "At its height in the 13th century, Mali stretched from the Atlantic Ocean coast in the west to beyond the Niger bend in the east, and from the goldfields of modern Guinea in the south to the major southern Saharan caravan stops in the north" (Microsoft Corporation 1997–2004a).

---

* *Asante sana* to Nzingha Helen Jones for her editorial assistance.

Mansa Musa was a devout Muslim and in 1324 and 1325, he made spiritual pilgrimages to Mecca. He and his entourage of thousands must have made a magnificent impression as they traveled across the Sahara toward one of the largest gatherings of people with a spiritual purpose in the world. In his retinue were military and medical personnel, scholars, political leaders, historical recorders, and servants. Each of his servants carried a baton of solid gold. Included in the entourage were one hundred camels, each carrying three hundred pounds of gold. As Mansa Musa traveled, he generously gave gold to the common people. In fact, he gave away so much gold that in Cairo, Egypt, the price of gold fell and consequently, Egypt's economy was deflated for more than twenty years afterward (Karenga 1993, 93–94; Microsoft Corporation 1997–2004b; Microsoft Corporation 1997–2004c).

When Mansa Musa returned to Mali after his hajj, his faith in Islam was strengthened, and his political, economic, and educational network was extended. He brought back Islamic scholars, books, and architects. He sent students to study in Morocco and became known for "the friendly relations he maintained with other African States, especially the Sultan of Morocco" (Boahen 1966, 18).

Mansa Musa's hajj became famous throughout Europe, Arabia, and Africa. In 1375, Majorcan cartographer Abraham Cresques drew a famous "Map of the World" on which was depicted a wealthy west African king. He was dressed in an elegant robe and a crown, and he held a scepter in one hand and a massive gold nugget in the other. "Mansa Musa and his kingdom appeared on the maps over a period of nearly 200 years up through that produced by Martin Waldseemuller in 1516, even though Mansa Musa himself died in 1332" (Carew 1993, 270). One of Mansa Musa's most lasting legacies was his sense of justice and impartiality (Boahen 1966, 18). Indeed, his hajj appears to have had a major effect on his personal life and his historical legacy.

Malcolm's Hajj

In 1964, Malcolm X made a hajj to Mecca. When Malcolm finished his pilgrimage, his faith in Islam was strengthened, and his political, economic, and educational network was extended. These results made reverberations that affected African people throughout the world. Unlike Mansa Musa, Malcolm did not give away gold and thus deflate Egypt's economy; but his connections with Egypt and other African countries deflated the negative image of African Americans. Like Mansa Musa, the information that Malcolm brought back transformed the image of Islam in the minds of thousands. Indeed, he helped to put the religious practice of many African Americans on a new path.

The Reasons for the Hajj

In the early part of 1964, Malcolm X began to realize that Elijah Muhammad would never reinstate him as a representative of the Nation of Islam. More important, he began to question whether he wanted to represent the Nation of Islam. He had doubts about its moral values and its leadership, and its connection with the Islamic religion. He was feeling spiritually bankrupt.

Malcolm X decided to investigate Islam himself. He went to Mecca with the same purpose as Makeda, Queen of Sheba, when she went on her pilgrimage to the court of King Solomon. Makeda wanted "to prove him with hard questions" (Budge 1932, chap. 24; Felder 1993, 1 Kings 10:1, 2 Chron. 9:1), and Malcolm wanted to "prove" Islam with hard questions. I have called this type of pilgrimage, in which one "sets out on a quest for wisdom" using the energy of both feminine-intuitive and masculine-rational thought processes, the search for "[t]he Shebanization of Knowledge" (Monges 2003, 199). Malcolm X wanted to Shebanize his knowledge base of Islam—that is, he wanted to investigate, ask challenging questions, expand his knowledge base, and nourish his spirit.

We sense some of this "Shebanization of Knowledge" in one of Malcolm's last interviews—this one with New York radio personality Les Crane:

> Crane: Your trip to Africa changed your thinking and your position to a great extent.

> Malcolm X: Yes. Travel always broadens one's scope.... I went in search of an understanding of the religion of Islam.... One of the things that Elijah Muhammad always taught us was that Islam is a religion of God. It was a religion in which no whites could participate. And he used—to prove his point, he told us that Mecca was a forbidden city. A city that was forbidden to non-Muslims. And since a white person couldn't be a Muslim in his teaching, he said that no white could enter Mecca. (Malcolm X 1989, 85)

One of Malcolm's first observations contradicted what he had been taught by Elijah Mohammed:

> Every specimen of humanity is represented there. It's an absolute brotherhood. So that when I saw this with my own eyes, and saw that people of all colors could practice brotherhood, it was at that point that ... I believed in Islam as a religion of brotherhood. (Malcolm X 1989, 85–86)

Indeed, Malcolm X saw that brotherhood was a possibility. However, he still had the reality of America in the forefront of his mind: "I believe that it is possible for brotherhood to be brought about among all people, but I don't delude myself into dreaming or falling for a dream that this exists before it exists" (Malcolm X 1989, 87).

The Role of Women

One of the results of Malcolm's transformation was a holistic analysis of the role of women. He became conscious of the pivotal role of women in true brotherhood. In one of his last speeches, he comments:

> One thing I noticed in both the Middle East and Africa, in every country that was progressive, the women were progressive. In every country that was underdeveloped and backward, it was to the same degree that the women were undeveloped, or underdeveloped, and backward. (Malcolm X 1989, 98)

Thus, women must be free to develop fully in order for a society to develop fully. Indeed, the role of women is interconnected and integrated with all aspects of a culture.

> In ... societies where they put the woman in a closet and discourage her from getting a sufficient education and don't give her the incentive by allowing her

maximum participation in whatever area of the society where she's qualified, they kill her incentive. And killing her incentive, she kills the incentive in her children. And the man himself has no competition so he doesn't develop to his fullest potential. (Malcolm X 1989, 98)

Transformation

During Malcolm's hajj, he participated in five days of rites and rituals in which he was interconnected with Muslims of all colors. He later told writer Alex Haley:

Pilgrims from Ghana, Indonesia, Japan, and Russia, to mention some, were moving to and from the dormitory where I was being taken. I don't believe that motion picture cameras ever filmed a human spectacle more colorful than my eyes took in.... It was like pages out of the *National Geographic* magazine. (Malcolm X 1965, 333)

Before they reached Mecca, all the pilgrims had entered a state of ritual purity by having performed ritual bathing. They then dressed in the *ihram*, which is a white seamless shroud they keep for the rest of their lives as their burial garb (Microsoft Corporation 1997–2005). Therefore, there were no visible indicators of class or status. Consequently, Malcolm X experienced the freedom of just being, or letting go of attachments. His higher self was given the space to rise.

Indeed, Malcolm X experienced a new phenomenon. Instead of being looked down upon because he was an African American, he received special treatment: "My being an American Muslim changed the attitude from merely watching me to wanting to look out for me. Now, the others began smiling steadily" (Malcolm X 1965, 335). Thus, he became an ambassador for Africans in America.

Malcolm X now began to look at the world through the prism of brotherhood, not racism. His perspective of humanity was beginning to change:

Dr. Omar Assam ... wrung my hand in welcome, a young, tall, powerfully built man.... In America, he would have been called a white man, but—it struck me hard and instantly—from the way he acted, I had no *feeling* of him being a white man.... I was speechless at the man's attitude, and at my own physical feeling of no difference between us as human beings. (Malcolm X 1965, 338)

Through relationships such as this, Malcolm X learned the potential of the human spirit.

After the Hajj

After the hajj, Malcolm X became El-Hajj Malik El-Shabazz. When he left Mecca, like Mansa Musa, he became known for the friendly relationships he established and maintained with African states. He widened his religious, political, economic, and social network. He visited "Egypt, Arabia, Kuwait, Lebanon and then Sudan, Ethiopia, Kenya, and what was then Zanzibar and Tanganyika, and is now Tanzania, also Nigeria, Ghana, Liberia, Guinea, and Algiers, or rather Algeria. Then in Europe: Geneva, Paris and London" (Malcolm X 1989, 91). These travels after the hajj solidified his transformation.

Space and Time

Transformations usually happen in a space and time that do not coordinate with clocks and the Western calendar. Malcolm X said that Mecca "seemed as ancient as time itself" (Malcolm X 1965, 343). The rituals in which he participated were the same ones in which Mansa Musa and others had participated for almost fourteen hundred years. In his *Autobiography*, Malcolm vividly describes these rituals:

> I saw the Ka'ba, a huge black stone house in the middle of the great Mosque. It was being circumambulated by thousands upon thousands of praying pilgrims, both sexes, and every size, shape, color and race in the world ... [praying] "O God, You are peace, and peace derives from You. So greet us, O Lord, with peace."
>
> My feeling there in the House of God was numbness. My *Matawaf* led me in the crowd of praying, chanting pilgrims, moving several times around the Ka'ba. Some were bent and wizened with age; it was a sight that stamped itself on the brain. I saw incapacitated pilgrims being carried by others. Faces were enraptured in their faith. (Malcolm X 1965, 343)

Both Mansa Musa and Malcolm X were inspired by the possibilities of brotherhood. After his hajj, Mansa Musa became known for his impartiality, expanded sense of justice, and an extensive, well-organized court system. He is still renowned in history as a great leader (Boahen 1966, 18).

After his hajj, when asked by other Muslims what part affected him the most, El-Hajj Malik El-Shabazz replied: "The *brotherhood!* The people of all races, colors, from all over the world coming together as *one*! It has proved to me the power of the One God" (Malcolm X 1965, 345). This exchange with other Muslims also gave him the opportunity to inform them of the plight of Black people in America. They were already aware that it was not a good one, but El-Hajj Malik El-Shabazz made them aware that it was, above all, "inhuman, that it was a psychological castration" (Malcolm X 1965, 345). Racism was so pernicious that it became a yardstick by which everything was measured, he informed them. The color blindness of the Muslim world that he had experienced changed his previous way of thinking (Malcolm X 1965, 345): he now saw the possibility of human brotherhood.

El-Hajj Malik El-Shabazz showed the world that transformation is always possible. He showed the world that the ability of the spirit to expand is limitless. After his hajj, his expanded view of true justice was reported around the world. The impact of his transformation is still reverberating in the world today and will echo as long as history is told.

References

Boahen, A. Adu. 1966. *Topics in west African history*. London: Longman Group Limited.

Budge, E. A. Willis, trans. 1932. *The Queen of Sheba and her only son Meneyelek (I) being the 'book of the glory of kings' (kebra nagast)*. London: Oxford University Press.

Carew, Jan. 1993. Moorish culture-bringers: Bearers of enlightenment. In *Golden age of the Moor*, ed. Ivan Van Sertima, 248–277. New Brunswick, NJ: Transaction Publishers.

Felder, Cain Hope. 1993. *The original African heritage study Bible*. Washington, DC: Winston.

Karenga, Maulana. 1993. *Introduction to Black Studies*. Los Angeles: University of Sankore Press.

Malcolm X. 1965. *The autobiography of Malcolm X*. With Alex Haley. New York: Ballantine.

Malcolm X. 1989. *Malcolm X: The last speeches*. Ed. Bruce Perry. New York: Pathfinder.

Microsoft Corporation. 1997–2004a. Africa. In *Microsoft Encarta online encyclopedia 2004*. http://encarta.msn.com.

Microsoft Corporation. 1997–2004b. Mali empire. In *Microsoft Encarta online encyclopedia 2004*. http://encarta.msn.com.

Microsoft Corporation. 1997–2004c. Musa. In *Microsoft Encarta online encyclopedia 2004*. http://encarta.msn.com.

Microsoft Corporation. 1997–2005. Hajj. In *Microsoft Encarta online encyclopedia 2005*. http://encarta.msn.com.

Monges, Miriam Ma'at-Ka-Re. 2003. The shebanization of knowledge. In *Afrocentricity and the academy*, ed. James L. Conyers, Jr., 199–200. Jefferson, NC: McFarland.

23

Malcolm X-isms and the Protest Poetry of Blas Jiménez: Liberation by Any Means Necessary

Antonio Tillis

One of the most controversial and most recently celebrated figures of the civil rights era in the history of the United States was Malcolm Little, later known as Malcolm X and later still as El-Hajj Malik El-Shabazz. Malcolm's original surname "Little," his full Arabic name, and the letter X (standing for "the unknown") as the surname by which he is most remembered represent his journey toward discovery and enlightenment. Virtually erased from the annals of recorded history and public discourse until the release of Spike Lee's film *Malcolm X* in 1992, Malcolm was vilified by a public which wrongly perceived as racist the ideologies and dogma he had espoused in public addresses, interviews, and published works. In the historical imagination of most Americans, the importance of Malcolm X to the successes of the civil rights movement has been minimized because of a national tendency to stereotype the revolutionary leader as a racist who preached a gospel of hate. Mainstream scholars of the historical moments of the 1960s have often failed to analyze the impact of Malcolm X and the Nation of Islam on the mobilization of mid-western and northern Blacks in urban spaces where attacks—which were aligned with racism, police brutality, and denial of rights—were just a vicious as those reported in the South. Generally, scholars have not pointed out that Malcolm X and the Nation of Islam advocated social justice, self-love, Black unity, and racial pride, like Dr. Martin Luther King, Jr., and others. However, what distinguished this "radical" leader was his central concern with those he considered responsible for Black angst in the United States and throughout the world. Unlike many Black revolutionaries of his time, Malcolm X was un-apologetic in his disclosure to Black Americans the primary source of their travail: American racism perpetrated by the white man and his long, continuous history of Black sub-jugation. Thus, in order to raise the social consciousness of Black Americans, Malcolm's public addresses focused mainly on his and the NOI's above-mentioned hopes for Black America while pointing out white America as the culprit for their absence. Malcolm's ide-ologies, or "X-isms" as I call them, were attempts to light fires in Black audiences that would incite civic action, revolution, mental reconditioning, and activism. Such was the focus of one his public addresses that serves as the primary interest of this essay.

In a North American—principally United States—context, Malcolm X, El-Hajj Malik El-Shabazz, represented the continuation of a late-nineteenth-century ideology that advocated the conversion of consciousness of people of African descent on a global scale. Forged by Jamaica-born revolutionary Marcus Garvey, Black Nationalism pro moted the creation of a new Black order apart from the systemically racist New World. Garvey's new order, his "Back to Africa" movement, called for the return of the prodigal sons and daughters to the motherland. Garvey believed that postcolonial, postemancipated geographical spaces in the New World, particularly the United States, were intrinsically infected with the epidemic of racism. Consequently, Garvey saw no hope for Blacks in the United States, Cuba, and Central and South America in overcoming the societal ills that relegated people of African descent to the lowest echelons of society.

One-half century later, Garvey's political, social, and economic ideologies were revived by many Blacks in their confrontation with the twentieth-century oppression of Blacks in South Africa, South America, the Caribbean, and the United States. The first chapter ("Nightmare") of *The Autobiography of Malcolm X* (1965) presents the renaissance of these ideologies that lay dormant in Malcolm's developing mind and body. The blood that was giving life to the future revolutionary was fused with the ideology of Black Nationalism since his father, Earl Little, was a Baptist minister and an avid follower of Marcus Garvey. In many of his public addresses, Malcolm X reiterated the need for Black Americans to undergo a psychological raising of consciousness in order to rid themselves of the destructive conditioning that resulted from racism. Whites, according to Malcolm, had thoroughly convinced Blacks of their worthlessness, thus producing Black self-hatred. In his advocacy of psychic conversion, Malcolm X called for an examination of self among Black Americans through their own lenses rather than the deceptive and poisoned ones of white America. Concerning the ideology of "psychic conversion," West (2001) states: "Malcolm X's notion of psychic conversion holds that black people must no longer view themselves through white lenses. He claims that black people will never value themselves as long as they subscribe to a standard of valuation that devalues them" (137).

Regarding the relationship between Malcolm X and Latin America, addresses such as his speech delivered in New York City's Audubon Ballroom on June 28, 1965, demonstrated the inclusive nature of his vision as it related to Black mobilization and unity. The Pan-Africanist vision in this address resulted from the broadening of his personal worldview after his journeys to Mecca, Ghana, and other countries. In fact, his speech on June 28 occurred roughly one month after his return from Ghana, where he had decided that there was a need of another nonreligious organization. Upon returning to Harlem, he founded the Organization of Afro-American Unity (OAAU) and made his first public address to the organization. The OAAU was modeled after the Organization of African Unity (OAU), whose primary role was the creation of a forum for African leaders to promote unity in their collective struggle against whites' oppression of minorities and whites' control of African nations and their precious natural and human resources. Malcolm's message advocated the unification of Blacks in the Western Hemisphere as he equated the struggles of Blacks in the United States with those of African descent in Central America, South America, and the rest of North America. He further stated that persons of African heritage inhabiting the "Americas" as well as the Caribbean island-nations (or the West Indies) were "Afro-Americans." Indeed, he stressed that such inclusiveness was appropriate because those designated "Afro-American" represented a people bound by the African blood forging through their veins and by the collective struggle to dismantle white oppression for the purpose of Black liberation. Malcolm's broadening of the definition of "Afro-American" created a space for those of African ancestry outside the United States. His inclusion of Caribbean island-nations allowed critics of his sociopolitical thought to include spaces such as the Caribbean island Hispaniola, home to Haiti and the Dominican Republic. Hence, the first part of this essay analyzes Malcolm's first public address to the OAAU in order to extract the ideologies, or "X-isms," within its text. The second part analyzes selected poems of the Dominican writer Blas Jiménez to demonstrate the similarities between the ideologies in Malcolm's address and the ideologies in the protest poetry of Jiménez.

In Malcolm's first public address to the OAAU, he initially revealed his Pan-Africanist ideology as the aim of the organization:

> So we have formed an organization known as the Organization of Afro-American Unity which has the same aim and objective—to fight whoever gets in our way, to bring about complete independence of people of African descent here in the Western Hemisphere, and first here in the United States, and bring about the freedom of these people by any means necessary. (Malcolm X 1970, 37)

Themes of Malcolm's address included an emphasis on Black solidarity, the unification of the masses, self-destination, freedom, justice, and equality—to name a few. Furthermore, the speech focused on the five-pronged agenda of the OAAU: Establishment; Self-defense; Education; Politics and Economics; and Social Support.

First, Malcolm X asserted that "establishment" clearly articulated the Black Nationalist (or Pan-Africanist) focus of the membership. Such a focus, he maintained, would reclaim all those of African descent dispersed throughout the world—first by unifying Blacks in North America and then by mobilizing Blacks on a global scale for the cause of liberation. Malcolm's assertion was a call for people of African descent in North America, beginning with those in Harlem, to "establish" themselves specifically under the OAAU. This U.S.-based branch of the OAU would, he claimed, eventually link to projected branches chartered throughout the Americas. As mentioned above, this notion of collective unification was reminiscent of Marcus Garvey's Black mobilization efforts.

Second, Malcolm X asserted that *any* means necessary to bring about this unified Black freedom would be appropriate—including self-defense. Since Black Americans lacked protection by and from white civil servants in the United States, Malcolm X called self-defense an act of exercising one's right of self-protection: "We assert that in those areas where the government is either unable or unwilling to protect the lives and property of our people, that our people are within our rights to protect themselves by whatever means necessary" (Malcolm X 1970, 41). Indeed, Malcolm urged Black people to cease declaring war on each other and instead to focus their aggression on the "cause" of the systemic ills that plagued them.

Third, Malcolm X stressed the importance of education. Indeed, he saw it as fundamental both to social, political, and economic mobility and to the fight for human rights and the reclamation of oneself:

> Education is an important element in the struggle for human rights. It is the means to help our children and our people rediscover their identity and thereby increase their self-respect. Education is our passport to the future, for tomorrow belongs only to the people who prepare for it today. (Malcolm X 1970, 43)

Malcolm's insistence on the importance of education and its reformation in the United States was an issue debated by leaders of African descent in *all* the Americas. This reformation included a revision of history that would comprise the rich heritage of Africa and her offspring in the Americas in order to promote ethnic pride and a sense of self-worth through attachment to this "stolen legacy." To institute education reform, Malcolm called for an increase in Afro-American principals and teachers to instruct and train Afro-American students.

Fourth, Malcolm X stressed the necessity for African Americans to combine politics and economics. He viewed them like conjoined twins, since they are attached to each other. Indeed, he stated that political and economic power were the only types of power that mattered in the United States and that the sum of the two was social power.

The fifth, and final, objective of the OAAU, as Malcolm maintained in the rally address, was social support within Afro-American communities:

> This organization is responsible only to the Afro-American people and community and will function only with their support, both financially and numerically. We believe that our communities must be the sources of their own strength politically, economically, intellectually, and culturally in the struggle for human rights and human dignity. (Malcolm X 1970, 49)

For the OAAU, social responsibility within the Afro-American community was crucial in establishing moral responsibility within the community. Indeed, according to Malcolm X, through such communal efforts Afro-Americans would rid themselves of the vestiges of years of exploitation, neglect, and apathy. As part of the community's moral responsibility, Malcolm X called for a reclamation of the lost sheep: those lost to chemical addiction, prostitution, crime, and other social problems caused by centuries of marginalization, disregard, and disfranchisement. I contend that Malcolm's declarations for the OAAU were indeed Pan-Africanist in scope, since the social plight of Blacks in the United States paralleled that of those of African descent throughout the Americas who had been displaced and exploited since the institution of slavery. In order to accomplish the five aims of the OAAU, Malcolm X advocated a cultural revolution for resocializing and reconditioning Afro-Americans who had been brainwashed by the propaganda of white supremacy. In summation, the ideologies, or "X-isms," coded into Malcolm's address at the initial rally for the launching of the OAAU include the following:

1. Black unification and mobilization
2. Self-defense
3. Education as a means of social mobility
4. Political and economic power
5. Social responsibility

The selected poems of Blas Jiménez thematically mirror the messages encrypted in Malcolm's first public address to those assembled at the first meeting of the OAAU. Poetic analyses of "Rumores de tertulias" ("Rumors of Rap Sessions"), "Canción negra para rifles y atabales" ("Black Song for Rifles and Kettledrums"), "Mi llanto" ("My Weeping"), "Filamentos, filamentos, filamentos" ("Follicles, Follicles, Follicles"), and "Todo negro" ("All Black") indicate the protest nature of Jiménez's lyric verse. Indeed, like Malcolm X, Jiménez speaks to audiences with messages of hope, liberation, *and* protest. Except for the first poem, which appeared in *El Nativo* (1996), the remaining come from the author's *Caribe, africano en despertar* (1984). This volume speaks for the elevation of social consciousness among Caribbean people in general and among people in the Dominican Republic in particular. The poems in the volume address the historical brainwashing of Caribbean Blacks, thus attesting to the current social position of those of African descent in Caribbean nations. In addition, many of the poems offer a course for postcolonial liberation.

The history of Africans and descendants of Africa in the New World comprises over five hundred years of xenophobia, oppression, and enslavement, as well as postcolonial, psychological conditioning. In nearly all nations outside Africa, Black people have struggled ferociously for basic rights. As a result, after the emancipation of many nations from their colonial rulers, rights afforded by their constitutions included the enfranchisement of those of African descent; however, their everyday lives were marked by a constant battle to ensure that they could continue to exercise such rights. Thus, many did not subscribe to racial identifications that would engender nationhood. Those that did realized that a mere racial identification did not afford them respect and an acknowledgement of their existence. As a result, Blacks existed on the margins of identity, since many nations did not fully embrace those of darker hues. Additionally, celebrating and accepting a Black identity resulted in hostility and a state of terrorism for many. Both Blas Jiménez and Malcolm X speak of these challenges in their work.

Regarding this global Black phenomenon, Bhabha (1994) suggests that the condition of Blacks in the world is like that of exiles. He argues that Blacks' separation from their culture and tradition has created a people lost in the world and lacking the richness of their heritage and ancestry. Indeed, according to Bhabha, New World Blackness represents a dispersed clan that wonders aimlessly in search of self and place.

For many postcolonial scholars like Bhabha, the term *New World* includes those territories that suffered European conquest and domination during the fifteenth century. The use of specific terminology serves to prove a particular point in my initial argument concerning white oppression and hegemony. For many North Americans, the term *New World* evokes the connotation "new versus old." Most scholars agree that in such a context, reference to the "Old World" is an Africanized one that carries with it mixed connotations. The word *old* (as in the phrase "the Old World") typically connotes that which is antiquated, no longer relevant; yet the word also suggests that the "Old World" existed—with its own set of cultural norms and traditions. Conversely, the term *New World* suggests an Aryan renaissance of sorts—the beginning of a "new" civilization that leaves behind barbarity and celebrates civility. The concept *New World* begins to be even more contested in the context of the late-twentieth and early-twenty-first centuries. In "modern" times, the term suggests the civilization in the Americas situated below the cartographical divide that separates the United States from Mexico. For most scholars, a revisionist historical account is at play in an attempt to remove North America from the history of genocide, barbarity, oppression, and enslavement that is often part of the historical discourse on fifteenth century conquest. The first objective of this essay is to reestablish that the concept *New World* includes *all* of the Americas, including the Caribbean. The "New World" is the enormous landmass that imperialistic European nations invaded, deceptively conquered, and ruled as separate colonies. Such imperialism marked the beginning of xenophobia, genocide, subjugation, exploitation, and hatred of self. In the discourse of New World ideology, the narration is cyclical, since the "bottom line" is the reverberation of Bhabha's critical assertions of exile.

As mentioned above, the primary focus of this essay is to engage the Black Nationalist ideologies in the chartering address for the OAAU and their appropriation in the revolutionary poetry of the Afro-Dominican poet, Blas Jiménez. Critical analysis of Jiménez's poetry reveals parallels with "Malcolm X-isms" as they relate to Dominican and Caribbean Blackness. Indeed, in his poetry, Jiménez uses imagery and other poetic devices that call to mind the tenants of social, economic, and political nationalism espoused by Malcolm X. Additionally, Jiménez's revolutionary verses advocate the same notion of psychic conversion for Dominicans of African descent that Malcolm X advocated for African Americans. The aim of this section of my analysis is to explore the Black Nationalist ideologies advocated by Malcolm X and to demonstrate how they are imbedded within the poetry of Jiménez. In addition, certain works will show how this unapologetic Afro-Dominican started a Black poetic revolution that resonated with the thoughts of Malcolm X.

Blas Jiménez is recognized by many scholars of the Afro-Hispanic literary tradition as one of the first poets, if not the first poet, in Latin America to self-identify as Black and to expose the complexities of race in Latin America—specifically in the Dominican Republic. These complexities are rooted in the long, historical denial by many Latin Americans of an African heritage within their biological composition. As a result, Jiménez confronts this denial of African heritage and identification in his poems. His poetry also protests the treatment of people of African ancestry in Latin America and incites revolution. Additionally, his verses criticize those citizens who try to mask their Blackness in their celebration of indigenousness or the eroticized Hispanic "other." Jiménez's work challenges society since it advocates social change "by any means necessary." This brief essay will demonstrate the parallel ideologies between those found in the expository work of Malcolm X and those embedded within the lyric work of Blas Jiménez. Plagued by racism, subjugation, and poverty, Jiménez constructed an evolutionary Black voice that journeyed toward self-expression, self-acknowledgment, self-identification, and a reclamation of African identity and thereby evoked a rise in Black consciousness through Black Nationalist thought strategically utilized in his poetry.

Jiménez was born in Santo Domingo in 1947. It is plausible that he later became quite familiar with the legacy of Malcolm X. In his late teens, he received his bachelor's degree from Texas A&M University in the late 1960s. Since Jiménez had distinguishable Negroid features, he must have encountered racism American style—and in Texas, no less. Additionally, the young poet must have been familiar with the history of the civil rights movement in the United States and its drum majors of social justice and human rights. I am sure the name "Malcolm X" reverberated in the recesses of Jiménez's mind. In his poem "Rumores de tertulias" ("Rumors of Rap Sessions"), the speaker refers to the need for a conscious awakening among Black-colorless poets. In the poem, Jiménez uses the word *colorless* to symbolize blindness of identity. The poem begins by asking whether or not those addressed in the work are indeed poets:

> ¿Poetas?
> Poco a poco llegan los negros.
> Incoloros de negros … ¿Poetas?
> Revolucionarios e incoloros.
> (Poets?
> Little by little Blacks arrive.
> Colorless blacks … Poets?
> Revolutionaries and colorless.) (Jiménez 1996)

The initial interrogative is of significance to the overall meaning of the poem. The question of whether or not aspiring Black poets are really "poets" speaks to the social responsibility of those who have the power to write, to create, to utilize their craft as propaganda for the cause of social revolution and reform. In addressing the role of Black artists in the struggle, Jiménez is ideologically in concert with the thought of many writers and activists of the 1960s and 1970s. The Dominican poet advocates a politically active role by Black writers in the fight for social change. As the poem continues, the "poets" are described as "colorless." Such a depiction shows their denial of their African past and their selective amnesia:

> De poesías incoloras,
> para divertir la sexualmente maniatada sociedad.

Llena está la noche de poetas negros incoloros ...
(From colorless poetry,
in order to sexually enjoy the tied hands of society.
Full is the night of Black colorless poets ...) (Jiménez 1996)

As victims of sadistic pleasure for the white majority, these "colorless," blind poets are raped. They are rendered defenseless, willing victims of the robbery of self. Stolen from these violated poets is the legacy of the richness of their African heritage, since "society" has "tied" their "hands," prohibiting them from expressing it. The result of such historical brainwashing and the loss of the power of self-awareness is a people who remain errant, trapped in poverty and self-hatred, and wandering in the blindness of self. The following stanza addresses this consequence:

Aquellos poetas de vida bohemia.
Los de pobrezas escogidas,
los de ...
Hombres pobres, aquellos poetas.
(Those poets of a Bohemian life.
Those of hidden poverties,
those of ...
Poor men, those poets.) (Jiménez 1996)

In the poem's final stanzas, reference is made to Malcolm X and the need for his revolutionary ideology:

Sin la retórica de un hombre sin nombre,
sin el hombre X ...
Aquel negro rojo de Harlem,
hombre lucha,
hombre X.
(Without the rhetoric of a nameless man,
without the man X ...
That Black red man of Harlem,
fighter man,
man X.)

Aquellos poetas necesitan
las riquezas de una visión
en la historia que hace futuros.
(Those poets need
the riches of a vision
in a history that makes futures.) (Jiménez 1996)

'Rumores de tertulias" is laced with imagery of Malcolm X and the need for Blacks in Caribbean nations like the Dominican Republic to embrace his ideology. Jiménez's desire is that one would rise from the masses like Malcolm X in order to mobilize a poetic Black revolution where poets would use their lyricism to instill revolutionary thoughts into Black audiences.

The first selection from *Caribe, africano en despertar* (1984) is "Canción negra para rifles y atabales" ("Black Song for Rifles and Kettledrums"). Like the aforementioned work, "Canción negra" advocates Malcolm's liberation ideology by any means necessary—even through the use of violence. The poem embraces the ideology of physical aggression in the pursuit of cultural revolution and unity among Blacks. Interesting is the symbolic use of the kettledrum, an instrument endemic to Caribbean culture. John

Mbiti (1990) and other scholars on African cosmological thought claim that drums serve many purposes within the community. One is congregating the clan for religious and ceremonial events or occasions of war. In "Canción negra," the onomatopoeia serves a dual purpose. First, it summons people of African heritage to action. Black political mobilization is a major theme of the poem since the speaker calls for unity in order to change the current situation. The poem begins:

> Tam, tam-tam tam-tam
> me tocan los atabales
> dicen acércate más
> vamos a unir nuestras manos
> vamos los tiempos a cambiar
> (Bam, bam-bam, bam-bam
> the kettledrum calls me
> beckoning me to come closer
> let us join hands
> let us change the times) (Jiménez 1984)

The revolutionary tone reflects the theme of social change as the beats of the kettledrum "beckon" the people of African heritage. The second and third stanzas reveal the second purpose of the use of onomatopoeia in the work. The "tam-tam" imitates the sound of discharging rifles as generations accomplish the revolutionary promise of liberation. And like willing soldiers, they come with their guns loaded, ready to carry out the act of self-liberation. In the third stanza, the emphasis is collective liberation as brothers and sisters both take part in the effort of pouring gunpowder into rifles in order to eradicate oppression and subjugation by "smoking" the "maggots."

> Tam, tam-tam, tam-tam
> los hijos de los negritos
> hicieron un compromiso
> para despertar al mundo
> traen los fusiles listos
> (Bam, bam-bam, bam-bam
> Sons and daughters of Black boys and girls
> made a promise
> to wake up the world
> they bring their guns loaded)

> Tam, tam-tam tam-tam
> ¿Qué puedes hacer hermano?
> tú puedes dar una mano
> echa pólvora en tu rifle
> quememos a los gusanos
> (Bam, bam-bam, bam-bam
> What can you do brother?
> You can lend a hand
> pour powder in the rifle
> we burn maggots) (Jiménez 1984)

The themes implied in the lines above reflect Malcolm's insistence on unity and collective participation in order to bring about cultural revolution. In Malcolm's first public address at the initial meeting of the OAAU, he stated: "Our cultural revolution must be the means of bringing us closer to our African brothers and sisters. It must begin in the community and be based on community participation" (Malcolm X 1970, 55). Collective participation is a primary theme in Jiménez's "Canción negra," since the preceding stanzas concentrate on unity in the struggle and on mobilization. The concluding stanza reeks of the ideology of freedom by "any means necessary." First, the onomatopoetic rhythm of the kettledrum signifies that the end justifies the means. Second, through various poetic devices, Jiménez asserts the importance of freedom and the need for acquiring it through force if necessary. Third, "Canción negra" implies that freedom from postcolonial oppression is desired and that after centuries of struggle, the time has drawn nigh as the kettledrum continues to forcibly send out the call for revolution.

> Tam, tam-tam tam-tam
> me tocan los atabales
> dicen acércate más
> que en este ritmo traemos
> traemos la libertad
> (Bam, bam-bam, bam-bam
> the kettledrum calls me
> beckoning me to come closer
> that in this rhythm we are bringing
> we are bringing freedom.) (Jiménez 1984)

In the next two poems, Jiménez focuses thematically on the question of nationalism, the loss of "national" identity, the loss of a historical sense of self, cultural brainwashing, and the need for psychic conversion. Black Nationalist ideology emanates from these works. In the first, "Mi llanto" ("My Weeping"), the speaker is saddened by the profound themes among Black people as mentioned above. The tone is ironic as the speaker begins with the rhetorical question, "Sing to a white god?" The irony implied is that people of African descent have no need to sing the praises of white humanity since the rich legacy of Africa was robbed by whites from their historical consciousness; thus, the irony signifies the urgency of a psychic conversion among the masses.

> ¿Cantar al Dios blanco?
> la historia soy yo
> vinculados a la tecnología de "desarrollo humano"
> para mejorar la existencia vacía del nacionalismo
>
> Cuando todos eran negros
>
> ¿Nacionalismo?
> pregunta un desplazado
> sin habitat (pero la historia soy yo)
>
> Incapacitados los líderes de ojos abiertos
> créense europeos-yanquis
> con su protección que les llega del
> infinito en naves o cuentos
> históricos de aculturación
>
> ¿Cantar al Dios blanco?
> la historia soy yo
> nace la nación en mis nietos
> Cuando todos eran negros
>
> ¿Cantar al Dios blanco?
> la historia soy yo

la muerte del presente cabalga
con los hombres insensibles
los llamados a ser papel higiénico
ajustados a condiciones de profetización perenne
nalgas en el extranjero
y una falsa participación

¿Cantar al Dios blanco?
cuando todos son negros

(Sing to a white god?
I am history
tied to the technology of "human development"
in order to better the empty existence of nationalism

When everything was Black

Nationalism?
asks a displaced and
homeless man (but I am history)

Open-eyed, incapacitated leaders
believing yourselves European-Yankees
with your protection that carries you from
infinity on slave ships or historical
tales of acculturation.

Sing to a white god?
I am history
the nation is born in my grandsons and granddaughters

When everything was Black

Sing to a white God?
I am history
the death of the present rides
on insensible men
those called to be toilet paper
adjusted to conditions of perpetual prophecy
in asses of forefathers
and a false participation [fake copartnership]

Sing to a white God?

When everything is Black.) (Jiménez 1984)

The harsh and ironic tone of "Mi llanto" cries out for Blacks to reconnect with the richness of the cultural heritage of Africa for obtaining self-worth through Black Nationalism. Their human soul and intellect must be challenged in order to rid themselves of the poisonous contamination and conditioning of hundreds of years of mental bondage. In the first stanza, the phrase "the empty existence of nationalism" refers to the displaced nature of Blacks as they are left out of the "nationalism" in societies where the cultural norm is Eurocentrism. The speaker further suggests that the participation in a "nation" by those of African origin is false because the society's "nationalism" does not include the "history" of Blacks who contributed to that "nation." Repeated throughout the poem are two refrains placed in binary opposition. The first is the rhetorical question, "Sing to a white god?" The second is the statement, "When everything was Black." Such placement in the poem begs the reader to consider the former in light of the latter. The speaker deals with the loss of national identity and the appropriation of whiteness through "acculturation" as descendants of kings and queens are reduced to toilet paper used to wipe the "asses of forefathers." Yet the speaker allows a third refrain to resonate: "I am history." This refrain reinforces the need for education regarding the lost self—the African self before assimilation and acculturation. Malcolm's insistence on the reclamation of self is embedded within "My Weeping," as is the ideology of psychic conversion. The poem addresses the urgent need to recapture lost heritage and identity through education about Africa and her legacy in the Americas. Through such education, the legacy of white supremacy and cultural brainwashing can be dissolved in order to bring about liberation. In Malcolm's address at the OAAU founding rally, he stated: "History is a people's memory, and without a memory man is demoted to the level of the lower animals. When you have no knowledge of your history, you're just another animal; in fact, you're a Negro; something that's nothing" (Malcolm X 1970, 55). Noting that the term *Negro* was an abstract populist construction void of meaning, Malcolm X challenged its use for defining *nationalism* for Afro-Americans, since the designation had no implications of Africa as a nation. The essence of Malcolm's statement is found in Jiménez's poetry. Like the revolutionary leader, Jiménez knows that the existence of a people is tied to the knowledge of their history. Thus, the repetition of "I am history" emphasizes the need to know oneself as history personified—as Africa extended into the Americas. Once this knowledge is accomplished, then the manifestations of liberation, such as self-love, self-reclamation, and self-celebration, are actualized.

The next poem manifests the aforementioned in the politics of the body. Entitled "Filamentos, Filamentos, Filamentos" ("Follicles, Follicles, Follicles"), the work deals with a reclamation of self and promotes self-love. Additionally, it demonstrates the process of psychic conversion as the soul and intellect of "Black folks" foster a reappropriation and celebration of corporal blackness.

Crece en mi piel negra
mi pelo
un pelo crespo cubre mi cuerpo
pelo de negro
negro filamento
filamento córneo
filamento fuerte
filamento bueno
filamento que crece en mi piel
como en la piel del abuelo
el pelo que no se lleva el viento
viento fuerte del trópico
pelo bueno del negro
cubriendo todo mi cuerpo
en el calor tropical
no me sofoca mi pelo
filamento córneo
filamento fuerte
filamento bueno

(Growing from my black skin
my hair
curly hair covers my body

Black hair
Black follicles
corneous follicles
strong follicles
good follicles
follicle that grows from my skin
like from the skin of my grandfather
hair that doesn't blow in the wind
the strong wind of the tropics
good Black hair
covering my entire body
in the tropical heat
my hair does not suffocate me
corneous follicles
strong follicles
good follicles) (Jiménez 1984)

In "Follicles," Jiménez challenges the historical disparagement of Black body character-istics. The tone of the poem responds to the negative image of corporal Blackness by re-defining beauty as the speaker accepts and celebrates the ethnic markers of skin color and hair texture. The poem contests the ideology of white supremacy concerning its prescribed norm of beauty and calls into question the historical use physical features to define *Blackness*. The speaker rejects the vilification of Black body characteristics and challenges the dominant historical paradigm regarding physical attributes. Thus, the in-trinsic beauty of the Black self is liberated—freed from white supremacist ideology. Furthermore, the speaker reclaims the "self" through the use of alliteration ("*filamento fuerte*" ["strong follicles"], for example) and thus transforms *Black*, *skin*, *body*, and *hair* into *beauty*, *strength*, *goodness*, and *pride*.

The final poem in this analysis is "Todo negro" ("All Black"). Of all the poems ana-lyzed in this essay, "All Black" most evokes a unified Black Nationalist ideology and a Black New World Order. Again, Jiménez begins with an interrogative and follows it with a declarative statement. The poem reads:

¿Todo negro?
sí, todo negro

las nubes negras tengo por alas
las noches negras son mi morada.

¿Todo negro?
sí, todo negro

vivo mis ritos que no comprendes
de ritmo traigo mi son candente.

¿Todo negro?
sí, todo negro

uniendo suerte con mis hermanos
creo mares negros, mares humanos.

¿Todo negro?
sí, todo negro

un mundo nuevo vamos tejiendo
un mundo negro sin los lamentos.

¿Todo negro?
sí, todo negro ...
(All Black?
Yes, all Black

Black clouds I have as wings
Black nights are my home.

All Black?
Yes, all Black

I live my rituals that you do not understand
for rhythm I bring my candescent son.

All Black?
Yes, all Black

Uniting destiny with my brothers and sisters
I create Black seas, human seas.

All Black?
Yes, all Black.

We weave a New World
a Black world without wailing.

All Black?
Yes, all Black ...) (Jiménez 1984)

After the interrogative and the declarative statement, which serve as a poetic reminder of the answer to the proverbial question, references to nature are used to symbolize components of the Black Nationalist ideology that is interwoven throughout the poem. "Black clouds I have as wings" contains a metaphor for the overarching scope of Blackness since "clouds" represent Blackness hovering over disparate terrain and "wings" represent its mobility. The phrase "Black nights" as a metaphor for "my home" connotes an affirmation of the natural comfort associated with the speaker's Blackness. Affirmation of Blackness continues as the unique characteristics of Black culture are celebrated. The tone is one of cultural pride and "ownership": those who do not reside within Blackness do not understand its "rituals" and "rhythm." Additionally, the theme of Black unification surfaces as "Black seas, human seas" are created as a result of Black mobilization. This global perspective is like the Pan-Africanist ideology of Marcus Garvey, Malcolm X, and others. As Malcolm envisioned the OAAU interweaving with the OAU, the speaker in "All Black" concludes with the revolutionary vision of unity among the "human seas" creating a "New World" that is all Black—and void of the wailings of oppression, subjugation, injustice, and white supremacy.

In conclusion, the protest poetry of Blas Jiménez is filled with messages of hope and liberation for people of African ancestry in the Caribbean, especially in the Dominican Republic. The themes of his poems selected for analysis in this essay focus on self-respect, cultural revolution, the reformation of education, political empowerment, economic liberation, and mobilization. Thus, Jiménez creates a revolutionary poetic trajectory that uplifts as it challenges the marginalization and oppression of Blacks while dismantling the dogma of white supremacy. These themes parallel those advocated by Malcolm X in his public addresses and published writings. This essay has championed the similarity in focus between the ideologies that define the legacy of Malcolm X and those that mark the poetry of Blas Jiménez. The message rendered by Malcolm to those assembled at the opening rally for the Organization for Afro-America Unity was unapologetically laced with his ideas on white supremacy, Black liberation, and revolution. Similar ideas are poetically rendered in the above selections from Jiménez's work. Malcolm's focus on cultural reformation and revolution is found in the work of Jiménez, as this poet of African descent designated poetry as the necessary means for cultural revolution and the transformation of sons and daughters of Africa situated in Caribbean nations.

References

Bhabha, Homi K. 1994. *The location of culture.* London: Routledge.

Jiménez, Blas. 1984. *Caribe, africano en despertar.* Colección Cimarrones, Santo Domingo: Editora Nuevas Rutas.

_____. 1996. *El nativo: Versos en cuentos para espantar zombies.* Santo Domingo: Editora Búho.

Mbiti, John. 1990, *African religions and philosophy.* 2nd ed. Oxford: Heinemann Educational Publishers.

West, Cornel. 2001. *Race matters.* 2nd ed. New York: Vintage.

Malcolm X. 1965. *The autobiography of Malcolm X.* With Alex Haley. New York: Ballantine.

_____. 1970. *By any means necessary.* Ed. George Breitman. New York: Pathfinder.

Further Reading

Bhabha, Homi K., ed. 1990. *Nation and narration.* London: Routledge, 1990.

Cambeira, Alan. 1997. *Quisqueya la bella: The Dominican Republic in historical and cultural perspective.* New York: M. E. Sharpe.

Cronon, Edmund David, and John Hope Franklin. 1969. *Black Moses: The story of Marcus Garvey and the Universal Negro Improvement Association.* Madison: University of Wisconsin Press.

Fanon, Frantz. 1963. *The wretched of the earth.* New York: Grove.

Malcolm X. 1965. *Malcolm X speaks: Selected speeches and statements.* Ed. George Breitman. New York: Grove Weidenfeld.

_____. 1971. *The end of white world supremacy: Four speeches by Malcolm X.* Ed. Benjamin Karim. New York: Arcade.

24

Globalizing African American Political Thought: A Case Study of Malcolm X

Godwin Ohiwerei

> If all of us are going to live as human beings, as brothers, then I'm for a society of human beings that can practice brotherhood. (Malcolm X, 2001, p. 28)

Local Politics and Disenfranchisement

The national group of African descent that can wield the most significant power on the international level for Black people is composed of African Americans. While it may be true that African Americans can play a vital role in the international arena for the interests of peoples of African descent, racism and the politics of disenfranchisement continue to cloud issues of identity and global positioning for Blacks in the United States. When political, social, and economic dilemmas among Africans are discussed on the international level, few African Americans are in key governmental positions from which they can promote Black interests on the international scene. The success of Jews in the Diaspora in articulating Jewish struggles anywhere in the world is a model for people of African descent to emulate. African Americans, who are United States representatives, tend to act in the interests of white Americans—mostly those of European descent.

When, in 2001 though 2005, the United States Secretary of State was an African American and when the United Nations Secretary General is currently an African, one would expect that the political and economic interests of continental Africans and of those in the African diaspora would be of central interest to the international community. However, this is not the case. Indeed, it is strange to note that the British Prime Minister Tony Blair and British pop stars like Bono have made a more significant push for African socioeconomic development by pressuring the developed countries (the Group of 8) to forgive the debts of Africa's poorest countries.

The tsunami disaster of late December 2004 and the quick response of the industrialized world motivated other countries to act in support of the dispossessed. Juxtapose that with the failure of the industrialized countries to recognize the situation in Darfur as one of genocide. In addition, no situation in recent memory has been as horrendous as the genocide in Rwanda and the world's neglect of a calamity that

329

claimed the lives of over 850,000 innocent people. Also, the war in the Congo has raged for over forty years (with brief periods of ceasefire), and until recently, apartheid in South Africa was an embarrassment to the international community. Africa continues to struggle alone, with minimal support from the global community. But when the Western world or the United States is in need of support from the world community, every other country is expected to support the industrial powers. In North America, Haitians are continually treated with disdain when they seek political-cum-economic asylum in the United States as compared with Cubans. The various pathologies of the African American poor and working class continue to be an ongoing debate. All over the world, the welfare of peoples of African descent tends to attract less attention from the world body as represented by the United Nations and the industrialized countries.

Paradigm Shift

Since the issues mentioned above are complicated on a macrosociological scale, this essay will deal with the issues on a smaller scale, using the life experiences of Malcolm X to show the relationship between the local and the international exposure of Malcolm to the United States' subjugation of African Americans. The key fact of Malcolm's experiences was that his travels outside the United States affected his social construction of race and racism in a very positive way. More significantly, Malcolm as a racist turned out to be a myth rather than a reality. Indeed, Malcolm's eventual understanding that the world was not just the United States reduced his initial anger against whites so that during the later part of his life, his answers to the adversities of African Americans were to move toward global justice and to conclude that global capitalism and social inequality, not mere whiteness, were the serious problems underlying those adversities.

The metamorphosis of Malcolm's life showed that his experiences outside the United States significantly influenced his views on the ability of nations worldwide to bring about change among African Americans. A review of Malcolm's life indicates that it took a significant turn when he changed from being a disenchanted Black youth to a street thug. During a term in prison, he became one of the most articulate and learned civil rights activists of the 1960s. Malcolm was a special civil rights activist because he did not see white dominance in the United States as solely an African American problem; rather, he saw that racism and class discrimination was global in character (Kahn, 2001; Morris, 2001; Muhammad, 2002).

Malcolm X seriously challenged the paradigm that people of African descent do not matter in international politics. When one talks about a paradigm shift, one can see it reflected in Malcolm's metamorphosis. One has to appreciate how an individual like Malcolm X, with long-held perceptions of localized politics and with anger and hatred against white people, was willing to change his perception to a broader vision of global understanding. The willingness to constantly seek the truth or to validate one's own belief was characteristic of Malcolm's political and social development.

By January 18, 1965 (approximately one month before he was murdered), Malcolm reiterated that he was not a racist and that he was against racism and discrimination in any form. He indicated that he believed strongly in human beings and that all people should be respected regardless of their race. A strong factor in this paradigm shift was his visit to Mecca where he experienced the brotherhood of man—that is, people of all races and colors from all over the world coming together as one (Burrow, 1996).

According to Malcolm, rectifying the psychological conditioning of Black people should begin with the proper education of Black people—an education addressed to Black children, as well as adults, and grounded in their history and culture before their enslavement in the United States (Morris, 2001).

This essay centers on Malcolm's attempt to change the focus of the struggle against racism and cultural injustice. It argues that the idea of localizing, within the United States, the issues of racism, prejudice, inequality, and support for racial justice by African Americans limited their significance and success. Malcolm emphasized that when African American social and political struggles became globalized, especially when continental Africans and those in the African diaspora became involved, there would be significant pressure on the United States government to respond positively. Malcolm believed that as long as African American racial and equality struggles were fought within the United States, African Americans could only acquire allies that were fellow Americans to rescue them—that is, whites who had earlier discriminated against them. He further stated that as long as issues related to racism were categorized as those of civil rights, they fell under the category of domestic (that is, United States) issues. In other words, since the United States government consisted of many segregationists and racists, especially from the South, positive outcomes on civil rights struggles would be unlikely.

At the beginning of 1965, Malcolm stated that it was not accidental that the struggle of African Americans had been a struggle for civil rights. He cautioned that as long as African Americans were struggling merely for civil rights, they were asking many racist segregationists who held positions of power in the U.S. Congress to rescue them (like the hen asking the fox for rescue). The most powerful racist and segregationist congressmen came from the South—the most racist part of the country. Consequently, African Americans could only achieve their goals of racial equality to the extent that these powerful congressmen allowed them (Malcolm X, 2002a).

Globalizing Pathologies Experienced by Continental Africans and Africans in the Diaspora

From 1954 to 1964 newly independent African nations began to emerge. The impact of those nations upon the civil rights struggle in the United States was tremendous. The African revolution and the militancy existing on the African continent were two major factors in the rapid growth of the Black Muslim movement. In turn, the Black Muslim movement pushed the civil rights movement (and the liberals) out into the open (Malcolm X, 2002a).

By the time of his death in 1965, Malcolm had visited Egypt, Saudi Arabia, Kuwait, Lebanon, Sudan, Ethiopia, Tanzania, Nigeria, Ghana, Liberia, France, England, Switzerland, and other countries (Malcolm X, 2002a; Malcolm X, 2003). By 1964, Malcolm had discovered a new approach in dealing with racism and oppression in the United States. He believed that globalizing the plight of African Americans would reduce the dependency of African Americans on their oppressors to solve the problem of disenfranchisement. The emergence of newly independent African nations had become the powers that the United States and the United Nations had to take seriously. Malcolm was perceptive enough to understand that the growing number of African nations in the United Nations could be used as a major political and economic means of embarrassing the United States government:

> It was not accidental that in the United Nations during the 1960s, African foreign ministers were openly accusing the United States of being an imperialist power and of practicing racism. In the past, these labels were always confined to the European colonial powers independently, but never was the United States itself singled out and labeled, identified as an imperialist power. (Malcolm X, 2004a, p. 89)

Malcolm further stated:

> [W]hen you get involved in a struggle for human rights, it's completely out of the jurisdiction of the United States government. You take it to the United Nations. And any problem that is taken to the United Nations, the United States has no say-so on it whatever. Because in the UN the largest bloc of votes is African; the continent of Africa has the largest bloc of votes of any continent on this earth. And the continent of Africa, coupled with the Asian bloc and the Arab bloc, comprises over two-thirds of the UN forces, and they are the dark nation. (Malcolm X, 2002b, p. 79).

The implication of the argument above was that Malcolm wanted to make the issue of racism against Blacks not only a civil rights issue but also a human right's issue because civil rights fell only within the jurisdiction of the U.S. government. Malcolm's argument was important because human rights is part of the charter of the United Nations and any nation that classifies its grievance under the label of human rights violations can present its case before the United Nations. Such a tactic, Malcolm believed, would globalize the problems of African Americans, who could then find allies in nations that find the treatment of African Americans unjust. The nations most likely to lobby for African Americans were independent African countries that were members of the United Nations. These countries could not directly challenge the U.S. government independently, but such a challenge would be much easier under the UN mandate. Malcolm discovered that African countries were always interested in supporting the struggle of African Americans for racial equality but that they saw themselves as handicapped by the notion that the struggle was a civil rights issue (Malcolm X, 2001; Malcolm X, 2002a).

Outcomes

If Black people were united, Malcolm argued, they could challenge racial oppression effectively; if Black people were united, they could advance economically; if Black people were united, they would represent a potent political influence (Painter, 1993).

> The Black community in the Western Hemisphere, especially in the United States and somewhat in the Caribbean area, realizing once and for all that we must restore our cultural roots, must establish contacts with our African brothers, we must begin from this day forward to work in unity and harmony as Afro-Americans along with our African Brothers. (Malcolm X, 2001, p. 40)

Malcolm X pursued a grand plan to alter the focus and forum of further debates about U.S. racism by internationalizing them. On July 17, 1964, he began a campaign to persuade the members of the Organization of African Unity (OAU) to bring the matter of U.S. racism before the UN, just as the OAU had done with South African apartheid. In taking the case of the Black man and the Black woman in the United States before the nations in the UN, Malcolm did not expect that that the UN would produce meaningful changes in U.S. society, but he believed that no forum could better internationalize the debate or provide such "perfect theater" for the "humiliation" of the United States. Had Malcolm succeeded more fully in this campaign before his death—as U.S. State Department and Justice Department officials were reported to believe—the United States would find itself in the same category as South Africa, Hungary, and other countries whose domestic policies had become issues for debate at the UN (James, 2003).

Malcolm X struggled to integrate the interests of continental Africans with those of the African diaspora. He consistently emphasized the similarities between the outcomes of the colonization of Africans and the African American struggle for full emancipation. He believed that when the struggles of African Americans and Africans became integrated, the resulting bond would strengthen the struggle of the two parties against their oppressors:

> Because the same beat, the same heart, the same pulse that moves blacks on the African continent—despite the fact that four hundred years have separated us from that mother continent, and an ocean of water has separated us from that mother continent—still, the same pulse that beats in the black man on the continent today is beating in the heart of the black man in North America, Central America, South America, and the Caribbean. Many of them don't know it is true. (Malcolm X, 2001, p. 56).

Indeed, Malcolm well articulated the need for an integration of ideas between continental Africans and those in the African diaspora when he stated:

> As long as we hated our African blood, our African skin, our Africanness, we ended up feeling inferior, we felt inadequate, and we felt helpless. And because we feel so inferior and so inadequate and so helpless, instead of trying to stand on our own feet and do something for ourselves, we turned to the white man, thinking he was the only one who could do it for us. That due to the fact that blacks have modeled themselves in the image of whites, it is not surprising that white is accepted as the personification of beauty and personification of success. (Malcolm X, 2001, p. 57)

Cheikh Anta Diop stated: "If only our traditional historians, ethnologists, and sociologists had fully realized, as one has a right to expect of them, that the essential need of a people is not so much to be able to glory in a more or less great past but rather to discover and realize the continuity of the past" (Jennings, 2002).

It is significant to note that African Americans represent both political and economic power when compared with continental Africans and those in the African diaspora. Uneven power distribution among Blacks and whites in U.S. society is no excuse for the low level of involvement of African Americans in the global discussions of the social, political, and economic issues of people of African descent.

Therefore, Black people's self-determination and challenges to the cultural supremacy of whites will be more successful when people of African descent all over the world join together to challenge the white hegemony. In order to challenge white culture, Blacks must understand the need for a collective consciousness—that helping

Blacks in one part of the world means helping Blacks all over the world. Indeed, the suffering of Blacks in one part of the world indirectly affects Blacks all over the world. The term *white hegemony* is generally used to describe the dominance of the United States and western Europe. There are serious limitations when African Americans localize their socioeconomic plight by focusing on U.S. sociopolitical dynamics between U.S. whites and blacks rather than seeing how these relationships exist globally.

Malcolm's argument that the United Nations should become a medium for integrating the struggles of Blacks worldwide was quite valid when he stated that it was no longer an accident in the United Nations that every time the Congo crisis or any problem on the African continent was being debated in the Security Council, its members coupled it with what was going on in Mississippi and Alabama. Malcolm surmised that the greatest accomplishment made in the struggle of the Black man and the Black woman in the United States toward some kind of real progress in 1964 was the successful linking together of the African American problem with the African problem, thereby making the Black problem a world problem (Malcolm X, 2002a; Malcolm X, 2004a).

When Malcolm traveled to Paris, he called on the Afro-American community in France and other parts of Europe to unite with the African community—a message that was consistent in his speeches during the later part of his life. Malcolm's interaction with and study of people in developing societies benefited him tremendously. Indeed, his social contact with the developing world fostered a better understanding of the subordination of African Americans. He was able to understand that there were people outside the United States with similar problems of subordination. He therefore issued a call for the marginalized peoples of the world to support each other in order to achieve global socioeconomic emancipation.

Malcolm was prophetic when he stated that both Blacks in the African diaspora and African Americans had a stake in the African revolution. For as long as the African continent was dominated by colonial powers, those powers were enemies of the African people. Indeed, they created a negative image of the African continent and the African people, and they projected an image abroad that was very hateful. And because it was hateful, over one hundred million people of African heritage in the West looked at that hateful image and did not want to be identified with it:

> We shunned it, and not because it was something to be shunned. But we believed the image that had been created of our own homeland by the enemy of our own homeland. And in hating that image we ended up hating ourselves without even realizing it.... You can't hate the roots of the tree without hating the tree, without ending up hating the tree. You can't hate your origin without ending up hating your self. You can't hate the land, your motherland, the place that you came from, and we can't hate Africa without ending up hating ourselves. (Malcolm X, 2001, p. 54)

The political clout of these newly independent African nations was an angle of strength to African Americans in terms of identity and political will. Malcolm further indicated:

> [N]either was the case of Black Africa in this country ever linked with what was happening to people in Africa. If there's any drastic departure from past procedures that have been reflected already in the present UN session, it's the tendency on the part of African representatives one after another to link what's happening in the Congo with what's happening in Mississippi. (Malcolm X, 2004a, p. 89)

The representation of African countries in the UN and their clear identification with the conditions of African Americans led a number of African American activists to travel to certain African nations to see what was actually going on in those countries as compared with the U.S. media perceptions of Africans. Malcolm indicated that African delegates to the UN did not allow themselves to be labeled as "Negros," and he further stated that only African Americans allowed themselves to be called "Negroes," since, according to Malcolm, African Americans had been misguided, mistaught, misled, and misinformed (Malcolm X, 2004b).

> And I say that this is a serious problem, because all of it stems from what the western powers do to the image of the African continent and the African people. By making our people in the Western Hemisphere hate Africa, we ended up hating ourselves. We hated our African characteristics. We hated our African identity. We hated our African features. So much so that you would find those of us in the west who would hate the shape of our lips. We would hate the color of our skin and the texture of our hair. This was a reaction, but we didn't realize that it was a reaction. (Malcolm X, 2001, p. 54)

Thus, Malcolm argued that African Americans had not succeeded in conquering racism because they had internalized the stereotypical image imposed on them (Malcolm X, 2004b, p. 90).

At the London School of Economics on February 11, 1965, Malcolm stated:

> [T]he African revolution must proceed onwards, and one of the reasons that the Western powers are fighting so hard and are trying to cloud the issue in the Congo is that it's not a humanitarian project. It's not a feeling or sense of humanity that makes them want to go in and save some hostages, but there are bigger stakes. They realize not only that the Congo is so situated strategically, geographically, that if it falls into the hands of a genuine African government that has the hopes and aspirations of the African people at heart, then it will be possible for the Africans to put their own soldiers right on the border of Angola and wipe the Portuguese out of there overnight. (Malcolm X, 2001, p. 53)

When the various African governments used the United Nations to criticize the United States for its role in the Congo and linked it to its treatment of Blacks in Mississippi in 1964, Malcolm saw that relationship as positive. During an interview at Columbia University, he indicated:

> I have never taken responsibility or credit, you might say, for the stance taken by African nations. The African nations today are represented by intelligent statesmen. And it was only a matter of time before they would have to see that they would have to intervene in behalf of 22 million black Americans who are their brothers and sisters. And it is a good example of why our problem has to be internationalized. (Malcolm X, 2001, p. 238)

Malcolm further stated that linking the problem of racism in the Congo and linking the problem of racism in South Vietnam to the racist U.S. treatment of Blacks were the same. They were all part of the vicious racist system that the Western powers had used to continue to degrade and exploit and oppress the people in Africa and Asia and Latin America during recent centuries (Malcolm X, 2002a, p. 238).

Issues that Malcolm dealt with are still very much the issues that we are dealing with today: the case of the Congo (now called the Democratic Republic of the Congo), African American sociopolitical conditions, and African political and economic stagnation. In addition, people of African descent have not heeded the call of Malcolm X for a close relationship in order to internationalize the plight of Africans on the continent and those in the African diaspora. The continued marginalization of the condition of Black people on the international level calls for the type of leadership that is not ethnic but global in ideology.

References

Burrow, Jr., Rufus. (1996). Malcolm X was a racist: The great myth. *The Western Journal of Black Studies, 20* (2).

Kahn, Joel S. (2001). *Modernity and exclusion.* London: Sage Publications, Ltd.

James, Branham Robert. (2003). I was gone on debating: Malcolm X's prison debates and public confrontations. *Argumentation & Advocacy, 31* (3).

Jennings, Regina. (2002). Cheikh Anta Diop, Malcolm X, and Haki Madhubuti. *Journal of Black Studies, 33* (2).

Malcolm X (2001). *February 1965: The final speeches.* New York: Pathfinder.

Malcolm X (2002a). *Malcolm X speaks: Selected speeches and statements* (George Breitman, Ed.). New York: Pathfinder.

Malcolm X (2002b). *Malcolm X talks to young people: Speeches in the United States, Britain and Africa* (Steve Clark, Ed.). New York: Pathfinder.

Malcolm X (2003). *By any means necessary.* New York: Pathfinder.

Malcolm X (2004a). *The last speeches* (Bruce Perry, Ed.). New York: Pathfinder.

Malcolm X (2004b). *Malcolm X on Afro-American history.* New York: Pathfinder.

Morris, Jerome. (2001). Malcolm X's critique of the education of Black people. *The Western Journal of Black Studies, 25* (2).

Muhammad, Elijah. (2002). *The divine sayings of Elijah Muhammad.* Maryland Heights, MO: Secretarius Publications.

Painter, Nell Irvin. (1993). Malcolm X across the genres. *American Historical Review, 98* (2).

25

Public and Shadow Values in the Thought of Malcolm X

Rhett Jones

Every society has a system of public values—ideas the society's people agree are good, right, proper, and worth striving for. The value system legitimates and supports all the activities which the society undertakes—from disciplining children to executing criminals convicted of capital crimes, to waging government-sponsored wars on other societies. The society uses the value system to both measure and evaluate the extent to which its reality matches its ideals. These values are public in the sense that they are routinely acknowledged and celebrated in the speeches of politicians, in the sermons of ministers, and in the instructions of schoolteachers. In the contemporary United States, for example, such values include democracy, love, happiness, and success. Of course, what persons actually do can be quite different from what they value or profess to value. Indeed, behavior and belief are linked, each having an impact on the other. Even those who systematically ignore or violate the values remain aware of them. In a multicultural, multiracial, and multireligious society such as that of the United States, some groups may reject the values, but most at least claim to be committed to them.

In addition to these public values, the United States also maintains a system of shadow values that have, over the course of its history, proven every bit as powerful as democracy, equality, freedom, and justice. People believe in these shadow values, too. Since they sometimes conflict with public values—for instance, the claim that the white race is superior to others cannot fit into a society committed to equality—shadow values are not often publicly celebrated. But they shape American behavior just the same. Malcolm X recognized the two types of values and explored both in his development of strategies for Black liberation. This essay is concerned with his explorations.

Based largely on Malcolm's speeches, commentaries, and responses to questions during the last months of his life, the essay begins with a discussion of how values fit his changing plans for Black liberation. Malcolm X was concerned with the hypocrisy characteristic of the United States' relations with its public values and the continuing power of its shadow values. The essay then examines the three most powerful and widely held of these shadow values—violence, the belief in the supremacy of whiteness, and greed. It concludes with a brief discussion of Malcolm's understanding of the implications of public and shadow values for the international Black struggle.

Values in Malcolm's Social Thought

Malcolm X freely shared his ideas about American values in the last months of his life. Indeed, Jones (2007) argues that it is possible to construct an entire sociology derived from his talks, interviews, and other materials in the months before his assassination on February 21, 1965. Malcolm's thought was in constant flux—a change that can be seen in his autobiography (Malcolm X 1966) as he moved into the Nation of Islam and in his last talks as he constructed his own system of social thought (Alkalimat and Associates 1986; Asante 1988; Karenga 1993). One way of tracing his evolution is to suggest that Malcolm, in changing his social analysis, inverted the direction of causality. While a Black Muslim he believed that the cause of Black people's problems was found in their ideology—particularly in their religious beliefs. The solution to their problems would emerge following a change in beliefs. Afro-Americans (Malcolm's preferred term) needed to abandon the false faith of Christianity and return to their original Islamic religion. They would then be able to recover a positive self-image, come to an understanding of their history, and, thus armed, defeat racism in the United States, obtain genuine independence for Africa, and restore persons of African descent to their rightful (and historic) position in the world.

After he broke with the Nation of Islam, Malcolm changed his stand: he began to focus on economic and political power, not religious belief. He declared in the 1964 founding rally of his Organization for Afro-American Unity (OAAU) that only two kinds of power counted in the United States, economic and political (Malcolm X 1970, 45–46). Epps goes so far as to claim that Malcolm became a kind of "primitive Marxist" (Malcolm X 1969, 92), while Alkalimat and Associates and Breitman agree that Malcolm, at the time of his assassination, was creating a new movement that, if not socialist, was certainly much influenced by socialism (Alkalimat and Associates 1986, 304) (Breitman 1967, 39). According to Breitman, Malcolm was on his way "to a synthesis of black nationalism and socialism" at the time he was assassinated (Breitman 1967, 69). Malcolm X suggested that Black Americans, in their struggle, might follow what Africans had done with socialism, fitting it into the African context and modifying it, but not simply importing it unchanged from Europe (Malcolm X 1970, 181). Whether or not he was a Marxist—and he never declared himself one—Malcolm believed that the subordinate position of Blacks was caused by economic and political forces. The public value system of the United States was a mere fig leaf for covering the brutal nakedness of economic exploitation and political oppression. In sharp contrast to his activities while in the Nation of Islam, Malcolm encouraged Black Americans to reject the false and specious values of white America and to focus instead on the economic realities that were responsible for their cruel treatment.

Malcolm's new approach, emphasizing the Afro-American struggle as economic rather than ideological, fit and complemented his methodological strategy. He thought the best way to understand and advance the struggle was for Blacks to learn from those most affected by bigotry; thus, he first urged Blacks to listen to one another. Black folk should never simply accept what others, even other Blacks told them; instead, they should cut through the web of shadow values to find out for themselves (Malcolm X 1965, 91, 102). Having listened to one another and investigated for themselves, they could then take action (Malcolm X 1965, 155). Later he began to urge his listeners to organize themselves formally into research groups to share their ideas and having shared them, to use them to free not only Afro-Americans but Black folk worldwide (Malcolm X 1971, 5). Study and reflection, he argued, could lead to a program that would shake the entire world (Malcolm X 1965, 43). He further believed that shared Black study would result in a shared plan of action (Malcolm X 1965, 118–119). During a question-and-answer session after a talk in December 1964, he said:

> My suggestion would be that young people, like yourselves, many of whom are still in school and are more flexible in matters where you have not yet come to a conclusion, sit back and weight the thing [racism] for yourself and analyze it. If you can ever find what it is in the very atmosphere here that brings out these things, then perhaps you might be able to save the country. You might be able to build a better society. (Malcolm X 1965, 214)

He also urged his audience to do what he was already doing himself: "I spend my time out there in the streets with people, all kinds of people, listening to what they have to say" (Malcolm X 1965, 75).

In addition, he urged African Americans to observe, speaking of the Black middle class:

> You ever watched them? You ever watched one of them? Do that—watch them, watch the real bourgeois black Americans. He never wants to show any real sign of emotion. He won't even tap his feet. You can have some of that real soul music, and he'll set there, you know, like it doesn't move him. I watch him and I'm telling you. And the reason he tries to pretend like it doesn't move him is that he knows it doesn't move them [whites]. And it doesn't move them be- cause they can't feel it, they've got no soul. And he's got to pretend he has none just to make it with them. This is a shame really. (Malcolm X 1972, 13)

Malcolm went on to inform his listeners that they could learn much about middle-class Blacks—what they thought of themselves and how they related to whites—by simply watching them. He urged Blacks to listen, watch, learn, reflect, conclude, then start the en- tire cycle over again. At almost any point in this cycle, Afro-Americans should discuss their ideas with other Black Americans. By this means, they would eventually agree collectively on a strategy for liberation. Malcolm argued that such a strategy would forcefully engage and enlist the masses of Blacks because it would derive from their own observations and plans, not from some theories originally developed in Europe and the United States.

In his now classic work, Stuckey (1987) finds that African American ideology in gen- eral and Black Nationalism in particular were built from the ground up, rooted in the traditions of central and west Africa and shaped by their slave experience in the United States. Influenced by these forces, Blacks gradually constructed a system of thought that embodied and reflected their life in the Americas. While Mintz and Price (1992) do not systematically examine ideology, they do argue that the slaves themselves constructed New World Black cultures—and not by simply imitating whites, as so much of the scholarship insists. Jones (1988) finds that Black Americans did not have sufficient au- tonomy to construct an ideology of their own; instead, they used white American ideol- ogy against white folk. Rael (2002) argues that the experiences of the masses of slaves in the United States was simply irrelevant to ideological construction because the slaves were not involved in political discussions. As he sees it, most of the slaves lived in the South, so the free Blacks living in the North were more influenced by the ideological de- bates among white elites than by the cultures created by the southern slaves.

Whether one sides with Stuckey or Mintz and Price or Jones or Rael in this impor- tant debate, values are central to understanding Afro-American culture. It can be ar- gued that Blacks first borrowed and then fully accepted white values or that Afro-Amer- ican values were derived from a slave consensus or that they were modeled on the paradigms created by Black elites and then accepted by the Black masses. But whichever argument one accepts, values played a role in how Blacks defined whites, Blacks, and the African American struggle. Though like many Black leaders, Malcolm X did not systematically (and sociologically) use the term *values*, he clearly concluded that what Blacks believed was important.

The public values of the United States are quite clear, but Malcolm X saw that there were two sets of problems which Black folk faced when they sought to commit to them: one had to do with white hypocrisy, the other with shadow values. First, the United States claimed to be committed to a certain system of values, but according to Malcolm, it behaved in a different way. In a 1964 address to the Organization of African Unity (OAAU), he observed that South Africa preached segregation and practiced segregation: "She at least practices what she preaches. America preaches integration and practices segregation. She preaches one thing while deceitfully practicing another" (Malcolm X 1965, 75). The United States, he pointed out, presented itself as the exemplar of freedom, trotting all over the world and telling other nations how to achieve freedom while denying the vote to its Black citizens (Malcolm X 1965, 50). This sort of hypocrisy made it difficult for African Americans to follow U.S. whites by simply behaving in ways that were directly and simplistically linked to the U.S. value system. Indeed, Malcolm put it: "I don't see any American dream. I see an American nightmare" (Malcolm X 1965, 26).

White U.S. authorities admitted no such hypocrisy. According to Malcolm X, the reason why they did not was that "[Y]ou and I are living in a very deceitful and tricky country, which has a very deceitful and tricky government" (Malcolm X 1965, 91). He also noted: "[The nation's white ruling authorities had] mastered the art of very deceitfully painting people whom they don't like in any image they know you won't like. So you end up hating your friends and loving [your] enemies" (Malcolm X 1965, 91). The use of the word *deceitfully* suggests a deliberate plan to mislead blacks. But whether most whites were aware of the nightmare they had created for Blacks or of their hypocrisy was not always clear, though Malcolm seemed to believe that most of them were. He did insist that the white leaders were. Their hypocritical behavior was not accidental but was deliberately planned and self-serving. In this regard, Malcolm's argument resembled that of the distinguished Black historian, Lerone Bennett (1970), who believed that racism was not the result of a natural recognition of differences among the races and was not an accident of circumstances. Instead, Bennett wrote, it was deliberately created by white elites over the course of the eighteenth century with the aim of dividing Black slaves from lower-class white workers. In his time, as had been the case with the white elites in the period Bennett described, Malcolm found that the white ruling class only pretended a commitment to U.S. values, profiting economically and politically from this pretense.

Violence — A Shadow Value

In addition to the set of problems caused by white hypocrisy regarding public values, a second set of problems confronted by Blacks resulted from shadow values. Three of these were important in the U.S. value system—violence, whiteness, and greed. The commitment of a clear majority of U.S. whites to these shadow values made it impossible for African Americans to follow U.S. public values to achieve their goals. Malcolm saw that a blind acceptance of the values of most U.S. whites and a reliance on them to achieve Afro-American liberation would not work: "A chicken just doesn't have it within its system to produce a duck egg. It can't do it. It can only produce according to what that particular system was constructed to produce. The system in this country cannot produce freedom for an Afro-American" (Malcolm X 1965, 68–69). If the system of beliefs which the United States had constructed had not worked and could not work for Black people, they obviously could not use it. As Malcolm often stated, they would have to develop their own sense of values based on their own observations and reflective discussions of these observations. One such strategy was developed by Martin Luther King, Jr., and others, who directly confronted the white U.S. shadow value of violence by using nonviolence. Malcolm often declared that he would become nonviolent only when the Ku Klux Klan, the White Citizens Council, and similar racist organizations became nonviolent. To a group of Mississippi teenagers visiting New York City late in 1964, he said: "I myself would go for nonviolence if it was consistent, if everybody was going to be nonviolent all the time. I'd say, okay, let's get with it, we'll all be nonviolent. But I don't go along with any kind of nonviolence unless everybody is going to be nonviolent" (Malcolm X 1965, 138). He often made it clear that he had great respect for the courage of King and his followers. Significantly, their nonviolent strategy was rooted in an un-American value system—a strategy that had been forged into a political instrument by Mohandas Gandhi during India's struggle for independence from Great Britain. Malcolm did not believe nonviolence could work in the United States, for, as James Farmer, leader of CORE points out (1968, v), "the crux of the problem of race in America today [is] not that black people are violent, but that the whole nation is wedded to the nation that 'the big fist wins,'" or, as H. Rap Brown declared in one of the 1960s most frequently cited provocative assertions, "[v]iolence is as American as apple pie." Just as white America celebrated a value system it would not transform into reality for Black America, so, too, did it transform its routine violence against Blacks into an unacknowledged value. According to Malcolm X, there was no need for Black people to follow white people into this convoluted system of denied values and shadow values; instead, they should work on developing their own system of values.

In so doing, it was not necessary for U.S. Blacks to incorporate revenge against most U.S. whites into their new value system: "The very conditions that whites created are already plaguing them into insanity and death. They are already reaping what they have sown" (Malcolm X 1970, 178–179). Malcolm shrewdly realized that in their self-serving hypocrisy and race-based cruelty, most U.S. whites were undermining their own value system. It was not working for Blacks, and as most U.S. whites continued to abuse and distort it, the U.S. value system would soon not work for them either. The system which the nation's leaders claimed to rest on values clearly spelled out in the Declaration of Independence did not rest on such values. Rather, it rested on brute power and the cheerful willingness of most whites to murder Blacks, crushing anyone who got in their way (Malcolm X 1965, 119). Malcolm argued that Blacks needed to reject this sham value system and instead meet white power with Black power (Malcolm X 1965, 150).

In order to do this, Blacks needed to admit to themselves that they were not part of U.S. society, or as Malcolm put it (1972, 14), "[y]ou are not of the west, you are in the west." This admission would both liberate them from a value system that had repeatedly failed African Americans and free them to develop a new system of their own. Malcolm observed that before Blacks could be Americans, they would have to enjoy the fruits of Americanism and that while African Americans had not enjoyed the fruits, they had experienced the thorns (Malcolm X 1965, 172). Part of the process of white domination of Blacks in the United States was that the nation's authorities had insisted that Blacks were American citizens but that, in fact, they had not treated them as such. As Malcolm often stated, by formally accepting Blacks as American citizens, the U.S. government had made bigotry an internal problem, thus preventing the United Nations from helping Blacks on the grounds that African Americans' human rights were being violated. Malcolm was not deceived by this hypocrisy: "Well I am one who doesn't believe in deluding myself. I'm not going to sit at your table and watch you eat with nothing on my plate and call myself a diner. Sitting at the table doesn't make you a diner, unless you eat some of what's on that plate" (Malcolm X 1965, 26). Thus, to extend this metaphor, since African Americans were never served, it was pointless of them to observe the rules of etiquette, as many respectable Blacks urged. Afro-Americans could display excellent table manners, but they would never be given anything to eat. They gained nothing by telling themselves they ought to accept white values and behave in ways acceptable to white folk. Having been born in the United States did not make a Black person a U.S. citizen; if it did, neither legislation nor amendments to the Constitution would have been necessary (Malcolm X 1965, 26).

One of the worst consequences of being a legal American but not being accepted as an American was that many Blacks worked hard to be Americans by following the white U.S. value system. Indeed, as Malcolm pointed out (1969, 182), "[t]he black man in America tries to be more American than anyone else." This behavior—often noted by sociologists of the time—was, as Malcolm saw it, pointless. Behaving like white Americans would not enable Black Americans to escape racism; rather, it shifted their energies away from developing tactics that would improve their lives. Black folk needed to spend their time watching, listening, and talking with one another about the real problems of the Afro-American community rather than trying to be like whites. In acting like white folk, they also appeared to legitimate white patterns of behavior even when these patterns manifested clear hatred and hostility toward Blacks. Blacks' emulation of whites was pathological as Malcolm saw it. Instead of looking at themselves and celebrating the great achievements of their ancestors in Africa, the Americas, and elsewhere in the world, too many Blacks were trying to be like whites and were thus behaving in ways they foolishly thought would win them acceptance by the white world.

Martin Kilson admitted in a discussion following Malcolm's talk at Harvard in March 1964: "I myself can see no basic, lasting or meaningful resolution to the terrible plight of most Negroes within the present political arrangements and modes of thought that the American market place of political ideas has given us" (Malcolm X 1969, 156). Kilson has long been right of center on matters of race relations, but here he agrees with Malcolm and concedes that the white U.S. value system offers Black folk no way to improve their position. However, as his writings since 1964 demonstrate, Kilson has generally urged Black Americans to be Americans and thus to work within and to use a value system that, at least as of 1964, failed to meet their basic human needs. Malcolm's position was quite different. In contrast, and up until his assassination, he did not believe that white U.S. values could be made to work for Blacks.

Whiteness—A Shadow Value

Malcolm often argued that one of the reasons for his position was the value most U.S. whites placed on whiteness itself. Whiteness, like violence, is not one of those public U.S. values listed along with democracy, freedom, liberty, and equality, yet it has proven every bit as important in U.S. history, culture, and society. Even at the height of the country's racism, which Rayford Logan (1965) recognized by originally subtitling his book on the period 1877–1901 *The Nadir of the Negro*, whiteness was not as frequently praised as equality, but it has always been a powerful belief. Early in the new nation's history, the Founding Fathers (all of them white) apparently decided that Blacks, Native Americans, and those persons of European ancestry who were not yet regarded as white could not be U.S. citizens. The requirement of whiteness for citizenship was not explicitly written into the Declaration of Independence, the Articles of Confederation, or the Constitution, yet it was implicit in those documents. Whiteness was indeed a powerful force which dictated that Black slaves would be counted as three-fifths of a person for purposes of apportioning representatives in the new democracy and that indigenous peoples were—despite considerable evidence to the contrary—incapable of participating in or contributing to U.S. civilization (McLoughlin 1986). In response to a question in December 1964, Malcolm X detailed America's commitment to whiteness: "This is true. This is the most racist nation on earth. There is no country on earth in which you can live and racism be brought out in you—whether you're white or black—more so than this country that poses as a democracy" (Malcolm X 1965, 214).

This shadow value of whiteness had a significance in the United States which it did not have elsewhere in the world, as Malcolm explained in a talk given in Detroit, less than a week before his assassination:

> In Asia or the Arab world or in Africa, where the Muslims are, if you find one who says he's white, all he's doing is using an adjective to describe something that's incidental about him, one of his incidental characteristics; there is nothing else to it, he's just white. But when you get the white man over here in America and he say's he's white, he means something else. You can listen to the sound of his voice—when he says he's white, he means he's boss. (Malcolm X 1965, 163)

Being white carried with it a higher status than any Black person could ever claim. Although most U.S. whites celebrated U.S. citizenship and its privileges and the U.S. government made immigrants who came to the United States complete certain requirements before they could become citizens, Europeans were already white. And whiteness was more important than citizenship. Blacks were citizens, but they were not white and so could not expect to advance beyond a second-class citizenship. Persons of European ancestry who "just got off the boat" were already white; hence, according to Malcolm, they were already well on the road to being accepted as U.S. citizens. Although Blacks had long been in the United States they "aren't Americans yet" (Malcolm X 1965, 25–26).

The origin of white persons did not matter; they had routinely been extended rights for which Afro-Americans were still fighting, as Malcolm declared in a 1964 meeting of his Organization of Afro-American Unity (OAAU):

> [P]eople who just got off the boat yesterday in this country, from the various so-called Iron Curtain countries, which are supposedly an enemy to this country, and no civil rights legislation is needed to bring them into the mainstream of the American way of life, then you and I should just stop and ask ourselves, why is it needed for us? ... [T]hough you have the right of birth in this land, you're still not qualified under their particular system to be recognized as a citizen. Yet the Germans, that they used to fight just a few years ago, can come here and get what you can't get. The Russians, whom they're supposedly fight-

ing right now, can come here and get what you can't get without legislation; don't need legislation. The Polish don't need legislation. Nobody needs it but you. Why?

These questions were rhetorical since Malcolm already knew the answers. But he urged his Black audiences to study and develop answers for themselves.

Since all these peoples were regarded as white, they just had to show up in the United States to be treated fairly. By merely doing so, they obtained what scholars now call "white-skin privilege." But since there was nothing Blacks could do to change their skin color, nothing they could do to obtain the shadow but all-important value of whiteness, they had nothing to gain by accepting the values of white folk. Many Blacks understood that whiteness was important; in fact, some remained formally Black but celebrated their European ancestry, while others passed as white. What some scholars (Russell, Wilson, and Hall 1993) are calling "the color complex" was important during Malcolm's era and remains just as important today. Malcolm observed Blacks "running around bragging about [their] Scotch blood or [their] German blood or this other kind of blood" (Malcolm X 1970, 119). Some Blacks adopted a pattern that led them to favor—as mates, employees, sorority sisters—Black persons who were European rather than African in appearance. They told one another that they ought to choose a marriage partner whose physical features would mean that any children would have European-like skin color, lip shape, and hair texture. These choices demonstrated that the shadow value of whiteness had a powerful impact even within the African American community itself.

In encouraging one another to make such choices, Afro-Americans were telling one another that they could better themselves, their families, and their children by making their offspring more white in appearance. Their preference for whiteness and their rejection of blackness was challenged by Black Americans who sometimes moved from a psychological rejection of such arguments to a political organization against them. The two most notable twentieth-century examples were Marcus Garvey's Universal Negro Improvement Association of the 1920s and the less well-organized Black Is Beautiful/Black Power movement of the 1960s. Whites, according to Malcolm, did not have to exercise choice. They had already achieved the value of whiteness simply by having been born white and thereby becoming eligible for everything that the United States had to offer. Malcolm believed that the lack of such choice gave Blacks a chance to be morally superior to whites (Malcolm X 1969, 108). After all, the essence of morality is that an individual chooses to behave in one way or another. Whites had created a system in which they had no choice: no matter how they behaved, they were always better than Blacks. No matter how cruel, brutal, or vicious a white person might be, he or she would always be superior to a Black one. By relying so heavily on their shadow value of whiteness, as David Walker (1965) made clear, most U.S. whites rejected such U.S. public values that had been derived from Christianity and the Declaration of Independence. They could not "do unto others," and they could not allow Blacks "liberty and the pursuit of happiness" so long as they believed that U.S. Blacks were an inferior species of humankind—if indeed they were part of humankind at all. For most U.S. whites, behavior was biologically driven, since white people would always be physically, intellectually, and morally superior to Blacks.

As a member of the Nation of Islam (NOI), Malcolm X inverted this belief by claiming that whites, as a people, were created by a renegade and evil scientific genius who then loosened them, like mad dogs, on Blacks. There was nothing Black people had to do to be superior to whites since they were already superior simply by having been born Black. As a Black Muslim, Malcolm believed that the only choice persons of African descent had to make was whether to choose to recover their rightful place in the world. In the theology of the NOI, no matter how Afro-Americans acted, they would always be superior to whites. Like white U.S. racism, this interpretation of human behavior was biologically driven, with little room for human beings to make meaningful moral choices. Blackness in this system was the mirror image of whiteness in that both were determined by race. The only change was that rather than being genetically inferior to whites, Blacks were now genetically superior. They did not have to make difficult moral choices; they merely had to have been born Black. As Malcolm saw it, the purpose of Black Nationalism was to enable persons of African ancestry to understand this reality and act accordingly.

In a 1965 interview Malcolm explained why he had changed his ideas about Blacks and Black Nationalism:

> But when I was in Africa in May, in Ghana, I was speaking with the Algerian ambassador who is extremely militant and is revolutionary in the true sense of the word (and has his credentials as such for having carried on a successful revolution against oppression in his own country). When I told him that my political, social and economic philosophy was black nationalism, he asked me very frankly, well, where did that leave him? Because he was white. He was an African, but he was Algerian, and to all appearances he was a white man. And he said if I define my objectives as the victory of black nationalism, where does that leave him? ... So he showed me where I was alienating people who were true revolutionaries, dedicated to overturning the system of exploitation that exists on this earth by any means necessary. So, I had to do a lot of thinking and re-appraising of my definition of black nationalism. Can we sum up the solution to the problems confronting our people as black nationalism? (Alkalimat and Associates 1986, 303–304)

In the last months of his life, Malcolm X was less and less likely to describe himself as a Black Nationalist, though he had not yet found an alternative label that accurately described his philosophy. In a 1965 interview Malcolm admitted: "And if you notice I haven't been using the expression [Black Nationalism] for several months. But I still would be hard pressed to give a specific definition of the overall philosophy which I think is necessary for the liberation of the black people in this country" (Malcolm X 1971, 15).

Clearly Malcolm X had rejected any sort of racial determinism, white or Black. In 1965 he stated: "I, myself, do not judge a man by the color of his skin. The yardstick that I use to judge a man is his deeds, his behavior, his intentions" (Malcolm X 1970, 171). Behavior and the moral choices that determined it, not race, became important to Malcolm. Much was being made then, as now, of the need for brotherhood, but Malcolm asserted that brotherhood should not be practiced with a person simply because his or her skin was white; rather, brotherhood should be offered to an individual on the basis of his or her actions and attitudes. In a Chicago speech in 1964, Malcolm made explicit his position on racial determinism:

> In the past I have permitted myself to be used to make sweeping indictments of all white people, and these generalizations have caused injuries to some white people who did not deserve them.... In the future I intend to be careful and not to sentence anyone who has not been proven guilty. I am not a racist and do not ascribe to any of the tenets of racism. In all honesty and sincerity it can be stated that I wish nothing but freedom, justice and equality; life, liberty and the pursuit of happiness for all people.

Malcolm's choice of words was curious since here he adopted the rhetorical values of the United States, which he had earlier (and often) declared were false and meaningless for U.S. Blacks. Since whites paid no attention to Blacks, there was no reason why Blacks should pay them any attention either.

Malcolm did not mean the Blacks should adopt bigotry. Racism, he declared, could not be defended by any intelligent person because there was no material evidence to support it (Malcolm X 1965, 215). But despite repeated and persistent governmental, intellectual, and religious condemnations, racial bigotry continued to exercise a powerful hold on both whites and Blacks in the United States. The ultimate cause of the coming planet-wide war was not, as Elijah Muhammad had often preached, the biologically driven hostility between white folk and Black, but a battle "between those who want freedom, justice and equality for everyone and those who want to continue the system of exploitation" (Malcolm X 1965, 216). Again, Malcolm's choice of words reflected the rhetorical values of the United States, but it is clear that Malcolm believed such a clash would be driven by the economic and moral choices consciously made by human beings and not by unconscious forces with their roots in race. In a letter written while in Saudi Arabia in 1964, Malcolm made clear his explicit rejection of racial determinism, adding: "You may be shocked by these words coming from me, but I have always been a man who tries to face facts" (Malcolm X 1965, 60). Race caused nothing, and it should certainly not be allowed to cause a war.

To stave off a race war, Blacks needed to free whites from the clutch of whiteness by affording them the opportunity to make choices rather than failing to provide them with a way to escape their belief in white supremacy. In response to a question in 1965, Malcolm X replied: "If you attack a man because he is white, you give him no out. He can't stop being white. We've got to give the man a chance" (Malcolm X 1965, 213). He went on to say that he did not believe most white folk would choose to reject whiteness. In this regard, he was very much like David Walker (1965), who believed that the history of the white race powerfully demonstrated its commitment to whiteness but believed that if its members were faithful to the U.S. value system, they could overcome racism.

Greed—A Shadow Value

When asked in an interview in January 1965 what was responsible for race prejudice in the United States, Malcolm X succinctly replied: "Ignorance and greed" (Malcolm X 1965, 196). Greed, Malcolm clearly understood, was a powerful force in U.S. society. The capitalist system celebrated and rewarded those who were economically successful, while placing few restraints on them. As a consequence, they were free to behave pretty much as they wished. According to Malcolm X, only two kinds of power counted in the United States—economic and political (Malcolm X 1970, 45–46). Social power was derived from these two, and neither it nor any of the U.S. public values such as equality, brotherhood, or justice stood a chance against the shadow value of greed. In a speech in November 1964, Malcolm X said:

> You know, you can't communicate if one man is speaking French and the other one is speaking German. They've both got to speak the same language. Well, in this country you're dealing with a [white] man who has a language. Find out what that language is. Once you know what language he speaks in, then you

can talk to him. And if you want to know what his language is, study his history. His language is blood, his language is power, his language is brutality, his language is everything that's brutal. And if you can't talk that talk, he doesn't even hear you. You can come talking that old sweet talk, or that old peace talk, or that old nonviolent talk—that man doesn't hear that kind of talk.

Indeed, nonviolence and other U.S. public values meant little. It was not possible—in a country worshipping greed and using force—to even have a serious conversation on nonviolence. Of course, most U.S. whites were perfectly willing to hold such discussions—mainly to persuade U.S. Blacks that most whites sincerely believed in their stated public values. But most did not. Instead, most U.S. whites responded only to economic and political power.

Not only did entering into peaceful dialogue with whites for Black rights mean nothing to most U.S. whites; they could not be talked into liberating Black folk anyway. Malcolm X believed whites could not give Blacks freedom, since it could not be given by one person to another (Malcolm X 1965, 111). If Blacks wanted freedom, they had to take it. Because Black people seemed to be so committed to a value system that had repeatedly failed them, Malcolm had reservations about some Black leaders. He suspected that those who were preaching the power of nonviolence had been bought off. In a meeting in Paris in 1964, he was asked why many Afro-Americans remained committed to nonviolence even when they were being attacked and when their nonviolent efforts seemed to have little impact on most U.S. whites. He responded: "That's easy to understand—shows you the power of dollarism. The dollar makes anything possible" (Malcolm X 1970, 114). Malcolm believed that the legitimization of greed and the celebration of wealth made it possible for anyone to be bought off, and he often warned his student audiences that as their organizations became more effective, efforts would be made to buy them off.

At the same time the United States was buying off its own dissidents, both white and Black, it was bribing dissidents outside the country. Malcolm concluded that all this corruption was taking place because while America was advocating its public values—attempting to convince countries all over the globe to become democracies—it was at the same time covertly following its shadow values of violence, whiteness, and greed. Long before others recognized the existence of global capitalism, Malcolm emphasized that the power structure was not only ruling Blacks in the United States but was also ruling others abroad (Barnes 1971, 27). Malcolm saw that the Black struggle in the United States was not only a conflict of Black versus white and a struggle limited to this country; he also saw that it was a worldwide struggle of the oppressed against the oppressors (Breitman 1967, 39). "Western interests," which Malcolm said might better be described as "imperialism, colonialism, racism and all these other negative isms or vulturistic isms" (Malcolm X 1965, 161), operated around the globe. In a speech in Detroit in 1965, Malcolm urged his audience to recognize:

> The interests in this country are in cahoots with the interests in France and the interests in Britain. It's one huge complex or combine, and it creates what's known not as the American power structure or the French power structure, but an international power structure. This international power structure is used to suppress the masses of dark-skinned persons all over the world and exploit them of their natural resources.... Mind you, the power structure is international, and its domestic base is in London, in Paris, in Washington, D.C., and so forth.

He often noted that just as the oppressor was international, so, too, did the freedom fight have to become international. U.S. Blacks could not hope to succeed in isolation.

There was no way in which they could comfortably benefit from the public values of the United States while the "masses of dark-skinned persons" remained subservient to the international cartel.

The United States had become the center of this imperialist organization (Malcolm X 1965, 149), but there were some tensions within this combine. All the other western nations, Malcolm X argued, had become satellites of the United States (Malcolm X 1965, 120), including France (Malcolm X 1970, 168). But France was not content with this role. It wanted the United States to be its satellite. But these disputes were essentially minor, in-family ones, since much of the Western world—which had accepted the U.S. shadow value of greed—was united around politics and economics, the only forces that really counted. The United States and Europe remained together because they needed each another to continue exploiting the non-Western world. The Europeans turned to Uncle Sam because the United States had not colonized Africa and so did not have a negative image in Africa (Malcolm X 1965, 170). As Africa (and Asia and other parts of the colonized world) awoke in the years after World War II, it became clear to European colonizers that they could no longer control these areas by force. Malcolm observed:

> Since their own economy, the European economy and the American economy, had been based upon their continued influence over the African continent, they had to find some means of staying there. So they used the friendly approach. They switched from the old openly colonial imperialistic approach to the benevolent approach. They came up with some benevolent colonialism, philanthropic colonialism, humanitarianism, or dollarism. Immediately everything was Peace Corps, Operation Crossroads. (Malcolm X 1965, 170)

Dollarism was an especially powerful force. In reply to a question put to him at the Militant Labor Forum in January 1965, Malcolm explained: "You can cuss out colonialism, imperialism, and all other kinds of isms, but it's hard for you to cuss out that dollarism. When they drop those dollars on you, your soul goes" (Malcolm X 1965, 199).

In a sense, the United States was practicing throughout the world tactics it had first tested on Blacks within its borders. Europeans could not readily hold on to economic and political power in Asia, Africa, the Caribbean, and other parts of the world because they were (rightfully) regarded by the peoples of these regions as racist colonizers. But except for the Philippines, Latin America, and Alaska, the United States had never been regarded as a colonizing power. It now entered into "non-Western" areas proudly bearing its public values of democracy, fair play, and justice. The nation made a great deal of its willingness to share and spread these values. It brought along, however, its shadow values. No matter what the U.S. government stated publicly, it continued to privilege whiteness and when deemed necessary, to use violence. It often justified military intervention. It sponsored attacks in the Congo, repeatedly threatened what was then called "Red China," and used its dollars to buttress brutal dictators throughout Latin America. Within its borders the United States had insisted that Blacks could make things better for themselves by pursuing public values in just the way whites had done. At the same time, the nation continued to exploit Black people no matter how they behaved. The United States was now—as the head of the "international combine" (Malcolm's phrase)—using the same tactics in the rest of the world.

Scholars such as McManus have argued that the United States never bettered the position of its Afro-American citizens out of a commitment to its own public values (McManus 1973, 197). Had he read their works, Malcolm would have agreed. Indeed, he declared that the nation only helped U.S. Blacks when such aid served its own interests

(Malcolm X 1965, 7). In an interview conducted after he spoke at a meeting of the Organization of African Unity (OAU) in 1964, Malcolm stated:

> It was the world pressure, brought about by Hitler, that enabled the Negro to rise above where he was [in 1939]. After Hitler was destroyed, there was the threat of Stalin, but it was always the world pressure that was upon America that enabled black people to go forward. It was not the initiative internally that the Negro put forth in America, nor was it a change of moral heart on the part of Uncle Sam—it was world pressure.

It was for this reason that when asked what he thought of "Red China," Malcolm said he thought it was good for U.S. Blacks that centers of power existed outside the United States (Malcolm X 1965, 215). According to Malcolm, the United States was incapable of acting within the framework of its own celebrated public values. The only language which most white people in the United States spoke was that of blood, power, and money. Pressure could be brought to bear internally by Blacks who made it clear they would have their freedom "by any means necessary," but for their struggle to be successful, they would have to have powerful economic and political allies from outside the nation. Ultimately, greed—the shadow value so well implied by Malcolm's term *dollarism*—was more important to most whites than any public value.

The importance of the dollar was true whether such whites lived in Africa or in America. According to Malcolm X, the "western imperialist nations" had deliberately subjugated Africans for economic reasons that were responsible for Africa's low standard of living (Malcolm X 1965, 127). The system, Malcolm argued, was simple enough. These nations used African raw materials to "feed the machines of the Europeans and make jobs for them" and then sold these goods back to the Africans as finished products. There was, according to Malcolm, nothing particularly complicated about this process, and it had little to do with the values which the international power elite claimed to be bringing to Africa (Malcolm X 1965, 127). A similar strategy was at work in the United States, where most Blacks had no control over land (Malcolm X 1965, 57). In both places, members of the ruling class were in reality serving their greedy appetites by denying Blacks any sort of economic power. And in both Africa and the United States, the solution was similar: Blacks had to gain control over their own land and develop their own industries (Malcolm X 1965, 39, 127).

Similar problems for Africans and Afro-Americans did not call for identical strategies. According to Asante, Malcolm understood what it meant for Blacks to live within the imperialist United States, and he understood the special economic and social position of African Americans (Asante 1988, 18). The primary responsibility of Afro-Americans, Malcolm often said, was to develop ways of working with and supporting not just Africans but other exploited peoples of the world. Malcolm X is often compared to his great Black Nationalist predecessor, Marcus Garvey, but unlike Garvey, he did not believe that a simple Black replication of the tactics, organizations, and ideologies which had served whites would solve Black problems. By the time of his assassination, Malcolm X was beginning to understand and to argue that the system of Europeans and U.S. whites had often not served them well either. Since it rested on greed and a ready willingness to use violence, only the most selfish and vicious whites profited from it. These whites understood the shadow values that drove U.S. society and took advantage of their understanding; consequently other whites were generally exploited almost as often as Blacks. According to Karenga, Malcolm saw a parallel between these selfish, vicious whites and the Black middle class. Like their white counterparts, many members of this Black group were selfish, self-serving, and willing to settle for tokenism, com-promise, and even attacks on Blacks themselves if these served their interests (Karenga 1993, 250).

These Blacks were just as greedy as their white counterparts, but like their fellow Blacks who were not so greedy, they were citizens of the United States. All these people—white, Black, rich, and poor—were caught in the web of an international car-tel that was greedy and vicious. In coming to understand the shadow value of greed, Malcolm did not lose sight of whiteness. This shadow value, in which virtually all Euro-peans and U.S. whites as well as many Africans and African Americans believed, was a powerful force in dividing U.S. society. Like violence and greed, whiteness had time and again in the history of the United States demonstrated that it was more powerful than such public values as equality, freedom, and justice.

Conclusion

Given Malcolm's understanding of U.S. shadow values, the reason for his reluc-tance—in the last months of his life—to use the term *Black Nationalism* in reference to himself and his program becomes clear. If Malcolm had lived long enough to read James E. Jackson, who wrote: "The opposite of racial nationalism is interracial equal-ity and justice, not the change of white nationalism to black nationalism" (Jackson 1974, 210), he might have agreed. Jackson was a Black leader in the Communist Party of the United States and was thus experienced in walking the fine line between race analysis and class analysis. Like the earlier Communist-linked African Blood Brother-hood (Draper 1970; Kuykendall 2002) Malcolm X recognized that both race analysis and class analysis were important and that sorting out the respective importance of each oversimplification had to be avoided. This avoidance was especially necessary if political action, and not just theoretical understanding, was sought. According to Malcolm, one example of such oversimplification was claiming that Black National-ism was a kind of racism. In a speech delivered at Harvard University, Malcolm ex-pressed his anger at those who took this position, observing that the European Com-mon Market excluded all who were not European but that it was not charged with racism (Malcolm X, 1969, 158). Malcolm was shrewd enough to recognize that white-ness, and the power whites had to present it in various guises, was among the most lethal weapons of the international combine. While Malcolm was a member of the Nation of Islam, his strategy had been to use blackness as a counterweight to white-ness, but like Jackson, he was beginning to recognize that the solution was far more complex.

Malcolm often confessed that he did not know all the answers, and just as often, he urged Blacks to work them out for themselves. They should do so by carefully observing whites and themselves, by frequent discussions among themselves, and by refusing to accept the interpretations of others. A small number of persons of European ancestry had constructed a powerful international cartel, and while Malcolm had not (yet) devel-oped a guidebook for its overthrow, he did realize that understanding the United States was the key. Indeed, according to Malcolm, the United States was not only far more powerful than the European nations; it had also constructed a value system that stood in sharp contrast to the status- and family-based system of the Europeans.

The system that the United States offered to the world consisted of egalitarian, humane, and libertarian public values, but this system was a false and hypocritical one, as Malcolm's reflective study of the nation's treatment of Blacks revealed. According to Malcolm, the U.S. government was urging other governments to strive for the very values it ignored. Moreover, it publicly denied the shadow values that were at the very core of its history and plans for the future. Just as the United States was the center of the international combine and of world power, U.S. Blacks were the center of the United States. Their actions repeatedly demonstrated the falseness of the United States' public values and revealed the power of its shadow ones. But according to Malcolm X, if Afro-Americans were to effectively challenge their nation's shadow values of violence, whiteness and greed, they would need first to understand them and themselves.

References

Alkalimat, Abdul, and Associates. 1986. *Introduction to Afro-American studies: A peoples college primer.* 6th ed. Chicago: Twenty-First Century Books.

Asante, Molefi Kete. 1988. *Afrocentricity.* Trenton, NJ: Africa World Press.

Barnes, Jack. 1971. In tribute to Malcolm X. In *Malcolm X talks to young people: Speeches in the United States, Britain, and Africa,* ed. Steve Clark. New York: Pathfinder.

Bennett, Lerone. 1970. The road not taken. *Ebony* 31 (August): 71–76.

Breitman, George. 1967. *The last year of Malcolm X: The evolution of a revolutionary.* New York: Merit Press.

Draper, Theodore. 1970. *The rediscovery of Black Nationalism.* New York: Viking.

Farmer, James. 1968. Introduction to *CORE and the strategy of non-violence,* by Inge Powell Bell. New York: Random House.

Jackson, James E. 1974. *Revolutionary tracings in world politics and Black liberation.* New York: International Publishers.

Jones, Rhett S. 1988. In the absence of ideology: Blacks in colonial America and the modern Black experience. *The Western Journal of Black Studies* 12 (Spring): 30–39.

_____. 2007. Methodology and meaning: The sociology of Malcolm X. In *Malcolm X: A Historical Reader,* ed. John L. Conyers, Jr., and Andrew P. Smallwood. Durham, NC: Carolina Academic Press.

Karenga, Maulana. 1993. *Introduction to Black Studies.* Los Angeles: University of Sankore Press.

Kuykendall, Ronald D. 2002. African Blood Brotherhood: Independent Marxists during the Harlem Renaissance. *The Western Journal of Black Studies* 26 (Spring): 16–21.

Logan, Rayford. 1965. *The betrayal of the Negro.* New York: Collier Books.

Malcolm X. 1965. *Malcolm X speaks: Selected speeches and statements.* Ed. George Breitman. New York: Grove.

_____. 1966. *The autobiography of Malcolm X.* With Alex Haley. New York: Grove.

_____. 1969. *The speeches of Malcolm X at Harvard.* Ed. Archie Epps. New York: William Morrow.

_____. 1970. *By any means necessary*. Ed. George Breitman. New York: Pathfinder.

_____. 1971. *Malcolm X talks to young people: Speeches in the United States, Britain, and Africa*. Ed. Steve Clark. New York: Pathfinder.

_____. 1972. *Malcolm X on Afro-American history*. New York: Pathfinder.

McLoughlin, William G. 1986. *Cherokee renascence in the new republic*. Princeton, NJ: Princeton University Press.

McManus, Edgar J. 1973. *Black bondage in the North*. Syracuse, NY: Syracuse University Press.

Mintz, Sidney W., and Richard Price. 1992. *The birth of African-American culture: An anthropological perspective*. Boston: Beacon.

Rael, Patrick. 2002. *Black identity and Black protest in the antebellum North*. Chapel Hill: University of North Carolina Press.

Russell, Kathy, Midge Wilson, and Ronald Hall. 1993. *The color complex: The politics of skin color among African Americans*. New York: Harcourt Brace Jovanovich.

Stuckey, Sterling. 1987. *Slave culture: Nationalist theory and the foundations of Black America*. New York: Oxford University Press.

Walker, David. 1965. *David Walker's appeal*. New York: Hill and Wang (Orig. pub. 1829).

26

"You Don't Call the Kittens Biscuits": Disciplinary Africana Studies and the Study of Malcolm X

Greg Kimathi Carr[1]

> Malcolm X was one of the most feared debaters on the American platform, capable of demolishing an opponent with a one-liner. In one debate, for example, his opponent, also black, kept insisting, "I am an *American*." Malcolm demanded that blacks call themselves black men and women and not Americans. His opponent persisted, and this led Malcolm to ask, "Why do you call yourself an American, brother?" "Because I was *born* in this country," shouted his irrepressible adversary. Malcolm smiled and spoke softly: "Now, brother, if a cat has kittens in the oven, does that make them biscuits?"[2]
>
> James Farmer, *Lay Bare the Heart*

> We used to bite the bullets with the pigskin casings
> Now we perfect slang like a gang of street masons
> Scribe check make connects
> True pyramid architects
> Replace the last name with the X

---

1. I wish to express my gratitude for the support and forbearance of Dr. James N. Conyers in urging this essay into print and for the constant inspiration and intellectual camaraderie of the students, faculty, and staff of Howard University.

2. James Farmer, *Lay Bare the Heart: An Autobiography of the Civil Rights Movement* (New York: New American Library, 1985), 224. Farmer relates this famous anecdote while discussing his experience "debating" Malcolm in 1961 and 1962. He notes that he was later advised not to appear again publicly in open discussion with Malcolm by Roy Wilkins, Whitney Young, and Martin Luther King, Jr., at a "Big Six"/Council of United Civil Rights Leadership meeting in the spring of 1963. King mentioned that he had declined to appear on a network television panel with Malcolm, and Young said: "I don't think we ought to appear with that guy; we can't win." He added: "I think all of us should agree here in CUCRL that none of the top leaders will appear on a platform, radio, or TV with Malcolm X because we just give him an audience" (ibid., 222). Farmer does not portray this group's withdrawal from discussions and debates with Malcolm X as a defeat of their generally integrationist politics and philosophies; however, the silence concerning Wilkins's, King's and Young's rationales, particularly given each man's keen intellect and erudition, may imply their begrudging awareness of the resonant chord Malcolm's analysis struck with the African-American public sphere.

The man's got a God complex
But take the text and change the picture
Watch Muhammad play the messenger like Holy Muslim scriptures
Take orders from only God
Only war when it's Jihad
See Ali appears in Zaire to reconnect 400 years
But we the people dark but equal give love to such things
To the man who made the fam' remember when we were kings[3]

Lauren Hill, "Rumble in the Jungle"

European Biscuits or African Kittens?: Epistemological Assumptions and Intellectual Genealogy in Africana Studies

Malcolm's metaphor, "you don't call the kittens biscuits," demonstrates the irreconcilable distance between subject positions in the study of Africana in the Western academy. This essay suggests that the academic study of Malcolm X might best be undertaken by the methodologies and techniques being developed in the academic discipline of Africana Studies.[4] It explains how such a study might be approached by first establishing the subject position of Malcolm X within the long-view genealogy of what Cedric Robinson has called "the Black Radical Tradition" (BRT). Robinson uses this term to describe the nature and character of collective African cultural and social life as well as the intellectual work produced by representative individuals drawing on it throughout its half-millennium response to the "oppression emergent from the immediate determinants of European development in the modern era."[5]

Africana Studies, as Daudi Azibo has written, is similarly grounded in its presumptions about the enduring and enabling centrality of Africana cultural texts and practices[6] to professional African intellectual work. Scholars within Africana Studies have promoted the use of the term "African-Centered" or "Afrocentric" Worldview (AWV) to describe this phenomenon. Through his life, oratory, and organizational work, Malcolm X represented the institutions and larger groups of African people who perpetu-

---

3. Fugees (Wyclef Jean, Prazwell, and Lauren Hill), Featuring A Tribe Called Quest, Busta Rhymes and John Forte, "Rumble in the Jungle," *When We Were Kings*, compact disc, Polygram Records, ASIN B000001ER9, (c) 1996 Polygram Records.

4. Africana Studies contains a range of disciplinary practices. See, among others, Conyers and Stewart. The anthologies are edited by Norment and Aldridge and Young.

5. Cedric J. Robinson, *Black Marxism: The Making of the Black Radical Tradition* (London: Zed Books, 1983), 96–97.

6. Azibo follows Wade Nobles, Linda James Myers, and many others in referring to this as the "African-Centered Worldview," which Azibo defines as "the irrefragable, enduring and original conceptual foundation for Black Studies." Daudi Azibo, "Articulating the Distinction Between Black Studies and the Study of Blacks: The Fundamental Role of Culture and the African-Centered Worldview," *The Afrocentric Scholar* 1, no. 1 (May 1992): 66.

ally (re)create the BRT/AWV[7] in response to what I will describe below as the "episodic horizontal challenges" of each generation's historical experience.

Malcolm's enduring resonance in the imagination of African public spheres is grounded in the authenticity of his archetype in the cultural grammar and vocabulary of the BRT/AWV.[8] This representative grounding also ensured his relationship as an "outsider" to the United States and Europe (his African "cat" and "kittens" to the "oven") and his rejection of U.S. and European domination from that African insider/U.S.-European outsider's perspective. Africana Studies is a set of disciplinary practices also grounded in epistemological and discursive postures residing inside the normative range of the African-Centered Worldview and outside the cultural and political sphere of Eurocentrism and is therefore best suited to undertake the accurate study of both Malcolm X and the broader cultural continuum out of which he was formed. Most academic discussions of Malcolm X outside Africana studies do not consistently declare or interrogate the ideological, epistemological genealogies in which they labor.[9]

Part One of this essay comments on the contemporary explosion of interest in the scholarly study of Malcolm X, culminating with the call for a break with the narrative frame that has guided the examination of his life. Part Two outlines an experimental methodology relying on a new approach to historiography within Africana Studies as a possible method of studying Africana, including the representative life and work of

---

7. Molefi Kete Asante accurately identifies Malcolm X as an archetypical figure in Africana history and culture, a "cultural hero" who was "pre-eminently a cultural spokesperson, a cultured person, an analyst and theorist of culture, a revolutionary cultural scientist." Molefi Kete Asante, *Malcolm X as Cultural Hero and Other Afrocentric Essays* (Trenton, NJ: Africa World Press, 1993), 25. Asante recognizes that Malcolm was part of a longer continuum of African historical experience who "did not stand outside of space and time. He was bound to the past, to the present, and to the future" (ibid., 31).

8. The existence of an African-Centered Worldview is the most contested assertion in contemporary Africana Studies. Robinson's now twenty-year-old articulation of a theory of the Black Radical Tradition, a more materialist-oriented framing of a similar assertion, has received little comment in the field, an indication by many thinkers of their lack of comfort with the concept of a corporate set of African cultural identity markers. That Malcolm X was an archetype within a normative range of Africana cultural markers is rejected by scholars such as E. Francis White and Patricia Hill Collins, among others, who assert that a) there is no defining normative range of African cultural identity and b) Malcolm X, the Nation of Islam, and its contemporary progeny, into which they group "conservative Afrocentrists" as proseletyzers of a Black Nationalist "civic religion," have been used to feed "heterosexisms" and masculinist domination. See E. Francis White, *Dark Continent of Our Bodies: Black Feminism and the Politics of Respectability* (Philadelphia: Temple University Press, 2001), 37–44, and Patricia Hill-Collins, *From Black Power to Hip Hop:Racism, Nationalism and Feminism* (Philadelphia: Temple University Press, 2006), 85–94. On the silences facing the initial reception of and subsequent engagement with Robinson's thesis, see Robin Kelley, "Foreword to 2000 Edition," *Black Marxism: The Making of the Black Radical Tradition*, by Cedric Robinson (Chapel Hill, NC: University of North Carolina Press, 2000), xviii, and Darryl C. Thomas, "Black Studies and the Scholarship of Cedric Robinson," *Race and Class* 47, no. 2 (October–December, 2005): 1–22.

9. I am indebted to the scholarship of Dr. Clyde Taylor of New York University, whose provocative text *The Mask of Art* calls for undertaking such a "break" with the Western epistemological and aesthetic contract. By challenging thinkers to induce a "crisis of knowledge" by becoming aware of the controlling cultural principles (the Master's Discourse) which guide their assumptions as the initial step in professional intellectual work, Taylor provides Africana Studies with a necessary set of techniques for "rendering the invisible visible." See Clyde Taylor, *The Mask of Art: Breaking the Aesthetic Contract—Film and Literature* (Bloomington: Indiana University Press, 1998), 3–69.

Malcolm X. Part Three uses a text from contemporary African American popular culture to illustrate how these techniques can reimagine basic narratives and lessons of Malcolm's life.

Contemporary Malcolm X Studies: Narrative Assumptions and Contested Epistemologies

The cache of documents, photographs, ephemera, and personal effects that form the corpus of the Malcolm X papers held by New York's Schomburg Center for Research in African-American History and Culture[10] and the exhibition of selected items from that cache,[11] from May 19 to December 31, 2005, signal the latest watershed moment in the continually evolving relationship of various public spheres with the image and meaning of the life and work of Malcolm X.[12] The "Malcolm Renaissance" is usually traced to Malcolm's emergence as a major figure in late-1980s popular cultural texts and practices among African American youth,[13] which, in turn, led to the convergence of commercial and African American populist mythmaking agendas, as illustrated by the 1992 Spike Lee motion picture *Malcolm X*.[14] In the past year, more sophisticated examinations of

---

10. Herb Boyd, "Schomburg Designated as Repository for Malcolm X Papers," *New York Amsterdam News*, January 9–15, 2003, 1, 40; Herb Boyd, "Looking Over Malcolm X's Shoulder," *New York Amsterdam News*, January 23–29, 2003, 30. Manning Marable has written that primary source materials on Malcolm X were located as of 2003 in at least seventy-three different U.S. archives and libraries, including the Schomburg. See Manning Marable, "Rediscovering Malcolm's Life: A Historian's Adventures in Living History," *Souls: A Critical Journal of Black Politics, Culture and Society* 7, no. 1 (Winter 2005): 29.

11. Herb Boyd, "Remembering Civil Rights Leader Malcolm X at 80," *New York Amsterdam News*, May 12–18, 2005, 4.; Herb Boyd, "Malcolm X Exhibit: 'Astounding,'" *New York Amsterdam News*, May 19–25, 2005, 1, 28. The Schomburg exhibition provided information which guided viewers to an online teacher's guide related to the exhibition at www.schomburgcenter.org. The narrative placards for the exhibition were assembled by a team led by Cheryll Y. Greene, the consulting editor for the late Henry Hampton and his Blackside Production team's 1994 PBS Documentary *Malcolm X: Make it Plain*. See Schomburg Center for Research in Black Culture/The New York Public Library, *Malcolm X: A Search for Truth* (exhibition placard) (New York: Schomburg Center for Research in Black Culture/The New York Public Library, 2005); and William Strickland, the Malcolm X Make it Plain Production Team, and Cheryll Y. Greene, eds., *Malcolm X: Make it Plain* (New York: Penguin, 1994), vii–viii.

12. For a useful treatment of the emergence of Malcolm X scholarship in the academy generally, see Robert Jenkins and Mfanya Donald Tryman, eds., *The Malcolm X Encyclopedia* (Westport, CT: Greenwood Press, 2002). Jenkins and Tryman's text attempts "an encyclopedic coverage of the world he helped shape and that helped shape him" (ibid., vii). It provides ten extensive thematic essays and hundreds of entries composed by over seventy contributors.

13. See, among others, Charise L. Cheney, *Brothers Gonna Work it Out: Sexual Politics in the Golden Age of Rap Nationalism* (New York: New York University Press, 2005), 81–86.

14. See Gerald Horne, "'Myth' and the Making of 'Malcolm X,'" *The American Historical Review* 98, no. 2 (April 1993): 440–450. In addition to providing an insightful historicizing of the film's content, Horne outlines the complex cultural, economic, and political interests that accompanied the appearance of the film. He notes that the range of Black Nationalisms symbolized by Malcolm, the Nation of Islam, and other groups was nurtured by a massive failure by the white Left to reject racism from the 1930s to the 1960s. Like Cedric Robinson before him, however, Horne does not reduce the phenomena of Black Nationalism or Pan-Africanism to a simple reaction to white racism. This lack of reductionism distinguishes the work of Horne, Robinson, and a handful of others from less culturally grounded interrogations of Africana radicalism. See Gerald Horne, *From the Barrel of*

Malcolm X have appeared, the most imaginative of which include Michael A. Gomez's reading of Malcolm according to the long-view genealogy of west-Atlantic Africana Islam, *Black Crescent*[15] and James Tyner's remarkable reading of the influence of Malcolm on cultural and physical geography, *The Geography of Malcolm X*.[16]

This scholarship will soon include a much-anticipated biography by Manning Marable to be published in 2008.[17] Marable has noted that the vast majority of Malcolm X scholarship does not rely on the largely underused and underanalyzed primary sources surrounding his life.[18] The discussion of the politics of Malcolm X scholarship underscores the burgeoning centrality of Malcolm X to contemporary discussions of U.S. citizenship and identity.

---

a Gun: The United States and the War Against Zimbabwe, 1965–1980 (Chapel Hill, NC: University of North Carolina Press, 2001), 38

15. Gomez's text links Malcolm to an extended reading of the African Muslim presence in the Western Hemisphere. Gomez divides that presence into two distinct phases: the pre-Columbian and enslavement-era migration of thousands of continental African Muslims westward and the (re)emergence of Islam as a vehicle for African empowerment in the twentieth century through the Noble Dru Ali and Elijah Muhammad movements. Gomez contends that Malcolm X closed a circuit that saw Africans enter the Western Hemisphere as orthodox Muslims, reinvigorate African Islam in the twentieth century by cleansing it from heterodox approaches, and, through Malcolm, achieve some wedding of nationalist and Pan-Africanist sentiment with more orthodox Islamic values. Michael A. Gomez, *Black Crescent: The Experience and Legacy of African Muslims in the Americas* (New York: Cambridge University Press, 2005).

16. James Tyner, *The Geography of Malcolm X: Black Radicalism and the Remaking of American Space* (New York: Routledge, 2006). Tyner contends that Malcolm transformed the way that physical and cultural space has been used—as a place in which to convene communities seeking social justice. He also explores the way that Malcolm seized on ideas of African American community solidarity to promote radical social transformation. Tyner concludes his book by evoking Cedric Robinson's definition of the Black Radical Tradition as the process by which successive generations of African people used their access to experiential data and historical memory to struggle to convene such liberated spaces (ibid., 163–64).

17. Marable's biography will rely on unrestricted access to the Schomburg materials and other sources. He has argued that through his brief perusal of the unpublished chapters of Malcolm's autobiography (currently in the hands of Detroit attorney Greg Reed), Malcolm envisioned a broad-based, pluralistic Black united front to attack oppression in the United States. Marable claims to have started work on the biography in 1987 by dividing the study of Malcolm into four research categories: (1) the Black organizations in which Malcolm X played a significant leadership role; (2) the surveillance of Malcolm X by the FBI and other governmental agencies; (3) the materials of Alex Haley; and (4) the family of Malcolm X, including their access to all otherwise inaccessible papers. See Marable, "Rediscovering Malcolm's Life," 29. Marable, who has called Malcolm X "the most remarkable historical figure produced by America in the 20th century," connects him to "a broad internationalist vision of emancipatory power" and "a kind of critique of globalization." See Manning Marable, interview by Amy Goodman, "The Undiscovered Malcolm X: Stunning New Info on the Assassination, His Plans to Unite the Civil Rights and Black Nationalist Movements and the 3 'Missing' Chapters From His Autobiography," Democracy Now!, http://www.democracynow.org.

18. Manning Marable, *Living Black History: How Reimagining the African-American Past Can Remake America's Racial Future* (New York: Basic/Civitas Books, 2005), 135–177. In a chapter of this book entitled "Malcolm X's Life After Death: The Dispossession of a Legacy," Marable brings to a larger public forum assertions that have circulated among small communities of Malcolm X scholars and associates for some time. Among these assertions are that his wife and family attempted to distance the memory of Malcolm from his "black nationalist" period and that Alex Haley collaborated with both Doubleday and the federal government to produce a posthumous version of *The Autobiography* that did not accurately represent the thinking or the composite figure of Malcolm X. On the portrayal of Malcolm X by his eldest daughter which lends support to Marable's analysis, see Attallah Shabazz, foreword to *The Autobiography of Malcolm X*, by Malcolm X (as told to Alex Haley) (New York: Ballantine Books, 1999), ix–xxiv.

With the possible exception of William Sales's work on the institutional significance of the Organization of Afro-American Unity[19] and the nationalist-oriented texts produced by authors such as Oba T'Shaka[20] and Zak Kondo,[21] most of the scholarship on Malcolm over the last decade and a half has emphasized the possibilities and failures of racial, cultural, and sexual hybridity;[22] critical antiracism; and the transcendent hu-

19. See William W. Sales, Jr., *From Civil Rights to Black Liberation: Malcolm X and the Organization of Afro-American Unity* (Boston: South End Press, 1994). Sales marks the year 1990 as "the year they re-discovered Malcolm" (ibid., 3), when Malcolm's sixty-fifth birthday and the twenty-fifth anniversary of his assassination was used by Preston Wilcox of AFRAM associates to call together a "Malcolm X Work Group" comprised of James Cone, Abdul Alkalimat, and others. From May 19 through May 25, a conference, "Malcolm X Speaks to the 1990s," was held in Havana. In November, the City University of New York hosted an international conference on Malcolm X. These events led to an explosion in publications on Malcolm X, discussed above, as well as the redoubling of efforts to inscribe the slain thinker in U.S. public ritual and memory. Mrs. Rowena Moore "established the Malcolm X Foundation and succeeded in having [his] birthplace in Omaha, Nebraska declared a national and state landmark" (ibid., 3). Perhaps the ultimate elevation to "secular state sainthood" occurred when the U.S. Postal Service issued a Malcolm X stamp on January 20, 1999. The Postal Service narrative that accompanies all issues of commemorative African American stamps erased Earl Little's status as a Garveyite; called Little "a Baptist preacher" who "was killed, probably murdered, because of his political and social activism"; linked Malcolm's emergence as a "militant activist" to the Nation of Islam; and stated that "after a trip to Mecca," Malcolm "came to believe that the world's people could live in fellowship." See United States Postal Service, "Malcolm X," in USPC Publication 354, "African Americans on Stamps" (Washington, DC: United States Postal Service, 2004), 17. As I will argue, this "official" narrative disconnects Malcolm from the organic Black Radical Tradition into which he was born and nurtured.

20. Oba T'Shaka, *The Political Legacy of Malcolm X* (Richmond, CA. Pan-Afrikan Publications, 1983) predates by nearly a decade the explosion of "Malcolmiana," mainly because of T'Shaka's work as a community organizer, including firsthand work with Malcolm as the 1963 chairman of the San Francisco chapter of CORE (ibid., 39–42). T'Shaka's thesis is that Malcolm X received his initial worldview from his family (ibid., 13–18) and never deviated from his basic analysis of white racial exploitation, using his broadening international perspective instead to strengthen his analysis of what he called "the worldwide system of white supremacy" (ibid., 214). Malcolm's potential to organize others to see and combat this system, T'Shaka contends, made Malcolm the leading enemy of a "broad, vicious, dirty and sophisticated attack against the Black Liberation Movement" (ibid., 217). In addition, T'Shaka links Malcolm to a long-view genealogy of internationalized African liberation struggles, including the Haitian Revolution, various "Back to Africa" movements, the Garvey Movement, and the Pan-African and Anti-Colonial movements. T'Shaka concludes with an organizer's handbook based on what he terms Malcolm's priority of establishing "powerful, broad-based mass movements" on the local and international levels (ibid., 257).

21. See Baba Zak Kondo, *Conspiracy: Unraveling the Assassination of Malcolm X* (Washington, DC: Nubia Press, 1993). Kondo's text, written over several years with the assistance of leading Malcolm X scholar Paul Lee, includes 1,2666 footnotes drawn from personal interviews, six separate sets of FBI files, and other materials to implicate the Nation of Islam in what he nevertheless concludes was a federal conspiracy to kill Malcolm X (ibid., 167–195). Like T'Shaka, Kondo frames the attack against Malcolm as part of a larger attack against African nationalist institutions, noting the ongoing FBI attack against the Nation of Islam after Malcolm's death and the Nation's inability to come to terms with "the importance of his [Malcolm's] internationalism," which Kondo reads as Pan-Africanism (ibid., 201–202).

22. Two of the more provocative theses advanced in the "hybridity" vein are the controversial "psychobiography" by Bruce Perry, *Malcolm: The Life of a Man Who Changed Black America* (Barrytown, NY: Station Hill Press, 1991) and Jan Carew's extended essay on his interaction with Malcolm in England in December 1964–January 1965, Jan Carew, *Ghosts in Our Blood: With Malcolm X in Africa, England, and the Caribbean* (Chicago: Lawrence Hill Books, 1994). Carew's indispensable book relies on discussions with Malcolm, his brother Wilfred, and relatives of his mother's family, and it is the first to extensively discuss Malcolm's Caribbean roots as a source of what Carew hypothesizes was an emerging internationalist perspective.

manism for which Malcolm allegedly had become a marker during the last eighteen
months of his life.[23]

This emphasis seems merely a reworking of the many biographical treatments which
appeared immediately after Malcolm's death and which established the narrative frame
of youthful innocence; tragedy, criminality, and fall; conversion and Black rage; and second conversion and nominal redemption[24]—a narrative frame that continues to guide
the historiography of Malcolm X.[25] Far less emphasis has been placed on considering the
historiographical assumptions that ask how and why Malcolm made his assessments of
self, the community, and the world—positions which vary much less than is immediately apparent from reading the vast secondary literature associated with him.

Adolph Reed has written that the deceased Malcolm, bereft of living agency, "is now
even more of a hologram of social forces" than he was for the generation that came of
age immediately following his death. He writes that "the inchoate, often apparently inconsistent trajectory of his thought makes him an especially plastic symbol in the present context."[26] While Reed does not engage in what he derides as playing the "what-

23. One of the earliest anthologies to highlight advocates of this posture in the 1990s "Malcolm
Renaissance" was Joe Wood, ed., *Malcolm X: In Our Own Image* (New York: St. Martin's Press,
1992.) Cornel West accuses Malcolm of a fear of "cultural hybridity" that he might have transcended
had he not been blind to class, gender, and sexual-orientation issues (ibid., 56). Arnold Rampersad
takes a professional biographer's issue with Perry's hybridity thesis in an essay, "The Color of His
Eyes: Bruce Perry's *Malcolm* and Malcolm's Malcolm" (ibid., 117–134).

24. When interest in Malcolm was reignited by Spike Lee's 1992 motion picture *Malcolm X*, *U.S.
News and World Report* strengthened the influence of this period of Malcolm X scholarship by separating Malcolm's life into the following episodes: Malcolm the Child (arguing that "Malcolm inherited his rage" from his father, "a one-eyed Baptist preacher named Earl Little"); Malcolm the Hustler;
Malcolm the Convert; Malcolm the Messenger; and Malcolm: His Own Man (when he "discovered"
that NOI teachings contradicted orthodox Islam). Lewis Lord, Jeannye Thornton, and Alejandro
Bodipo-Memba, "The Legacy of Malcolm X," *U.S. News and World Report* 113, no. 20: 76. For a critical acceptance of this period that sees it as the inevitable stage of "falsified racial consciousness" leading to "racial self-identification" and, ultimately, the basis for racial, class, and human liberation, see
the Marxist-Freudian psychoanalytic treatment, Eugene Victor Wolfenstein, *The Victims of Democracy: Malcolm X and the Black Revolution* (Berkeley: University of California Press, 1981).

25. One of the earliest framings of Malcolm's life outside the genre of autobiography was George
Breitman, *The Last Year of Malcolm X: The Evolution of a Revolutionary* (New York: Schocken Books,
1968), which elaborates on the text of a speech, "Malcolm X: The Man and His Ideas," delivered
shortly after Malcolm's death in 1965. Breitman, who never met Malcolm, frames him as a potential
American savior. He writes that if white Americans "adopt Malcolm's strategy, accept his legacy and
develop it in accordance with the logic of the direction in which he was moving during his last
year … the day will come when all decent Americans will look back on Malcolm with gratitude and
love" (ibid., 95). This "last year transformation" thesis, now an accepted part of Malcolm X hagiography, has been challenged by a number of Malcolm's contemporaries. Breitman himself was challenged by Rev. Albert Cleage in an essay in the September–October issue of the *International Socialist Review*. The essay was republished in *Myths About Malcolm X: Two Views*, Albert B. Cleage and
George Breitman, 3–12, 26–30 (New York: Pathfinder, 1968). Cleage's remarks are also included in
what has been called the most effective early anthological canonization of "Malcolm X as African
Hero," John Henrik Clarke, ed., *Malcolm X: The Man and His Times* (New York: Collier Books,
1969). The first full-length political biographical treatment to emerge was Peter Goldman, *The
Death and Life of Malcolm X* (New York: Perennial/Harper and Row, 1974), which focuses on Malcolm's late and post-NOI periods. Goldman, who knew Malcolm as an interviewer and a correspon-
dent, interviewed nearly one hundred of Malcolm's associates and related persons on several conti-
nents, read the substantial primary and secondary literature available at the time, and crafted an
account that attempts to discern Malcolm and African America in its full humanity.

26. Adolph Reed, Jr., "The Allure of Malcolm X and the Changing Character of Black Politics," in
Stirrings in the Jug: Black Politics in the Post-Segregation Era (Minneapolis: University of Minnesota

Malcolm-would-do-if-he-were-alive game," he summarizes as follows his extended critique of what he sees as the uses (and misuses) of Malcolm X by African American intellectuals to evade the particulars of critical Black politics:

> One irony in the present appropriation of his image does stand out, however.
> Despite Malcolm's own ambivalence about his status as a race spokesman and
> the legitimacy of black leadership as a category (and notwithstanding his
> rhetoric about unity), Malcolm made his reputation by attacking entrenched
> elites and challenging their attempts to constrain popular action and the vox
> populi. Now he is canonized as an icon, an instrument of an agenda that is just
> the opposite of popular mobilization.[27]

The inability of the range of scholarship to come to consistent terms with Malcolm's
outright rejection of the idea of Africans as full-fledged "Americans," as well as the similar
posture assumed by his intellectual predecessors and descendants,[28] stems from the lack of
epistemological space that can accommodate the African-Centered Worldview/Black Radical Tradition. Disciplinary Africana Studies[29] provides the most viable professional and

---

Press, 1999), 223. Reed has been consistently suspicious of analytical frameworks that depend on
"presumption of a universal, consensual or somehow otherwise singularly definitive and authentic
state" of group experience or perspective. He argues that "the abstract and hermetic language of po-
sitionality, difference and otherness fixes the interpretive lens at a point so remote from the ways that
people live their lives and form themselves in the everyday world we all share" that it never confronts
how inadequate essentializing notions of identity can be. See Adolph Reed, Jr., *Class Notes: Posing as
Politics and Other Thoughts on the American Scene* (New York: The Free Press), xvi–xvii. Reed's argument places him at epistemological odds with the Afrocentrists, who have nevertheless failed (so far)
to demonstrate the essentializing elements in all intellectual postures. It also, however, places him at
odds with other Malcolm interpreters who have sought to build frameworks of meaning to advance
their own ideological agendas. For example, Michael Eric Dyson accuses Reed, whose disdain of
Dyson's analytical skills is widely known, of influencing Joe Wood to reject Dyson's submission to
Wood's anthology, *Malcolm X: In Our Image*. Dyson says that, ironically, this rejection led first to the
publication of his essay in *The New York Times Book Review* and then to his writing his own Malcolm
book, Michael Eric Dyson, *Making Malcolm: The Myth and Meaning of Malcolm X* (New York: Oxford University Press, 1994). Dyson's text portrays Malcolm as everything from a public moralist to a
potential emerging socialist, while challenging future scholars to give his life a "comprehensive and
critical examination" designed to eschew hagiography and romanticism. See Michael Eric Dyson, ed.,
The Michael Eric Dyson Reader (New York: Basic Civitas Books, 2004), 261–286.
    27. Reed, "The Allure of Malcolm X," 223.
    28. This inability is by no means total. Nikhil Pal Singh, *Black Is a Country: Race and the Unfinished
Struggle for Democracy* (Cambridge: Harvard University Press, 2004) provides the most provocative recent analysis of the status of Africans in the U.S. civic polity outside Africana Studies. Singh argues that
U.S. "mythic nationalism" and the "fictive ethnicity" which it generates rests on the perpetuation of
Africans as an "anti-citizenry," a group that can never fully be "integrated" into the narrative or the
polity. He deftly distinguishes Malcolm's struggle for "gaining civic recognition and equalizing material
distribution" from a less important—and ostensibly unattempted—quest to question "the constitutional morality of racial integration or separation" (ibid., 209–210). Singh's apprehension of this fundamental element of African-American cultural identity—namely, the ambivalence about and/or the lack
of interest in group racial/cultural assimilation—has been quantified in part by Michael Dawson's recent study of a national survey which focused on the ideological and political beliefs of Africans in the
United Statesd, Michael Dawson, *Black Visions: The Roots of Contemporary African-American Political
Ideologies* (Chicago: University of Chicago Press, 2001), 85–134. Singh's thesis also supports the assumptions raised by Michael Gomez and Cedric Robinson discussed earlier and later in this essay.
    29. "Disciplinary Africana Studies" must be distinguished from other epistemological postures
in the field (namely, multi- or interdisciplinary analyses of phenomena) as a body of knowledge
with "a reasonably logical taxonomy, a specialized vocabulary, an accepted body of theory, a systematic research strategy, and techniques for replication and validation." See, among others, Greg Kimathi Carr, *Blacks Studying: Genealogy, Contexts and Techniques in Disciplinary Africana Studies*

intellectual space for considering Malcolm's commitment to African people and their group development.

Within the field of Africana Studies, however, the assertion that a set of disciplinary techniques has sufficiently emerged to apply to the study of phenomena is not settled.[30] Even the most consistent and prolific proponents of the study of Malcolm X with self-asserted academic allegiance to Africana Studies often approach the topic by embracing political rather than epistemological investigative postures.[31]

There are very few—if any—moments in the record of Malcolm's life that are inconsistent regarding how he viewed himself and other Africans vis-à-vis the United States. As a perpetual outsider, a "victim of democracy," Malcolm traced the coordinates of a preexisting set of African public memories. Any rhetorical "kitten" born of African parentage into a U.S. "oven" would be linked to a set of identity coordinates that precede, transcend, and, arguably, will endure and survive both the U.S. experiment with democracy and the moment of Western dominance in world history. This long-view genealogy of African—and human—global identity forms the foundation of disciplinary Africana Studies and sets the context for the study of Africana, including the life and work of Malcolm X.

(Dubuque, IA: Kendall Hunt, forthcoming) and Janet Gail Donald, *Learning to Think: Disciplinary Perspectives* (San Francisco: Jose-Bass, 2002), 8.

30. See Schomburg Center for Research in Black Culture/The New York Public Library, *Malcolm X: A Search for Truth* (exhibition placard).

31. The Africana Studies scholar with perhaps the most well-developed record of institutionalizing the study of Malcolm X, Abdul Alkalimat, nevertheless approaches the study from a sociologist's perspective, choosing to link Malcolm's development to a materialist philosophy of history. See, among others, Abdul Alkalimat, ed., *Malcolm X: A Research Site* (Toledo, OH: University of Toledo and Twenty-First Century Books, 1999), http://www.brothermalcolm.net; and Don Murphy and Jennifer Ratke, eds., *Malcolm X in Context: A Study Guide to the Man and His Times* (New York: School Voices Press, 1992). The latter text, a study guide for high school, undergraduate, and autodidactic study groups as well as individual students, categorizes Malcolm's life into the familiar narrative phases, promotes his antiimperialist commitments, and links him genealogically to contemporary antiimperialist groups such as the Black Panthers. More recently, Andrew P. Smallwood has raised the implications for Africana Studies of linking Malcolm's autodidactic education and debate style to the emergence of the field of Black Studies. He emphasizes that "Malcolm X's public exploration of Black Nationalism served as an ideological model for activism that led to the establishment of Black studies as an academic discipline in higher education." He also links this phenomenon to Nathan Hare's famous 1974 charge that Black Studies must develop community-centered sites of academic knowledge production that are "relevant to the community." Andrew Smallwood, "The Intellectual Creativity and Public Discourse of Malcolm X: A Precursor to the Modern Black Studies Movement," *The Journal of Black Studies* 36, no. 2 (November 2005): 260–261.

Disciplinary Africana Studies and a
Paradigm of Historical Memory[32]

Africana Studies can be described as "the systematic professional study of Africa when and wherever you find her."[33] It emerges out of what Cedric Robinson has called "the Black Radical Tradition," the range of lived cultural, historical, and political systems that African people have improvised to help them navigate their most recent series of historical challenges. For Africana Studies scholars, these improvised techniques connect with each other to provide the guideposts for making their work relevant to the larger African community.[34] Accordingly, the contribution of all representative scholars to an academic discipline derived from that tradition rests on the accuracy with which they a) represent the lived experience of African people and b) link their interpretations to a long-view genealogy that observes the rules generated by Africans across time and space.[35]

That a theory of history provides the foundation for the epistemology of Africana Studies is well settled in the field.[36] What theories of history should receive the most acceptance, however, is not well settled.[37] Winston Van Horne has observed that within the field of Africana Studies (which he refers to as "Africology"), contesting paradigms must be articulated and refined. Those that are better able to withstand "free, open, unencumbered and searching critical inquiry" will propel the discipline forward provided

---

32. A greatly expanded discussion of the model introduced in this essay can be found in Greg Kimathi Carr, "Inscribing African World History: Intergenerational Repetition and Improvisation of Ancestral Instructions," in *The Association for the Study of Classical African Civilizations African World History Project*, ed. Asa Hilliard III, vol. 2, *Historiography* (Los Angeles: ASCAC Foundation, forthcoming).

33. I use this broad definition to frame the nature of Africana intellectual work beyond the academy while simultaneously acknowledging the existence of standards and techniques for assessing the reliability of knowledge production. James Stewart's "Jazz Model" of Africana Studies provides a useful comparative metaphor for achieving a similar—albeit more academically oriented—result. See James Stewart, "Reaching for Higher Ground: Toward an Understanding of Black/Africana Studies," *The Afrocentric Scholar* 1, no. 1 (May 1992): 51–52 and James Stewart, *Flight: In Search of Vision* (Trenton, NJ: Africa World Press, 2004), 191–202.

34. William F. Santiago-Valles refers to this process as "praxis research," a form of dialectic pedagogy that relies on continuous interaction between scholars and the communities they labor on behalf of. W. F. Santiago-Valles, "Producing Knowledge for Social Transformation: Precedents from the Diaspora for Twenty-First Century Research and Pedagogy," *The Black Scholar* 35, no. 2 (Summer 2005): 54. Terry Kershaw identified a similar interactive process between Africana Studies scholars and the communities they seek to assist in improving life chances. Terry Kershaw, "Afrocentrism and the Afrocentric Method," *The Western Journal of Black Studies* 16, no. 3 (Fall 1992): 163.

35. For a representative survey of the genealogy of disciplinary Africana Studies, see Nathaniel Norment, Jr., ed, *The African-American Studies Reader* (Durham, NC: Carolina Academic Press, 2001) and Delores Aldridge and Carlene Young, eds, *Out of the Revolution: The Development of Africana Studies* (Lanham, MD: Lexington Books, 2003).

36. Stewart, *Flight*, 33.

37. Lucius Outlaw has correctly observed that "racial identity and common experiences, cultural commonalities and shared sites of origin, do not, automatically and necessarily, provide the essential unifying coherence of a disciplinary enterprise, its norms, agendas and strategies." Lucius T. Outlaw, "African, African-American, Africana Philosophy, in *African-American Perspectives and Philosophical Traditions*, ed. John Pittman, 88 (New York: Routledge, 1997).

one assumes there will never be a one-to-one correspondence between the discipline and any of the many contesting paradigms that organize its subject matter.[38]

The search for historical context and frameworks to explain human experience underlies even the most irrational human behavior.[39] The larger frameworks built to interpret reality may sometimes seem invisible or intuitive. This characteristic is the direct consequence of repetition, which embeds them deeply into group consciousness and which, once so embedded, makes the frameworks ubiquitous and powerful.[40] Society is anchored in networks of ritual repetition in concert with symbolic markers of human memory such as shrines, icons, and totems.[41] These networks extend outward and in concentric circles from the most immediate and pervasive markers of individual identity. From birthdays to anniversaries to ritual gatherings such as worship, family reunions, and public holidays (for example, those celebrating the birthdays of Martin Luther King, Jr., and in Africana nationalist communities, of Malcolm X), what Evitar Zerubavel calls "the social structure of memory"[42] relies on ritual repetition as an anchor for the reinforcement of collective memory.

Inscribing an African world historical narrative as the foundation for disciplinary Africana Studies requires integrating the African-Centered Worldview and the Black Radical Tradition in a balance of the relationship between historical events and narratives of those events. Over the last half-millennium, African memory spread regionally and then globally in the wake of episodic experiences of voluntary and forced migrations, labor appropriation, violence and the responses to it by re-creating syncretistic cultures, and the tactical adaptation of Africans to local circumstances.[43]

---

38. Winston Van Horne, "Africology: A Discipline of the Twenty-First Century" (paper, the Sixth Annual Cheikh Anta Diop Conference, Temple University, Philadelphia, October 7, 1994), 12.

39. See *Thinking and Knowing* (Danbury CT: Grolier Educational Corp., 2002), 6–23.

40. Evitar Zerubavel has called this process and phenomenon "socio*mental* topography," or "how the past is registered and organized *in our minds*." Evitar Zerubavel, *Time Maps: Collective Memory and the Social Shape of the Past* (Chicago: The University of Chicago Press, 2003), 2 (italics in the original).

41. Robert Farris Thompson, *Face of the Gods: Art and Altars of Africa and the African Americas* (New York: Prestel, 1993).

42. Zerubavel, *Time Maps*, 1–10. The interaction of rituals, shrines, totems, and icons to build the "mythic nationalism" of U.S. identity is widely acknowledged. See, among others, Carolyn Marvin and David W. Ingle, *Blood Sacrifice and the Nation: Totem Rituals and the American Flag* (New York: Cambridge University Press, 1998), 1–2; Alessandra Lorini, *Rituals of Race: American Public Culture and the Search for Racial Democracy* (Charlottesville: University of Virginia Press, 1999), 208–256; and Patricia Nelson Limerick, *To Die For: The Paradoxes of American Patriotism* (Princeton: Princeton University Press, 1999). Nelson's book traces the origins and meaning of holidays such as Memorial Day and Independence Day as ritualized anchors of collective memory. For the similar function of Savior's Day in Nation of Islam public memory, see Clifton E. Marsh, *The Lost-Found Nation of Islam in America* (Lanham, MD: Scarecrow Press, 2000), 69 and Robert L. Jenkins, "Savior's Day Convention," in *Malcolm X Encyclopedia*, ed. Robert L. Jenkins and Mfanya Donald Tryman, 489–90 (Westport, CT: Greenwood Press, 2002). Many of the ritual gatherings and texts in the African community utilize images, speeches, and other texts associated with Malcolm X as part of the building of collective African American memory. See William Van DeBurg, *New Day in Babylon: The Black Power Movement and American Culture, 1965–1975* (Chicago: University of Chicago Press, 1992), 6.

43. The patterns of the globalization of Africans in the contemporary era have become clearer with advances in demographic and historical research in areas as diverse, but interconnected, as human geography, genetics, and cultural anthropology. See, among others, Dirk Hoerder, *Cultures in Contact: World Migrations in the Second Millennium* (Durham, NC: Duke University Press, 2002) and Ronald Walters, *Pan Africanism and the African Diaspora* (Detroit: Wayne State University Press, 1994). For representative case studies of relinkages among group-oriented African intellectual elites,

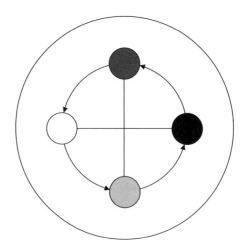

Figure 1

Ki-Kongo "Tendwa Nza Kongo" Cosmogram. (Figure courtesy of Robert Farris Thompson, *Flash of the Spirit: African and Afro-American Art and Philosophy* [New York: Vintage, 1984], 109.)

A central African epistemological device, the Ki-Kongo "Tendwa Nza Kongo" Cosmogram,[44] can usefully represent this triple concept of historical memory, repetition, and improvisation (see Figure 1). The symbol charts what the Ki-Kongo call "the four moments of the sun," symbolizing the cyclical dimensions of reality, including the daily, group, and historical human experience as microcosm. The Ki-Kongo trace the movement of history/reality from sunrise (birth) to the apogee of material power and strength (noonday sun), the waning of physical reality (sunset), and the apogee of spiritual power and strength (the midnight sun). This process repeats as process while it differs experientially for each individual and social/ "national" group which undertakes its journey around the cycle. The Ki-Kongo used the seashell of the Kodya crustacean to represent the cosmogram in three dimensions, thus adding the necessary understanding that historical time does not repeat itself but spirals and extends dynamically.[45]

Thus, while each successive generation of Africans encountered distinct and unique challenges to its historical episode, it contributed a distinct improvisational engagement with those challenges based on a received/learned storehouse of historical memories

---

see J. Lorand Matory, *Black Atlantic Religion: Tradition, Transnationalism and Matriarchy in the Afro-Brazilian Candomble* (Princeton: Princeton University Press, 2005) and Kamari Clarke, *Mapping Yoruba Networks: Power and Agency in the Making of Transnational Communities* (Chapel Hill: University of North Carolina Press, 2004).

44. Historians of the trafficking in African humanity known as "The Transatlantic Slave Trade" agree that over one-third of all Africans arriving in the Western hemisphere during this period were forcibly removed from west-central Africa, the region out of which came Ki-Kongo, Lingala and other cosmogram-using African national ("ethnic") groups. Their disproportionate influence in crafting the spiritual traditions of the West Atlantic (including Candomble, Vodun, Voodoo, Hoodoo, and Santeria) relied on the flexibility of their belief system, which, in turn, relied on their relationship to their land and immediate ancestors and on their belief in a universe balanced in the divinely ordered motions represented by the cosmogram. See Robert Farris Thompson, *Flash of the Spirit: African and Afro-American Art and Philosophy* (New York: Vintage, 1983), 108–116.

45. From a different vantage point, but possessing a similar epistemological understanding, Molefi Kete Asante evokes supporting concepts of time and space in an essay, "Dancing Between Circles and Lines." See Molefi Kete Asante, *The Afrocentric Idea*, rev. ed. (Philadelphia: Temple University Press, 1998).

preserved from the experiences of previous generations. This relationship between historical memory (the vertically spiraling genealogy of collective experience) and immediate historical experience (the horizontal journey through the cycle) forms the idea of collective historical memory that anchors this particular paradigm in disciplinary Africana Studies.[46]

The final critical elements of the modified Ki-Kongo cosmogram paradigm are the apprenticed reception of historical memory (repetition) and the contribution to the ongoing accumulation of memory (improvisation). The human being who thinks historically develops multiple literacies: the ability to enter various human communities with senses attuned to the particular cultural grammar and vocabulary used by a particular community to create and interpret cultural meaning.[47] At each episodic turn, Africans have had to improvise solutions to challenges such as the suppression of language, cultural texts, and practices; the creation of "blackness" as the primary marker for power relations; and the intellectual bifurcation between European and non-European knowledge-producing institutions.

Africans have preserved and extended discrete group identities in their institutions (e.g., family, community, spiritual/religious, and educational organizations) and in the internal governance mechanisms that, through them, have shaped individual personality development in the African community. They have also passed on the "ground rules" for improvising solutions to the "horizontal episodic challenges" each generation has faced. Scholarship on Malcolm X and others is disproportionately influenced by a class-based epistemology that privileges the moments and sites where those individuals interacted with Western educational and other socializing institutions.[48] Accordingly, the process of recognizing enduring African-Centered Worldview markers in the thought and actions of Malcolm X[49] and others is filtered through a methodological process that does not yield optimal understanding.

---

46. It is critical to note that collective historical memory as a function of selective preservation and extension of the past is germane to all human societies. Additionally, historians have begun to reconcile the search for historical accuracy and truth with the observation that "the search for historical truth brings with it not a rejection but rather a greater awareness of the cultural specificity and the necessary limitations of historical practice." Ann Curthoys and John Docker, *Is History Fiction?* (Ann Arbor: University of Michigan Press, 2005), 6.

47. The most systematic work done to date on the importance of grammar and vocabulary in Africana meaning-making communities is, unsurprisingly, studies of speech communities. In her provocative book, Lisa Green, *African-American English: A Linguistic Introduction* (New York: Cambridge University Press, 2002), Green suggests the possible transdisciplinary importation of ideas about lexical, grammatical, syntactical, and other speech terms to the study of the making of cultural meaning.

48. The recent Schomburg exhibition is no exception. One of the earliest documents exhibited is an eighth grade "opinion book," containing brief comments written by Malcolm's classmates. Malcolm was the only African American in his class. Many of the one-line entries refer to him as "tall, dark and screwy" and "swell"—with one interesting exception. Entry # 7 contains the three-word warning: "don't get personal." I imagine that an entire article can—and likely will—be written attempting to trace Malcolm's conflicted racial identity to this preteen "opinion book" in which one young male chronicles his encounters with, among others, perhaps a young white female (or male?) classmate in whom he showed particular interest. At the top of the "opinion book," Malcolm had written his name as "Malcolm 'Harpy' Little." This might well serve as the metaphor—the "Harpy"—for the idea that Malcolm was always, like the mythical Harpy, a hybrid who never fit in and was "othered" by all communities.

49. An interesting exception to and example of drawing on the influence of Africana institutional socializing agents as the source of Malcolm's intellectual work is Hank Flick and Larry Powell, "Animal Imagery in the Rhetoric of Malcolm X," *Journal of Black Studies* 18, no. 4 (June 1988):

Accessing the Ki-Kongo cosmogram as the paradigm for framing a disciplinary inter-rogation of Malcolm's life and context causes us to raise several first-order questions. What were the long-view genealogies of African historical memory that Malcolm was introduced to through the institutions of family and community throughout his life? Were there ordered techniques drawn from the same cache of African historical mem-ory that governed the process of his individual improvisational contributions to future generations? How have the generations since his death incorporated his memory and the memory of his improvisational techniques into the longer genealogy of Africana historical memory, the Black Radical Tradition, and the African-Centered Worldview?

Malcolm's improvised trajectory as "public outsider" and critical interpreter of African life in both the United States and the larger world provides one of his most salient contributions to the ongoing genealogy of Africana memory. His life's trajectory mirrors that of most African intellectuals who base their analyses on the lived culture and experiences of African people. The clarity of his goal of separating from whites stems from his lived experiences as a highly literate child with self-sufficient, Pan-Africanist parents;[50] as a young adult surrounded by the class aspirations of the lower-middle[51] and upper-middle[52] classes of the post-War African American community; as

---

435–451). The authors, rhetoricians by training, contend that Malcolm used animal imagery to unite African Americans in understanding how to view whites as well as in understanding what ani-mal behavior to emulate vis-à-vis whites. What is not discussed — and what would be illuminated if the analysis used an Africana Studies disciplinary frame grounded in a theory of African-Centered historical memory — is the common experiences and worldviews shared by Malcolm and other Africans that provided the resonance of his metaphors. Malcolm, who grew up in farmland Ne-braska and Michigan, connected to the rural and animal-relationship experience of Africans. Many discussions of his rhetoric completely miss this point while nonetheless emphasizing his use of ani-mal metaphor in comments such as his famous remark, "chickens coming home to roost," on De-cember 1, 1963. See Robert E. Terrill, *Malcolm X: Inventing Radical Judgment* (Lansing: Michigan State University Press, 2004), which links Malcolm's rhetorical style to what Terrill calls "trickster consciousness," an experimental awareness that allows the rhetor to tap into the "nomadic restless-ness" between two or more well-defined social categories (ibid., 171–172). Terrill does not, however, trace this "trickster consciousness" through its logical Africana genealogy of historical memory: the Yoruba-derived, West Atlantic, syncretic, reconfigured practice of "esu," the supremely conscious manipulator of speech and irony.

50. Earl and Louise Little's Garveyite roots have been well discussed. According to Jan Carew, Malcolm's oldest brother Wilfred insisted that their father had never been a Baptist preacher but was "a Garveyite activist whom sympathetic Black ministers allowed to address their congregations from time to time." Carew, *Ghosts in Our Blood*, x. Malcolm's youthful academic aptitude has also been documented, though troublingly eschewed in favor of the hagiographical embrace of the well-re-hearsed conversions narratives. A review in the Schomburg exhibition of the letters written to his siblings while he was working in Massachusetts, on the trains, and while he was incarcerated shows solid literacy, a commitment to perfection in penmanship, and a preoccupation with punctuality and time.

51. Malcolm's work on trains put him in intimate contact with arguably the largest network of progressive African labor in the United States, the Brotherhood of Sleeping Car Porters and Cham-ber Maids. See Beth Tompkins Bates, *Pullman Porters and the Rise of Protest Politics in Black Amer-ica, 1925–1945* (Chapel Hill, NC: University of North Carolina Press, 2001).

52. Malcolm's work as a hustler, thief, and pimp placed him on the outer edges of hard core crime (e.g., assault, murder, etc.). As a numbers runner, he learned the value of intellectual skill prized in the African-American community at the time (witness his remarks on West Indian Archie). The Haley *Autobiography* and subsequent discussions of this phase in Malcolm's life did not focus on the rich cultural tapestry and humanity of the Africans he interacted with. For example, shortly before his death in 1998, Malcolm "Shorty" Jarvis coauthored an autobiography in which he sought to "redeem" the caricatured image he had acquired as the "sidekick" of Malcolm during his preprison Roxbury days. Malcolm "Shorty" Jarvis, with Paul D. Nichols, *The Other Malcolm:*

well as through his interactions with family and community and the institutional influence of the UNIA.

The masses of Africans in the United States have a conditional and relative relationship to the nation. Malcolm's famous "house negro/field negro" comparison from his November 1963 "Message to the Grassroots[53]" should be viewed not as a historically accurate depiction of skin-color privilege and plantation-era politics among enslaved Africans but as an epistemological technique for framing the attitude of most U.S. Africans toward the nation. Similarly, his best-known speeches and public pronouncements—including the ones made closest to his assassination—preserve his identity and politics as a Black Nationalist with a developing interest in international coalition politics centered on a Pan-African political and cultural coalition[54].

That Malcolm X developed the vast majority of his public analyses in dialogical interaction with Africans from beyond the small category of "professional intellectuals" suggests that any analysis of his life and work should view his speeches, pronouncements, letters, and ancillary materials in the context of the worldviews of the communities he resonated and interacted with. According to his friend and confidante Peter Bailey, Malcolm was first and foremost a "master teacher" whose classrooms were often the street.[55] As a master teacher, Malcolm convened what Donald Phillip Verene has identified as the three authorities that exist in a learning space (i.e., a classroom): the text, the teacher, and the student.[56] What he learned and put immediately into im-

---

"Shorty" Jarvis (Jefferson, NC: McFarland, 2001). Hakim A Jamal, who met Malcolm as a teenager on the same Roxbury streets, provides a similarly redemption-minded personal account of their relationship (before, during, and after the Nation of Islam years) in Hakim A. Jamal, *From the Dead Level: Malcolm X and Me* (New York: Warner, 1973). Redd Foxx reveals a tantalizing slice of conversation he had with his old acquaintance from their days working on the railroad in a little-known semiautobiography and history of Black comedy penned in the late 1970s. Foxx writes: "Malcolm X was a friend of mine and he was having a hard time getting people to listen to him. So I suggested that he try telling people a funny incident. Before you get down to the nitty gritty, you got to get them to laugh first. Then, when you've got their attention, drop your spiel on them. He tried it and it worked." Redd Foxx and Norma Miller, *The Redd Foxx Encyclopedia of Black Humor* (Pasadena, CA: Ward Ritchie Press, 1977), 239–240. Malcolm's deft ability to wed humor and criticism, two dimensions of irony, was no doubt aided by the series of rhetorical strategies he gleaned from various African speech communities. Robert Terrill acknowledges the indirect influence on Malcolm of the rhetorical strategies of the UNIA and the Moorish Science Temple. Terrill, *Malcolm X: Inventing Radical Judgment*, 65–108. Although Malcolm never met Paul Robeson, his worldview, analytical approach, and even his speaking style were greatly influenced by listening to the famous intellectual, performer and human rights activist on the radio and reading newspaper accounts of his work. Robert L. Jenkins, "Paul Robeson," in *The Malcolm X Encyclopedia*, ed. Robert Jenkins and Mfanya Donald Tryman, 472–474 (Westport, CT: Greenwood Press, 2002) and Martin Duberman, *Paul Robeson* (New Brunswick, NJ: Rutgers University Press, 1989), 528.

53. Malcolm X, *Malcolm X Speaks: Selected Speeches and Statements*, ed. George Breitman (New York: Pathfinder, 1965), 11–13.

54. In one of his final public pronouncements, Malcolm contended that the Nation of Islam under Elijah Muhammad was not pro-African (and was indeed anti-African); that its Black Nationalism was extremely U.S. centered; and that, in contrast, he (Malcolm) was seeking a coalition with the emerging nations of independent Africa. See "The Black Muslim Movement: An Assessment" (panel discussion, WINS Radio, February 18, 1965), in Malcolm X, *February, 1965: The Final Speeches*, ed. Steve Clark, 184–229 (New York: Pathfinder, 1992).

55. Peter Bailey, quoted in *Malcolm X: Make it Plain*, eds. William Strickland, the Malcolm X Make it Plain Production Team, and Cheryl Y. Greene, 115 (New York: Penguin, 1994).

56. Donald Phillip Verene, *The Art of Humane Education* (Ithaca, NY: Cornell University Press, 2002). According to Verene, the most effective teachers are able to convene communities of learning

provisational practice was how to reconcile his own developing sense of global politics with the lived, experiential group dimensions of the Black Radical Tradition.

Framing the Study of Malcolm X in Africana Studies: Clues From Hip-Hop

As academy-sited intellectuals continue to struggle to generate appropriate models for studying Africana in general and Malcolm X in particular, intellectual work linking Malcolm's life and work to preceding and succeeding genealogies of Africana intellectual texts and practices have appeared in places more consistent with the theory that the Black Radical Tradition is a set of intra-African group (as distinct from elite, Western-oriented) practices. An excellent example of a textual analysis of Malcolm X and the continuum he extends from and contributes to that responds well to the paradigm of Africana historical memory discussed earlier is "Rumble in the Jungle," a collaborative musical rumination on the 1974 Muhammad Ali-George Forman boxing match of the same title.[57]

Surprisingly little academic attention has been paid to the Ali-Foreman moment, particularly given its major significance in the annals of Africana popular culture.[58] Like his friend and one-time close associate Malcolm X, Ali was a political and cultural "outsider." He was also a convert to the Nation of Islam who, like Malcolm, ultimately eschewed the parochial nationalism of the group for a broader, internationalist perspective and politics. Much like Malcolm, his anti-Vietnam War, pro-"Black is Beautiful" stances, improvised through an experientially southern U.S. cultural Africanness that availed himself of the cultural texts and grammar of distinctly Africana ironic rhetorical style, earned him the love and admiration of the African American community and the contempt of the white American community.

When, twenty three years later, the film producer Leon Gast released his footage of the fight and concert in a feature-length film entitled *When We Were Kings*, a new gener-

---

on the basis of their wide knowledge of subject matter and how that knowledge interacts with the lived experience of their students.

57. For a discussion of the February 1997 Radio City Music Hall release of the documentary *When We Were Kings* and the live performance of "Rumble in the Jungle" by the Fugees et al., see Ethan Smith, "Rumble Rap," *New York*, February 2, 1997, 143.

58. This is sure to be remedied shortly; over the last half-decade, a small stream of books addressing the cultural significance of African American sports performances has appeared, following in the tradition blazed by contemporary analysts such as Harry Edwards and an intermediate generation led by Richard Lapchick and others. Among the most significant are case studies, Douglass Hartmann, *Race, Culture and the Revolt of the Black Athlete: The 1968 Olympic Protests and Their Aftermath* (Chicago: University of Chicago Press, 2004) and Amy Bass, *Not the Triumph but the Struggle: 1968 Olympics and the Making of the Black Athlete* (Minneapolis: University of Minnesota Press, 2004). Ironically, George Foreman won widespread acclaim in the U.S. white community—and contempt in the U.S. African community—for hewing to a "mythical nationalist" line, avoiding the politics of protest undertaken by the Africans on the U.S. team and cementing his image in the historical narrative by waving a U.S. flag after winning the heavyweight division boxing gold medal. In that respect, many African Americans saw the Ali defeat of Foreman six years later as a measure of group vindication. The ironic convergence of a Pan-African disdain for Foreman (precipitated in part by his parading a German shepherd around Kinshasa, thereby earning the contempt of Zairians who equated the animal with the dreaded Belgian colonial authorities) still awaits an earnest and perceptive historical chronicler.

ation was introduced to the politics and symbolic conflict of the time.[59] Much less attention was paid to a CD compilation of live performances from the artists on the Kin-
shasha concert bill. The first track on the CD, however, was a hip-hop text that brought
together several of the most influential voices from the internationalist genre of hip-hop:
the Haitian/American trio The Fugees; the Caribbean-influenced Busta Rhymes, and the
proto-Afrocentric pioneers from the "Native Tongues" crew, A Tribe Called Quest.

A general survey of the songs' lyrics, with particular attention to the song performed
by Lauren Hill, reinforces the themes outlined in the paradigm of the making of
Africana historical meaning—namely, that any analysis of Africana phenomena must
view individuals first as representative types of the communities they emerge from; that
these communities congeal in episodic fashion around improvised cultural texts and
practices that are linked by institutionally guided repetition to preexisting deep wells of
African memory; and, finally, that the endurance of salient features of historical memory—and the mechanisms for determining reliability and authenticity when judging
the accuracy of descriptions of that memory—rely upon accessing an epistemology
drawn from the grammar and vocabulary of the African-Centered Worldview.[60]

The lyrics of "Rumble in the Jungle" transcend a critique of the racial politics of the
moment to position the Ali-Foreman fight as part of an extended manifestation of the
Black Radical Tradition. Malcolm X looms as a heavy presence in the text of the fight
and the surrounding political space convened to insulate it from critics.[61] The song begins with a sample of an interview Ali gave in Zaire, where he stated that he wanted to
win back the heavyweight championship on behalf of the poverty-stricken and historically unaware Black people of the United States. Ali's voice fades, and Lauren Hill is
heard singing the song's refrain:

> Block's on fire (Block's on fire tonight)
> Fiends getting higher (uh-huh)
> Robbing blue collar (Hey yo we rob them blue collars)
> Killing for a dollar (Stick 'em up)
> Youths get tired (Ali ah yeah)
> We're dealing with them liars (We're dealing with too many liars)
> From Brooklyn to Zaire (uh-huh ah yeah)
> We need a ghetto Messiah (ah yeah come on)

While these lyrics refer directly to Ali, they also evokes the improvisational shift from
group-centered Africana governance systems to more strictly hierarchical and individu-

---

59. See Richard Corliss, "Long Live the King," *Time*, February 17, 1997.

60. Historiographical methodology stemming from the Western historical method (i.e., the Ger-
man-influenced, primary print source documentation-oriented method of the making of meaning
practiced by Leopold von Ranke and others) would seek a literal connection between the subjects of
the songs, Ali and Malcolm X. Ironically, while recording the song, Fugees leader Wyclef Jean stated
that "you got to know where you're coming from to know where you're going, Muhammad Ali is
where we came from, and a lot of kids are forgetting it, so we're telling them that this is what was
and this is where we're going." In response to this statement, Ali said: "Rap music has become a
mainstay of black music today, and I'm honored that rappers of this stature consider me the original
rapper. But I'm particularly honored that they all wanted to rap with me on '*Rumble* In The *Jungle!*'" Jim Bessman, "Mercury Ready to Rumble with Ali Film's Soundtrack," *Billboard*, January 18,
1997, 9.

61. This space included, significantly, the convening of a coterie of African American popular
performers from North America (The Spinners, Bill Withers, James Brown, B. B. King),
Caribbean/Latin America (Celia Cruz), and Africa (Miriam Makeba) to perform at what was billed
"The Black Woodstock."

ally oriented ones[62] to better meet the above-mentioned episodic challenges of cultural assault, racializing of power relations, and bifurcation of knowledge attendant to the West Atlantic sojourn. These challenges are enumerated in the description of the material circumstances (drug abuse, robbing, murder, destruction, despair) attendant to the Pan-African ("Brooklyn to Zaire") call for help from within ("a ghetto Messiah"). A major improvisational figure to access previous African icons of divine intelligence (from Djehuty in classical east Africa to Esu in medieval west Africa) is the "badman," the figure capable of outsmarting and thereby transcending both the oppressed and the oppressor.[63]

Beyond conventional readings of African-U.S. religious history that might equate the call for a "ghetto Messiah" primarily or exclusively with Liberation Theology or conventional Euro-Christian theology, this call fits firmly with the idea of a representative figure who embodies the "trickster"/"badman" Africana cultural location occupied by Ali and, before him, the man referred to by Ossie Davis as "Our Black Shining Prince"[64]: Malcolm X.

Hill's lyrics are preceded by lyrics from Wyclef Jean and Q-Tip of a Tribe Called Quest and are followed by an astonishing metaphysical rumination by Busta Rhymes that links the Ali-Forman conflict to everything from DNA to Blacks performing White-face cultural identities. Jean's lyrics assert that "you versus me/That's like Ali versus Foreman," positioning the Olympian as the stand-in for European interests in defeating Ali. This use of a Black stand-in reveals the distinction between race and culture that Malcolm evoked on many occasions, particularly near the end of his life when he responded to criticisms that he was fighting with a Black man (Elijah Muhammad) in public by stating: "[N]o white man can put words in my mouth, no white man can sic me on another Black group. When I have analyzed the man and the group with my own understanding, and feel that it is detrimental to the interests of the Black community, then I'm going to attack it with that same intensity."[65]

Jean then sings that the match is "God's act/Stand back and watch/Devil's time out/Can't be timed with no swatch watch," thus removing the event from the strictures of linear time and inserting it firmly into a cyclical temporal frame easily appre-

---

62. The relationship of representative individuals as leaders to various preenslavement systems of African governance is complicated and extends beyond the present essay. Michael Gomez has observed that large groups of Africans, such as the Ibo of present-day southeast Nigeria, had governance systems that relied on much more diffuse sites of governing power; accordingly, the emergence of minister-academic-political individual leadership structures was an improvisational adaptation, not a "natural" result of the assertion of African political will. See Michael Gomez, *Exchanging Our Country Marks: The Transformation of African Identities in the Colonial and Antebellum South* (Chapel Hill: University of North Carolina Press, 1998).

63. Useful historiographies of the "badman" figure in U.S. African intellectual life include John W. Roberts, *From Trickster to Badman* (Philadelphia: University of Pennsylvania Press, 1990) and Cecil Brown, *Stagolee Shot Billy* (Cambridge, MA: Harvard University Press, 2003).

64. Ossie Davis, "Our Shining Black Prince," in *Malcolm X: The Man and His Times*, ed. John Henrik Clarke, xi–xii (New York: Collier Books, 1969). Davis writes elsewhere in the volume that Malcolm X was an uncompromisingly honest man, which for an Black man in the United States, was a rare and precious thing. Davis's description prompted his assertion that "Malcolm was our manhood, our living Black manhood!" (ibid., xii)—a quotation that has earned him the disdain by other African American intellectuals of those who seek to depict Malcolm X as a symbol of Black patriarchy and hypermasculinity. See Ossie Davis, "Why I Eulogized Malcolm X," in *Malcolm X: The Man and His Times*, ed. John Henrik Clarke, 128–131 (New York: Collier Books, 1969).

65. John Henrik Clarke, "The Black Muslim Movement," in *Malcolm X: The Man and His Times*, ed. John Henrik Clarke, 225 (New York: Collier Books, 1969).

hended through the use of the Ki-Kongo paradigm. This paradigm also establishes a sense of inevitability attendant to cyclical models of historical time. The three-dimensional, spiral nature of the model, however, insulates the idea of "destiny" in many Africana cultural traditions from the charge of static, unchanging views of reality. The fight is far from settled: it will be won or lost on its merits. The confidence shown by Ali mirrors that shown by Malcolm and referenced by Jean. It is a confidence in the durability of the values and techniques of the long-view African historical genealogy.

Jean finishes his lyrics by boasting of taking "an extra bar/as I spar with literature/Taking kingdoms from the Tsars/Winning more wars than the Moors." In this closing, he links the Ali moment to the long-view genealogy of African Islam recently outlined in Michael Gomez's *Black Crescent*, discussed above. The pivotal figures in the exponential resurgence of Islam in the United States are, of course, Elijah Muhammad and Malcolm X.

The imagery of long-view genealogies of African history returning cyclically to inform the improvisational moment of Ali-Foreman is evoked by the next two lyricists, John Forte and Q-Tip. Forte rehearses a minihistory of the Nation of Islam, claiming to have witnessed "The Devil spar with Allah" and asserting that "Mathematics is the key/To set my whole race free." He reveals the allure of the Nation of Islam-era Malcolm to those in younger and even more improvisational extensions of the Nation, such as the Nation of Gods and Earths (the Five Percenters), the Hebrew-Israelites, and other spiritually oriented nationalist groups which rely heavily on symbolism, ritual, and iconography. The study of Malcolm as a possible figure of divination may yield a deeper understanding of the Africana connections to these organic movements—at least as deep an understanding as the distancing act of viewing him as a "secular saint."[66]

Q-Tip's lyrics almost serve to herald Hill's, encapsulating the actual fight and climaxing with the triumphant combatant anticipating the observer(s) who will make sense of the triumph. Into this prepared space, Hill empties her analysis in one of the most memorable lyrics in recent hip-hop historiography:

> We used to bite the bullets with the pigskin casings
> Now we perfect slang like a gang of street masons
> Scribe check make connects
> True pyramid architects
> Replace the last name with the X
> The man's got a God complex
> But take the text and change the picture
> Watch Muhammad play the messenger like Holy Muslim scriptures
> Take orders from only God
> Only war when it's Jihad
> See Ali appears in Zaire to reconnect 400 years
> So we the people dark but equal give love to such things
> To the man who made the fam' remember when we were kings

In the initial couplet, Hill evokes the major episodic challenges of the enslavement and postenslavement eras (literal and metaphorical "bullets" encased in anti-African sheaths represented by a central symbol in Nation of Islam instruction: the pig) and an-

---

66. Dyson, *Making Malcolm*, 270.

nounces their defeat in the form of waves of ever-improvising generations (a slang-perfecting "gang of street masons"). Each generation of Africans introduced, through the
popular culture, templates that were harnessed to the service of political action. Robin
D. G. Kelley has written persuasively of Malcolm's use of his own familiarity with the
popular culture of African Americana—from bars and music to dance and other forms
of entertainment.[67] In his way, Malcolm raised in the Nation and in its/his progeny a
slang-perfecting "gang of street masons" with an internal lingo. Anyone who has heard
or used the phrase "by any means necessary" understands the culturally encoded meaning of the concept.

Hill's use of the bullet metaphor echoes the combative imagery of Malcolm's speech
in Cleveland, Ohio, on April 3, 1964, "The Ballot or the Bullet." The text of his speech
deals substantially with the bleak economic, political, and social conditions faced by
Africans locally and globally and calls for them to unite, taking the fight "into the
United Nations, where our African brothers can throw their weight on our side, where
our Latin-American brothers can throw their weight on our side, and where 800 million Chinamen are sitting there waiting to throw their weight on our side."[68] Malcolm
concludes the speech by outlining the philosophy of Black Nationalism, which he describes as the antidote to the political impotency of the U.S. Democratic and Republi-
can parties.

The next three lines push the vertical genealogy many cycles backward, connecting
the efforts to retrieve African historical memory systematically undertaken in the era of
Malcolm X (the "[s]cribe check" which "make[s] connects") with a foundational classical Africa ("True pyramid architects") that compels African Americans to take the next
distancing step from the cultural and institutional contexts of their oppressors ("Replace the last name with an X"). One of the most enduring admonitions uttered by
Malcolm was to "study history, which rewards all research." This admonition underscores Malcolm's unyielding commitment to connect the lived experiences of contemporary African communities both to other contemporary African communities and to
all historical African communities.

The "X" Malcolm took as a condition for membership in the Nation of Islam was a
marker of racial independence as distinct from a marker of the connection to an African
cultural interdependence. The latter connection is evidenced in his receipt of the name
"Omowale" in Trenchard Hall at the University of Ibadan in Nigeria in May, 1964,
which Malcolm recounts in the following passage from the *Autobiography*:

> Afterward, in the Student's Union, I was made an honorary member of the
> Nigerian Muslim Students Society. Right here in my wallet is my card: El-Hajj,
> Malcolm X. Registration No. M-138. With the membership, I was given a new
> name: "Omowale." It means in the Yoruba language, 'the son who has come
> home.' I meant it when I told them I had never received a more treasured honor.[69]

67. Robin D.G. Kelley, "The Riddle of the Zoot: Malcolm Little and Black Cultural Politics During World War II," in *Malcolm X: In Our Own Image*, ed. Joe Wood, 155–182 (New York: St. Martin's Press, 1992.)
68. Malcolm X, "The Ballot or the Bullet," in Malcolm X, *Malcolm X Speaks: Selected Speeches
and Statements*, ed. George Breitman, 35 (New York: Pathfinder, 1965).
69. Malcolm X (with Alex Haley), *The Autobiography of Malcolm X* (New York: Ballantine
Books, 1999), 357. See also T'Shaka, *The Political Legacy of Malcolm X*, 63–85. Ironically, while Malcolm was in Ghana, Muhammad Ali (whom Haley refers to in the *Autobiography* as "Cassius Clay")
was in the country as well. Malcolm made sure to avoid Ali so as not to "put him on the spot." He
recounts: "I knew that Cassius would have been forbidden [by the NOI] to associate with me. I

Hill's recognition that the erasure of the last names of the slave masters did not completely restructure African reality is made apparent in the next two lines. While whites would hardly abandon their cultural, political, economic, and, for some, spiritual "God complex," the "text," which all inhabitants of the United States have shared familiarity with, nevertheless exists in different cultural and social spaces, depending on the worldview (the "picture" evoked by Hill). Changing the worldview allows for coexistence to cease as a barrier for the (re)connection of transcending and enabling cultural identities. With identity intact, the inevitable day of reckoning is secured.

Louis A. DeCaro, Jr., has written extensively on Malcolm's commitment to the principle of redemptive spiritual traditions, arguing that he linked religious action with the program of uplift for African people. Taking the "text" of the Abrahamic faith traditions (Judaism, Christianity, and Islam) but changing the picture, DeCaro argues that Malcolm used his Nation of Islam years to reinforce what he had received from his Garveyite upbringing regarding the equating of racial hatred with evil and the equating of the struggle against oppression with divine order.[70]

Consequently, Malcolm witnessed his own Muhammad (Elijah) "play the messenger like Holy Muslim scriptures," replacing any idea of white superiority with the irreducible concept of God as the only authority. Malcolm's reticence to use violence, even in the face of personal attacks on his family and his person, is consistent with Africana worldviews that do not seek to initiate conflict. Cedric Robinson reads this relationship with violence as an essential part of the Black Radical Tradition, arguing that the tradition is "motivated by the shared sense of obligation to preserve the collective being, the ontological reality."[71]

This obligation, which, Robinson observes, "proceeded from the whole historical consciousness of Black people and not merely from the social formations of capitalist slavery or the relations of productions of colonialism," caused Africans to develop a different relationship to violence. Preserving the physical self or property was not a priority; rather, the priority was "the preservation of the ontological totality granted by a metaphysical system that had never allowed for property in either the physical, philosophical, temporal, legal, social or psychic senses." For Africans, "defeat or victory was an internal affair."[72]

For Malcolm, then, the loss of physical property (such as his firebombed Queens house), intellectual property (i.e., the *Muhammad Speaks* newspaper he had founded), and social property (his membership status in the Nation of Islam) were not important relative to his obligation to preserve the collective self. In his final interview with Gordon Parks, he observed: "It's a time for martyrs now. And if I'm to be one, it will be in the cause of the brotherhood. That's the only thing that can save this country. I've learned it the hard way—but I've learned it. And that's the significant thing."[73] This statement has been read a number of ways—from a death wish to exhaustion to mes-

---

knew that Cassius knew that I had been with him, and for him, and believed in him, when those who later embraced him felt that he had no chance" (Malcolm X, *Autobiography*, 365).

70. See Louis A. DeCaro, Jr., *On The Side of My People: A Religious Life of Malcolm X* (New York: New York University Press, 1996), 262–293. After this work (which DeCaro called "the first religious biography to focus exclusively on Malcolm X"), he wrote a treatment of Malcolm's relationships with Christianity, Louis A. DeCaro, Jr., *Malcolm and the Cross: The Nation of Islam, Malcolm X, and Christianity* (New York: New York University Press, 1998).

71. Robinson, *Black Marxism*, 170.

72. Ibid., 168.

73. Malcolm X, interview by Gordon Parks, "One Big Force Under One Banner," February 19, 1965, in Malcolm X, *February, 1965: The Final Speeches*, ed. Steve Clark, 231 (New York: Pathfinder, 1992).

sianism to rhetorical bombast. However, when placed in the long-view genealogy of the African-Centered Worldview and the Black Radical Tradition, Malcolm's statement begins to open a different set of possibilities.

Of course, the Muhammad of Lauren Hill's lyrics is specifically Muhammad Ali (though the function of Ali in Zaire is only enhanced when viewed through the episodic, cyclical framework of the Ki-Kongo paradigm). Ali's refusal to go to war with the Vietnamese internationalizes the stance assumed by Malcolm and, before him, by Elijah Muhammad (vis-à-vis World War II).[74] Ali's "Jihads," then, like Malcolm's, acknowledged a divine rather than a human superiority. They included Ali's war to stay off the battlefields of Southeast Asia and, symbolically, his struggle to assert a sense of trans-African hope through his triumph in Zaire, in self-stated service to his collective African family.

Hill concludes her song with a temporally harmonizing recognition of the enduring cyclical importance of Ali and, by extension, the people and institutions that gave nurture, instruction, and license to him—including Malcolm X, the Nation of Islam, the Garvey Movement, and the entire genealogy of the Black Radical Tradition as it emerged over several centuries. Standing beyond the episodic, horizontal challenges of any immediate moment are "we the people dark but equal," who retain the presence of self and culture to have love to give to assessed exertions on their behalf. Her final salute, "to the man who made the fam' remember when we were kings," applies equally to any link in the genealogical chain, including, of course, Malcolm X.

Lauren Hill's lyrics capture one of the ways that subsequent generations have acknowledged the contributions of Muhammad Ali, of Malcolm X, and, by extension, of all those firmly recognized in the genealogy of African historical memory. The improvisational contribution of this current generation of young Africans—hip-hop—is most powerful when it accesses long-view African memory. So, too, is disciplinary Africana Studies. The example of Malcolm X provides a rich field of cultural texts and practices to study and to emulate epistemologically. There is much work to be done.

The Meaning of Malcolm X for Africana Studies

The United States is less a nation than an improvisation, a convening of extensions of cultures. Malcolm X endures primarily as a signifier of Africa in the West—as the anticitizenry, or "Black" people. Furthermore, he endures not as the discursive opposite and definer of "whiteness" but as the self-conscious outsider, the "victim of democracy." Manning Marable quotes one of his graduate students in making a qualitative distinction between the perceptions of two representative figures in the genealogy of African historical memory outside the African community: "Martin Luther King, Jr. belongs to everybody. Malcolm X belongs to us."[75]

74. See Gerald Horne, *Race War! White Supremacy and the Japanese Attack on the British Empire* (New York: New York University Press, 2004), 48; see also Ernest Allen, Jr., "When Japan was 'Champion of the Darker Races': Satokata Takahashi and the Flowering of Black Messianic Nationalism, *The Black Scholar* 24, no. 4 (Winter 1994): 23–46.

75. Manning Marable, *The New Black Renaissance: The Souls Anthology of Critical African American Studies* (Boulder, CO: Infinity Publications, 2005), 3.

The reproduction of Malcolm by contemporary scholars extends the profound class split between academics and larger communities of African people which emerged full blown at the nexus of the nineteenth century and widened in the wake of the secularization of intellectual work in the late nineteenth and early twentieth centuries. Most African people—and, arguably, these intellectuals themselves—are aware of how Africans view themselves and how they are viewed by others; however, the political choices the elite make are consistent with two beliefs: first, that African people cannot survive and thrive in this polity on their own political, economic, and cultural terms; and, second, that the genealogy of Africana history and culture is inferior to the traditions extending out of Europe, traditions that they would rather be junior partners to than being with their own.

These two beliefs are evidenced in the (re)productions of Malcolm X in the scholarship and the interpretation of both Malcolm's words and the more popular representations of Malcolm by nonelites. In doing this work, the elite mediate a public sphere that is never entirely under their control; their audience, then, is multiple and, thereby, compromised with regard to the most enduring of Malcolm's messages. Africana Studies came into existence at the behest of the same Africans who have "given love to such things" over the 400-year course of the West Atlantic encounter. It is a field and a discipline fit only for the "kittens"; no biscuits need apply.

Contributors

Adisa A. Alkebulan (Ph.D., Temple University) is Assistant Professor of Africana Studies at San Diego State University. He is currently working on a book on language and colonialism in Africa. He is a major contributor to the upcoming *Encyclopedia of Black Studies*, and his work appears in anthologies on rhetoric, literature, and Malcolm X.

Katherine O. Bankole (Ph.D., Temple University) is an Associate Professor of History at West Virginia University. She is the author of *Slavery and Medicine: Enslavement and Medical Practices in Antebellum Louisiana*.

Scot Brown (Ph.D., Cornell University) is Associate Professor of History and African American Studies at the University of California at Los Angeles. He is the author of *Fighting For Us: Maulana Karenga, The US Organization, and Black Cultural Nationalism*.

Greg Kimathi Carr (Ph.D., Temple University; JD, The Ohio State University) is Assistant Professor of African American Studies at Howard University. He is the author of the essay, "The African and African American Studies Curriculum Guide," prepared for the Association for the Classical Study of African Civilizations. He has published numerous articles in the areas of Africana Historiography, Research Methods, and Africana Nationalist Movements.

James L. Conyers, Jr. (Ph.D., Temple University) is Director of the African American Studies Program, Director of the Center for African American Culture, and University Professor of African American Studies at the University of Houston. He is the editor of *Engines of the Black Power Movement*.

Malachi D. Crawford (ABD, University of Missouri at Columbia) is a doctoral candidate in the Department of History at the University of Missouri at Columbia. His areas of interest are Africana religion, research methods, and womanism.

Paul Easterling is a doctoral student in Religious Studies at Rice University. His areas of interest are West African Religions, theory, methods, and Africana Historical Studies.

Mekada Graham (Ph.D., University of Hertfordshire, England) is Associate Professor of Social Work at the University of Oklahoma at Tulsa. She is the author of *Black Issues in Social Work and Social Care*.

Robert L. Harris, Jr. (Ph.D., Roosevelt University) is Professor of Africana Studies and Vice Provost for Diversity and Faculty Development. He is the coeditor of *The Columbia Guide to African American History Since 1939*.

Rhett Jones (Ph.D., Brown University) is Professor of Africana Studies and History at Brown University. His areas of specialty include African American history before 1800, African American theater, Black/Native relations before 1800, Caribbean history before 1840, and race relations in the colonial Americas.

Maulana Karenga (Ph.D., University of Southern California) is Professor of Black Studies at California State University at Long Beach. He is the Chair of the US Organization. He is also the author of *Maat, The Moral Ideal in Ancient Egypt.*

Maghan Keita (Ph.D., Howard University) is Director, Center for Arab and Islamic Studies, and Professor of History and Africana Studies at Villanova University. He is the author of *Race and the Writing of History: Riddling the Sphinx.*

Miriam Ma'at-Ka-Re Monges (Ph.D., Temple University) was Associate Professor of Social Work and Africana Studies at California State University at Chico. She is the author of *Kush — The Jewel of Nubia: Reconnecting the Root System of African Civilization.*

Godwin Ohiwerei (Ph.D., Louisiana State University) is Chair of the Department of Sociology and Anthropology and Professor of Sociology at New Jersey City University. He is the author of *Developing Strategies for Excellence in Urban Education.*

Victor O. Okafor (Ph.D., Temple University) is Professor of African American Studies, Eastern Michigan University. He is the author of *Towards an Understanding of Africology.*

Reiland Rabaka (Ph.D., Temple University) is Assistant Professor of Ethnic Studies at University of Colorado at Boulder. He is the author of *W.E.B. Du Bois and the Problems of the Twenty-First Century: An Essay on Africana Critical Theory.*

Larry Ross (Ph.D., University of Missouri) is Associate Professor of Sociology and Anthropology at Lincoln University in Jefferson City, Missouri. He is the author of *African-American Jazz Musicians in the Diaspora.*

Andrew P. Smallwood (EdD, Northern Illinois University) is the Director of the African American Studies Program and Assistant Professor of African American Studies at Austin Peay State University. He is the author of *An Afrocentric Study of the Intellectual Development, Leadership Praxis, and Pedagogy of Malcolm X.*

James B. Stewart (Ph.D., University of Notre Dame) is Professor of Labor Studies and Employment Relations and African American Studies and Management Organization at Pennsylvania State University at McKeesport. He is the author of *Flight in Search of Vision.*

Christel N. Temple (Ph.D., Temple University) is Associate Professor of Africana Studies at the University of Maryland at Baltimore County. She is the author of *Literary Pan-Africanism: History, Contexts, and Criticism.*

Julius E. Thompson (Ph.D., Princeton University) is the Director of the Black Studies Program and Professor of History and Black Studies at the University of Missouri at Columbia. He is the author of *Lynchings in Mississippi: A History, 1865–1965.*

Antonio Tillis (Ph.D., University of Missouri) is Associate Professor of Spanish and African American Studies at Purdue University. He is the author of *Manuel Zapata Olivella and the "Darkening" of Latin American Literature.*

Ahati N. N. Toure (Ph.D., University of Nebraska at Lincoln) is the Assistant Director of the African American Studies Program and adjunct instructor at the University of Houston.

Akinyele K. Umoja (Ph.D., Emory University) is Associate Professor of African American Studies at Georgia State University. He is the author of numerous articles and has a research expertise in Africana cultural resistance movements.

Shirley N. Weber (Ph.D., University of California at Los Angeles) is Associate Professor of Africana Studies at San Diego State University. Her research areas of interest are Mar-

cus Garvey and the UNIA, Nationalist Movements, Black women in Nationalist movements, Africana Curriculum, and Service Learning in Africana Studies.

Index

A

Abu-Jamal, Mumia, 50
accommodation, 44, 133
activism, Black
    in Britain, and histories of black communities, 55–56
    history of, and social welfare in Britain, 57–63
    and successful struggle strategies, 79–82
Adefumi, Oserjiman, 51
Adoro, Theodor, 284
Aelane, Yahne, 58
Africa. *See also* Afrika; back to Africa
    and Black heritage and identity, 334–35
    liberation movement, international, 45–46
    main concerns of, 1960–1967, 128
    Malcolm and African life, 366–67
    Malcolm as global leader of, 152–53
    and paradigm of ancestor creation, 167–69
    subjugation of, for economic reasons, 78–79
    underdevelopment in, and neocolonialism, 121–22
"Africa, A Nation for the Negro Peoples of the World," 133–34
"African," 201
African American
    Afrocentric consciousness for, 222
    identify formation, 187–88, 201–3
    and international independence, 8–10
    leadership, twentieth-century, 4
    in the New World, history of, 318–19
"African American Mysteries: Order of the Men of Oppression," 209
African American Summit, 123
African Children's Fund, 59
African Methodist Episcopal Church, 4
African People's Socialist Party, 71

African Progressive League, 59
African Summit Conference, 127, 230
Africana Critical Theory. *See* Critical Theory, Africana
Africana Social Movement. *See* Social Movement, Africana
Africana Studies. *See also* Africana Studies, Disciplinary; Critical Theory, Africana; worldview, African-centered
    contemporary Malcolm X studies, 356–61
    definition of, 355, 362
    Enlightenment contextualization of Malcolm, 240–42
    and his intellectual life, 244–49
    historical contextualization of Malcolm, 242–43
    intellectual construct of Malcolm, 240–43
    intellectual foundation of, 236–40
    intellectuality of, 238–44
    and "Jazz Model," 362n33
    meaning of Malcolm in, 374–75
    and moral construction of intellectual life of Malcolm, 244–49
    overview, intellectual and moral constructs, 235–40
    overview of, 167–69, 187–89, 354–56
    philosophy/critical theory compared, 285–86
    and "praxis research," 362n34
    research and protocols of, 210
    and Ujima paradigm, 20–29
Africana Studies, Disciplinary, 360
    and collective historical memory, 365
    definition of, 360–61n29
    global identity as foundation of, 361
    and paradigm of historical memory, 362–68
    and viewing Malcolm's speeches in context, 367–68

Africanity, 73, 76
Africanization, 122
"Africology," 362–63
Afrika
    "Afro-American" or "Afrikan," 43
    definition of, 31n
    shifting view of continental, 42–43
Afrikan Business and Culture, 61
Afrikan Liberation Day, 47
Afrikan Liberation Movements, 207–12
Afro-American
    Association, 48
    definition of, 84
    to include Caribbean island-nations, 316
    Institute, 48
Afrocentrism, 149–50
    and "conservative Afrocentrists," 355n8
    and Eurocentrism, 285
    theory, and areas of argumentation, 190
afterlife, 174–75
Ahmed, Akbar Muhammad, 49
Akan, 171
    dirge attributes, 176
    funeral ceremony, 167–68
    funeral dirge, 175
Aklkebulan, Adisa A., 299
Al-Amin, Jamil, 51
Ali, John, 33
Ali, Muhammad
    and George Forman boxing match, 368–74
    as rapper, 369n60
Ali, Nobel Drew, 37, 150–51
Alkalimat, Abdul, 69, 71, 338, 358n19
    and study materials developed by, 361n31
"All Black," 327
    ("Todo negro"), 318
All God's Children Need Traveling Shoes, 180–81
Allen, Richard, 4, 120
American Revolution, 23
Amini, Johari, 272
Ammere, Cojoh, 58
ancestor, 182
    "elder" and "old age," definitions of, 172
    list, associated with Malcolm by poets, 175
    Malcolm as ancestor, 173–82
    and "material opulence," 173
    paradigm of creation of, 167–68
    type of death of, definition of, 172
"And if it wasn't for," 275

"And Shine Swam On," 170
Anderson, Carol, 212
Anderson, Talmadge, 67, 69, 71
Angelou, Maya, 180–81
Ani, Marimba, 206n6
anti-imperialism, 45
apartheid, 330
    as domestic issue of South Africa, 127–28
    and US racism at UN, 128, 333
Aptheker, Herbert, 207n10, 208n11
Asante, Molefi Kete, 21, 60, 68, 69, 71, 72, 169, 190, 283, 338
    and "Afrocentric idea" of critical theory, 284
    on Black status in U.S., 349
    functional paradigm, definition of, 219
    Malcolm as "cultural analyst," 189
    Malcolm as cultural hero, 223, 355
    Malcolm as extremist in press, 221
    Malcolm in context of time and space, 203
    Malcolm on "objectivism," 196
Asante stool, 25
assassination, 231. *See also* FBI
    of Malcolm, 20, 68, 72
    of Malcolm, and influence on black middle-class, 200, 219
    of Malcolm and NOI, 142, 179
    of Malcolm X, in drama and other literary genres, 178–82
    of Malcolm X and Black Arts Movement, 170, 177–78, 273
    and premonition of, by Black leaders, 182
    and undelivered petition to United Nations, 128–30
atonement, 227
Autobiography of Malcolm X, The, 35, 71, 111, 118, 135, 171
    essay on, web site, 264
    as evidence of reformation project of NOI, 198
    first chapter, "Nightmare," 316
    as inspiration for plays, drama, 179
    and missing three chapters from, 357n17
    responsible for hero dynamic, 168
    teaching guide for educators, web site, 264
Awoonor, Kofi, 181–82
axiology, 20, 24–25
Azibo, Daudi, 354
Azikiwe, Naomi, 231

B
back to Africa, 222, 289–91, 316, 358n20
    and emancipation, 133
    Malcolm on, 289–90
    and Marcus Garvey, 133–34
    symbolic meaning of, for Malcolm, 222
Bagwell, O., 215, 220, 223
Bailey, Harry A., Jr., 199
Bailey, Peter, 34, 39, 367
Baldwin, James, 179, 223, 251, 252n74, 255,
    256n91
"Ballad to the Anonymous," 174
"Ballots or Bullets," 117, 131–32, 135–36,
    256, 372
("Bam, bam-bam bam-bam"), 322–23
Bandung Conference, 8, 22–23, 37, 104–5
Banka, Bob, 265
Bankole, Katherine O., 187
Banneker, Benjamin, 241, 245
Baraka, Amiri, 11, 51, 176, 178, 202, 251, 281
Baraka, Res, 272
Barn, R., 57
Barnes, Jack, 68, 73, 347
Bass, Bernice, 38, 118
Bell, Inge Powell, 80
Bennett, Lerone, 340
Berg, Bruce L., 29
Berry, Mary Frances, 72, 85
Beshti, Bashir M. El, 18
Best, Steven, 282n2, 284n5, 285n6
Bhabha, Homi K., 319
bigotry, 86
Billingsley, A., 58
Black
    and "Negro," 141
Black/Africana Studies, 10–11
Black Afrika, 42
Black Arts Movement, 5–6, 11, 47, 355n9
    assassination as catalyst for, 170
    and Black Studies Movement, 10–12
    influence of Malcolm on, 168
    Malcolm X as inspiration for, 267–80
    and revolutionary poetry, 319–28
    and themes linked to Malcolm X, 12
Black Belt, 128–29
Black Bourgeoisie, 81
"Black Bourgeoisie," 199
Black Common Market, 120
Black Crescent, 357, 371
Black Economic Summit, 120
Black English, 132
Black Fire, An Anthology of Afro-American
    Literature, 169–70

Black Freedom Movement, 48, 94. See also
    role
    role of women in, 40–42
Black Governmental Conference, 50
"black internationalism," 149
"Black is beautiful," 241n23, 244, 252,
    257–58, 344, 368
Black Liberation Movement, 4, 132
    Army, 144
    characteristics of, 100
    as economic, 338
    history of armed struggle, 207–12
    and Malcolm, 93, 94
    and need for collective strategy, 339
    redefinition of, as human rights, 103–4
    and religion, 99
    and secret order during slave era, 209
    and separate system of values for Blacks,
        341
    and values, 337
"Black Man's History, The," 192
Black Muslim, 141, 300
    Malcolm as, 338
    movement, growth of, 331–32
    and white media/FBI connection, 307
Black Muslims in America, The, 8, 135
Black Nationalism, 5–6, 69, 228, 315–16. See
    also Kwanzaa; self-determination
    in African American Studies, 187
    and Christianity, 113, 135
    and continental Afrikans, 42–43
    definition of, 138
    and economic philosophy of, 117,
        134–35
    generally, 137–46
    ideology of, 131–32
    interchangeable use of "Black" and
        "Afro-American," 100
    Malcolm as model for, 94–95
    and Malcolm on youth, 107
    and Malcolm X, 31–32, 70–71
    and Marcus Garvey, 8
    and "Message to the Grass Roots,"
        19–20, 24–25
    and NOI, 7, 44–46
    and Pan Africanism and socialism,
        289–90
    purpose of, 345
    and racism, 350
    and revolutionary nationalism, 45
    and revolutionary poetry, 318–28
    and role of women in, 40–42
    term first introduced, 135–36

Black Nationalism, *continued*
  with traditional roots in Africa, 339
  two forms of, 32
  and white racism, 356n14
Black Nationalism: A Search for an Identity in America, 31
"black neo-nationalism," 254n82
Black/Note, 12
Black Panther Party, 6, 31, 72, 136, 138, 144
  history and ideology of, 50
Black Power: The Politics of Liberation in America, 131–32
Black Power Movement, 5–7, 31, 47–48, 77, 132
  as Black Nationalist resurgence, 137–38
  and cultural nationalism, 144
  and popularity of African culture, 122
  and rejection of whiteness, 344
  and sexism in, 47
Black Protest Movement, 188
Black Radical Tradition, 354–56, 357n16, 362. *See also* worldview, African-centered
  and black radicalism, 282
  as contested assertion, 355n8
  Malcolm as a Black radical, 289–91
  and "official" narrative disconnect, 358n19
  and violence, 373–74
Black Reconstruction, 228, 229, 251
"Black Revolution, The," 193
"Black Shining Prince, The," 177
"Black song for Rifles and Kettledrums" ("Canción negra para rifles y atabales"), 318
Black sovereignty, 3–4
Black Star Line, 134
Black Studies Movement, 5–6. *See also* Africana Studies
  and Black Arts Movement, 10–12
  department at San Francisco State College, 10–11
blackness, 74, 193
  in Discciplinary Africana Studies, 365
  and Dominican and Caribbean, 319–20
  and "epistemology of Blackness," 253
  as fundamental reality, 102
  and Hispanic "other," 320
  meaning of, 84, 258
  and new knowledge users and producers, 252
  rejection of, 344–45
  in revolutionary poetry, 326–27

and solidarity, 85
Blair, Tony, 329
Blassingame, John W., 72, 85, 248
Blaustein, A, 120
"Block's on fire (Block's on fire tonight)", 369
Blues for Mister Charlie, 179
Blumberg, Rhoda, 3
Boateng, Felix, 168, 169
Boigny, Houphouet, 123
Bono, 329
bourgeoisie, black, 23–24, 81–82. *See also* class
Bradley, Ed, 51
Braidwood, S., 58
Breakout, The, 179
Breitman, George, 22, 45n61, 68, 74, 85, 179, 222, 239, 281, 338, 359n25
  global struggle against oppessors, 347
Brooks, Gwendolyn, 167, 270
"Brother Freedom," 175
"Brother Malcolm's Echo," 176
brotherhood, 118, 345–46
  of all men, 201, 331
  and greed, 346
  of humanity, 224
  Malcolm on, 329
  and martyrdom, 373
  in Muslim tradition and in US, 98–99
  and women, 311–12
Brotherhood of Sleeping Car Porters and Chamber Maids, 366n51
Brown, Elaine, 200
Brown, H. Rap, 51, 341
Brown, Scott, 137
Brown, William Wells, 207, 208, 211
Brown v. Board of Education, 6
Browne, R., 122
Budge, E.A. Willis, 311
Bullins, Ed, 178
Burroughs, Margaret G., 170–71, 175, 177, 270
Burrow, Rufus, Jr., 331
business development
  and black community, 120
  curbed by fear-based social climate, 194
  by the UNIA, 134–35
Butler, Broadus, 291
"by any means necessary," 122, 235, 256, 269, 281, 317, 372
  in Dominican poetry, 320
  freedom, 107–9, 323, 349
  and mission of OAAU, 219
  as rallying cry to confront racism, 52–53
  strive for success, 63

C
Cabral, Amilcar, 286, 287, 289, 290
"Canción negra para rifles y atabales"
    ("Black Song for Rifles and Kettle-
        drums"), 318
and violence for Black unity, 321–23
"¿Cantar al Dios blanco?", 323
capital, cultural, 60
capitalism
    black, 120
    colonialism and racism tied to, 69
    and colonialism criticized, 289
    global, 347–48
    and greed as shadow value, 346–50
    as impediment to African American lib-
        eration, 288–89
    Malcolm on, 288
    monopoly, and black-owned business,
        120
    as vulture, 46, 95
Carew, Jan, 203, 281, 358n22, 366n50
Caribe, africano en despertar, 318
Carlton-LaNey, I., 55
Carmichael, Stokely, 72, 131–32, 136, 257
Carr, Greg Kimathi, 353, 362n32
Carr-Damu, Samuel, 143
Carson, Clayborne, 155, 305
Castro, Fidel, 37
CBS Television, 308
Central Intelligence Agency (CIA), 303
Charles, Ray, 268
"chickens coming home to roost," 20, 33,
    93–94, 218. *See also* Kennedy, John F.
Christianity, 140, 206n6
    clergy and armed resistance by slaves,
        208
    and Du Bois on, 237
    hypocritical, 242
    and links to suffering and oppression,
        140–41
    and racism, 73, 81
    rejection of, 101
    as "white man's religion," 32
church, black, 4–5, 117, 135
Churchill, Ward, 304
Cinque, Joseph, 274
civil rights
    and human rights, 48–49, 79, 103–4,
        156, 187, 219
    and human rights, before the OAU,
        126–28
    and human rights, web site contrasting,
        265

leaders and black middle class, 199–201
leadership's refusal to debate with Mal-
    colm, 353n2
and "separate but equal" doctrine, 130
Civil Rights Act, 126, 130
Civil Rights Congress, 229
Civil Rights Movement, 4
    as "black protest movement," 215
    emphasis of, 7
    impact of Malcolm on, 9–10
    infiltrated by FBI, 152
    King and Malcolm compared, 236
    and Malcolm X, 315
    origins of, 6–8
    and Pan Africanism, 9–10
    social ecology of, 26–27t2
"Claims of the Negro Ethnologically Consid-
    ered, The," 242
Clark, Kenneth, 237, 244, 255
Clarke, John Henrik, 34, 39, 68, 94, 206,
    218, 223, 281, 282, 359n25
Clasby, Nancy, 21, 24, 251, 253, 254
class. *See also* "Black is beautiful"
    analysis and race analysis, 350
    behavior and consciousness, 95
    black middle, 82–83, 193, 199–201, 339,
        349–50
    discrimination, global, 330–31
    and economic and political power,
        82–86
    Malcolm as epistemologist, 250–54
    struggle, and Marxism, 287
Cleage, Albert, 359n25
Cleaver, Eldridge, 50, 72, 85, 247n47, 257
Clegg, Claude A., 7
Clifton, Lucille, 274
COINTELPRO, 51–52, 152, 206, 299, 304
    definition of, 304
Colaiaco, James A., 4
Colfax, J. David, 75
Collins, Patricia Hill, 282, 289, 355n8
colonialism, European, 8, 23, 37
    and capitalism criticized, 289
    and the Caribbean Blacks, 318–28
    changed to benevolent philanthropy,
        348
    combating, 9–10
    and "God's Judgment of White Amer-
        ica," 118
    as international power structure, 86–87
    persistence of, and current African
        economies, 122–23
Color and Democracy: Colonies and Peace, 228

"color complex," 81–82. *See also* skin color
Coloured Seaman's Industrial League, 59
Coltrane, John, 268
Comes the Voyager At Last: A Tale of Return to Africa, 181–82
communication
    ethnography of, 25–29
    with whites, 77
"Communication and Reality," 303–4
Communist Party, 69, 305, 350
communitiy, black
    seeking social justice, 357n16
community, black. *See also* activism, Black
    activism, 19, 60–62, 95
    and Africana Studies, 362n34
    and black business development, 120
    and black church in, 117
    and Black Panther Party programs in, 136
    in Britain, and welfare interventions in, 55–63
    and community-development corporations, 120
    and community service of the NOI, 301
    empowerment, 6, 7
    empowerment, in Britain, 59–62
    empowerment, strategies for, 62–63
    and ghetto economic development, 114–17
    MMI and moral reformation in, 100
    and need for academic sites located in, 361n31
    organizer's handbook, 358n20
    Police and the Black Community, 193
    and rites-of-passage programs, 62–63
    and slum status, 117
    and social support within, 318
Comparative Sociology, 78
Condit, Celeste, 24, 191, 248n53, 254, 255
Condo, Baba Zak, 8
Cone, James H., 4, 152–54, 281, 282, 358n19
Conference of Independent African States, 127
confrontation, tactic of, 44
Congo, 330, 334
Congress of African People (CAP), 31, 138
Congress of Racial Equality (CORE). *See* CORE
"Conservation of Races," 252
Constitution, U.S.
    Afrikans incorporated into, 209
    and Declaration of Independence, 341
    self-defense guaranteed by, 107–9

"Context, Form and Poetic Expressions in Igede Funeral Dirges," 171
Convention on the Prevention and Punishment of Genocide, 213
Conyers, James L., 17
Cooks, Carlos, 42–43n51, 291
Cooper, Thomas, 58
CORE, 7, 80
cosmology, 20, 22
Council of African Organizations, 232–33
Council of United Civil Rights Leadership, 353n2
Counterintelligence Program, FBI. *See* COINTELPRO
Crane, Les, 311
Crawford, Malachi D., 227
"Crece en mi piel negra," 325–26
Creswell, John W., 20, 25
Critical Theory, Africana, 281–91
    and Afrocentric ideology, 287
    definition of, 282, 282n2, 283–85
    overview, 281–82
critical thinking, 40, 95
Cruse, Harold, 289
Cuffee, Paul, 133
Cugoano, Ottobah, 58–59
cultural celebration, 6
    Malcolm X's birthday, 144
culture
    adaptations in, 169–82
    and Africana Studies, 354–56
    Akan, applied to Malcolm lecture, 25
    Black cultural nationalism, definition of, 138
    component of UNIA, 134–35
    definition of, 172
    and impact on Black ideological constructions, 339
    of involuntary immigrants, study of, 20
    Malcolm as cultural icon, 203, 290–91, 355
    Malcolm's precepts on, and Black resistance, 145
    popular, and Malcolm X, 237
    reestablishment of African, by Garvey, 135
    and role of women in, 311–12
    Schomburg Center for Research in African-American History and Culture, 356
    separate, of Afro-American, 132, 360n28
    and tradition of "ancestor," 167–68, 172–73

Cummings, R., 122
Curthoys, Ann, 365n46
custom. *See* culture

D
Danner, Margaret, 272
Darkwater: Voices From Within the Veil, 228
Davenport, Christian, 24
Davidson, N.R., Jr., 178–79
Davis, Angela, 167, 289
Davis, Darren, 24
Davis, Ed, 11
Davis, Miles, 268
Davis, Ossie, 94, 190, 370
Davis, T., 60, 63
Dawson, Michael, 360n28
Day of Absence, 168
"Days After," 177
De Baptiste, George, 209
Death of Malcolm X, 178
Death of White Sociology, The, 67
DeCaro, Louis A., Jr., 8, 148, 152, 155, 282
    principle of redemptive spiritual tradi-
        tions, 373
Declaration of Independence, 341
Dei, G., 57, 60, 61
Delaney, Martin, 133, 138, 170, 291
democracy
    criticism of, 291
    radical, 39–40
Detroit Red. *See also* X, Malcolm
    as "hustler," 4
    hustling and street life of, 115–16
    legal and illegal employment ventures,
        115–17
    and life as petty criminal and prisoner,
        68
Dhabihu service, 143
diaspora, 3–4, 8, 60
    African, and continental Africans, 333
    and Africana Critical Theory, 283
    and Afro-American cultural deficiency,
        140
    and Marxism, 288–89
    and New World, 319
    and New World Black "exiles," 318–19
    and Old World, 319
    and Pan-African racism, 331–32
    and Pan-Africanism, 105–7
    and theory of liberation relating to, 284
    and unity, 9–10, 43, 154–55
Diem, Ngo Dinh
    assassination of, 34n12

Diggs, Charles C., 229
Dillare, J.L., 132
Diop, Cheikh Anta, 182, 333
dirge, funeral, 167–68. *See also* oratory
    attributes, 176
    as cultural legacy, 175
    defining and reintroducing, 171–77
    definition of, 171–72
    and *Funeral Dirges of the Akan People*,
        173
    grouped as themes, 171
    lineage segmentation and clan disper-
        sions, 175
    and significance of traditions,
        177–78
discrimination theory, 283–86
"Do not speak to me of living.", 177
"Do you listen now," 176
Docker, John, 365n46
dollarism, 347–49
domination
    definition and context for, 285n6
    theory critical of, 283–86
"Don't Buy Where You Can't Work," 135
Douglass, Frederick, 4, 167, 175, 208, 242
    as mythoform, 170
    on necessity of armed struggle,
        210n21
drama, 178–82
Draper, Theodore, 281, 350
drum, 322
    Djembe, 25
Du Bois, Shirley Graham, 12–13, 181
Du Bois, W.E.B., 196, 212, 213, 228, 235–38,
    247, 250, 257–58
    consciousness of Black knowledge and
        experience, 251
    and integration, 133
    and King, compared, 235–38
    and moral construction of race, 243
    as mythoform, 170
    "Talented Tenth," 4
    worked against Garvey, King, and Mal-
        colm, 154
Duneier, Mitchell, 76
Durant, Will, 196
Dyson, Michael Eric, 18, 238, 239, 282,
    360n26

E
ecology, social, 20, 25, 28*fig*1
economy, 119, 318. *See also* liberation, eco-
    nomic; politics

education
    of Blacks, grounded in history and cul-
        ture, 331
    as defense from conflict of interest be-
        tween races, 72–73
    Malcolm on, 44–45, 317
    and Malcolm's dream of studying law, 115
    moral, oral traditions as, 168–69
    political, and ideology, 286
    and prison as metaphor, 246
    provided by NOI, 217
    in "the science of politics," 290
    as tool for liberation, 246–47
    and universities, 73
Education of the Black People, The, 246
Edwards, Harry, 368n58
Egedde, 171
Eissien-Udom, E.U., 7, 31
El-Beshti, Bashir, 198
El Hajj Malik: A Play About Malcolm X,
    178–79
elegy. *See* dirge, funeral
emancipation. *See* slavery
emigration, Black
    and Black Nationalist Movement, 7–8
    and Garvey ideology, 113
Emmanuel, James A., 170
employment, 45
empowerment, Black, 7
*End of White World Supremacy: Four Speeches
    by Malcolm X, The*, 190
Engels, Frederick, 287
Enlightenment, 240–43, 245n41
    separations of mind/body and
        intellect/action, 257
Ephirim-Donkor, Anthony, 172–73
epistemology, 20, 23–24
Epps, Archie, 68, 70, 82, 239, 250, 338
Equiano, Olaudah, 58, 241, 242, 245
Essien-Udom, E.U., 37, 104
"establishment," 317
"esu," 366n49
eulogy. *See* dirge, funeral
European Common Market, 83
Evans, Mari, 272
Evanzz, Karl, 150, 306, 307
Everett-Karenga, Ron. *See* Karenga, Maulana
Evers, Medgar, 167, 274
    assassination of, 34n12

F
Fabio, Sarah Webster, 272
fable, 169

Faisal, King, 125
"Fall yearning down, my hopes shall compass
    yours," 176
Fanon, Franz, 21, 85, 100, 254–56, 258,
    286–87
    on education, 290
    as mythoform, 170
    racism and class struggle, 287
Fard, Wallace D., 243, 305
Farmer, James, 341, 353
Faux, G., 120
FBI, 152. *See also* COINTELPRO
    and Black leaders, 200
    file on Malcolm, 155
    infiltration of political organizations by,
        145
    investigations of Malcolm increased,
        231
    and media tactics, 303–8
    memorandum on Malcolm, 232
    and NOI in conspiracy to kill Malcolm,
        358n21
    slandering NOI leadership, 305–7
    surveillance of Malcolm by, 299
Felder, Cain Hope, 311
Ferdinand, D., 57
Ferguson, Herman, 49, 51
fiction, speculative, 168
Field Negro, 23, 95
"Fight the Power," 12
"Filamentos, filamentos, filamentos"
    ("Follicles, Follicles, Follicles"), 318
    promotion of self-love, 325–26
"Five Faces of Malcolm X, The," 258
Flick, Hank, 21, 190
"Follicles, Follicles, Follicles," 325–26
    ("Filamentos, filamentos, filamentos"),
        318
"For Malcolm, A Year After," 173
*For Malcolm: Poems on the Life and Death of
    Malcolm X*, 170–71, 270
"For Malcolm X," 175
Ford, Clyde W., 203
Forman, George
    and Muhammad Ali boxing match,
        368–74
    and Pan-African disdain for, 368n58
Forman, James, 49
Foucault, M., 60
Foxx, Redd, 367n52
France, 86
    interchangeable use of "Arab" and "Al-
        gerian," 100

Frankfurt School of Critical Theory, 282n2, 284
   definition of, 283–84
   and history of, 284–85
Franklin, John Hope, 190, 207
Franklin, V.P., 210
Frazier, E. Franklin, 81, 199
freedom. *See also* Black Power Movement
   "by any means necessary," 94, 349
   fight, need to be international, 347–48
   Malcolm on international freedom fight, 347–48
   necessity to take, 347
   and peace, 108–9
"freedom from mental slavery," 57, 60
Freedom of Information Act, 304
French Revolution, 23
Friere, Paulo, 251–52
From Civil Rights to Black Liberation, 9
Fruit of Islam (FOI), 33
Fryer, P., 57–59
Fugees, The, 369
Funeral Dirges of the Akan People, 167–68, 173

G
Gallen, David, 155, 282
Gandhi, Mohandas, 341
Garnet, Henry Highland, 208–9
Garrison, William Lloyd, 210
Garvey, Marcus, 4, 131, 175, 291, 315–16.
   See also back to Africa
   and access to media, 153
   compared to Malcolm X, 349
   deportation of, 150
   influence on Black Nationalism, 133–35
   influence on Elijah Muhammad, 150–52
   influence on Little family, 149–50, 216
   influence on Malcolm, 112, 147
   influence on UNIA ideology, 133–35
   as messianic leader, 38
   as mythoform, 170
   and self-reliance, 80
Garvey Movement, 19, 56, 113, 358n20
Garveyism, 93, 147, 148–50
Gast, Leon, 368
Gates, Henry Louis, 239, 254n82
genocide, 49, 213
   cultural, 217
   definition of, 213n31
   economic, 129–30
   and Genocide Convention, 128
   and New World, 319

   and petition to UN by Malcolm, 94, 128–30
   in Rwanda, 329
Geography of Malcolm X, The, 357
Gerzina, G., 58
Ghana, 24, 43, 154
   and the Akan, 171
   and Maya Angelou, 180–81
   as progressive country, 118
   University of, 164
Gilbert, Zack, 275
Giovannoni, J., 58
Giroux, Henry A., 251–52
Godlas, Alan, 265
"God's Judgment of White America," 118
Gold Coast, 24
Goldman, Peter, 7, 223, 249, 281, 359n25
Gomez, Michael A., 357, 370, 370n62
Gordon, Charles, 179–80
Gottlieb, Roger S., 287
Graham, Le, 177
Graham, Mekada, 55–58, 62
Gravitts, Joseph X., 33
Gray, Cecil Conteen, 190
"gray propaganda," 305
greed, 346–50
Greek, William, 58
Green, Lisa, 365n47
Greene, Cheryll Y., 356n11
Griffiths, Bernard Elliot, 58
griot (storyteller), 12
Group on Advanced Leadership (GOAL), 48, 50–51
"Growing from my black skin," 325–26
Guevara, Che, 9, 144, 232
Gwaltney, John Langston, 76
Gwynne, James B., 171

H
Habermas, Jurgen, 284
Haiti, 330
Haitian Revolution, 210, 358n20
hajj, 125. *See also* pilgrimage; transformation
   of Malcolm, reasons for, 310–11
   of Mansa Musa, 309–10
   purpose and definition of, 309
   and transformation from, 312–13
   web site, "Hajj as a Shift against Racism," 265
Haley, Alex, 35, 45, 216, 239, 312
   and inaccuracy in *Autobiography*, 357n18
Halifu, Tommy. *See* Jacquette-Mfikiri, Tommy

Hall, Raymond L, 281
Hall, Ronald, 81, 344
Hamer, Fannie Lou, 105
Hamilton, Charles V., 72, 131–32, 136
Hammer, M.C., 12
Hampton, Henry, 356n11
Hampton, Lionel, 268
Harambee, 143n29
Harding, Vincent, 146
Hare, Nathan, 361n31
Harlem, 7
     and Cuban delegation with Malcolm X,
          37
     and "Detroit Red," 115–16
     and Malcolm X Commemoration, 52
     oral tradition of, 11
     in play, 178–79
     and voting registration drive in, 223
Harper, Frederick, 17
Harris, Donald, 9
Harris, Leonard, 282
Harris, Robert L., 61, 73, 125
"hate mongering," 223
Hate That Hate Produced, The, 223–24,
     299–300
Hayden, Robert, 170, 272
hegemony, white, 334
Held, David, 282n2
"Help the Children," 12
Henderson, David, 170
Henry, Milton, 50
Henry, Richard, 50
Herskovits, Melville, 251
Hill, John Henry, 210
Hill, Lauren, 354, 369–74
Hinton, Johnson, 7
Hip-Hop Movement, 5–6
     and Africana historical meaning, 369
     and Africana Studies, 368–74
     and long-view African memory in, 374
     and oratory style of Malcolm X, 12
     and race and culture in lyrics, 370
     and rap music, 11–12
"His name was simply X,", 174
history
     of Africa, near destruction of, 73
     Black, web site, 265
     and collective historical memory,
          365n46
     to determine social values, 346–47
     genealogy of Africana, 375
     "I am history," in revolutionary poetry,
          324–25

     as key social science, 95
     and Ki-Kongo "Tendwa Nza Kongo"
          Cosmogram, 364–68
     and knowledge as necessary tools, 253–54
     Malcolm on, 192, 196–97, 346–47
     metaphysical view of, 44
     misuse of, 284–85n5
     need to study, 372
     and origin of slaves from Africa, 364n44
     and reformation project of the Nation of
          Islam, 198
     religious, and Liberation Theology, 370
     Schomburg Center for Research in
          African-American History and Cul-
          ture, 356
     theory of, Black Radical Tradition,
          362–68
     and Third World peoples' role, 105
     and undelivered petition to UN, 130
     web sites of historic moments, 263–65
Hodgett, Colin, 178
Holiday, Billie, 268
holiday, public
     origin and meaning, 363n42
Holly, James Theodore, 210
Honderich, Ted, 287, 290
hooks, bell, 289
Hoover, J. Edgar, 232, 306
Horkheimer, Max, 283, 284
Horne, Gerald, 20, 239, 240, 242, 243,
     254n82, 258, 356n14
House Negro, 23, 95
housing, 45
Howard-Pitney, David, 225
Hoyt, Charles Alva, 195, 239, 258
human rights
     and civil rights, 48–49, 79, 330–31
     and civil rights, before the OAU, 126–27
     and civil rights, before the UN, 219
     and civil rights, in African American
          Studies, 187
     and civil rights, web site contrasting,
          265
     civil rights as international, 212–13
     influences on Malcolm's perception of,
          230–31
     Malcolm on, 103–4
     Malcolm on human rights violations, 156
     Malcolm X as advocate for, 153–55
     and UN petition charging genocide in
          US, 128–30
     violations by the US, Malcolm statement
          on, 156

Human Rights, Universal Declaration of, 129, 130
humanism, 22
Humphrey, Hubert, 301
hybridity, cultural, 359n23
"hybridization," 202

I
icon, 189, 360, 363
    Malcolm as, 236–43
identity, Black, 97, 189–90
    construction, 191–92, 202–4
    formation, 201–3
    global, and disciplinary Africana Studies, 361
    Malcolm on, 193, 334–35
    Malcolm on class, 195
    Malcolm on search for, 201–2
    and reformation project of the Nation of Islam, 197–99
    with respect to concept of nationalism, 196
ideology, 287
    and X-ism, 315, 317, 319
Idoma Alekwu, 173
Igede, 171
Illo, John, 248–49
Imani, 139
"Immortal now, he sits in fine company," 175
imperialism, 6, 23
    and Africana Critical Theory, 286
    as international power structure, 86–87
    as racism, 83
    US as imperialist power, 332
    and weakness of ideological deficiency, 287
incarceration. *See* prison
independent thinking, 40
Indonesia. *See* Bandung Conference
"Inscribing African World History," 362n32
integration
    desire for, 132–33
    as hoax, 19
    of ideas, Malcolm on, 333
    Malcolm on, 205n1
    as tokenism, 22
    and W.E.B. Du Bois, 133
International Conference of Black Writers and Artists, 255
International Foundation for Education and Self Help (FESH), 123
International Monetary Fund, 122
Islam, 140

Africana, 357n15
and Black Nationalism, 32
image of, transformed, 310
key to Black moral regeneration, 100–101
Malcolm on role of, 194
and Mansa Musa, 309–10
and Mecca, 309
Muslims and religious reevaluation of whites, 98–99
in the NOI, 151
religion of brotherhood, 311, 313
rituals of hajj, 313
and role of women, 311–12
"It Was A Funky Deal," 273–74

J
Jackson, George, 247n47
Jackson, James E., 69, 350
Jacquette-Mfikiri, Tommy, 142–43
Jahn, Janheinz, 132
jailhouse intellectual, 248
Jamal, Dorothy, 142–43
Jamal, Hakim (Allen), 51, 142–43, 367n52
    critical of US Organization, 143n30
James, C.L.R., 287, 289
James, I.R., 60
James-Wilson, S., 60
Jarvis, Malcolm "Shorty," 366n52
"Jazz Model," 362n33
Jean, Wyclef, 369n60, 370
Jenkins, Robert L., 5, 8, 9
Jennings, Regina, 333
Jeremiad, 225
Jews, 106
Jiménez, Blas, 317
    biography of, 320
    protest poetry of, 315–28
Joans, Ted, 270
Jogensmel, Broughwar, 58
Johnson, Christine C., 272, 275–76
Johnson, Lyndon B., 306
Jones, J.T., IV, 11
Jones, Leroi. *See* Baraka, Amiri
Jones, Rhett S., 67, 69, 76, 80, 337–39
Jungle Music, 12

K
Karenga, Brenda Haiba, 143
Karenga, Maulana, 10, 11, 51, 69, 71, 93, 190, 281–83, 338
    and armed Black resistance to state, 144–45
    and black churches, 4

Karenga, Maulana, *continued*
    and "context as text," 188
    influence of Malcolm on, 139–42
    Malcolm on history, 192
    Malcolm on whites and Black middle
        class, 349–50
    on Malcolm's oppositional logic, 204
    and US Organization, 138–39, 142–43
Karim, Benjamin, 5, 190, 197–98
    web site on Malcolm X, 264
Karumanchery, L., 60
Kawaida theory, 284
Kelley, Robin D.G., 23, 372
Kellner, Douglas, 282n2, 283, 287
Kennedy, John F., 152
    and "chickens coming home to roost,"
        20, 33, 93–94, 218
Kenya, 37, 127
Kenyatta, Jomo, 127, 140, 231, 268
Kershaw, Terry, 362n34
Key-Hekima, Karl, 142–43
Kgositsile, K. William, 176
Ki-Kongo
    paradigm, 371
    "Tendwa Nza Kongo" Cosmogram,
        364–68
Killens, John Oliver, 34, 39
Killian, Lewis M., 199–200
Kilson, Martin, 342
King, B.B., 268
King, Don, 69
King, Martin Luther, Jr., 72, 167, 353n2
    on armed struggle, 209
    "bankrupt" white folk, 237
    and civil rights movement, 236
    compared/contrasted with Malcolm, in
        literature, 180
    compared to Malcolm, 205–7
    compared with Malcolm, 180
    "dream" or "nightmare," 256n89
    and fabricated dichotomy with Mal-
        colm, 154
    Malcolm on, 200
    Malcolm on American dream, 340
    and Malcolm X compared, 205–7, 269t1
    and nonviolence, 300
    in play as antithesis of Malcolm, 179
    as poetic inspiration, 268
    and reparations, 205n2
    and role of FBI in assassination of, 206
    and violence with nonviolence, 341–42
Kiswahili, 139, 140
Kly, Yusuf Naim, 24, 300

Knight, Etheridge, 170, 173, 273
knowledge
    of Africa and self-love, 73
    cultural, affirmation of, 60
    and intellectual life of Malcolm X,
        244–49
    Malcolm as creator of body of knowl-
        edge, 252–53
    Malcolm as epistemologist, 250–54
    Malcolm on identify formation and, 192
    and Malcolm's anti-intellectualism, 238n
    of past, Afro-Americans to develop,
        80–81
    and power of the Black mind and intel-
        lect, 245–46
    self, and Black identity, 202
    "the Shebanization of," 311
    of white behavior, shared in songs, 74
Kondo, Zak, 358
Ku Klux Klan, 52, 76, 156, 221
    attack on Little home, 19, 149, 215–16
    and UN petition charging genocide in
        US, 128
    as violent bigots, 224–25
Kujichagulia, 139
Kuumba, 139
Kuykendall, Ronald D., 350
Kuzaliwa (Malcolm X's birthday), 144
Kwanzaa, 47, 51, 143–44

L
Ladner, Joyce, 67
Lambert, William, 209
land ownership, 113
language, 132, 171
Lapchick, Richard, 368n58
Latimore, Jewel C., 272
leadership, Black, 23–24
    call for global, 336
leadership, merit-based, 38, 46–52
    Malcolm as "good shepherd," 45–46
leadership, messianic, 46–47
    Malcolm as messiah, 371
    model of, 37–38
League of Black Revolutionary Workers, 138
League of Coloured Peoples, 59
League of Revolutionary Black Workers
    (LRBW), 31
LeBlanc, Keith, 12
Lee, Paul, 358n21
Lee, Spike, 12, 35, 125, 238, 239, 254n82,
    265, 315, 359n24
    and "Malcolm Renaissance," 356–57

Leedy, Paul D., 148
legacy
 and Africana Social Movement, 5–6
 and Black Nationalism, 97–100
 cultural, 47, 60–61
 dirge as, 175
 of enslavement, 193–94
 international, 49–52
 political, 9–10, 46–52
 practical, 94–95
 of self-determination, 52–53
LeMelle, Sidney, 239
Levine, Daniel, 68
Lewis, John, 9
Lewis, Stanford, 73
liberation, economic. *See also* genocide, economic
 Malcolm on, 223
 repudiation of separate nation-state
  model for, 114
 and role of women, 122
 and separate Black nation model,
  112–14
 theory with wholesale changes in economic order, 111–12
 Ujamaa, in US Organization, 139
Lincoln, C. Eric, 8, 9, 104, 135, 189
literacy. *See* education
literature, and poetry, 169–82
Little, Earl, 19, 147, 316
 biography of, 358n19
 Christianity and black Nationalism, 113
 death of, 114–15
 and his strategy for independence,
  112–13
 influence on Malcolm, 215–16
 and Marcus Garvey, 148–50
Little, Louise, 19, 115, 119, 149, 216
 and Caribbean background of, 358n22
Little, Malcolm, 315
 and early childhood, 68, 93, 112,
  114–15
 early childhood of, 19, 148, 215–16
Little, Philbert, 216
Little, Wilfred, 19, 115, 216
Logan, Rayford W., 229, 343
Lomax, Louis, 300
"Looking Homeward, Malcolm," 174
Lorde, Audre, 282, 289
Lorimer, D., 57
Louis, Joe, 268
Lucaites, John, 24, 191, 248n53, 254, 255
Lucas, James R., 272

Lumpkin, Katharine DuPre, 209
Lumumba, Patrice, 144, 152, 218, 274
 assassination of, 34n12, 49–50, 231
Lynch, Willie, 154
lynching, 4, 178, 197
Lyotard, Jean-Francois, 252–53, 256

M
Madhubuti, Haki R., 225
Major, Clarence, 272
"Malcolm," 274
*Malcolm: The Life of a Man Who Changed
 Black America*, 358n22
"Malcolm Renaissance," 356–57
Malcolm X, 12, 35, 125, 238, 254n82, 315,
 359n24
 and "Malcolm Renaissance," 356–57
 web site for film, 265
"Malcolm X," 270
Malcolm X: Justice Seeker, 171
Malcolm X: Make it Plain, 356n11
Malcolm X: Nationalist or Humanist
 web site, 265
"Malcolm X: No Sell Out," 12
*Malcolm X: The Life of a Man Who Changed
 Black America*, 182
"Malcolm X—An Autobiography," 174
*Malcolm X—The End of White World Su-
 premacy*
 web site, 265
"Malcolm X Doctrine," 51
Malcolm X Foundation, 51, 143n30, 358n19
Malcolm X Grass Roots Movement
 web site, 264
Malcolm X Institute of Black Studies
 web site, 264
Malcolm X/Malik Shabazz Study Guide
 website, 263
*Malcolm X Speaks: Selected Speeches and
 Statements*, 179
"MALCOLM X SPOKE TO ME and sounded
 you," 270
Malcolmian Method, 189–92, 203
Malcolm's Life and Death
 web site, 264
Mali, 309–10
"Malik's flowers fade," 177
Mandela, Nelson, 167
Mandeville, George, 58
manhood, 94
*Manual for Writers of Term Papers, Theses,
 and Dissertations, A*
 web site, 263–64

Maquet, Jacques, 83
Marable, Manning, 12, 17, 289, 374
    and lesser known scholarly assertions,
        357n18
    pending biography with new materials,
        357n17
Marcuse, Herbert, 283, 284, 286
marriage, interracial, 129
Marsh, Robert, 78
Marx, Karl, 287
Marxism, 69, 239
    and addressing racial realities in U.S., 76
    class struggle as thesis of, 287
    and critical theory, 282n2
    Malcolm as "primitive Marxist," 338
    sociological ideology of, 70
materialism, dialectical, 25–26
Mau Mau Rebellion, 37
mayor, 120–21
Mbiti, John, 321–22
M'Buyinga, E., 121
McLoughlin, William G., 343
McManus, Edgar J., 349
Mecca, 309
media
    Afro-American Broadcast Company, 233
    and dichotomy of "good Blacks vs. bad
        Blacks," 200
    distortion, 198, 220, 222, 299–308
    and documentary "The Hate That Hate
        Produced," 223–24, 299–300
    and Malcolm at TV interview, 237
    Malcolm on propaganda and media tac-
        tics, 301–4
    and power of establishment over, Mal-
        colm on, 193
    as surveillance tool for FBI, 307–8
Meeting: A One Act Play, The, 180
"Message to the Grass Roots," 180, 367
    Africana cultural analysis of, 17–29
    as alternative body of knowledge, 23–24
Message to the Grassroots, 143
metaphor
    Malcolm reduced to, 254
    taught by, 94–95
    used by Malcolm X, 22
methodology, historical analysis, 148
methodology, Ujima paradigm, 25–29
"Mi llanto," 323–25
    ("My Weeping"), 318
Militant Labor Forum, 289
Mill, John Stuart, 132
Mills, C. Wright, 75

Minority Small Business Investment Compa-
    nies, 120
minority status, 154
Mintz, Sidney W., 339
Mis-Education of the Negro, The, 246
"mixed blood theories," 202
MMI, 9, 20, 94
    founded, 218
    and moral reformation in the Black
        community, 101
    purposes of, 34–35
model Maulana, 94–95
Modern Black Convention Movement, 144
Monges, Miriam Ma'at-Ka-Re, 309
Montgomery, Wes, 268
Moore, Queen Mother, 51
Moore, Rowena, 358n19
Moorish Science Temple, 32, 151
morals
    construction of race, 252
    Malcolm as moral guide, 168
    moral and intellectual constructions,
        244–49
    and skin color, 344
    social and moral responsibility, 318
Morganthau, Henry III, 237
Moritz, Elke, 264
Morris, Jerome, 331
Morris, P., 57
Morrison, Toni, 251–52
Morrow, Raymond A., 282n2, 283
Moss, Alfred A., Jr., 207
mourning, public. See dirge, funeral
Muhammad, Elijah, 19. See also Black Na-
    tionalism
    forbids participation in political activi-
        ties, 6–7
    and Garvey influence on, 150–52
    as Garveyite, 135
    infidelity of, 152, 217
    influence on Malcolm, 93, 151–52,
        190
    Malcolm as follower of, 68
    as messianic leader, 38
    and separate Black nation-state model,
        112, 113–14
Muhammad, Elijah, Jr., 33
Muhammad, Ford, 151
Muhammad Speaks, 9, 93, 117, 120
Mullane, Deirdre, 225
MUNTU, 11
Musa, Mansa
    hajj of, 309–10

Muslim Mosque Incorporated (MMI). *See* MMI
"My Ace of Spades," 270
"My Weeping"
  ("Mi llanto"), 318
Myers, Linda James, 354n6
Myers, N., 58
Myrdal, Gunnar, 77–78
myth
  definition of, 20–21
  making, and Malcolm X, 240
  making, and speculation, 168
  Malcolm as a racist, 330
  and "Malcolm Renaissance," 356–57
  and political stereotype, 21–22
"Myth of Black Capitalism," 120
mythoform, 169, 182
  definition of, 167
  examples of, 170
  Malcolm as, 170

N
NAACP, 4
  and civil rights movement, 199–201
  and petition to UN with Du Bois, 228
  and racism, 301
Nadir of the Negro, The, 343
NAO, 80
narrative. *See also* oratory
  and animal imagery in speeches, 366n49
Nasser, Gamal Abdel, 231
Nation of Islam (NOI)
  and Black Nationalism, 44–46
  dissension among leadership, 33–34
  and early association with Malcolm X, 32–33, 93–94, 117
  and emigration proposal of, 113
  FBI slandering leadership of, 305–7
  and Garvey's influence on, 4, 135
  implicated in death of Malcolm, 178–79, 358n21
  influence of Malcolm on, 5, 139–42
  and its intellectual foundations, 244
  Malcolm on nonengagement policy of, 151
  and Malcolm's rhetorical style, 190
  and Malcolm's rift with, 20, 33–37, 93–94, 299–300, 306–7
  now known as the World Community of Islam, 135
  organization of temples, 6t1
  Original Men and diabolical derivatives, 104–5

periodical of the, 9
and politics of Black identity, 141
and prisoners, 5
promoted self-sufficiency, 216–17
the reformation project of, 197–99
and role of women in, 41, 118–19
and Savior's Day, 363n42
and small business ventures of membership, 117
sociological study of, 8
and superiority of blackness, 223, 344–45
and traditional beliefs of, 44
was not pro-African, 367n54
National Afro-American Organization, 48
National Association for the Advancement of Colored People (NAACP). *See* NAACP
National Coalition of Blacks for Reparation in America (NCOBRA), 47
National Negro Congress, 228
nationalism, 132–33, 135
  and destructive influence of Christianity, 206n6
  in Dominican revolutionary poetry, 323–25
nationalism, black. *See also* identity, Black
  and "black neo-nationalism," 254n82
  in literature and poetry, influence of Malcolm, 170–82
  Malcolm on being an American, 197
  Malcolm's social philosophy, 223–24
  Marcus Garvey and Elijah Muhammad, 150–52
nationalism, cultural, 98, 144
nationalism, revolutionary, 45, 49, 50, 69, 97
Native Americans, 85–86, 343
Neal, Larry (Lawrence P.), 11, 169–70, 174, 272
Negro
  Convention, 133
  death of term, 201
  definition of term, 325
  in Little household, 216
  Malcolm as "anti-Negro," 195
  "so-called Negro," 141, 194–95
Negro Factories Corporation, 134
Negro World, The, 216
Nell, William Cooper, 211
neocolonization, 119, 121–22, 126
Neuman, W. Lawrence, 283
"New Afrikan Creed," 51
New Afrikan Peoples Organization, 52
New Plays from the Black Theatre, 178

Newton, Huey P., 50, 85, 257

Ngao Damu, Samuel. *See* Carr-Damu, Samuel

Nia, 139

Nigeria, 171, 180

nigger, 100, 115, 258
　discouraged word in Little household, 216
　good, 195
　Malcolm as "bad nigger" leader, 200
　"smart," 216

"Night of the Living Baseheads," 12

Nixon, Richard, 120

Nketia, J.H, 167–68, 176–77
　on death, dirge, and ancestor acknowledgment, 174–75
　and dirge, 171
　significance of traditional dirges, 177–78

Nketsia, Nana, 43

Nkrumah, Kwame, 37, 118, 126, 154, 164, 231
　audience between Malcolm and, 181
　nonalignment strategy to avoid neocolonialism, 121
　and petition before the UN, 229

Nobles, Wade, 354n6

"nobody mentioned war," 274

Nommo, 172, 225

nonviolence, 269
　and Afrikan liberation movements, 207–12
　citizenship rights and international human rights, 212–13
　and combat with Indians, 212
　Malcolm on, 341
　meaning of, 347
　origin of, 210
　and participation by Afrikans in war efforts, 211–12
　and right to self-defense, 85, 107–9
　slaves response to, 210–11
　and violence as shadow value, 340–42
　web site, contrasting King and Malcolm X, 264

Norfolk Prison Colony, 248

norm, 70

Norman, George, 274

Nower, Joyce, 239n17, 256

Nyerere, Julius K., 121, 231

Nyeusi, Sanamu, 143

O

OAAU, 9, 20
　addressed identity in charter, 202
　and black community development, 117–18
　and community unity, 102
　dedicated to defense, unity and liberation struggle, 94
　formation of, after Africa trip, 230
　history of, 50
　and new leadership, 39–40
　objectives of, 317–18
　as organizational alternative, 22–23
　and power, 77
　to promote unity, 316
　purposes of, 34–35
　raises freedom struggle to international level, 126–27
　and role of women in, 41–42
　to serve the unification of New World Africans, 218–19
　as vehicle for unity and solidarity of American Africans, 35

OAU, 45
　attendance at, 126
　criticism of, 121
　emulated to form OAAU, 106
　Malcolm on international pressure and status of Blacks, 349

Obadele, Gaidi, 50

Obadele, Imari, 50

Obote, Milton, 127, 231

Ofari, E., 120

Ogede, Ode S., 171, 173, 176

Ohiwerei, Godwin, 329

Ohmann, Carol, 240, 247, 248

Okafor, Victor O., 215

Okoli, Emeka J., 73

Okunor, Shiama, 73

"Old Negro and the New Negro, The," 193, 195

Omowale, 153 *See also* Shabazz, El-Hajj Malik El
　meaning in Yoruba, 372

"On Black Power," 265

On the Side of My People: A Religious Life of Malcolm X, 148

One Day when I Was Lost, 179

ontology, 20, 22–23

Opportunities Industrialization Centers, 120

oratory, 11–12
　and "active" voice, 249
　and argumentation styles, 95
　civil rights leadership's refusal to debate Malcolm, 353n2

and importance of grammar and vocabulary, 365n47

Malcolm on American race relations, 221

and Malcolmian Method of oppositional rhetoric, 189–92

methodology to include anger, 75–76

and oral traditions as moral education, 168–69

style, Malcolm, 24

and traditional narratives, 167

"Order of Emigration," 209

Organization of African Unity (OAU). *See* OAU

Organization of Afro-American Unity (OAAU). *See* OAAU

"Original.", 270

"Our Black Shining Prince," 370

"Our People Identify with Africa," 118

"out of place," 58

Outlaw, Lucius T., Jr., 283, 285, 362n37

Outline of History, 196

Ouverture, Toussaint L., 274

Owolo, Obaboa, 51

Oxford Companion to African American Literature, The, 167, 168

P

Painter, Nell, 238, 244–46

Pan-African, 3

Federation, 59

leadership qualities of 1960 Black leaders, 180

Movement, 153–55

movement, 358n20

vision, 316–17

Pan-Africanism, 45, 147–64, 289–90. *See also* Ghana

advocated by Malcolm, 222–23

and "down home" rather than "back home," 80

ideology, 317

influences on black leadership, 150–52

and international independence, 8–10

liberation movements' support of, 47–52

and link between black Americans and Africans, 79

and Malcolm, 105–7, 152–53, 227–28

and need to act, 83–84

need to understand exploitation of Africans, 72

and paradigm shift from domestic to, 330–31

and racism in Britain, 56

and racism in U.S., 126–27

and Third World solidarity, 104–5

two schools of thought, 229–30

and white racism, 356n14

paradigm

and ancestor creation, 167–68

functional, definition of, 219

of historical memory, 362–68

Paris, Peter, 256

Parker, Charles, 268

Parks, Rosa, 6

Patterson, James, 174

Patterson, William L., 213

Pennington, James W.C., 211n25

Perry, Bruce, 5, 7, 111, 114, 116, 182, 239, 281, 358n22

Philadelphia Negro, 252

philosophy. *See also* Pan-Africanism

Afrocentricity and Eurocentrism, 285

Black Nationalism, economic, 134–35

and Christianity, 140–41

and criticism, definition of term, 290

and goals of UNIA, 133–34

and ideology, definition of term, 290

Little family and impact of Garvey's, 149–50

Malcolm on, 289

and Malcolm's, 24–25, 96–97, 223–24

political, and American ideal, 300

pilgrimage, 125–26, 218. *See also* hajj; Mecca; transformation

and brotherhood, 224, 331

by Malcolm, 35

and transformation of Malcolm, 98

web site, Malcolm's own words and timeline of life, 264–65

and "white" Muslims, 230

Pinkney, Alphonso, 7, 94, 132, 281

Play of Giants, A, 180

plebiscite, 50

Plessy v. Ferguson, 130

"Poem for Black Hearts, A," 176

"¿Poetas?", 320

poetry

alternate names for Malcolm, 176

dirge as mournful poem, 171–72

inspirational Black figures for Black poets, 268

and literature influenced by Malcolm X, 167–82, 267–80

poetry, *continued*
  and poets on "Aftermath," 274–75
  and poets on "Death," 273
  and poets on "Life," 272
  and poets on Malcolm X, 276–77
  and poets on "Rage" and sorrow,
    274–75
  protest, of Jiménez, 318–28
  and social background of poets, 277,
    278–79*t*3, 280*t*4
  use of elements of Igede dirge in Black,
    173–74
"Poets?", 320
Police and the Black Community, 193
police brutality, 126, 136, 220
politics
  and deceitful government, 340
  of disenfranchisement, overview,
    329–30
  and economic power, after NOI, 338
  and economics, as types of power, 318
  embarrassing U.S. at UN, 332, 333
  of Malcolm, 121, 224–25
  and paradigm shift from domestic to in-
    ternational, 330–31
Poole, Elijah. *See* Muhammad, Elijah
Powell, Adam Clayton, Jr., 37, 135, 196
Powell, Adam Clayton, Sr., 135
Powell, Larry, 190
power, 77
  Black, synonymous with "Black Nation-
    alism," 132
  for black Americans, 79
  and class, 82–86
  and corruption, 347
  economic and political, after NOI, 338
  as global, 105
  and greed, 346–50
  Malcolm on international, 233–34
  politics and economics, as types of,
    318
  social, from economic and political
    power, 346–47
  UN, and Afro-American solutions to
    racism, 79–81
  white, as international, 78
praise poem, 174. *See also* dirge, funeral
press. *See also* media
  and Malcolm as threatening force, 190
  and propagandistic tactics of, 193
Price, Leontyne, 268
Price, Richard, 339
prison, 4

as educational facility for civil rights ac-
    tivist, 330
  and fatherhood prison program, 63
  and jail, definition in drama, 179
  Malcolm as paradigm of prison intellec-
    tual, 246–47
  Malcolm in, 216, 304–5
  Malcolm's readings in, 235n3
  as metaphor, 246
  and Nation of Islam in, 19, 93
  Norfolk Prison Colony, 248
Progressive Labor Party, 69
propaganda. *See* media
property
  of self, and "stealing" property, 241
Prosser, Gabriel, 175, 274
Provisional Government of the Republic of
  New Afrika (PGRNA), 31
  history and ideology of, 50–51
Public Enemy, 12
"public intellectual," 189
public value. *See* value

Q
Q-Tip, 370
Quaison-Sackey, Alex, 232
Quigless, Helen, 177

R
Rabaka, Reiland, 281
race
  analysis and class analysis, 350
  Malcolm on American race relations,
    221
  moral construction of, 243–49, 252
  as prison, education the key, 246–47
racial determination
  Malcolm on, 345–46
racism, 45. *See also* human rights
  basic causes of, 77
  black, Malcolm as apostle for, 237
  and black middle-class, 82–83,
    199–201
  in Britain, 56–57
  and civil rights movement, 48
  and class struggle, 287
  in Congo and South Vietnam, 335
  and defeat by black-derived strategies,
    75
  in Dominican poetry, 320
  early forms of resistance to, in Britain,
    59
  exposed at OAU by Malcolm, 126–27

as fictions organized by imperialists, 80–81

globalizing debates on, 333

institutional, in Britain, 57

and internalization of stereotypical image, 335

and international human rights, 330–31

and link between black Americans and Africans, 79

Malcolm on intergenerational Black phobia, 220–21

Malcolm on "the white man," 196–97

Malcolm on white immigrant and Black citizenship, 343–44

and oral tradition as response to, 169

as psychological castration, 313

as responsible for Black angst, 315

and secondhand citizenship, 343

shared by Africans and Afro-Americans, 331–32

as taught in African American Studies, 187

and "The Hate That Hate Produced," 299–300

transformation of Malcolm after hajj, 312–13

before the UN, 125–30

as violation of human rights, 156

violence as shadow value, 340–42

violence as solution, 85

white, 98, 301, 340

white, and "Malcolm Renaissance," 356n14

and whiteness, 74

Radical Sociology, 75

radicalism, 282, 289–91

Rael, Patrick, 339

Rainey, Ma, 268

Randall, Dudley, 170–71, 177, 268

Randolph, A., 60

Ranke, Leopold von, 369n60

rap music, 11–12

"Red China," 86

Red Feather Institute for Advanced Studies in Sociology, 75

Reed, Adolph, 359–60, 360n26

religion. *See also* Islam

    and afterlife, in dirge, 174–75

    and Karenga, 140

    Malcolm on liberation through use of, 151–52

    and police brutality, 220

    as support of social struggle, 101

reparations, 51, 205n2

Republic of New Africa, 6

resistance, 208–9, 255

resources, 70

restitution, 205n2

revenge, 341

revolution. *See also* assassination; Tocqueville, Alexis de

    African, 331–32

    African, and Black heritage and identity, 334–35

    African, liberation struggles on continent, 230

    Black, criticisms of, 253

    and Black political mobilization in poetry, 322–23

    and Black resistance, 144–45

    cultural, Karenga's assertion of, 142

    definition of, 256

    differences in Black and Negro, 23

    first to conceptualize then to organize, 241

    Haitian, 210

    Malcolm as model revolutionary, 94

    and nuanced analysis of, 247–48n53

    and poetry of Afro-Dominican poet, 319–28

    and prison revolutionaries, 246–47

    right to freedom and privilege to peace, 108

    summarized, 256

    and white revolutionaries, Malcolm on, 345

    and white revolutionaries and Black Nationalism, 98–99

revolution, cultural, 47. *See also* Black Nationalism

    in freedom struggle, 97–100

    Malcolm on, 322–23

Revolutionary Action Movement (RAM), 6, 31, 48, 49, 138

    as guerilla fighting force, 144

    politics of, 36–37

rhetoric

    as epistemological shifts, 247–48

    example, Malcolm on skin color, 220

    Malcolm as master rhetorician, 248–49

    Malcolm's style and "trickster consciousness," 366n49

    oppositional, Malcolmian Method of, 191t1

    style of Malcolm X, 189–92

    and uses of irony and humor, 367n52

Rhymes, Busta, 370
Rivers, Conrad Kent, 174
Roach, Jack L., 75
Robeson, Paul, 128, 213, 367n52
Robinson, Cedric J., 289, 356n14, 362, 373
    and Black Radical Tradition, 354, 355n8,
        357n16
Robinson, Jackie, 268
Rogers, J.A., 196
role
    definition of, 82
    of women, 31, 40–42, 46–47, 118–19,
        122, 311–12
    of women, and patriarchy, 258
    of women, in NOI, 217
Roosevelt, Eleanor, 212, 229
Ross, Larry, 263
Rueter, Theodore, 225
"Rumble in the Jungle," 354, 368
"Rumores de tertulias"
    and need for social awakening,
        320–21
    ("Rumors of Rap Sessions"), 318
"Rumors of Rap Sessions"
    ("Rumores de tertulias"), 318
Russell, Bertrand, 140–41
Russell, Kathy, 81, 344
Russia
    and human rights violations, 106
Russian Revolution, 23
Rustin, Bayard, 68–69, 251, 255

S
Sales, William, 9, 39, 282, 289, 304, 358
San Francisco State College
    Black Studies department at, 10–11
Sanchez, Sonia, 177, 223
Santiago-Valles, William F., 362n34
Schilling, Marcel, 264
Schmitt, Richard, 287
Schomburg Center for Research
    in African-American History and Cul-
        ture, 356, 365n48
SCLC, 7–8, 199–201
Seale, Bobby, 50
Seaton-Msemaji, Ken, 142–43
segregation, 4
    compared in South Africa and America,
        86
    and growing activism, 36–37
    and Malcolm on race relations, 224
    and "moral separation," 242
    and "separate but equal" doctrine, 130

self-defense, 48, 281
    as assertion for the common good, 245
    Malcolm on, 221–22, 317
    and the struggle for freedom, 107–9
"Self-Destruction," 12
self-determination, 6, 48, 227, 281, 317
    and community empowerment, 7
    Garvey's self-help and, 149–50
    and involvement in politics by Blacks,
        223
    Kujichagulia, in US Organization, 139
    more successful with Black unity,
        333–34
self-determination, community, 61–62
self-sufficiency, 112–13
Sellers, Cleve, 48
"separate but equal," 130
separation
    and Henry Turner, 133
    Malcolm on, 201
    and states granted as partial reparations,
        51
    tactic of NOI, 44
Sex and Race, 196
Shabazz, Betty, 13, 19, 51, 143
    description of assassination, 265
Shabazz, El-Hajj Malik El, 315. See also hajj
    after hajj, 312–13
Shabazz, Omowale Malik, 35, generally
        31–53
    and Afrikan liberation struggle, 46–52
    and changing epistomological perspec-
        tive, 44–46
    period, radical nationalist, 36–37
    and role of women, 40–42
    shift in leadership style, 37–38
    shift in perspective on continental
        Afrikans, 42–43
    shift in political ideation, 39–40
    transformation of Malcolm X to, 19
shadow value. See value
Shah, Yusuf. See Gravitts, Joseph X.
Shakur, Mutulu, 52
Sharpeville Massacre, 127–28, 176
Sharrief, Raymond, 33
Shaw, Yusuf, 8–9
"Shebanization of knowledge," 311
Shifflet, Lynn, 34, 39, 42
shrine, 363
Shyllon, F., 57
simile, 22
Sinclair, R., 57
"Sing to a white god?," 324–25

Singh, Nikhil Pal, 360n28
Skellington, R., 57
skin color, 81–82
    and Garvey's opposition to bleaching
        creams, 134–35
    Malcolm on, 220, 335
    Malcolm on white, 333
    and passing as white, 344
    and "white-skin privilege," 344
slavery. *See also* dirge, funeral; X
    African people as "property" and poor
        relief, 58
    and apologist justification for, 125
    armed resistance during time of, 207n10
    cause of, 45
    concept of property and self, 373–74
    control of Africa through disunity, 154
    demographics of, 58
    and emancipation of slaves, 133
    during the Enlightenment, 241
    and "freedom from mental slavery," 57,
        60
    in hip-hop lyrics, 371–72
    historians of, 146
    Malcolm on "house slave" and "field
        slave," 195
    menial jobs as "slave labor," 114
    and New World, 319
    and oral traditions of slaves, 168–69
    and origin of slaves from Africa,
        364n44
    and psychosocial control of black
        masses, 192–94, 203
    and research of "militant abolitionism,"
        208n11
    and self-determination, 132–33
    slaves and New World Black cultures,
        339
"Sleep Bitter, Brother," 176
Small, S., 56, 61
Smallwood, Andrew P., 3, 11, 203
    and Black studies, 361n31
Smith, Charles U., 199–200
Smith, R.C., 225
SNCC, 7, 48–49, 76
"so-called Negro," 201
    Malcolm on, 194–95
"Social Background of the Black Arts Move-
    ment, The, 11
Social Movement, Africana, 3–4
    and definition of Africana socialism, 28
    and Malcolm as ideological influence, 47
    reasons for studying, 10–11

socialism, 45
    and Third World struggles for liberation,
        105
    and values in social thought, 338–40
Socialist Workers Party, 69
sociology, 70
    and evolution of sociological thought,
        68–71
    Malcolm and paradigm for, 76–77
sociology, Black
    and Malcolm X, 68–71
    overview of, 67
    and race role, 82–86
    and research strategies of, 71–76
solidarity, African/Black, 58, 104–5, 317,
    357n16
"Solitude of Change, The," 175–76
sons of Africa, 58
Souls of Black Folk, 196, 236, 252
"Souls of White Folk, The," 258
South Africa, 86
    and apartheid, 127–28, 330, 333
Southern Christian Leadership Conference
    (SCLC). *See* SCLC
Soyinka, Wole, 180
Spriggs, Edward S., 177
Stanfield, J., 56
Stanford, Max, 51
status, 82
    of Africans in US., analysis of, 360n28
    assigned by racists and imperialists, 86
    of being white, 343
    of Blacks and racism, 193
    and debate of naming using "X," 194–95
    definition of, 70
    differences in occupational as barrier,
        114
    Malcolm on international pressure and
        Black, 349
    Malcolm on minority, 154
Stetson, Jeff, 180
Stewart, James B., 10, 111, 114, 120, 362n33
"Stillborn Pollen Falling," 177
Stokes, Ronald, 7, 220
Stop the Violence Movement, 12
Story of Civilization, 196
Strickland, William, 5, 7, 9
Structuration theory, 20
Stuckey, Sterling, 146, 339
Student Non-Violent Coordinating Commit-
    tee (SNCC), 31
Stull, Bradford, 248n53, 250, 251, 258
Sullivan, Leon, 120, 122–23

Sundiata, 169
supremacy, white, 301. *See also* white
    contested in revolutionary poetry, 326–27
    critic of, 281
    as danger to Black family, 225
    as "morality" problem, 242
    replaced with God as only authority, 373
    taught in African American Studies, 187
    and worldwide system of, 358n20

T
Taiwan, 86
"Tam, tam-tam tam-tam," 322–23
Tanzania
    socialism with Ujamaa village, 121
Taylor, Clyde, 355n9
Teddlie, Abbas, 25
Teddlie, Charles, 25
temple
    financial situation stabilized, 117
    Muslim, organized by Malcolm, 217–18
    in Nation of Islam, organization of, 6*t*1
Temple, Christel N., 167
Temporary Alliance of Local Organizations, 139
"Tendwa Nza Kongo"
    Cosmogram, Ki-Knogo, 364fig1
Terrell, Mary Church, 213
Terrill, Robert, 247, 258, 366n49, 367n52
territory, 132
    issue of, in NOI, 135
Thewel, Michael, 248
Thomas, Lizzie, 257
Thomas, Tony, 239
Thompson, Julius E., 267
Till, Emmett, 6
Tillis, Antonio, 315
"To Malcolm X," 274
Tocqueville, Alexis de, 241, 245n41
"Todo negro"
    (All Black"), 318
    evokes unified Black Nationalist ideology, 326–27
¿Todo negro?, 326–27
tokenism, 22, 350
totem, 363
Toure, Sekou, 231
tradition, 373
    African, 10–12, 167
    African, and slavery, 168–69
transformation, 35–37, 309–13, 316
    "last year transformation" thesis, challenge to, 359n25

political, of Malcolm, 44–46
    through travel, 99
travels, 10*t*2
    to Africa, 12–18, 218, 230–31
    and African leaders, 153–55
    after hajj, 312–13
    chronicled by Angelou, 180–81
    encouraged, 45
    to Europe, 232, 334
    new strategies based on, 154–55
    and paradigm shift from focus on domestic issues, 330–31
    and shaping of concept of Third World, 105
    and shifting view of Afrikans, 42–43
triangulation, 25
trickster, 168, 370
Trotter, Monroe, 170
Trout, Lawana, 188
"True Remedy for the Fugitive Slave Bill, The," 208
Truth, Sojourner, 242
Tryman, Mfanya Donald, 5, 8, 9
T'Shaka, Oba, 277, 358
Tshombe, Moise, 231
Tubman, Harriet, 242
Turabian, Kate L., 263 64
Turner, Henry, 133, 167
Turner, James, 8
Turner, Nat, 4, 175, 211, 242, 274
    as mythoform, 170
Turner, Richard Brent, 1718
Tyner, James, 357

U
Uganda, 127
Ujima, 139
Ujima paradigm, 20–29
    axiology, 24–25
    cosmology, 22
    epistemology, 23–24
    methodology, 25–29
    ontology, 22–23
    social ecology, 25
UMBRA, 48
Umoja, 139
Umoja, Akiniyele K., 31
Uncle Tomism, 179, 195
underground
    Afrikan movement, 209
    movements, and violent resistance, 144–45
    railroad movement, 210–11

UNIA, 32
    and Earl Little, 216
    and female leaders in, 41
    in Little household, 148–50
    philosophy and goals of, 133–35
    and rejection of whiteness, 344
United Nations
    and apartheid in South Africa, 128
    Covenant on Human Rights, 104
    delegates not called "Negroes," 335
    and focus on women, 122
    human rights and racism, 79–81, 332
    and Malcolm on international power
        structure, 233–34
    as model for integration of Black global
        issues, 334
    and petition by Malcolm to, 94, 128–30,
        155–56, 212–13, 228–29
    and Russian human rights violations,
        106
United States
    as agent of neocolonialism, 119
    as center of imperialist organization,
        348
    need to understand, 350
    Post Office, Malcolm X stamp, 358n19
    preaches integration and practices segre-
        gation, 340
    and public values of, 337, 338
    and secondhand citizenship, 343
    whiteness and violence justified by, 348
unity, Black, 7, 45–46, 157, 227, 323
    advocated by Malcolm, 222–23
    and class, 82–86
    community organization as requirement
        of, 102–3
    as emphasized by Malcolm X, 39–40
    link between black Americans and
        Africans, 79
    Malcolm on, 152–53, 332, 333, 335
    Malcolm on shared Black study and ac-
        tion plan, 338–39
    and need to act, 83–84
    promoted by Earl Little, 216
    promoted in drama, 179
    and Third World conferences increasing,
        104–5
    and transformation, 316
    Umoja, in US Organization, 139
    and "working unity," 85
Universal Negro Improvement Association
    (UNIA). See UNIA
urban development

based on collective ownership, 117
and black political control, 120–21
and community service of the NOI, 301
and global perspective of, 119–23
small entrepreneur-based model of,
    119–23
US Organization, 6, 31
    and alternative cultural rituals and prac-
        tices, 145
    decline of, 145–46
    founders of, 142–43
    influence of Malcolm on, 142–45
    overview of, 138–39
    value system of, 139

V
value
    and Black self-hatred, 316
    in Declaration of Independence, and vi-
        olence, 341
    definition of, 70
    greed as shadow, 346–50
    life-affirming, 187
    Malcolm as "vessel of cultural values,"
        168
    Malcolm on hypocrisy of American val-
        ues, 342
    public and shadow, overview of, 337
    relativity of, 24–25
    reorient, towards self-love and self-re-
        spect, 134–35
    schools of thought on Black value con-
        struction, 339–40
    system, American, 77
    system, United States and European,
        350–51
    system, US Organization, 139
    violence as shadow, 340–42
    and white hypocrisy, 340
    whiteness as shadow, 342–46
Van Deburg, William, 281
Van Horne, Winston, 362
Verene, Donald Phillip, 367
Vesey, Denmark, 211, 274
violence, 281
    and Afrikan liberation movements,
        207–12
    and Afrikan "manhood" rights, 209
    "as American as apple pie," 341
    black-on-black crime as shameful, 84
    and FBI slandering of NOI leadership,
        305–7
    Malcolm as apostle of, 254

violence, *continued*
    Malcolm on, 198, 221–22
    Malcolm X as inspiration for, 144–45
    between police and Black citizens, 193
    and revenge, 341
    as shadow value, 340–42
    as unanticipated continuous acts, 255
voting rights, 45
    and Black Panther Party, 136
    and justification of genocide in US, 129
    and OAAU, 96
    and voting registration drive in Harlem,
       223

W
Walker, Alice, 272
Walker, David, 208, 241, 245, 344
Walker, Margaret, 175
Wall, Jim Vander, 304
Wallace, Mike, 223–24, 300
Walton, H. Jr., 225
Ward, Douglas Turner, 168
warfare, 22–23
warrior, 202, 204, 225
Washington, Booker T., 133, 170
Washington, Dinah, 268
Washington, James M., 206
Washington, Madison, 211
Washington, Margaret, 146
Watts, 176
We Charge Genocide, 128, 129
"We used to bite the bullets with the pigskin
    casings," 353–54, 371
*We Will Suffer and Die if We Have To: A Folk
    Play for M.L. King*, 178
Weber, Shirley N., 131
Wells, H.G., 196
Wells-Barnett, Ida B., 4
West, Cornel, 289, 316
    and "cultural hybridity," 359n23
Western Journal of Black Studies, The, 69
Wheatley, Phyllis, 241, 245
When We Were Kings, 368–69
"When You Died," 275
"When you died, Malcolm,", 275–76
white. *See also* skin color
    behavior, knowledge of in song, 74
    hegemony, definition of, 334
    as "moral monsters," 256n91
    Muslim, 230
    people, Malcolm on, 215
    as problem, 256n91
    religious reevaluation of, 98–99

White, E. Francis, 355n8
"White Man is God For Cult of Islam," 305–6
white supremacy. *See* supremacy, white
whiteness, 141, 237, 374
    as covert requirement for citizenship,
       343
    important to study, 74
    Malcolm on, 343
    as powerful value, 350
    in revolutionary Dominican poetry,
       323–25
    as shadow value, 342–46
    social perception of, in US, 343
    status of, and benefits from, 82
"Why I'm Not a Christian," 141
Wilkins, Roy, 68, 69, 72, 353n2
Williams, George Washington, 211
Williams, Robert, 291
Williams, Robin, 274
Wilson, Joseph T., 211
Wilson, Midge, 81, 344
Wintersmith, Robert, 193
Wolfenstein, Eugene Victor, 281, 282
women
    as contextualizations in Malcolm's life,
       242
    oppression of Black, 130, 258
    role of, 31, 40–42, 46–47, 118–19, 122,
       311–12
Wood, Joe, 282, 360n26
Woodson, Carter G., 192, 246
Woodward, Komozi, 144
World Bank, 122
World Book Multimedia Encyclopedia, The
    digital sourse on Malcolm X, 264
World Community of Islam, 135
worldview, African-centered, 71–76, 369, 374
    "African-Centered," definition of, 354
    "Afrocentric," 354
    and Black Radical Theory, 374
    as contested assertion, 355n8
    and recognizing markers, 365–66
Worley, James, 176, 272
Wright, Jay, 176
Wright, Richard, 255
"Written After Thinking of Malcolm," 275

X
X, Malcolm. *See also* Detroit Red; Little,
    Malcolm; Shabazz, El-Hajj Malik El
    biographical profile of, 21*t*1
    emergence as independent theoretician,
       68

and King, politics, principles and leadership style compared, 269t1
lectures by, in 1963, 29t3
as model teacher and student, 94–95
as "postmodern man," 252–53
"Progress is healing the wound.", 3
repository of historic documents on, 356
and research strategy of, 74–75
stamp of, 358n19
undiscovered materials of, 357n17
web sites on, 263–65
X-ism, 315, 318
XXX
as cultural symbol, 122, 174, 175
as indication of racial independence, 372
and loss of identity through slavery, 194–95
as name change, 19, 217
standing for "unknown," 315

Y
Yeshitela, Omali, 71
Young, Whitney, 72, 353n2
youth, 107

Z
Zerubavel, Evitar, 363
Zine, J., 60
Zinn, Howard, 76
Zulu, 140